A
CHANGING
IMAGE:
American
Perceptions of
the Arab-Israeli Dispute

by
RICHARD H. CURTISS

Published by the
American Educational Trust

For Raymond Holden Curtiss
1963 - 1981

A brave and concerned idealist
whose causes were those of compassion, not of anger

Published in the United States of America
by the American Educational Trust
P.O. Box 53062
Washington, D.C. 20009

Library of Congress Catalogue Card Number 83-149825

Library of Congress Cataloging-in-Publication Data

Curtiss, Richard H., 1927–
  A changing image.

  Includes bibliographical references and index.
  1. Near East—Foreign relations—United States.
  2. United States—Foreign relations—Near East.
  3. Jewish-Arab relations—1949–   . I. Title.
  DS63.2.U5C87   1986   327'.56073   83-149825
  ISBN 0-937165-00-X

Preface

The first edition of this book, finished early in 1982, predicted that continuing unrestricted American economic and military support of Israel inevitably would bring to power there increasingly extremist leaders. Those Israeli extremists would, in turn, commit acts that would force Americans to reassess their initial tilt in the Israeli-Palestinian dispute. Americans would recognize that since there are moderates and extremists in both camps, only adoption of an even-handed U.S. policy eschewing all extremists, Israeli and Arab, would eventually bring moderates to power on both sides simultaneously who could negotiate a lasting peace.

The 1982 Israeli invasion of Lebanon began validating the first prediction while the book was still on the presses. Rekindled interest in the Middle East, and adoption of the book as a text or collateral reading for university courses all over the United States, resulted in it being sold out in less than two years. Meanwhile many of the leaders mentioned in that first edition were providing valuable new insights through publication of their own memoirs, and all three living ex-Presidents of the United States sent me encouraging letters concerning the accuracy and fairness of the book.

My own work and travel as a consultant to a number of U.S. Government and private non-profit institutions prevented me from including these insights and updating the book for nearly four years. The delay, however, has given me time to ponder reactions to a book which sought to provide Americans what they need to know in order to make intelligent decisions about the Israeli-Palestinian dispute, and at the same time provide Arab and Israeli readers with evidence that moderate policies by their leaders will generally evoke a positive response by Americans.

One thing that became evident to me is that few Americans realize that ever since 1967 every U.S. administration has supported the same, simple blueprint for Middle East peace, based upon the inadmissability of the acquisition of territory by war. It is United Nations Security Council Resolution 242's land-for-peace formula, which over the years has been agreed to by the U.S., the USSR, all of the Arab confrontation states and the Israeli government of Golda Meir. Since its adoption in 1967, the various U.S. administrations have also addressed the resolution's principal ambiguities. The Nixon Administration noted that when the Israelis return to their pre-1967 borders in return for Arab and international guarantees of peace, territorial adjustments must be "insubstantial." The Reagan Administration has insisted that the resulting Palestinian state should be created in confederation with Jordan. The Carter Administration said that Jerusalem should not be divided and that Christians, Jews and Muslims should have unimpeded access to their own Holy places. This was also envisioned in the original UN partition plan which divided Palestine into independent Jewish and Palestinian states, but specified that Jerusalem would be internationally administered. None of the provisions of Resolution 242, or the U.S. positions taken before or after it, would prevent either the Israelis or the Palestinians, or both, from making Jerusalem the capital of their respective states after a settlement is reached.

Other reactions to the first edition of this book followed two distinct tracks. Virtually every American, regardless of ethnic or religious background, who had spent time personally in the Middle East or who had followed Middle East affairs closely in the United States, welcomed the book enthusiastically. The only critical comments I heard from such "old hand" readers were that in some cases I had "pulled my punches," had not put sufficient emphasis on the original injustices suffered by the Palestinians, and was too optimistic about the accessibility of the U.S. media and the support of Congress for an even-handed position.

Reactions from Americans who do not know the Middle East at first-hand, or whose only Middle Eastern exposure has been through brief visits to Israel, were puzzling. They were neither particularly favorable nor critical. On call-in talk shows any objections offered to my comments generally were based upon vague questions about Israel's "strategic" value to the U.S., inaccurate historical assumptions about occupancy of the Holy Land in past ages, or politicized interpretations of Holy Writ that seemed to trivialize the Creator of the Universe.

After pondering it all, I have reluctantly decided that reservations of the "old hands" concerning Congress and the media are valid. Although individual journalists by the dozens have replaced their personal ignorance with understanding about the Middle East, their influence has hardly been felt in the mainstream U.S. media. Partly as a result of this, and even more because of the increasing vulnerability of our legislative processes to corruption by immense quantities of "lobby" money, Members of Congress seem ever less-inclined to represent the interests of their own constituents in Middle Eastern matters. These interests, it is obvious to me, are maintenance of constructive relations with *all* moderate, like-minded nations through adherence to our own moral traditions and scrupulous respect for international law, human rights, self-determination and fair play. Above all, our interest is in a lasting Middle East peace.

I have been encouraged by one observation. First-hand acquaintance with the Middle East clarifies the thinking of virtually every intelligent American so exposed. Sometimes in only a few weeks or less, a life-time of misinformation, stereotyping and prejudice is swept away. I am well aware that every intelligent American citizen cannot have first hand exposure and that *I* cannot produce, in this book, the three-dimensional impact that seems to make even short-term personal visitors to the Middle East suddenly, blindingly, "see the light." But I can present, to the best of my ability, the facts I have learned about the U.S. and the Middle East in 30 continuous years of dealing with them. Perhaps they will help readers reach their own conclusions, and give them the courage to insist that their own voices be heard.

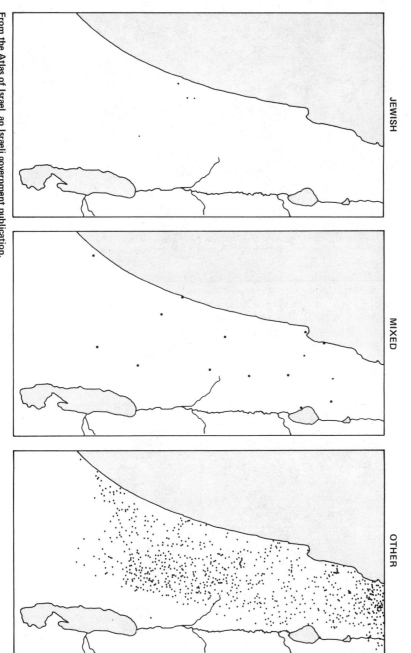

SETTLEMENTS, 1878

JEWISH

MIXED

OTHER

From the Atlas of Israel, an Israeli government publication.

Many turn-of-the-century Jewish immigrants who had been attracted by the Zionist promise of "a land without people for people without land" were chagrined to find Palestine already settled with Christian and Muslim villages. The indigenous Palestinians were descended not only from the seventh century A.D. Muslim Arab conquerors but from Christian Byzantines, Romans, Greeks, Persians, Hebrews, Philistines, Caananites, Amorites and even earlier inhabitants of a land that has been continuously occupied since the stone age. These photos, taken between 1900 and 1920, show an Arab village (above) surrounded by citrus and olive trees, and an Arab man and his daughter picking Jaffa oranges.

Acknowledgments

In the fall of 1956, after foreign service tours in Europe and the Far East and while preparing in Washington for my first Middle Eastern assignment, I underwent the "revelation" familiar to nearly every American who becomes involved in Middle Eastern affairs. In a year that encompassed U.S. withdrawal of support for Egypt's Aswan Dam, President Nasser's nationalization of the Suez Canal, the surprise Israeli, French and British attack on Egypt, and President Eisenhower's bold intervention to stop it, I was stunned by the contrast between what I read in the diplomatic telegraphic traffic from the Middle East on the one hand, and in the U.S. press on the other. Even more surprising was the contrast between the scholarly orientation material I was reading on the Middle East and virtually all of my preconceptions. I had imagined an area of hostile, volatile people dominated by irrationally anti-American mobs. I learned instead about more than a century of uniformly harmonious and productive cooperation between Americans and Arabs that had brought great benefits to both. I had not merely been ignorant about the region, I had been shockingly misinformed.

Upon arrival in the Middle East, I found that my American foreign service colleagues there bore special burdens. In my previous experience, colleagues had generally approved of American policies in the areas in which they served. Helping to explain and carry out such policies had been something of a holy crusade for us all. In the Middle East, however, the atmosphere was totally different. Patriotic American foreign service officers there considered our developing policies a prescription for disaster. Their efforts were devoted to compiling evidence that U.S. policy should be reconsidered in Washington before it was too late. Although there was not unanimity concerning responsibility for the tragic cycle of violence that already had claimed so many lives in the Middle East, there was general agreement that blind American partisanship on the side of the Israelis was complicating efforts to settle the problems underlying that violence. Most unsettling to Americans in the Middle East at that time was the one-sided picture of events that Americans at home received from the American media, and sometimes from official American statements, particularly during national election campaigns.

Some foreign service officers, not liking what they saw, completed their tours and transferred to other areas. Others, however, steeped themselves in knowledge of the area so that, while they might be ignored, they could not be refuted when they spoke out to correct American public misperceptions of the area, its peoples, and their problems. Long association with such foreign service officers in the Middle East, who repeatedly have put their country's interest ahead of their own career advancement, has been one of the most inspiring aspects of my foreign service career. Conversations with such colleagues, and with the American educators, businessmen, missionaries and journalists in the Middle East who fought similar battles within their own disciplines, reinforced my own deep misgivings and strengthened my determination not to acquiesce silently in actions that I perceived to be against the best interests of the people of the United States.

It is, therefore, those thoughtful and patriotic colleagues and associates who have inspired this book. To name them would in many cases do them a disservice. They know who they are. I am deeply indebted to them all, as all Americans should be.

Parts of this manuscript took shape after I had served as Deputy Director in the U.S. Information Agency's office of Near East, North African and South Asian Affairs and during an assignment to the Department of State's Executive Seminar in National and International Affairs. My case study for that assignment provided me the opportunity to visit government agencies, journalists, embassies, universities, think tanks, and lobbying groups concerned with the Israeli-Palestinian problem. Thanks to recommendations and introductions developed during such conversations in Washington, I then was able to visit Middle East and public opinion specialists throughout the United States for more off-the-record conversations.

In 1980 I retired from my last foreign service assignment as Chief Inspector of the U.S. Information Agency. With the active encouragement of former foreign service colleagues, I then set out to turn my case study into this book. I have donated both the first and second editions to the American Educational Trust, a non-profit foundation dedicated to furthering mutual understanding between Americans and Middle Easterners and headed by my friend and colleague of more than 20 years, Andrew I. Killgore, former U.S. Ambassador to the State of Qatar.

Friends have asked why my wife, Donna Bourne Curtiss, and I undertook a task that, based on the experiences of other Americans, may expose us to personal and professional harassment. My wife, who shared all of the formative years, accompanied me on all of the travels for this book, analyzed the findings and critiqued my presentations of them, prepared the index, typed much of the first edition and entered and coded all of the second edition on a word processor, has devoted thousands of hours to the thankless tasks that made publication of both editions possible. She spoke for us both when she responded that we had no choice.

Our four children spent most of their formative years in the Middle East, and all came to terms with the fact that their foreign friends often blamed the United States for the tragedies that occurred around them. Each, however, remained aware of the extraordinary basic decency and fairness of the American public. If Americans at home perceived Middle Eastern events differently than did Americans who grew up in the Middle East, our children were willing to ascribe the differences to lack of accurate information, not to lack of human compassion.

Our youngest son, Raymond Holden (Denny) Curtiss, having lived most of his first 13 years overseas, had developed an intense patriotism that perhaps only other young expatriates can fully understand. He hoped for a military or civilian career with the U.S. government. Having personally experienced some of the tragedy of lives and dreams wasted in the Lebanese Civil War, he was also an extraordinarily concerned and idealistic person. He directed his hard-earned dollars to the causes of wildlife conservation and wilderness preservation, and his thoughts and actions to the creation of international understanding to avert future wars.

In high school in Virginia he was bothered by the fact that even his closest American friends had some of the same biases and hostilities toward Arabs that his Middle Eastern friends had had toward Americans. He brought some of those American high school students to talk with me about it. After one such session, to prepare Denny and his friends to represent Jordan in a mock United Nations debate, they told him it was the first time they had realized the Israeli-Palestinian problem could be solved peacefully and that there were moderate and reasonable people on both sides capable of doing it.

"Dad," Denny said that night, "you should write a book so that other people can read some of the things you told my friends."

"I'll try," I promised, "when I have the time to do it."

"Okay," he answered, "but what if by then it's too late?"

A very few months after that conversation, Denny was killed in an accident. If it now is too late for him to read this book, it is not for other Americans like the concerned friends who meant so much to him. So this book is for Denny from both of his parents: A promise kept, and perhaps not altogether too late.

SETTLEMENTS
BY TYPE AND NUMBER OF INHABITANTS
1931

▲ JEWISH   ● NON-JEWISH

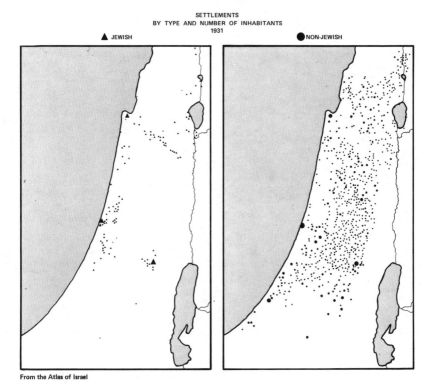

From the Atlas of Israel

Above, General Allenby leads the British army into Jerusalem during World War I, ending four centuries of Turkish rule. The British column pictured had pushed north along the coast from Egypt while Arab irregulars harassed inland Turkish Army outposts and communications in a campaign that became familiar to two generations of British and American readers through the writings of Lawrence of Arabia. Below, Sir Herbert Samuel, British Governor General, poses in 1925 with heads of religious communities in Jerusalem.

Contents

1. Why Perceptions Matter   **1**
2. President Wilson's Fourteen Points and the Palestine Mandate   **11**
3. President Roosevelt and the European Holocaust   **21**
4. President Truman and the Creation of Israel   **27**
5. President Truman's Second Term and Post-Partum Depression   **35**
6. President Eisenhower and the Build-up to Suez   **39**
7. President Eisenhower's Second Term
   and the Coca Cola Invasion   **53**
8. President Kennedy and Good Intentions Deferred Too Long   **63**
9. President Johnson and the Six-Day War   **71**
10. An Awkwardness for President Johnson   **87**
11. President Nixon and the Rogers Plan   **101**
12. The War of Attrition   **109**
13. The Build-up to October   **115**
14. The October War   **123**
15. Ceasefire, Cheating and Confrontation   **141**
16. Step by Step from President Nixon to President Ford   **151**
17. President Carter and a Christian Approach   **165**
18. Camp David   **185**
19. After Camp David   **195**
20. President Reagan and Strategic Consensus   **203**
21. The Invasion of Lebanon   **219**
22. The Reagan Plan   **237**
23. The Revolt of the Moderates   **249**
24. A Word About Lobbies – Carrots and Sticks   **261**
25. The Israel Lobby – Where Goliath Works for Little David   **267**
26. Jewish Dissenters – Cranks or Prophets?   **273**
27. The Arab Lobby – Wherever It Is   **279**
28. American Business and the Arab Cause   **289**
29. Arab Diplomatic Activities   **295**
30. Christian Churches – Peace or Armageddon?   **299**
31. The Media – Copout or Conspiracy?   **307**
32. The Universities – The Great Fear   **327**
33. Congress – For Sale or Rent   **339**
    Appendix: The Evidence of the Polls, 1946-1986   **355**

PLO

Bloodshed begins. Above, British troops disperse Palestinian protest demonstration in old city of Jerusalem in 1928. Below, David Ben Gurion speaks to newly-arrived Jewish immigrants in Jerusalem in 1924

Zionist Archives

CHAPTER I

Why Perceptions Matter

"Since the war in 1973 the United States has agreed to over $10 billion in military and economic support for Israel. Under the Carter Administration, one fifth of all our economic and military assistance around the world has come to this nation. In next year's budget, nearly half of all our sales credits and grants will go to Israel. This is an unprecedented amount, but we have no regrets."[1]

Vice President Walter F. Mondale, July 5, 1978
(address in Jerusalem)

"Four Arab-Israeli wars have not only brought bloodshed and untold suffering to the peoples of the Middle East, they have also cost the United States and the rest of the world incalculable billions. At several points the conflict has threatened world peace itself."[2]

Ambassador-at-Large Alfred L. Atherton, Jr., April 3, 1979

"One miscalculation and the flames of war could sweep the entire Mideast region. And it is not known how far the sparks of this fire could scatter."[3]

Leonid I. Brezhnev, May 22, 1981

"From the time of Israel's founding, the United States has served as its indulgent protector. In the past four years alone we have provided assistance exceeding $11 billion. Our current annual subsidy of over $2 billion (the equivalent of more than $3,500 a

---

1. Mondale, Vice President Walter F., in remarks at State Dinner, Israeli Knesset, Jerusalem, July, 5, 1978.
2. Atherton, Alfred L., Jr., Assistant Secretary of State for Near Eastern and South Asian Affairs, in address entitled "Examination of U.S. Vital Interests in the Middle East" before the World Affairs Council of Pittsburgh, Pa., April 3, 1979.
3. Brezhnev, Leonid I., Chairman, Presidium of the Supreme Soviet, USSR, in remarks broadcast from Georgian Soviet Republic, May 22, 1981.

year for each Israeli family of five) is . . . one of our few sacrosanct budget items. In addition to official aid from American taxpayers, Israel receives massive sums from its generous American friends.[4]

Former U.S. Under Secretary of State
George Ball, June 15, 1981

"If all forms of support are lumped together, Israel draws somewhere around $10 billion a year from the U.S. and its citizens."[5]

Joseph C. Harsch, August 11, 1983

"Regular FY 1986 U.S. aid to Israel will total at least $3.75 billion: $1.8 billion in military credits, $1.2 billion in economic aid and $750 million in the form of a supplemental cash transfer. Israel will get from the U.S. during the next fiscal year $400 million more than it got in FY 1985, and a whopping $1.14 billion more than it got in FY 1984. Furthermore, all of the FY 1986 aid is in so-called 'forgiven' loans, which is another way of saying that the Israeli government does not have to repay them."[6]

Dennis Wamsted, December 2, 1985

These statements illustrate the extraordinary nature of America's relationship with Israel, and hint at its significance to American relationships with the rest of the world. Although, as Ambassador Atherton says, the Arab-Israeli wars have cost the United States and the rest of the world "incalculable billions," the costs of direct U.S. government assistance to Israel *can* be calculated. Between 1949 and September 30, 1986 Israel, with some three million Jewish citizens in residence there, will have received more than $35 billion ($35,684,000,000) in direct U.S. government grants and loans. This means that every man, woman and child in the U.S. has contributed $159 toward a total of $11,897 per Israeli. Or, to follow George Ball's example above, each American family of five has contributed $795 to subsidize each Israeli family of five to the tune of $59,485.

These figures do not include the substantial losses to the U.S. treasury from tax-free contributions by U.S. citizens to Israel, probably a larger item in Israel's earlier years than were direct U.S. treasury grants and loans. Neither do these totals reflect the rapidly accelerating rate of U.S. payments to Israel. Of the nearly $36 billion allocated to Israel in the first 37 years of its existence, more than $11 billion was allocated within the last four years. The FY 1986 direct U.S. government contribution has reached some $1,250 per Jewish Israeli.

The 1980 Presidential election campaign was conducted against a background of local tax revolts and a one trillion dollar national debt. It culminated in massive but totally unsuccessful efforts to balance the federal budget by cutting non-military expenditures. The 1984 campaign was overshadowed by a massive U.S. national debt, rapidly approaching an incomprehensible two trillion dollars. It might seem remarkable,

4. Ball, George W., former U.S. Under Secretary of State, *Washington Post*, June 15, 1981.
5. Harsch, Joseph C., *Christian Science Monitor*, August 11, 1983.
6. Wamsted, Dennis, *Washington Report on Middle East Affairs*, December 2, 1985.

therefore, that during those campaigns, no Presidential and few Congressional candidates mentioned that a country with less than one tenth of one per cent of the world's population was, in the last year of the Carter Administration, receiving more than 22 per cent of total direct U.S. foreign assistance, and substantial additional amounts via various government subsidies and tax-exempt donations. Instead, after the advent of the Reagan Administration, Israel's military aid total was significantly increased. Clearly, the relationship with Israel flows outside the current of normal partisan politics. Throughout the past decade each administration, whether Republican or Democratic, has regularly increased Israel's aid total, while also increasing its assistance to neighboring countries willing to keep the peace with Israel, particularly Jordan and Egypt. This in turn brings the percentage of U.S. aid devoted directly to Israel or to its immediate neighbors close to 40 per cent of the total world-wide American military and economic foreign assistance effort.

What is the explanation for this uncomplaining acceptance by taxpayers and their elected representatives of a heavy, rapidly-increasing, and obviously perilous burden of support for Israel? Most Americans would unhesitatingly answer that they support Israel because it is the right thing to do. In fact, over the years many — perhaps most — Americans have maintained that the U.S. has a "moral obligation" to protect Israel, regardless of cost, from destruction at the hands of its neighbors.

There have always been some American critics of Israel who question both the morality of and the obligation for American support. They contend that the Jewish state in Palestine was founded with total disregard for the rights and welfare of the Arab majority which then inhabited the land, and that the sense of obligation has been built up in the United States only by many years of intense media manipulation and political pressure. When such objections to the idea of a U.S. "moral obligation" are raised, Israel's defenders are less likely to defend the premise than to shift to a second rationale for extensive U.S. support of Israel. For many years this rationale concerned Israel's image as an embattled "friendly democracy" surrounded by hostile and unstable dictatorships. Very recently, and particularly under Republican administrations, it has been suggested that the U.S. has a "strategic interest" in defending Israel. The implication is that states hostile to Israel are also likely to be hostile to the U.S., and that Israel thus somehow has a role in keeping them at bay on behalf of the United States. This explanation, however, does not withstand scrutiny. The American tradition of friendly relations with all the major Arab states, as well as with the Ottoman Empire which once administered most of them, goes back without interruption for more than a century and a half. The only significant issues of contention between the U.S. and any major Arab countries in this century have all in one way or another derived from U.S. support for Israel. In short, the U.S. had no enemies in the Middle East or in the Islamic world until it sponsored the creation of a Jewish state in a land occupied by Muslim and Christian Arabs.

What is remarkable, then, is that for 38 years Americans have willingly shouldered the burdens of supporting Israel, at steadily and rapidly-increasing costs to themselves, regardless of the shifting circumstances in the Middle East and without ever reaching a national consensus on specific reasons for this militarily and politically perilous support.

A foreigner, seeking to make sense of the variety of conflicting explanations offered, could be forgiven for examining the common political interest or "strategic ally" explanations first. Would a great power, locked in a hideously expensive, frequently bloody, and seemingly endless struggle with the Soviet Union for world-wide power and influence, commit so much of its military and financial capability to the support of Israel except for political or military advantage? One way to approach this question is through the writings of American experts over the past several years.

Perhaps predictably, a critic of Israel, Professor Alan R. Taylor of American University, asserts that America's support for Israel is not a political advantage, but a liability. He writes:

"The political cost of America's special relationship with Israel has been to place in serious jeopardy the political leverage of the United States in an area of primary strategic and economic importance. The relationship has also placed a far greater strain on the Soviet-American search for detente than any other factor in contemporary international affairs. In these respects, Israel is more of a liability than an asset and there is an imperative need for the United States to re-evaluate what it is getting – or losing – from its patronage of Israel."[7]

Even a sympathetic observer of Israel, Professor Robert Tucker of Johns Hopkins University, notes that although Israel's dependence upon the U.S. is increasing, the common political interests of the two countries are diminishing. He writes:

"The congruence of interests that might make so increasingly dependent a relationship tolerable – if never desirable – no longer exists. Indeed, it has never really existed, though it more nearly approximated the ideal in earlier years."[8]

Still more bluntly, shortly before Egyptian President Sadat's death, syndicated columnist Joseph Kraft assessed the consequences to the United States of Israel's political course under Prime Minister Menachem Begin. Kraft, an occasional critic of Begin but no enemy of Israel, wrote:

"As matters now stand, Begin threatens American ties with moderate states, especially Saudi Arabia. He could drive Egyptian President Sadat away from the peace accord with Israel, and force Syria further into Soviet arms. Even war cannot be excluded."[9]

Both friends and foes of Israel seem to agree that America's popular, but expensive, special relationship with Israel is not based upon common political interests, and is in fact a growing political liability to the United States. Therefore, foreigners schooled in the maxim that in international relations there are "no friendships, only interests" may be pardoned for assuming that if the U.S. does not subsidize Israel for political

---

7. Taylor, Alan R., Professor of International Relations at The American University, Washington, D.C., "The Meaning of U.S. Aid to Israel," published by the National Association of Arab Americans.
8. Tucker, Robert W., Professor of International Relations at Johns Hopkins University, "Israel and the United States: From Dependence to Nuclear Weapons?", *Commentary*, November 1975, p. 30.
9. Kraft, Joseph, *Washington Post*, July 14, 1981.

advantages, it must do so for military purposes. Both influential Republicans and Democrats have made statements to this effect. For example, in a 1977 article, Dr. Eugene V. Rostow, Under Secretary of State in the Johnson Administration from 1966 to 1969, defined a "strategic" motive for supporting Israel:

"(I)f we face, as we may, a showdown some day with the oil-producing states, Israel would be an indispensable ally. In addition, Israel is the only sure access point we have between Western Europe and our partners in the Far East, Australia, New Zealand, Korea and Japan."[10]

The validity of this thinking is as questionable now as it was then. The Arab oil producers are dependent upon U.S. allies in Western Europe and Japan to purchase their oil, and these same Arab oil producers are major markets for U.S. exports. Therefore the only conceivable cause of a "showdown" would be U.S. support for Israel.

Edward Sheehan is an author and Middle East expert with little affinity for the kind of thinking represented by the Rostow quotation. He indicates, however, that there was also a "strategic" motive in U.S. support for Israel in the minds of at least some officials of the first Nixon Administration. This was between 1969 and 1972 when Henry Kissinger was President Nixon's national security adviser, before Kissinger became Secretary of State and assumed the dominant role in U.S. Middle Eastern policy. Sheehan writes:

"Kissinger accepted and in fact helped to promote the conventional strategic wisdom of the first Nixon Administration—that, in the absence of fruitful negotiations, a strong Israel, militarily much superior to its Arab foes, would prevent war and serve as the surest sentinel of American interests in the Middle East."[11]

Kissinger himself later wrote, however, that Nixon believed it was the harsh treatment of the Arabs by John Foster Dulles that had enabled the Soviet Union to get a foothold in the Middle East, and achievement of an Arab-Israeli peace was the best way to edge the Soviets back out of the area.

Therefore, whatever the conventional wisdom of the era prior to the October 1973 war, by 1975 Dr. Tucker, despite his sympathy for Israel, was prepared to dismiss Israel's "strategic" value to the U.S. as categorically as he dismissed its political value. He wrote:

"In the best of circumstances Israel is not an attractive ally, and the present circumstances are evidently not the best."[12]

In 1979 George Ball, Under Secretary of State in the Kennedy and Johnson Administrations from 1961 to 1966 and U.S. Ambassador to the UN in 1968, took this view of American strategic interests in the Middle East:

10. Rostow, Eugene V., Former Under Secretary of State, in "The American Stake in Israel.", *Commentary*, April 1977, p. 37.
11. Sheehan, Edward, Harvard University Research Fellow, in "Step by Step in the Middle East," *Foreign Policy*, Spring 1976, pp. 8-9.
12. Tucker, Robert W., "Israel and the United States: From Dependence to Nuclear Weapons?" *Commentary*, November, 1975, p. 38.

"We need to keep the Middle East out of the communist orbit. That requires not only that there be peace between Israel and the Arab world, but that we avoid those divisive issues that set Arab states against one another, and thus invite them to play one superpower against the other . . . So long as Iran was governed by the Shah, who was friendly to Israel, it was at least arguable that the military power of Israel, in tandem with Iran's, was a general force for stability. Today, however, with Iran in a militantly anti-Israeli posture that is unlikely soon to change, there is no possibility whatever of Israel playing any useful part in the direct military or strategic sense. The blunt fact then is that so long as it seems to be seeking to consolidate its hold on the West Bank for the long term, its impact on the stability of the Middle East will be wholly negative."[13]

Most such assessments dating to the end of the Carter Administration agreed that Israel was a net strategic, as well as political, liability to the U.S. The Reagan Administration, however, initially signaled a new attitude. On February 13, 1981, only a month after he assumed office, the new U.S. Secretary of State's approach to the Middle East was bluntly described in the *Washington Post* by the syndicated columnists, Rowland Evans and Robert Novak:

"(Alexander) Haig looks at Israel not in terms of American constituency-group politics but as an American ally with strategic strength to offer Washington, much like Saudi Arabia and other U.S. allies in the Arab world."[14]

Only four months later, after Menachem Begin had taken advantage of the resuscitation of this concept of Israel as a U.S. "strategic ally" to pick fights with virtually every Arab nation friendly to the U.S., however, the Reagan Administration's newly-appointed Ambassador to the U.N., Jeane Kirkpatrick, declared:

"The security of this nation and our allies is bound up with the peace and security of the Middle East. Our own broad foreign policy interests do not permit us to ignore the interests and sensibilities of Egypt, Saudi Arabia, Jordan and other states in the area. Neither do we desire to do so."[15]

Therefore, when a U.S.-Israel "strategic cooperation agreement" was announced in October, 1981, a month after the assassination of President Anwar Sadat of Egypt, it was Israel that had pressed hard for what was simply a reluctant U.S. payoff to induce Israel to follow through on its final Sinai withdrawal commitment under the Camp David treaty with Egypt.

The divergence in interests is as apparent to Israeli leaders as it is to their U.S. counterparts. On December 15, 1981, after Israel stunned the U.S. by "annexing" territory it had taken in 1967 and 1973 from Syria, Israeli Foreign Minister Yitzhak Shamir brushed aside U.S. criticism that Israel's actions violated the fundamental principle of international law barring acquisition of territory by force of arms by saying:

---

13. Ball, George W., "The Coming Crisis in Israeli-American Relations," *Foreign Affairs*, Winter 1979/80, p. 250.
14. Evans, Rowland and Novak, Robert, *Washington Post*, February 13, 1981.
15. Kirkpatrick, Jeane, U.S. Ambassador to the United Nations, in remarks on June 21, 1981.

"Much as we want to coordinate our activities with the United States, the interests are not identical. We have to, from time to time, worry about our own interests." [16]

Regardless of changes in both American and Israeli leadership, the strategic, military, and political facts have remained immutable for several years. Israel is a country literally too small to contain a U.S. military base that could not be neutralized in short order by Soviet weapons from adjacent Arab lands or Mediterranean waters. The Israeli army, though superbly trained, equipped, and motivated, demonstrated in 1973 that it cannot sustain a full-scale war against its Arab neighbors for more than a few days without almost total resupply from the outside. Even in the absence of open hostilities, Israel cannot maintain full mobilization for much more than a month without bringing the economy to a halt. Moreover, so long as Israel's political problems with the Palestinians and its Arab neighbors remain unresolved, American use of Israeli facilities or support of an Israeli military effort would seriously undermine U.S. relations with most or all of 21 members of the League of Arab States. These states extend in a 5,000-mile belt from the Straits of Gibralter to the Straits of Hormuz, straddling air and sea routes between Europe and Africa, and between Western Europe and South and East Asia. A simple glance at the map confirms that, until Israel and its Middle Eastern neighbors compose their differences, the strategic advantages in the bilateral U.S.-Israel relationship accrue to Israel, not to the U.S.

If, then, even Israel's faithful friends admit an increasing divergence between U.S. and Israeli political interests, and cannot substantiate vague statements that Israel is a "strategic asset" by explaining how the relationship could confer a net political or strategic advantage upon the U.S., then the real basis of American support for Israel must lie elsewhere.

Friends of Israel might cite consistent and overwhelming support from virtually all segments of U.S. public opinion for an "outpost of democracy" in the Middle East. In the words of Washington Director Hyman Bookbinder of the American Jewish Committee:

"Israel's cause is in substantially good shape today not because of the 2 percent of Americans who are Jewish and have demonstrated their support for Israel, but because another 50 or 60 or 70 percent of non-Jewish Americans have manifested this support." [17]

Skeptics describe "persistent and increasing domestic political activity" by American Jewish organizations on behalf of Israel. In the words of *Washington Post* columnist Philip Geyelin:

"U.S. aid to Israel gets bigger every year, systematically, thanks to an endlessly energetic Israeli lobby." [18]

---

16. Claiborne, William, "Israel Moves to Smoothe Ties with U.S., Others After Golan Action," *Washington Post*, December 16,1981.
17. Bookbinder, Hyman, statement at 54th General Assembly of the Council of Jewish Federations, reported in Jewish Telegraph Agency daily bulletin for November 21, 1985.
18. Geyelin, Philip, "One Too Many Gifts for Israel?," *Washington Post*, November 11, 1985.

Both viewpoints have merit. The polls attest to the former. Candidates for national elective office attest to the latter. In every state and in a majority of Congressional districts, large blocs of influential Americans can be organized rapidly to protest in harsh and politically damaging terms any signs of wavering support for Israel. They can also reward or punish initiatives concerning Israel by increasing or withholding campaign contributions. Bloc votes in key industrial states can influence Presidential elections, sometimes decisively.

How has such overwhelming public support and political influence been developed? Is it largely due to the commitment, energy, and high achievement of America's Jewish citizens, who number a little more than six million people, but less than three per cent of a national population of nearly 240 million? Or can it be attributed largely to the sentiments of other Americans: Democrats and Republicans, Catholics and Protestants, old and young, Northerners, Southerners and Westerners, who rarely turn their attention to the Middle East, but who will always lean toward an Israel they perceive as having been born out of the Holocaust that wiped out European Jewry, shaped by the lonely struggle for an independent Jewish state, and tempered in five wars?

Expert opinion supports both views. In an article in *Commentary*, the monthly organ of the American Jewish Committee, a political scientist, Earl Raab, emphasizes the support of the general public. He writes:

"The fulcrum of popular American support for Israel has nothing to do with Israel as a Jewish state, It is, rather, the belief that Israel is a small democratic nation which is trying to preserve its independence." [19]

Also writing in *Commentary*, Professor Seymour Martin Lipset, a long-time close observer of U.S. public attitudes toward Israel, and Professor William Schneider of Harvard University emphasize the key role of Zionist organization:

"The only 'veto group' in the American electorate concerned with the Middle East is composed of those dedicated to the survival of Israel. This group, which includes almost all Jews along with many non-Jews, has been ready to bombard Congressmen and the administration with letters, telegrams, phone calls and personal visits to present their case. Many of them have been willing to contribute generously to the campaign funds of politicians who support Israel. Conversely, they will vote against those who oppose Israel, a fact of which office-holders are well aware." [20]

In *The Nation*, journalist David Caploe writes that the most important element of American public opinion support for Israel is "a widely and deeply held perception

---

19. Raab, Earl, "Is Israel Losing Popular Support? The Evidence of the Polls," *Commentary*, January, 1974, p. 27.
20. Lipset, Seymour Martin, Professor of Political Science and Sociology and Senior Fellow of the Hoover Institution, Stanford University, and Schneider, William, Associate Professor at Harvard University, "Carter vs Israel: What the Polls Reveal," *Commentary*, November 1977, p. 29.

of Israel's reasonableness, moderation and desire for peace, contrasted with the extremism, bellicosity and irrational blood lust of the Arabs."[21]

Other observers cite negative reactions by the American public to the sometimes shrill tones of third world critics of the U.S. in general, and to traditional Arab hyperbole in particular, as an important element in U.S. public support for Israel. In an interview in the *Journal of Palestine Studies*, veteran Washington journalist James McCartney cites "differences between the essentially European culture of Israel and Arab culture," noting that in America "for the most part Arabs have not really been understood very well."[22]

Even more succinctly, Rabbi Arnold Jacob Wolf, a prominent Jewish critic of present Israeli policy, notes in the American Jewish newsletter, *Sh'ma*, that "The PLO has also worked hard to make Begin's intransigence credible and legitimate."[23]

It appears that the authors of these varying assessments, like most persons closely concerned with U.S. Middle Eastern policy, see the strong U.S. military, economic, and political support of Israel directly linked, through effective domestic political activity, to the strong pro-Israel sentiment that has traditionally dominated U.S. public opinion.

Experts may still disagree whether U.S. policy vis-a-vis the Arab-Israeli dispute is in America's self-interest. The point on which virtually all do agree, however, is that self-interest is not the factor motivating that American policy. The critical factor, from the creation of Israel to the present day, has been a strong pro-Israel bias in American public opinion. To understand that bias, it is appropriate to review the historical record, its American interpreters, and the U.S. opinion polls to see how American perceptions of the Arab-Israeli dispute developed, what they are today, and where they may be moving.

21. Caploe, David, Fellow of the Trans-National Institute, "New Look at Israel," *The Nation*, July 23, 1977, p. 71.
22. Ghareeb, Edmund, excerpts from interview with James McCartney, Knight Newspapers, in "American Media and the Palestine Problem," *Journal of Palestine Studies*, Autumn 1975/Winter 1976, p. 138.
23. Wolf, Rabbi Arnold Jacob, "Israel – The Futility of Dissent," *Sh'ma: A Journal of Jewish Responsibility*, November 30, 1979, p. 9.

From 1936 to 1939 the Arab inhabitants of Palestine revolted against what they perceived as Britain's betrayal of its World War I pledges to the Arabs and its seeming acquiescence in Zionist plans to turn Palestine into a Jewish state. In these two 1936 photos, Palestinian Arab villagers and gendarmes pose with a variety of weapons at the beginning of the fighting while (below) British soldiers patrol in Haifa.

Zionist Archives

CHAPTER II

President Wilson's Fourteen Points and the Palestinian Mandate

"His Majesty's Government view with favor the establishment in Palestine of a national home for the Jewish people . . . it being clearly understood that nothing shall be done which may prejudice the civil and religious rights of the existing non-Jewish communities in Palestine, or the rights and political status enjoyed by Jews in any other country."
British Foreign Secretary Arthur Balfour in letter
to Lord Lionel Rothschild, November 2, 1917

"The other nationalities which are now under Turkish rule should be assured an undoubted security of life and absolutely unmolested opportunity of autonomous development."
Twelfth of President Wilson's Fourteen Points
promulgated to the U.S. Congress, January 8, 1918

"It was the anti-Semitism of continental Europe in the nineteenth century that turned the minds of modern, secular Jews towards the Holy Land and aroused in them the desire to create not only a 'spiritual centre' but a Jewish nation. The founder of modern Zionism was the Viennese journalist Theodor Herzl, who created the Zionist Organization in 1897. He believed that the institution of a Jewish nation in Palestine would solve the Jewish problem, put an end to anti-Semitism, and unite the Jews of all countries in a semi-religious, semi-political homogeneity. His ideas of practical politics were nebulous, and he never seems to have faced the fact that the country was already inhabited by a settled population that had been there for thirteen hundred years."[1]
Vincent Sheean, 1935

---

1. Sheean, Vincent, *Personal History*, Doubleday, New York, 1935.

11

"No other problem of our time is so deeply rooted in the past."
Report of the Peel Royal Commission
to Palestine, 1937

"The passions aroused by Palestine have done so much to obscure the truth that the facts have become enveloped in a mist of sentiment, legend and propaganda, which acts as a smokescreen of almost impenetrable density."[2]
George Antonius, 1938

Israelis believe that a Jewish presence remained in Palestine even after the Jewish revolt in 135 A.D. that led to Roman destruction of the Second Temple; throughout the subsequent occupations of Palestine by Christian Byzantines, Muslim Arabs, and Crusaders; and then during a succession of Muslim dynasties that culminated in four centuries of Ottoman Turkish rule. Arabs dispute the continuity of this presence, citing the massacres of both Muslims and Jews by the Crusaders as examples of periods when Jews would have had to vacate Palestine in order to avoid annihilation. Both sides agree, however, that before the late 19th century the Jewish presence in Palestine was minute. There were tiny, impoverished colonies of Orthodox Jews, almost totally dependent upon donations from fellow Jews in the European diaspora; and perhaps a few Sephardic Jews, whose ancestors had been expelled from Spain in 1492, found sanctuary under the Ottomans, and established relatively prosperous communities in various parts of the far-flung Ottoman Empire.

A return to the Promised Land has figured prominently in Jewish rituals and prayers through the ages. The modern political Zionist movement that made a large-scale return a reality dates, however, only to 1896, when an Austrian Jewish journalist, Theodor Herzl, made the somewhat obscure Zionist cause his own. Although he was not personally religious and was well integrated into his own society, Herzl was profoundly shocked at the anti-Semitism he saw manifested in France in the course of the infamous Dreyfus affair. He concluded that, if such virulent anti-Semitism could arise in the first European country to grant Jews the full rights of citizenship, there was little hope for Jews anywhere until they obtained a land of their own. His message was not popular with the integrated Jews of Western Europe, and particularly not with the most successful members of Jewish communities in those countries, but Herzl's charismatic leadership caught the imagination of many Jews in Eastern Europe just at a time when Czarist pogroms were driving large numbers of Jews out of their communities in Russia and Poland. The vast majority of these displaced Jews were emigrating to the United States. Small groups went to Palestine, however, supplementing the earlier Jewish religious colonies, where they began heavily subsidized experiments with new agricultural crops and techniques.

Zionism's slogan was "a land without a people for a people without a land." However, the Jews of Zionism's "First Aliyah" who began arriving in the late 19th century found

---

2. Antonius, George, *The Arab Awakening*, London, 1938.

that the slogan was based on a false premise: The land in question was already inhabited by a half million Muslim and Christian Arabs. Although most were living at the subsistence level under administrators who had grown increasingly corrupt and venal as the once-powerful Ottoman Empire decayed, their natural rate of increase vastly exceeded the early trickle of Zionist settlers.

Nevertheless, starting in 1905, the year of Herzl's death, the influx of Jewish immigrants increased as revolutionary movements were put down by the Czarist authorities. Numerous disappointed young idealists, inspired more by political Socialism than by religious Judaism, began arriving in Palestine. This "Second Aliyah" increased the Jewish population of Palestine from 23,000 in 1882 to some 80,000 at the outbreak of World War I in 1914. It also set the political and moral tone in Israel for generations to come. Until the Begin era, virtually all of Israel's incumbent leaders traced their origins to the "Second Aliyah" immigration of young political activists from 1905 to 1914.

Leadership of the World Zionist movement was assumed during World War I by Dr. Chaim Weizmann, a brilliant British chemist of Russian Jewish origin. He was a flexible and effective political tactician whose faith in moderation, and in his own ability to obtain a Jewish homeland in Palestine from the British government, never wavered. He developed many allies in the British establishment, among both Britain's increasingly influential Jewish community and British Christians. Many of the latter, including Winston Churchill, shared the almost mystical belief current in 19th century British literature that Britain was somehow destined to help the Jews find their way to their Promised Land in Palestine. Prominent Britons, Jewish and Christian, who supported Zionist goals for purely religious or philosophical reasons, became adept at offering pragmatic explanations of why attaining those goals would also be in the British national interest. This phenomenon, so familiar in the United States today, is clearly illustrated in the debates which accompanied the Balfour Declaration. This was the pledge in 1917 by British Foreign Secretary Arthur Balfour to a private British Jew, Lord Lionel Walter Rothschild, that the British government "view with favor the establishment in Palestine of a national home for the Jewish people . . . it being clearly understood that nothing shall be done which may prejudice the civil and religious rights of the existing non-Jewish communities in Palestine. . . ."

The Declaration was justified to skeptical members of Parliament (and to strong opponents among Britain's Jewish community who feared it could jeopardize the relatively secure status of Britain's Jewish subjects) by Lord Balfour, an enthusiastic supporter of Zionism, on shifting grounds. In earlier, unsuccessful drafts, it had been presented as a shrewd step to ensure support for the Allied war effort not only by the large Jewish communities of Europe, but also by the newly-important Jewish community of the United States. It was argued that American Jews, given their strong antipathy to Czarist Russia, from which so many had recently fled, might oppose America's entry into the war on the Allied side. The promise of a national home for the Jews in Palestine if the Allies won might help neutralize that opposition. However, by the time the Balfour Declaration was formally promulgated in 1917, America had already entered the war on the Allied side, and the proponents of Zionism had smoothly shifted to a new rationale. They said that a strong, European-oriented Jewish community in proximity to the Suez

Canal would protect that lifeline of the British Empire from interdiction by volatile and hostile local populations.

Strangely, in the long run, it was only the Arab community that really accepted this tortured "strategic" rationalization for the establishment of a Jewish homeland. In their subsequent efforts to oppose that homeland, alternating between periods of relatively meek submission to British authority and violent outbursts when they felt threatened by additional Jewish immigration, the Arabs always missed the key to the persistent support for Zionism in British political life. They alternately invoked or threatened British national interest in the Middle East, when a direct appeal to Britain's traditional sense of fair play might have been far more effective.

During and immediately after World War I, however, British fair play was little in evidence. The Balfour Declaration was only the last of three conflicting World War I commitments entered into by Britain during its campaign to defeat the Central Powers and their Turkish partner. The first was the secret Sykes-Picot agreement to divide the Ottoman Empire into spheres of influence administered by the European Allies. Russia's withdrawal from the war invalidated much of this agreement, which nevertheless left a residue of confusion concerning what international control had been planned for the various regions of Palestine. More important was the correspondence between Sir Henry McMahon, British High Commissioner in Egypt, and the Sherif Hussein, Guardian of the Muslim Holy Places in the Hejaz province of present-day Saudi Arabia. These letters formally promised British support for Arab independence in return for Arab support of the British war effort against the Turks. The pledges in the three sets of British documents were mutually irreconcilable, and the long story of British vacillation among the conflicting demands (again best known to westerners through the moral dilemma of the conscience-stricken Lawrence, who found himself playing an active role in his country's betrayal of its wartime Arab allies) is outside the scope of this study, except as American perceptions are involved.

In fact, Americans were involved at several stages as the backdrop of this century's Middle Eastern tragedies unfolded. American medical and educational missionaries had come to the Middle East in significant numbers starting in the 1820s. Some stayed only for a tour of duty and returned to the United States or left for other missions. Others spent a lifetime of service in the area. The result was a remarkable network of American schools that laid the foundations for the modern educational systems in several Middle Eastern countries, and the establishment of hospitals that endure to this day as some of the finest medical facilities in the world.

During World War I, such institutions in Palestine literally saved many of the indigenous communities from extinction by providing them with food and medicine. These were gathered not only through the sponsoring Christian religious institutions but also by an official U.S. government relief program administered under the direction of the U.S. Ambassador in Istanbul, Henry Morgenthau, Sr., a distinguished non-Zionist American Jew.

By the end of the war, as the irreconcilability of British and French purposes with local self-determination became apparent, both Arab and Turkish leaders sensed that President Wilson's Fourteen Points, promulgated to the U.S. Congress on January 8, 1918, held the best promise for the Arabs to achieve their independence, and for the Turks to retain theirs.

His twelfth point read: "The other nationalities which are now under Turkish rule should be assured an undoubted security of life and absolutely unmolested opportunity of autonomous development." Six months later, on July 4, 1918, he added the statement that every question should be settled "upon the basis of the free acceptance of that settlement by the people immediately concerned."

The faith of Middle Eastern leaders in Wilson's words on this score was reinforced by their own first-hand experiences during the preceding century with America's missionary and diplomatic representatives. (It is interesting to note that, during World War I, neither Turkey nor the United States declared war upon one another, despite Ottoman participation in the war on the side of the Central Powers and American participation on the side of the Allies.) These Middle Eastern leaders wanted America to accept League of Nations mandates to administer the area. But by then Wilson, weakened politically at home, was losing his battle to have the United States join the League. As a result, the U.S. retreated into an isolationism that was only ended by the 1941 attack on Pearl Harbor.

Britain's World War I pledge to the Sherif Hussein eventually was redeemed in part by the installation of two of his sons as rulers of Iraq and Jordan. Palestine, however, became a British Mandate. There the British doggedly tried to fulfill the obviously contradictory Balfour pledges to establish "a national home for the Jewish people" without prejudicing "the civil and religious rights of the existing non-Jewish communities in Palestine."

A relic of American involvement in the struggles of the time is the report of Dr. Henry C. King, president of Oberlin College, and Charles Crane, an American businessman. They were sent to the Middle East in 1919 by President Wilson with the approval of the Supreme Council of the Paris Peace Conference.

The King-Crane Commission report made grim reading, not only for Zionists, but also for British and French politicians planning to divide the area. The Americans found that the Arabs of Palestine wanted their homeland to remain part of Syria, with the Sherif Hussein's son Faisal as head of state. The King-Crane report warned against "the extreme Zionist program for Palestine of unlimited immigration of Jews looking finally to making Palestine a Jewish state." It concluded that, although some of the Zionist proposals were praiseworthy, implementing the Zionist plans as a whole would be unfair to the Arab majority and could only be effected by application of military force. The American report was ignored by Europe's "peacemakers," and not even made public until 1922.

The prescience of the King-Crane Commission was amply borne out by events throughout the Mandate period. There were widespread disturbances pitting Arab against Jew in 1920, 1921, and 1929.

A noted American writer, Vincent Sheean, who had gone to Palestine at the expense of the Zionist organization to write about the Jewish settlements, witnessed the 1929 riots. A moving chapter, entitled "Holy Land," in his *Personal History*, published in 1936, describes the horrors he saw; his subsequent testimony to a British commission of inquiry that they were deliberately provoked by Zionist militants, one of whom had confided the strategy to him in advance; and the eventual attempt by his erstwhile sponsors to discredit both his testimony and himself.

Early in his visit his words echoed those of his American predecessors on the King-Crane Commission. Sheean wrote in his diary:

"I am coming, or have already come, to two conclusions: that the difficulty of Zionism is essentially one thing only, its attempt to settle a country that is already settled; and second, that the Balfour Declaration is a document that really guarantees only one thing, the permanence of the British occupation of Palestine."[3]

Then, at the height of the disturbances, he reported: "However ferocious the Arab mobs might be, however ghastly the results of their fanatical fury, I could never lose sight of the fact that they had been goaded beyond endurance . . . If they had killed me by mistake during these days (as they easily might have done), I should have protested with my dying breath that it was not their fault. No matter how deeply I was moved by the sufferings of the Jews, I had to retain what intelligence nature and experience had given me; and that intelligence represented the disasters as a plain, inevitable result of the Zionist policy in an Arab country."[4]

Summarizing the experience, which brought about his temporary nervous collapse, and his permanent "deconversion" from Zionism, Sheean concluded:

"To fight anti-Semitism on its own ground was the duty of every civilized human being, but that duty could never be fulfilled by attempting to expropriate a part of the Arab world. Two wrongs, in the twentieth as in other centuries, were still two wrongs."[5]

Finally, in 1936, an Arab strike against the British authorities led to three years of anarchy and Arab guerrilla warfare against the British forces. Of this period, it can be said that there were extremists and moderates in both the Arab and the Jewish camps. Among the Jewish settlers, the relative moderates, led by David Ben Gurion, followed the course charted by Zionist leader Chaim Weizmann who insisted on obtaining Zionist goals through cooperation with the British. They consistently prevailed over the Revisionists, led by Vladimir Jabotinsky, a brilliant orator who advocated militant methods to obtain a revision of the terms of the British Mandate as a first step toward the establishment of a Jewish state embracing all of Palestine and present-day Jordan. The struggle, though intense, was primarily political and involved only sporadic violence and bloodshed within the Jewish community.

On the Arab side, both the tactics and results were different. The extremists were led by the Grand Mufti of Jerusalem, Al-Haj Muhammad Amin al-Husayni. Interesting-

3. Sheean, Vincent, *Personal History*, Doubleday, New York, 1936, p. 344.
4. *Ibid.*, p. 370.
5. *Ibid.*, p. 392.

ly, the Grand Mufti owed his 1921 appointment, despite his prominent role in the 1920 anti-Jewish riots, to the first British Governor of Palestine, Sir Herbert Samuel, a Jew. The Grand Mufti's rivals were the relative moderates of the Nashashibi clan, and eventually also supporters of the Abd al-Hadi clan.

The result was a long and violent three-cornered struggle within the Arab community of Palestine, characterized by extensive intimidation and even assassinations. Each bout generally concluded with victory for the more extremist elements and the temporary flight from the country of many of the most responsible Palestinian leaders. After each upsurge of violence, Royal investigative commissions would arrive in Palestine. The Grand Mufti's response was not only a boycott of such commissions, but also intimidation of other Arabs invited to testify before them. He thus ensured that, although the Jewish case received a full hearing, the Arab case was presented only by well-meaning local British officials, not by the Arabs themselves. Despite what by western standards can only be described as perversely inept Arab leadership, the commissions generally returned to London calling for corrections to curb Zionist plans and protect the Arab community. But in London politicians were exposed to a patient and effective Zionist campaign to water down such recommendations, led as always by the brilliant and effective Dr. Weizmann, whose devotion to his adopted country was ultimately and dramatically demonstrated by the death of his RAF pilot son in World War II.

Israel today honors Theodor Herzl, the charismatic journalist who popularized Zionism; Chaim Weizmann, the patient and persistent scientist and political tactician; and David Ben Gurion, the stubbornly optimistic leader of its fight for independence, as its founding fathers. Yet knowledgeable Israelis should also offer up an occasional secret prayer of thanks to the Grand Mufti, Al-Haj Muhammad Amin al-Husayni, who topped even his own record for pre-war self-destructive leadership of the Palestinian community when World War II began by publicly supporting the losing side. When the United States entered the Palestine political scene after World War II, friends of Israel in the United States were thus able to describe the leader of the Palestinian Arabs as an admirer of America's defeated enemy, Adolf Hitler.

Aside from the contributions of Israel's Jewish founders and their Arab opponents, the ultimate responsibility for Israel's existence in its present form must be assigned to Hitler himself. At the time he assumed power in Germany, Jewish immigration into Palestine had slowed. Economic stagnation there was not only discouraging prospective immigrants to Palestine but was encouraging an even higher number of Jews to emigrate *from* Palestine in search of better economic conditions. They either returned to the European countries from which they had come, or re-emigrated to the United States, where most of their relatives had originally traveled.

Only the sudden flight of Jews from Hitler's Germany and from other European countries conquered or threatened by his legions turned the immigration tide back in favor of Palestine's Jewish community. The flight from Germany also had another effect. It neutralized the rising chorus of Jewish concern about the effect a Jewish state would have on the hard-won status and rights of Jews in their many other homelands in both the Old and New Worlds. Particularly in the United States and England, where second-, third-, and fourth-generation Jews were not only successful in business, but had entered the various professions in numbers exceeding their percentage in the population, Jewish leaders expressed concern. If every Jew were now to have a second country, would he still be accepted as a loyal citizen or subject in the country of his birth? While some non-Zionist Jews opposed the establishment of a Jewish homeland on such political grounds, others opposed it on purely religious grounds, believing that the Promised Land was intended to be a religious Kingdom of God, not a political state ruled by man.

Regardless of individual feelings, however, the Jewish Holocaust in Europe stilled almost all non-Zionist voices, first for the duration of the war and then, more permanently, as the State of Israel became immutable reality.

Meanwhile, the stream of Jews fleeing Nazi persecution and seeking to enter Palestine had become a flood. The Arab inhabitants remained thoroughly aroused, as they saw the lands and jobs they occupied disappearing at a faster rate than ever. The British, looking toward the war they saw approaching and fearing not only continued resistance by the Arab Palestinians but also the hostility of Muslims throughout the Arab world and Asia, once again set up a Royal Commission to investigate the problem. This time competing Palestinian elements combined forces to testify, and were supported by delegates from five independent Arab states. The results of the investigation were contained in a "White Paper" that did not suffer the usual London political dilution. It guided British policy throughout most of World War II. The "White Paper" laid down a final quota of 75,000 Jewish immigrants over five years, after which the doors to Palestine would be closed, not to be reopened except in the unlikely case of mutual consent by Palestine's Arab and Jewish communities. It also restricted land sales to Jews in some areas, and banned them completely in others. The lines were now drawn.

Inside Palestine the Revisionist movement of Jabotinsky gave rise after his death in 1940 to two secret armed organizations. The smaller of the two was known as Lehi by Israelis and as the Stern Gang by the British. Israel's subsequent Prime Minister, Yitzhak Shamir, played a leading role in the organization, which never really stopped fighting the British, even as Rommel's Afrika Korps rolled closer to Palestine. Among its accomplishments were the 1944 assassination in Egypt of Lord Moyne, Britain's wartime Minister of State; and the 1948 murder in Jerusalem of the Swedish United Nations mediator, Count Folke Bernadotte. The larger of the two secret Revisionist armies, the Irgun Zvai Leumi, led by another future Israeli Prime Minister, Menachem Begin, remained quiescent until after the Nazi tide had been turned back at Al Alamein. However, it then launched a terrorist war against the British authorities which continued with few interruptions until the British withdrew from Palestine.

Meanwhile the bulk of the Jewish population in Palestine, led by David Ben Gurion, followed the moderate course laid down by Weizmann and supported the British war effort. More than 43,000 Palestinian Jews enrolled for service with British forces by 1944, even before Britain agreed to set up a separate Jewish Brigade. It was in an action by British-trained Jewish soldiers against the Vichy French in Lebanon that the future Israeli Defense Minister, Moshe Dayan, lost an eye.

On the Arab side there was a similar division. The Palestinian population, still demoralized after its revolt against the British, and stripped of much of its leadership either through death in action, assassination or exile, gave ostensible support to the British. By 1943 some 8,000 Palestinian Arabs were serving with the British forces. But at the same time the Grand Mufti made negative headlines as he moved from one Axis front to another. He started in 1941 with support for a short-lived revolt by Iraqi military officers supported by German aircraft, and continued almost to the end as he lent his moral support to German efforts in the Balkans to recruit Muslims to fight on the Russian front.

British attempts after World War II to limit the immigration of Jewish refugees into Palestine, in keeping with commitments made to the Arab majority there, encountered political opposition from the U.S. and armed resistance from rapidly-growing Jewish irregular armies. After the Exodus, above, seeking to land undocumented Jewish immigrants, was turned back by the British, Jewish displaced persons (below) awaiting transportation from the former Bergen-Belsen concentration camp in Germany demonstrated in 1947 against the forced return of the Exodus and its passengers from Palestine to Hamburg.

Zionist Archives

Zionist Archives

Above: David Ben Gurion reads the proclamation of the State of Israel at the first meeting of the Provisional Council, forerunner of the Knesset, in the Tel Aviv museum on May 14, 1948. Members of the provisional government on platform are, from left, Bechor Shitreet, David Remez, Pinhas Rosen, Perez Bernstein, Rabbi Y.L. Maimon, David Ben Gurion (standing), Moshe Shapiro, Moshe Sharett, Eliezer Kaplan, Mordecai Bentov and Aharon Zishing.

Below Left: Young members of the Orthodox Christian club in Jerusalem sign on as volunteers for a militia to defend Palestinian Arab neighborhoods and villages in 1947.

Below Right: David Ben Gurion, about to become Israel's first Prime Minister, signs Israel's proclamation of statehood as his old friend, Moshe Sharett (right), holds the document. Sharett, a moderate who sought peace with the Arab states, became Israel's second Prime Minister. His strong opposition forced postponement of plans by Ben Gurion and Moshe Dayan to expand Israel's borders into Southern Lebanon, the West Bank and Syria's Golan Heights.

CHAPTER III

President Roosevelt
and the European Holocaust

"Your Majesty will recall that on previous occasions I communicated to you the attitude of the American Government toward Palestine and made clear our desire that no decision be taken with respect to the basic situation in that country without full consultation with both Arabs and Jews. Your Majesty will also doubtless recall that during our recent conversation I assured you that I would take no action, in my capacity as Chief of the Executive Branch of this Government, which might prove hostile to the Arab people. It gives me pleasure to renew to Your Majesty the assurances which you have received regarding the attitude of my Government and my own, as Chief Executive, with regard to the question of Palestine and to inform you that the policy of this Government in this respect is unchanged."[1]

President Roosevelt in letter to King Abd al-Aziz Ibn Saud
of Saudi Arabia, April 5, 1945

"Give me a chance, dear Manny, to talk with Stalin and Churchill. There are all sorts of schemes, crackpot and otherwise, being advanced. Perhaps some solution will come out of this whole matter. I don't want to see war between the one or two million people in Palestine and the whole Moslem world in that area — 70 million."[2]

President Roosevelt in letter
to Representative Emmanuel Celler, 1945

---

1. *Foreign Relations of the United States, 1945*, Volume VIII, p. 698.
2. Wilson, Evan M., *Decision on Palestine: How the U.S. Came to Recognize Israel*, Hoover Institution Press, Stanford, California, 1979, p. 49.

"The Arabs, individually and collectively, regard the future of Palestine as a matter of life and death."[3]

Prince Abd al-Illah, Regent of Iraq
in letter to President Roosevelt, 1945

"You know, Eleanor, I've seen so much now of the Middle East, when we get through here I believe I'd like to go there and live. I feel quite an expert. I believe I could help to straighten out the Near East."[4]

President Roosevelt, 1945

Midway in World War II the Palestine problem began to appear increasingly on the American domestic political scene. As war spread throughout Europe, the center of World Zionism necessarily moved to the United States. In 1942, at a conference of the main Zionist groups in New York, the "Biltmore program," named after the conference site, was adopted. It urged, in terms more militant than had ever been voiced publicly outside revisionist circles, that "the gates of Palestine be opened" and "that Palestine be established as a Jewish commonwealth integrated into the structure of the new democratic world." Ben Gurion adopted the militant American Zionist program, openly aiming at Jewish statehood for Palestine, as his own. The stage was set for the Zionist entry into American politics.

It seems remarkable, in view of the importance of the "Jewish vote" in political calculations of that period, that there is so little mention of Palestine in the annals of the early years of President Franklin D. Roosevelt's incumbency. After the Biltmore program was adopted, however, and particularly during the last year of Roosevelt's life, the issue gained significance very rapidly.

As a former New York Democratic Party leader, Roosevelt had always maintained close ties with New York's Jewish community leaders. In a joint effort with one such leader, Morris Ernst, an attorney, he first encountered the increasing divergence between American Jews whose first concern was Zionism and those who were more concerned with the immediate rescue of Europe's endangered Jews. Very early in World War II Ernst went to London on Roosevelt's behalf to see if England and the Commonwealth countries would join the United States in taking a half million Jewish refugees. Ernst returned with the British agreement to match the U.S. in granting up to 150,000 visas each. With Canadian, Australian and some South American participation, at least 500,000 Jews could be saved.

According to Ernst, a week after he reported the success of his mission to President Roosevelt, the President informed him that the initiative was off, noting that "the dominant vocal Jewish leadership of America won't stand for it." Convinced that the President was wrong, Ernst then sought in vain to garner support himself among influential Jewish friends. Most declined to support the rescue initiative, he reported, on the grounds

---

3. Wilson, Evan M., *Decision on Palestine—How the U.S. Came to Recognize Israel*, Hoover Institution Press, Stanford, 1979, p. 52.
4. Bishop, Jim, *FDR's Last Year, April 1944-April 1945*, Morrow, New York, 1974, p. 526.

that it would undermine the Zionist movement. The story is related in detail by the anti-Zionist author, Alfred Lilienthal, in his 1979 book, *The Zionist Connection: What Price Peace?"* [5]

By 1944, sentiment had crystallized sufficiently within the U.S. Jewish community so that pro-Zionist planks were included in both major party platforms. American diplomats sought to assure Arab leaders that these pro-Zionist statements were electoral politics, and not statements of U.S. foreign policy. Most Arab leaders accepted these assurances at the time. After his re-election, however, President Roosevelt found himself holding off Zionist leaders who sought to nail down the campaign pledges in the form of a Palestine Resolution in Congress. Roosevelt said that such a resolution would undermine the Allied war effort in the Middle East. It was introduced nonetheless and defeated only after a personal appeal by Secretary of State Edward R. Stettinius, Jr.

The pressure on President Roosevelt escalated rapidly on both sides. On February 14, 1945, en route home from the meeting at Yalta with Winston Churchill and Josef Stalin, the U.S. President met aboard a U.S. naval ship with Saudi Arabia's King Abd al-Aziz Ibn Saud. The King was an imposing figure, well over six feet tall and already a legend for the military audacity and political genius he had exerted to unify the Arabian peninsula under his banner. His meeting with the polio-crippled U.S. President was a fantastic success, in the tradition of many equally unlikely Arab-American encounters both before and since. The American destroyer commander charged with transporting the Saudi Monarch from Jeddah to the Great Bitter Lakes, midway in the Suez Canal, had at first been horrified to learn that the King's party was greater than the number of empty berths on the ship. King Abdul Aziz solved this by having erected on the ship's deck a large tent under which he could hold court by day and sleep at night. The next problem was the arrival in advance of the King of quantities of rice, vegetables and live sheep. By the end of the three-day voyage, however, the American crew had learned that the King's purpose had been to introduce them to the delights of traditional Saudi guest fare of roast lamb and rice, as well as to tip each crew member royally with $40 and to present the senior officers with gold daggers and swords.

Although the actual meeting between the U.S. President and the King aboard a U.S. cruiser was brief, the royal gestures continued from both sides. Although he was normally a chain smoker, Roosevelt refrained from smoking at all in the King's presence. When the King, crippled with arthritis, expressed interest in the wheelchair to which Roosevelt was confined, the U.S. President immediately presented him with a spare chair that normally accompanied him. Subsequently, Roosevelt sent the King a DC-3 transport plane with the free service of an American crew for a year. This favor to the Saudi Monarch ultimately grew into a mutually beneficial commercial contract under which Trans World Airlines organized and then helped operate the Saudi national airline for many years.

The King, upon learning that there was no time to present the U.S. President with a full Arab meal, insisted upon having his own retainers brew Arab coffee for the Presi-

5. Lilienthal, Alfred, *The Zionist Connection – What Price Peace?* Middle East Perspective, Inc., New York, 1979, pp. 35-6.

dent as at least a token of Arab hospitality. This was followed with a gift to the President of gold daggers and swords, and jewels and expensive Arab clothing for the President's family.

In their conversations, President Roosevelt described the plight of the Jews of Europe under the Nazis. When he finished an eloquent, if obvious, attempt to enlist the King's support for more Jewish immigration into Palestine, the Saudi Monarch's response was both logical and laconic:

"Give the Jews and their descendants the choice lands and homes of the Germans . . . Amends should be made by the criminal, not by the innocent bystander."[6]

King Ibn Saud also exacted assurances from the President that he would "do nothing to assist the Jews against the Arabs and would make no move hostile to the Arab people."

By the time he returned to the U.S., President Roosevelt apparently had undergone the conversion so familiar from the earlier days of Royal Commission investigators to Palestine, and subsequently from the reactions of Americans who have lived and worked in the Middle East. He told friends that in a few minutes of conversation with the Saudi Monarch he learned more about the Palestine situation than he had learned in all of his previous life.

His new knowledge did not prevent him, however, from authorizing a U.S. Zionist leader to state that the President still favored a Jewish state and unrestricted Jewish immigration into Palestine. Then, as the Arabs reacted with angry questions, he authorized the Department of State to reaffirm his pledge to Ibn Saud and other Arab leaders that there would be prior consultation with the Arabs as well as the Jews before the U.S. took any action related to Palestine. Any maneuvering room between Jews and Arabs on Palestine was narrowing dramatically. President Roosevelt's death on April 12, 1945 left unresolved the ultimate stand he might have taken on that too-often-promised land.

The President's widow, Eleanor Roosevelt, later became such an ardent and articulate supporter of Israel that her actions as a U.S. delegate to the United Nations, bordering on intimidation of weak nations needing American support, would have provoked cries of outrage in the present international political climate. However, that was after her husband's death. During Roosevelt's lifetime the White House adviser in charge of Zionist concerns was David Niles. In the State Department the role was assumed by Under Secretary of State Sumner Wells. Wells, an intimate friend and former schoolmate of the President, was a Christian, but he supported the concept of a Jewish homeland for Palestine as ardently as did Niles and other American Jews in key positions at that time. Because there is no clear distinction between the actions that Niles and Wells took on the President's initiative, and on their own, not enough evidence exists to determine clearly how Roosevelt himself felt about the Zionist goals. Niles said in 1962 that had President Roosevelt lived longer, Israel probably would never have come into existence. Whatever his feelings, Roosevelt was an adroit politician

---

6. Eddy, William, *FDR Meets Ibn Saud*, American Friends of the Middle East, New York, 1954, p. 34.

who knew how to keep himself publicly uncommitted. He also was sophisticated enough to know that America's Jewish leaders needed his support as much as he needed theirs.

That was not the case after President Roosevelt's death, less than a month before the May 8, 1945 Allied victory in Europe and four months before the victory over Japan. The hard decisions about Palestine devolved upon a man who was conspicuously ill-prepared for the role in terms both of his knowledge of the Middle East and of his domestic political support.

After members of the United Nations, strongly lobbied by the United States, voted in November, 1947, to partition Palestine into an Arab and a Jewish state, fighting spread among Arab villagers and Jewish settlers and militias in the countryside and in the cities and towns as well. Arab volunteers (above) at Tulkarm, near Nablus, practice marching with World War I bolt action rifles in February, 1948, while (below) newly arrived Jewish immigrants to Palestine practice firing automatic weapons.

Zionist Archives

Zionist Archives

The violence that broke out almost immediately after the United Nations November, 1947 vote to partition all of Palestine except Jerusalem between its Arab and Jewish inhabitants almost cooled President Truman's enthusiasm for that solution. However, against the advice of Secretary of State George C. Marshall, Middle East experts in the Department of State and U.S. Ambassadors in the area, and in response to pleas of U.S. Jewish leaders and Domestic Political Adviser Clark Clifford, he again threw U.S. support behind the plan which brought Israel into existence in May, 1948. Above, the scene after a truck bomb explosion at the offices of the Palestine Post in Jerusalem February 2, 1948. Below, Palestinian fighters with Abd al-Kader al-Husseini, cousin of the Grand Mufti and a highly respected leader whose death at Kastel in April, 1948, caused Palestinian loss of the position and the opening of the road connecting the Jewish forces in the coastal areas to those in Jerusalem.

PLO

CHAPTER IV

President Truman and the Creation of Israel

"The fate of the Jewish victims of Hitlerism was a matter of deep personal concern to me."[1]

Former President Harry Truman, 1955

"As the pressure mounted, I found it necessary to give instructions that I did not want to be approached by any more spokesmen for the extreme Zionist cause."[2]

Former President Harry Truman, 1955

"I'm sorry, gentlemen, but I have to answer to hundreds of thousands who are anxious for the success of Zionism: I do not have hundreds of thousands of Arabs among my constituents."[3]

President Harry Truman, Nov. 10, 1945

"The inescapable conclusion of my examination of our Palestinian policy during these six years is that many of our present problems in the Middle East must be attributed to Truman's decisions regarding partition and recognition—decisions that have drastically affected American interests in the area to this day. I began this study with the opinion, which I had held since my days on the Palestine desk, that Truman's principal motivation had been humanitarian, but after examining all the evidence, including data that were not available to us in the State Department at the time, I have been

---

1. Truman, Harry S, *Memoirs*, Doubleday, Garden City, New York, 1955, Vol.II *Years of Trial and Hope*, p. 132.
2. *Ibid.*, p. 160.
3. Eddy, William A., *F.D.R. Meets Ibn Saud*, American Friends of the Middle East, New York, 1954.

27

forced reluctantly to the conclusion that on certain key occasions (October 1947 and May 1948) he was more influenced by domestic political considerations than by humanitarian ideals."[4]

Evan M. Wilson, 1979

"I am confident that the American people, who spent their blood and their money freely to resist aggression, could not possibly support Zionist aggression against a friendly Arab country which has committed no crime except to believe firmly in those principles of justice and equality, for which the United Nations, including the United States, fought and for which both your predecessor and you exerted great efforts."[5]

King Abd al-Aziz Ibn Saud of Saudi Arabia
in Oct. 15, 1946 letter to President Truman

"We do not wish at all to believe that Zionist influence in America can reverse facts so as to make right wrong and wrong right."[6]

Prime Minister Nuri al-Said of Iraq in note
to U.S. Charge d'Affaires, Baghdad, 1945

"One injury cannot be removed by another even more harmful . . . In this case we shall be face to face with the Zionist Nazism against the Arabs instead of a German Nazism against the Jews."[7]

Syrian Ministry of Foreign Affairs note
to American Legation, Damascus, 1945

As a freshman Vice President under a President in his fourth term, Harry Truman was not likely to know what his predecessor really thought about the struggle shaping up in Palestine. Yet, when he succeeded to the Presidency, Truman was conscientious about accepting the responsibility that was thrust upon him. He was a stubbornly decisive man, and this quality has enshrined him in the minds of Israelis as perhaps their truest friend among American Presidents. At the same time, probably no American President has ever disregarded expert advice so thoroughly and with such relish. In acting to establish and later to support the Jewish State in Palestine, Truman ignored the objections of his Secretary of Defense, James Forrestal, and three of his Secretaries of State: James Byrnes, General George Marshall, and Dean Acheson.

With the war over, and Jewish terrorism against British forces and in support of illegal Jewish immigration increasing, Truman lent himself to what could only be construed by disgusted British observers as cheap shots aimed at a war-drained great power still trying to maintain some semblance of law and order in a land wracked with communal violence between Jews and Arabs.

4. Wilson, Evan M., *Decision on Palestine: How the U.S. Came to Recognize Israel*, Hoover Institution Press, Stanford, California, 1979, p. 149.
5. *Ibid.*, p. 100.
6. *Ibid.*, p. 65.
7. *Ibid.*, p. 65.

He pressed the British hard to allow an additional 100,000 Jews to enter Palestine from Europe. Given America's horror over the Nazi concentration camps, it would be ridiculous to attribute this solely to a desire for Jewish electoral support. A somewhat less charitable view must be taken, however, of the simultaneous actions of various American Zionists. In conversations with the leaders of America's wartime ally, these Americans strongly implied that a failure to raise the immigration quota would greatly lessen Britain's chances of post-war cooperation with the United States. It was, unfortunately, not the last instance when private but influential American citizens used the American treasury as both carrot and stick to convince reluctant foreign nations to support the interests of the Jewish State.

President Truman's next decision was far less understandable from a humanitarian point of view. When Britain set May 15, 1948 as the date for its withdrawal from Palestine, Truman decided to support a United Nations plan to partition it between its 1,300,000 Arab and 650,000 Jewish occupants. The plan was a masterpiece of gerrymandering. It awarded 56.4 per cent of the country to the Jews, who comprised 33 per cent of the population and owned less than 6 per cent of the land. The plan to give such a huge portion of Palestine to a minority of its inhabitants made for a strange division of population between the two enemies. Even after partition, under the U.N. plan the Jewish portion would contain 497,000 Palestinian Arabs, a certain recipe for trouble, while the Arab portion would contain only 10,000 Jews. Despite virtually unanimous opposition to the plan from State and Defense Department experts on the Middle East, President Truman put United States support behind it. When it appeared that the plan could not obtain the necessary two-thirds vote in the UN General Assembly, even with U.S. support, private Americans lobbied small and weak states, particularly countries from the under-developed world which were heavily dependent upon U.S. investment, aid and good will, to support the partition.

General Carlos Romulo, a staunch supporter of the United States through the dark years of World War II in the Pacific, headed the Philippine delegation to the UN. He spoke out against the plan and finally returned to his country rather than vote for it. But the newly-independent Philippine Government, dependent upon U.S. support while it rebuilt its war-destroyed economy, had received a telegram supporting the partition from 26 pro-Zionist U.S. Senators. It ordered its UN delegation to support the plan. The same telegram, sent to several countries, was reported to have changed four votes to yes and seven votes from no to abstentions. Other countries reported both blackmail and bribery attempts in the campaign that elicited a final vote of 33 to 13 in favor of the resolution.

Shocked by the bloody conflict that broke out in Palestine between the Arab and Jewish communities after UN adoption of the partition plan, President Truman gave closer attention to his foreign affairs experts who had accurately predicted this tragic turn of events. When Britain refused to take any measures to implement the partition and other Security Council members expressed similar opposition, the State Department began searching for an alternative plan. Having obtained President Truman's agreement, the Department now advocated postponing partition in favor of a UN trusteeship over Palestine to commence when the British withdrew.

However, neither Secretary of State Marshall nor the head of the U.S. delegation to the UN, former Senator Warren Austin, were aware of the drama taking place in the White House. In his *Memoirs,* published in 1955, President Truman described the atmosphere at the time:

"The matter had been placed in the United Nations and, true to my conviction that the United Nations had to be made to work, I had confidence that a solution would be found there."[8]

However, according to Merle Miller, author of *Plain Speaking: An Oral Biography of Harry Truman,* pressure from the various American Zionist groups was intense. Mr. Truman told Miller:

"Well, there had never been anything like it before, and there wasn't after. Not even when I fired MacArthur, there wasn't. And I said, I issued orders that I wasn't going to see anyone who was an extremist for the Zionist cause, and I didn't care who it was . . . I had to keep in mind that much as I favored a homeland for the Jews, there were simply other matters awaiting . . . that I had to worry about."[9]

Then on March 13 the President received a telephone call from Eddie Jacobson, his close friend from World War I army service and from a haberdashery partnership they had once had in Missouri. Mr. Jacobson said he was in Washington and wanted to see the President. Mr. Truman has described to Miller what followed:

"I said to him, 'Eddie, I'm always glad to see old friends, but there's one thing you've got to promise me. I don't want you to say a *word* about what's going on over there in the Middle East. Do you promise?' And he did."

But, when Mr. Jacobson was ushered into the Oval Office, Mr. Truman recalled:

"Great tears were running down his cheeks and I took one look at him, and I said 'Eddie, you son of a bitch, you promised me you wouldn't say a word about what's going on over there.' And he said, 'Mr. President, I haven't said a word, but every time I think of the homeless Jews, homeless for thousands of years, and I think about Dr. Weizmann, I start crying. I can't help it. He's an old man, and he's spent his whole life working for a homeland for the Jews, and now he's sick, and he's in New York and wants to see you. And every time I think about it, I can't help crying.'

"I said, 'Eddie, that's enough. That's the last word.'

"And so we talked about this and that, but every once in a while a big tear would roll down his cheek. At one point he said something about how I felt about old Andy Jackson and he was crying again. He said he knew he wasn't supposed to, but that's how he felt about Weizmann.

"I said, 'Eddie, you son of a bitch, I ought to have you thrown right out of here for breaking your promise; you knew damn good and well I couldn't stand seeing you cry.'

"And he kind of smiled at me, still crying, though, and he said, 'Thank you, Mr. President,' and he left.

8. Truman, Harry S, *Memoirs*, Doubleday, Garden City, New York, 1955, Vol.II *Years of Trial and Hope*, p. 157.
9. Miller, Merle, *Plain Speaking — An Oral Biography of Harry S Truman*, Berkley Books, New York, 1974, p. 234.

"After he was gone, I picked up the phone and called the State Department, and I told them I was going to see Weizmann. Well, you should have heard the carrying-on."[10]

Five days later, on March 18, Dr. Weizmann came into the White House through the east gate for an unannounced visit during which President Truman apparently assured him that the U.S. was supporting partition. The next day, Ambassador Austin, proceeding with the policy previously agreed to by the President, read a statement calling for a postponement of the partition resolution and the substitution of a UN trusteeship over Palestine.

President Truman stated in his diary entry for that day:

"The State Department pulled the rug from under me today. . . . In Key West, or en route there from St. Croix, I approved the speech and statement of policy by Senator Austin to the UN meeting. This morning I find that the State Department has reversed my Palestine policy. The first I know about it is what I see in the paper. Isn't that hell? I am now in the position of a liar and a double-crosser. . . . "

There has been a great deal of controversy about this ever since, with partisans of Israel, and of President Truman, claiming that he was the victim of treachery by lower echelon officers at the State Department. However, as the documents agreed to by the President have been declassified over the years, it has become apparent that a postponement of the partition plan and substitution of a UN trusteeship was suggested by the State Department and agreed to by the President. Apparently his concern was over the fact that it contradicted statements he subsequently made during the two private visits to the White House, one by his Jewish former haberdashery partner and one by the leader of the World Zionist Organization.

The fact that President Truman could approve a policy, fly into a rage when it was officially announced, and later blame his rage not on the substance of the announcement but on its timing, indicates that he faced the same problem that had begun inexorably closing in on President Roosevelt in the weeks prior to his death. The aspirations of American Zionists, which by the end of World War II had become the aspirations of a great majority of American Jewish voters, simply were not compatible with American interests in the world in general and in the Middle East in particular. Further, and this apparently was understood at the time only by American diplomats, and the soldiers, educators, and other Americans who had lived and worked in the Middle East, these Zionist aspirations were incompatible with the principles for which the United States had stood from the time of the American Revolution. The great humanitarian impulse to settle Europe's surviving Jews in Palestine clashed directly with President Wilson's insistence that every international question should be settled "upon the basis of the free acceptance of that settlement by the people immediately concerned."

President Truman's Secretary of State knew that two thirds of the "immediately concerned" people in Palestine were Arabs. The President's domestic political advisers were only interested in the fact that nearly all of America's Jewish community also

---

10. Miller, Merle, *Plain Speaking — An Oral Biography of Harry S Truman*, Berkley Books, New York, 1974, pp. 234-5.

felt "immediately concerned," and these Americans could vote, make speeches, write editorials, and provide or withhold campaign contributions.

President Truman was fully aware of both dimensions of the problem. As early as 1945, a group of foreign service officers who headed U.S. missions in the Middle East was brought to Washington to report directly to the President on the problems his policies were creating for the entire U.S. position there. The U.S. Minister to Saudi Arabia, Colonel William Eddy, recounts that the President listened to their individual reports, then dismissed them with the words:

"I am sorry, gentlemen, but I have to answer to hundreds of thousands who are anxious for the success of Zionism. I do not have hundreds of thousands of Arabs among my constituents."[11]

It was certainly this concern that determined the President's policy after the Weizmann meeting and the blow-up over Ambassador Austin's speech. Weizmann followed up his meeting with a letter to President Truman on April 9, 1948 urging that partition be implemented without delay because "the choice of our people is between statehood and extermination." David Niles, a Jewish aide who had been President Roosevelt's White House liaison with Jewish groups and who had remained in that position under President Truman, now found a strong backer in Clark Clifford, who already was mapping out the strategy for the Truman 1948 re-election campaign. Clifford had been shocked at the results of a special Congressional election in the Bronx. In a district where 55 per cent of the voters were Jewish, the Democratic Party candidate had lost. Among the campaigners for the victorious American Labor Party candidate had been Truman's predecessor as Vice President, Henry Wallace, who had declared that "Truman still talks Jewish but acts Arab."

The plan to postpone partition and substitute a UN trusteeship over Palestine was foundering, and Clifford sensed that U.S. support for it had cost Truman domestic support. Clifford's strategy for recouping that domestic electoral support was to have President Truman recognize the new Jewish state even before the partition plan went into effect with the May 15, 1948 withdrawal of the British from Palestine. At a meeting called to discuss the subject on May 12, Secretary of State Marshall vehemently opposed premature recognition of a state that had not even defined its own future boundaries. He not only refused to endorse the idea but added some angry words which are surely unprecedented in a conversation between a President and his Secretary of State. In General Marshall's own memorandum of the conversation, he noted:

"I said bluntly that if the President were to follow Mr. Clifford's advice and if in the elections I were to vote, I would vote against the President."

No decision was made at that meeting, but on May 13 Dr. Weizmann wrote the President a letter asking that the U.S. "promptly recognize the Provisional Government of the new Jewish State." The following day Clifford, not the Secretary of State, informed Eliahu Epstein, the Washington representative of the Jewish Agency for

11. Eddy, William A., *F.D.R. Meets Ibn Saud*, American Friends of the Middle East, New York, 1954.

Palestine, that the White House would need a formal request for recognition in order to take the desired action. Epstein, who was shortly to change his name to Eliahu Elath and become Israel's first Ambassador to the U.S., explained that the request could not be made until the new state came into existence at midnight, May 14, in the Middle East, which would be 6 p.m. Washington time. Nevertheless, a draft request was prepared in Washington. Since the Jewish Agency representative did not yet know the name of the state to be, it was referred to simply as "the Jewish State." While an Agency representative was driving to the White House with the request, another Agency employe heard on the radio that the state was to be named "Israel." This second employe sped to the White House and in pen substituted "State of Israel" for "the Jewish State" on the request for recognition.

Secretary Marshall was informed late in the afternoon of the President's decision to recognize Israel; Ambassador Austin was notified at 5:40 p.m. At 6 p.m. the British Mandate expired. At 6:01 Israel came into existence. And at 6:11 the U.S. announced its recognition of the new state.

There are many postscripts to this amazing sequence of events. It has been reported that Secretary of State Marshall had to send his then Under Secretary Dean Rusk, to New York to talk the U.S. delegation to the UN out of resigning en masse. Ambassador Austin retreated to his hotel room rather than appear with the delegation he headed when it announced U.S. recognition of Israel. Even Eleanor Roosevelt, the Jewish State's most active partisan on the delegation, later wrote to Secretary Marshall to complain that the manner of U.S. recognition had caused "consternation" among the other UN delegations.

Mrs. Roosevelt's concern about "consternation" among other UN delegates in New York, rather than bloodshed in the Middle East, illustrates the innocence of many active American partisans of the new state, who had never doubted that they were pushing the United States along a humanitarian course. In the Middle East the realities were clearer. At the time of the UN vote in favor of partition, when Jews were dancing in the streets all over Palestine, David Ben Gurion had written:

"I cannot be among the dancers. I am like someone in mourning at a wedding. I am filled with an awful fear at the sacrifice that awaits our people."[12]

By May 14, 1948, when Ben Gurion arose before the new nation's leaders in a small auditorium in the Tel Aviv Museum of Art to proclaim the birth of the new state, deaths from fighting between Arab and Jewish irregulars were already in the hundreds, up to 300,000 Arabs were reported to have fled or been forced from their homes, and the armies of four Arab states were poised for what they considered a rescue operation to restore displaced Arabs to their homes and lands, and the west perceived as an invasion to eliminate the new state by force.

The outcome is well known. Jewish settlers, under the leadership of officers trained and seasoned by service with the various Jewish armed groups and with British forces

---

12. Derogy, Jacques and Carmel, Hesi, *The Untold History of Israel*, Grove Press, New York, 1979, pp. 75-6.

in World War II, fought the multi-pronged but badly coordinated Arab attacks. Using motley but sizable collections of secretly stockpiled arms, the Jewish militias gained more territory than they lost before running short of ammunition.

A truce arranged by the UN on June 11 ended after a month when the Arabs refused to extend it. But it had given the Israelis sufficient time to bring in a large number of new fighters. Some were foreign volunteers with essential military skills, others simply raw manpower hurriedly culled from the refugee camps of Europe. These reinforcements were flown or ferried to Israel in a clandestine air and sea fleet assembled from surplus and "liberated" military equipment from the battlefields of Europe, and manned by demobilized Jewish airmen, sailors and soldiers from virtually every Allied army. Equally important, the Israelis bought arms and ammunition from many countries, particularly Czechoslovakia. The Czech deal was brokered by the Soviet Union, which at the time had suddenly become not only a faithful supporter of the new Jewish state, but also a considerably more effective one than the United States, which was futilely seeking to enforce an arms embargo on all parties to the conflict.

The embargo seemed most effective, however, against the Arabs. They did not use the brief truce period to resupply and regroup their strained armies or to train the Palestinian guerrillas, who at the time functioned more as a mob than an army. When all-out fighting resumed, Israel had between 60,000 and 100,000 fighters armed and ready to face between 35,000 and 45,000 Arab regular troops. The superior Israeli numbers and the intensive preparations during the truce rapidly paid off during the next ten days of fighting.

This time, when the United Nations imposed a cease-fire, the territory controlled by the Israeli fighters had been enlarged to 77 per cent of the entire mandate. Jerusalem, which under the partition resolution was to remain under international control, now was about evenly divided between Israeli and Jordanian forces. Jordan's largely British-officered Arab Legion, which during the fighting had purposely refrained from moving into areas given to Israel under the partition plan, now remained in place after the fighting ended. This gave Jordan *de facto* control over what remained of what had been planned as the Palestinian portion of the partitioned mandate, with the exception of the Gaza area which now was controlled by Egypt. Thus both the planned international area and the planned Palestinian portions of the partitioned land remained under Israeli, Jordanian or Egyptian control.

Meanwhile, some 750,000 Palestinians, having fled before or been forced out at gunpoint by Israeli soldiers, were barred from returning to their homes inside the vastly extended Israeli lines. Now, as refugees without homes or a country of their own, most found themselves in camps living under even more primitive conditions than had the post-war Jewish refugees of Europe, to alleviate whose suffering President Truman had helped to create the State of Israel.

Troops of the Arab Liberation Army (above) made up of hastily-recruited Palestinians, augmented by Syrian and Lebanese volunteers, check their guns under a crossroad sign prior to attack on Affula, June 4, 1948. Israeli defenders (below) dig in behind barricade of rocks. Nearly 40 years later Arabs and Israelis still have profoundly different perceptions of the 1947–1949 fighting. Israelis think of the fighting that followed the May, 1948 creation of the State of Israel as an invasion by outside armies from Egypt, Jordan and Iraq, turned back by the bravery of outnumbered Jewish settlers augmented by newly-arrived Jewish World War II veterans and refugees from Europe. Arabs see the 1948 fighting as a desperate rescue attempt by ill-equipped units from weak and newly-independent or only semi-independent neighboring Arab states to save unprepared Palestinian Arabs who were being pushed out of their ancestral lands by European Jews in a well-prepared military action enjoying clandestine support from the U.S., USSR, and Eastern and Western Europe. The bitterness of those early, bloody encounters has permeated subsequent mutual perceptions.

PLO

Palestinian fighters (above) under fire in 1947 fighting near Hebron.

Jewish supply convoy (below, left) halts during fighting along road to Jerusalem.

Arab volunteer (below, right) training in hills near Nablus Feb. 11. 1948, in interval between UN partition resolution and British evacuation of Palestine.

CHAPTER V

President Truman's Second Term and Post-Partum Depression

"Perhaps they were wrong in pursuing this aim, perhaps their efforts were bound to create new and intractable problems. However, several decades ago Zionism moved out of the realm of the history of ideas, good, bad or indifferent, into the field of action. It has resulted in the birth of a nation to the joy of some and the distress of others."[1]

Walter Laqueur, 1972

"Every Israeli knows in his heart of hearts what injustice to the Palestinians the establishment of Israel has involved."

Walid Khalidi, American University of Beirut, 1981

"The very real admiration and respect which all Arabs held for America is evaporating rapidly and may soon disappear altogether, along with our many mutual interests and cooperation."

Saudi Arabian Foreign Minister Prince
(and later King) Faisal, 1945

"It is no exaggeration to say that our relations with the entire Arab world have never recovered from the events of 1947-48 when we sided with the Jews against the Arabs and advocated a solution in Palestine which went contrary to self-determination as far as the majority population of the country was concerned."[2]

Evan M. Wilson, 1979

---

1. Laqueur, Walter Z., *A History of Zionism*, Holt, Rinehart and Winston, New York, 1972, p.xv.
2. Wilson, Evan M., *Decision on Palestine: How the U.S. Came to Recognize Israel*, Hoover Institution Press, Stanford, California, 1979, p.154.

It is ironic, but perhaps fitting, that after a victorious 1948 election campaign in which his seminal role in the creation of Israel was a major asset, President Truman spent his second term worrying about the 750,000 Palestinian refugees, who now considerably outnumbered the Jewish refugees who had been in Europe's post-war displaced persons camps. As the Israelis stoutly resisted UN resolutions to withdraw from territory captured in their war of independence, or to repatriate the Palestinian refugees who had fled or been ejected from their homes, President Truman's impatience grew.

In May, 1948, he told the Israelis that if they persisted in their refusals, "the U.S. Government will regretfully be forced to the conclusion that a revision of its attitude toward Israel has become unavoidable." The State Department advised him to pressure Israel to return to the partition lines by halting U.S. technical, financial and diplomatic assistance and lifting the tax exempt status of Jewish organizations raising funds for Israel. Nevertheless, in a foretaste of what every subsequent American President has at some time experienced, Israel formally rejected the American request. Also anticipating diplomatic experiences to come, the American Ambassador to Israel then explained that the tone of the President's note had "embittered Israeli opinion" and that Israeli concessions on the refugees might only be possible if the request were "not put in the form of a demand." The border adjustments, the Ambassador added, were not possible at all. Truman made no more demands, but no Israeli concessions on refugees followed.

Many of those who worked with, or against, President Truman have eloquently summed up their feelings about his Middle East decisions. In his book *Plain Speaking*, based on President Truman's dictated reminiscences, Merle Miller records a memorable event in 1949:

"The Chief Rabbi of Israel came to see the President and he told him, 'God put you in your mother's womb so that you could be the instrument to bring about the rebirth of Israel after two thousand years.' At that, great tears started rolling down Harry Truman's cheeks."[3]

In his book, *Present at the Creation: My Years at the State Department*, Dean Acheson revealed his own feelings:

"I did not share the President's views on the Palestine solution to the pressing and desperate plight of great numbers of displaced Jews in Eastern Europe. The numbers that could be absorbed by Arab Palestine without creating a grave problem would be inadequate, and to transform the country into a Jewish state capable of receiving a million or more immigrants would vastly exacerbate the political problem and imperil not only American but all Western interests in the Near East. From Justice Brandeis, whom I revered, and Felix Frankfurter, my intimate friend, I had learned to understand, but not to share, the mystical emotion of the Jews to return to Palestine and end the Diaspora. In urging Zionism as an American Government policy, they had allowed, so I thought, their emotion to obscure the totality of American interests."[4]

---

3. Miller, Merle, *Plain Speaking—An Oral Biography of Harry S Truman*, Berkley Books, New York, 1974, p. 236.
4. Acheson, Dean, *Present at the Creation: My Years in the State Department*, Norton, New York, 1969, p. 169.

In a letter to the anti-Zionist author, Alfred Lilienthal, in 1977, former Secretary of State Dean Rusk said of Mr. Truman:

"He, as all Americans, had been deeply shocked by the full exposure of the frightful atrocities of the Hitler regime. Mr. Truman was strongly impelled toward a homeland for the Jews where such things could not be repeated, and this view was politically reinforced by a large, active and dedicated group in this country who were working very hard on behalf of a Jewish State in Palestine. It would be naive to think that these domestic political considerations played no part in Mr. Truman's own thinking and decisions."[5]

In his *Study of History*, British historian Arnold Toynbee also provides a mixed assessment:

"The Missourian politician-philanthropist's eagerness to combine expediency with charity by assisting the wronged and suffering Jews would appear to have been untempered by any sensitive awareness that he was thereby abetting the infliction of wrongs and sufferings on the Arabs."[6]

Britain's post-war Prime Minister, Earl Clement Attlee, was not at all charitable in two recorded comments after he left office. He said that "U.S. policy in Palestine was molded by the Jewish vote and by party contributions of several big Jewish firms," and "there is no Arab vote in America."

Perhaps the best explanation of the era is provided by President Truman himself. In a memorandum to his Jewish affairs adviser, David Niles, on May 13, 1947, a year to the day before his decision to recognize Israel against the advice of his foreign and military affairs advisers, he wrote:

"We could have settled this Palestine thing if U.S. politics had been kept out of it. Terror and Silver [U.S. Zionist Leader Rabbi Abba Hillel Silver] are the contributing cause of some, if not all, of our troubles."[7]

---

5. Lilienthal, Alfred M., *The Zionist Connection: What Price Peace?*, Middle East Perspective, Inc., New York, 1978, p. 96.
6. Toynbee, Arnold J., *A Study of History*, Oxford University Press, New York, 1956, vol. XIII, p. 308.
7. Lilienthal, Alfred M., *The Zionist Connection: What Price Peace?*, Middle East Perspective, Inc., New York, 1978, p. 95 from Truman to Niles memorandum dated May 13, 1947, in files of Harry S Truman Library, Independence, Missouri.

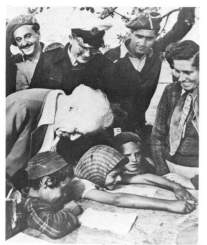

Israel Information Office   UNRWA

The fighting that swept Palestine from 1947 to 1949 left the country divided psychologically as well as physically. Above left, Israeli Prime Minister David Ben Gurion visits Jewish students at the Faradiya immigrant camp. Above right, a Palestinian Arab refugee child in UNRWA's Sbeineh emergency refugee camp in Syria. Below left, Palestinian refugee girls at the UNRWA school in Jabalia camp in the Gaza strip. Below, right, a Palestinian student teacher in the West Bank's UNRWA women's training center in Ramallah.

UNRWA   UNRWA: Kay Brennan

Iraqi artillerymen (above) fire at Israelis in 1948 fighting. King Abdullah of Jordan (below) inspects a Jordanian artillery unit at Mafraq before it departs for Palestinian front. Lack of coordination was only one of the problems of troops sent from Egypt, Jordan and Iraq to help the Palestinian Arabs. Egyptian soldiers, still under the rule of King Farouk, found their weapons inferior and ammunition defective. Iraqi troops, under a British-influenced government, were withdrawn after seeing little action. Jordanian troops fought tenaciously but their British officers were under orders not to press the attack into areas that had been awarded by the Partition Resolution to Israel. This made it possible for their opponents, after a defeat, to withdraw, regroup and resupply in safety, and attack again. The Palestinian humiliation suffered by Arab troops in 1948 led directly to the coup that overthrew King Farouk in Egypt, and to strong anti-western feelings that were a major factor in the overthrow of the Iraqi monarchy 10 years later.

United Nations

United Nations

Beginning their diaspora: Palestinians are evacuated under U.N. protection from the "Faluja Pocket" where Egyptian troops, including a young Major Gamal Abdel Nasser, were trapped after Israeli forces took advantage of an Oct. 14, 1948 ceasefire to surround the area held by Egyptian forces. The U.N., which could not induce the Israeli besiegers to withdraw to the original cease-fire line, evacuated civilians trapped in the surrounded area. After a general armistice was signed February 24, 1949, Egyptian forces returned to Egypt, but the Israelis would not allow these Palestinians to return to their homes. They were now trapped in the Gaza strip where they and thousands like them have remained as homeless refugees from 1948 to the present.

CHAPTER VI

President Eisenhower
and the Build-up to Suez

"The Suez debacle not only ended British and French pretensions to great power status, it drove Nasser toward the Soviet Union and titillated Israel's expansionist ambitions. But Eisenhower and Dulles were evenhanded. If our European allies had to withdraw, so had the Israelis. By threatening to cut off America's public and private subsidies to Israel, they forced Ben Gurion—kicking and screaming—to pull the Israeli army back from Sinai. It was the last time America applied the same rules to Israel that it applied to other allies or other friendly countries. Thereafter, when Israel embarked on adventures in total disregard of American views or interests, it risked little more than a gentle pro forma rebuke *from Washington."[1]*

George Ball, 1981

"During the campaign, some political figures kept talking of our failure to 'back Israel.' If the Administration had been incapable of withstanding that kind of advice in an election year, could the United Nations thereafter have retained any influence whatsoever?"[2]

President Dwight D. Eisenhower, 1965

"With the exception of the Eisenhower Administration, which virtually compelled Israel's withdrawal from Sinai after the 1956 war, American Presidents, and to an even greater degree Senators and Representatives, have been subjected to recurrent pressures from what has come to be known as the Israel lobby. For the most part they have been respon-

---

1. Ball, George, *Washington Post*, June 15, 1981.
2. Eisenhower, Dwight D., *The White House Years: Waging Peace 1956-1961*, Doubleday, Garden City, New York, 1965, p. 99.

sive, and for reasons not always related either to personal conviction or careful reflection on the national interest."[3]

Senator Charles McC. Mathias, Jr., 1981

The election of General of the Armies Dwight D. Eisenhower to the Presidency brought more than a change of parties to the White House. After the Allied victory in World War II, Eisenhower had accepted the Presidency of Columbia University and returned to civilian life. But as the U.S. and Western Europe grew increasingly fearful of Soviet intentions, America's hero of World War II returned to Europe to organize NATO and its defenses. By the time this task was completed, he was so popular with the American public that he could have had the Presidential nomination of either party. He chose the Republicans, who then passed over their expected nominee, Senator Taft, to hand the General the nomination. He easily defeated the Democratic candidate, Adlai Stevenson. As a result, when he entered the White House, Eisenhower was his own man, with a personal political base so secure he could not seriously be challenged by any single interest group. Eisenhower was also a West Pointer who had come up the peacetime army career ladder. Unlike his predecessor, he preferred to delegate authority, and he listened carefully to those who did the staff work before he made any decision. Strangely, these traits almost brought about a complete change in U.S. Middle Eastern policy, but they eventually resulted in the undoing of Eisenhower's plans for the Middle East.

While Eisenhower was accepting the Presidential nomination in July, 1952, Egypt was undergoing a revolution. Given the predelictions of its playboy King Farouk, the revolution probably was inevitable. But Egypt's 1948 debacle in Palestine was, at the very least, the catalyst for a coup by army officers humiliated at the Egyptian defeat, and outraged by the high-level sloth and corruption it had revealed. In 1954 Colonel Gamal Abd al-Nasser, the driving force behind the original coup, deposed its ostensible leader, General Mohammad Naguib, and assumed power himself. To the credit of Arab affairs experts both in the United States and in Israel, they had early on picked the handsome, fiery colonel as the Egyptian to watch. In each country secret chains of events were set in motion, but at least one of the Israeli plans was diametrically opposed to the plan of the United States.

Eisenhower understood the unique potential for flexibility of a charismatic leader with a strong political base. Assured by his Middle East advisers that Nasser was such a leader, he set out to woo the Egyptian leader through Kermit Roosevelt, grandson of President Theodore Roosevelt. To keep the press off the track, U.S. and Egyptian intelligence channels were used. The idea was to make it clear to this Arab reformer that the U.S. was ready to adjust its Middle East policies to Nasser's new politics if the Egyptian leader was willing to make peace with Israel and thus to remove at one stroke both the greatest single strain on Egypt's budget and the only serious irritant in U.S.-Arab relations.

---

3. Mathias, Senator Charles McC. Jr., "Ethnic Groups and Foreign Policy," *Foreign Affairs*, Summer, 1981, pp. 992-3.

Meanwhile, without the knowledge of the United States, several operations in Israel were initiated at the same time. One of them was eventually destined to become a cancer in the Israeli body politic, called the "Lavon Affair" and considered by some to be "Israel's Dreyfus case." At the time there were two main forces in Israeli politics. The dominant figure was David Ben Gurion, Israel's first Prime Minister, who had originally proclaimed the independence of the Jewish State and whose Old-Testament patriarchal mien was the symbol of Israel's war of independence and the years of defiance that followed. Throughout his career, Ben Gurion had moved steadily away from the moderation and flexibility of Chaim Weizmann toward the hardline stance that had become so familiar to Arab opponents and Western mediators. As Prime Minister, he stubbornly refused to accept or comply with repeated UN resolutions calling on Israel to return the territory it had seized in the 1948 fighting, and repatriate or compensate the Arab refugees who had fled or been expelled. Faced with Palestinian guerrilla activities from Gaza and the West Bank, he backed a policy of strong reprisals.

The other force was Moshe Sharett, Ben Gurion's Foreign Minister in 1953, who then succeeded him as Prime Minister during one of the convulsions that increasingly wracked Israel's ruling coalition of labor and non-communist leftist parties. Sharett believed that a policy of Israeli moderation in the face of Arab guerrilla attacks, Israeli compensation of Arab refugees, and an understanding with Egypt on boundaries could ultimately bring about a peaceful acceptance of Israel by its Arab neighbors.

First Ben Gurion, and later Sharett, attempted to contact the new Egyptian leader. With Ben Gurion's blessing, Israel's military hero, Yigael Allon, then a private citizen, had sought to re-establish communication with Nasser. Allon had first met Nasser after the UN cease-fire in 1948, when Allon's troops surrounded and held in place in the Falluja pocket a large Egyptian force which included Nasser. Subsequently, when Sharett became Prime Minister, he also attempted to make indirect contacts with Nasser, hoping that they might eventually lead, if not to face-to-face negotiations between the two leaders, at least to serious discussions between their representatives.

Unknown to the U.S., however, and apparently unknown to Sharett as well, the Israeli Army Intelligence organization – which at that time operated independently of the Mossad, Israel's equivalent of the CIA – was laying the groundwork for its own secret plan. Both before and since Nasser's time, the greatest concerns of many hardline Israeli leaders have focused not on the radical Arabs, but rather on moderate Arab leaders who have sought to establish or maintain close ties with the West. Obviously, if the West ever reached an agreement with the Arabs at the expense of Israel's territorial ambitions, it would be with just such a moderate Arab leader. Therefore the efforts by the Eisenhower Administration to cultivate the charismatic Egyptian colonel had not gone unnoticed in Israeli intelligence circles. Nor had the forthcoming British-Egyptian negotiations on the withdrawal of British forces from the Suez Canal, scheduled for July 1954.

Two Israeli journalists, Jacques Derogy and Hesi Carmel,[4] relate that early in

---

4. Derogy, Jacques and Carmel, Hesi, *The Untold History of Israel*, Grove Press, New York, 1979, pp. 101-128.

1954 Israeli Army Intelligence conceived a plan to attack British personnel inside Jordan. The purpose was to increase suspicion between Britain and Jordan, or Britain and Egypt (which would have been blamed for the attack), or possibly both. Shortly afterward, the same organization initiated a similar plan in Egypt, activating two networks of resident Egyptian Jews. These young people had been recruited in Egypt, secretly trained in Israel, and then sent back to Cairo and Alexandria to await orders to carry out acts of sabotage in case of war between Egypt and Israel. The networks were instructed to explode small incendiary bombs in American installations in Egypt, presumably to set off a chain of mutual recriminations that might spoil the budding American-Egyptian courtship. After completing the sabotage of American installations, the networks were also to bomb various public places in Cairo and Alexandria in order to exacerbate tensions between Nasser and the Muslim Brotherhood, which had backed the ousted General Naguib, and thus establish a general climate of Egyptian instability during the British-Egyptian Canal Zone negotiations.

The plan was set in motion by an Israeli spymaster sent to Cairo posing as a German businessman. On July 14, while Alexandrian Egyptians were observing Bastille Day as a symbol of the overthrow of Monarchist tyranny, incendiary devices were planted in U.S. Information Service libraries and other U.S. government institutions open to the public in both Cairo and Alexandria. A week later, on July 23, during Egypt's national day celebrations, Israeli agents sought to repeat their success with explosions in the Cairo railway station and in movie theaters in Cairo and Alexandria. In Alexandria, however, an incendiary device went off prematurely in the pocket of one of the young Egyptian Jews, Philippe Nathanson, as he stood in front of a theater and he was seized by the police. Within days the members of both the Cairo and Alexandria sabotage networks, along with one additional unaffiliated Israeli spy, were seized. Only the Israeli spymaster escaped the country.

Though the plan misfired, the denouement was rapid, and it succeeded beyond the wildest dreams of its Israeli planners in extinguishing all hopes of moderation, but in Israel rather than in Egypt. The arrested provocateurs were brought to trial in Cairo on December 11, 1954. They included an attractive Egyptian Jewish girl, Victorine Ninio, who was reported to have twice tried to commit suicide while under interrogation and who was brought, wounded, into the courtroom. The Egyptian press reported that the unaffiliated spy, Max Bennett, had been more successful in avoiding interrogation. He had killed himself with a rusty nail pried from his cell door. As the trial opened, the Israeli press seethed with indignation at what it assumed was an Egyptian show trial on baseless charges intended to terrorize Egypt's remaining Jewish community.

British and French politicians, assuming the same thing, begged Nasser to stop the proceedings, but to no avail. Seemingly most indignant of all was the first moderate Prime Minister in Israel's brief history, Moshe Sharett. This, the two Israeli journalists maintain, was because when the plan failed, the Israeli Army Intelligence chief, Colonel Benjamin Gibli, had so carefully covered his tracks that Sharett, too, at first believed the accused Egyptian Jews to be innocent. There were others who knew the truth, including General Moshe Dayan, Gibli's immediate superior, who seems to have assisted

Gibli to assure that ultimate blame for the operation would fall on Dayan's own direct superior, Defense Minister Pinchas Lavon.

On December 12, 1954, the second day of the Cairo trial, Sharett angrily denounced "these calumnies designed to strike at the Jews of Egypt." Later, when death sentences were handed down, Sharett publicly vowed, "We will not negotiate in the shadow of the gallows." At that moment at least four separate efforts, including one initiated by President Eisenhower, to initiate direct or indirect contacts between Colonel Nasser and Israel's heretofore moderate Prime Minister Sharett started to unravel. By the time the Prime Minister and others who apparently had been ignorant of the plot realized that there was substance to the Egyptian charges, the damage was done. Egyptians, angry at the seeming hypocrisy of the Israeli Prime Minister's scathing denials and never dreaming that he might truly be uninformed, had also begun to break off contacts.

By January 20, two of the conspirators had been hanged in Egypt and hopes among moderates for an Israeli-Egyptian rapprochement had died with them. The plot and coverup are known as the "Lavon Affair" to Western journalists, who have given it virtually no American press coverage in all the years since; and as the "Haessek Habish" or "Ugly Affair" to Israeli journalists, who have written thousands of words about the coverup, but very few words to reveal that the original act was a secret Israeli provocation against American diplomatic and cultural offices in Egypt.

The affair lingered on for a decade as a running sore in Israeli political life. Pinchas Lavon, the Defense Minister who had been hounded from office with forged documents and perjured testimony, was eventually rehabilitated. His ultimate persecutor, the by-then embittered and irascible David Ben Gurion, retired for the last time from public office in 1964. Four years later, the surviving four Jewish provocateurs, including Victorine Ninio and the luckless Nathanson, were handed over by the Egyptians to the Israelis as part of the general exchange of prisoners which took place after the 1967 Arab-Israeli war. Their arrival in Israel received low-key coverage in the Israeli press, and virtually none in the United States.

Even in the wake of the bitter exchange of recriminations in December 1954 and January 1955, some members of the Eisenhower Administration hoped that the situation could be salvaged. However, after the disgrace and resignation of Lavon, on February 17 Ben Gurion himself replaced Lavon as Defense Minister in the government of Ben Gurion's rival, Prime Minister Sharett. Ben Gurion immediately initiated drastic acts of retaliation for guerrilla raids, including a massive Israeli incursion into the Gaza strip and the assassination by letter bomb of an Egyptian military officer in Gaza who was said to be directing the guerrillas. The political fallout from the Lavon Affair had opened the way for Ben Gurion's policy of ten eyes for an eye and ten teeth for a tooth, which delivered the *coup de grace* to Sharett's dream of Egyptian-Israeli negotiations.

Shaken by the massive Israeli raid into Gaza, which he had been powerless to stop, Nasser turned to the U.S. with a request for $27 million in arms. The State Department, mindful of an agreement by Britain, France, and the United States in 1950 to maintain an arms balance between Israel and the Arabs, and confident that Egypt was short of funds, informed Nasser that he would have to pay for the arms in cash.

"Our attitude," President Eisenhower subsequently wrote, "may, with the advantage of hindsight, appear to have been unrealistic."[5]

It was. The Russians, with astonishing speed, moved into the breach with an offer of their own. They were able to offer arms rapidly, and on barter rather than cash terms, because after the death of Josef Stalin, Moscow had adopted a new political policy. Rather than working through communist parties abroad, the Soviets sought to encourage collaboration with countries which might be pulled out, or kept out, of Western alliances. This policy was to be followed regardless of the political system of the collaborating country, or of the status of local Communists.

President Nasser did nothing about the Soviet offer for a time. In September 1955, however, when the Israelis jarred him with another strong and successful raid on an Egyptian outpost, he made good his threat of the previous June and accepted the Russian proposal. He struck a deal to accept large quantities of arms, ostensibly from Czechoslovakia (the transaction is reminiscent of the Soviet-brokered airlift of Czech arms to the beleaguered Israelis in 1948), in exchange for Egyptian cotton.

The arms sale had an immediate effect on negotiations then under way for the World Bank, the U.S. and the U.K. to provide the foreign exchange required to construct the Aswan High Dam. These negotiations already seemed to be in the same kind of trouble that had overtaken the request for U.S. arms. Nasser objected to requirements by the World Bank that Egypt tighten its belt economically as a condition for receiving the money to build the dam, saying that such requirements infringed on Egypt's sovereignty. Now, however, an even larger problem arose in the U.S. Hostile questions were raised by hard-core cold warriors unwilling to use U.S. economic aid to help a country that was not clearly an ally; by Senators from cotton-producing states who had their own doubts about the political wisdom of appropriating tax money from their constituents to increase the cotton-growing capacity of Egypt; and by friends of Israel, who played effectively on both of the other concerns. But, regardless of their motivations, all of the American critics asked the same hard question: How was Egypt to meet its share of the High Dam's cost now that its cotton crop was mortgaged for years to come to pay the cost of Soviet arms?

Event followed event to worsen Egyptian relations with Britain, France and the U.S., and once again the Soviets moved adroitly, this time offering to replace Western financing of the High Dam with their own. Israel, meanwhile, had expressed alarm at the pace of Egyptian rearmament. It pressed its major supplier, France, for additional weapons and also opened a campaign for U.S. military assistance.

Sensing that things were getting out of hand, the U.S. again tried to initiate high-level secret contacts with Egypt in order to lower the tension. President Eisenhower sent a trusted personal emissary, former Secretary of the Navy Robert Anderson, to speak first with Nasser and then with Ben Gurion. It was the American hope that Anderson, shuttling between Israel and Egypt via third countries such as Greece and Italy (in a secret version of the highly visible Kissinger shuttles eighteen years later) could

---

5. Eisenhower, Dwight D., *The White House Years: Waging Peace 1956-1961*, Doubleday, Garden City, New York, 1965, p. 24.

develop enough common ground between Nasser and Ben Gurion to justify eventual Egyptian-Israeli negotiations.

Vastly complicating the problem was Nasser's insistence that a personal meeting was unthinkable in the current Arab political climate (some of it of his own making), and that communication could therefore continue only through intermediaries. Yet Ben Gurion insisted that only in a face-to-face meeting could he reveal the full extent of the Israeli concessions he was prepared to deliver. The impasse was a paradigm for recurrent failures in the years to follow, with most Arab leaders unwilling to meet their Israeli counterparts in the absence of specific advance Israeli concessions, and the Israelis unwilling to make the concessions except in a face-to-face meeting. By the end of February 1956, the Anderson mission had failed. The Egyptians continued to stockpile Soviet arms and Israel, after the U.S. rejected its arms request on April 3, initiated the arrangements that soon resulted in huge secret deliveries of French planes, tanks and munitions to its ports.

U.S. Secretary of State John Foster Dulles was preoccupied with building bulwarks against Communism and seemed insensitive to Nasser's determination to remove all vestiges of foreign domination—including military or economic aid with political or even financial strings attached. Similarly, the quick-tempered Egyptian leader displayed little sensitivity to the political problems of an American administration clearly and openly eager to help him. U.S. politicians and journalists with a pro-Israeli bias found that the best way to undermine American public support for Egypt was simply to draw attention to some of the more extreme statements or contradictory actions of its President, who was seeking to achieve undisputed Pan-Arab leadership.

The Aswan High Dam negotiations, therefore, were not helped when Nasser announced his recognition of the Chinese People's Republic without a warning even to Egyptian Foreign Ministry professionals, much less to the Nationalist Chinese or to the dean of the Cairo diplomatic corps—who happened to be the U.S. Ambassador. The gesture was tied largely to Egyptian arms procurement efforts. But Americans in general, and perhaps Dulles as well, saw this as a direct slap not only at the Nationalist Chinese but also at the Americans themselves, who had so recently fought the Communist Chinese in Korea. One immediate repercussion was a unique Senate rider to the Mutual Security Act of that year requiring "that none of the funds provided in this Act shall be used for assistance in connection with the construction of the Aswan Dam."

Eisenhower appeared willing to defy Congress, or at least to test the constitutionality of the rider, by continuing the negotiations. But he was ill on July 19 when, only days after the Senate action, the Egyptian Ambassador met with Dulles and brought the Egyptian request to a head. Dulles claimed he had just a few days earlier warned the Egyptians against bringing up the matter, given the Congressional sentiment of the moment. He probably was further incensed when the Egyptian Ambassador mentioned in the same conversation the Soviet offer to finance the dam. Without consulting Eisenhower, Dulles withdrew the American offer on the spot. On the same day, he confirmed what seems to have been an abrupt or, at the very least, a graceless decision with a formal announcement that the U.S. would not participate in Aswan financing.

Nasser interpreted the public American rejection as an invitation to the Egyptian people to bring down his regime. On July 24, 1956 he responded with a harsh speech against the United States. Two days later he announced that he was nationalizing the Suez Canal. Even as he spoke, Egyptian technicians who had quietly entered the Canal area earlier in the day seized its key installations from Canal company employees. The takeover occurred just a month after the last British forces, pushed by Egyptian nationalism and pulled by American anti-colonialism, had been withdrawn from the Canal zone.

Egypt's July 24, 1952 revolution had set in motion several chains of events aimed at mediating the Arab-Israeli dispute. The arrest of a Jewish provocateur in Alexandria on July 24, 1954 ultimately brought those initiatives to a halt. Now, after Dulles' withdrawal of U.S. financing for the Aswan Dam, the Egyptian President's July 24, 1956 verbal attack on the U.S., followed by his nationalization of the Canal, set the stage for a new pattern of violence that would plague the Middle East for at least a generation to come.

President Eisenhower, who seldom criticized his Secretary of State, clearly understated his feelings when he wrote:

"I have never doubted the wisdom of cancelling our offer, but I was concerned, in view of the events of the following weeks, that we might have been undiplomatic in the way the cancellation was handled."[6]

In retrospect it seems clear that the Israelis abandoned serious attempts to reach agreement with Egypt around the time that Sharett stated in January 1955 that he refused to negotiate "in the shadow of the gallows," and Ben Gurion launched his massive raid of February 1955 into the Gaza Strip. The raid convinced Egypt that it must obtain arms, Western if possible and Russian otherwise. Egypt's success in obtaining Soviet arms in turn provided the rationale for Israel's request to the U.S. and France for arms.

The French Prime Minister, Guy Mollet, faced with a full-scale rebellion in Algeria after November 1954, and growing anti-French movements in Morocco and Tunisia, blamed all three on the Egyptian President's propaganda and material support. As a result, he was ready to listen to Israel. French arms began reaching Israel in quantities that clearly violated the 1950 tripartite agreement against weapons shipments that would upset a rough Arab-Israeli arms balance. At one point the French notified Eisenhower of their desire to ship 12 Mystere jet fighters to Israel. He replied that he had no objection. Much later, on the eve of hostilities, American photo reconnaissance flights over Israel revealed that the 12 Mysteres had somehow become 60, displaying, in Eisenhower's words, "a rabbit-like capacity for multiplication." Some time after the secret weapons shipments had begun, secret French-Israeli military planning began as well.

As Churchill's Foreign Secretary, Anthony Eden had agreed not to try to bring Jordan into the Baghdad Pact, in return for which President Nasser had suspended propaganda attacks against Britain and Jordan. After he became Prime Minister himself,

---

6. Eisenhower, Dwight D., *The White House Years: Waging Peace 1956-1961*, Doubleday, Garden City, New York, 1965, p. 33.

however, Eden did attempt to enlist Jordan, and Egypt unleashed a violent and effective propaganda barrage. To defend his reputation, King Hussein did more than abandon any idea of joining the Pact. He also dismissed the British commander of his Arab Legion, Glubb Pasha, despite that distinguished officer's long record of service. The new British Prime Minister was so outraged that, according to British statesman and author Anthony Nutting, Eden vowed "the world was not large enough to hold him and Nasser."

In Anglo-American discussions in Washington in February, 1956, even as the renewed Eisenhower attempt to start Egyptian-Israeli negotiations fizzled out, British and U.S. differences emerged clearly. The British were deeply concerned about preserving what remained of their imperial traditions. The Americans, by contrast, found it natural and even inevitable that the last of the 19th-century colonial structures should decay. They were more concerned about the kinds of nationalist leadership that would arise around the fallen pillars of empire. The British saw Nasser as a mortal danger to Western interests, and their concern centered on how best to bring him down. The Americans, on the other hand, were particularly eager to preserve and protect strong and independent leaders like Egypt's charismatic President, and they focused their energies, albeit not always effectively, on keeping him from being drawn into the Russian orbit.

Eisenhower's speechwriter, Emmet John Hughes, records Dulles' comments as they worked together on a speech in 1956, at a time when the gap between the U.S. and its erstwhile western allies was widening. Dulles told Hughes:

"The concepts and words that matter, in all we say, I think, are simply *peace* and *change*. We live in an age of deep change. You can't stop it. What you can do is to bend every effort to direct it – to see that it is evolutionary rather than revolutionary – and to retain, in the process, all that is good in the past. Most particularly, this is true of the whole Afro-Asian problem. What the Western world is moving toward is a new role with these peoples – a role of partnership rather than rule."[7]

Secretary Dulles' action precipitately withdrawing – without consulting the President – U.S. support for Egypt's Aswan Dam was, therefore, a negation of the whole Eisenhower policy of flexibility. At the same time, Nasser's subsequent retaliatory action in nationalizing the Suez Canal was a confirmation, in British and French minds, of their own more rigid stand.

Both Eden and Mollet wanted to use force to restore international control over the Canal and to humiliate, and if possible destroy, Nasser. President Eisenhower would not condone military action, but Dulles' attempts to bring the Canal under international control may not have made this initially clear to the British and French. They proceeded with plans to halt Canal traffic by withdrawing European pilots. This, they reasoned, would throw the dispute into the United Nations, where they counted on a Russian veto to prevent UN action. The stage then would be set for their own recourse to force.

---

7. Hughes, Emmet John, *The Ordeal of Power: A Political Memoir of the Eisenhower Years*, Atheneum, New York, 1963, pp. 208-9.

Dulles knew that, in a U.S. election year, a UN debate would reawaken all the domestic interests that had plagued Roosevelt's last days and Truman's first term. Whether the U.S. supported its old wartime allies or followed its postwar inclination to accommodate new nationalist leaders, Eisenhower was bound to alienate one or another segment of the voters. Dulles suggested that the Canal be run by an association of the maritime powers that used it. He persuaded Eden to sponsor the idea at a conference of maritime powers in London and the conference adopted it. But meanwhile the European pilots had walked out of the Canal zone on September 14, 1956 and the Egyptians had taken it over. The Canal continued to run smoothly and efficiently, and thus the rationale for the users' association vanished. Therefore, as soon as Dulles left London, Eden and Mollet threw the dispute into the UN Security Council according to their original plan.

President Nasser by now was aware that the British and French were preparing for a showdown. He astonished them both by agreeing at the UN to a set of six British principles to settle the Canal dispute. But by then, France, Israel, and Britain had other plans, which did not include a settlement with Egypt. The British introduced more conditions, precipitating more UN debate, and eventually a Soviet veto.

A French-Israeli plan against Egypt had matured in early October. The Israelis suggested that it begin with a preliminary Israeli diversion against Jordanian forces in the West Bank. King Hussein, seeing what the Israelis were up to, appealed for help to Iraq, ruled by his second cousin, the young Faisal II, and to Britain. Iraq sent troops and Jordan's British allies indicated they were prepared to use their aircraft against any Israeli attempt to seize the West Bank. Only then, it seems, did the French and Israelis inform the British that the Israeli move toward Jordan was a feint, and that the ultimate joint goal was the Suez Canal. British participation in the plan against Egypt was approved by the British cabinet on October 25, 1956.

Eisenhower, after his long association with the British, became more and more upset as fragmentary clues to the French-British plan began to emerge. "My conviction was that the Western world had gotten into a lot of difficulty by selecting the wrong issue about which to be tough," Eisenhower later wrote. "To choose a situation in which Nasser had legal and sovereign rights, and in which world opinion was largely on his side, was not in my opinion a good one on which to make a stand. Accordingly I drafted a reply to this effect."[8]

He was equally concerned about Israeli intentions:

"Both Foster [Dulles] and I suspected that Ben Gurion might be contemplating military action during these pre-election days in the United States because of his possible overestimate of my desire to avoid offending the many voters who might have either sentimental or blood relations with Israel. I emphatically corrected any misapprehension of this kind he might have."[9]

---

8. Eisenhower, Dwight D., *The White House Years: Waging Peace 1956-1961*, Doubleday, Garden City, New York, 1965, p. 50.
9. *Ibid.*, p. 56.

And to his assistant, Hughes, he had trenchant comments on each of the conspirators, starting with Israel:

"I just can't figure out what the Israelis think they're up to. . . . Maybe they're thinking they just *can't* survive without more land. . . . But I don't see how they can survive without coming to some honorable and peaceful terms with the whole Arab world that surrounds them. . . ."[10]

He was even more critical of France:

"Damn it, the French, they're just egging the Israelis on—hoping somehow to get out of their *own* North African troubles. Damn it, they sat right there in those chairs three years ago, and we tried to tell them they would repeat Indochina all over again in North Africa. And they said, 'Oh, no. That's part of metropolitan France'—and all that damn nonsense."[11]

However, prophetic as he was on Israel and France, his comments on his old friend and ally, Britain, make ironic reading nearly three decades later, now that British and American roles with regard to Israel have reversed:

"I just can't believe it. I can't believe they would be so stupid as to invite on *themselves* all the Arab hostility to Israel. . . . What are they going to do—fight the whole Muslim world?"[12]

On October 29, as Dag Hammarskjold, Secretary General of the United Nations, initiated private negotiations on Britain's six principles, Israeli paratroops dropped over Sinai, landing close to the Mitla Pass and only 40 miles east of the Suez Canal. At the same moment Israeli armored columns roared westward across the Sinai peninsula to link up with the paratroops and southward into Sinai in the direction of Sharm al-Shaikh on the Straits of Tiran.

Eisenhower has commented that "the Presidency seldom affords the luxury of dealing with one problem at a time." That was amply demonstrated the day Israeli paratroopers dropped into the Sinai passes. The Polish people and government had just faced down the Soviet Union. Since 1949 the Russians had forced Poland to include a Russian Marshal in the Polish Cabinet as Secretary of Defense. On October 19, 1956 the Poles had told Khrushchev in Warsaw that Soviet Marshal Konstantin Rokossovsky had to go. Khrushchev reportedly informed the Poles that at that moment a Soviet division was moving toward their borders and, "if you don't obey, we will crush you." The Poles stood their ground and Khrushchev angrily returned to Moscow. When he got there, however, the Russians called off the invasion.

Unfortunately, in Eisenhower's words, "the fire ignited in Poland brought a holocaust to Hungary." When Hungarians sought to emulate the Polish success against the Russians, street fighting broke out in Budapest between Russian tanks and Hungarian youths wielding Molotov cocktails. By October 29, most of the Hungarian armed forces had

---

10. Hughes, Emmet John, *The Ordeal of Power: A Political Memoir of the Eisenhower Years*, Atheneum, New York, 1963, p. 212.
11. *Ibid.*, p. 212.
12. *Ibid.*, pp. 212-3.

gone over to the rebels and had brought huge sections of the country under rebel control. Though casualties were heavy, it appeared that the Hungarians were also succeeding in facing down the Russians.

Eisenhower dealt hourly with the ticklish problem of how to dissuade the Russians from further repressive moves, and the Poles and Hungarians from further violence that would make Russian repression inevitable. Meanwhile, he had a heavy schedule of speeches and appearances around the country in his second bid for the Presidency. The election was just seven days away.

Hughes was in almost constant contact with Eisenhower as they put together carefully worded statements on all three of the President's concerns: Hungary, the Middle East, and the election. Hughes recorded his own impressions of the situation a few hours before the Israeli paratroop drop was confirmed:

"The pieces of the picture fit together fairly clearly . . . through all the fog of uncertain information. From the viewpoint of Israel, the timing looks superb: Russia is deep in satellite trouble, Britain and France are straining at the leash for a crack at Nasser, and the U.S. is in the middle of a national election. Thus, the chance looks golden. . . . "[13]

However, Eisenhower was a President who was capable of telling Eden in a telephone conversation: I don't give a darn about the election." [14] The President immediately called for UN Security Council action. Ignoring the U.S. call, the British and French issued an ultimatum to Egypt and Israel, giving each twelve hours to cease hostilities and withdraw to positions 10 miles on either side of the Canal. This meant, of course, that Egypt would have to evacuate its own territory east of the Canal, and give up the Canal as well, while Israel would move forward 20 miles to take up positions within striking distance of the Canal. If anyone still thought the British-French ultimatum was truly designed to protect the Canal, this illusion was dispelled on October 31, when British planes swooped in from Cyprus to bomb the Canal's Ismailia headquarters and its Port Said terminal, along with airfields and other installations in both Cairo and Alexandria. It was a reprise of 19th century gunboat diplomacy.

Egypt reacted by sinking ships in the Canal, blocking further navigation. Syria later responded by sabotaging the pipelines carrying oil across its territory from Iraq to the Mediterranean, interrupting the flow of oil to Western Europe. When the British and French vetoed a cease-fire resolution in the UN Security Council, the United States introduced a resolution in the General Assembly calling for a cease-fire and for the dispatch of UN soldiers to enforce it. Surprisingly, not only Egypt but Israel too accepted it. This pulled the rug out from under the Anglo-French invasion force, still steaming from Malta toward Egypt. The British and French, however, announced that their troops would land to keep order until the UN force could arrive.

By this time the combination of blunt Soviet threats, unyielding U.S. opposition, and strong domestic criticism in Britain had thoroughly shaken Eden. He informed

---

13. Hughes, Emmet John, *The Ordeal of Power: A Political Memoir of the Eisenhower Years*, Atheneum, New York, 1963, p. 213.

14. *Ibid.*, p. 92.

Mollet that Britain was withdrawing from the operation. The word, however, apparently did not get to his military commanders, and 20 hours later British and French paratroops and infantry landed, broke through fierce Egyptian opposition, and assumed positions along the now totally-blocked Canal.

Israel, having first stunned her fellow conspirators by accepting the UN cease-fire, now abruptly decided to risk new U.S. disapproval in order to fulfill a long-standing national objective. Israel broke the cease-fire and resumed military operations just long enough to seize Sharm al-Shaikh, commanding the entrance from the Red Sea into the Gulf of Aqaba. It then accepted the cease-fire once again. (This tactic of waiting until after a cease-fire agreement has been reached and then mounting an offensive to attain major military objectives has been used by Israel in virtually every war it has fought. It had also been used by Israel in the fighting of 1948 to seize vital objectives and surround enemy forces at the Falluja pocket.)

Eisenhower meanwhile rejected a Soviet plan for joint action as "unthinkable" and warned that the entry of any new troops into the Middle East would oblige all members of the United Nations, including the United States, to take effective countermeasures. Both countries continued to apply pressure separately, however, and the British and French agreed to withdraw. Eden, whose political career was ended by the debacle, as a last act delivered his own scathing denunciation of the hypocrisy of the Soviet Union's entry into the Middle East as a peacemaker while its hands were still stained with Hungarian blood.

On November 8, 1956, after receiving reports that Ben Gurion had rejected the UN order to withdraw his forces, Eisenhower informed the Israeli leader that the U.S. viewed Israel's refusal with "deep concern." Ben Gurion rapidly reconsidered and, after meeting with his cabinet for nine hours, informed Eisenhower that Israeli forces would withdraw after all since "we have never planned to annex the Sinai Desert." When the fighting was over, Britain admitted to 16 dead, and France to 10. Press reports put the Israeli dead near 200 and the Egyptian dead at 1000.

In Hungary, where the Soviets had feigned withdrawal and then, on November 4, launched a major tank assault to crush the rebels, 25,000 Hungarians were dead. By the end of the year, another 150,000 Hungarians had fled their country. The Soviets had given Imre Nagy, the Prime Minister of Hungary during its short-lived rebellion, a pledge of safe conduct. They then seized and executed him.

Secretary Dulles, already afflicted with the cancer that would soon kill him, realized that the West had fallen into disarray over the Middle East at the very moment he had awaited in Eastern Europe for all the years since World War II. He sadly told the President on November 1:

"It is nothing less than tragic that at this very time when we are on the point of winning an immense and long-hoped-for victory over Soviet colonialism in Eastern Europe, we should be forced to choose between following in the footsteps of Anglo-French colonialism in Asia and Africa, or splitting our course away from their course."[15]

15. Eisenhower, Dwight D., *The White House Years: Waging Peace 1956-1961*, Doubleday, Garden City, New York, 1965, p. 83.

Eisenhower, writing later, added:

"I still wonder what would have been my recommendation to the Congress and the American people had Hungary been accessible by sea or through the territory of allies who might have agreed to react positively to the tragic fate of the Hungarian people. As it was, however, Britain and France could not possibly have moved with us into Hungary."[16]

Finally, speaking more boldly on the Middle East than almost any U.S. President since, Eisenhower summed up his thoughts on Suez and the 1956 Presidential campaign:

"During the campaign, some political figures kept talking of our failure to 'back Israel.' If the administration had been incapable of withstanding this kind of advice in an election year, could the United Nations thereafter have retained any influence whatsoever?"[17]

Israel Office of Information
Israeli soldier hands out packets of cigarettes to Egyptian prisoners from the 1956 campaign being returned to Egypt.

---

16. Eisenhower, Dwight D., *The White House Years: Waging Peace 1956-1961*, Doubleday, Garden City, New York, 1965, p. 88.
17. *Ibid.*, p. 99.

CHAPTER VII

President Eisenhower's Second Term and the Coca Cola Invasion

"Eisenhower sought to preserve U.S. influence in the developing world, even at the risk of alienation from European allies. While he continued the general policy of support for Israel, he angrily opposed the British-French-Israeli attempt of October 1956 to topple Egypt's Nasser by military action. He would not permit France and Britain to renew their colonial hegemony. The United States even joined with the Soviet Union in a UN resolution condemning the invasion. Eisenhower compelled the NATO allies to withdraw from the Suez Canal and the Israelis to pull back from Sinai and Gaza. It was a rare case in modern history of a Great Power acting in the name of a principle against what appeared to be its own strategic interests—against its allies and in concert with its adversaries. The deviation was short-lived. Nasser proved an ungrateful recipient of American protection. He acted against U.S. interests in every part of the globe, and the landings of the U.S. forces in Lebanon in 1958 were directed against Egypt—to the sardonic satisfaction of Britain, France and Israel."[1]

Abba Eban, 1983

"Ironically, instead of bringing peace nearer, the Sinai War, by increasing Arab hatred and fear, by giving the Arabs still another reason for wanting revenge, and by further humiliating them, made the Arabs even more adamant in their refusal to come to terms with Israel. Besides, by exaggerating the extent of Israel's military victory and of Egypt's defeat in the Sinai, the Israelis became, as the New York Times *reported on November*

---

1. Eban, Abba, *The New Diplomacy: International Affairs in the Modern Age*, Random House, New York, 1983, p. 36.

12, 1956, more overconfident and cocky, and, therefore, 'more difficult to handle' and less willing to make concessions. "[2]

Fred J. Khouri, 1968

"To prevent an outbreak of hostilities I preferred a resolution which would call on all United Nations members to suspend not only governmental but private assistance to Israel. Such a move would be no hollow gesture. "[3]

Dwight D. Eisenhower, 1965

The Suez crisis ended as raggedly as it began. The British and French withdrew in December 1956 and the Egyptians had agreed by the end of the same month to start clearing the Canal. The Israelis, however, still hoped to drive a hard bargain. For a time after the 1948 war, Israeli-chartered ships carrying cargoes for Israel had passed through the Canal flying the flags of their country of registry. After 1950, however, the Egyptians had brought this to a halt. They linked their refusal to allow Israeli cargoes to transit either the Canal or the Straits of Tiran, controlling the Gulf of Aqaba, with Israel's refusal to comply with UN resolutions concerning withdrawal from territory seized during the 1948 fighting and the repatriation or compensation of Palestinians made homeless at that time.

The Israelis now made it clear that they were not going to complete their withdrawal from Sinai until they secured guaranteed access through the Canal and the Tiran Straits. They also said that they would not permit Egyptian authorities back into the Gaza Strip at all.

The U.S., concerned that Britain and France were now considered allies of Israel, and hoping to position itself as an impartial mediator, did not want the issue to go back to the UN, where the U.S. would have to stand up and be counted on one side or the other. Messages were exchanged between the U.S. and Israel, but Ben Gurion grew increasingly outspoken in his rejection of U.S. requests that he withdraw his forces. When Israel sent the U.S. a refusal in writing, and the U.S. delegate to the UN told Eisenhower there was no further way to delay a UN discussion, the President began a series of meeting with his advisers on February 15. He later wrote about the discussions:

"Secretary Dulles strongly expressed the view that we had gone as far as possible to try to make it easy for the Israelis to withdraw. To go further, he said, would surely jeopardize the entire Western influence in the Middle East, and the nations of that region would conclude that United States policy toward the area was, in the last analysis, controlled by Jewish influence in the United States. In such event the only hope of the Arab countries would be found in a firm association with the Soviet Union."[3]

Like Truman before him, Eisenhower considered stronger action than has ever been threatened since to make Israel withdraw so that he could get on with his program to stabilize the post-Suez situation in the Middle East:

---

2. Khouri, Fred J.,*The Arab Israeli Dilemma*, The University Press, Syracuse, N.Y., 1976, p. 218.
3. Eisenhower, Dwight D., *The White House Years: Waging Peace 1956-1961*, Doubleday, Garden City, New York, 1965, p. 185.

"In considering various possible courses of action, I rejected, from the outset, any more United Nations resolutions designed merely to condemn Israel's conduct. Once more, I rejected also any new resolution like that of October 30, 1956, which had called only for a suspension of governmental support of Israel. Indeed, such a suspension against both Israel and Egypt was already in effect by the United States. To prevent an outbreak of hostilities I preferred a resolution which would call on all United Nations members to suspend not just governmental but private assistance to Israel. Such a move would be no hollow gesture. As we discussed it [Treasury Secretary] George Humphrey put in a call to W. Randolph Burgess, Undersecretary of the Treasury for Monetary Affairs, who gave a rough estimate that American private gifts to Israel were about $40 million a year and sale of Israel's bonds in our country between $50 and $60 million a year."[4]

To gain time, Eisenhower then made public earlier messages he had sent to Israel, predictably unleashing a storm of domestic protest. He writes:

"In a special White House conference with congressional leaders of both parties two days later, politics was in the back of many of the conferees' minds. In 1956 the Republican national ticket had carried New York by more than one and one-half million votes—the largest margin in the history of the Empire State. But faced with the possibility of having to take a stand for strong American action against Israel, some of those present were more than a little nervous."[5]

Congressional leaders at the meeting on February 20 were doubtful. One of them, Senator Lyndon Johnson, argued that in "cracking down" on Israel the U.S. was using a double standard, following one policy for weak countries like Israel and another for strong countries like the Soviet Union, since the Soviets were not complying with a UN resolution on Hungary. Johnson also had reservations about any Congressional statement on the matter, unless it was certain that such a statement would cause Israel to withdraw.

As the Eisenhower Administration pursued its double confrontation, with Israel on the one hand and with Israel's domestic supporters in the U.S. on the other, the UN moved inexorably toward calling for world-wide sanctions against Israel. Finally, on March 1, 1957, Israeli Foreign Minister Golda Meir went before the UN General Assembly to announce Israeli readiness for a "full and complete withdrawal" of military forces, and Eisenhower was free to pursue his own Middle Eastern plans.

Even before the British and French withdrawals from the Suez Canal, Eisenhower had outlined what later became known as the Eisenhower Doctrine, to fill the vacuum he believed the decline of British and French power had created, "before it is filled by Russia." To the Arabs, however, it looked like the substitution of one kind of Western tutelage for another. Harold Macmillan, Britain's new Prime Minister and Eisenhower's old wartime colleague and friend, was also unenthusiastic at a British-American meeting held March 21, 1957 in Bermuda. Afterward Eisenhower wrote:

"Foster and I at first found it difficult to talk constructively with our British colleagues about Suez because of the blinding bitterness they felt toward Nasser. Prime Minister Harold Mac-

---

4. Eisenhower, Dwight D., *The White House Years: Waging Peace 1956-1961*, Doubleday, Garden City, New York, 1965, pp. 185-6.
5. *Ibid.*, p. 186.

millan and Foreign Minister Selwyn Lloyd were so obsessed with the possibilities of getting rid of Nasser that they were handicapped in searching, objectively, for any realistic method of operating the Canal."[6]

Prior to the Suez crisis British Prime Minister Eden had concluded that either he or Nasser must go. His prediction was fulfilled with his own resignation. The Egyptian President, on the other hand, had emerged from the affair with enormously enhanced prestige. Some Arab countries were still struggling with colonial rule, and most others with its psychological and economic after effects. Therefore, Nasser's success in turning back both of the major colonial powers made him a symbol of the aspirations of Arabs almost everywhere.

It was a time of increasing turbulence in the Arab world, as individual leaders and political parties, appealing alternately to Pan-Arabism and to regional rivalries or separatist traditions, struggled among themselves. The era is now known as the "Arab Cold War." Nearly all of it lies outside the parameters of a study of U.S. perceptions of the Arab-Israeli dispute. Yet the events of this period reinforced a growing impression among Americans in general that the entire Middle East was an area of shifting, unstable alliances and of emotional, volatile people.

The Eisenhower Doctrine sought to focus U.S. economic and military aid on strengthening those leaders the U.S. considered moderate, while ignoring those the U.S. considered too dependent upon the Soviet Union, or too weak and unpopular within their own countries to rule without eventual Soviet help. Implicit in the doctrine was the possibility of U.S. military action if a country requested armed assistance against an internal or external threat. Liberal critics complained that Eisenhower's Administration was becoming too much like the ousted colonial regimes, insensitive to the new nationalist aspirations not only of the Arabs, but of all emerging countries. Conservative critics, on the other hand, attributed increasing turbulence and Soviet infiltration into the Arab countries to Eisenhower's original decision to oppose the French, British, and Israelis at Suez. Nasser became the focus of much of this debate in the U.S. as well as among other Western powers. Critics on either side found it convenient to cite the words and actions of the Egyptian leader to prove their points.

U.S. diplomats and military officers serving in Egypt had fallen under Nasser's charismatic sway even before he emerged as the undisputed leader of the officers who overthrew King Farouk. By now, some of those who supported Nasser and the Arab nationalist tendencies he personified had risen to important second- and third-echelon positions in the U.S. foreign affairs establishment. On the other hand, diplomats whose foreign service assignments had given them a more European orientation saw Nasser as the original wrecker of the Western Alliance, whose influence should be ended as soon as possible.

Friends of Israel, by no means all of them Jewish, were also influential in governmental circles. In addition, Israel had partisans in media and in academic circles.

---

6. Eisenhower, Dwight D., *The White House Years: Waging Peace 1956-1961*, Doubleday, Garden City, New York, 1965, p. 122.

Although journalists and scholars could not make U.S. policy, their words could raise or lower the fortunes of both career and elected government officials, and they were willing to ally themselves with anyone who opposed the Egyptian President. The result was a running series of battles within the foreign affairs establishment and an extraordinary policy in which the U.S. repeatedly prepared for possible military action, as happened in Jordan early in 1957, in Syria later the same year, and then in Lebanon in 1958.

In the first two cases the situation appeared to stabilize before any overt U.S. action was taken. All contenders for influence in the U.S saw this as a vindication of their own recommendations. Those among the State Department's Middle East hands who had counseled moderation could say that, by not intervening, the U.S. had enabled the Arabs to work things out themselves. Those who had wanted the U.S. to intervene militarily in coordination with conservative Arab states argued from the same events that, if even the threat of force persuaded Egypt's ruler to adopt policies of conciliation, a demonstration of real force might bring him down.

The Israeli influence was most overtly demonstrated during the 1957 events in Syria. U.S. officials, eventually including the President, became convinced that a government of Communists and leftists, with none strong enough to assert mastery, made Syria ripe for Soviet plucking. From Israel, Ben Gurion tossed gasoline on the embers of U.S. doubt and suspicion, cabling Eisenhower that "it is impossible to distinguish between Syria and Russia" and that "the establishment of Syria as a base for international Communism is one of the most dangerous events which has befallen the Free World in our time."

State Department officials and other Americans who counseled moderation were soon reinforced by the clear reluctance of such conservative Arab regimes as Saudi Arabia, Iraq, and Jordan to become directly involved. The latter two countries, along with Lebanon, had raised the alarm in the first place and would be most threatened by the Soviet penetration of Syria. As a result U.S. hawks, who by then had President Eisenhower's ear, could say little that would justify U.S. intervention.

A combination of Syrian army officers and political leaders, some fearing the rise of Soviet influence and some dismayed by Syria's isolation from all other Arab countries, eventually requested a union with Nasser's Egypt. The United Arab Republic came into existence on February 22, 1958, and soon was expanded to include northern Yemen in a confederation known as the United Arab States.

American diplomats who feared that use of U.S. military force would create far more problems in the Arab world than it would solve pointed to this as vindication of their stand. Nasser had without bloodshed closed the hole through which Soviet influence might have entered Syria. Other Americans, who by then had developed a distaste for Nasser reminiscent of Anthony Eden's statements on the eve of Suez, depicted the Egyptian as a "dictator" brandishing Soviet arms to intimidate Arabs into joining his makeshift empire, one certainly destined to fall under Soviet sway when he had sufficiently overextended himself. The dynamic Egyptian could speak extemporaneously for hours at a time in a simple, highly-personalized style that combined colloquial Egyptian Arabic with the melodic classical Arabic of the Koran. He mesmerized not only his countrymen but also Arabs throughout the Middle East. As a result, in the United States Nasser's supporters and detractors both could generally find something in his speeches to quote in support of their differing viewpoints.

The political confusion in the Middle East, and the divisions in the U.S. over how or whether to deal with it, finally intersected in Lebanon in 1958. When the French created Lebanon as a largely Christian entity carved out of predominantly Muslim Greater Syria, they unwittingly built in a time bomb. The tiny country is centered on the mountain range where Maronite Christians and Druze (the followers of a secretive religion which branched off from Islam after the 11th century A.D.) have lived for centuries, aloof from domination by the Muslims who inhabit the coastal and inland plains around them.

The French wanted to make the Christian enclave as economically viable as possible. They therefore attached to the mountain territory not only the port of Beirut, which had many Christian and Druze residents, but also coastal Tripoli, Sidon, and Tyre, which had virtually none. As the years went by a higher birthrate among the Muslims, and extensive emigration to the U.S. and Latin America by the Christians, began to alter the religious balance. The Christian-dominated Lebanese government refused to authorize any further census after 1934. The influx of a predominantly Muslim Palestinian refugee population in 1948 increased the imbalance. The Muslims already were restive with their slightly inferior share of official positions and other governmental benefits. They also were strongly attracted to Nasser's Pan-Arabism. When rumors spread that the conservative Maronite President, Camille Chamoun, was going to seek to amend the Lebanese Constitution to permit himself an unprecedented second six-year term, the large Muslim quarters of both Beirut and Tripoli, as well as many all-Muslim towns and villages, began to defy the President's rule. On May 13, 1958, Chamoun appealed to Eisenhower, charging that the arms and ammunition being used by the Muslims were being smuggled over the mountains from Nasser's new Syrian province.

Eisenhower informed Chamoun that U.S. troops invoked under the Eisenhower Doctrine would not come to Lebanon to give him a second presidential term, and would not come at all unless Lebanon's request had the concurrence of a second Arab nation. Eisenhower had managed to remain somewhat detached from his immediate advisers' strongly negative feelings about the Egyptian President. Yet even Eisenhower was surprised when Nasser quickly agreed with an American suggestion to send in UN observers to investigate the infiltration of weapons and men. The Egyptian President went considerably further, suggesting that the U.S. and Egypt jointly sponsor new Lebanese elections that would make it possible for the Army commander, General Fuad Chehab, to assume the Presidency. Lebanon's National Pact specifies that the President must be a Maronite Christian and by tradition the commander of the Army also is a Maronite. Therefore Chehab was eligible so far as the Pact and the Christians upholding it were concerned, while his actions in keeping the Lebanese army out of the incipient civil war (and thus avoiding a split between its Muslim and Christian soldiers) had made him readily acceptable to Lebanon's Muslims.

Eisenhower declined Nasser's suggestion of joint action but welcomed what he later described as the "puzzling" favorable Egyptian attitude toward UN intervention. The Lebanese crisis seemed to be simmering down.

Three months earlier—when Egypt and Syria had formed the United Arab Republic—Iraq and Jordan, ruled by second cousins, had reacted by forming a Hashemite Union, uniting the two Kingdoms into one, with the stipulation that the ruler of the considerably larger, richer and more populous Iraq would have specified prior rights. The Union was unpopular among many of the thousands of Palestinian refugees to whom King Hussein had granted full Jordanian citizenship, but who looked to Nasser as the Pan-Arab leader who might some day restore their Palestinian homeland.

The Iraqi Prime Minister, Nuri al-Said, offered to redeploy some of his troops from the Iranian border to the Jordanian border in case Jordan's Arab Legion could not handle the resulting instability. Normally, troop movements in Iraq were carried out via circuitous routes in order to bypass Baghdad completely. When troops had to pass through the Iraqi capital, it was customary for them to unload their guns. This was an emergency deployment, however, and the old Iraqi strongman, whose career had started in the Ottoman army before World War I, had grown blatantly overconfident about his power and luck. For some time he had ignored the public's discontent over his use of oil revenues, deferring immediate benefits—such as rapid expansion of public education—to build an infrastructure of dams, canals and power plants for expanded agricultural production. His program was not widely understood, and neither Nuri al-Said nor the unpopular Regent, Prince Abd al-Illah, had made a serious effort to explain it to the people of Iraq. Now Nuri ignored urgent warnings by his security police about the troop movement. As a result, two ambitious army officers, Brigadier Abd al-Karim Qasim and his popular chief of staff, Colonel Abd al-Salam Arif, found themselves moving their entire motorized force with loaded guns by night through the streets of Baghdad.

By mid-morning of the next day, July 14, 1958, the Regent, the King and their immediate relatives, both male and female, were dead. Brigadier Qasim had taken over the government, jubilant mobs ruled the streets, and Nuri al-Said was in hiding. A few days later, Nuri tried to escape disguised as a veiled, black-robed pious woman. He is said to have been spotted by a small boy who noted a man's shoes under the woman's robe, and to have been killed on the spot. Brigadier Qasim's politics were a mystery—and remained so—to Westerners, but Colonel Arif was known to be a great admirer of Nasser. Arif made this manifestly clear by taking a trip to Cairo immediately after the coup.

Although these events aroused anti-Nasser sentiment among leaders of both Britain and the U.S., Eisenhower continued to insist that a rescue effort for Chamoun would need another Arab country's blessing. Britain immediately consulted with Hussein, who was shocked and angered over the fate of his Iraqi relatives and also of members of a Jordanian delegation visiting Baghdad who were killed by a mob in the first hours of the revolution. Shortly afterward, still on July 14, the British Prime Minister was able to report to the U.S. President that requests for military assistance had been received from both President Chamoun and King Hussein.

The day after the Iraqi revolution, the U.S. called for an emergency meeting of the UN, and U.S. Marines went ashore in full battle gear on a long sandy beach south of Beirut bordering the international air field. In view of the Lebanese army's neutrality, Eisenhower was not sure whether his Marines would be welcomed or met with army gunfire. Nevertheless, demonstrating the political caution that characterized all of his military actions, he had decided not to land in a secure Christian area. Instead, the U.S. force would limit itself to securing the capital and its airport adjacent to the landing site. He later explained:

"The decision to occupy only the air field and capital was a political one which I adhered to over the recommendations of some of the military. If the Lebanese army were unable to subdue the rebels when we had secured their capital and protected their government, I felt, we were backing up a government with so little popular support that we probably should not be there."[7]

There was a tense moment, however, as the troops prepared to drive slowly into the city. They were met on the road by an official party composed of Lebanese Army Commander Chehab, the U.S. Admiral in charge of the operation, who had flown into Lebanon in advance of his troops, and by the U.S. Ambassador. There was a lengthy period of negotiations as the Marines waited all along the landing area. Lebanon's beaches normally are jammed in July with crowds of bathers, among whom move vendors of soft drinks, ice cream, and various Lebanese foods. There were no bathers on July 15, 1958, but while the U.S. troops waited, vendors who had been watching the invasion from their nearby houses warily approached. By the time the order to drive on into the city was given, the U.S. Marines and the Lebanese soft-drink vendors had had their first mutually satisfactory encounter. Twelve hours later, when the landing craft of the next Marine battalion hit the beach, Marines were mobbed by vendors of soft drinks, ice cream and spicy foods. The entire three-stage Marine landing has gone down in both U.S. and Lebanese history as "the Coca Cola invasion." It presaged the commerical bonanza enjoyed by the merchants of Beirut for three months until they waved farewell to the last members of the 14,000-man U.S. force on October 21, 1958.

In Jordan, just two days after the U.S. Marines had landed in Beirut, British troops were airlifted into Amman in support of King Hussein and found a similar welcome. The main concern throughout their brief stay in Jordan was the awkward fact that the only available supply route for their forces lay through the air space of Jordan's enemy, Israel.

After the U.S. landing in Lebanon, there was no lack of advice from Americans in the area. Some conservative U.S. businessmen resident in Beirut strongly backed Chamoun. Most diplomats were gravely concerned about hostile Arab reactions to direct U.S. intervention. Eisenhower characteristically sent his own emissary, Robert Murphy, a diplomat whose association with Eisenhower went back to World War II and the Allied landings in North Africa. After talking to everyone he could contact, including Nasser in Egypt and Qasim in Iraq, Murphy concluded that only a special Lebanese election giving General Chehab an opportunity to assume the Presidency would restore consensus rule.

---

7. Eisenhower, Dwight D., *The White House Years: Waging Peace 1956-1961*, Doubleday, Garden City, New York, 1965, p. 175.

The election was held July 31 and General Chehab was elected with the support of both Muslims and Christians in Lebanon. It was exactly the solution Nasser, depicted by many British and American opponents as the chief agent of international Communism in the Arab world, had proposed to the U.S. President three months earlier.

A year after the Lebanon landing Eisenhower was visited in Washington by Rashid Karami, Prime Minister of Lebanon (where under the National Pact the Prime Minister is a Sunni Muslim), and one of the two main "rebel" leaders of 1958. Eisenhower has recorded his impressions of the visit:

"I enjoyed that conversation. In the course of it I happened to mention the landings in Lebanon the year before; Mr. Karami said with a laugh that it would have been better had the United States held off sending troops but had merely sent Mr. Murphy to straighten out the situation. I was highly pleased with the implicit compliment to Bob Murphy . . . who was participating in our talk. But . . . no one man could possibly have composed the differences that were then tearing Lebanon to pieces. . . . However, as our conversation ended, I could not completely smother the thought that if our visitor's statement had been true, everyone in my Administration could have been saved a lot of anxious hours."[8]

Israel Office of Information

Israeli soldiers drive through Al Arish after taking it from Egyptian army in 1956 war.

---

8. Eisenhower, Dwight D., *The White House Years: Waging Peace 1956-1961*, Doubleday, Garden City, New York, 1965, p. 189.

Zionist Archives

All smiles: The 1956 Israeli surprise attack on Egypt, timed to begin just before U.S. Presidential elections and supported militarily by France and Britain, was an easy one for Israel. Even though it was broken up by U.S. and Soviet threats to intervene, and President Eisenhower eventually forced the Israelis to withdraw from Sinai, it was the beginning of Israel's self-image of military invincibility. Above left Israeli soldier reads Egyptian newspaper. Above right an Israeli poses with his automatic weapon in Sinai desert. Below four Israelis captured during the campaign celebrate their return to Israel in exchange for captured Egyptians.

Israel Office of Information

CHAPTER VIII

President Kennedy and Good Intentions Deferred Too Long

"Kennedy's impact on the international community closely paralleled his domestic reverberation. His youth and style, which separated him from the previous generation, excited the hope of innovation and initiative . . . The group that he gathered around him included men such as Adlai Stevenson, Chester Bowles and Kenneth Galbraith who would have been happy with an America showing a more accomodating face to the nonaligned world, but the dominant memory in Kennedy's mind was of how appeasement led to danger and how unchecked aggression grew from small to large arenas until it went beyond control. The mechanical application of these lessons from European history to the remote areas of Southeast Asia led to an embarrassing conclusion. America's greatest international error—Vietnam—was committed under the aegis of the presidential team most versed in the ways of the world and most at home in the concepts and traditions of diplomacy."[1]

Abba Eban, 1983

"Once countries had gained their independence, Kennedy believed that the sensible thing was to try to live with the new nations and their new leaders. Not domination or preachment, but adjustment and rapprochement seemed to him the fruitful relationship. He saw this as a long-term investment and was ready in the meantime to put up with a certain amount of nonsense."[2]

Arthur M. Schlesinger, Jr., 1965

1. Eban, Abba, *The New Diplomacy: International Affairs in the Modern Age*, Random House, New York, 1983, p. 42.
2. Schlesinger, Arthur M., Jr., *A Thousand Days—John F. Kennedy in the White House*, Houghton Mifflin, Boston, 1965, p. 564.

"Nasser liked Kennedy's Ambassador, John Badeau, and he liked Kennedy's practice of personal correspondence. Kennedy put off, however, an invitation for a Nasser visit until improved relations could enable him to answer the political attacks such a visit would bring from voters more sympathetic to Israel."[3]

Theodore Sorensen, 1965

Since President Eisenhower was not eligible for a third term, the election contest in 1960 was between his vice president, Richard Nixon, and Senator John F. Kennedy. Kennedy, the candidate of the liberal, eastern wing of the Democratic Party, had wrested the nomination from Senator Lyndon Johnson, who was supported by its southern, conservative elements. Kennedy courteously offered the older, more seasoned Johnson the Party's vice presidential nomination, and reportedly was shocked and disappointed when Johnson swallowed his pride and accepted it.

The only remarkable aspect of the campaign itself was the fact that Nixon, already well known, unwisely agreed to a series of televised debates with the relatively unknown Kennedy. Fearing the still-unexplored potential of the new medium, both candidates largely avoided the controversial issues that would have given substance to their debates. Instead they competed with ringing declarations on non-controversial issues. Most of the foreign policy debate concerned the need to get tough with America's favorite enemy, Cuba's Fidel Castro. Israel was praised by both candidates, loudly and often, both on television and in personal appearances before Jewish groups. As always, when the electoral campaign turned to the Middle East, the challenger had the advantage. He could take the previous administration to task for not doing more for the Jewish State. At that time it probably made little real difference what either candidate said on Israel, so long as each made the ritual pledges of support and devotion. For historical reasons, most of the Jewish vote went to the Democratic candidate in any case. In this election, the vote was even less likely to go to Nixon. His outspoken conservatism, his aggressive tactics in the searches during the 1950s for real or fancied Communist influence in the U.S. government, and his defense—as Vice President—of Eisenhower Administration policies during the 1956 Israeli attack on Egypt had made Jews frankly uneasy.

The television debates introduced a crucial new factor to what clearly was going to be a very close election, and to what the press had been calling a Tweedledum versus Tweedledee campaign. Senator Kennedy was indisputably better looking than Vice President Nixon. Platitudes delivered with a touch of humor by a fresh-faced Irishman from Massachusetts sounded more promising than similar lines delivered by a somber Californian with five o'clock shadow. Pundits generally agreed that the debates were a draw on substance, but that Kennedy had won them on style. The voters subsequently confirmed that judgment.

It was such a close victory that, had Nixon chosen to follow up serious charges of fraud in the decisive Illinois vote, he might have thrown not only the election results but the country into chaos. Kennedy could not be expected, therefore, to launch his Administration with controversial new foreign policy initiatives that could erode his

---

3. Sorensen, Theodore C., *Kennedy*, Harper and Row, New York, 1965, p. 540.

already uncomfortably narrow political base. His first foreign initiative, the Bay of Pigs landing by anti-Castro Cubans, backfired. In that operation each party had good reason to blame the other. Eisenhower, a Republican, had initially approved a military operation that was politically unsound. When Kennedy, a Democrat, took office, he had made it militarily unsound as well by denying it U.S. air cover.

Therefore, it is surprising to realize, with the benefit of hindsight, that from the time Kennedy entered office as the narrowly-elected candidate of a party heavily dependent upon Jewish support, he was planning to take a whole new look at U.S. Mideast policy. He obviously could not turn the clock back and undo the work of President Truman, his Democratic predecessor, in making the establishment of Israel possible. Nor, perhaps, would he have wanted to. Kennedy was determined, however, to develop good new personal relationships with individual Arab leaders, including those with whom the previous Administration's relations had deteriorated. As a result, various leaders of newly independent countries were surprised to find their *pro forma* messages of congratulation upon Kennedy's assumption of office answered with personalized letters from the young American President.

The explanation was simple. As a child in a proudly Irish-American family, Kennedy had listened with fascination to the tales of Ireland's struggle for independence. As the son of a U.S. Ambassador to the Court of St. James's, he had seen more of other countries during school vacations than most Americans see in a lifetime. He was also a member of the World War II generation that had personally paid the price for international greed and shortsightedness between the wars. He was an authentic war hero who had come back. His older brother, Joseph, had been killed in the air war over Europe. John Kennedy had been hospitalized repeatedly for back injuries sustained when the torpedo boat he commanded was cut in half by a Japanese destroyer. He had had a lot of time to read and think about the false pride of the old that has so often sent the young off to war.

Kennedy had visited Indochina in 1951. By 1957, as a freshman member of the Senate Foreign Relations Committee, he thought he recognized the same tragedy of colonial inflexibility unfolding in Algeria. Already one of the congressional library's heaviest borrowers, he now spent additional time in conversation with William J. Porter, an Arabist and the director of the State Department's Office of North African Affairs. Porter feared that Washington's uncritical support of its NATO ally, France, in the increasingly brutal French repression of the Algerian nationalists, threatened the whole future of the United States in North Africa. Kennedy also talked to members of the Algerian FLN delegation at the United Nations.

In July 1957 he rose on the Senate floor to deliver his first major foreign policy speech. He told his colleagues:

"No amount of mutual politeness, wishful thinking, nostalgia or regret should blind either France or the United States to the fact that, if France and the West at large are to have a continuing influence in North Africa . . . the essential first step is the independence of Algeria."[4]

---

4. Schlesinger, Arthur M., Jr., *A Thousand Days—John F. Kennedy in the White House*, Houghton Mifflin, Boston, 1965, p. 564.

The speech prompted more mail than any other he delivered as a Senator. The foreign policy establishment in New York, a bastion of Atlantic solidarity, expressed righteous indignation. The bumptious young Senator had publicly criticized America's oldest ally. The French were irritated and Republicans professed shock. (Kennedy's words, however, were akin to Eisenhower's private comments of the same period.) Even the arbiters of his own Democratic Party establishment, Adlai Stevenson, the twice-defeated Presidential nominee, and Dean Acheson, the former Secretary of State, criticized Kennedy's irresponsibility in undermining an ally. Yet, as Chairman of the Africa Subcommittee of the Senate Foreign Relations Committee, the young Senator continued to speak in the same vein, warning that "the word is out – and spreading in a thousand languages and dialects – that it is no longer necessary to remain forever poor or forever in bondage."[5]

Not everyone was critical, however. Secretary of State Dulles privately told the young Senator from the opposing party that he had used Kennedy's speech in arguing for moderation in Paris. French moderates similarly welcomed the speech as support for their futile attempts to prevent extremists from taking over both camps in the Algerian conflict. Three years later, an American journalist who had visited the rebels in Algeria told the Senator that his weary, battle-hardened hosts had astonished him by asking about Kennedy's chances for the Presidency.

Kennedy became President in January 1961, and Algeria achieved its independence on July 3, 1962. That was only five years and one day after Kennedy had given his Senate speech calling for independence. But what tragedies had unfolded in the meantime: Algeria had lost a tenth of its population and it now had a ravaged economy presided over by a radicalized leadership. However, despite their suffering, much of it at the hands of soldiers wielding American-made arms supplied to France under NATO auspices, Algeria's FLN leaders had not forgotten the American Senator who had championed their cause and they publicly hailed his election.

Kennedy in turn sent William Porter, the U.S. Foreign Service officer who had explained to him the Algerian cause, as the first U.S. Ambassador to Algeria. Ahmad Ben Bella visited Washington the same year. Afterward, in the words of Ambassador Porter, Ben Bella "ascribed to Kennedy everything he thought good in the United States." Unfortunately, to Kennedy's baffled disappointment, the Algerian leader proceeded directly from his visit with Kennedy in Washington to Havana for a visit to Castro, and then signed his name to a communique calling, among other things, for the U.S. to withdraw from its base in Guantanamo.

In discussing their struggle with Israel, Arabs frequently remind Americans of the Arabic proverb that "the friend of my enemy is my enemy." Kennedy was learning that in practice the Arabs sometimes forget that their proverb cuts both ways.

Kennedy also struck up a warm friendship with Tunisia's Habib Bourguiba, which was reinforced by friendly ties between the Tunisian Ambassador to Washington, Habib Bourguiba, Jr., and many of the young White House advisers.

5. Schlesinger, Arthur M., Jr., *A Thousand Days – John F. Kennedy in the White House*, Houghton Mifflin, Boston, 1965, p. 553.

Kennedy's relationship with Nasser was more tentative. It probably was not helped by the fact that one of the two White House staffers responsible for Middle Eastern matters was also a major White House liaison with the U.S. Jewish community. Nevertheless, the Kennedy White House was preoccupied with the question of whether better relations were possible with the Egyptian leader, whose standing with the Eisenhower White House seemed to have fallen in direct proportion to his rising prestige in the Arab world.

John Badeau, a man who had invested his entire life in educational and charitable work in the Middle East and who had served as President of the American University in Cairo, was sent to Egypt as the new U.S. Ambassador. A long and personalized response by Nasser to a fairly routine message that Kennedy sent to the Arab chiefs of state initiated a serious correspondence between the two leaders.

Kennedy had made strong public commitments to Israel during the election campaign and he was under great pressure to follow through on them. Nevertheless, in 1961, when Kennedy recognized the new government in Syria that had broken away from the union with Egypt; and in 1962, when Kennedy sent Hawk anti-aircraft missiles to Israel, he was careful to inform Nasser in advance of the impending actions and the reasons for taking them.

In 1962 there was a coup in Yemen. The ensuing struggle pitted Egyptian troops and Egyptian-supported Yemeni Republicans against British and Saudi-supplied forces loyal to the Imam Badr and created chaos not only in the Middle East but also in relations between the Middle East and the United States. Kennedy recognized the new Yemeni Republic. In doing so he followed the instincts he had first exhibited on the Senate floor, as well as the advice of those State Department area specialists who had always seen Nasser as the pan-Arab portent of the future in the Arab world. But Kennedy's immediate motive was to secure an Egyptian withdrawal in order to prevent an Egyptian clash with Saudi Arabia, the traditional U.S. ally in the area. The Saudis, and the British who at that time were still in Aden, considered Nasser's occupation of Yemen a prelude to direct attacks on their own territory. The ensuing confusion in U.S. Middle Eastern policy interrupted Kennedy's efforts to cultivate the Egyptian leader, although limited U.S. programs of grants and loans to Egypt continued.

In his biography of Kennedy, Theodore Sorensen has written of the incipient Kennedy-Nasser relationship:

"Nasser liked Kennedy's Ambassador, John Badeau, and he liked Kennedy's practice of personal correspondence. Kennedy put off, however, an invitation for a Nasser visit until improved relations could enable him to answer the political attacks such a visit would bring from voters more sympathetic to Israel."[6]

As with most good intentions deferred, the invitation to Nasser for a personal meeting with Kennedy was never issued. On November 22, 1963, President Kennedy was assassinated in Dallas, Texas, by Lee Harvey Oswald, an American deeply concerned

---

6. Sorenson, Theodore C., *Kennedy*, Harper and Row, New York, 1965, p. 540.

with U.S. policy toward Cuba, who had lived for a time in the Soviet Union and then returned to the United States. The assassin was almost immediately killed by Jack Ruby, an American Jew with gangster connections.

The circumstances gave rise to many conspiracy theories, including one believed by virtually all Arabs that the assassination was to prevent an impending U.S. policy change in the Middle East. No Middle East connection of any sort has ever been discovered, however. Instead, ironically, the assassination five years later by an Arab-American in California of President Kennedy's younger brother, an outspoken supporter of Israel, made Robert Kennedy the first American victim of the Palestinian-Israeli dispute to be killed on U.S. soil.

Americans will, therefore, never know whether the course of U.S. policies in the Middle East might have been altered by a young President eager to reexamine any problem, and with a demonstrated understanding of colonialism and its psychological aftermath. They were too stunned to ask any such questions as they looked at photographs of their new President, taking the oath of office while at his side stood the widow of their fallen leader, her clothing still stained with his blood. They watched grief-stricken as Kennedy's young son saluted his father's funeral cortege and the world statesmen who walked behind it.

Only later did Americans learn with amazement about the spontaneous outpouring of grief all over the globe. In divided Berlin, lighted candles were placed in darkened windows. In Poland, church bells tolled throughout a funeral half way around the world. And in Ireland, a kinsman of the fallen President reported that "they cried the rain down that night." In Belgrade, Marshal Tito telephoned the American Ambassador and then was too overcome to speak. In Guinea, President Sekou Toure said, "I have lost my only true friend in the outside world." And in Algiers, Ahmad Ben Bella telephoned Ambassador Porter to express his incredulity, adding: "Believe me, I'd rather it had happened to me than to him."

The mourning stretched across the Arab world, where to this day faded photographs on humble walls depict the young hero who, though grievously wounded in war, had set out again in peacetime to slay the dragons of bigotry, exploitation, ignorance and poverty and who, at the beginning of his political quest, had risked his future to speak up for Algerian patriots fighting their own lonely battle against crushing odds.

Even in Iraq, where fighting between Baathist and Nasserist elements in the government and army was putting Nasserist President Abd al-Salam Arif in undisputed control, residents under a nighttime curfew cried before the television sets that brought them the tragic news. Later, by daylight, a young American woman checking on the welfare of isolated American citizens and protected by her diplomatic license plates drove slowly through the deserted Baghdad streets. As she turned into a side street, she found her progress blocked by a huge tank, its guns leveled at a barricaded building across the Tigris River. When she tried to back away, the tank left its station and lumbered over to her car. A turret opened and an Iraqi officer, sweating in oil-spattered coveralls, clambered down to confront the American woman as she nervously gripped her steering wheel.

"Don't be frightened," the officer said gently. "I have only come to tell you how sad we all are about the death of your President." There were tears in his eyes as he clambered back into his tank.

"I started crying too," the woman reported. "He was crying for the young President we'd lost, before any of us really knew what he stood for. But when I looked at that Iraqi soldier who took time out from a battle in which he could have been killed himself to comfort an American, I realized I was crying for all of us. For Arabs and for Americans in the Middle East. Not just for what we'd lost in Dallas that week, but for what we'd been losing in the Middle East for a whole generation."

PLO

Cross-border terrorism continued before and after the 1956 Sinai invasion. Often, regardless of where Arab guerrillas came from, Israeli "reprisals" were aimed at West Bank Palestinians, apparently in hopes of provoking fighting with King Hussein's Jordanian troops stationed there. In 1953 Ariel Sharon's elite paratrooper Unit 101 killed 60 civilians in the West bank village of Qibya (above) by blocking up the doors and blowing up the houses with the inhabitants inside. At that time Israel blamed the raid on "border settlers" enraged by Arab attacks. The truth gradually emerged, however, as Unit 101 troopers boasted to the press about their exploits all over the West Bank. On November 13, 1966, 15 Jordanian soldiers were ambushed and killed while trying to stop an Israeli assault on the West Bank village of As-Samu where several civilians also died. Egyptian troops were stationed near As-Samu and other villages being attacked, but they were separated from Israeli forces by a screen of U.N. troops on Egyptian (not Israeli) territory. Egyptian President Nasser found the pressure building up to do something about the U.N. troops stationed on Egyptian territory.

Israel accepted a ceasefire at the end of its French and British-supported Suez campaign in 1956. Then Israel broke the ceasefire just long enough for its mobile units (below) and paratroopers under the command of Colonel Ariel Sharon to seize Sharm Al-Sheikh on the southern tip of Sinai, allowing Israeli ships to pass through the Straits of Tiran (above) to Israel's port of Eilat. When Israel withdrew from Sinai in 1957 under pressure from President Eisenhower, the United Nations took over Sharm Al-Sheikh to ensure that the straits remained open to ships of all nations. It was the UN withdrawal from that position in 1967 that set the stage for the next Egyptian-Israeli war.

Israel Office of Information

CHAPTER IX

President Johnson
and the Six-Day War

"In 1967, Johnson and his advisers watched the imminent Arab-Israeli war as bemused spectators. Their main goal seemed to be avoidance of any military commitment that might affect the U.S. effort in Vietnam. In 1957, the United States, on obtaining Israel's withdrawal from Sinai, had undertaken to support Israel's right of free passage in the Gulf of Aqaba and the Straits of Tiran and to regard a renewal of the Egyptian blockade as an agressive act which Israel had a right to resist by force. After a vain attempt to organize an international naval force to break the blockade, Johnson ceased to oppose self-help by Israel, and he gave Israel strong support in the United Nations discussions."[1]

Abba Eban, 1983

"Lyndon, and Sam Rayburn too, were very much opposed to the Eisenhower Doctrine, which was so clearly designed to placate the Arabs early in 1957, and Lyndon in the Senate managed to defuse some of the sanctions John Foster Dulles wanted to impose on Israel."[2]

Merle Miller, 1980

"You have lost a very great friend, but you have found a better one."[3]

President Lyndon Johnson
(in comment to Israeli diplomat), 1963

1. Eban, Abba, *The New Diplomacy: International Affairs in the Modern Age*, Random House, New York, 1983, p. 46.
2. Miller, Merle, *Lyndon: An Oral Biography*, Ballantine, New York, 1980, p. 476.
3. *Ibid.*, p. 475.

"However tantalizing the initial U.S.-Arab relationship in the early fifties—and the hopes of renewal during the first Kennedy months—Arab nationalism was irritatingly and increasingly cramping the governing American style by the mid-sixties; and for men like President Johnson and his advisers—the Rostows—irritations are dealt with by a 'bold' course of action."[4]

Abdullah Schleifer, 1972

Lyndon Johnson had spent all of his adult life striving toward power, including the Presidency. He filled Washington with "Lyndon's people," parking political aides who could help him at campaign time in "Schedule C" political positions all through the government. Johnson himself was an astute professional politician. Therefore, as he took the oath of office, standing with John Kennedy's widow in the airplane that was about to take his slain predecessor's body back with them to Washington, he was well aware that this was a horrible way to take over the job he had wanted so long.

One of the first things President Johnson did was solicit advice from his two living predecessors, Harry S Truman and Dwight D. Eisenhower, both of whom were generous with their time and thoughts. It is a moving commentary on the strength of U.S. institutions to read Johnson's account of his interview with former President Eisenhower, whom he had asked to come to Washington. Johnson, as the Democratic Senate Majority Leader, had often helped Republican President Eisenhower to prepare bi-partisan legislation. Now Eisenhower gave Johnson suggestions for quickly pulling a deeply divided Congress behind his efforts, some notes on what to say, and, interestingly, a list of Eisenhower's own three or four most trusted advisers in government. The top name on the list was that of Robert Anderson, the former Secretary of the Navy and later of the Treasury, who had so frequently served as a personal emissary from Eisenhower to the rulers of the Middle East and who had conducted the secret U.S. attempt in 1956 to get the Israelis and Egyptians negotiating instead of arming for war.

Johnson, the defeated candidate for his party's presidential nomination only three years earlier, was soon deeply resented by the liberal wing of the Democratic Party. He faithfully carried out Kennedy's domestic programs, but the Kennedy partisans could never forget that Johnson was not their own fallen leader. The Kennedy mixture of intellectuals, artists and backroom power brokers had in their minds become an American "Camelot." The often crude and coercive style of the Johnson White House was not an acceptable substitute, and one by one the Kennedy advisers left. Few of their successors appeared to be men of international vision. None exhibited much patience with seemingly unpredictable Arab leaders. It would be charitable to say that Johnson failed to follow up what had seemed to be promising Kennedy initiatives with the new leaders of Arab nationalism because he feared the political opposition would endanger his important domestic programs. It would be charitable, but it would not be true.

In fact, Johnson put Kennedy's domestic programs through Congress far more rapidly than would have been possible if their originator had not been martyred. Also, as time and Vietnam unfortunately proved, Johnson was not afraid of controversial foreign

---

4. Schleifer, Abdullah, *The Fall of Jerusalem*, Monthly Review Press, New York, 1972, p. 94.

policy initiatives. It appears that he let the initiatives with Nasser, the Algerians and others lapse simply because neither he nor some of his blatantly pro-Israel advisers thought they were a good idea.

In the thirties, the lanky, hard-working congressman from Texas had been unswerving in his commitment to the programs of the New Deal and had become something of a protege of Franklin D. Roosevelt. President Roosevelt, as a former governor of New York, had close ties to what was then called "the New York Jewish community." This was before Adolf Hitler's persecutions of German Jews had had such a searing impact in the U.S., and long before the birth of Israel. The "community" was a network of wealthy, and in many cases highly influential, persons in New York. What distinguished them from the big rich in many other parts of the country was their strong attraction to the kind of liberal causes personified by President Roosevelt and, in her own right, by his wife Eleanor.

In his informative book, *Lyndon: An Oral Biography*, Merle Miller quotes Edwin Weisl, Jr., the son of one of the influential members of that New York Jewish community of the 1930s:

"Our family relationship with President Johnson arose over thirty years ago through my father's relationship with President Roosevelt's personal adviser and assistant [Harry Hopkins]. Roosevelt, it is well known, took a liking to Johnson and wanted to make sure that he got a broader acquaintance with people throughout the country, and he asked Hopkins to put Johnson in touch with someone in New York who could introduce him around, and Hopkins picked my father.

"Johnson got to know him, used to come up frequently and stay at our house or our apartment in New York, and we involved ourselves in many ways throughout his career, with helping him in his campaigns, helping him get newspaper support in Texas, and became very friendly with Johnson. We worked on his preparedness committee at one point, and in his campaign for the presidency in '60, and then in '64, we of course were very active."[5]

When Eisenhower and Dulles threatened to remove the unique tax-free status of donations to Israel in order to make the Israelis withdraw from the Sinai, Democratic Senator Johnson and Republican Senator William Knowland of California, the most prominent member of the "China lobby," had been two of the most persistent and powerful senators blocking the Administration's plan.

It came as no surprise, therefore, that when Johnson assumed the Presidency, he remained strongly sympathetic to Israel. Isaiah "Si" Kenan, Israel's chief American lobbyist of the time, later told Merle Miller:

"One of Johnson's first statements concerning Israel was when he said to an Israeli diplomat shortly after the assassination of Kennedy, 'You have lost a very great friend, but you have found a better one.' And I would say that everything he did as president supported that statement."[6]

The Israeli diplomat probably was Ephraim "Eppy" Evron, then the second man in Israel's embassy in Washington. Evron had been personal assistant to the ill-starred Pinchas Lavon. To Evron's credit, he had remained unswervingly loyal to his chief

5. Miller, Merle, *Lyndon: An Oral Biography*, Ballantine, New York, 1980, p. 475.
6. *Ibid.*, p. 475.

when Moshe Dayan, Shimon Peres and others reportedly had sought to enlist Evron in a campaign to pin the blame on Lavon for the 1954 Israeli order to provocateurs in Egypt to place incendiary devices in American Embassy and Consulate libraries in order to upset relations between Eisenhower and Nasser. Evron would have nothing to do with the forgery of evidence and, when Lavon was forced to resign, Evron went too. Evron's subsequent success was proof that in the politics of any country, demonstrated loyalty to the boss is a cardinal virtue when applicants are being interviewed for a new job.

In 1963 Evron was in Washington in charge of Israeli intelligence. He was developing, with James Angleton of the CIA, perhaps the closest partnership U.S. intelligence services have ever had with any country other than Britain. In a way it was closer. Starting in the time of the Eisenhower Administration, the U.S. had dispensed with most of its own intelligence resources in Israel. The CIA, therefore, became increasingly dependent on the Mossad and other Israeli intelligence services for information about both Israel and the countries around it. Most Americans are familiar with some of the harmful side effects of the close intelligence collaboration with Britain, which resulted in many U.S. secrets finding their way to the Soviet Union. They may not be aware of the results of similar collaboration with Israel.

Long after the British spies, Burgess, McLean and Philby, had defected to the Soviet Union, America's secrets continued to follow them to Moscow. It is particularly ironic that Angleton, who had had a leading role in establishing the intimate U.S-Israeli intelligence collaboration, subsequently became personally identified with the theory that only the presence of a high-level mole in the CIA could explain this persistent, continuing leakage of U.S. intelligence information to the USSR.

In fact, the mole almost certainly was the Israeli connection itself. As early as 1954 the Israelis were working at cross purposes with the U.S. in the Middle East, seeking to spoil or abort U.S. alliances with any Arab country they considered a threat to themselves. What better way could be devised to keep the U.S. and the Arabs apart than to let the Russians know who in each Arab government was favorably disposed toward the United States? Moscow in turn could drop hints, or even manufacture evidence, that such a person was a U.S. "agent," and his political career, and perhaps his life, ended.

Also, so long as the U.S. kept losing its own friends or intelligence resources in the Middle East, it remained dependent upon Israel, which could screen the information it passed on to the U.S. to affect U.S. policy. The lengths to which Israel was prepared to go to keep the U.S. blind in the Middle East were eventually to be made clear to President Johnson during the 1967 war by the tragic incident described in the next chapter.

Meanwhile, however, Evron's presence in Washington in 1963 and 1964 was highly visible proof that, if the CIA then had little intelligence capability in Israel, the arrangement was not reciprocal. Evron (who at the beginning of the Reagan Administration was the Israeli Ambassador to the U.S.) did not confine himself to his frequent meetings with Angleton to exchange intelligence with the CIA. He also became a close personal friend of President Johnson.

Harry McPherson, Johnson's longtime friend, has described the relationship to Merle Miller:

"Eppy is five foot three with a quintessential Jewish face . . . and one of the most marvelous people I have ever known. I think Eppy felt what I've always felt, that some place in Lyndon Johnson's blood there are a great many Jewish corpuscles. He really reminds me of a six-foot-three-inch slightly corny Texas version of a rabbi. . . . He is just as likely to spill out all of his woes, his vanity, his joy. . . . He is not afraid of making a fool of himself – as Martin Buber describes – the kind of divine foolishness."[7]

Everyone talked to Miller about the warm feeling Lyndon Johnson had for Israel, even Evron himself. Miller quotes him as follows:

"Johnson's feeling about Israel came out very early in the crisis of 1957 when he was a majority leader. When at that time President Eisenhower and Secretary of State Dulles wanted to force us to withdraw from Sinai, they threatened us with economic sanctions. Johnson persuaded Senator William Knowland of California, who was then minority leader, to come with him to the White House and tell the President that it just wouldn't do."[8]

Miller summarized what he heard about Johnson's role in blocking the Eisenhower initiatives as follows:

"Lyndon, and Sam Rayburn too, were very much opposed to the Eisenhower Doctrine, which was clearly designed to placate the Arabs early in 1957, and Lyndon in the Senate managed to defuse some of the sanctions John Foster Dulles wanted to impose on Israel."[9]

All these words reflect the golden first years of the Johnson Administration, when the domestic ideas of the Kennedy "New Frontier" were incorporated in the legislation of the Johnson "Great Society." They characterize the period before a few moves in Southeast Asia to help the South Vietnamese government escalated into Johnson's guns-with-butter war in Vietnam, and they reflect the kind of superficial faith in any self-proclaimed U.S. ally that seemed to guide Johnson's early foreign policy initiatives.

What played well in the U.S. polls could not be all bad. Therefore, a President who carried the latest polls in his jacket pocket did not have to look ahead. If he took an action and it played in Peoria, he could do it again. In the Johnson era, as in the Truman era, Attlee's comments about the U.S. still held true: "There is no Arab vote in America."

For a few days in May and early June of 1967, however, Johnson seemed to wish that he had not so conspicuously depicted himself as Israel's great American friend. To understand the ensuing crisis in U.S.-Israeli relations, it is necessary to sketch in some intervening history.

When Nasser found he no longer had even a tentative suitor in the White House, his relationship with the Soviet Union began to flourish. The Soviets sent him arms, dumped his cotton all over the world at any price they could get for it, used his ports

---

7. Miller, Merle, *Lyndon: An Oral Biography*, Ballantine, New York, 1980, pp. 475-6.
8. *Ibid.*, p. 476.
9. *Ibid.*, p. 476.

and airfields for secret missions of their own, and undoubtedly gave him more advice than he thought he needed. What he probably did not realize at the time was that Soviet adventurism in the Middle East had become a key issue in a power struggle within the Kremlin. Hardliners, led by Leonid Brezhnev, were determined to retaliate against – or take advantage of – the growing American involvement in Vietnam, which followed the seemingly successful U.S. venture in the Dominican Republic. The U.S. appeared to be becoming progressively more reckless, playing for higher and higher stakes at increasing distances from home. The Brezhnev faction believed it could call the U.S. hand in the Middle East, an area where the Americans now seemed to be doing everything wrong.

For some time the Syrians had been supporting Palestinian guerrilla raids across Israel's borders. The Israelis complained to the Syrians and threatened them. But, true to their policy of retaliating against moderate Arab regimes, the Israeli reprisal raids were against Jordan, and more specifically against the Palestinian West Bank villages under Jordanian rule.

In November 1966, an Al Fatah mine planted on an Israeli road near the Jordanian frontier killed three and wounded six Israeli soldiers. A column of Israeli tanks and armored vehicles, supported by Mirage aircraft, crossed the frontier and destroyed the West Bank village of As-Samu. Eighteen Jordanians were killed and 134 wounded in the fighting, which involved both the villagers and lightly-armed Jordanian soldiers who tried to come to their rescue.

At this time King Hussein was the only really effective spokesman for the Arabs before U.S. audiences. His English was excellent and he had become a familiar television personality on his frequent visits to the United States, stating the Palestinian and Arab cause moderately and effectively time and time again. The U.S. had joined in condemnation at the UN of the Israeli raid. President Johnson, however, did not ask the Israelis why, if they were angry with Syria, they kept pounding Hussein's subjects on the West Bank. With little U.S. intelligence capability in Israel, perhaps there was no one with easy access to the President to tell him that Israeli planners had calculated that, if Hussein appeared too weak to defend his subjects, those subjects sooner or later would find a way to replace him. Nor was there anyone to warn Johnson that the new ruler probably would be more like Nasser or the rulers of Syria. Then the Israelis would have an excuse to do what they wanted to do in 1956: Move into Jerusalem and the West Bank, expel Jordan's Arab Legion, and hope that as many of Jordan's Palestinian subjects as possible would go with it.

However, exactly what the Israelis were going to do to realize this plan suddenly became immaterial. The power play in the Kremlin momentarily preempted all other plans in the Middle East, and in the end accomplished the Israeli purpose far more gracefully than they could have done it for themselves.

The Russians told the Syrians that the Israelis were massing troops on their border for a major strike. It made sense, since the Israelis in April, 1967, had lured the Syrians into an aerial dogfight in an incident that began when Israel sent an armored tractor into a demilitarized zone. By the end of the day six Syrian planes had been shot out of the skies, some over Damascus, others over Jordan. Syrian peasants, believing Syrian radio claims that the planes being shot down were Israeli, had even taken prisoner one of the Syrian pilots as he walked in from the desert where his parachute had taken him. While the Syrians were denying losses of their own, Jordanian television, which can be seen in Syria, showed downed Syrian pilots being treated in an Amman hospital. It all had been very embarrassing for the extremist Syrian government of that time and it was easy for the Syrians in May, 1967, to believe that the Israelis were massing on their borders for the long-threatened ground retaliation. There was only one problem: It was not true. Either the Israelis had fooled the Russians with fake messages or the Russians had simply made it up.

The Syrians, who had long since ostensibly mended their fences with Nasser after their break from the United Arab Republic, now demanded his assistance. By this time taunts against the Egyptian President from many parts of the Arab World had become nearly unbearable. Egyptian troops, separated from the Israelis by a screen of UN forces on Egyptian territory, had done nothing in November, 1966, while a short distance away in Sammu Israeli tanks were leveling Palestinian homes with the occupants still in them. Again in April, 1967, Egyptian forces did nothing as Israeli planes shot down Syrian planes over the Syrian capital. The Syrians now demanded to know whether Egyptian forces would hide behind the UN screen while Israeli tanks ran over Syrian villages as well. Nasser had always vowed that the moment for Egypt to strike at Israel would come, but that it should be at a time and place of his own choosing. Could he stand by, however, doing nothing during a major Israeli attack on Syria, and still claim to be a leader of all the Arabs? He asked the Russians if the Syrian reports of Israeli troop concentrations on their borders were true. The Russians confirmed the reports, which of course Nasser did not know the Russians themselves had originated.

Nasser then made one of the theatrical gestures which in the past had helped him capture Arab minds and hearts, and which had also made him increasingly dependent on the Soviet Union. He asked the UN Secretary General to remove the UN forces "from the international frontier between Egypt and Israel." The Israelis are depicted in the U.S. as eternally on the defensive. In fact, however, they had never permitted UN forces to be stationed on Israeli territory. That meant that the only UN forces separating Egypt and Israel were on Egyptian territory. When they were removed, Egyptian forces would be free to strike against Israel's southern borders if Israeli tanks and planes crossed their northern borders against Syria. UN Secretary General U Thant, however, decided to remove UN forces from all Egyptian territory, not just the forces on the border with Israel. Unfortunately for Nasser, the UN withdrawal meant that his troops were perfectly free to move back into their former position on the Egyptian side of the Straits of Tiran. The position had been occupied in 1956 by the Israelis, who violated the cease-fire they had already accepted just long enough to seize it. Facing Eisenhower's displeasure, and the threat of UN sanctions which the U.S. obviously would not veto, the Israelis reluctantly turned the position over to UN forces when they withdrew from Sinai.

Now, UN forces were gone and Egyptian forces were back on the Straits. It is not clear whether Nasser was trapped by circumstances and by his own rhetoric or whether he really believed he could use political means to win a decisive strategic victory over

the Israelis. Whatever the reason, he announced that he would not permit Israeli shipping to enter the Gulf of Aqaba, Israel's only outlet to Asia and the Far East.
It was obvious to the U.S. that the Israelis would not accept this, even though very
few Israeli ships actually used the Gulf of Aqaba at that time. President Johnson realized he had to watch while Israel took back the Straits by force, or else try to head
off the war by organizing an international fleet to steam into the Gulf of Aqaba and
break the blockade. President Johnson set about organizing such an action, which became
known as "the Red Sea regatta" by White House aides. Meanwhile, the Israelis were
organizing their own forces, which had all the necessary strike plans meticulously worked
out.

Did the Israelis plan military action all along, setting up a screen of false military
communications to deceive and alarm the Russians? Or was it planned Russian disin-
formation to the Arabs that made war inevitable? No clear answer emerges from reading
memoirs of the Americans involved with the situation. They simply do not jibe. They
only demonstrate that in fact there were many forces at work. Not only were different
groups working at cross purposes within the Arab camp, but also within the governments of both Israel and the United States.

One such memoir is Louis Heren's book on the Johnson Presidency, *No Hail, No
Farewell*. If one believes the Heren version, when the Israelis seemed to be in trouble,
Johnson the friend of Israel began to depict himself as Johnson the prisoner of commitments to Israel made by a Republican predecessor. Heren's book omits the fact that,
as a Senator, Johnson had fought all U.S. efforts to use a big stick to make Israel withdraw
from Sinai in 1956. It depicts Johnson as shocked and surprised that the U.S. had been
compelled to offer carrots instead. Heren writes:

"There was a quick flight to Ottawa for discussions with Lester Pearson, the Canadian prime
minister, and Harold Wilson flew from London to Washington. The two discussed joint action
by the maritime nations to ensure the free passage of the Strait of Tiran, as Anthony Eden and
Eisenhower had once discussed joint action for keeping open the Suez Canal. Into this rather
uninspired diplomacy, Abba Eban, the Israeli foreign minister, dropped a bombshell. He arrived in May and told a horrified Johnson that there was a secret American commitment guarantee-
ing free access of shipping through the Strait of Tiran to Aqaba. Eban produced copies of documents
so secret that they were not in the State Department's files.

"The first commitment was made by Eisenhower's Secretary of State, the late John Foster
Dulles, after the 1956 war in an effort to persuade the Israelis to withdraw from Sinai, and especially
Sharm el Sheikh. He had assisted in the writing of Israel's final statement in the United Nations
debate in 1957. It said that interference in shipping in the Strait of Tiran would be regarded
as an act of war. I understood at the time that Eban produced a copy of the statement with corrections written in Dulles' hand. He also produced a personal letter from Eisenhower to Ben-Gurion,
thanking the then Israeli prime minister for agreeing to the arrangement and strongly emphasiz-
ing the American commitment. Johnson was naturally appalled, and without corroborative
documents in the White House and State Department files fobbed off Eban while a search was
made. He knew that presidential papers are not the property of the state but the personal papers
of the president concerned. Since FDR, presidents had followed the custom of putting their papers
in special libraries, and that Friday night Tom Hughes, of the State Department, was sent to
Gettysburg to go through the Eisenhower papers. He returned the following day, exhausted but

with the evidence. Without the benefit of a treaty, and senatorial advice and consent, the United States was fully committed to keeping the Strait of Tiran open and morally committed to go to Israel's help in the event of war." [10]

In Heren's version of the situation, Johnson is not hoisted on his own pro-Israel petard, but instead gamely struggled to uphold secret commitments unwisely made by Eisenhower and Dulles, closet pro-Israelis all along. But if Heren is correct and that was the view from the Johnson camp early in May, by the end of the month things apparently looked different to President Johnson. By that time he certainly had been informed by every branch of U.S. intelligence that the Israelis would win any Middle East war, no matter how or where it started. Merle Miller interviewed John P. Roche, Johnson's White House speech writer, about the atmosphere at the time. As Roche tells it:

"Of course his [Johnson's] purpose at the time was to try to keep the Israelis from attacking and try to bring some pressure on Nasser to open the straits, and at the same time make it clear that he was not going to support the Arabs, that we were going to support Israel if it came to a crunch.

"The State Department had prepared a draft for him which was the most incredible document. It was a completely 'on the one hand' and 'on the other hand' thing. It didn't cut any ice at all. It didn't have one declarative sentence in it as to what we were going to do.

"I worked until about two or three o'clock in the morning on May 23, using some quite tough operational language regarding the fact that the closing of the Straits of Tiran had been a violation of international law and norms and so forth. I called Walt Rostow and I read it to him, and Walt said, 'That sounds fine to me but mark it for the president'. . . .

"The next day there was tremendous pressure brought on Johnson to get him to come out for Israel. Jewish pressure groups in this country were lined up all the way from Washington to California, and Johnson engaged in one of his malicious little games. The various Jewish groups would call him and what he did was he'd fish out the State Department draft and read it to them and say, 'Well, how do you feel about that? They think this is the kind of thing I ought to say. How does it sound to you?'

"So boom! The phones are ringing. The Israeli ambassador Avraham Harmon is over in Humphrey's office with Eppy Evron, who is practically in tears. So Humphrey calls me up and he says, 'What do you know about this?' It was very embarrassing, because I happened to know that what I had written the night before had already gone on speech cards, and he was going on television. He'd approved it, signed it, everything else. . . .

"All day Johnson went on doing this. I called Rostow. I said, 'For God's sake, what is he doing?' Walt said, 'Oh, he's just getting a little therapy for all this pressure they put on.' " [11]

President Johnson did read the message that evening, declaring that "the right of free, innocent passage of the international waterway is a vital interest of the international community" and stating his hope that the UN Security Council "can act effectively."

Miller records that, when the Israeli Foreign Minister, Abba Eban, visited him in Washington on May 26, Johnson told Eban, "I want to see that little blue and white

10. Heren, Louis, *No Hail, No Farewell*, Harper and Row, New York, 1970, pp 162-3.
11. Miller, Merle, *Lyndon: An Oral Biography*, Ballantine, New York, 1980, p. 479.

Israeli flag sailing down the Strait of Tiran." However, in order to avoid a confrontation with the Soviet Union, Johnson added that the U.S. must remain above it all. Roche recalled for Miller a White House discussion following the same meeting.

"That night I was working and around nine thirty or ten o'clock the phone rang and he said, 'Come on down.' I went down. Walt Rostow was there, and the president had some of that poisonous low-cal Dr. Pepper, and I had a cup of coffee. He told a little bit about his visit with Eban. You know he was a great mimic, Johnson was. He did a takeoff on Eban, and he said, 'What do you think they're going to do?' We sat around and talked about what we thought the Israelis were going to do. . . . I said, 'I think they'll hit them.' He [Johnson] said, 'Yes, they're going to hit. There's nothing we can do about it.' " [12]

In his own book, *The Vantage Point*, Johnson recalls the May 26 meeting with the Israeli Foreign Minister:

"Our conversation was direct and frank. Eban said that according to Israeli intelligence, the United Arab Republic (UAR) was preparing an all-out attack. I asked Secretary McNamara, who was present, to give Mr. Eban a summary of our findings. Three separate intelligence groups had looked into the matter, McNamara said, and it was our best judgment that a UAR attack was not imminent. 'All of our intelligence people are unanimous,' I added, 'that if the UAR attacks, you will whip hell out of them.'

"Eban asked what the United States was willing to do to keep the Gulf of Aqaba open. I reminded him that I had defined our position on May 23. We were hard at work on what to do to assure free access, and when to do it. 'You can assure the Israeli Cabinet,' I said, 'we will pursue vigorously any and all possible measures to keep the strait open. . . .'

"Abba Eban is an intelligent and sensitive man. I wanted him to understand the U.S. position fully and clearly, and to communicate what I said to his government. 'The central point, Mr. Minister,' I told him, 'is that your nation will not be the one to bear the responsibility for any outbreak of war.' Then I said very slowly and very positively: 'Israel will not be alone unless it decides to go alone.' " [13]

After Eban's return to Israel, he cabled Johnson on May 30 that the Israeli Cabinet had decided two days earlier to postpone military action and to "await developments for a further limited period." Eban added, however, that "it is crucial that the international naval escort should move through the Strait within a week or two." On June 2 an Israeli diplomat told the President's aide, Walter Rostow, that nothing would happen before "the week beginning Sunday, June 11."

Johnson was not overwhelmed by nations volunteering their ships to join a U.S.-led flotilla to break the blockade of the Straits of Tiran. He believed, however, that he had lined up the Netherlands and Australia as well as the British. He therefore planned to go to Congress with the plan during the week of June 5. Meanwhile, both Ambassador Charles Yost and President Eisenhower's long-time confidant and occasional secret emissary to the Middle East, Robert Anderson, were in Cairo. Initially they suggested a visit to Cairo by Vice President Hubert Humphrey. Then it was decided that Vice

12. Miller, Merle, *Lyndon: An Oral Biography*, Ballantine, New York, 1980, p. 480.
13. Johnson, Lyndon B., *The Vantage Point: Perspectives of the Presidency 1963-1969*, Holt, Rinehart and Winston, 1971, p. 293.

President Zakaria Mohieddin of the UAR would first visit Washington on June 7 to confer on the crisis. Neither of those plans to avert war was to be tested, however. Instead, some American Middle East specialists believe that the scheduled visit to Washington by the Egyptian Vice President caused Israel to move the date of the attack forward by one week.

In yet another interview about the feverish days before June 5, Miller quotes a Democratic political leader, Abe Feinberg:

> "Finally, on the night of June 4 we had a Democratic rally in New York, and Johnson was the main speaker. I had gotten word that afternoon and I went up to where he was sitting. I remember Mary Lasker was on one side and Mathilde Krim, who was then a professor at the Weizmann Institute, was on the other. And I whispered to him, on the side where Mrs. Krim was sitting. I said, 'Mr. President, it cannot be held any longer. It's going to be within the next twenty-four hours.' Well, he made a speech that night that absolutely brought the house down, completely extemporaneous. About Israel and about its survival." [14]

The Israeli aerial attack that followed on June 5, 1967 was such a masterpiece of meticulous planning that, given the exigencies of war, any unexpected action from the other side should have spoiled it all. But nothing did. The date was known only to a few senior officers. As a deception, Defense Minister Moshe Dayan sent several thousand Israeli soldiers on leave. They were photographed for the press as they relaxed on the beaches of Tel Aviv over the weekend. The time was carefully fixed, but not at either of the traditional times for a military attack: It was not sunrise, as might have been expected in order to maximize the daylight hours available to the attackers. Nor was it a few hours before sunset, which would permit the attack to be completed just before darkness and eliminate the possibility of rapid retaliation. Instead, the attack was set for 8 a.m. Israeli intelligence had established that the Egyptian armed forces remained on alert all night long. Then, starting at 7:30 a.m., Egyptian watch officers began going to breakfast. Therefore, at 6 a.m. on June 5, Israeli air force planes had engaged in routine maneuvers, landing back at their bases at 7:30. As the Egyptian radar operators who had been watching them land relaxed and headed off to breakfast, wave after wave of Israeli aircraft took off from Israeli bases. Some flew west out to sea, some headed south toward Elath. The last waves to take off streaked straight toward Egypt. All of these Israeli planes, whether they had turned south from the Mediterranean, west from the Negev desert, or were flying directly from Israeli bases, thundered into Egyptian airspace at exactly the same moment. The fastest planes were targeted at the most distant Egyptian airfields; the slowest struck closest to Egypt's borders with Israel.

Within minutes, every major military airfield in Egypt was under simultaneous attack. Waves of planes dove to unleash bombs or rockets on grounded Egyptian aircraft, and then rose to circle and dive again. Only minutes, and sometimes seconds, after each attack ended and the last Israeli planes vanished into the clear skies, a new wave would roar in over the same battered Egyptian fields. The turnaround time on Israeli airfields for rearming and refueling was down to as little as four minutes. The

---

14. Miller, Merle, *Lyndon: An Oral Biography*, Ballantine, New York, 1980, p. 480.

result was that most Egyptian airfields stayed under almost continuous attack all morning, unable to activate their anti-aircraft defenses or to get their own planes airborne before all were destroyed.

Egypt's air force was permanently out of action by 1 p.m. Then it was Syria's turn. Six separate waves of Israeli fighter bombers swooped in to destroy the Damascus international airport in the course of a seemingly endless afternoon, while Damascenes stood on their flat rooftops watching in glum astonishment. Each wave came in high from the east and then one by one the planes dove at top speed through a cloud of black anti-aircraft bursts from batteries ringing the airport. As each wave departed it left behind dense clouds of black smoke from gasoline storage tanks and airport buildings, as well as the planes caught on the ground. The same tactics that had worked so well in Egypt throughout the morning were followed in Syria throughout the afternoon. The planes made pass after pass until every rocket and shell was gone, and then darted back through mountain passes to Israel to make way for the next group of attackers. Syrians on the high mountains above Damascus could see columns of smoke rising far out across the desert, each one marking the site of a destroyed Syrian military airfield. The fastest Israeli planes struck distant bases near Aleppo in the north, and in the eastern desert and along the Euphrates River near the Iraqi border. The older, slower planes meanwhile continued the shorter bombing shuttle between the Syrian capital and Israeli bases less than 100 miles away.

Having achieved total mastery of the air on Monday, the first day of the war, Israel knew that the Egyptian forces in Sinai stood no chance. It became a twice-fought war. Israeli armored columns repeated the 1956 race to Suez as Israeli aircraft carried out disabling attacks against vehicles on the narrow winding roads of the Mitla and Gidi Passes. This stopped reinforcements or supplies from reaching the Egyptians in Sinai, and cut off their retreat. When the race was finished, what might have been at least an Egyptian delaying action became a rout.

There were unexpected occurrences all through the first day of the war, but they seemed to favor only the Israelis. When the first Israeli planes struck Egyptian airfields while many of the radar operators were at breakfast, the top Air Force base commanders were not even at their commands. Nearly all had assembled at one airfield to welcome the Egyptian Air Force Commander back from an inspection trip. In retrospect, it seems incredible that with Israel poised for an attack for days, and with foreign residents being evacuated from virtually every Middle Eastern capital, the officers in charge of Egypt's air defenses would assemble in any one place, no matter what the occasion. The absence of the military commanders was particularly serious because the Egyptian military organization of the time was extremely centralized, with little initiative expected or permitted from below. If, when the attacks began, middle level officers did not defy tradition and take the initiative, there literally was no one at some bases to order the pilots to scramble their planes, or what was left of them after the first attack.

King Hussein of Jordan had flown secretly to Cairo May 30 and in a six-hour visit had patched up things with President Nasser. Jordan's army was placed under a unified Arab command and token Egyptian units were flown to Jordan. It should have been a day of celebration for Israeli military planners because, six days later, on the morning of the Israeli strike at Egypt, Jordanian guns opened up against the Israelis in Jerusalem. They thus gave the Israelis the long-awaited grounds to move against Jordanian-occupied Jerusalem and the West Bank.

A little later on June 5 came another self-destructive decision for the Arabs. President Nasser and King Hussein together accused the U.S. and Britain of participating in the Israeli aerial attacks. This was precisely the moment when the Arabs most needed their viewpoints conveyed to an unreceptive administration in Washington. One of their best means was through the generally sympathetic chiefs of U.S. diplomatic missions in the Arab World. Yet, just when these ambassadors should have been burning up the wires to Washington describing the carefully-planned Israeli attacks they were witnessing and trying to explain to the Johnson Administration the catastrophic consequences that might befall U.S. interests in the Middle East if the war continued, each American embassy was coming under attack by hostile Arab mobs. Acting on the false reports of U.S. complicity in the attacks, several Arab governments, including Egypt, Syria, Iraq, Algeria and the Sudan, broke diplomatic relations with the U.S. and ordered the embassies' American employes to depart within 48 hours. Thus ambassadors who might have counseled the U.S. to put pressure on Israel to stop the attacks were engrossed in protecting the lives and property of their employes, burning classified files and destroying cryptographic equipment. A near tragedy occurred in Aleppo, Syria, where a mob stormed the American Consulate General and set fire to the building. Syrian guards escorted the wives of the staff members safely through the mob, but the American officers locked themselves into an upstairs vault in order to destroy cryptographic equipment. When they had finished and emerged from the vault they found the entire lower floor a sea of flames. Only with the help of Syrian guards outside the building were they able to slide down a rope, one by one, and avoid being burned to death.

Neither before nor since have Americans encountered such hostility in the Middle East as in those terrible days when nearly every Arab believed "the big lie," namely that American and British naval aircraft had helped the Israelis carry out the first attacks of the Six Day War. Fortunately, however, no American was killed or seriously injured by a mob in an Arab country as thousands of U.S. citizens were evacuated from cities throughout the Middle East.

Many of these Americans had devoted their entire lives to the Arab World and were probably as exasperated with Israel's friend in the White House as they were with any combination of Arab leaders. From their safe havens in Athens, Rome, Tehran and Madrid, the evacuees sought explanations for the bizarre circumstances in which they found themselves. First, the logistics of the attack might really have fooled Nasser. As his incredulous radar operators recorded the makeup of each wave of incoming planes, they soon had counted far more planes than the total possessed by the entire Israeli Air Force. Moreover, large numbers of the planes were attacking from the sea, where units of the Sixth Fleet were known to be patrolling. What no one realized was that meticulously trained Israeli air and ground crews had reduced the time required for some round trips to less than 40 minutes.

Given Nasser's record for emotional reactions in the past, this explanation of his self-destructive charges against Britain and the U.S. made sense in 1967. In retrospect, however, it appears that the picture may have been somewhat more complicated.

There were many things happening on Middle Eastern airwaves that day, some of which will be examined in the next chapter. In addition, Israeli pilots themselves may have contributed to Nasser's confusion. Israeli pilots of "oriental" origin, many of whom were born in Arab countries and speak unaccented Arabic, have since described some of their incidental activities while engaged in dogfights over Egypt. They had been fully briefed, even down to the voices and names of the Egyptian pilots they might face. If an Egyptian pilot told his ground controllers or squadron commander that he thought he was hit, a quick-witted Israeli pilot might come in on the same radio frequency, shouting in Arabic, "You're on fire, jump before you explode."

The airwaves were full of chatter that day. Many of Israel's best pilots were, and are, native-born Americans or Englishmen. They learned to fly in the armed services of their native countries, and only later entered the service of Israel. Some of them admit that, when they fly in Israel's wars, they keep their U.S. or U.K. passports with them, just in case they are shot down over enemy territory.

Unlike the Arabic-speaking Israelis, however, none of the English-speaking Israeli pilots have since seen fit to boast about what they were doing or saying over their aircraft radios that day. It is quite possible, however, that they were speaking to each other, in English, in the U.S. Air Force and RAF jargon they knew so well. Something made the Egyptians and Jordanians believe some of the aircraft destroying Egypt's airfields that day had been launched from U.S. and British carriers, rather than from Israel.

Although no Americans died by violence in the Arab countries in those dramatic days, there were heart attacks and an untreated case of appendicitis killed an American evacuee in Egypt. The Voice of America was very slow to deny the charges of American intervention, a mistake it has not made since. It subsequently blamed the delay on a lack of policy guidance from the White House. Fortunately, a State Department spokesman did not not wait. He affirmed America's neutrality during the Department's press briefing, and the local U.S. embassies eagerly picked up and distributed his words.

President Johnson, whose aides have often since described the tough messages being exchanged over the hot line between the Kremlin and the White House that day, does not seem to have cared about the thousands of Americans trapped in the Middle East. He later wrote:

"Our problems that day were complicated by an error made by a briefing officer in the State Department. Pressed for a statement of American policy, he began well: 'I am in no position to speak specifically beyond the President's statement of May 23.' But as he continued, speaking in the context of anti-American riots in Arab countries and of danger to American citizens there, he said: 'Our position is neutral in thought, word, and deed'. . . . This remark stirred unnecessary resentment among many Americans."[15]

---

15. Johnson, Lyndon B., *The Vantage Point: Perspectives of the Presidency 1963-1969*, Holt, Rinehart and Winston, 1971, pp. 298-9.

Johnson seemed oblivious to the fact that, however much the words may have offended his Jewish political supporters in the U.S., they probably saved the lives of many American diplomats and businessmen serving their country in the Middle East. There was still more fighting to come. The Israelis have made much of their efforts to dissuade King Hussein from coming into the war at Egypt's side. They warned him against committing his forces, they point out, and they did not attack him first. The moment his guns opened fire on them, however, Israeli troops were poised. Israeli General Mordechai Gur, whose paratroops spearheaded the breakthrough in Jerusalem, described in his book *The Battle for Jerusalem*, some of the planning:

"We had been in the Israeli-held sector of Jerusalem a week before, on May 30, to discuss various contingencies if war were to break out. . . . The Jordanians we thought were too vulnerable to attack us. But the possibility did exist that they might try to prevent convoys from going up to Jerusalem. . . . These assessments had led us to concentrate, at the time, on the northern Jordanian sector; we had looked for a springboard from which we could join up with the police garrison on Mount Scopus. Now that Hussein had elected to join in the war and had attacked us, the objective had changed: we were thinking suddenly not only of Mount Scopus, but of the liberation of the whole of Jerusalem." [16]

Gur's book implies that the plan for a general attack was hurriedly improvised when events on the first day of the war made such an attack politically possible. Other passages of the same book, however, indicate how long the Israelis had awaited this opportunity and the enormous amount of advance planning and preparation involved on Israel's side of the line dividing Jerusalem:

"The houses in the immediate vicinity of the boundary had been prepared in advance as battle sites. On every roof positions for weapons had been constructed. Now we found that the iron gates to the roofs were locked. The rapidity with which the battle plan had evolved made it impossible to coordinate all necessary details, and the men with the keys couldn't be found." [17]

Even more revealing is this passage by General Gur:

"Suddenly Colonel David came in, brimming over, as always, with energy and smiles . . . Behind us we had years of working together. Long ago he and I had planted charges of explosives to undermine the wall of the Old City, hoping that some day we would have a chance to set them off." [18]

The Israeli attack began after dark June 5. It was quick and deadly. The Arab Legion resisted, but both Jerusalem and the West Bank, which the Israelis had fought so hard to occupy in 1948, and which they had come so tantalizingly close to obtaining with French cooperation in 1956, finally fell to the Israeli Army. Who can forget the dramatic photos of sweat-stained, powder-blackened Israeli soldiers, who had just broken through the dense cluster of stone houses around Jerusalem's Wailing Wall, weeping with exaltation as they pressed themselves in prayer against the ancient rocks of the most sacred

---

16. Gur, Lt. Gen. Mordechai, *The Battle for Jerusalem*, Popular Library, New York, 1974, pp. 18-9.
17. *Ibid.*, p. 28.
18. *Ibid.*, pp. 31-2.

site of Judaism? For them, the time-honored religious vow, "Next year in Jerusalem," had finally been fulfilled.

As Israeli troops on Wednesday mopped up the last defenses of the Suez Canal, and even allowed a few dazed or lightly wounded Egyptian stragglers to swim across to their own lines, attention shifted to Syria. The defenses of the Golan Heights overlooking Israel's Hula Valley seemed impregnable. But the Israeli Air Force, which totally dominated the skies, had already stopped harassing the fleeing Egyptians and had begun softening up the Syrian positions with bombs, rockets, and napalm. An attack scheduled for Thursday was postponed for 24 hours. Finally, at a heavy price in blood, Israeli infantrymen climbed up the hills, fighting from one fortified bunker to the next, while Israeli armored bulldozers scraped a road out of one of the steepest hillsides. After the infantrymen and the bulldozers finally reached the crest, hundreds of Israeli tanks were free to roll across the rocky but level terrain of the Golan Heights. All day Friday cease-fires with the Egyptians were being violated and reinstated. In Syria, however, the Israelis ignored all of the UN Secretary General's cease-fire proposals and kept moving forward. It appeared that they might try to drive their tanks down from the heights against Damascus itself, where the Syrians were digging anti-tank ditches across southern approaches to the sprawling, oasis capital.

On the morning of Saturday, June 10, Soviet Chairman Kosygin asked that Johnson personally come to the hot line. He told Johnson flatly that if the Israelis did not stop their thrust into Syria the Soviets would take "necessary actions, including military."

Incredibly – though perhaps not, in light of what was already going on in Vietnam – Johnson's first reaction was not to call off the Israelis. Instead he ordered the Sixth Fleet, which had been steaming in circles 300 miles west of the Syrian coast, to change course and proceed directly toward Syria. Later in the day, the Israelis agreed to a cease-fire with Syria through UN negotiators, thus sparing President Johnson and Chairman Kosygin, who had exchanged additional hot line messages throughout the day, from rushing into a decision about whether or not to begin World War III.

Israel Information Services

Israeli armored personnel carriers pause in their 1967 invasion of Sinai to await an airdrop of gasoline and supplies.

Israel Information Services

Israeli Mirage aircraft (above) en route to attack Egyptian airfields. Egyptian MIG fighters (below) on the airstrip after the lightning attack the morning of June 5, 1967. On the first day of the Six-Day War Israel destroyed much of the Egyptian Air Force in the morning and then attacked Syrian airfields in the afternoon, using its fastest aircraft against more distant targets in Egypt and Syria and slower aircraft against airfields closest to Israeli borders. Although Israel claimed that its strike was pre-emptive, U.S. intelligence had told the Israelis there was no evidence that Egypt was planning an attack. President Johnson told the Israelis he would send U.S. ships to lead those of a number of European countries through the Straits of Tiran to assure that Egyptian takeover of the U.N. position there would not interfere with international access to that waterway.

Zionist Archives

Zionist Archives   PLO

Four Faces of the 1967 War. *Exaltation* (upper left): Israeli paratroopers break through to the Wailing wall in Jerusalem. *Desperation* (upper right): A Palestinian father driven out of his West Bank home and carrying his two children and their remaining possessions on his back negotiates a broken bridge across the Jordan river. *Humiliation* (lower left): Egyptian soldiers sit under guard where they were captured after Israel's surprise attack, the second across the same border in 11 years. *Despair* (lower right): An old Palestinian woman who lost her first home in 1948 and her second in 1967 weeps in a Jordanian refugee camp.

PLO   UNRWA

CHAPTER X

An Awkwardness for President Johnson

"Israel continues to insist that the attack was a case of mistaken identity. This claim simply does not hold water. There is simply no way that the Israeli pilots and torpedo boat crews could have concluded that it was anything other than a U.S. ship . . . Before as well as subsequent to the attack on the Liberty, *the U.S. Congress has investigated in depth just about every incident of a similar nature in which the military forces participated. At the very least the Congress, in deference to the families of the men who died on board the* Liberty, *should once and for all clear up the uncertainties, speculations, and the unanswered questions surrounding this tragedy, which still is thought by many to be a deliberate coverup on the part of the Government of Israel as well as the Government of the United States."*[1]

Admiral Thomas H. Moorer, former Chief of U.S. Naval Operations,
and Chairman of the U.S. Joint Chiefs of Staff, 1985

"As for the attack on the defenseless Liberty, *the Israeli government claimed that the converted freighter had been mistaken for an Egyptian warship. A U.S. naval board of inquiry found that the daylight attack had been unprovoked and deliberate. Then the U.S. government shrouded the entire* Liberty *matter in secrecy under a cloak of 'national security' considerations, where it remains even now."*[2]

Wilbur Crane Eveland, 1980

1. Moorer, Thomas, H., (Chief of Naval Operations, 1967-70, Chairman, Joint Chiefs of Staff, 1970-74), *Washington Report on Middle East Affairs*, May 27, 1985, pp. 1,3.
2. Eveland, Wilbur Crane, *Ropes of Sand: America's Failure in the Middle East*, Norton, New York, 1980, p. 325.

"Whatever [Admiral] Kidd or Admiral John McCain or [Commander] McGonagle or the Joint Chiefs of Staff in Washington or every surviving member of the crew of the Liberty thought—and they all knew damn well they had been attacked in cold blood— they had to accept they had lost the game. Because of political expedience and a frightened presidential administration in Washington, its eye on the next election and the powerful pro-Democratic Jewish vote, absolutely nothing would be done to repair the damaged honor of the U.S. Navy and the personal hardship the killing of 34 American sailors and the maiming of another 171 had brought to so many innocent families. "[3]
Anthony Pearson, 1978

"Not surprisingly, Israel claimed that nearly everything she did was in self-defense. The preemptive strikes of the fifth of June were in self-defense. The capture of El Arish, the naval and paratroop assault on Sharm al-Sheikh, the sweep through Sinai, and the armed penetration of Jordan were all in self-defense. Now, with the war virtually over and with the world crying for peace, could Israel put troops in Syria without being seen as an aggressor? Probably not. Not with the USS Liberty so close to shore and presumably listening. Liberty would have to go. "[4]
James M. Ennes, Jr., 1979

"We in the Department of Defense cannot accept an attack upon a clearly marked noncombatant United States Naval ship in international waters as 'plausible' under any circumstances whatever. The implications that the identification markings were in any way inadequate are both unrealistic and inaccurate. The identification markings of U.S. Naval vessels have proven satisfactory for international recognition for nearly 200 years. "[5]
U.S. Department of Defense Statement, 1967

The euphoria that gripped the Israelis after the June 1967 war may well stand as a high water mark in the nation's history. It certainly marks the moment when Israel peaked in world esteem. Only a year earlier, in 1966, Israel's economy had slowed to a standstill in the absence of serious external pressures, and the essential foreign subsidies they generated. More Jewish Israelis were leaving Israel than were coming in, an impossible situation for a country whose public image was that of a refuge for all of the world's homeless Jews. In 1966 even Israel's Jews had been heading for the promised lands of Australia and North and South America.

Now again, in 1967, the world rang with deserved praise for the courage of Israeli fighting men and women, the brilliance of Israeli leaders, and the spirit of Israeli reserv-

---

3. Pearson, Anthony, *Conspiracy of Silence: The Attack on the U.S.S. Liberty*, Quartet Books, London, 1978, p. 61.
4. Ennes, James M., Jr. *Assault on the Liberty. The True Story of the Israeli Attack on an American Intelligence Ship*, Random House, New York, 1979, p. 212.
5. Goulding, Phil G., *Confirm or Deny—Informing the People on National Security*, Harper & Row, New York, 1970, p. 124.

ists abroad who had rushed to book air passage back to their country to join their units at the front.

The Russians had supplied both Syria and Egypt with false information so elaborate that it even included an Israeli military planning document, stolen years earlier by a highly-placed Russian spy in Israel. The date was altered to corroborate Russian reports of Israeli preparations for an imminent attack on Syria. The Russian plan had produced the very Middle East war that the hardline Brezhnev faction had wanted, but the war had produced the wrong results. Instead of pushing the U.S., busy with Vietnam, out of the Middle East and more firmly implanting Soviet influence in the Eastern Arab countries, it had produced a humiliating defeat for Russian arms. Much of the Israeli armament was still French. However, the sophisticated weapons that Israel increasingly had received from the United States, as American concern grew over Soviet arms shipments to Egypt and Syria, had triumphed over the Russian tanks that lay scattered in vast junkpiles from the Mitla Pass to the Golan Heights and the charred Russian planes that marked every airfield in Egypt and Syria.

After the Israeli victory, Johnson expressed regret that the Israelis did not wait (though he seems to have made no serious effort to compel them to do so) for his own actions to open the Straits of Tiran. He wrote:

"I have always had a deep feeling of sympathy for Israel and its people, gallantly building and defending a modern nation against great odds and against the tragic background of Jewish experience. I can understand that men might decide to act on their own when hostile forces gather on their frontiers and cut off a major port, and when antagonistic political leaders fill the air with threats to destroy their nation. Nonetheless, I have never concealed my regret that Israel decided to move when it did. I always made it equally clear, however, to the Russians and to every other nation, that I did not accept the oversimplified charge of Israeli aggression."[6]

Although Johnson regretted the Israelis' moving forward on their own, he was relieved at the way things turned out. In the U.S., only he and his immediate aides fully realized how close the Israeli actions had again brought the world to the brink of a disastrous Soviet-U.S. confrontation. He wrote:

"Aside from the tragic accident involving the *Liberty*, no American died in the Middle East war in 1967. But the peace of the world walked a tightrope between June 5 and June 10, 1967, as it does today."[7]

The "tragic accident involving the *Liberty* " however, merits some attention. At the time, it was dismissed by much of the U.S. press as simply an erroneous attack by Israeli war planes and torpedo boats on a U.S. Navy intelligence-gathering vessel which the Israelis said they had mistaken for Egypt's only military transport ship. Nearly every American aboard was killed or wounded. After considerable prompting by the U.S. government and Israel's friends in the U.S., Israel paid the families of the victims a total of $6.8 million. It also promised at first to pay for the material damages, but

---

6. Johnson, Lyndon B., *The Vantage Point: Perspectives of the Presidency, 1963-1969*, Holt, Rinehart and Winston, 1971, p. 297.

7. *Ibid.*, p. 304.

then ignored the U.S. government's claim of $7.6 million for the ship. A U.S. Naval Board of Inquiry was convened, but it sought to limit its investigation to any failures in U.S. performance that might have contributed to the disaster.

The whole matter might have rested there except for one awkward detail: The ship had not sunk. As a result there were survivors, more than two hundred of them, all U.S. Navy or National Security Agency personnel. The father of one of the dead American officers was a retired Navy captain who had served in U.S. Naval intelligence. He interviewed many of the survivors, then went back and talked to his old Navy colleagues about the limits imposed on the inquiry. It is one thing to pass on without comment a report that you believe is a whitewash. It is another thing to look an old wartime buddy in the eye, and pretend to him that you believe it, especially when you know the incident it describes cost him his son.

It was difficult, but not completely impossible, to believe that the Israelis could, in the heat of the Six-Day War, have briefly mistaken a U.S. vessel for an Egyptian one. Alternatively, it was not too difficult to believe that the Israelis suddenly found that they had a reason of such national importance that it overrode all moral objections to the sinking of an American Navy ship gathering electronic intelligence on the edges of the most successful war in Israeli history. What still is difficult to believe, however, is that, if the United States subsequently discovered the true nature of the Israeli action, and the reason why it was taken, it would itself seek to withhold this information.

Among rational Americans, talk of high-level plots and high-level coverups always, and rightly, strains credulity. Therefore, before continuing with the story it is perhaps best to digress with Richard Deacon, a pro-Israel English writer, who was formerly Foreign Manager of the London *Sunday Times*. The British author's book, *The Israeli Secret Service*, gives a brief account of the incident and offers its own explanation for the Israeli action. A passage in Deacon's book also vividly describes the attitude toward Israel in the Washington of the Lyndon Johnson era, sketching in the background against which otherwise responsible Americans might have gone along with a coverup, and why it might have worked — for a while. Deacon writes:

"For a brief period Ephraim Evron was Israel's most powerful figure in Washington, more highly regarded than the Ambassador, and welcomed as a collaborator and Mossad liaison officer to the CIA. For years the tentacles of the Israeli Secret Service had reached out into all walks of American life, not in any sinister way, as was sometimes alleged by her enemies, but in a quietly persistent manner which embraced making friends and influencing people, establishing opinion lobbies and gathering intelligence. This influence extended into the U.S. Congress and the Senate, the Pentagon, the defense and electronic industries, the research laboratories and such Jewish-oriented organizations as the Anti-Defamation League, the Jewish Defense Committee, Bonds for Israel and the Federation of Jewish Philanthropies. Some of these bodies have served as fronts for intelligence-gathering and there are few of the important Congressional Committees which do not possess one member or staff assistant who does not feed the Israeli network material."[8]

---

8. Deacon, Richard, *The Israeli Secret Service*, Taplinger, New York, 1980, pp. 169-70.

That, from a pro-Zionist author, is perhaps the best preparation for what follows. These are the words of the mother of Lt. Stephen Toth, who was killed on the *Liberty*, and whose retired intelligence officer father, Navy Captain Joe Toth, had insisted on pursuing the matter. Reports Mrs. Toth:

"They killed my husband. . . . First my son, then my husband. The harassment took the form of threats and claims that Joe was damaging national security, and there was surveillance and pressure from people like the IRS. It was too much for his bad heart. It took a year to kill him, but it did."[9]

She spoke these words to a British journalist, Anthony Pearson. His book, *Conspiracy of Silence: The Attack on the U.S.S. Liberty* relates the stories of the survivors, and the by now fairly successful efforts of many well-meaning people in and out of the U.S. government to put together a coherent version of what happened, possible reasons for it, and the coverup that followed.

Like most tragedies, it started out routinely. The *Liberty* was a Navy ship used by the U.S. National Security Agency to monitor foreign communications. Such "snooper ships" or "ferrets," flying the flags of the Soviet Union, the U.S., and other countries and laden with antennae and electronic gear, are familiar sights to all sailors and to those who live in the ports used by the world's principal navies. Their function was relatively unknown to the American public until the North Koreans seized one of the *Liberty's* sister ships, the *Pueblo*, in 1968. Today, nearly every American recalls the *Pueblo*. Yet very few Americans recall the *Liberty*, despite the grievous losses suffered by her crew.

On May 24, 1967, 19 days before hostilities broke out on June 5, the National Security Agency ordered this U.S. Navy spy ship, with a complement of 297 men aboard, to leave its normal station off West Africa and travel to the Middle East. By the night of June 7, the ship was proceeding cautiously toward the Gaza Strip and the Sinai coast, relaying the findings of its array of sophisticated monitoring equipment. The equipment was operated solely by personnel of the National Security Agency. Even the ship's U.S. Navy commander was not allowed to enter the restricted portions of the hold, where the equipment functioned day and night, pulling in a variety of information that traveled across the area's radio waves.

Some authors claim that as early as June 7, the third day of the war, Washington had become aware of a highly disturbing fact. Whatever the Israelis had been doing overtly to keep King Hussein from committing his forces to the war, Israeli intelligence wizards were doing something else entirely. Using highly sophisticated equipment, they reportedly had devised a means to intercept, change, and then relay onward communications between Cairo and Amman. They were "cooking" the messages to lure King Hussein into committing his forces fully to attacks in support of the Egyptian Army and draw them away from defense of the West Bank and Syria. This is Deacon's version of the still-murky details:

---

9. Pearson, Anthony, *Conspiracy of Silence: The Attack on the U.S.S. Liberty*, Quartet Books, London, 1978, p. 132.

"Now once war had been launched the Israelis had one tremendous advantage over the Egyptians in that they had broken Egyptian and Jordanian ciphers. Thus the Israelis, thanks to their superior intelligence, were in a position to exploit this advantage by feeding false information by signals to the enemy. In a relay station in Sinai, radio messages from Cairo to Amman were being blocked by the Israelis and, in the jargon of the intelligence world, 'cooked' before being swiftly rerouted to Amman. The Israeli plan was to create the impression that the war was going well for the Egyptians. Throughout the first day of the war the aim was to feed these false signals to the enemy, thereby creating the maximum confusion in their ranks, and to black out and jam messages from Cairo to Amman telling King Hussein that the Israelis were gaining ground. Later Israel falsely informed Jordan by 'cooked' messages that the Egyptians were counter-attacking in Sinai and needed support from Hussein by an attack on Israeli positions in the Hebron area." [10]

That day, Deacon asserts, Eugene Rostow reportedly called the Israeli Ambassador, Avraham Harman, to the Department of State and told him that the U.S. knew about the "cooked" messages, and understood that they were intended to draw King Hussein further into the war and to keep his forces fighting long enough for Israel to seize all of Jerusalem and the West Bank.

Deacon's version of the story does not make clear whether Rostow discussed with the Israelis how the U.S. was able to monitor their messages. It probably did not make any difference. If Ambassador Harman could not find out, his popular deputy, "Eppy" Evron, almost certainly could.

The morning of June 8 dawned bright and Mediterranean-clear as the *Liberty* steamed off Al Arish. Immediately after sun-up, a French-built "Noratlas" transport circled the ship three times and then flew off toward Israel. The *Liberty's* crew was not concerned, since the ship was showing a huge American flag 100 feet above its flying bridge. The number 5 on both of its bows was twelve feet tall and had been freshly painted a few weeks earlier. Its name was lettered on the stern in English. On such a clear day, and in such calm weather, everything should have been going well, but it was not. According to some reports, the *Liberty's* receivers were encountering such loud jamming that it prevented the ship from receiving any other radio signals. At first, the chief radioman thought that it was because his own transmitters were malfunctioning, but a check proved otherwise. Significantly, perhaps, the jamming was loud enough to make radio transmission from the ship very difficult.

The *Liberty* had just made a turn on its roughly circular course at 8:50 a.m. when a single unidentified jet circled her, and then flew toward the mainland. There was no attempt at communication either way. At 10:56 the Noratlas transport appeared again and circled three or four times, apparently photographing the *Liberty* from a low altitude. It repeated this scrutiny again at 11:26 a.m. and 12:20 p.m. Also during the morning, two unidentified jets circled the ship twice and flew off toward the south.

The ship's captain, Commander William McGonagle, was puzzled and concerned at this almost continuous Israeli aerial surveillance but, in the absence of further orders from his base, he stayed in his own pattern while the NSA technicians continued their monitoring operations. Commander McGonagle did not know that three separate

---

10. Deacon, Richard, *The Israeli Secret Service*, Taplinger, New York, 1980, p. 180.

messages had been dispatched from Washington ordering the *Liberty* to leave the area. None of the messages reached him. All had been misrouted somewhere along the chain of communications, even though all had been given the highest priority designation in order to assure instant transmission.

Suddenly, shortly before 2 p.m., the ship's radar picked up the tracks of both planes and ships racing toward the *Liberty*. It was just about the time the last message had been sent from Washington. The planes, Israeli Mirage fighters, one by one dove without warning toward the ship in an attack pattern. Their concentrated rocket, cannon, and machine gun fire rapidly swept away virtually everything above deck—sunbathing off-duty crewmen, lookouts, sailors seeking to man the four pedestal-mounted 50-caliber machine guns that would have allowed the ship to protect itself, and the antennae needed to get off a distress signal. For five to six minutes according to Commander McGonagle, and as long as 20 to 30 minutes according to some officers, the Israeli planes made pass after pass. Their armor-piercing shells left more than 800 holes in the hull and superstructure.

In the first minutes nearly everyone above deck was down—dead or wounded. Lieutenant James Ennes, electronics material officer on the *Liberty*, in his book *Assault on the Liberty*, describes the scene:

"Blood flowed, puddled and coagulated everywhere. Men stepped in blood, slipped and fell in it, tracked it about in great crimson footprints."[11]

Lieutenant Stephen Toth was killed as he climbed to the lookout station to identify the attacking planes. Although painfully wounded himself, Commander McGonagle used those first few moments well. At 2:10, while still under the initial attack, he reported that he got off an all-channel distress message: "Mayday! Mayday! Am under attack from jet aircraft." Seconds later the jets silenced his radio and took out his antennae, so that he never heard the response from the Sixth Fleet aircraft carrier *Little Rock* confirming the receipt of his only transmission and reporting that it was dispatching jet aircraft to his assistance. Lieutenant Ennes, whose memory of the duration and details of the attack differs in several respects from Commander McGonagle's, describes it in these words:

"The first airplane had emptied the gun mounts and removed exposed personnel. The second airplane, through extraordinary luck or fantastic marksmanship, disabled nearly every radio antenna on the ship, temporarily preventing our call for help. Soon the high-performance Mirage fighter bombers that initiated the attack were joined by smaller swept-wing Dassault Mystere jets, carrying dreaded napalm-jellied gasoline. The Mysteres, slower and more maneuverable than the Mirages, directed rockets and napalm against the bridge and the few remaining topside targets. In a technique probably designed for desert warfare but fiendish against a ship at sea, the Mystere pilots launched rockets from a distance, then dropped huge silvery metallic napalm canisters as they passed overhead. The jellied slop burst into furious flame on impact, coating

11. Ennes, James M., Jr. *Assault on the Liberty. The True Story of the Israeli Attack on an American Intelligence Ship*, Random House, New York, 1979, p. 62.

everything, then surged through the fresh rocket holes to burn frantically among the men inside."[12]

As is the case with most dramatic events, many discrepancies exist among the recollections of eyewitnesses to the attack concerning the number of planes participating, the duration of the attack, and even how many distress messages the *Liberty* was able to get to Sixth Fleet units, and whether or not the *Liberty* heard responses to its messages. Whether or not Commander McGonagle heard the responses to his SOS, a lot of other people probably did, and that may have saved his ship from going to the bottom with all hands.

As armed Sixth Fleet jets streaked eastward toward the *Liberty* (and the war zone), Johnson informed Kosygin on the hot line that they were on a reconnaissance mission to investigate the distress call, and were not planning any hostile activity against the Arab forces. The point was to keep the Russians, fearing an attack, from mounting a counterstrike. The U.S. Embassy in Moscow later reported that Johnson's precautionary measure had convinced the Russians more than anything else that he really was trying to keep the Arab-Israeli war from developing into a general holocaust. At the same time, however, Americans have reported that impromptu preparations were being made for a punitive strike at Egypt if it turned out that Egyptian planes were attacking the U.S. ship. An unhappy postscript to this is that, on orders from Washington, the carrier-based planes were recalled immediately after they were launched. The recall of a mission which could have arrived in time to fight off the torpedo boat attackers has never been explained, despite recent requests by surviving crew members and by Admiral Thomas Moorer, former Chairman of the Joint Chiefs of Staff, for a formal U.S. Government investigation.

While all of this was happening around the globe, and the surviving crew members of the *Liberty* were battling fires all over the ship, three Israeli motor torpedo boats were bearing down upon her to open an all-out attack. While 20 and 40-millimeter guns riddled the ship, some six torpedoes were launched, one of which struck the communications room dead center in the number three hold. The entire communications center was destroyed, and its commander and most of his staff were killed by the explosion or trapped by the rush of water that filled the hold.

Here again, recollections differ as to what happened next. It would be immaterial except that some of the recollections of Commander McGonagle, as related to the Naval Board of Inquiry, were subsequently published in unclassified, summary form. Shortly afterward, "eyewitness" accounts by Israeli military personnel appeared in the Israeli press which closely matched the published recollections of the U.S. ship's commander and which attributed the attack to mistaken identification. It was only later, when detailed recollections by other ship's officers began to leak out, that the wide discrepancies between the Israeli version of events, and accounts of many of the American eyewitnesses became glaringly obvious.

---

12. Ennes, James M., Jr. *Assault on the Liberty. The True Story of the Israeli Attack on an American Intelligence Ship*, Random House, New York, 1979, p. 67.

McGonagle recalled that as he awaited another salvo from the torpedo boats, the firing stopped and one of the torpedo boats blinked out the question, "Do you need assistance?" Torn between astonishment and fury, McGonagle declined assistance.

However, Ennes recalls the attack by the torpedo boats as continuing for a protracted period after the torpedo struck. He writes:

"Petty Officer John Randall was knocked off his feet by the impact of the torpedo . . . Randall burst out of his shop and onto the main deck in time to see torpedo boat *Tahmass* drift slowly down the ship's starboard side, her guns trained on *Liberty's* bridge. Randall extended the middle finger of his right hand in a universal gesture of contempt—and then watched the 40 mm cannon swing around until it came to bear squarely on his chest. But Randall was too angry to be frightened and too proud to move; he stared defiantly at the gunner while the boat drifted past. Luckily for him, that gunner had no stomach for firing at such an easy target. Moments later all three boats commenced circling *Liberty* at high speed while firing at the waterline and at any men they could see moving. . . . An engineman brought the news the bullets were whistling over the ship's boilers: 'The boats are firing at the waterline. They're trying to explode the boilers!' he yelled. But most of the bullets were passing harmlessly through the ship. . . .

"Thomas Smith, the ship's laundry operator . . . waited for the sound of the machine guns to stop. When the torpedo boats finally pulled back, he raced to his abandon-ship station where he was alarmed to see sticky rubber sealant leaking from the life rafts . . . Finally, at a life-raft rack on the ship's port quarter, Smith found several apparently sound rubber rafts. When he pulled cords on the CO_2 cylinders, only three rafts held air. These he secured with heavy line and dropped over the side, where they would be ready if the abandon-ship order came. Lurking lazily a few hundred yards away, patiently waiting for *Liberty* to sink, the men on the torpedo boats watched the orange rafts drop into the water. Smith saw someone move on the center boat as her engine growled and her stern settled lower in the water. The boat moved closer to *Liberty*. When within good machine-gun range she opened fire on the empty life-rafts, deflating two and cutting the line on the third, which floated away like a child's balloon on the surface of the water. Smith cursed helplessly as a torpedo boat stopped to take the raft aboard. Then the boats added speed, taking the raft with them, and turned toward their base at Ashdod, sixty-five miles away."[13]

Whether the sea attack continued long after the torpedo hit as recalled by Ennes or stopped almost immediately afterward as recalled by McGonagle, there is little disagreement about other events occurring after the torpedo hit and before the boats left the area. Two large Hornet helicopters embellished with the Star of David insignia began circling the ship at a distance of only 100 yards. They made no offer of rescue, nor did they attack. The American crew could see, however, that they contained armed Israeli troops in battle dress. The torpedo boats then closed in again and at the same moment the surviving *Liberty* crew members braced themselves as two jets swept toward the ship in attack formation. But nothing happened. The aircraft departed without firing, the helicopters left without trying to put their soldiers aboard and, according to Ennes, it was at this time that the *Tahmass*, one of the torpedo boats, blinked out a message which the *Liberty's* crew could not understand. The *Tahmass* came still closer,

---

13. Ennes, James M., Jr. *Assault on the Liberty. The True Story of the Israeli Attack on an American Intelligence Ship*, Random House, New York, 1979, pp. 91-2, 95-6.

according to Ennes, and the Israeli commander inquired with a bullhorn, "Do you need any help?" Commander McGonagle declined the offer and after an hour the torpedo boats departed as well.

The attack was over although the ship was approached once more, as it limped away, by an Israeli helicopter apparently offering to assist with casualties, some of whom were still lying dead on the shattered decks. Having lost its radio, the ship could not establish communication and, recalling the armed troops on the previous helicopters, Commander McGonagle refused to let this one land. By this time Washington officials had established voice contact with the *Liberty*, knew that Israeli planes and ships were responsible for the attack and had dropped the idea of a retaliatory attack against Egypt.

Many mysteries and some inconsistencies still exist concerning the *Liberty*. It seems certain that the Israeli Defense Minister, Moshe Dayan, personally ordered the attack. A charitable interpretation of what followed is that, once the area containing the electronic monitoring equipment and its crew had been wiped out by the first torpedo, the attackers saw no reason to continue. The *Liberty* obviously would discover nothing more. However, given the jamming of the *Liberty's* radio frequencies and the violence and coordination of the combined air-sea attack, which seemed aimed at knocking out all of the ship's communications in the first few seconds, and which was followed up with a torpedo at the water line, it seems likely that the object was to sink the ship without a trace. One can only speculate on why the attack stopped so suddenly, just short of completion. It is hard to imagine that Dayan, who 13 years earlier at the time of the "Lavon affair" had not balked at approving the order to carry out provocations against American installations in Cairo, would have missed this chance to kill two birds with one stone. If he had already decided that the communications monitoring must be stopped, even at the cost of the lives of the American crew, why not send the ship to the bottom? That way, Egypt would be blamed and the U.S. might be provoked into a move that would accomplish Israel's (and the USSR's) long-standing aim of once and for all alienating the U.S. from Egypt.

There are various possible explanations of why the attack stopped. One, of course, is that the Israelis really had just discovered for the first time that they were sinking an American ship. This is the official Israeli explanation, but it is not accepted by the Americans actually involved in the attack or in the naval inquiry that followed.

A second explanation is that, at some point after the attack began, an Israeli officer rebelled against the order to sink the ship and refused to allow it to continue. That is at least consistent with the evidence. It is also supported by a CIA information report which, with the informant's name deleted, was declassified and released into the public domain under the Freedom of Information Act. (It should be noted that in preparing such reports the U.S. government agency involved does not necessarily authenticate the information they contain. It simply transmits the report, rumor or theory which has been presented to the drafting officer by an informant.) The CIA message read:

"(Sources deleted) commented on the sinking of the US Communications ship *Liberty*. They said that Dayan personally ordered the attack on the ship and that one of his generals adamantly opposed the action and said, 'This is pure murder.' One of the admirals who was present also disapproved the action, and it was he who ordered it stopped."[14]

Still a third explanation is simply that the Israelis suddenly realized, or were told, that they had been caught. Whether they were aware that the initial distress message had not identified the attackers is not clear. Nor is it clear whether they thought they could finish the job before the arrival of American jets at the scene. What is certain is that other American ships were in the general vicinity and were therefore able to monitor the attack on the *Liberty* via their own radios. If at some point in the action the Israelis became aware of this, they would know that the game was up. In any case, they had already destroyed electronic evidence of their prior actions, and any capability of the *Liberty* to monitor those actions further.

Another possibly relevant factor is the report by British journalist Pearson that pilots of two of the attacking Israeli aircraft were in fact dual-nationality American-Israelis. In a conversation Pearson reports he had in Israel with one of those pilots, who learned to fly in the U.S. Air Force, Pearson quotes the pilot as saying that when he and his comrade, a former U.S. Navy flyer, first saw the U.S. Navy markings on the *Liberty*, they twice asked for reconfirmation of the attack orders. The orders were reconfirmed and the attack began. The pilot told Pearson that his father, who had emigrated from the U.S. to Israel, had denounced him for "carrying out orders" to kill his own former countrymen just as had members of the Nazi S.S. Although Pearson reported this conversation in detail in his book, no further evidence of the existence of either of these two dual-national pilots has surfaced. Other experts on the subject, therefore, now tend to discount Pearson's report.

Whatever the reasons for the Israeli orders to start and to stop the attack, it is the attitude of the U.S. government in impeding investigation into the matter that most puzzles subsequent investigators.

In his book, Lieutenant Ennes articulates this concern:

"There *were* a number of perfectly legitimate security issues that had to be reckoned with: the mission and capabilities of the ship; the reaction time of the fleet; the deployment and control of nuclear weapons; the deployment of submarines. All of these things are sensitive and could provide useful information for a potential enemy. However, the coverup went far beyond that."[15]

The allusion to nuclear weapons and deployment of submarines refers to the presence of the nuclear attack submarine *Andrew Jackson* at the scene. In addition to its other duties the *Liberty* was functioning as the submarine's eyes and ears. It has been suggested that the combined presence of the two ships was a clear warning to the Israelis not to deploy the atomic weapons they had assembled themselves, using technology obtained from France and fissionable material stolen from an American uranium-processing plant in Pennsylvania. By blinding the submarine, the Israelis would

14. Ennes, James M., Jr. *Assault on the Liberty. The True Story of the Israeli Attack on an American Intelligence Ship*, Random House, New York, 1979, p. 214.
15. *Ibid.*, pp. 203-4.

have been demonstrating that they would have no compunctions about taking out a U.S. nuclear submarine as well if it served their purposes. The weakness in this explanation is the fact that by this time the war already was going so well for the Israelis that it had no need to deploy atomic weapons which it presumably would use only as a last defense.

Former CIA agent Wilbur Crane Eveland advances his own explanations both for the motive behind the attack, and for U.S. government reluctance to investigate it. He reports in his book:

"Message intercepts by the *Liberty* made it clear that Israel had never intended to limit its attack to Egypt. Furthermore, we learned that the Israelis were themselves intercepting communications among the Arab leaders. The Israelis then retransmitted 'doctored' texts to encourage Jordan and Syria to commit their armies in the erroneous belief that Nasser's army had repelled the Israeli invaders. To destroy this incriminating evidence, Moshe Dayan ordered his jets and torpedo boats to destroy the *Liberty* immediately. . . . The Israeli government claimed that the converted freighter had been mistaken for an Egyptian warship. A U.S. naval board of inquiry found that the daylight attack had been unprovoked and deliberate. Then the U.S. government shrouded the entire *Liberty* matter in secrecy under a cloak of 'national security' considerations, where it remains even now. Individual claims of compensation for the ship's dead and wounded were paid by the U.S. government, supposedly on behalf of Israel. Even moves by Congress to stop all aid to Israel until $7 million in compensation for the *Liberty* was paid succumbed to White House and Department of State pressure. Why? Defense Minister Dayan had stated his government's position bluntly: Unless the United States wished the Russians and Arabs to learn of joint CIA-Mossad covert operations in the Middle East and of Angleton's discussions before the 1967 fighting started, the questions of the lost American ship and how the war originated should be dropped. That ended the U.S. protestations."[16]

The U.S. Government's motivation for continuing to withhold information about the attack continues to bother well-intentioned Americans. If their own government does not tell the truth about the transgressions of its allies, what about its own sins of omission or commission? How can decent and respected Americans, sworn to protect and preserve the Constitution of the United States, act in a manner so inconsistent with both its letter and its spirit? Is it not better to admit the truth, no matter how damaging to the U.S. relationship with Israel, than go on telling new lies to cover it up?

The significance of the Dreyfus affair was not the fact that an innocent Jewish army officer was convicted on trumped-up charges of treason against the France he served and loved. What shocked the world (and launched Zionism as a serious movement) was the fact that, when his innocence was proved, the authorities tried to disregard the truth in order to protect the French institutions under which he had been convicted.

In Israel's Lavon affair, it was not the stupidity or immorality of the plan to incite the U.S. against Egypt that ultimately shocked Israelis. It was the fact that, years later, when it was revealed that Pinchas Lavon had been blamed on the basis of forged documents, Ben Gurion not only refused to accept the evidence but intensified his

---

16. Eveland, Wilbur Crane, *Ropes of Sand: America's Failure in the Middle East*, Norton, New York, 1980, p. 325.

persecution of Lavon in order to protect the political fortunes of his Labor party proteges, Dayan and Peres.

After the Gulf of Tonkin incident, and the Watergate coverup, Americans reluctantly realized that the leaders of both U.S. political parties in recent decades have persuaded themselves that, under certain circumstances, fabricated evidence or outright lies are justified. Many well-intentioned Americans would say that withholding facts or even lying is permissible if it is demonstrably in the national interest. Others, equally well-intentioned, would disagree, saying that the lie becomes a spreading cancer in the body of mutual trust upon which all democratic societies must rest, and that, in the end, the cancer is far more destructive than the evil the lie originally was devised to counter.

Whatever the answers to those abstract questions, in the case of the *Liberty* it appears that any withholding of facts or lying that may still be taking place is in the national interest of Israel, not the United States, It certainly is not in the interest of the hundreds of Americans personally bereaved or afflicted by this tragedy.

In the prologue to his book about the attack, Ennes summarizes the entire case nicely:

"Even before the wounded were evacuated, a news lid went down over the entire episode. This story was not to be told. The Navy's own failures were never exposed or acknowledged, and Israel's fragile alibi was nurtured and protected. Israel claimed that the ship was at fault for being near the coast, for 'trying to escape' after being fired upon by jets, and for not informing the Israeli government of her location; and our government tolerantly kept those assertions from public knowledge. Israel claimed that the attack resulted from mistaken identity, and our government quietly accepted that excuse."[17]

Some have called this a whitewash, but that is not entirely true. When pressed, various government departments eventually released documents pointing to Israeli guilt, as for example the CIA document quoted previously. Nor has there been a permanent total news blackout, as the number of books already published concerning the attack on the *Liberty* indicates. But the reluctance of the Congress, the Navy, or any other government agency to examine the evidence, and offer its own opinion as to whether the attack was deliberate and, if so, the probable motive for it has been very effective in making the incident gradually recede from public consciousness. For anyone who doubts the all-pervasive effect of this information "brown-out," it may be instructive to complete this chapter with President Johnson's own account of the attack on the *Liberty*, written long after the facts had been studied and published, at least in classified form. His description of the *Liberty* affair in his own book, *The Vantage Point*, reads:

"Thursday, June 8, began on a note of tragedy. A morning news bulletin reported that a U.S. Navy communications ship, the *Liberty*, had been torpedoed in international waters off the Sinai coast. For seventy tense minutes we had no idea who was responsible, but at eleven o'clock we learned that the ship had been attacked in error by Israeli gunboats and planes. Ten

---

17. Ennes, James M., Jr. *Assault on the Liberty. The True Story of the Israeli Attack on an American Intelligence Ship*, Random House New York, 1979, pp. 3-4.

men of the *Liberty* crew were killed and a hundred were wounded. This heartbreaking episode grieved the Israelis deeply, as it did us."[18]

The true toll of the attack on the *Liberty*, as President Johnson already seemed to have forgotten, was 34 men killed and another 171 men wounded.

Israel Information Services

Major General Uzi Narkiss, Defense Minister Moshe Dayan, and Chief of Staff Yitzhak Rabin stride through the Lion's Gate into the conquered Old City of Jerusalem in June, 1967. Israel's victory over all of its neighbors in only six days gained it world esteem. Thoughtful Israelis, however, mark this victory as the beginning of a new self-image of invincibility which has made many of their leaders reluctant to make the territorial compromises necessary if they are to enjoy peace with their Middle Eastern neighbors.

---

18. Johnson, Lyndon B., *The Vantage Point: Perspectives of the Presidency, 1963-1969*, Holt, Rinehart and Winston, 1971, pp. 300-1.

CHAPTER XI

President Nixon
and the Rogers Plan

*"The Middle East is volatile, vulnerable, crucial to the conflict be-
tween East and West, and caught in shifting political crosscurrents that can be more
explosively emotional than those in almost any other part of the world."*[1]

Richard M. Nixon, 1982

*"The Rogers initiative . . . was the first American step on the correct path . . . There
were two factions in the U.S. who had sponsored the initiative: Rogers and a group
of State Department experts who were fully convinced of the need to establish peace
in the area in order to safeguard American and Western interests. There was, however,
an opposing faction led by Henry Kissinger which believed that it was in the interest
of the U.S. to support Israel totally . . . Kissinger was able to persuade Nixon to adopt
his views under the pretext of confronting Soviet infiltration in the area. This was the
real beginning of the failure of the initiative."*

Mahmoud Riad, Former Egyptian Foreign Minister, 1981

*"Spite played a major role in America's foreign policy in the Middle East in 1969 and
1970. Nixon had assigned the Middle East to Rogers, in part because of concern about
Kissinger's Jewishness but also out of a belief that Rogers, whose office was being
systematically stripped of its authority, should be left with some area of responsibility.
In the early months of the Nixon presidency, Kissinger, whose NSC would still have
prior review of all State Department policy papers on the Middle East, accepted the*

---

1. Nixon, Richard M., *Leaders*, Warner Books, New York, 1982, p. 279.

division of power. Kissinger nonetheless did not hesitate to move in on Middle East policy shortly after the inauguration."[2]

Seymour Hersh, 1983

"When I entered office I knew little of the Middle East. I had never visited any Arab country; I was not familiar with the liturgy of Middle East negotiations. The first time I heard one of the staple formulas of the region's diplomacy was at a dinner at the British Embassy in February 1969. Someone invoked the sacramental language of United Nations Security Council Resolution 242, mumbling about the need for a just and lasting peace within secure and recognized borders. I thought the phrase so platitudinous that I accused the speaker of pulling my leg. It was a mistake I was not to repeat. By the end of my time in office I had become like all other old Middle East hands; word had become reality, form and substance had merged. I was immersed in all the ambiguities, passions, and frustrations of that maddening, heroic and exhilarating region."[3]

Henry Kissinger, 1982

With every year that passes it becomes clearer that during the first two years of the Nixon Administration a true Middle East peace might have been achieved. The opportunity was presented by a sea change in Arab public opinion as even militant Arab leaders began to accept publicly the idea of a permanently-divided Palestine. The window of opportunity was brief, however, since even the most moderate Israelis were beginning to believe, privately, that they could keep it all.

Why was the opportunity lost? At the time, Americans blamed Russian deceit and Egyptian gullibility. The Arabs blamed Israel and its persistent supporters in the Nixon Administration.

Only the Israelis felt no need to assess blame, since the lack of a settlement left them in possession of all the territories they had seized in 1967. In retrospect, however, the euphoria that followed that smashing military victory, and the resulting world acclaim, was a disaster for the Israelis. For the first time in their history they seemed to lose all touch with the realities of demographic and territorial weakness and external dependence that once had governed their every move. Thus the opportunity to make peace with their neighbors and become an accepted and productive member of the Middle Eastern community of states was lost, at least for a generation, and perhaps forever. When the magnitude of this disaster is finally understood by all Israelis, it will be interesting to see whom they blame. It may be Henry Kissinger. Or it may be simply themselves.

At the beginning of the Nixon Administration prospects for Middle East peace could not have looked better. President Nixon probably came into office better prepared on foreign policy than any other President of this century. His first concern was extricating the U.S., "with honor," from the no-win situation in Vietnam. That was the assign-

---

2. Hersh, Seymour, *The Price of Power: Kissinger in the White House*, Summit Books, New York, 1983, p. 213.
3. Kissinger, Henry, *White House Years*, Little Brown and Company, Boston, 1979, p. 340.

ment he gave to Henry Kissinger, his new National Security Adviser. Kissinger, a German-born Harvard professor, had been for some time a well-paid consultant to Nelson Rockefeller.

From his new White House vantage point, Kissinger rapidly demonstrated an ability to articulate his point of view with impressive erudition, an unmatched skill at press manipulation, and a seemingly compulsive need for no-holds-barred bureaucratic self-aggrandizement. All of these qualities played a role in his relentless campaign to denigrate the State Department and, especially, the new Secretary of State, William Rogers. Soon Kissinger, rather than Rogers, had a Presidential license to attack, single-handedly, U.S. problems virtually anywhere in the world.

Except in the Middle East. Although Kissinger repeatedly sought to take over direction of U.S. policy in that area, about which, by his own admission, he was almost totally ignorant, President Nixon stubbornly resisted each move. The Middle East was the one area left solely to Rogers. Former White House Aide John Erlichman says Nixon felt that "Henry, being Jewish, simply could not gain the required confidence from Arab leaders."[4]

Or, it may be that Nixon already had recognized that the Middle East might lend itself to his proclaimed intention to seek a new era of negotiation rather than confrontation with the Soviet Union. Even before his inauguration he had sent former Pennsylvania Governor William Scranton on a Middle East fact-finding mission. In the Middle East Scranton had said that Nixon favored an "even-handed" policy there.

This caught the favorable attention of Arab leaders, but it set off a storm of protest from Jewish supporters of Israel in the United States. During the 1968 election campaign most Jewish voters had supported the Democratic candidate, former Vice President Hubert Humphrey, who had a long record of apparently sincere support for Israel over many years in the Senate. Nixon, on the other hand, had drawn special criticism from Jewish friends of Israel as early as the 1954 campaign when, as Vice President, he had accused them of misrepresenting American Middle East policies abroad.

Israel's American friends also remembered Nixon's support of the Eisenhower policies at Suez and after. Nixon, therefore, had entered the White House with few Jewish supporters, despite his fervent campaign statements in support of Israel. That may explain why, even with Kissinger excluded, the Nixon Middle East policy often seemed to be running on two tracks. One was to build up some confidence in Israel (and, perhaps, support for Nixon among its American friends) by giving Israel sophisticated weapons. The White House official in charge of this effort was Leonard Garment, a former Nixon law partner who was Nixon's liaison with the Jewish community and a low-key, moderate man who got along with almost everyone.

On the other track, however, Rogers was familiarizing himself with the remarkable changes that were taking place in the Middle East. The Arabs had been able to blame their 1948 defeat on indifferent and corrupt rulers. The 1956 defeat had resulted from

---

4. Erlichman, John, *Witness to Power: The Nixon Years*, Simon and Schuster, New York, 1982, p. 299.

a conspiracy and combined sneak attack by Israel, France and Britain. But in 1967 there was no one to blame. Egyptian President Nasser had believed and acted on erroneous information received from his friends, the Russians.

Whether the Russians actually intended to deceive Nasser and provoke a war, or whether they were deceived themselves by their electronic interception of a gradually rising, and perhaps carefully orchestrated, level of Israeli military communications, is still disputed. Certainly the Israelis were remarkably well prepared to strike when Nasser made his fatal misstep.

His reckless rhetoric had swept away the protecting U.N. presence and given the Israelis the only excuse they needed for their carefully-prepared and devastating attack. Nasser's charges of U.S. and British collaboration with Israel were not widely believed for long. He accepted the consequences, and resigned. In a truly spontaneous outpouring, however, Egyptians had poured into the streets to demand that he remain in power.

Nevertheless, self-esteem had been grievously wounded throughout the Arab World. The first reaction was a meeting of Arab leaders in Khartoum at which they vowed, in the strident language of the past, no peace and no recognition of Israel. At the same time, however, King Faisal of Saudi Arabia and President Nasser of Egypt met quietly and accepted a Sudanese compromise proposal to settle their Yemeni dispute, which had polarized inter-Arab relations and tied down forces that might better have been employed in defending against the Israeli attack.

The Arabs were finally shocked out of some of the dreams into which they had retreated when their past glories had faded centuries earlier. Behind the facade of intransigent slogans issuing from Khartoum, there began to emerge a new current of moderation. The June, 1967, defeat had awakened Arabs who, until that moment of truth, had accepted the political slogans that for so long had been a substitute for rational thought, careful planning, and hard work.

In Israel, however, the victory had set a reverse process into motion. Revisionists, once regarded as fanatics, were now listened to more respectfully as they articulated the belief that Jerusalem and the West Bank (and modern Jordan, as well) were God-given parts of Israel. They were determined that not an inch would go back to the Arabs—ever. Moderates, who before 1967 might happily have settled for the 1948 cease-fire lines as a permanent boundary, now devised the "Allon Plan" to give only the barren hills and populous West Bank towns back to the Arabs, while keeping a network of "strategic settlements" in the Jordan valley and on the heights above to act as a "trip-wire" against future invasions.

Neither extremists nor moderates in Israel talked about giving back any part of Jerusalem, despite its role as third holiest city for the world's 800 million Muslims. Instead, Israel, with a Jewish population probably not exceeding three million, set out on a high-speed campaign to shut off all of Jerusalem from Islamic rule forever. The former Jewish quarter of the old city was virtually leveled, to remove its Arab residents, and then rebuilt and resettled with Jewish occupants. Huge new apartment buildings for Jewish families were constructed on hills all around the city. Jerusalem's city limits were extended far into the countryside.

Aware that Israel was making it as difficult as possible for peace-makers to undo the results of its military victory, the Arabs took their case to the United Nations. Israel, however, refused to withdraw from territory taken from any of the three Arab belligerents in the absence of direct negotiations for a permanent peace. For their part, the Arabs unwisely declined to negotiate directly with Israel from their self-perceived position of weakness.

Finally the impasse was broken. The Western powers, the Soviet Union, and eventually all of the Arab confrontation states and the Israeli government of Prime Minister Golda Meir agreed to UN Security Council Resolution 242 of November 22, 1967, whose principal author was Lord Caradon, British representative to the United Nations. In slightly ambiguous language it set out as the basis for a final settlement Israeli withdrawals from lands occupied during the 1967 war in return for Arab acquiescence in Israel's right to exist within secure and recognized boundaries.

The ambiguity was created by a difference in the French and English language versions of one provision of the resolution. The English version specifies "withdrawal of Israeli armed forces from territories occupied in the recent conflict."

The French version specifies "retrait des forces armées Israéliennes des territoires occupés lors du récent conflit." Arab signatories cite the French text's call for withdrawal from "*the* territories occupied" while Israelis cite the English text's "territories occupied." The Arabs say Resolution 242 specifies that Israel must withdraw from *all* occupied territories, while the Israelis say it leaves the extent of the withdrawals to be negotiated.

The ambiguity of the two versions is not accidental. Authors of the resolution had decided that this was the only way to secure the agreement of all parties to Resolution 242 as a framework for settlement.

The most significant change that confronted Rogers when he assumed office was the evolution of more moderate public positions among leaders of the Arab confrontation states. First their external statements, and then their internal statements as well, began to reflect the understanding that, in accepting Resolution 242, they were limiting Arab claims to the lands first occupied by Israel in 1967, and were relinquishing claims to the lands awarded by the UN Partition Plan to Israel in 1947, and the additional lands seized by Israel in 1948.

Rogers had the Assistant Secretary for Near Eastern Affairs, Joseph Sisco, draw up in utmost secrecy a plan of action to implement Resolution 242's land-for-peace formula. The key provision was that there would be only "insubstantial" alterations between the pre-1967 boundaries and the final, permanent national boundaries.

Nixon called an all-day session of the National Security Council and obtained strong backing from other members of his new foreign affairs team, including Defense Secretary Melvin Laird, Under Secretary of State Elliot Richardson and CIA Director Richard Helms, for an activist policy aimed at implementing the Rogers plan. The mood of the meeting was expressed by one participant who declared: "It is high time that the United States stopped acting as Israel's attorney in the Middle East."

There was a contradiction inherent in implementing the plan, however. It depended not only on Israeli and Arab cooperation, but also on support from the Soviet Union. Yet, from Nixon's point of view, the primary reason for pursuing the plan was to secure withdrawal of the Russians from their new position of power in the Mediterranean.

Nixon felt that errors by John Foster Dulles in dealing with Egypt had provided the original opening through which the Russians had first slipped into the Mediterranean. France, Italy and other U.S. Mediterranean allies openly blamed the close U.S.-Israeli relationship that had developed during the Johnson Administration for Russia's continuing influence, deriving from its role as principal arms supplier to both Egypt and Syria. Clearly the way to get the Soviets back out of the Mediterranean area was to settle the Arab-Israeli dispute so that the Arabs would no longer feel they needed Soviet help. The problem was how to get the Soviets to cooperate in a scheme aimed at ultimately reducing their own influence in the Middle East.

Meanwhile, Israelis, who were content with a status quo which left them in possession of all of the conquered Arab territory as well as recipients of an increasing supply of U.S. weaponry, were receiving full information from well-placed American friends on the activities over which Nixon had clamped the tightest security measures he could devise. Israel orchestrated a rising crescendo of complaints that the U.S., in concert with the U.K., France and the USSR, was preparing to "impose" a Middle East settlement which would force it to give up battlefield conquests essential to its security in exchange for paper promises from the Arabs.

As U.S. Jewish groups and media personalities picked up their cues, however, Kissinger skillfully directed their ire toward Rogers and away from Nixon. In confidence he pointed out to Jewish journalists that, since the new President had been elected without significant Jewish support, personal attacks on the President rather than on the State Department could arouse an alleged latent anti-Semitism in Nixon which might have consequences no American or Israeli Jew could foresee.

The President himself was convinced that Israel would never enjoy real security until it signed a peace agreement acceptable to its Arab neighbors. But instead of going to the American people with this obvious truth he let the State Department quietly pursue the Rogers plan, working first through the Soviet Ambassador in Washington. Rogers felt that once the U.S. and USSR settled on general guidelines, the agreement would receive quick backing from the U.K. and France and the resulting "Big Four" agreement could be handed to UN Middle East negotiator Gunnar Jarring of Sweden to present to Egypt, Jordan, Israel and, eventually, Syria.

Kissinger, however, had begun quietly denigrating the plan via "back channel" communications using members of his own staff, cooperative CIA officials, and even Ambassadors willing to carry messages without informing their own superior, the Secretary of State. He was in frequent personal contact with Soviet Ambassador Anatoly Dobrynin and Israeli Ambassador Rabin in the course of his world-wide responsibilities, and was in back channel communication with the Nasser government in Egypt. All received the impression that the President was virtually disengaged from Roger's persistent Middle East peace efforts and that the U.S. had no serious intention of proceeding with any plan strongly opposed by Israel.

In fact, Nixon was giving Rogers a great deal of flexibility in hopes that an agreement on the Middle East plan would provide a strong start toward negotiations on armaments and other East-West issues crucial to all of the Nixon Administration's foreign policy plans. When the Russians objected to ambiguous U.S. language concerning Egyptian and Israeli boundaries, Rogers accepted the Russian position, and ruled out any retention of Sinai territories by Israel. It was agreed that the Egyptian-Israeli border would be the same as before the Six-Day War. When the draft agreement was finally completed through negotiations between Sisco and Dobrynin in Washington, it was forwarded to Moscow. There, however, in October, 1969 the Russians flatly turned it down, although it contained the language upon which they had insisted throughout the preliminary Washington talks. The Soviet rejection was promptly echoed by Egypt.

Kissinger made the most of the setback, telling anyone who would listen that it had been naive of Rogers to expect the Soviets to cooperate in a plan aimed at ejecting them from the Mediterranean. The Israelis, though delighted, did not relax their campaign of defiance. American Middle East experts were perplexed. They had anticipated the extreme Israeli resistance but had not expected Nasser to unleash the Cairo media to denounce a plan that would have achieved the very goal he sought, recovery of all Egyptian territory, and virtually all other Arab territory seized in 1967 as well.

Rogers and his staff kept working, hoping that eventually the Russians would recognize the plan as the only sure way to reduce the risk of nuclear confrontation in the Middle East, and that the Egyptians would soon come to their senses. Since Kissinger kept working as well, Nixon perceptibly began to lose confidence in both the feasibility of the plan and the competence of its authors. The President, nevertheless, did not rein in Rogers.

On December 9, 1969, Rogers made his plan public, convinced that since the Israelis knew all the details anyway, a closer examination by the Arabs might result in a reversal of their opposition. Rogers made it clear that the plan was not limited to an Israeli-Egyptian settlement, but also called for Jordanian-Israeli negotiations involving the West Bank, Jerusalem and the Palestinian refugees. The result was a renewed storm of public Israeli opposition. In an emergency meeting, the Israeli cabinet formally rejected the plan. By this time the religiously-motivated desire to keep all of the West Bank and Jerusalem had taken firm root in Israel, although in their public arguments Israeli Labor coalition leaders continued to stress only security considerations.

Public discussion of the plan by Rogers provided Kissinger with an opportunity to bring his own opposition to it into the open. He told his staff that Rogers had not cleared the December 9 speech in advance with him, and that as a result the President was caught unawares. Joseph Sisco, Roger's principal Middle East assistant at the time, who subsequently held the same position under Kissinger, states flatly that Kissinger not only saw the speech in advance but even made substantive comments and recommendations for changes.[5] The White House staff, however, and perhaps President Nixon as well, presumably believed the Kissinger version of the affair at the time.

On the day after the speech, Kissinger openly criticized the Rogers plan at a National Security Council meeting. At the same time he advanced his own diametrically-opposed Middle East strategy, which was to delay settlement for as long as needed

---

5. Hersh, Seymour, *The Price of Power: Kissinger in the White House*, Summit Books, New York, 1983, p. 213.

to win the Arabs away from their Soviet mentors. The longer the stalemate lasted, Kissinger said, "the more obvious it would become that the Soviet Union had failed to deliver what the Arabs wanted."[6]

On December 17, Nixon ordered Leonard Garment to give private assurances to Israeli Prime Minister Golda Meir that the State Department initiative would not have his full backing. On January 25, 1970, Nixon sent a message to an emergency meeting of Jewish leaders assembled in Washington to protest the Rogers plan. The Nixon message backed away from the unambiguous language in the Rogers plan about the necessity for Israeli withdrawal from the occupied territories, and Nixon promised to continue supplying necessary military equipment to Israel.

The Rogers plan for peace in the Middle East had become moribund, rejected first by those who might have benefited most from it, and now even by the President under whose sponsorship it was prepared.

Whether the ultimate responsibility lies with the Russians, radical Arabs, increasingly intransigent Israelis or U.S. bureaucratic in-fighting, the way was opened to three more of the most violent years in the bloody history of the Israeli-Palestinian dispute.

Israel Information Services

Destroyed Egyptian vehicles attest to the ferocity of the Israeli aircraft strikes that preceded the Israeli armored thrust through Sinai in June, 1967.

6. Evans, Rowland and Novak, Robert, *Nixon in the White House*, Random House, New York, 1971, p. 88.

CHAPTER XII

The War of Attrition

"The Nixon-Ford-Kissinger years are the surprise story of American diplomatic history. The two Presidents came to office with a reputation for mistrust and suspicion of America's adversaries and strong reservations about America's friends. Theirs was a confrontationist mood. Kissinger's writings revealed a profound historical sense and an impulse to evolve new ideas and concepts; but his somber view of man's political nature and his skeptical attitude toward anything that could be described as utopianism seemed to augur a tenacious defense of existing stabilities rather than an impulse to look beyond them. Yet this unlikely union of disparate characters left American policy after eight years more thoroughly transformed in scope and spirit than any corresponding period before or since."[1]

Abba Eban, 1983

"What Israel wanted from the United States was two nearly irreconcilable courses of action: unconditional support of Israel's negotiating position, which Israeli domestic politics usually drove toward the tactically intransigent; and influence on the Arab countries to accept the State of Israel and conclude a peace. To fulfill the first role, we would have to act in effect as Israel's lawyer; to achieve the second objective, we would have to gain Arab confidence and a reputation for fairness. If we were serious about the peace process we had to take Arab views seriously; on occasion we would have to dissociate from Israeli positions or actions we considered unreasonable."[2]

Henry Kissinger, 1982

1. Eban, Abba, *The New Diplomacy: International Affairs in the Modern Age*, Random House, New York, 1983, pp. 62-3.
2. Kissinger, Henry, *Years of Upheaval*, Little, Brown and Company, Boston, 1982, p. 620.

"The future of the Middle East, including that of Israel, hinges on the achievement of an honorable overall settlement of the Arab-Israeli conflict . . . A perpetually destabilized and turbulent Middle East is no lasting asset to the Israelis or the world."[3]

Walid Khalidi, Professor of Political Studies,
American University of Beirut, 1981

"The Middle East crisis had had its origin in Palestine, but all parties showed extraordinary ambivalence in their approach to the Palestinians. In 1973 they were still treated as refugees in the UN, as terrorists in the United States and Western Europe, as an opportunity by the Soviets, and as simultaneous inspiration and nuisance by the Arab World."[4]

Henry Kissinger, 1982

Rebuffed at home, William Rogers nevertheless moved to quiet a rapidly deteriorating situation in the Middle East, the only area left to the Secretary of State after President Nixon had delegated primary responsibility for U.S. relations with the rest of the world to National Security Adviser Henry Kissinger. For some time Egyptian artillery had been pounding Israeli positions along the Suez Canal in what the Egyptians called the "war of attrition." In return, the Israelis, besides using their own artillery to pound the Egyptian cities along the canal into rubble, made devastating commando raids into isolated Egyptian positions, and harassed Egyptian installations from the air.

On January 7, 1970, Israel launched the first of a series of "deep penetration" air raids on Cairo suburbs. Although ostensibly targeted on Egypt's arms industry, the raids hit residential areas and in one case a school was destroyed in mid-day, killing the students inside. If the Egyptians sought to erode Israeli determination to hold on to the Sinai with a daily toll of death and destruction along the front lines, the Israelis were prepared to shock the Egyptians into an acceptance of the status quo by making even the quiet streets of suburban Cairo subject to sudden terror strikes from the air.

Egypt demanded Soviet help to stop the deep penetration raids and soon new Russian interceptor aircraft combined with Soviet-built SAM missiles to challenge Israeli domination of Egyptian skies. The Israelis claimed that Russian instructors who came to supervise Egyptian use of the new planes were also flying some of the fighters in combat. As casualties mounted, possibly including Israelis killed by Russians and Russians killed by Israelis, tension in Washington mounted as well. If the battle turned decisively against the Israelis, they would soon be calling for U.S. planes and pilots to bail them out of a war they could not afford to lose. Kissinger's scenario of letting the Middle East bleed until the Arabs tired of Russian medicine seemed perilously close to involving the U.S. in direct combat with Russians.

Nixon may secretly have enjoyed seeing Russian pilots under fire from American weapons in Middle Eastern skies, just as U.S. pilots and soldiers were under fire from Russian weapons in Vietnam. But he supported an increasingly activist policy by Rogers

---

3. Khalidi, Walid, *Conflict and Violence in Lebanon*, Institute of Palestine Studies, Washington, D.C.
4. Kissinger, Henry, *Years of Upheaval*, Little, Brown and Company, Boston, 1982, p. 625.

to bring about a Middle East cease-fire. In June, 1970, Rogers presented the combatants with a cease-fire proposal based on a "standstill" of all weapons and forces in an area extending 50 kilometers on either side of the Suez Canal. Egypt accepted the proposal on July 23 and Israel accepted on July 31. But when the standstill cease-fire went into effect on August 7, the U.S. did not carry out a key element of its enforcement responsibility.

There were American U-2 photo-reconnaisance planes in the Mediterranean area and, as a guarantor along with the Russians of the agreement, the U.S. should have been flying over the area to record the exact position of every weapon in the 100-kilometer-wide zone at the moment the agreement went into effect. No photographs were made, however, and partisans differ as to the reasons. Israelis say the U.S. neglected its duties. Americans say Israel had for some time threatened to shoot down reconnaisance planes of any nationality that passed over the area. Almost immediately, therefore, Israel charged that the Egyptians were continuing to move their newly-received SAM missiles into the standstill zone to secure it against the Israeli planes that up to then had dominated the skies along both sides of the Canal.

The U.S. at first assumed the night-time Egyptian moves resulted from orders issued the day before the cease-fire went into effect, and that they would stop within hours. When the Israelis claimed the Egyptians had violated the standstill cease-fire for two nights running, there still were no aerial photographs to prove or disprove the Israeli claims. Whatever the reason that kept U.S. planes from making a routine photo-reconnaisance flight for more than 48 hours, it left a residue of bad feeling on all sides. The Israelis charged that the forbidden movements had greatly altered the balance of weaponry along the Canal, and this theme was picked up rapidly and effectively by Israel's articulate supporters in the United States. The Israeli grievance was assuaged with the usual medicine—new shipments of expensive U.S. military equipment.

Meanwhile Kissinger was able to say that the alleged Egyptian breech of faith only proved that the U.S. could expect nothing but betrayal in the Middle East from the Russians and their friends. As for the Russians, they answered this complaint by blandly telling the U.S. that although they were Egypt's principal source of weapons and funding, they had no more control over their Egyptian client's actions than did the U.S. over those of its Israeli client state. The standstill agreement lowered the casualties, but it increased suspicion between Egypt and Israel on one hand, and between the USSR and the U.S. on the other.

While the Arab-Israeli lines were clearly drawn along the Suez Canal, another less easily defined battlefront was forming all around Israel. The Arab moderation that had gradually emerged after the 1967 war was to some extent offset by another new element resulting from that wrenching Arab defeat. That was an armed Palestinian national movement which, if not totally independent of the competing Arab countries that sponsored it, was at least strong enough and wily enough to play one Arab country against another for its own benefit.

In 1948, 1956 and 1967 the Palestinians had watched the armed forces of neighboring Arab countries do the bulk of the fighting for them. The simultaneous defeat in 1967 of all three major Arab states bordering Israel shocked many Palestinians into the belief that if there were ever to be any lasting military victories against the Israelis, they would have to be set in motion by the Palestinians themselves.

Major elements of this Palestinian armed movement, although still individually sponsored by various Arab countries and by the Soviet Union, began coming together under the umbrella of the Palestine Liberation Organization, which until after the 1967 war had been little more than an ineffective debating society sponsored largely by Egypt. Many of the new component organizations had little in common other than a burning desire to keep the Middle East pot boiling until the Israelis finally either lost a war or tired of fighting and offered a reasonable peace to their Palestinian neighbors. All of these emerging Palestinian groups rejected UN Security Council Resolution 242, but for differing reasons. Some were true irredentists, seeking to take back all of the land of Palestine to create a "democratic secular state" with equal rights for all Jews, Muslims and Christians born in Palestine or born of parents who had lived there. Others, although they were reluctant to admit it publicly, were increasingly willing to settle for the "two state" solution under which the old Palestine Mandate would be divided between a Jewish and an Arab state as envisaged by the UN partition plan in 1947. The main objection by these moderates to Resolution 242 was that it treated the Palestinian question as a refugee problem and made no clear provision for an independent Palestinian state separate from both Jordan and Israel.

By far the largest, and perhaps the most moderate, of the Palestinian armed groups was Al Fatah, which initially took much of its support from Kuwait, and later from Saudi Arabia as well. Its Leader, Yassir Arafat, who had long represented the "military option" but whose politics were rightist rather than leftist, became chairman of the PLO. He completed the metamorphosis of the former political forum, noted chiefly for strong rhetoric, into a Palestinian bureaucracy, administering schools, hospitals and a fighting force, and gearing up for ever larger-scale, cross-border infiltration into Israel.

In Jordan, where most of the PLO groups were headquartered, tension built steadily between the Palestinians and the Jordanian army. Before 1967, whenever any Palestinian group attacked Israel, or Jews or Israelis anywhere else in the world, terrible Israeli military retribution was most likely to be visited upon the Jordanian-administered West Bank, and after that upon Jordan itself. The Jordanian army could do nothing to stop Palestinian raids into Israel from Lebanon or Syria, but it sought increasingly to prevent any Palestinians from crossing into Israel from Jordanian territory. Fights, shootings and robberies marked the deterioration of relations between King Hussein's soldiers and the PLO irregulars, particularly the leftist groups which openly declared that a social revolution against traditional Arab regimes was a necessary prelude to Arab unity and the eventual liberation of Palestine.

In September, 1970, the Marxist Popular Front for the Liberation of Palestine, headed by a Christian Palestinian physician, George Habash, hijacked five passenger aircraft. One, a Jumbo Jet, was taken to Cairo, one of the few Middle East airports large enough to receive it. After the passengers were released it was destroyed on the ground. In a blatant challenge to King Hussein's authority, the other airliners were landed at Dawson's Field, a remote former British military airfield in the Jordanian desert. There, after standing off surrounding Jordanian troops for days, the PFLP hijackers released the passengers but, before the Jordanians could move in to protect the planes, blew them up.

It was the straw that broke the camel's back. Hussein had been in continuous touch with leaders of the western countries, as they pleaded for him to do something to rescue their nationals from the Marxist hijackers. Now he ordered his army into action against the Palestinian armed groups on his territory, shelling their camps in the Amman suburbs and in remote areas of the country as well.

As the fighting increased, Nixon's foreign affairs team in Washington shifted from wondering whether American intervention was needed to save the airline passengers to wondering whether intervention was needed to save Hussein's kingdom.

Israel said yes. Since the U.S. still had virtually no ground surveillance capability in the area, and no relevant satellite intelligence for the area in the period concerned, it was heavily dependent upon Israeli intelligence for a view of what was happening in Jordan. The Israelis reported that Syrian tanks were crossing the Jordanian border and heading in the direction of Amman.

The Israelis wanted to send their own tanks across the Jordanian border, to thwart what they told the U.S. was a Syrian invasion of Jordan. The U.S. for a time considered authorizing an Israeli airstrike. The Israelis insisted the Syrian armored force would have to be stopped by Israeli ground forces. The U.S. refused to permit this. To this day it is not clear whether a large force of Syrian tanks entered Jordan as alleged by Israel, or whether the vehicles allegedly spotted from inside Israel were simply some armored troop carriers or other military vehicles manned by the Palestine Liberation Army, which was based in Syria, going to the aid of the Palestinians under fire in Jordan. There were divisions within the Syrian government as to what action to take, and it is a matter of record that Hafez Al Assad, the Air Force commander who took over the Syrian government only a few weeks later, prohibited any intervention in Jordan by aircraft based in Syria. Since there was no Syrian air support for the beleaguered Palestinians, Jordan used its own air, armored and artillery units promptly and effectively to overcome all Palestinian opposition on its territory.

While this was occurring, however, President Nixon was tensely pondering the Israeli reports of an invasion of Jordan by 250 Syrian tanks which could only be stopped by a counter-invasion of Israeli tanks and aircraft. He, Kissinger and Sisco, who up to then had been wrestling with the problem of whether or not to use U.S. forces to seek to rescue the hijacked aircraft passengers, now put out strong warnings to the Soviet Union that may have brought the two countries as close to war as they had been on the fourth day of the 1967 Arab-Israeli war when Johnson briefly believed that Soviet-supplied Egyptian aircraft were attacking the USS Liberty. If Nixon had permitted an Israeli attack across the Jordanian border to thwart an imagined Syrian "invasion," the Russians might well have permitted or even participated in a *real* Syrian attack, putting the U.S. and USSR eyeball to eyeball in an area of primary concern to each of them.

Jordanian army and air force successes dissipated whatever "invasion" force there was, however, while President Nixon was still warning Israel in the strongest possible terms that he was not yet ready to permit its forces to take either ground or aerial action in Jordan. Once again World War III was averted, but with no thanks to U.S. intelligence, which by agreement with Israel more than a decade earlier remained blind in the area; no thanks to the Soviet Union's client Palestinian group, the PFLP, which had precipitated the entire operation in obvious hopes of bringing down King Hussein and perhaps setting off a new Middle Eastern War; and no thanks to America's Israeli client, which sought to use the opportunity to slash across the Jordan River and seize East Bank territory, from which it almost certainly would have been unwilling to withdraw.

The Jordanian crisis of September, 1970, went down in history as "Black September." It had lasted less than a month but it left the Middle East changed in two respects. Thanks to Dr. Habash's extremist PFLP, the entire Palestinian armed movement lost its Jordanian base. Many of the fighters were driven across the border into Syria during the September, 1970 fighting and all of the rest were pushed after them in July, 1971. Nearly all eventually found their way to Lebanon, helping to set the stage for the tragic civil war that overwhelmed that country less than four years later.

Meanwhile, Egyptian President Gamal Abdel Nasser, the personification of Pan Arabism, while working night and day to reconcile the Arab antagonists fighting in Jordan, had suffered a heart attack and died. Although from abroad both his rhetoric and his actions had sometimes made him seem as much a divider as a unifier, his death came as a profound shock to all Arabs and to most knowledgeable westerners as well. Most agreed he had restored to the Arabs some of the dignity and the unity of purpose they had lost through defeat and division more than four hundred years earlier. He symbolized the dream that unites all Arabs psychologically, and underlies both their radical political rhetoric and their cultural and linguistic conservatism. That dream is the certainty that one day the Arabs will again be politically unified—as they were in the Golden Age that followed the prophet Mohammad's call to Islam—and that the act of reunification will once again thrust them to the forefront of human history, culture and achievement.

With Nasser's death, however, there seemed to be no other Arab leader suited to assume his role as the symbol of Pan Arabism. The Israelis breathed more easily as they strengthened their grip on the newly-conquered territories; the Arabs seemed to go back, at least for a time, to dreaming; and the U.S. Middle East diplomatic momentum, that for a time seemed so close to bringing about real movement for peace, subsided.

CHAPTER XIII

The Build-up to October

"All Israeli leaders I have known have agreed almost instinctively on one proposition: never to accept the first proposal put forward by the United States, whatever its merit. If Israel submits without a struggle—never mind the substance— the United States may come to think of it as a docile client and God knows what we then might take it into our heads to impose."[1]

Henry Kissinger, 1982

"What is . . . likely, it seems to me, is that even the conservative and basically pro-Western Arab states such as Saudi Arabia will be forced by the pressure of the more radical Arabs to use oil as a political weapon and to threaten a freeze on expansion or a slow-down or cut-back not merely for conservation reasons but as the basis for a political ultimatum. No longer will they expend their production to satisfy growing Western demands unless the West changes its policies toward the Arab-Israeli struggle . . . Though I know of no easy solution to the problem, it is essential that we face this calamitous prospect not as a remote possibility but, in my view, as almost a certainty. It does no good to deny reality. It is something for which we should be urgently planning."[2]

George Ball, August 14, 1973.

"The city of Cairo . . . has almost twice the population of Israel. Every three years Egypt's population grows by the size of all of Israel's. It was a nearly insoluble dilem-

---

1. Kissinger, Henry, *Years of Upheaval*, Little, Brown and Company, Boston, 1982, pp. 538-9.
2. Ball, George, Lecture at Aspen Institute, Colorado, Aug. 14, 1973.

ma: Israel had the power but not the faith for peace. The Arabs were still at a military disadvantage but they had the numbers and the time. They could wait for the Israeli mistake that would prove fatal. And the consciousness of this danger was what made Israeli diplomacy tense and rigid. "3

Henry Kissinger, 1982

Anwar Sadat, the new President of Egypt, was a combination of tactician and dreamer. An army officer from humble circumstances, he had been a member of Gamal Abdel Nasser's conspiratorial circle of reformist officers who overthrew King Farouk in 1952. Most of Sadat's colleagues in the Egyptian government thought of him as a trusted Nasser henchman rather than as a leader in his own right. They saw him, therefore, as a "transitional" figure who would hold the government together until a new strong leader emerged to fill Nasser's roll as the hero of Pan-Arabism. Sadat, however, had no intention of letting power slip from his hands, and he concluded from the beginning that his most dangerous rivals were the leftist Egyptian officers, led by General Ali Sabri, who were closely identified with the Soviet civilian and military presence in their country.

In February, 1971, within five months of assuming power, Sadat was making both long-term and short-term overtures of the kind sought by the U.S. from the beginning of the Nixon Administration. For the short term, in return for an Israeli withdrawal from the East Bank of the Suez Canal and back into the Sinai, Sadat said, he would clear and reopen the Suez Canal. For the long term, if Israel would withdraw to its 1967 boundaries, Egypt would become the first Arab country to sign a peace treaty with the Jewish state.

The short-term proposal was not made in a vacuum, since Sadat knew that Moshe Dayan was already arguing for a partial Israeli withdrawal from the Sinai on the grounds that Israeli positions along the Canal would be too difficult to defend militarily against a determined Egyptian attack. Sadat's imaginative concept was to make a step that he believed Israel was willing to take in its own military interest into a first tangible move toward permanent peace. Sadat knew that it would be difficult for both Arabs and Israelis to acquiesce to Resolution 242's land-for-peace formula. He realized, however, that it was the only possible compromise even remotely acceptable to *both* sides.

Further, Sadat asked Donald Bergus who, in the absence of an American Ambassador in Cairo since the 1967 break in diplomatic relations, headed the U.S. interests section of the Spanish Embassy there, to tell President Nixon that if Egypt and the U.S. could come to an agreement about an Israeli withdrawal to permit Egypt to reopen the Canal, Sadat would remove the Russians from Egypt.

It would be unrealistic to attribute this almost incredible Sadat offer solely to an abstract desire for peace. He undoubtedly feared a coup by leftist Egyptian army officers, whose prospects of success would be weakened if their Russian mentors were no longer in the country. Nevertheless, Bergus and the State Department Arabists recognized this as an almost sure-fire first step toward a permanent Middle East settle-

---

3. Kissinger, Henry, *Years of Upheaval*, Little, Brown and Company, Boston, 1982, p. 634.

ment. Sadat's investment in rebuilding the Canal and the cities along it would immensely raise Egypt's stake in keeping the peace.

The offer arrived in Washington at about the same time that Democratic Senator Stuart Symington was declaring in the Senate that Kissinger had become "Secretary of State in everything but title," and that Rogers was, as a result, being "laughed at" throughout the government. Nixon was making public efforts to demonstrate that Rogers still had a free hand in the Middle East, and Kissinger—preoccupied with the Far East— for a time seemed to limit his guerrilla warfare against the State Department.

While Rogers and Sisco moved rapidly to set up a dialogue with Sadat that would pin down his offers and Israel's responses, Kissinger sounded out the Israelis, using back channel messages via Israeli Ambassador Yitzhak Rabin. In Israel, however, the situation was almost uniquely unfavorable.

Dual aspects of David Ben Gurion's legacy to the country he had come to personify were two political proteges who faithfully mirrored two different aspects of his own complex character. The pragmatic but ruthless and deceitful aspect was personified, and magnified, by Moshe Dayan, whose mercurial changes of political position and total disregard of principle were beginning to be seen by his countrymen less as manifestations of a supple intellect than as symptoms of amoral opportunism. Called back into a national unity government on the eve of the 1967 attack, he had been politically resuscitated by the lightning victory. The aplomb with which he assumed credit for a victory based on meticulous military planning by others before his return, however, only increased the distrust felt for him by other Labor coalition leaders.

Golda Meir, on the other hand, represented the solid, persevering, and crowd-pleasing aspect of the Ben Gurion image. If he was the personification of an Old Testament prophet, she was Israel's national Jewish mother: Tough, sentimental, down to earth and clearly willing to subordinate her personal needs to those of her country. Unfortunately, she was also extraordinarily unimaginative, inflexible, and stubborn. It was she who had blandly responded to an interviewer who wondered if she didn't feel some guilt about the thousands of Palestinians displaced by the Israelis by saying: "What Palestinians? There are no Palestinians!" Years later, asked by Italian Journalist Oriana Fallaci if she didn't feel pity for the dispossessed people who by then filled refugee camps all around Israel's expanding borders, she had snapped back: "Of course I do, but pity is not responsibility, and the responsibility for the Palestinians isn't ours."

Her attitude toward Sadat's extraordinary offers was so non-committal and inflexible that, according to her Ambassador in Washington, Yitzhak Rabin, an exasperated Kissinger had once complained to him that "no one knows what you want" and "there is serious fear that what you *really* want is to evade any settlement that requires concessions on your part so that you can remain along the lines you hold at present."

As usual during the Nixon Administration, U.S. policy responded to Sadat's extraordinary offer by moving down two different tracks. While Rogers sought to shape the Egyptian overtures into an irresistible peace offer, Kissinger began to act as if they had never been made. Kissinger made a point of playing down Sadat's importance in background interviews with the press, depicting him as merely a transitional figure, not to be taken seriously. Even in Kissinger's subsequent memoirs he continued to depict

Sadat's effort in that period as "a complicated maneuver strengthening his position in the Arab world while inching Egypt toward a more realistic, nationalist posture."[4] It is obvious from Kissinger's memoirs that he, and presumably President Nixon as well, were aware that with elections scheduled the following year, mutual friendly gestures between the U.S. and an Arab nation, and U.S. pressure on Israel to show flexibility, would arouse dangerous hostility among Israel's powerful American supporters. Speaking of the remainder of 1971, Kissinger says in his book *Years of Upheaval* :

"My principal assignment was to make sure that no explosion occurred to complicate the 1972 election, which meant that I was to stall."[5]

A persistent critic of Henry Kissinger, Seymour Hersh, puts it more bluntly:

"On its face, forcing Israeli disengagement in the Sinai posed immense political risks for the President, who was counting so heavily on Jewish financial and electoral support in the 1972 elections—support he had never had before. And yet Sadat was giving the United States and its President a chance for a wondrous triumph—the kind of opportunity Kissinger and Nixon had seized in other parts of the world. Middle East peace would isolate the Soviet Union and further disarm the administration's antiwar critics."[6]

Although Golda Meir did not have the imagination to reach for peace, both she and Dayan knew very well how to fight effectively and get their way in the United States. When Rogers suggested that an international peacekeeping force, including Soviet troops, be assembled to protect Israel's borders, Israel's oldest friend in the U.S. Senate, Henry Jackson of Washington, accused the Nixon Administration of "courting disaster." Both Israel's Embassy and the potent lobby comprised of Israel's American supporters began to threaten that if Nixon encouraged Sadat on his present course by putting pressure on Israel to consider the offers seriously, there would be serious repercussions on Nixon's 1972 re-election campaign.

The contrast between Nixon's two principal foreign policy aides was never more obvious than in their differing assessments of their chief. Rogers thought Nixon would rise above domestic political considerations to the possibility of an historic breakthrough toward peace in the Middle East—an opportunity never presented so clearly before. Kissinger concluded that Nixon would not take the risk of antagonizing Israel and potential Jewish contributors to his campaign. Nixon has little to say on the matter in his own memoirs. His subsequent statements, however, reveal that although he recognized the opportunity, and perhaps even understood Kissinger's self-serving efforts to play down its significance, he resolved first to win re-election and then—with no further electoral hurdles to face—deal firmly with the Middle East.

The next two moves from Egypt only strengthened the various players in their divergent courses. With Rogers scheduled to visit Cairo in May, 1971, Sadat suddenly purged his principal rival within the government, Ali Sabri, who was Secretary General of the country's only legal political party, the Arab Socialist Union, and widely con-

---

4. Kissinger, Henry, *Years of Upheaval*, Little, Brown and Company, Boston, 1982, p. 201.
5. *Ibid.*, p. 196.
6. Hersh, Seymour, *The Price of Power: Kissinger in the White House*, Summit Books, New York, 1983, p. 407.

sidered the Soviet Union's most influential friend in the government. Shortly after that, Sadat signed a friendship treaty with the Soviet Union.

Rogers and the State Department Arabists correctly interpreted this as a delicate balancing act. Sadat had effectively wiped out a potent base of Soviet influence in his government. To balance this in the public eye he had signed a treaty with the Soviets that had no practical import whatsoever.

Kissinger, on the other hand, seized upon the Egyptian-Soviet treaty to resume full-scale bureaucratic warfare against what he called "erratic American diplomacy" which had encouraged "Soviet boldnesss." In June, 1971, a bizarre incident gave him an opportunity to turn what would otherwise have been simply a typical and minor example of Arab and U.S. cultural differences into another blow against Rogers and the Department of State.

After a Sisco visit to Cairo, Mahmud Riad, Sadat's increasingly skeptical Foreign Minister, gave Donald Bergus a written summary of Egypt's reactions to Israeli intransigence. Bergus told him it was written in such a negative manner that it would inevitably provoke an unfavorable reaction in Washington. Bergus offered to re-draft it to show Riad how to make the tone more acceptable while leaving the substance unchanged. Riad agreed and Bergus handed him back a draft which Sadat eventually approved, almost unchanged, for Bergus to send to Washington. Later, when Washington did not react to the message, Sadat leaked it to the press, hinting that a message actually prepared with U.S. approval was now being ignored in Washington. Bergus had to explain to Riad that he had re-drafted the message personally, and with no reference to Washington. Since it was an act difficult for the hierarchical Egyptians to understand, they didn't try. Instead Riad made the Bergus explanation public.

The Israelis, who had always distrusted State Department Middle East experts, understood exactly what had happened and they seized upon the Egyptian blunder. They expressed outrage, through their friends in the U.S. media, at what they depicted as evidence of collusion—behind Israel's back—between U.S. diplomats and Egypt. Kissinger seized upon the whole incident as a further means to discredit Roger's State Department with Nixon.

The guerrilla warfare continued in Washington for the rest of the year, with Kissinger calling upon the Middle East experts in the National Security staff, to their despair, not for advice on the issues, but only to draft arguments for Kissinger to present to the President as to why State Department advice should be disregarded. Meanwhile Rogers and his staff continued to labor, almost desperately, to keep what they saw as a sure-fire Egyptian peace initiative on track while they sought to build up U.S. pressure to wring some concessions from the Israelis, who, with the exception of Dayan, had no intention of making any at all.

Sadat, who later became a master at manipulating not only the U.S. Government but even the Israeli-influenced American media, showed in the first two years of his Presidency very little understanding of or patience with what was going on in the U.S. He had proclaimed that 1971 would be the "year of decision." Either the Israelis would accept his peace overtures, or there would be war. When, by the end of 1971, there was no war, Kissinger again argued that this only vindicated his policy of letting the

120   A CHANGING IMAGE

Middle East bleed. Sadat's threats, he said, had been typically empty Arab rhetoric.
By the end of 1971, therefore, Sadat was thoroughly disillusioned. He had offered
the U.S. for nothing everything it could not get from Nasser at any price. Rogers and
Sisco came and went, but nothing happened. When Sadat sought to set up the secret
"back channel" communications so favored by the conspiratorial Kissinger, Kissinger
virtually ignored him. Meanwhile Sadat was coming under increasingly heavy pressure
from Riad and others who were skeptical that the U.S. could ever free itself from Israel's
influence. They felt that only the use of force would shock the U.S. out of its dream
that the Arab world would continue to tolerate Israeli occupation of huge tracts of Egyptian, Syrian and Palestinian land without eventually beginning to exact a price from
Israel's only remaining sponsor, the United States.

By mid-1972 Sadat was desperate. On July 18, even in the absence of any U.S.
response to his offer, he played his last card and expelled the huge corps of Soviet
military advisers from Egypt. Nixon, meanwhile, had focused his full attention upon
the fall election campaign. There was no Washington reaction at all to this Mideastern
diplomatic victory. Sadat then proposed via "back channel" a meeting between Kissinger and his Egyptian opposite number, Hafiz Ismail. Kissinger, pleading the press
of Vietnam negotiations, postponed it.

Even after Nixon was re-elected Sadat was ignored, although the murder of Israeli
Olympic athletes in Munich by Palestinian terrorists in September, 1972, and a series
of retaliatory Israeli raids on Palestinian camps in Lebanon and Syria, made the level
of Middle Eastern violence hard to overlook.

In January, 1973, Arab foreign and defense ministers convened in Cairo and appointed an Egyptian commander-in-chief for the Jordanian, Syrian and Egyptian fronts.
In April the Israelis landed terrorists of their own in Beirut, the capital of Lebanon,
where they assassinated three PLO leaders and a woman who got in the way. The level
of violence was escalating dangerously.

Sadat repeatedly made it clear that he now was preparing in earnest for the war
he had been threatening for more than two years. In retrospect, it seems inexplicable
that neither the U.S. nor Israel took him seriously.

The explanation, however, lies in the fact that by then only two people were directing U.S. Middle East policy. The first was the unimaginative Golda Meir, who as yet
had no reason to believe she could not control any American President. The second
was Henry Kissinger, who in Nixon's second term had taken over as Secretary of State.
Four years earlier, Kissinger had admitted that he knew nothing about the Middle East.
At the beginning of the second Nixon term there is ample evidence that he still knew
nothing about its Arab inhabitants.

It was not the way Nixon had planned it. After his re-election Nixon had penciled
a note on a Kissinger memorandum recommending continued U.S. inaction:

"I have delayed through two elections and this year I am determined to move off dead center—I
totally disagree (with inaction). This thing is getting ready to blow." [7]

---

7. Kissinger, Henry, *Years of Upheaval*, Little, Brown and Company, Boston, 1982, p. 211.

Further, in another appended comment to Kissinger, he indicated which way he expected to move:

"K – you know my position of standing firmly with Israel has been based on broader issues than just Israel's survival – Those issues now strongly argue for movement toward a settlement. We are now Israel's *only* major friend in the world. I have yet to see *one iota* of give on their part – conceding that Jordan and Egypt have not given enough on their side. This is the time to get moving – and they must be told that *firmly* . . . The time has come to quit pandering to Israel's intransigent position. Our actions over the past have led them to think we will stand with them regardless of how unreasonable they are."[8]

Why, then, with Nixon apparently determined at last to follow the even-handed policy first enunciated by his emissary, William Scranton, four years earlier, did nothing happen? The answer can be stated in one word: Watergate. Increasingly Nixon was preoccupied with keeping the illegal entry to wiretap telephones in the Democratic national campaign headquarters during the 1972 election campaign by paid employes of Nixon's own re-election committee from casting a shadow over the results of the election and the second term it provided him. By involving himself in details of the cover-up, however, he had implicated himself personally, and feared exposure. Under these circumstances, he increasingly left Kissinger to run U.S. foreign policy, and Kissinger's mandate now unmistakably included the Middle East.

In two meetings with Sadat's foreign policy adviser, Kissinger offered nothing in exchange for Egypt's moderation. Sadat, in turn, by the obviousness of his preparations for war, seemed almost to be begging the U.S. to stop him. In his memoirs Kissinger offers a disingenuous explanation for his refusal to listen to anyone but himself and Golda Meir on the Middle East, and his amazing refusal to draw even the most elementary conclusions from intelligence reports of increasing Syrian-Egyptian contacts and increasing military activity on both the Syrian and Egyptian fronts.

First, however, he blames Golda Meir. Kissinger reports that during her March 1, 1973 visit to the White House Nixon told her that his previous Middle Eastern visitor, King Hussein of Jordan, had just warned Nixon that if he continued to ignore Egyptian offers to make peace, and Hussein's own willingness to reach a generous diplomatic solution with Israel as well, Sadat would have no recourse except war.

"No," Golda Meir, said. "The Arabs would not attack because they could not win." "Israel," she said, knew that "we never had it so good."[9]

Kissinger describes the Israeli position matter of factly:

"Golda had two objectives: to gain time, for the longer there was no change in the status quo, the more Israel would be confirmed in the possession of the occupied territories; and to achieve Nixon's approval of a new package of military aid for Israel."[10]

Further Kissinger describes the by then well-documented consequences of giving in to the Israelis:

---

8. Kissinger, Henry, *Years of Upheaval*, Little, Brown and Company, Boston, 1982, p. 212.

9. *Ibid.*, p. 220.

10. *Ibid.*, p. 221.

"The situation was further complicated by the perennial problem of military deliveries for Israel. One of the weaknessss of our military supply relationship with Israel was that it came up for renewal every year or two. Inevitably, each new delivery provided a focal point for Arab resentment and led to an internal debate within our government about priorities. Regularly, as domestic pressure reinforced strategic necessities, the outcome was a favorable decision on a new arms package (for Israel), fueling a new outburst of outrage in the Arab world." [11]

It is when he accounts for his own failure to heed U.S. intelligence warnings that Kissinger offers his unique explanation of one of the most dramatic intelligence failures in American history, which in turn led to a war which no one wanted, and which no one won:

"For Sadat was moving toward war, using an extraordinary tactic that no one fathomed: If a leader announces his real intentions sufficiently frequently and grandiloquently, no one will believe him. Sadat had first declared 1971 as the 'year of decision.' We had believed him . . . Sadat made no military move that year or in 1972. Ominous threats continued to issue from Cairo, but as of December 20, 1972, our assessment was that Sadat had few, if any, military options." [12]

From a man whose family prudently had fled Germany after Adolf Hitler "grandiloquently" announced his real intentions toward Germany's Jews, the excuse seems remarkably feeble. In a published interview with "this incredible, inexplicable, unbearable personage" Henry Kissinger, who "pretends to change our destiny, and does not change it" Oriana Fallaci wrote: "He is a man who lives in the past, without understanding the present and without divining the future." Possibly that is why in 1973, on the 14th day of the Muslim holy month of Ramadan, which also happened to be Yom Kippur, the Jewish Day of Atonement, no one — except perhaps Golda Meir — was more surprised than Henry Kissinger when the Egyptians opened a massive attack against Israeli positions along the Suez Canal at the same moment that Syrian tanks rolled across Israeli lines on the Golan Heights.

---

11. Kissinger, Henry, *Years of Upheaval*, Little, Brown and Company, Boston, 1982, p. 221.
12. *Ibid.*, p. 206.

CHAPTER XIV

The October War

"The Egyptian-Syrian attack was a classic of strategic and tactical surprise. But the surprise of the October War is not explained fully by either background 'noise' or deception. It resulted from the misinterpretation of facts available for all to see, unbeclouded by any conflicting information. Sadat boldly all but told what he was going to do, and we did not believe him. He overwhelmed us with information and let us draw the wrong conclusion. October 6 was the culmination of a failure of political analysis on the part of its victims."[1]

Henry Kissinger, 1982

"In the Middle East, the Arabs' surprise attack on Yom Kippur marked a watershed in the Arab-Israeli conflict. Israel eventually triumphed, but the war proved, to the astonishment of many, that Israel could be caught by surprise and that Arab forces could wield sophisticated weapons effectively. The war also pointed up Israel's dependence on U.S. arms and ammunition, and Israel's increasing isolation in the world community because of the Arab's oil weapon. In addition, the Soviet ultimatum and the threat of unilateral intervention on October 24 illustrated graphically the risks of a superpower showdown in any future war in the Middle East. Each of these factors contributed to the new U.S. perception that a resolution of the Arab-Israeli conflict was vital to the American national interest."[2]

Abba Eban, 1983

---

1. Kissinger, Henry, *Years of Upheaval*, Little, Brown and Company, Boston, 1982, p. 459.
2. Eban, Abba, *The New Diplomacy: International Affairs in the Modern Age*, Random House, New York, 1983, p. 60.

"In effect, the October war made it possible for Secretary Kissinger to pose as the savior of both sides. When the Israelis were in trouble, the American resupply effort made it possible for them to continue the battle on a scale commensurate with their needs. When the Egyptians were in trouble, American pressure on Israel enabled them to avert a defeat which would have fractured the Egyptian army and shaken the Sadat regime. Throughout the Nixon years, the administration had been straining to achieve 'even-handedness': By force of circumstances, that blessed state was reached in practice in October 1973. "[3]

Theodore Draper, April 1975

"An agreement to separate military forces has been implemented on the Egyptian-Israeli front and now a similar accord has been negotiated between Israel and Syria. For the first time in a generation we are witnessing the beginning of a dialogue between the Arab states and Israel. "

Richard Nixon, June 5, 1974

Israelis speak of the Yom Kippur War, Arabs of the Ramadan War, and Westerners call it the October War. All can agree it was a turning point in the long struggle between Jew and Arab. After demonstrating the near-total lethality of modern tank, aerial, and missile warfare, the fighting subsided into a stalemate, with Egyptian forces in former Israeli positions and Israeli forces in former Egyptian positions on both sides of the Suez Canal. The Golan Heights between Damascus and northern Israel became a vast junkyard of burned-out Syrian and Israeli tanks and missiles marking the advances and retreats of both armies. In fact, none of the armies had been able to continue for more than a few days without an airborne resupply effort by their superpower sponsors, and those Soviet and U.S. rescue efforts came closer to touching off World War III than any events since the Berlin blockade of 1948 and the Cuban missile crisis of 1962. Meanwhile, the Arab oil producing countries had imposed an oil embargo to protest the U.S. resupply of Israel. That Arab political embargo was to transform the economy of the entire world for the remainder of the 20th century.

The Soviet Union had warned the U.S. of the likelihood of war in May and again in June, 1973. On October 4 it began an airlift of Soviet diplomats from Egypt and on October 5 Soviet naval ships put to sea from Port Said and Alexandria.

For Henry Kissinger, however, the October War began at 6:15 a.m. October 6, 1973, when "Joseph J. Sisco . . . barged into my bedroom all but shouting that Israel . . . Egypt and Syria were about to go to war."[4] Kissinger was staying at the Waldorf Towers in New York for the annual session of the UN General Assembly. Two hours earlier Golda Meir had summoned the U.S. Ambassador in Tel Aviv to her office and told him "we may be in trouble." The Israelis had belatedly decided that what they had been dismissing as Egyptian and Syrian military exercises were about to turn into

---

3. Draper, Theodore. "The United States and Israel: Tilt in the Middle East", *Commentary*, April . 1975, p. 31.
4. Kissinger, Henry, *Years of Upheaval*, Little, Brown and Company, Boston, 1982, p. 450.

an afternoon attack on Israel. Mrs. Meir was calling up Israeli reserves, but wanted the U.S. to tell both the Soviet Union and Israel's Arab neighbors that Israel was not planning to initiate hostilities with a pre-emptive attack as it had in 1967.

Kissinger called Soviet Ambassador Anatoly Dobrynin at 6:40 a.m. and, when Dobrynin protested that his communications were not fast enough to permit the Soviets to act in time to stop the attack, Kissinger put the White House switchboard at Dobrynin's disposal. At 6:55 Kissinger called the Israeli Charge d'Affairs and asked him to inform Meir that her assurance had been passed to Moscow. At 7 a.m. he telephoned the Egyptian Foreign Minister, who was attending the UN General Assembly in New York, and read him the Israeli message verbatim. The Egyptian said he would relay the message to Cairo. Next Kissinger tried to reach the Syrian Deputy Foreign Minister, but Syria's UN Mission did not answer its telephone. By 8:15 Kissinger had an answer from Egypt charging Israel had attacked Egyptian positions along the Gulf of Suez. It was clearly only a cover story, because by then Egyptian and Syrian planes were attacking Israel on both fronts. Their attack had begun at 2 p.m. Eastern Mediterranean time.

With President Nixon ever more deeply enmeshed in the toils of Watergate, Kissinger and his former NSC deputy, General Alexander Haig, who was now White House Chief of Staff, were given a remarkably free hand to deal with the crisis. Kissinger sprang into a purposeful frenzy of activity.

He first alerted the U.S. Sixth Fleet in the Mediterranean. He then turned his attention to preventing the United Nations from calling for a cease-fire in place, since he knew that both the Egyptian and Syrian armies were penetrating deeply through Israeli lines.

Kissinger contacted the Soviets and suggested a joint call for a return to the lines from which the conflict had started. He reasoned, he admits in his memoirs, that if the Soviets agreed, the Arabs would accuse them of betraying Arab interests to improve Soviet ties with Washington. "If the Soviets refused, as was probable," Kissinger continues, "we would have gained the time for Israel to restore the status quo ante by military means."[5]

Meanwhile Kissinger was telling others that if the Soviets agreed to work with the U.S., the war would end quickly. If they refused, the U.S. would let Israel "beat up" the Arabs for a day or two and that would quiet the Soviets. The only problem with his strategy was that it was the Israelis who continued to be beaten up.

It seems fairly certain that Sadat's plan was to penetrate the lightly-held Israeli fortifications along the Canal, advance a few miles into the desert, and stop before his lines became so extended that they would be vulnerable to Israeli air power. Similarly, the Syrians apparently expected heavier resistance and had no plans beyond regaining some of the territory taken from them in 1967. After their tanks crashed through Israeli defense lines on the Golan Heights they stopped, rather than pushing down into Israel proper. It was increasingly clear that the purpose of the Egyptian and Syrian-initiated war was to puncture Israel's self-image of military invulnerability, and then seek a negotiated settlement. The Israelis, however, seemed unable to comprehend this. All

---

5. Kissinger, Henry, *Years of Upheaval*, Little, Brown and Company, Boston, 1982, p. 471.

they could see was that the Egyptian Army was consolidating its bridgeheads on the east side of the Canal, and the Syrian army was in position to sweep down from the heights and literally cut Israel in two.

From the day of the attack, Israel began pressing the U.S. for a speedup of military supplies already in the pipeline and for special equipment, such as Sidewinder heat-seeking antiaircraft missiles. Israeli commercial planes with markings painted out were sent to pick up the materials requested, and Kissinger told Defense Secretary Schlesinger to make arrangements to load them at an out-of-the-way military base. A debate began within the U.S. Government as to whether the U.S. really wanted to play the role of ammunition passer to Israel in the heat of battle, and thus perhaps alienate the Arabs once and for all. Kissinger, however, argued that the Arabs must not be allowed to win with Soviet weapons or they would become intractable.

Kissinger gradually became aware that he was not the only one stalling a U.N. vote. The Soviet reply to his invitation for joint action spoke more about joint political action after a cease-fire than about the cease-fire itself, while a friendly message from Cairo reiterated Egypt's terms that Israel should withdraw from the occupied territories as the prelude to a peace conference to discuss such matters as freedom of navigation in the Strait of Tiran.

"We do not intend to deepen the engagement or widen the confrontation," Sadat's foreign policy adviser, Hafiz Ismail, informed Kissinger in the first of a series of almost daily messages sent back and forth during the war through Kissinger's beloved "back channels."

In his memoirs Kissinger admits that "until this message, I had not taken Sadat seriously. Because of the many threats to go to war that had not been implemented, I had dismissed him as more actor than statesman. Now I was beginning to understand that the grandiloquent gestures were part of a conscious strategy. They had guaranteed surprise."[6]

Although perhaps only he had been surprised, Kissinger's next observation indicates that he had begun, at last, to respect the Egyptian leader he had so carelessly dismissed so long as Sadat was in contact with Rogers rather than himself. Kissinger writes:

"Sadat's ability from the very first hours of the war never to lose sight of the heart of his problem convinced me that we were dealing with a statesman of the first order. Hafiz Ismail's message, while avowing sweeping terms, stated a modest and largely psychological objective 'to show,' so the message said, 'that we were not afraid or helpless.' That objective Sadat achieved brilliantly. It was the precondition of his subsequent peace diplomacy."[7]

By Monday evening, at the end of the third day of the war, Kissinger found things going very well, from his point of view. Israeli Ambassador Simcha Dinitz had just assured him that Israel needed three full days to mobilize completely, but then would require only 48 hours to "complete military operations already in train" and push the Egyptians and Syrians back to their starting points. Kissinger warned Dinitz against new territorial acquisitions, pointing out that when the U.S. moved, with or without

6. Kissinger, Henry, *Years of Upheaval*, Little, Brown and Company, Boston, 1982, p. 482.
7. *Ibid.*, p. 482.

the Russians, in the Security Council it would be with a resolution for a cease-fire and return to the positions of October 5. Both the Russians and the Egyptians seemed equally willing to postpone actually introducing any motion, however, so no significant moves were made in either the General Assembly — which Kissinger feared since the U.S. could not veto its resolutions — or in the Security Council. Kissinger already had noted that "it was becoming apparent even at this early stage that we were the only government in contact with both sides. If we could preserve this position we were likely to emerge in a central role in the peace process."[8]

Picking up his optimism, Kissinger recalls, Nixon told him "the one thing we have to be concerned about, which you and I know looking down the road, is that the Israelis, when they finish clobbering the Egyptians and the Syrians, which they will do, will be even more impossible to deal with than before and you and I have got to determine in our own minds, we must have a diplomatic settlement there."[9]

Reality began to set in for Kissinger when a telephone call from Dinitz woke him at 1:45 a.m. Tuesday, October 9. Dinitz wanted to talk about resupply. Kissinger suspected that perhaps the Israelis wanted to commit the U.S. to an increased schedule of weapons deliveries before the tide of battle turned in their favor, and he told Dinitz they could discuss it in the morning. At 3 a.m. Dinitz called again, with the same concern. It was agreed they would meet at 8:20 a.m. in the White House. There Kissinger learned, for the first time, that Israel had already lost a staggering 500 tanks, 400 on the Egyptian front alone, and 49 aircraft. Fourteen of these were Phantoms, which at that time were being produced at the rate of only one per month in the United States.

It was suddenly clear that Israel no longer had the aircraft or the armor to roll back either the Egyptians or Syrians, but instead faced a war of attrition in which the Arab armies would stay within the cover provided by their Soviet surface-to-air missiles and bleed Israel to death. There was no need for either the Egyptians or Syrians to surge forward again, since Israel could not possibly win a battle of attrition. Dinitz told Kissinger that Prime Minister Meir, now quite desperate over Israel's plight, was prepared to travel secretly to the U.S. for an hour to plead with President Nixon for urgent arms aid. Meanwhile the Israelis were concentrating on breaking the Syrian lines before doing anything further against the Egyptian forces. Defense Minister Moshe Dayan, in fact, was recommending a withdrawal deep into the Sinai, in keeping with his long-held view that Israel did not have the strength to keep the Sinai peninsula from being turned into a death trap which would engulf the entire defending Israeli army just as it had engulfed Nasser's defending armies in 1956 and 1967.

Less than an hour after his meeting with Dinitz, Kissinger met with Secretary of Defense James Schlesinger and CIA Director William Colby. Colby suspected that Israel's plea for rescue was in fact a trick to stockpile as many weapons as possible for the future. Schlesinger pointed out that the U.S. was not being asked to send weapons to defend Israel from invasion, but rather to maintain Israeli occupation of Arab lands seized in 1967. Other participants concurred.

---

8. Kissinger, Henry, *Years of Upheaval*, Little, Brown and Company, Boston, 1982, p. 487.
9. *Ibid.*, p. 490.

Meanwhile, Dinitz had been playing skillfully the traditional role of Israeli Ambassadors in Washington, stirring up Israel's friends in the media and on the Hill. Among the many Congressmen, therefore, who called Kissinger to tell him to stop dragging his feet on arms for Israel was one of Israel's most faithful friends, Senator Frank Church of Idaho. Church, a fierce opponent of the American war in Vietnam, and a consistent critic of the CIA and of deceit in foreign policy, was now urging Kissinger to "slip in" a few phantoms to Israel without asking anyone's permission.

Although Dinitz later denied that he had orchestrated a telephone assault on the U.S. Secretary of State, Kissinger probably didn't at all mind being told by Congressmen to disregard future problems with the Arabs, who inevitably would make the U.S. pay dearly for helping Israel retain its hold on illegally-occupied Arab lands. It meant that he could later blame Congressional pressure when Americans began to ask why the costs of driving their cars and heating their homes and offices had increased several-fold.

That this might occur was no longer speculation. Already Kissinger had received reports from U.S. Ambassadors in the Middle East that Saudi Arabia had asked but been denied permission by King Hussein to move the Saudi Brigade stationed in Jordan into Syria and that Soviet ambassadors were relaying messages from Moscow to King Hussein and to President Houari Boumedienne of Algeria urging them both to enter the war.

Nevertheless, after a meeting with Nixon, Kissinger told Schlesinger the decision was to speed the supply of ammunition and aircraft to the Israelis. He told Dinitz that the U.S. would approve all special equipment the Israelis had requested except laser bombs, and that all aircraft and tank losses during the war would be replaced. There was no limitation put on this replacement commitment. The Israelis were, therefore, free to throw all of their aircraft and tank reserves into battle immediately, a luxury no other nation at war has been able to exercise in modern times.

Wednesday, October 10, brought evidence that Syria was also feeling hard-pressed. Twenty Soviet transport aircraft were en route to resupply the Syrian army. At the same time the Soviet Union informed the U.S. that it would not block "adoption of a cease-fire resolution in the Security Council." Kissinger did not yet want such a resolution, which would consolidate the Egyptian and Syrian victories. It would have destroyed the entire structure of his Middle East diplomacy, which was to convince the Arabs that only the U.S. could produce progress toward getting their lands back. U.S. Vice President Spiro Agnew was resigning under pressure that same day, and Kissinger used President Nixon's preoccupation with this unprecedented domestic event as an excuse to delay answering the Russians. Meanwhile, within the U.S. Government, opposition to the policy of no-strings support for Israel was becoming more open. There were reports that King Hussein was under heavy pressure to enter the war and that King Faisal had decided to fly a Saudi brigade directly from Saudi Arabia to Syria. Other U.S. officials tried to tell Kissinger that resupply of Israel would arrive too late to affect the battle, but that it would turn all of the moderate Arab nations permanently against the U.S. They urged that instead of resupplying Israel, Kissinger press for an immediate cease-fire. Kissinger therefore urged the Israelis to make a maximum military effort within the coming 48 hours in an attempt to recoup as much territory as they could and, if possible, to go past the original lines in at least one place in order to improve the chances for a final bargain providing a return by both sides to all of the original lines.

Meanwhile Israel was no longer able to transport the flood of American equipment being offered if it continued to use only seven unmarked jets from the El Al fleet. The U.S. agreed to pay the cost of private air charter flights to carry additional equipment. No charter company, however, would undertake the job.

The rapidly increasing doubts, now being expressed throughout the Pentagon and State Department, of the wisdom of resupplying Israel on such a scale only compounded the confusion. The Israelis, and their American friends in Congress and the media, were becoming almost hysterical in their efforts to pin the blame for the delay on Kissinger, Schlesinger, or on the "middle level officials" to whom Kissinger generally attributed each new problem or unpopular move.

By Thursday, October 11, two decisive events had occurred. With an all-out tank assault the Israelis had broken through the Syrian lines and, in the words of Moshe Dayan, "were heading for Damascus." And the Russian airlift by then was reaching not only Syria but also, on a more limited scale, both Egypt and Iraq. The fact that the military tide seemed to be turning didn't lessen the din in Congress or the media however. Senator Henry Jackson of Washington, Israel's reliable spokesman in the Senate, now was charging that the Administration was deliberately procrastinating on resupply, and that the Soviet Union was exploiting the spirit of detente to persuade the U.S. not to rearm its beleaguered client. Israel's faithful chorus among American syndicated columnists was by now singing in key on both themes. President Nixon told Kissinger to warn Dinitz he would hold the Israeli Ambassador "personally responsible" if the obviously orchestrated outcry continued any longer. It was "one of the emptiest threats imaginable", according to Kissinger, who doesn't indicate in his memoirs whether or not he passed it on to Dinitz.

Also by October 11 Israel had begun aerial bombardments in the Nile Delta and, according to a message from Sadat to the U.S., more than 500 civilians had been killed. Hussein meanwhile informed the U.S. that he was moving a Jordanian Brigade into Syria to bolster Arab defenses in the Golan area.

The following day, Friday, October 12, the U.S. learned that seven Soviet airborne divisions had been put on alert. Meanwhile, both the U.S. and Soviet Mediterranean fleets were steaming in circles near Crete, each indicating a readiness to proceed eastward if a client state began to get the worst of it, or if the other fleet moved. Israel indicated it would now like the U.S. to call for a cease-fire, preferably in 24 hours.

That evening, however, the Soviet Union delivered two protest notes. One complained about continued Israeli bombing of civilian areas in both Egypt and Syria. A bomb had actually destroyed much of the Soviet Embassy in a residential section of Damascus, killing Soviet civilians. Israeli torpedo boats had also attacked a Soviet merchant ship in a Syrian harbor. The second note protested the U.S. weapons resupply project which had been under way almost from the beginning of the war. Kissinger, meanwhile, was seeking to persuade the British to introduce a cease-fire resolution. He did not tell them that he was acting on Israel's behalf. At the same time Nixon was announcing his choice for a new Vice President. Gerald Ford, who had represented a Michigan constituency in the House of Representatives for many years, was sworn in that evening.

At 11:20 p.m. Kissinger met once more with Dinitz in what he later described as "one of the decisive encounters of the week." Dinitz provided a military briefing, and Kissinger noted that the Israeli forces which Dayan had said were rolling toward Damascus had in fact not advanced. Kissinger asked whether the Israelis still planned an offensive or, if not, "do you want us to start the diplomacy (toward a UN cease-fire resolution) tonight?"

"I must tell you," Dinitz told him, "our decision whether to start a new offensive or not depends on our power. We thought we would have by now in Israel the implements to do it—the bombs, the missiles, etc."

Dinitz complained that promised U.S. heavy equipment was coming too late and that the charters carrying ammunition needed for a counter offensive had been delayed for three days. Israel, he said, was running out of ammunition.

By this time Kissinger clearly was no longer seeking to provide Israel with arms to defend itself, but rather with arms to enable Israel to mount a new offensive to recover and hold lands that the U.S. recognized as Arab territories. It was this that was engendering increasing bureaucratic resistance, particularly among U.S. military officers, who saw U.S. readiness stocks being rapidly and dangerously depleted not to defend Israel but to enable it to retake territory the U.S. had long since declared Israel must return to the Arabs. These actions are still highly controversial, with many officers charging, then and now, that in stripping U.S. Army and Air Force units of essential equipment and ammunition, Kissinger jeopardized U.S. national security only to preserve Israel's 1967 territorial conquests.

Kissinger spent most of what remained of the night discussing with Schlesinger and Haig alternatives to speed up the airlift. Then on the morning of Saturday, October 13, Kissinger conferred with Nixon, who was exuberant over the reception his surprise appointment of Ford had received from Washington leaders and the press.

Armed with Nixon's authority, Kissinger then convened a Saturday meeting of the Washington Special Action Group (WSAG), where all matters pertaining to the Middle East war were discussed before alternatives were submitted to the President for decision. Kissinger opened this meeting by telling the participants that the President had already made the decision to step up the airlift, and that he was speaking for the President in demanding the immediate resignation of anyone in the room who disagreed with this policy.

When word of this tough stance reached the press it would, of course, stop Congressional and journalistic complaints about the delays in airlifting materials to Israel. But it was equally effective in stopping any further discussion of the wisdom or morality of resupplying Israel with U.S. weapons which Israel no longer needed for defensive purposes, and thereby inevitably bringing down upon the United States the heaviest punishment the Arab oil producers could devise.

As a result of Kissinger's blunt threat to the other WSAG participants, the remainder of the October 13 meeting was devoted solely to the mechanics of the airlift. The charter project, which had literally never gotten off the ground, was abandoned in favor of direct transport of weapons and ammunition from the U.S. to Israel by American military planes of three types.

The U.S. was unable to secure the agreement of any NATO power to refuel such a U.S. military airlift, however. Finally, after President Nixon threatened to cut off all of its military aid, Portugal reluctantly gave permission for the resupply planes to refuel in the Azores. In addition, it was decided at the October 13 meeting to deliver 14 F-4 Phantom aircraft to Israel during the following two days.

Coincidentally, on the same day Kissinger gave his ultimatum to support the airlift or be fired to the WSAG participants — who besides Schlesinger and Colby also included Undersecretary of Defense William Clements, Admiral Thomas Moorer, and Undersecretary of State Kenneth Rush — the U.S. detected 67 Soviet airlift flights, the bulk of them to Egypt, and Sadat began moving more artillery across the Canal. Both Soviet and American officials were soon able to claim their resupply efforts were only a reaction to escalation by the other side.

The war that Kissinger had worked so hard to keep going for a few more days in order for the Israelis to take back the territory they had lost during the first week now was beginning to look like a major U.S.-Soviet confrontation. The President of the United States, however, was so deeply preoccupied with saving his ravaged Presidency from domestic opponents that he had turned over most of the strategic thinking about the escalating war to Henry Kissinger. Kissinger, in turn, was so obsessed with Soviet-U.S. power politics, that he seemed oblivious to the fact that hundreds of Middle Easterners were dying under a torrent of deadly and sophisticated Soviet and American munitions, now being flown by two air bridges of giant transport planes almost up to the front lines.

For the record, the resupply was begun by the United States on Sunday, October 7, the second day of the war, via five El Al aircraft shuttling between Israel and the U.S. The Soviet airlift began Wednesday, October 10 with flights to Syria. Resupply flights to Egypt started Thursday, October 11 and the first substantial arrival of Soviet supplies in Egypt was on Saturday, October 13. The U.S. had tried to step up the El Al airlift on Thursday, October 11, but was unable to obtain charters to do it. It began using U.S. military aircraft on October 13, and steadily increased the aircraft involved each day thereafter.

By Saturday, October 13, the day of Kissinger's ultimatum to the other American officials involved, alarm bells were ringing all over the globe. British Foreign Secretary Sir Alec Douglas-Home telephoned Kissinger to say that the U.K. would not be introducing a simple return-to-your places cease-fire resolution along the lines desired by Israel and the U.S. Instead, he proposed a cease-fire in place, sending in an international police force to patrol the rest of the occupied territories, and then an international conference. Kissinger, although he later justified his stand in terms of cold-war politics, clearly was speaking for Israel when he told Douglas-Home the British proposal was "too complicated" and, in a second message, that if the British introduced it, the U.S. would veto it. Home later called again to ask Kissinger bluntly whether the U.S. had lost interest in detente with the Soviet Union. Kissinger, by his own account, told the British Foreign Secretary that "detente is not an end in itself. I think developments now are going to drive us toward a confrontation." In his memoirs Kissinger explains:

"We had no alternative anyway. If the Soviet-armed states won, the Soviets would control the post-war diplomacy. If Israel did not force a decision, it would be enmeshed in a war of attrition in which courage and ingenuity even in Israeli measure could not overcome a population ratio of 30 to 1 arrayed against it."[10]

Kissinger, it seemed, was now prepared to intervene openly in the Arab-Israeli war to keep Israel from losing more of the Arab lands it had seized in 1967. And if the Soviets tried to stop him, he was prepared to risk war with the Soviet Union. In short, having silenced every other ranking U.S. official with a threat of instant dismissal that morning, Kissinger was, by that afternoon, seemingly having the time of his life.

He writes that on that same afternoon the British Ambassador to the U.S. had asked him "What will be your posture when the Arabs start screaming oil at you?" Kissinger had answered: "Defiance."

It would be interesting to know how many of the day's conversations he recounted to President Nixon that evening. Kissinger reports only that they had "a lengthy review" and that Nixon "agreed we were now in a test of wills, saying that this was 'one of those times' and 'that's what we are here for.' " Still later that evening, Kissinger received what he called "an unmistakable signal"[11] that Moscow was not prepared to push matters to a confrontation. This was a message from Brezhnev via Ambassador Dobrynin that Moscow had been prepared for two days to implement a cease-fire, but that when the United States had procrastinated, the Arabs had changed their minds.

On Sunday, October 14, Egypt launched a new attack into Sinai, largely to relieve the pressure on Syria, and in doing so made its first major tactical error of the war. As Egyptian tanks left their anti-aircraft missile screen they became vulnerable to Israeli air power. Some 250 were destroyed. In the U.S., meanwhile, as he stepped up the airlift, Kissinger began to think about mending some of his Arab fences. In a message to Sadat he acknowledged "the unacceptability to the Egyptian side of the conditions which existed prior to the outbreak of recent hostilities" and promised that "the U.S. will make a major effort as soon as hostilities are terminated to assist in bringing a just and lasting peace to the Middle East."

Two messages were sent to King Faisal of Saudi Arabia, for whom Nixon had a particular measure of regard. The first, signed by the President, asked for the Saudi monarch's understanding of U.S. efforts to reach a permanent and just peace and cited a Nixon press conference statement a month earlier that the U.S. was neither pro-Israel nor pro-Arab. The second, from Kissinger, notified Saudi Arabia of the U.S. airlift to Israel. A message was also sent to the Shah of Iran which thanked him for denying permission for the Soviet airlift to over-fly Iran. The message urged the Shah "not to be swept along by tactical considerations of the moment." This was meant to discourage the Shah from joining in any Islamic ground swell of support for the Arab combatants.

---

10. Kissinger, Henry, *Years of Upheaval*, Little, Brown and Company, Boston, 1982, p. 518.
11. *Ibid.*, p. 521.

By Monday, October 15, the U.S. airlift comprised 20 flights a day, including some by huge C-5A Starlifters, and was moving 1000 tons of equipment per day. Already it had surpassed the total of equipment delivered to Egypt, Syria and Iraq by the Soviet airlift up to that date. Referring both to Defense Secretary James Schlesinger's direction of the resupply effort and his initial reluctance to undertake it, Kissinger remarked: "I must say when you want to work you are terrific. You are equally awe-inspiring when you don't."

That day Kissinger received a surprisingly conciliatory message from Hafiz Ismail, Sadat's foreign policy adviser. After urging Kissinger to re-double his efforts to link a political solution with a military solution to the war, and denouncing the resupply of Israel, the message invited the U.S. Secretary of State to visit Egypt. Kissinger also received a message from the future King of Saudi Arabia, Prince Fahd, then Deputy Prime Minister, warning the U.S. that the situation was deteriorating to the point where it would soon become impossible for any Arab to say he was America's friend. This was followed the next day, October 16, by a message from King Faisal of Saudi Arabia warning that if the U.S. did not end its support for Israel, Saudi-U.S. relations would become lukewarm. In case President Nixon and Secretary Kissinger were not sure what "lukewarm" meant, they could read in the newspapers that Saudi Arabia was telling ambassadors of the European Community that unless they pressed the U.S. to change its policy, Saudi Arabia would reduce its oil production. Meanwhile, Saudi Minister of Petroleum Sheikh Ahmed Zaki Yamani was meeting with other Arab oil producers in Kuwait.

Kissinger promised Sadat "to make every effort to assist in achieving a final, just settlement once a cease-fire is reached" and added that "progress could be made on the basis of a cease-fire in place, accompanied by an undertaking by the parties to start talks under the aegis of the Secretary General with a view to achieving a setttlement in accordance with Security Council Resolution 242 in all of its parts."

But while his language was conciliatory, Kissinger gave orders that the U.S. resupply remain at least 25 percent ahead of the Soviets, and that a U.S. sealift, which had begun along with the airlift, be increased until it more than matched a Soviet sealift which was being prepared in Black Sea ports.

On that same day the U.S. learned that a force of 25 Israeli tanks had crossed to the west bank of the Suez Canal at the Great Bitter Lake and was racing to knock out the Egyptian surface-to-air missile sites protecting Egyptian advanced positions along the Canal's east bank.

By Wednesday, October 17, the Israeli Canal-crossing operation had grown to a full-fledged counter offensive, and Soviet Premier Alexi Kosygin was in Cairo, talking to the Egyptians about accepting a cease-fire. Brezhnev had sent a message to the U.S. reiterating the Soviet position that if Israel would return to its 1967 borders, its security could be guaranteed by the superpowers or by the Security Council. Almost overlooked in the tumultuous events in the Middle East was the arrival in Washington of a delegation of foreign ministers from Algeria, Kuwait, Morocco and Saudi Arabia. They told President Nixon that, in the words of Saudi Foreign Minister Omar Saqqaf, "Israel is not being threatened by the Arabs with annihilation," and that the Arabs "want no more than a return to the 1967 borders and respect for the rights of refugees to return to their lands or be compensated for what they have lost. This would be enough to guarantee the stability and integrity of Israel."

Nixon in turn made a promise:

"I will work for a cease-fire, not in order to trick you into stopping at the cease-fire lines, but to use it as a basis to go on from there for a settlement on the basis of Resolution 242 . . . You have my pledge. I can't say that we can categorically move Israel back to the 1967 borders, but we will work within the framework for Resolution 242." [12]

In the same conversation Nixon struck a theme that Arab leaders were to hear repeated with increasing frequency not only during the remainder of Nixon's Administration, but also during that of his successor. Kissinger, he promised the Arab foreign ministers, would become the negotiator of a lasting Middle East peace. As a Jew, Nixon told them, Kissinger would not be subject to the domestic pressures that the Israel lobby could exert on other U.S. politicians by calling them anti-Semitic. Saqqaf, including Kissinger with the other Arab foreign ministers present, diplomatically observed, "We are all Semites together."

Kissinger came away from Nixon's meeting with the Arab foreign ministers convinced that the U.S. airlift to resupply Israel had not seriously impaired the American relationship with the Arabs. It was not the last time he would mistake the habitual Arab courtesy and avoidance of confrontation for acquiesence. It was to be a lesson paid for, in hard currency, by oil consumers throughout the western world.

At his daily WSAG meeting on October 17, Kissinger told his colleagues "we have to keep the stuff going into Israel. We have to pour it in until someone quits." Afterward, the entire group went into the Oval office where Nixon, that week preoccupied with his coming confrontation with Watergate Special Prosecutor Archibald Cox, took time out to inform them that "no one is more keenly aware of the stakes: Oil and our strategic position." But, he added, in words that were clearly influenced by Kissinger's thinking and far from the attitude he had expressed at the beginning of his Presidency: "This is bigger than the Middle East. We can't allow a Soviet-supported operation to succeed against an American-supported operation. If it does, our credibility everywhere is severely shaken."

At the same moment, in Kuwait, the Arab oil producers were announcing an immediate petroleum production cutback of 5 per cent, to be followed by an additional 5 per cent cutback each month until Israel withdrew to its 1967 frontiers. Iran and five Arab states of the Gulf further announced a unilateral 70 per cent increase in the price of their oil from $3.01 to $5.12 a barrel. The production cut and price increase squeeze was beginning as a purely political gesture to make the U.S. desist from the airlift resupply of Israel, but its economic consequences were to change the history of the globe, and to swing the balance both of world opinion and world economic power further against Israel and what was soon to be Israel's only remaining friend, the United States.

European countries, which had been openly uneasy about the American policy of defending Israel's hold on Arab territories seized by force, now made haste to dissociate

---

12. Kissinger, Henry, *Years of Upheaval*, Little, Brown and Company, Boston, 1982, p. 525.

themselves publicly from the United States. The U.S. had oil resources of its own, and access to Venezuelan and other non-Arab oil. A cutoff from Middle Eastern oil would be a disaster, however, for most of America's European allies. Full recognition of this was only beginning to dawn on Kissinger, still absorbed in dreams of 19th century-style U.S.-Soviet power confrontations, and Nixon, hoping desperately for some major development to divert American public attention from the mortal wounds suffered by his Presidency.

The next day, October 18, Saudi Arabia turned the screw another notch by announcing that it had doubled to 10 per cent its own production cutback announced the day before by the Arab oil ministers. At the same time, King Faisal responded to Nixon's earlier message with three points of his own: (1) Prolongation of the war was only helping the Soviet Union; (2) The war could be ended if Israel would return to its 1967 borders; and (3) U.S.-Saudi friendship risked "being diminished" if the U.S. continued to support Israel.

Ironically, Golda Meir's response to a U.S. query about a cease-fire linked only to Resolution 242 arrived on the same day. In it she demurred from the cease-fire she had asked for only a week earlier, and specifically rejected linkage with Resolution 242, which had been the basis of Israel's negotiating posture for the previous six years. While the Arabs were reluctantly chipping away the economic underpinnings of the industrialized western world, and almost begging the U.S. to stop them, Israel was pursuing a game of one-upmanship with the U.S. so obscure that even the normally conspiratorial Kissinger was losing patience. His only response, however, was to urge Israel to speed up its military operations in anticipation of a cease-fire within 48 hours.

What he thought as he did it, however, is summed up in his own memoirs:

"We had seen Israel through two weeks of mortal peril. We had stalled at the UN when it served our common strategy; we had proposed a cease-fire when Israel was ready; we had poured in supplies during Israel's extremity. We could not now jeopardize relations with Europe and Japan, tempt an oil embargo, confront the Soviets, and challenge our remaining Arab friends either by forever delaying a cease-fire proposal or by jettisoning Resolution 242, in the name of which we had fought off Soviet and radical Arab pressures for six years. Nor would it have been in Israel's interest that we do so. Without Resolution 242 there would be no legal basis for any future negotiation." [13]

That evening Brezhnev sent the U.S. a three-part proposal drafted for Soviet submission to the UN Security Council. It called for a cease-fire in place, a phased Israeli withdrawal "from the occupied Arab territories to the line in accordance with Resolution 242" and "appropriate consultations" toward establishing a just peace. Kissinger in turn sent a message to Cairo, reiterating a U.S. offer to support a cease-fire linked to a reaffirmation of Resolution 242.

By Friday, October 19, the Israeli bridgehead on the Canal's west bank had grown to 300 tanks, moving both north and south of the crossing point to cut off the Egyptian forces that had crossed the Canal into Sinai from their sources of supply. If the Arabs, formerly confident of their ability to win any war of attrition, had been stalling about

---

13. Kissinger, Henry, *Years of Upheaval*, Little, Brown and Company, Boston, 1982, p. 539.

a cease-fire before, the reverse was now true. With the entire industrial might of the U.S. supporting the Israelis, and U.S. air and sealifts pouring in military supplies at a rate at least 25 percent higher than the Soviet supplies going to their Arab opponents, Golda Meir was stalling in order to take as much Egyptian territory as possible on both sides of the original cease-fire lines.

The Russians now sent an urgent message to Nixon calling for prompt joint decisions to forestall "harm" to Soviet-U.S. relations. They suggested that Kissinger come "in an urgent manner to Moscow to conduct appropriate negotiations."

Kissinger was delighted to assume the lone ranger role he had already played in negotiations concerning China and Vietnam. He convinced President Nixon that the time that would be required for him to reach Moscow would enable the Israelis to consolidate their military gains on the western side of the Canal before the combined U.S. and Soviet call for a joint cease-fire that would inevitably result from his Moscow visit.

Kissinger was actually en route to Moscow on Saturday, October 20, when Saudi Arabia announced that along with the other Arab oil producers it was cutting *all* oil sales to the United States. He also received two military reports from Israel, indicating that Israeli exhaustion might limit further advances, regardless of whether or not he continued to delay the impending cease-fire.

Two things were happening in Washington while Kissinger was flying to Moscow. First, in the absence of the overwhelming presence of his Secretary of State, Nixon was having some second thoughts about the U.S. support which was making Israel's continuation of the war both possible and profitable, but which every day seemed to be undermining the economic future of the U.S. and its European allies. He sent instructions to Kissinger to negotiate a cease-fire as rapidly as possible. When Kissinger telephoned General Haig from Moscow to ask what had prompted Nixon's message, he learned that the Watergate political cancer was spreading even further within the Administration. Unable to reach a compromise with Special Investigator Archibald Cox, Nixon had fired him. In protest, Attorney General Elliot Richardson had resigned.

Kissinger decided that instead of seeking to change the President's mind he would accept the instructions quietly and negotiate a cease-fire before the Soviets began to consider the possibilities that the U.S. government's total disarray opened before them. When he met with the Soviets on Sunday, October 21, he found them so eager to reach agreement that there was virtually no negotiation at all. Moshe Dayan had declared in a radio broadcast that, although Israel's military position was bound to continue improving, nevertheless Israel was prepared to accept a cease-fire based either upon a return by both sides to lines occupied prior to the war, or upon a cease-fire in place. Sadat had also indicated in a message to Washington that he was willing to separate a cease-fire from an overall settlement, if the U.S. and the USSR would "guarantee" both the cease-fire and a subsequent Israeli withdrawal.

In four hours of negotiation, including translations, checking of texts, and frequent consultations within each of the two delegations, an agreement was reached based upon a cease-fire in place and calling upon all parties to begin implementation of Security Council Resolution 242, in all of its parts. Immediate negotiations were to begin between the parties concerned "under appropriate auspices."

Ironically, the result of only four hours of negotiations took another four hours to transmit to Washington and thence to U.N. headquarters in New York. Apparently Soviet or other intelligence services were attempting to penetrate or harass U.S. communications, both in the U.S. Embassy and in Kissinger's aircraft on the ground. The result was a delay in transmissions between Moscow and Washington, as urgent to the Soviet Union as they were to the U.S. Nevertheless, at 12:50 a.m., New York time, Monday, October 22, the text agreed upon in Moscow became United Nations Security Council Resolution 338. The USSR had wanted the cease-fire to take effect the moment the resolution was passed. Kissinger, still delaying on behalf of Israel, had insisted that it become effective only 12 hours after the resolution was adopted.

So it was that Kissinger, who after completing the negotiations had accepted an invitation from Golda Meir to return to the U.S. from Moscow via Israel, found himself flying Monday morning, October 22, into a war zone, escorted by attack planes from the U.S. Sixth Fleet, which was still patrolling off Crete. It was the kind of dramatic entrance into Israel dear to the heart of the flamboyant U.S. Secretary of State, and it is obvious from his description of the event that he expected to be welcomed as the saviour of Israel in its hour of need. He describes his arrival emotionally:

"Much was written after the war about how eager Israel was to continue the war and how painful it found the cease-fire. No one would have guessed that from our reception. Soldiers and civilians greeted the approaching peace as the highest blessing. Israel was heroic but its endurance was reaching the breaking point. Those who had come to welcome us seemed to feel viscerally how close to the abyss they had come and how two weeks of war had drained them. Small groups of servicemen and civilians were applauding with tears in their eyes. Their expression showed a weariness that almost tangibly conveyed the limits of human endurance. Israel was exhausted, no matter what the military maps showed. Its people were yearning for peace as can only those who have never known it . . .

"Deep down, the Israelis knew that while they had won the last battle, they had lost the aura of invincibility. The Arab armies were not destroyed. The Arab nations had not won but no longer need they quail before Israeli might. Israel, after barely escaping disaster, had prevailed militarily; it ended up with more Arab territory captured than lost. But it was entering an uncertain and lonely future, dependent on a shrinking circle of friends. What made the prospect more tormenting was the consciousness that complacency had contributed to that outcome." [14]

Kissinger met three times with Golda Meir for a total of two hours that Monday afternoon. Much of her conversation consisted of probing to detect whether or not the U.S. and USSR had made a secret agreement to impose an Arab-Israeli peace based upon the 1967 borders. With a permanent Middle East settlement now so obviously attainable, she apparently could not believe the U.S. had not obtained it. Instead, Kissinger sought to explain to her that the prize he had extracted had been on behalf of Israel, not on behalf of the U.S. In Kissinger's words:

"For twenty five years, Israeli diplomacy had striven for direct negotiations. Now that this achievement was at hand, Golda was nearly overwhelmed by the realization, still mercifully

---

14. Kissinger, Henry, *Years of Upheaval*, Little, Brown and Company, Boston, 1982, pp. 560-1.

obscure to her colleagues, that the agenda for these negotiations would face Israel with the awesome dilemmas it had avoided for too long . . .

"In short, Israel's insecurity was so pervasive that even words were daggers. Golda knew very well that not even the attainment of its stated goals could compensate for the altered psychological balance. I asked whether she thought Sadat could survive the military setbacks of the last phase of the war. Golda replied matter-of-factly: 'I do. Because he is the hero. He dared.' She was right. Israel was at a disadvantage, even though the war ended in success, because (Israel's) task was beyond the human scale. It could not prevail by force simply by defeating its enemies; it had to crush them so that they could not revive. Given the disparity in numbers – the city of Cairo alone having twice the population of the entire State of Israel – no nation, however heroic, could sustain such a task indefinitely. This is why for Israel peace is as necessary as it is terrifying." [15]

While Kissinger was at lunch with Israeli officials in Tel Aviv, a message arrived saying Egypt had accepted the cease-fire, effective at 5 p.m. Cairo time, two hours ahead of the deadline. None of the Israelis present knew whether Cairo, capital of a country bordering Israel and, supposedly, Israel's major preoccupation for the previous 25 years, was in the same time zone as Tel Aviv. Kissinger had a member of his staff telephone Washington to find out, and suggested that the Israelis solve the issue by setting their own compliance with the cease-fire for 6:52 p.m., just 12 hours after Resolution 338 had been passed in the Security Council. Kissinger also learned what he had been trying for a week to extract from the Israelis: The exact disposition of their forces on the west bank of the Suez Canal. They had cut all supply routes to the Egyptian Third Army on the east bank except for one secondary road in the extreme south.

Before he left Tel Aviv, Kissinger received an invitation to visit Cairo next. He demurred, stopping in London just long enough to learn from the British press that talk of impeaching President Nixon was rising in the U.S. He landed in Washington at 3 a.m. Tuesday, October 23.

When he arrived in his office only a few hours later he found two messages awaiting him. One was from Hafiz Ismail in Cairo complaining that the Israelis had already broken the cease-fire and were seizing new positions, and inquiring what the U.S. and USSR were doing to ensure Israeli compliance. The other was from U.S. Ambassador to Israel Kenneth Keating, a former New York Senator, who seemed never to have abandoned the pro-Israel public and private statements and attitudes that had served him so well in the New York state political arena. Keating relayed complaints from Golda Meir of Egyptian cease-fire violations. Even the normally pro-Israeli Keating could not resist adding to his message the comment that, since the Israeli forces seemed to be gaining ground, some might view the Israeli claim that it was the Egyptians who were continuing the fighting with skepticism.

The events that followed, escalating rapidly into an historic Soviet-U.S. confrontation, are a case study in how the client comes to dominate the patron in any such relationship between nations. A parent might also recognize them as a case study in how not to handle a spoiled child.

---

15. Kissinger, Henry, *Years of Upheaval*, Little, Brown and Company, Boston, 1982, p. 564.

PLO

Israeli Occupiers. (Upper left) Israeli soldiers search Palestinian village of Karame, March 25, 1968. (Upper right) Israelis on West Bank patrol near Jericho, 1969. (Lower left) Israeli gendarmes pick through debris in bombed Jerusalem supermarket. (Lower right) Israeli border police mark an Arab shop in East Jerusalem which closed during a strike protesting Israeli annexation moves. Owners of shops which closed were either locked out or subjected to interrogation.

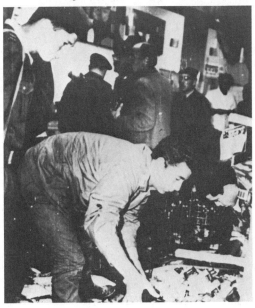

PLO   PLO

Jeffrey Blankfort   PLO

Armed Palestinians. (Upper left) Palestinian militiawomen. (Upper right) PLO fighter looking into Israel. (Lower left) Soldiers of the Palestine Liberation Army based in Syria drill with Kalashnikov automatic rifles. (Lower right) Palestinians with truck-mounted machine gun and Kalashnikovs.

PLO   Jeffrey Blankfort

CHAPTER XV

Ceasefire, Cheating and Confrontation

"'Golda called primarily to assure me that Egypt had been the first to break the cease-fire. I mumbled something about my impression that her soldiers were obviously not heartbroken by that unexpected turn of events. Having proved my skill at repartee, I explained my thinking on the UN resolution. I suggested that Israel pull back a few hundred yards from wherever it was now and call it the old cease-fire line. 'How can anyone ever know where a line is or was in the desert?' I said. Golda's melancholy at my obtuseness was palpable even at a distance of 6,000 miles. She replied: 'They will know where our present line is, all right.' Now I understood. Israel had cut the last supply route to the city of Suez. The Egyptian Third Army on the east bank of the Canal was totally cut off. A crisis was upon us."[1]

Henry Kisssinger, 1982

"The situation was now assessed by the Russians and the Americans, and both came to a similar conclusion. although not for the same reasons. The Soviets realized that the destruction of the Egyptian Third Army would mean a clear-cut defeat for a country they had supported. Russian prestige would suffer if such a client country, armed with Soviet weapons and equipment, were again to suffer a decisive military defeat. Kissinger, for his part, now appreciated that rescuing the army could be an important bargaining factor in achieving an ultimate arrangement between the sides."[2]

Chaim Herzog, 1982

---

1. Kissinger, Henry, *Years of Upheaval*, Little, Brown and Company, Boston, 1982, p. 571.
2. Herzog, Chaim, *The Arab-Israeli Wars: War and Peace in the Middle East*, Random House, New York, 1982, p. 283.

*"The Israelis refused to let the United Nations Emergency Force Contingent enter Suez
. . . We asked to send blankets and pullovers to our men of the Third Army. The Israelis
refused . . . When Cairo complained to Washington about Israel's intransigence,
pressure merely increased. On December 4 our Foreign Minister, Ismail Fahmy, got
a letter from Kissinger which said: Negotiations between Egypt and Israel at Kilometer
101 should resume 'on a business-like basis'. . . Kissinger did not define what he meant
by 'business-like basis.' But if it meant 'give and take' we were without doubt the ones
destined to go on giving. The oil embargo was beginning to bite. Now Kissinger was
forcing Egypt to persuade its Arab allies to abandon it. The whole Arab world was
now to pay the price for the encirclement of the Third Army."*[3]

Lt. General Saad El Shazly, 1982

The cease-fire went into effect on Oct. 22 after Secretary of State Henry Kissinger had
stopped in Tel Aviv en route home from his visit to Moscow where, with the Russians,
he had negotiated what became UN General Assembly Resolution 338, ending the October War. He arrived in Washington at 3 a.m.

An unpleasant surprise awaited him when he arrived in his office a few hours later.
It was a complaint from Egypt that the Israelis had broken the cease-fire and were seizing new positions. Since Kissinger had told the Israelis in Tel Aviv that he would understand if there were a few hours slippage in meeting the cease-fire deadline, he admits
in his memoirs that he "had a sinking feeling that I might have emboldened them."

It was now more than 20 hours beyond the deadline, however, and a message from
Soviet Chairman Brezhnev had also arrived saying that Israeli forces had crossed the
cease-fire line and were moving rapidly southward along the west bank of the Suez Canal.
Brezhnev wanted a meeting of the U.N. Security Council.

Kissinger called Israeli Ambassador Simcha Dinitz who assured him on behalf of
Prime Minister Golda Meir "personally, confidentially and sincerely that none of the
actions taken on the Egyptian front were initiated by us." Kissinger writes:

> "With all my affection for Golda, I thought she was imposing on my credulity with her defini-
> tion of 'initiate.' It was not plausible that the Egyptian Third Army should launch attacks after
> a cease-fire that had saved it from being overwhelmed."[4]

When Golda Meir telephoned a few minutes later Kissinger learned, to his horror,
that the commander of the Israeli force on the west (Egyptian) side of the Suez Canal,
Ariel Sharon, had taken advantage of the cease-fire to move his tanks forward and cut
the last remaining road linking Egypt's Third Army, east of the Canal, to Cairo. By
cutting Egypt's army off from its base, Israel was seeking to accomplish by trickery
after the cease-fire what it had not been able to accomplish during the fighting: The
surrender of Egypt's entire Third Army. Further, the Israelis flatly refused to withdraw.

A new message arrived from Brezhnev offering assurance that the Arab leaders

---

3. El Shazly, Lt. Gen. Saad, *The Crossing of the Suez*, American Mideast Research, San Francisco, 1980, pp. 285-7.

4. Kissinger, Henry, *Years of Upheaval*, Little, Brown and Company, Boston, 1982, p. 571.

were observing and would continue to observe the cease-fire, despite Israeli "treachery." Kissinger responded that the U.S. would support a new U.N. Security Council resolution calling for a return to the positions that had been occupied by the two sides when the cease-fire went into effect, but that the location of that line in the desert would have to be negotiated between Egypt and Israel. He suggested that Egypt release Israeli prisoners taken during the just-concluded war. The Russians seemed satisfied but Israel was not. Kissinger writes:

"Israel wanted what we could not grant: a veto over all our decisions regardless of the merits of the issue and a free hand to destroy the Egyptian Third Army. That Tuesday afternoon, October 23, we received a blistering communication from Golda . . . She chose to construe the proposed new Security Council resolution as an Egyptian Soviet imposition growing out of an Egyptian violation of the cease-fire: 'It is impossible for Israel to accept that time and again it must face Russian Egyptian ultimatums which will subsequently be assented to by the United States.' . . . Golda informed us that Israel would not comply with the proposed resolution or even talk about it. Israel seemed determined to end the war with a humiliation for Egypt. We had no interest in seeing Sadat destroyed—even less so via the collapse of a cease-fire we had co-sponsored . . . For if Sadat fell, the odds were that he would be replaced by a radical pro-Soviet leader . . . and sooner or later there would be another war reviving the same dilemmas we had just barely surmounted."[5]

Egyptian President Sadat, meanwhile, had sent the U.S. a request that the U.S. intervene to stop the Israeli violations, even if it meant the use of military force. The U.S. responded that it had urged the Israelis to observe the cease-fire. At the end of the day the U.N. Security Council passed Resolution 339 calling for a return to the original cease-fire lines and a new cease-fire.

Awaiting Kissinger the next morning, Oct. 24, when he arrived at his office was a message from Sadat reporting that Sharon's forces were once again attacking, seven hours after imposition of the newest cease-fire. It was followed by a sharp message from Brezhnev asking what the U.S. planned to do about the new violations by its client.

This time White House Chief of Staff Alexander Haig telephoned the Israeli Ambassador on behalf of President Nixon, asking for an explanation. The response from Israel was that the Israelis were trying to "absorb fire without answer."

Sadat, meanwhile, bluntly asked for troops or observers from both the United States and the Soviet Union to come to Egypt to implement the cease-fire. Kissinger had already told the Soviet Ambassador in Washington that the U.S. would veto any U.N. resolution calling for the introduction of troops into the Middle East by permanent members of the Security Council. Now Soviet Ambassador Anatoly Dobrynin informed him that the Soviet Union was going to support just such a resolution if some other country, like Egypt, introduced it.

Kissinger was in the process of warning the Soviet Ambassador that the U.S. would not agree when he was interrupted by a telephone call from President Nixon, who was preoccupied with the ongoing Watergate problem. Kissinger writes:

---

5. Kissinger, Henry, *Years of Upheaval*, Little, Brown and Company, Boston, 1982, p. 573.

"Nixon was as agitated and emotional as I had ever heard him. Talk of his possible impeachment increased daily . . . He spoke of his political end, even his physical demise."[6]

After this conversation Kissinger instructed John Scali, the U.S. Ambassador to the U.N., to veto any condemnation of Israel that could provide a pretext for intervention. He then resumed his conversation with the Russian Ambassador. Dobrynin told him that the Soviet government was so upset with U.S. permission for "the Israelis to do what they wanted" that it wanted to send troops to Egypt, with or without American participation.

Within a few minutes a message arrived from Brezhnev confirming this. Meanwhile the CIA reported that the Soviet airlift to the Middle East had stopped early on Oct. 24th, indicating that the aircraft were being assembled to carry some Soviet airborne divisions that had already been put on alert. There were other reports of Soviet warships heading for Alexandria.

Kissinger decided to hold a 10:30 p.m. meeting of the Washington Special Action Group (WSAG). Based upon the earlier telephone conversation with Nixon, who by then had retired for the night, Kissinger reports that he and Haig decided the President was too distraught to be awakened. Kissinger, who has been strongly criticized for this decision, writes in his memoirs:

"There has been some discussion since of whether it was a 'proper' National Security Council meeting if the President did not attend. (We were also without a Vice President, since Gerald Ford, nominated by President Nixon on October 12, had not yet been confirmed by the Senate.) It was in effect the statutory membership of the National Security Council minus these two men."[7]

At the meeting the participants decided that the Soviet Union was on the verge of a major decision and that it could only be influenced if the U.S. Government made clear its own determination to resist a unilateral move by the Soviets into Egypt. It was decided to raise the status of U.S. forces around the globe to DefCon III, the highest state of alert in peacetime conditions.

The U.S. had asked Israel how to deal with the Soviet invitation for joint action. The Israeli Ambassador brought the Israeli response to the White House during the meeting. It was a plan for Israeli forces to withdraw to the east side of the Canal, Egyptian forces to the west side, and for creation of a 10-kilometer demilitarized strip on either side. In effect Egypt was being asked to vacate 10 more kilometers of its own territory because Israel had violated the cease-fire. Kissinger judged it would so infuriate Sadat that he would insist on great power intervention. Kissinger gave up looking to the Israelis for help and sent a message to Sadat asking him to withdraw his request for Soviet troops.

Meanwhile reports reached the WSAG meeting that eight Soviet transport planes capable of carrying 200 troops each were slated to fly from Budapest to Cairo in the next few hours and that East German military units were being alerted. Participants

---

6. Kissinger, Henry, *Years of Upheaval*, Little, Brown and Company, Boston, 1982, p. 581.
7. *Ibid.*, p. 586.

at the WSAG meeting decided to alert the 82nd Airborne Division for possible movement, order the U.S. aircraft carrier Franklin Delano Roosevelt to move from Italy to join the carrier Independence off Crete, and the carrier John F. Kennedy and its task force to move from the Atlantic into the Mediterranean.

In case Moscow missed these signals, participants in the meeting then decided to order a delay in the return to the U.S. of troops participating in an annual NATO exercise in Europe and ordered the return from Guam of B-52 bombers stationed there. All of this saber rattling was part of an electronic game of chicken in which the Russian radio scanners were expected to detect and report these secret orders and Soviet officials to conclude from them that the U.S. was preparing to go to war if Soviet troops were dispatched to Egypt.

In his memoirs Kissinger records that for the second time he interrupted the meeting from which these orders were being issued to receive another message from Golda Meir, brought to the White House by Israeli Ambassador Dinitz. This message urged that the U.S. not ask Israel to pull back to the line it occupied at the time the original ceasefire went into effect.

The response by Kissinger is mystifying. He writes:

> "I assured (Dinitz) that we had no intention of coercing Israel in response to a Soviet threat."[8]

A few minutes later, when the WSAG meeting had concluded, Kissinger spoke to Dinitz again. This time, Kissinger writes:

> "I told Dinitz that we had completed our reply to Brezhnev. We would offer no new proposals except to augment the UN observer force. We would unequivocally reject joint military action and we would resist unilateral intervention by force, if necessary. I also asked Dinitz, for my information, how long it would take Israel to destroy the Third Army if a showdown became unavoidable."[9]

The meeting concluded and Kissinger went to bed while American forces were being put on alert all over the world. By the next morning it was clear that the bluff had worked. Egypt withdrew its request for Soviet and U.S. intervention, and no Soviet troops departed for Egypt. The U.N. Security Council passed a resolution calling only for an increase in the number of truce observers. The U.S. press, which had learned of the flurry of military orders during the night, attributed the crisis either to a Russian attempt to take advantage of Watergate-induced disarray within the U.S. Government, or a Nixon Administration attempt to manufacture a global crisis to divert attention from Watergate.

Had any newsman suggested the possibility that Kissinger and Haig would prefer to risk nuclear war with the Russians rather than insist that Israel return to the ceasefire line it had violated on the same day the October war ended, the idea would have seemed ludicrous. Therefore there was also no need pursue further the question of why

---

8. Kissinger, Henry, *Years of Upheaval*, Little, Brown and Company, Boston, 1982, p. 590.
9. *Ibid.*, p. 590.

neither Nixon nor Ford were informed of the meeting, even though one was required to chair it and the other might better have been given the opportunity to decide for himself whether or not he should stay away because of a legal technicality.

The U.S. Government returned to normal posture late Thursday, October 25 after the last vestige of the mutual alert, a Soviet force of 12 naval ships steaming southward, finally pulled up 100 miles short of the Egyptian coast and dispersed. Incredibly, however, the Israelis still were determined, under cover of the mutual wariness that followed the world-wide alarm, to bring about the Egyptian Third Army's surrender. Israeli troops prevented the medical convoy arranged by the U.S. from passing through.

Then, on Friday, October 26, Sadat complained to Nixon that Israel was preventing UN observers from reaching the area. Even the long-suffering Kissinger betrays impatience in his summation of the situation:

"We had supported Israel throughout the war for many historical, moral, and strategic reasons. And we had just run the risk of war with the Soviet Union, amidst the domestic crisis of Watergate. But our shared interests did not embrace the elimination of the Third Army. The issue of the Third Army was quite simply that Israel had completed its entrapment well *after* a cease-fire (that we had negotiated) had gone into effect. But while Israel could do this much, it could not cause the Third Army to surrender. Late the preceding night (October 25) Israel had replied to my query that it would take three or four more days of fighting along the *entire* front *and* the assurance of large quantities of modern equipment to destroy the Third Army. There was no way this could take place without another major crisis with the Soviet Union, the permanent enmity of all the Arab states and the humiliation of Sadat.

"Nor would the final destruction of an Egyptian army after the cease-fire have been in Israel's long-term interest. Maddened by the fact that they had been surprised, beside themselves with grief over the high casualties, deeply distrustful of Sadat, who had engineered their discomfiture, Israel's leaders wanted to end the war with his destruction. Their emotion was understandable. But one of our interests was to give Arab leaders an incentive for moderation. Our exchanges with Cairo had convinced us that Anwar Sadat represented the best chance for peace in the Middle East." [10]

The Defense Department submitted a plan to resupply the Egyptian Third Army using American military aircraft. Those who had been uneasy with the huge airlift that had made Israel's military offensive possible now suggested shutting it down. Kissinger resisted both ideas. Instead he spent a great deal of time trying to persuade Israel to allow food and water to reach the trapped Egyptian troops. He urged Israel to allow UN observers to travel to points between the two armies to monitor the cease-fire and permit convoys of food, water and medical supplies to pass through.

Nixon was for stronger warnings to the Israelis. Referring to U.S. agreements with Egypt he said "Let's keep our side of the bargain." The Israelis refrained from answering the U.S., except for a "personal" idea submitted by the Israeli Ambassador in Washington that any Egyptian wishing to leave the Third Army might be permitted to pass through Israeli lines so long as he left his equipment behind. Kissinger reports

---

10. Kissinger, Henry, *Years of Upheaval*, Little, Brown and Company, Boston, 1982, p. 602.

he told Dinitz "you will not be permitted to capture that army . . . I frankly think you will make a mistake if you push into a total confrontation." [11]

Later on the 26th Sadat reported that the Israelis were once again attacking on the ground and in the air. When the Israelis responded, it was clearly a stall, while they sought more time to batter the Egyptians into submission. Even the generally compliant John Scali at the UN told Kissinger, "I think unless we get the Israelis to back up we are not going to have a friend in the house." A long but ambiguously threatening message arrived from Brezhnev.

In his memoirs Kissinger describes his state of mind when, at 11 p.m. he called Dinitz on behalf of Nixon:

> "I had resisted the bureaucracy's pressures to undertake an American resupply of the Third Army . . . But it was becoming clear that Israel was in no position to make a decision. It seemed to prefer being coerced to release its prey rather than relinquishing it voluntarily. My ultimate responsibility was as Secretary of State of the United States, not as psychiatrist to the government of Israel. With the utmost reluctance I decided that my duty was to force a showdown." [12]

Kissinger told Dinitz that Nixon wanted by 8 a.m. a plan for getting non-military supplies to the Third Army or the U.S. would go back to the UN for enforcement of resolutions 338 and 339.

"I have to say again," Kissinger reports he told Dinitz, "your course is suicidal. You will not be permitted to destroy this army. You are destroying the possibility for negotiations." [13]

Golda Meir responded early Saturday October 27 in a message to Kissinger. He comments in his memoirs:

> "Even though I had transmitted our demand in the name of Nixon, Golda was too surefooted to tackle the President head-on. She made sure that her quarrels were always with subordinates. Placing the President on a pedestal gave him one more opportunity to change course by disavowing those who were undermining the harmony Golda postulated. And, if this failed, an ultimate concession to the President, with some skill and luck, could at least be turned into a claim for a future favor. . . ." [14]

> "Her message was one of aggrieved martyrdom: 'I have no illusions but that everything will be imposed on us by the two big powers . . . There is only one thing that nobody can prevent us from doing and that is to proclaim the truth of the situation; that Israel is being punished not for its deeds, but because of its size and because it is on its own.' " [15]

Her letter still had no proposal to relieve the seige of the Egyptian army her forces had trapped 48 hours after the U.S.-negotiated cease-fire. Egypt solved the problem by accepting a U.S. proposal for direct talks between Egyptian and Israeli officers under UN supervision at Kilometer 101 on the Cairo-Suez road. The only conditions the Egyp-

11. Kissinger, Henry, *Years of Upheaval*, Little, Brown and Company, Boston, 1982, p. 604.
12. *Ibid.*, p. 608.
13. *Ibid.*, p. 609.
14. *Ibid.*, p. 609.
15. *Ibid.*, p. 610.

tians imposed were that the Israelis stop firing two hours before the meeting, proposed for 3 p.m. Cairo time Saturday, October 27 and that they permit the passage of one convoy carrying non-military supplies to the Third Army under U.N. and Red Cross supervision.

Even then, Israeli soldiers stopped the Egyptian military representative at Kilometer 85. More back and forth messages between Cairo and Jerusalem, through Washington, followed and eventually Egyptian and Israeli officers met for direct talks for the first time in 25 years at 1:30 a.m. local time Sunday, October 28. The Israelis, however, delayed the passage of the supply convoy until Monday, October 29.

In fact, Kissinger admits, only his trip to the Middle East "marked the real end of the Middle East war." On November 9, Israeli and Egyptian agreement was announced to a six-point plan providing for movement of food, water and medicine to the town of Suez and to the east bank; replacement of Israeli checkpoints on the Cairo-Suez road with U.N. checkpoints; and an exchange of prisoners. By November 14 Egypt and Israel had worked out a detailed accord at Kilometer 101 for implementing the six-point plan. By then Kissinger had visited a number of Arab countries for the first time and was beginning to see for himself what Rogers had tried to tell him years earlier. The "moderate" Arab countries he was visiting, Egypt, Saudi Arabia, Jordan, Morocco and Tunisia, were ready to make a permanent peace whenever Israel could be persuaded to return to its pre-1967 borders.

Aided and abetted at every turn by Anwar Sadat, whom he had almost succeeded in destroying through years of denigration, and opposed and undercut at every turn by Golda Meir, whom he later professed to "love," Kissinger then set in motion his own personal peace shuttle. Eschewing the comprehensive solution envisaged in Resolution 242 and aiming instead for piecemeal solutions, it was what the world came to know as "step by step."

Israeli Information Services

Egyptian supply trucks link up with United Nations escort for drive through Israeli lines to the besieged Egyptian Third Army. Israeli forces under the command of General Ariel Sharon broke the Oct. 22, 1973 ceasefire to seize all of the roads linking the Egyptian Third Army, east of the Suez Canal, with its supplies. When Israel sought to force the trapped Egyptian force to surrender, the Soviet Union threatened to send its forces to halt Israeli defiance of the U.N. Resolution ending the war. The incident was one of the most serious U.S.-Soviet confrontations since World War II.

UNRWA

Black September: A half million of the one and a half million Palestinian refugees registered with the U.N. Relief and Works Agency (UNRWA) lived in Jordan at the time fighting broke out between the Jordanian Army and most of the armed Palestinian commando organizations in September, 1970. The fighting was provoked by the radical Popular Front for the Liberation of Palestine which at that time was a component group within the PLO. (It has since broken with Yassir Arafat's Al Fatah and left the PLO.) By the time the fighting had ended with the defeat of the armed Palestinians, many of the refugees, dispossessed first in 1948 and subsequently in 1967, had again lost their homes to the heavy artillery used in the fighting. Here survivors seek to resume normal life among the ruins of their concrete block shelters.

UNRWA

Israeli incursions into Lebanon: As armed Palestinians expelled from Jordan moved into Lebanon, their raids into Israel attracted extremely harsh retribution on themselves and their Lebanese hosts. Above, elderly Lebanese couple in the ruins of their home in the Arqoub, dynamited in 1969 by Israelis. Inset, children killed during Israeli air attack on Palestinian refugee camp in Lebanon in 1973. Below, wreckage of Lebanese civilian automobile carrying six passengers which was crushed by an Israeli tank during a 1972 armored thrust into Southern Lebanon.

PLO

CHAPTER XVI

Step by Step from
President Nixon to President Ford

"To the nations of the Middle East I pledge continuity in our vigorous efforts to advance the process which has brought hopes of peace to that region after 25 long years as a hot-bed of war."
Gerald Ford, August 12, 1974

"Although I said publicly that I welcomed the letter as an expression of Senate sentiment, in truth it really bugged me. The Senators claimed the letter was spontaneous, but there was no doubt in my mind that it was inspired by Israel . . . Because of the letter, however, the Israelis didn't want to budge. So confident were they that those 76 Senators would support them no matter what they did, they refused to suggest any new ideas for peace. 'Concessions will have to be made,' they were saying in effect, 'But we will make none of them. Sadat will have to make them all. And if Ford disagrees, we will show him who's boss.' "[1]
Gerald Ford, 1982

"For the past twenty-five years the philosophical underpinning of U.S. policy toward Israel had been our conviction – and certainly my own – that if we gave Israel an ample supply of economic aid and weapons, she would feel strong and confident, more flexible and more willing to discuss a lasting peace. Every American President since Harry Truman had willingly supplied arms and funds to the Jewish state. The Israelis were stronger militarily than all of their Arab neighbors combined, yet peace was no closer than it had ever been. So I began to question the rationale for our policy. I wanted

---

1. Ford, Gerald, *A Time to Heal: The Autobiography of Gerald R. Ford*, Harper and Row, New York, 1979, p. 287.

the Israelis to recognize that there had to be some quid pro quo. If we were going to build up their military capabilities, we in turn had to see some flexibility to achieve a fair, secure and permanent peace. "[2]

Gerald Ford, 1982

Once during the dramatic months that lay ahead, Henry Kissinger is said to have turned wearily to an aide and remarked that the Israelis and the Syrians are two peoples in the Middle East who really *deserve* each other.

His ordeal with repeated cease-fire violations had finally ended when Golda Meir became alarmed that continuing disregard of the various cease-fire agreements by her military commander on the east bank, General Ariel Sharon, might finally turn even America's first Jewish Secretary of State against Israel.

Sharon was a man who combined an outspoken racism and a total lack of human compassion with burning political ambition. He realized that his reckless actions on the west bank of the Suez Canal, whether or not they precipitated World War III, would certainly provide the Israeli press with crowd-pleasing images of the swashbuckling derring-do with which he planned someday to propel himself into the Israeli Prime Ministership. He had started successfully cultivating his ruthless, strong-man image many years earlier. One night in 1953 he had led his Unit 101 into the West Bank village of Qibya. His paratroopers shot all of the villagers who tried to escape from their houses, blocked up all of the doors, and then blew the houses and their remaining occupants to smithereens. International observers counted 60 bodies of men, women and children in the devastated village the next day, but with no one left alive in the village to report the missing, the full toll would never be known.

The Israeli Government claimed for a long time that the massacre had been committed by "frontier settlers," only admitting its official responsibility two years later after the men of Sharon's Unit 101 began bragging to the press about how they were killing Palestinians in terror raids all over the West Bank. The victims included both Jordanian soldiers and any civilians the paratroopers could lay hands on. One case is carefully documented in the diary of Former Israeli Prime Minister Moshe Sharett, who deplored both Sharon and the growing Israeli mood of public ruthlessness that made his rise possible. Sharon's troopers slipped into Jordanian territory and seized six Palestinian shepherd boys. They forced one boy to watch while they methodically stabbed each of the other five teenagers to death. Then they released the survivor to tell the families of the victims how their sons had died.

Now, in 1973, Golda Meir knew that she could not rein in Sharon, and that he still planned to capture or destroy Egypt's entire Third Army even though it was now weeks rather than days after the cease-fire was supposed to have taken effect. She therefore summoned a helicopter and, in her bedroom slippers according to the version of the story she told British TV correspondent Alan Hart, flew off into Egyptian territory on the east bank of the Canal. There she quite literally dropped down among

---

2. Ford, Gerald, *A Time to Heal: The Autobiography of Gerald R. Ford*, Harper and Row, New York, 1979, p. 245.

Sharon's tanks and ordered him to stop his depredations. It seemed an extraordinary way to end the war. Based upon Sharon's prior and subsequent demonstrations of what he is willing to do to anyone who stands in his way, it is likely that during her personal incursion into Egyptian territory Israel's Prime Minister was in at least as much danger from her own military commander and his "elite paratroopers" as she was from the surrounding Egyptian forces.

Henry Kissinger's ordeal by Syria began almost as soon as Golda Meir's helicopter trip into Egypt ended his ordeal by Israel. UN Resolution 338, drafted in Moscow with the Russians by Kissinger, had called for the holding of a conference "under appropriate auspices" to negotiate a just and lasting Middle East peace. The U.S. and USSR agreed to invite UN Secretary General Kurt Waldheim to host the conference in Geneva at the end of December. The European nations were to be excluded. It would be the first formal direct negotiation between the Arab nations and Israel in 25 years. Egypt and Jordan agreed to attend.

Israel, seeking as usual to extract some tangible reward or concession from the U.S., and Syria, generally the hard-line spoiler in the Middle East, both had to be persuaded. It eventually was clear that if Syria attended, Israel would attach impossible conditions concerning Israeli POWs held by Syria to its own attendance. Conversely, if Israel attended, then Syria would demand impossible prior commitments as to the results even before negotiations started.

Golda Meir and Moshe Dayan were absorbed in a domestic political minuet which had followed the total loss of confidence among the electorate in the Prime Minister and Defense Minister who had allowed Israel to be surprised by the Egyptian-Syrian attack. They were obviously not concerned with how things in Israel appeared to the outside world, but rather with the advantages which hard-line posturing might bring them with the electorate at home. Kissinger's main concern was that, if only one of the two prima donna states could be expected to attend, it be Israel. If Israel abstained, he reasoned, his opponents in the U.S. Government, and among all of America's allies as well, would be vindicated in their increasingly open assessment of Israel as simply America's spoiled child.

The result, finally, was a Geneva conference from which Syria abstained. It was convened on December 21, 1973. The first session adjourned three days later, and the conference has never yet reconvened.

In January, 1974, however, Kissinger began the first of his famous shuttles, and brought about an Egyptian-Israeli disengagement the same month. There followed an interval in which the Golda Meir government fell, and Israeli leaders vied with each other to express suspicion of what they depicted as a revival of the "even-handedness" which Governor Scranton had proclaimed at the beginning of the first Nixon term. Cited as evidence was the U.S. Government's participation in international condemnation of Israeli raids on Southern Lebanon, and U.S. efforts to arrange large-scale economic assistance for Egypt.

Most important for Americans, however, was the announcement by Arab oil ministers on March 18 that they were lifting the oil embargo against the U.S. The following month Kissinger began a new shuttle between President Assad of Syria and a Golda

Meir caretaker cabinet. At the end of May, after Kissinger had made 13 visits to Damascus, President Nixon announced the disengagement of Syrian and Israeli forces in the Golan Heights, ending seven months of bloody Israeli-Syrian skirmishing.

This was a period when hopes again began to rise in the Middle East. Although in retrospect it appears that Kissinger was simply reaping the harvest that could have been had for the asking a year earlier, without the bloody October war, it did not appear so at the time.

Americans, who had been watching television scenes of Middle East bloodshed for too long, were ecstatic at the image of their "Super K", defying death threats to shuttle persistently between intransigent Arabs and stubborn Israelis and finally emerge, first with a disengagement between relatively relaxed Egyptian and Israeli forces, and then between the bitter opponents on the Syrian-Israeli front.

Arabs were from the first skeptical about whether Kissinger was interested in the substance or simply the appearance of achieving peace. They repeatedly were assured by well-meaning Americans that, although so far they were only recovering territories the Israelis had no capability of defending in any case, encouraging precedents were being set.

The Israelis, now in such political disarray, had shifted from a heedless reliance on the U.S. Secretary of State to protect their interests – despite their own short-sighted statements and actions – to a growing suspicion that there might be some substance to what the Arabs were being told by Americans: That a Jewish Secretary of State, immune to the charge of "anti-Semitism" which was traditionally leveled at any American official seriously seeking to settle Middle Eastern problems, might be able to focus strong U.S. pressure on Israel when the time for serious negotiations finally came.

Richard Nixon was also watching the growth of the Kissinger legend with some frustration. As his shuttling Secretary of State became the darling of the U.S. media, none of the credit seemed to rub off on the domestically beleaguered U.S. President.

The Middle East, therefore, became the scene of a desperate, last-throw-of-the-dice attempt to rescue the Nixon Presidency via a Nixon tour to the countries that had been involved in the October War. Sadat, by now aware of the realities of U.S. domestic politics, saw a completed second Nixon term as his best hope for a final settlement with Israel. Therefore, since Egypt was Nixon's first stop, Sadat arranged for literally millions of spectators to line the railroad tracks to cheer a truimphal procession by train from Alexandria to Cairo of two Presidents whose countries had not even had diplomatic relations only seven months earlier.

Subsequently, on his visit to Damascus, President Nixon joined President Hafez Al-Assad in restoring the Syrian-U.S. diplomatic relations broken seven years earlier during the 1967 war. Nixon received a similarly warm welcome in Jordan from King Hussein and in Israel a somewhat restrained greeting from Golda Meir.

The extensive U.S. television coverage of Arabs and Israelis cheering him in their streets, however, did not save Nixon from the consequences of Watergate. Within weeks of his return from the Middle East it became known that there was evidence on tape that, even if he had not ordered the actual Watergate break-in, the President was personally involved in the subsequent cover-up. The tapes were subpoenaed by a federal judge, and Nixon resigned. His successor, Gerald Ford, had known Nixon for some 25 years since they were junior members of Congress. In his memoirs Ford provides his own assessment of his predecessor:

"Nixon had a brilliant mind, a great sensitivity to the public's political mood and a unique ability to analyze foreign policy issues and act decisively on them. Big decisions were his strength, and his batting average was excellent. But he abhorred details, and rather enjoyed pushing them off on subordinates. And that, it seemed to me, was one of several reasons he had come to this point of having to resign."[3]

The transition from a Nixon to a Ford Administration, on August 8, 1974, took place during what Washington diplomats later called "Middle East month." Between July 28 and September 10, King Hussein of Jordan and two Prime Ministers and four Foreign Ministers representing Egypt, Israel, Saudi Arabia and Syria trooped into the U.S. capital.

As a Congressman from Grand Rapids, Michigan, Gerald Ford had generally voted a straight pro-Israeli line. As Richard Nixon's second term Vice President, however, Ford had been part of an Administration so deeply involved in Middle East matters that it had actually tried to save itself by exploiting them. Combining the insights gained from the two different roles, Ford sought to keep the change in the White House from slowing the momentum in the Middle East.

His first visit, with newly-elected Prime Minister Yitzhak Rabin, Israel's former Chief of Staff, broke no new ground at all. Ford had known Rabin during Rabin's service as Israeli Ambassador in Washington. Ford considered him then "a dour, very serious man who dressed conservatively and spoke in a soft, almost inaudible voice." Ford now learned Rabin was also "a tough negotiator." In his memoirs, Ford writes:

"Toughness, I was convinced, was not the only ingredient needed to resolve the Middle East impasse. Flexibility – on both sides – was essential as well, and I wasn't sure how flexible Rabin could be."[4]

When Ford made it clear that he hoped the initial disengagement agreements with Egypt and with Syria would be followed by an agreement between Israel and Jordan, Rabin made it equally clear that he had no intention of negotiating with King Hussein. Although the King was the most moderate of all of the leaders of Arab states bordering Israel, the land taken from him was the land Israel was most reluctant to return.

The outlines of a hard-line Israeli policy, which envisioned no withdrawals at all from either Jerusalem or the West Bank, were beginning to show clearly through increasingly intransigent Israeli statements.

Nevertheless, Rabin clearly preferred the continuation of Kissinger-brokered step-by-step negotiations to a return to Geneva for negotiations under United Nations auspices. Kissinger accordingly undertook two lengthy visits to the Middle East in the fall of 1974.

---

3. Ford, Gerald, *A Time to Heal: The Autobiography of Gerald R. Ford*, Harper and Row, New York, 1979, p. 35.
4. *Ibid.*, p. 183.

Meanwhile, events in the Arab World had complicated Kissinger's task. On October 28, 1974, at a meeting of Arab heads of state in Rabat, Morocco, the PLO was designated as the sole legitimate spokesman for the Palestinians. It was a major triumph for Yassir Arafat and a setback for King Hussein, who thus lost his license to negotiate on behalf of the Arabs for return by the Israelis of the West Bank lands taken from him in the 1967 war.

Although Americans were quick to point out that by delaying any meeting with King Hussein the Israelis had lost the chance to reach an agreement with the most moderate of the Arabs concerning the West Bank, the Rabat decision in fact removed a major and growing point of tension between the Ford Administration and Rabin's new government. It lifted from Israel's shoulders the public responsibility for obstructing Kissinger's disengagement time-table. The next blow, from the point of view of those in the U.S. who hoped to keep pressure on Israel for some momentum toward peace, came after PLO Chairman Yassir Arafat was invited to speak before the United Nations General Assembly.

In his speech, Arafat offered either a gun or an olive branch, and described his dream of "one democratic state where Christian, Jew and Muslim live in justice, equality and fraternity." It was pitched to his own sharply-divided constituency, and to Europeans looking for evidence that Arafat's quarrel was not with Jews but with the Jewish State. On both of those counts it was successful. But those in the United States who were looking for some evidence of Arafat's willingness to accept the existence in Palestine of a Jewish state side by side with an Arab state could find in his words no hint of a two-state solution to the Palestinian-Israeli dispute.

Kissinger was meanwhile encouraged to see that President Sadat seemed willing to risk the suspension of Soviet arms shipments to Egypt by encouraging further step-by-step negotiations rather than a resumption of the Geneva conference. As a result, Kissinger launched an "exploratory" trip to the Middle East in February, 1975, extracting a promise from the Shah of Iran to supply oil to Israel in compensation for the oil that it would lose in any further withdrawal in Sinai.

Ford, meanwhile, was giving interviews in the U.S. pointedly focused upon American concern at the lack of interest in Israel in further disengagement. "Every day that passes," Ford told *Time* magazine, "becomes more dangerous." Therefore, he added pointedly, "in the final analysis, we have to judge what is in our national interest above any and all other considerations."

In an NBC interview, Ford said that if the current "step-by-step" approach failed, then the U.S. would have no alternative but to look for an overall settlement via a Geneva conference.

Kissinger returned to the U.S., telling Ford that Sadat was trying to be flexible but that the Israelis were being hard-line and tough in their demands. In March, Kissinger resumed his shuttle between Cairo and Jerusalem and again he reported flexibility from the Egyptians but resistance from the Israelis. Ford describes what followed:

"Finally, agreement was reached on the *framework* for a new accord. Israeli forces would pull back about 35 miles from the eastern bank of the Suez Canal, and the new dividing line between the two adversaries would be in the vicinity of the strategic mountain passes of Gidi and Mitla in the Sinai desert. The Israelis would return the oil fields at Abu Rudeis on the Gulf of Suez, and the Egyptians would be able to use a road that linked those fields to the rest of the country. Even though Sadat and Rabin acknowledged that this was only a first step and that eventually the Israelis would have to give up more of the territory they now occupied, both leaders seemed satisfied in principle with what had been worked out.

"Then the fragile agreement threatened to come apart. Once an agreement had been reached in *principle*, the Israelis insisted that they wouldn't move back past the crests of the two passes. That seemed fair enough, except that they couldn't—nor could anyone else—show us a map and say where those crests were, or precisely where the oil field road lay. As the talks dragged on, Rabin became less flexible. He fought over every kilometer. I wouldn't call it nitpicking—I didn't doubt for a minute that he really wanted peace. I recognized that the Israelis had a fundamental reluctance about giving up any territory in return for what they saw as only promises of good will—but he didn't seem to understand that only by giving do you get something in return.

"The Israelis kept stalling. Their tactics frustrated the Egyptians and made me mad as hell. Both Henry and I had received firm assurances from Rabin that a line could be drawn that would be acceptable to Israel. But Rabin now seemed afraid of his Cabinet's response. He would not— or could not—deliver on commitments he had made."[5]

As a result of Rabin's backsliding, on this one trip Kissinger shuttled eight times to Israel and five times to Egypt, with side visits to Turkey, Syria and Saudi Arabia while Rabin took Kissinger proposals back to his cabinet. Egypt wanted Israel to withdraw from the Sinai oil fields and both mountain passes, and Israel insisted that Egypt issue a statement of non-belligerency in return. Sadat protested that he could not renounce belligerency while Israel still occupied other Egyptian lands. Proposals for lesser withdrawals in exchange for lesser normalization actions foundered. Finally, the shuttle broke down.

"This is a sad day for America, which has invested much hope and faith," Kissinger said as he left Israel, "and it is a sad day also for Israel, which needs and wants peace so badly."

Ford made a point of greeting Kissinger personally when his helicopter touched down on the White House lawn. Ford describes what followed:

"Kissinger returned from the Middle East shuttle on the evening of March 23 . . . deeply disappointed by the Israeli attitude. He was worried that Sadat, who had gone along with many of our suggestions, would never work with us again. He might be driven into the radical Arab camp along with hotheads like Colonel Muammar Qaddafi of Libya, and if that ever happened, it would damage not only Israel's interests, but our own as well.

"Next morning in the Cabinet Room we briefed Congressional leaders of both parties on the results of Kissinger's trip. Asked about the meeting later by reporters, Senator Mansfield said that the Administration had decided to 'reassess' its policies in the Middle East. When (Presidential Press Secretary Ron) Nessen asked me what I thought he should say about that, I told him that he could call Mansfield's remarks 'correct' and that, in an indirect way, he could indicate that we thought the Israelis had been dragging their feet.

"Predictably, our 'reassessment' jolted the American Jewish community and Israel's many friends in Congress. The Israeli lobby, made up of patriotic Americans, is strong, vocal and

5. Ford, Gerald, *A Time to Heal: The Autobiography of Gerald R. Ford*, Harper and Row, New York, 1979, pp. 246-7.

wealthy but many of its members have a single focus. I knew that I would come under intense pressure soon to change our policy, but I was determined to hold firm. On March 27, I met in the Oval Office with Max Fisher, a prominent Detroit businessman who was chairman of the Jewish Agency for Israel. Max was a lifelong Republican and a close friend. He had served as an unofficial ambassador between the United States and Israel for years, and his contacts at the highest levels of both governments had often helped us bridge over misunderstandings. I said I thought it was imperative that we see new momentum toward peace in the Middle East, that my comments about reassessing our policies there weren't just rhetoric. I was not going to capitulate to pressure, and if the impasse continued, I might have to go public on where we stood and why. I didn't have to ask Max to get the message back to the Israelis. Word would spread very quickly that I meant what I said."[6]

Ford did not publicly place the blame for the breakdown on Israel. But, in an effort to move the problem away from the domestic political arena, he talked to a number of Democrats including former Supreme Court Justice Arthur Goldberg, Former Undersecretary of State George Ball, Eugene Rostow and former Senator J. William Fulbright. He also met on several occasions in the White House with various leaders of the American Jewish community.

An official of his Administration described the reassessment of the Administration's policy in the Middle East as "one part an effort to bring about more Israeli negotiating flexibility and three parts a serious look at our objectives and options." The Administration also announced that, although arms in the pipeline for Israel would go forward, the U.S. would be "reluctant" to enter into new arms procurement contracts.

Clearly Ford's purpose was to give Israel time to consider the disadvantage of a decreased arms supply and a probable return to Geneva, where Israel and the U.S. might face all of the Arab countries simultaneously, rather than one by one under Kissinger's auspices. It was a reminder of efforts by both Eisenhower and Truman to substitute the stick when the carrot no longer sufficed in U.S. dealings with Israel.

While arms shipments to Israel were frozen, the battle for U.S. public opinion was heating up rapidly. Israel was stung by news stories from Washington blaming Israeli intransigence for the new Middle East impasse. Over a two-month period, Israel sent nine high-level officials to the U.S. for separate speaking engagements blaming Cairo for the shuttle breakdown.

In return, Egypt sent a parliamentary delegation to the U.S. to tell Egypt's side of the story. In April, 1975, Clovis Maksoud, an editor from Beirut, started a three-month speaking tour of the U.S. under the sponsorship of the Arab League to explain the Palestinian viewpoint, while in May and June Saudi Arabia launched speaking tours of the U.S. by a six-member "truth squad."

Although major American Jewish organizations provided audiences and produced the media for attacks on the Administration by Israeli speakers, officially they refrained from direct criticism of President Ford or Secretary Kissinger. "Generally the leadership of the Jewish community has been trying to act as responsibly as it can under the

---

6. Ford, Gerald, *A Time to Heal: The Autobiography of Gerald R. Ford*, Harper and Row, New York, 1979, pp. 247–8.

circumstances," Bertram Gold, executive vice president of the American Jewish Committee, told *Time* magazine. He continued:

"It has been trying not to make the Administration the enemy. On the other hand, there is an apprehensive feeling that the Administration's reassessment is being used as a form of pressure on Israel. If 1975 turns out to be the year of intense pressure on Israel, there will be a very serious reaction among American Jews. We will go directly to Congress, and 1976 is not that far away."[7]

Local organizations were more outspoken. The New York United Jewish Appeal took advertisements in the *New York Times* and *New York Post* warning: "The price of silence was the Warsaw ghetto, Bergen-Belsen, Auschwitz, Dachau, Buchenwald." An ad hoc group called American Jews Against Ford proclaimed in newspaper advertisements that "American Jewry is called upon to work tirelessly to change the Administration and the kind of thinking that leads to sellouts. . . . Learn what you can do to oust Kissinger and Ford by joining A.J.A.F."

Although he seemed unruffled at the time, Ford in his memoirs speaks frankly of the bitterness the actions by American Jewish supporters of Israel aroused in him.

"What bothered me most," Ford writes," was the claim by some of those leaders that inasmuch as I was suggesting the possibility of a reassessment of our policy toward Israel, I must be anti-Israel or even anti-Semitic. That was just not true and I told those groups . . . it is because of my affection and admiration for the Jewish people and the state of Israel that I'm so concerned about the lack of progress toward peace in that part of the world. We *must* have progress soon if we are to avoid another war, the fifth in 30 years. Quite frankly, Israel's leaders have not been as quick to recognize this as I had hoped they would be. They have not been as forthcoming as I wanted them to be. Now, I have always believed in maintaining the national integrity of Israel, but always within the context of maintaining world peace and — above everything else — within the context of protecting the national interests of the United States. What this means is that the leaders of Israel and the American Jewish community here simply can't hold up a legitimate settlement and expect me as President to tolerate it."[7]

Ford is also caustic about the pressure put on Kissinger by Israel's supporters:

"For the past several weeks, the Israelis had been engaged in a not very subtle campaign to discredit Kissinger. He had been their hero after the 1973 war; now, all of a sudden, he was their adversary. Because Henry was a Jew, the Israeli hard-liners said, he was bending over backward to be 'fair' to the Arabs. He was 'out-Gentiling the Gentiles': he was 'sabotaging' Israel's interests. The charges were utterly false, of course. No one had worked harder to achieve a just and lasting peace in the Middle East than Henry Kissinger, and to see him attacked that way was reprehensible."[8]

However, the most significant event of the propaganda battle occurred in May, 1975. It followed a visit to Washington by King Hussein and preceded a trip by President Ford to Geneva for a meeting with President Sadat and a trip to Washington by

---

7. Ford, Gerald, *A Time to Heal: The Autobiography of Gerald R. Ford*, Harper and Row, New York, 1979, p. 286.
8. *Ibid.*, p. 287.

Prime Minister Rabin. Right at that point, 76 U.S. Senators signed a letter to President Ford urging him not to let the military balance shift against Israel, "to be responsive to Israel's urgent military and economic needs," and to seek a settlement "on the basis of secure and recognized boundaries that are defensible."

The letter, signed by three-fourths of the members of the Senate, effectively cut the ground out from under the President at the worst possible moment for U.S. diplomacy. On the one hand, he was engaged in a battle of wills with Israel. And on the other, he was trying to persuade Arab leaders that he could deliver meaningful Israeli concessions in exchange for meaningful concessions of their own.

In retrospect, it may have been the high water mark for the pro-Israel lobby in the United States. Some of the Senators who had signed the letter told journalists privately that they had been pressured to vote against their own best judgment, and expressed admiration for the few Senators who had resisted. Others were indignant at charges that, with one stroke of the pen, they had cracked, if not completely shattered, a carefully orchestrated Middle East peace initiative that had concerned much of the U.S. foreign policy establishment for most of the first year of the Ford Administration.

Ford is considerably more outspoken in his out-of-office comments than he was at the time:

"Although I said publicly that I welcomed the letter as an expression of Senate sentiment, in truth it really bugged me. The Senators claimed the letter was 'spontaneous,' but there was no doubt in my mind that it was inspired by Israel. We had given vast amounts of military and economic assistance to Israel over the years, and we had never asked for anything in return.

"Quite apart from that, the letter—especially its tone—jeopardized any chance for peace in the Middle East. For the past several weeks, Kissinger and I had been urging the Israelis to come up with new ideas for a just settlement of the Sinai dispute, ideas that I could present to Sadat when I met him in June. At that meeting I planned to make the same request of the Egyptian president. Once I had *his* ideas, I could relay them to Rabin and we could get the negotiations back on track again. Because of the letter, however, the Israelis didn't want to budge. So confident were they that those 76 Senators would support them no matter what they did, they refused to suggest any new ideas for peace. 'Concessions will have to be made,' they were saying in effect, 'but we will make none of them. Sadat will have to make them all. And if Ford disagrees, we will show him who's boss.' I thought they were overplaying their hand. For me that kind of pressure has always been counterproductive. I was not going to capitulate to it."[9]

On June 1, 1975, in Salzburg, Ford and Sadat met personally for the first time. Sadat was frank with Ford, explaining that his ejection of the Soviet military presence had cut off his supplies of arms and spare parts. His generals now were telling him that without such supplies the military couldn't defend the country. Further, his economy was in even more desperate shape. He needed peace, and he asked Ford what ideas he had brought with him.

Ford said he had brought none, because the Israelis had said they had none to give. As Ford recounts the conversation:

---

9. Ford, Gerald, *A Time to Heal: The Autobiography of Gerald R. Ford*, Harper and Row, New York, 1979, pp. 287-8.

"Sadat's expression didn't change. He puffed on his pipe and was silent for a while. Then he looked me in the eye. 'All right,' he said, 'We are willing to go as far as you think we should go. We trust you, and we trust the United States.' "[10]

Sadat proposed that a buffer zone be created around the disputed Gidi and Mitla passes. It would be patrolled by non-military American personnel who would warn either side of an impending attack. Ford liked the idea, but knew "that if the Israelis had discovered that the proposal to station civilian technicians in a Sinai buffer zone had come originally from Sadat, they might have rejected it out of hand."[11]

On June 2, 1975 prior to Rabin's visit to Washington, Israel announced it was thinning its forces in the vicinity of the Suez Canal. On June 5, the eighth anniversary of the war that had closed it, Egypt reopened the Suez Canal.

It was an auspicious prelude to the Rabin visit during which Ford planned to offer the plan to station Americans in Sinai without mentioning that it already had Egypt's blessing. Ford writes:

"Fortunately the press didn't ferret out the news, and on June 11 Israeli Prime Minister Rabin arrived in Washington. For the first time since the collapse of the Kissinger mission in March, I sensed that we were about to make progress. Clearly, Rabin had been shaken by our decision to 'reassess' our policies in the Middle East. Instead of arguing over which country was to blame for the breakdown of the talks in March, he wanted to move forward. He asked if I had any ideas as to how peace could be achieved. I replied that 'one suggestion we have been considering' involved stationing civilian technicians in a Sinai buffer zone. We'd have to get the Egyptians to agree, I said, and we'd also have to gain the backing of the Congress. Still, it was an idea that might break the current impasse. Rabin seemed intrigued. He said he'd take the idea back to Israel and let me know his government's response."[12]

While Rabin considered the plan, the Ford Administration kept the pressure on Israel. Ford's meeting with Rabin was described by U.S. press spokesmen as cool and reserved. Later that month, after an Israeli version of the latest negotiating position had leaked to the *New York Times*, the State Department branded the accompanying maps "inaccurate and highly misleading" and denounced "competitive leaks of confidential diplomatic exchanges."

On June 27, President Ford and Secretary Kissinger met with Israeli Ambassador Dinitz to present what the Israeli press called an "ultimatum" that Israel reconsider its negotiating position. On July 5, Kissinger suggested in an interview on ABC that the degree of U.S. support for Israel would be linked to Israel's response to Egypt's negotiating position. Egypt added to the pressure by announcing that it would not extend the mandate of the UN Expeditionary Force separating its troops from Israel's beyond July 24, 1975 in the absence of progress toward agreement.

---

10. Ford, Gerald, *A Time to Heal: The Autobiography of Gerald R. Ford*, Harper and Row, New York, 1979, p. 290.
11. *Ibid.*, p. 291.
12. *Ibid.*, pp. 291-2.

Under the growing pressure, contacts were intensifying. On August 21, Kissinger resumed a shuttle which, despite hostile demonstrations in Israel, took him seven times each to Egypt and Israel, with side trips to Syria, Saudi Arabia, and Jordan.

The hard bargaining which accompanied each visit to Israel has been subsequently described by Ford:

"The Israelis wanted to address each occupied area separately, and even before they would discuss a new Sinai pact, they demanded two concessions from us. The first was a written promise – a memorandum of understanding – that before the U.S. moved in any direction affecting the future of the region, we would notify them. I had no problem agreeing to that. The second concession was more troublesome. The Israelis were always insisting that we supply them more military equipment than our own experts thought they needed and far more than I thought we could afford. Initially, we had agreed to provide them $1.5 billion worth of arms. They would have to pay us back half that amount; the rest would be a loan with an understood forgiveness feature. The Israelis, however, wanted more. Their shopping list included sophisticated weaponry that even our own forces hadn't received yet. Pentagon officials urged me to refuse this new request. Israel, they pointed out, already had the third-largest air force in the world. She could destroy all her neighbors. It was a tough call. Nothing was more important to the Israelis than their own military security. If we provided the hardware, we could convince the Israelis that they were secure. Then they might be willing to accept some risks in the search for peace. In the end, I decided to approve a larger initial increment than the Pentagon recommended." [13]

Whether it was the earlier stick, the present carrot, or that Sadat's idea was simply too sensible to ignore, this time an agreement was reached. The "Sinai II" agreement was initialed on the same day, September 1, 1975, in both Alexandria and Jerusalem. Kissinger was present for both ceremonies, dramatizing the proximity of the two cities. On September 4 it was signed in Geneva by representatives of both Egypt and Israel.

It is axiomatic that U.S. initiatives on the Middle East grind to a halt in an election year. If an incumbent President undertakes anything more than courtesy-level communication with Arab countries, his opponent may depict him as selling out Israel. Compliments from Arab countries can be especially damaging at such a time, and most Arab leaders are aware of this. For Israel, U.S. election years are opportunities to carry out with minimum risk actions that in other years might seriously jeopardize Israel's relations with the United States.

Election years also bring Israel unsolicited commitments from American candidates. Israeli leaders have learned to garner these side benefits by making low-key, courteous comments about the incumbent administration. They refrain from heavy-handed statements that could be interpreted as overt interference in U.S. domestic affairs, or could discourage competing candidates from pursuing Jewish votes through ardent promises of support to Israel.

The 1976 national election campaign followed the script. However, Egypt's preference for the Ford Administration was obvious. Israel's distrust of both the Ford-Kissinger team, based on recent experience, and the born-again-Christian candidate, Jimmy Carter, based on uncertainty, was also obvious. As in past elections, American

---

13. Ford, Gerald, *A Time to Heal: The Autobiography of Gerald R. Ford*, Harper and Row, New York, 1979, pp. 308-9.

Jews contributed generously to both candidates but most tended to vote the Democratic ticket. Their support in key states certainly was an important element in the close Carter victory.

Meanwhile, in the Middle East, all initiatives toward a peaceful solution had been halted by the civil war in Lebanon. The traditional division of power there, which slightly favored the Christians over the Muslims, had become increasingly unstable as more Muslims than Christians were born, and as more Christians than Muslims emigrated from the country.

The dominant Maronite Christian community was becoming increasingly intransigent about any re-division of power, saying it would rather control a smaller, all-Christian Lebanon than divide power equally in a Christian-Muslim federation. It is likely that some of this intransigence was fed by secret contacts with Israel pursued first by the Maronite former President, Camille Chamoun, and later by Bashir Gemayel, younger son of a Maronite rival to Chamoun, Pierre Gemayel.

Israeli encouragement of a separatist Maronite state in Lebanon had first been advocated by David Ben Gurion and Moshe Dayan in the 1950s. It is not clear when the Maronite-Israeli relationship changed from flirtation to conspiracy. Palestinian and Sunni Muslim leaders began exhibiting U.S.-made arms that they claimed to be finding in mysterious caches along the Lebanese coast from the early 1970s, and both Chamoun's "Tiger" militia and Gemayel's Falange Party militia were well-armed with expensive, American-manufactured weapons by 1976. Starting in that year the visits to Maronite-controlled areas of Lebanon by Israeli military leaders and advisers were open and documented.

From 1969 on the presence in Lebanon of some 400,000 Palestinian refugees, many of them trained and heavily armed, had been sufficient justification to the Maronites for their own mobilization. It obviously also tempted leaders of the Sunni Muslim and Druze communities. They sought to use the threat of Palestinian arms and fighters to back up their own demands for redistribution of power. The Lebanese civil war, therefore, was a direct result of the Palestine problem. The clandestine Israeli arms shipments to the Maronite militias, and the all-too-overt presence of the Palestinians as an increasingly permanent and possibly threatening presence on Lebanese soil, provided the two catalysts for open resumption in 1975 of a Christian-Muslim Lebanese power struggle that had first flared into widespread fighting in 1860 and then again in 1958.

In 1975, however, unlike in 1958, what started as a series of battles between conservative Lebanese Maronite militias and leftist Palestinian armed groups gradually became full-fledged, merciless warfare. It pitted a loose and shifting alliance of Christians and a very few conservative, mostly Shia, Muslims against an equally unstable alliance of Palestinians, Muslims, Druze and "Progressive" leftist party contingents of mixed Muslim and Christian membership.

Virtually every major country in the Middle East, even non-Arab Iran, backed one or more of the contending militias with money, arms, and even manpower. U.S. Middle Eastern diplomacy was, therefore, fully occupied with attempts to halt the fighting in Lebanon. Because of its duration and the fact that it ranged from one of the biggest cities in the Middle East to tiny mountain villages, this fighting was far more costly in human lives than any of the earlier fierce but brief Arab-Israeli encounters. The country-wide phase of the Lebanese civil war finally was frozen in late 1976 when the Syrian regular army entered Lebanon, pushed aside advancing Palestinian forces, and took over policing the divided country. By that time all progress toward settling the basic Arab-Israeli dispute, in the U.S., the United Nations, and the Middle East itself, had come to a halt.

UNRWA

UNRWA

The first waves of Palestinian refugees in 1948 had lived in tent camps for many months before more permanent shelters could be built. After the Arab debacle of 1967, a new influx of 80,000 refugees from the West Bank and Gaza flooded into camps in Jordan, Syria and Lebanon, where thousands found themselves once again living in tents like these at the huge Nahr al Barid camp in Northern Lebanon.

CHAPTER XVII

President Carter and a Christian Approach

"After meeting with these key Arab leaders, I was convinced that all of them were ready for a strong move on our part to find solutions to the long-standing disputes and that with such solutions would come their recognition of Israel and the right of Israelis to live in peace. I agreed with their most important premise — that the Palestinian question would have to be addressed. But I was quite concerned that Israel, with its choice of a new prime minister, would not respond favorably to the peace effort I was contemplating."[1]

Jimmy Carter, 1982

In the Carter and Vance years there was no major conspiracy against us. Vance was really a good man and he tried very much to help us. Perhaps we didn't help him enough . . . I'm not sure."[2]

Yassir Arafat, 1984

"The Clinton pronouncement indicated that an American administration had finally focused on the core of the Middle East problem and had begun to approach it clearly and publicly, in a manner consistent with the concept of openness which Mr. Carter promised during his campaign. . . . The President of the United States called for an idea which, after all, is based on the same United Nations resolution which established a state for the Israelis."[3]

Sabah Kabbani, Syrian Ambassador to the U.S., March 17, 1978

---

1. Carter, Jimmy, *Keeping Faith: Memoirs of a President*, Bantam Books, New York, 1982, pp. 287-8.
2. Hart, Alan, *Arafat: Terrorist or Peacemaker?*, Sidgwick & Jackson, London, 1984, p. 450.
3. Kabbani, Ambassador Sabah, "Carter, the Palestinians and Israel," *New York Times*, March 17, 1978.

"There was an easy and natural friendship between us from the first moment I knew Anwar Sadat. We trusted each other. Each of us began to learn about the other's family members, hometown, earlier life and private plans and ambitions, as though we were tying ourselves together for a lifetime. Rosalynn and Sadat's wife, Jihan, sensed this special relationship and joined it easily. The news reporters often referred with some amusement to my claims of friendship with other people, but when I called President Anwar Sadat 'my close, personal friend,' both he and I—and perhaps even they— knew it to be true."[4]

Jimmy Carter, 1982

Jimmy Carter's victory resulted from a widespread perception by Americans that the U.S. establishment, and its institutions, had failed them. The U.S. had withdrawn in disarray from a war in Vietnam which half of the American people thought it should never have begun and the other half thought it should have finished. The Watergate scandal only strengthened the widespread revulsion against Washington "insiders" who seemed to be running the country into the ground. The result was Jimmy Carter, a small-town Georgian who had graduated from Annapolis and later became governor of Georgia, but whose experience on the national scene had ended when he resigned his Navy commission.

Carter had obvious strengths. He was extremely intelligent. He did not shrink from details. Instead, he relied upon his ability to concentrate on any complicated question, absorb the fine print, and make up his own mind about it. That was a tremendous strength for him when he was an engineering officer on a nuclear submarine, a small businessman, and governor of Georgia. But the White House was something else. A President who is his own Secretary of Defense and Secretary of State can get wonders done while he is concentrating on a problem. But when he is hit by hundreds of problems at once, he has to delegate most of them to his cabinet members. If they haven't really been in charge of the policy through its formative period, they may not be qualified when they are suddenly called upon to take over.

Fortunately, however, the Middle East was high on Carter's agenda from his first days in office. His campaigning on the subject had seemed to Ford supporters to be shameless pandering to Jewish contributors and voters. He got the "Jewish vote," although most thoughtful Jews were uncomfortable with a "born again Christian" who made no effort to soft-pedal his fundamentalist views.

Once Carter was ensconced in the White House, he made no secret of his determination to define and cut whatever Gordian knots were blocking real progress toward Middle Eastern peace. In 1973, when he was still governor of Georgia, Carter, his wife Rosalynn, and his press secretary, Jody Powell, had visited Israel. Spurred by a profound interest in the Bible, they had spent an intensive week traveling with an Israeli government vehicle, driver and guide through "the surprisingly tiny country on a route which we had been permitted to choose ourselves."[5]

---

4. Carter, Jimmy, *Keeping Faith: Memoirs of a President*, Bantam Books, New York, 1982, p. 284.
5. *Ibid.*, p. 273.

The result was exactly what governments seek to accomplish through such relatively unprogrammed tours, whether they are funded by the United States, its communist rivals, or skilled public relations experts in Israel. In his memoirs of four years in the White House, Carter describes his convictions on the Middle East at the time he assumed the Presidency. Although a mixture of fact and misinformation, they reflect the views of many Americans of the time, based partly upon deep religious conviction and partly upon systematic American media presentation of Israel in its best light, and the Arabs in their worst.

"In my affinity for Israel, I shared the sentiment of most other Southern Baptists that the holy places were revered and should be preserved and made available for visits by Christians, and that members of other religious faiths should have the same guaranteed privileges concerning their sacred sites. I remembered that prior to the 1967 war there were no such assurances; under Jordanian rule, the areas were often closed, and some of the sacred burial sites and other holy places were vandalized.

"The Judeo-Christian ethic and study of the Bible were bonds between Jews and Christians which had always been part of my life. I also believed very deeply that the Jews who had survived the holocaust deserved their own nation, and that they had a right to live in peace among their neighbors. I considered this homeland for the Jews to be compatible with the teachings of the Bible, hence ordained by God. These moral and religious beliefs made my commitment to the security of Israel unshakable.

"Another significant factor in my thinking was that both the United States and Israel are democracies. Israel's relatively small size and the number of her adversaries aroused in me a sense of responsibility to keep the Israelis able to defend themselves. Most Arabs had never accepted the 1947 vote of the UN General Assembly to partition the British Mandate of Palestine into a Jewish and an Arab state—but despite four wars the Israelis survived. I admired their courage, and was thankful for their success in establishing and sustaining their country."[6]

Carter was a highly intelligent man who eventually came to realize that there was more to the Middle East than just Israel. Therefore, of his prior convictions he writes:

"These were thoughts I shared with many other Americans, but now I had been elected President and needed a broader perspective. For the well-being of my own country, I wanted the Middle East region stable and at peace; I did not want to see Soviet influence expanded in the area. In its ability to help accomplish these purposes, Israel was a strategic asset to the United States. I had no strong feelings about the Arab countries. I had never visited one and knew no Arab leaders."[7]

Carter, therefore, threw himself into a cram course on the entire Middle East, and particularly the Arab-Israeli problem, almost from his first day in the White House. As he had already said while campaigning, he believed that the Kissinger step-by-step approach had run its course. He wanted to test the prospects for a comprehensive settlement. He took as a guide a report entitled "Toward Peace in the Middle East" issued by a group convened at the Brookings Institution in late 1975. The group had included

---

6. Carter, Jimmy, *Keeping Faith: Memoirs of a President*, Bantam Books, New York, 1982, p. 274.
7. *Ibid.*, p. 275.

Zbigniew Brzezinski, whom Carter made his White House National Security Adviser, and William Quandt, who became the National Security Council Middle East specialist. One month after he took office, Carter sent his new Secretary of State, Cyrus Vance, to the Middle East to sound out opinions and issue a series of invitations to leaders of the five Middle East countries most deeply involved in the Arab-Israeli problem.

Jimmy Carter wrote in his personal diary on March 7, 1977, the day he met with the first of his Middle Eastern visitors:

"Prime Minister Rabin came over from Israel. I've put in an awful lot of time studying the Middle East question and was hoping that Rabin would give me some outline of what Israel ultimately hopes to see achieved in a permanent peace settlement. I found him very timid, very stubborn, and also somewhat ill at ease. At the working supper Speaker Tip O'Neill asked him, for instance, under what circumstances he would permit the Palestinians to be represented at the Geneva talks, and he was adamantly opposed to any meeting if the PLO or other representatives of the Palestinians were there. When he went upstairs with me, just the two of us, I asked him to tell me what Israel wanted me to do when I met with the Arab leaders and if there were something specific, for instance, that I could propose to Sadat. He didn't unbend at all, nor did he respond. It seems to me that the Israelis, at least Rabin, don't trust our government or any of their neighbors. I guess there's some justification for this distrust. I've never met any of the Arab leaders but am looking forward to seeing if they are more flexible than Rabin."[8]

Carter later wrote in his memoirs that he "found this first meeting a particularly unpleasant surprise. I had thought that among the Israeli leaders he would be the one most committed to exploring new ideas and discussing the prospects for progress with me. His strange reticence caused me to think again about whether we should launch another major effort for peace."[9]

Nevertheless, with the Middle East very much on his mind, Carter's statements on the subject during speeches and press conferences seemed to be letting fresh air into U.S. policy, which had been a closed room since the 1976 election campaign had started gearing up, and the Kissinger shuttles had wound down.

Carter proposed two separate boundaries for Israel, an inner one based upon actual national sovereignty, and an outer one forming a defense perimeter patrolled by Israeli or international forces to guard against the possibility of suprise attack. The land between the two borders would be governed as a demilitarized zone. Carter also advocated Israel's ultimate withdrawal to the 1967 borders, with minor adjustments for security purposes, termination of belligerence, recognition of the rights of all countries to exist in peace, and freedom of trade, travel and cultural exchanges.

Carter had come to Washington as a no-frills populist and he cultivated that image. He liked to carry his own suitcases. On his inauguration day, with his family, he had climbed out of his limousine to walk back from the ceremony along Washington's Pennsylvania Avenue toward the White House. Therefore he recorded with obvious amusement in his diary a March 17 visit to the UN:

8. Carter, Jimmy, *Keeping Faith: Memoirs of a President*, Bantam Books, New York, 1982, p. 280.
9. *Ibid.*, p. 280.

"There was quite a flap about whether or not I would stand in the receiving line and meet the representative of the PLO, who are not recognized by us. When I got there I . . . went ahead and shook hands with everybody who came in, including the PLO representative, who was very embarrassed. It didn't hurt anybody." [10]

The pronouncement that caught the attention of Arab leaders, however, was also made in March, 1977, at Clinton Massachusetts. There President Carter declared that the Palestinians were entitled to a homeland, and that Israel eventually must return captured Arab territory. The Israelis were alarmed, and they expressed it through a series of visits by highly-placed Jewish Americans to both the White House and the State Department.

The hostile reaction by American Jews did not dampen the new President's determination to address Middle East problems seriously, and he has vividly recorded the hope aroused by his next Middle Eastern visitor in Washington.

"Then, on April 4, 1977, a shining light burst on the Middle East scene for me. I had my first meetings with President Anwar Sadat of Egypt, a man who would change history and whom I would come to admire more than any other leader. . . . When I asked him about Israel's withdrawal from occupied territories, he responded that 'some minimal deviation from the 1967 borders might be acceptable,' . . . an important concession and, so far as I knew, unprecedented for an Arab leader. We had a long discussion about Jerusalem – the most sensitive issue of all – and he agreed that the city should never be divided again . . . But he insisted that Arabs must have control over the area encompassing their own holy places, and that worshipers of all faiths needed free access to their shrines, without first having to obtain Israeli permission . . . We were in a good mood, and argued without restraint, even on the most delicate points. It was obvious that he was tired of war . . . I pushed him hard on the open borders and diplomatic recognition points, reminding him again that he and I might not be in office long and could not leave this kind of progress to others. He reminded me of the great political pressures in the United States on me and Congress, and I tried to convince him that I was willing to face any necessary political risks to reach a peace settlement. He finally said, 'It may be possible to have a clause at the end of an agreement saying that, if things go well, diplomatic recognition of Israel would come after five more years.' All this was much more than I had hoped to get. After Sadat left, I told Rosalynn that this had been my best day as President." [11]

The next Arab visitor was a long-term friend of the United States. King Hussein of Jordan had devoted a lifetime to displaying the moderate face of the Arabs to Americans. Although he had little to show for it other than the longest term in power of any leader in the Eastern Arab countries, he hadn't lost the knack. He was experienced in helping newly-elected American Presidents unlearn most of what they thought they already knew about the Middle East, and thereby preparing them to begin dealing realistically with its problems. Carter's diary recorded:

"We all really liked him, enjoyed his visit, and believe he'll be a strong and staunch ally for us as we approach the time for a Mideast conference later on this year . . . He said that for

---

10. Carter, Jimmy, *Keeping Faith: Memoirs of a President*, Bantam Books, New York, 1982, p. 281.
11. *Ibid.*, pp. 282-4.

the first time in 25 or 30 years he felt hopeful that this year we could reach some agreements. I feel the same way."[12]

Subsequently, in his memoirs, Carter deals both more substantively and more emotionally with his first encounter with the Jordanian monarch, propelled by tragedy (assassination of his grandfather, mental illness of his father) directly from childhood to kingship.

"Hussein accepted the principles of my public proposals for resolving the Middle East disputes, but emphasized that the basic rights of the Palestinians would have to be honored. He described the freedom of movement that was now routinely permitted between Jordan and the West Bank, but in deference to the Palestinians, he did not seem to be pressing any claims of Jordanian sovereignty over the territory being occupied by Israel . . . Late that night, Hussein, Rosalynn, and I sat on the Truman balcony, watching the planes land and take off from National Airport, and talked about both diplomatic affairs and personal matters. He was still emotionally drained by the recent death of his beautiful young wife in a helicopter accident. When he started telling Rosalynn how much he had appreciated my handwritten note, he started to weep, and our hearts went out to him . . ."[13]

Meanwhile, in the Middle East, an incident during the Rabin visit to Washington had suddenly brought down his government. The issue had nothing to do with Carter's obvious rapport with Egypt's President and Jordan's King, and the lack of it with Israel's Prime Minister. Instead, typically for Israel where U.S. support is taken for granted or considered to be the responsibility of the U.S. Jewish community rather than Israel's leaders, the issue that caused Rabin's downfall was a purely domestic one. Reporters accompanying Mrs. Rabin during her visit with her husband to the U.S. had noted that she visited a U.S. bank. This led to the revelation that ever since their diplomatic tour in Washington, the Rabins had kept a personal U.S. bank account. Personal bank accounts outside Israel, although common among Israelis, are illegal under Israeli law. The incident brought to the fore Israeli domestic resentment against what was increasingly perceived as a privileged and somewhat corrupt class of European-descended Jews, whose connections outside Israel alleviated some of the severe economic problems suffered by the so-called Oriental Jews. The latter had been for the most part unenthusiastic immigrants to Israel, uprooted from their ancient communities all over the former Ottoman Turkish Empire by Arab and Muslim resentment engendered by the establishment of Israel in 1947 and 1948. They had left middle class or better status in such far-flung countries as Morocco, Yemen, Iraq and even India to begin a new existence as part of a permanent underclass in the Jewish state.

The May, 1977 elections that followed Rabin's resignation brought to power for the first time Menachem Begin, the leader of the underground terrorist organization Irgun Zvai Leumi during the British Mandate, who had spent the 29 years since Israel's creation in unyielding opposition to any signs of territorial compromise by successive Labor Coalition governments. He was the direct political heir to the Revisionist Vladimir Jabotinsky, who stood for an Israel that included not only all of Palestine but also the

---

12. Carter, Jimmy, *Keeping Faith: Memoirs of a President*, Bantam Books, New York, 1982, p. 285.
13. *Ibid.*, p. 285.

lands east of the Jordan River comprising present-day Jordan. Withdrawal from the West Bank or Jerusalem would be, for Begin, a denial of his entire life's work.

The general disaffection among Israel's under-educated, under-employed and under-esteemed Oriental Jews was the immediate cause of the first Labor Coalition defeat in Israel's history. An important contributing factor, however, was the defection from the Labor Coalition of a new group, the Democratic Movement for Change, led by an archeologist and military hero, Yigael Yadin. It had campaigned against alleged Labor Coalition corruption and economic mismanagement but also against the hawkish views of the new Labor Coalition leader, Shimon Peres. Peres was perceived as wanting to hold the West Bank on security rather than religious grounds. Intelligent and articulate Israelis of the Democratic Movement for Change believed that a return of the West Bank to Arab control was essential if Israel was ever to enjoy peace, and if it was to remain a Jewish State rather than a state in which Jews dominated by brute force an eventual majority population of Arabs.

Leaders of major American Jewish organizations greeted the Begin victory with perceptible apprehension. They knew that his vociferous support of West Bank settlements for religious rather than security reasons would be hard to explain to an American public anxious for peace in the Middle East. Members of the American Jewish community flooded the White House with telegrams, however. Their message was that the new Prime Minister deserved a chance not only to speak for himself in Washington, but also to negotiate directly with the Arabs rather than be confronted with an imposed American solution.

Meanwhile Jimmy Carter was still meeting Middle Eastern leaders. Next was President Hafez Al-Assad of Syria, who was not interested in coming to Washington. It was arranged that, after attending a London economic summit, Carter would meet the Syrian President in Switzerland. In London, even before the meeting, however, Carter received a new insight at a private breakfast with President Valery Giscard d'Estaing of France. It was perhaps his first intimation of how deeply most of the leaders of Western Europe resent what they see as a U.S. tendency to treat the Arab-Israeli problem as primarily a matter of U.S. domestic politics. For Europeans, dependent upon unimpeded access to Middle Eastern oil and markets, it is literally a matter of economic survival.

Carter found the French President "a brilliant and strong man, very confident of himself, somewhat autocratic in demeanor, but personable and cordial toward me." Giscard d'Estaing, however, "did not waste words, and had a clear and analytical approach to the many issues we covered. We agreed on most of them, but I was troubled by his extremely antagonistic attitude toward Israel. He seemed quite convinced that the Israelis were international outlaws and that all the Arab positions were proper."[14]

Soon afterward Carter met for three and a half hours with President Assad. The U.S. President's diary entry for May 9, 1977 recorded:

"It was a very interesting and enjoyable experience. There was a lot of good humor between us, and I found him to be very constructive in his attitude and somewhat flexible in dealing with some of the more crucial items involving peace, the Palestinians, the refugee problem, and borders.

---

14. Carter, Jimmy, *Keeping Faith: Memoirs of a President*, Bantam Books, New York, 1982, p. 286.

He said that a year or two ago it would have been suicidal in his country to talk about peace with the Israelis, but they've come a long way and were willing to cooperate."[15]

In his memoirs, however, Carter notes wryly that "this was the man who would soon sabotage the Geneva peace talks by refusing to attend under any reasonable circumstances, and who would, still later, do everything possible to prevent the Camp David accords from being fulfilled!" Carter continues:

" The more I dealt with Arab leaders, the more disparity I discovered between their private assurances and their public comments. They would privately put forward ideas for peace and encourage us in any reasonable approach. However, the peer pressure among them was tremendous. None of them – apart from Sadat – was willing to get out in front and publicly admit a willingness to deal with Israel . . . There was also a private-public disparity, though of a different nature, among the leaders of the many organized groups in the American Jewish community. In our private conversations they were often supportive and, like the Arab leaders, urged us to explore every avenue that might lead to peace. They would deplore Israeli excesses, travel to Jerusalem to seek out moderate leaders who shared the same goals, and give generously of their time and money to any peaceful or benevolent cause. But in a public showdown on a controversial issue, they would almost always side with the Israeli leaders and condemn us for being 'evenhanded' in our concern about both Palestinian rights and Israeli security. I presumed that with all the other condemnations of Israel in the United Nations and from many individual countries, American Jews, even feeling critical, did not want to make their criticisms public."[16]

Because of Carter's sensitivity to the U.S. Jewish community's tendency to side publicly with Israel against him, even when individual Jews privately seemed to understand his desire to bring about a Middle East peace agreement, he increasingly used Vice President Walter Mondale as the Administration's contact with both Israel and the American Jewish community. Mondale had a long record of pro-Israeli statements and votes in Congress. When Mondale made what was supposed to be a conciliatory speech in San Francisco, however, Israel's American partisans seemed only to note that he reiterated Administration support for a Palestinian homeland and Israeli territorial withdrawals. Mondale also publicly expressed a new Administration confidence that the current leadership of the moderate Arab countries sincerely wanted peace.

This was demonstrated clearly when Crown Prince Fahd of Saudi Arabia arrived in Washington May 24, 1977, to discuss the Palestine problem. His extensive duties in assisting his ailing brother, King Khaled, included overseeing foreign affairs. The Kingdom of Saudi Arabia, in addition to its role as guardian of Mecca and Medina, places of pilgrimage sacred to some 800 million Muslims scattered all over the globe, was a major source of funding for Egypt, Syria, Jordan and the PLO, and thus in a crucial position to help or hurt peace initiatives among the confrontation states. Carter was clearly astonished and pleased by his encounter with this future King of Saudi Arabia and the other members of the Saudi Royal Family who accompanied him to Washington. He wrote:

15. Carter, Jimmy, *Keeping Faith: Memoirs of a President*, Bantam Books, New York, 1982, p. 286.
16. *Ibid.*, pp. 286-7.

"They were very frank and spoke freely about the intractable issues in the Middle East. Because the Saudis looked on atheism and communism with abhorrence, they despised and distrusted the Soviet Union. They considered the United States to be among their reliable friends. Above all, they were interested in the Palestinian question more than in any other.

"After a working supper with about 20 members of Congress as guests, Fahd and I went upstairs for a half-hour talk about the Palestinians. I reminded him that we were bound by a commitment not to recognize the PLO nor to negotiate with its leaders unless they would accept United Nations Resolution 242 and acknowledge Israel's right to exist; only then would the PLO be able to participate in the on-going peace process. Fahd agreed to help in every way he could with this problem.

"After meeting with these key Arab leaders, I was convinced that all of them were ready for a strong move on our part to find solutions to the long-standing disputes and that with such solutions would come their recognition of Israel and the right of Israelis to live in peace. I agreed with their most important premise – that the Palestinian question would have to be addressed. But I was quite concerned that Israel, with its choice of a new prime minister, would not respond favorably to the peace effort I was contemplating." [17]

Carter began preparations to meet with the newly-elected Menachem Begin. He writes:

"I had them replay the 'Issues and Answers' interview with Menachem Begin, chairman of the Likud party and the prospective Prime Minister of Israel. It was frightening to watch his adamant position on issues that must be resolved if a Middle Eastern peace settlement is going to be realized.

"In his first answer he stated that the entire West Bank was an integral part of Israel's sovereignty, that it had been 'liberated' during the Six Day War, and that a Jewish majority and an Arab minority would be established there. This statement was a radical departure from past Israeli policy, and seemed to throw United Nations Resolution 242, for which Israel had voted, out the window. I could not believe what I was hearing. He went on to say that there were absolutely no circumstances under which any Israelis would consider participation by members of the PLO in a Geneva conference, even as members of the Jordanian delegation. Other answers of this tenor made it clear that if he maintained these positions, there was no prospect of further progress in the Middle East." [18]

Carter set out to blunt what he was slowly coming to realize was a campaign among American Jews, orchestrated by the new government in Israel, to deflect his peace initiative even before his meeting with Israel's new leader. Carter writes:

"During this time, I was increasingly concerned about criticism of our peace initiatives from within the American Jewish community. My own political supporters were coming to see me. Groups were meeting with Cy Vance, and stirrings within Congress were becoming more pronounced. They were already nervous about the Begin election and the replacement of the well-known leaders of the Israeli Labor Party, which had governed Israel for so many years. Additionally, they were troubled about some of our proposals concerning the Palestinian issue and

---

17. Carter, Jimmy, *Keeping Faith: Memoirs of a President*, Bantam Books, New York, 1982, pp. 287-8.
18. *Ibid.*, p. 288.

'dual borders,' and my highly publicized and apparently friendly series of meetings with Arab leaders."[19]

Carter turned to Senator Hubert Humphrey, one of Israel's best friends in Congress, for support and Humphrey provided it both publicly and by bringing more Congressional leaders into the White House for meetings on the Middle East. "I made good progress with all except Senator Javits," Carter recalls, "who informed me in the Oval Office that he would make a critical speech about my policy on the Middle East. At least he was kind enough to send me a copy of the text just before he issued it to the press."[20]

What Javits did not tell Carter, however, is that the speech probably was written by paid lobbyists for Israel, working at the American Israel Public Affairs Committee (AIPAC). At that time, as now, it was common for such lobbyists to call Congressmen and volunteer to prepare a text for them on the Middle East. If it was delivered on the Senate or House floor, it strengthened the Congressman with potential campaign contributors. If it was delivered to a Jewish religious or civic group, the Congressman collected a hefty speaking fee. If he couldn't deliver in person the speech ghostwritten for him, AIPAC would obligingly find someone to deliver the speech in the Congressman's name. Either way the speech made the newspapers, the Congressman collected, and the pressure built up on the President of the United States to look elsewhere for foreign or domestic policy accomplishments.

It didn't work with the persistent optimist from Plains, Georgia, however, who records that "although many other issues claimed my attention, the Middle East question preyed on my mind."

Therefore the opposition only strengthened his determination to cut the Gordian knot. He writes:

"I had to repair my damaged political base among Israel's American friends, and in the process build further support for our peace effort. Before Begin arrived, I held sessions with Jewish leaders from all around the nation, explaining my policies as I had to the Congressional leaders. In most cases, their concerns seemed to be at least partially alleviated, giving me a little breathing room to prepare for the upcoming talks."[21]

Carter's preparations paid off. On July 19 he recorded in his diary:

"We welcomed Prime Minister and Mrs. Begin, having done a great deal of preparation for this visit. There have been dire predictions that he and I would not get along, but I found him to be quite congenial, dedicated, sincere, deeply religious . . . I think Begin is a very good man and, although it will be difficult for him to change his position, the public-opinion polls that we have from Israel show that the people there are quite flexible . . . and genuinely want peace. My own guess is that if we give Begin support, he will prove to be a strong leader, quite different from Rabin."[22]

19. Carter, Jimmy, *Keeping Faith: Memoirs of a President*, Bantam Books, New York, 1982, p. 288.
20. *Ibid.*, p. 289.
21. *Ibid.*, p. 290.
22. *Ibid.*, p. 290.

Carter had done his homework and this may have been one of the reasons Begin treated him with kid gloves on the first visit. The polls Carter referred to showed that 63 per cent of Israelis wanted peace with the Arabs, and 51 per cent were willing to give up significant parts of the West Bank to get it. On the more sensitive issues concerning the Palestinians, 52 per cent of Israelis thought the Palestinians deserved a homeland, 43 per cent thought it should be on the West Bank, and 45 per cent, half of those who had any opinion at all, endorsed direct talks with PLO leaders who would acknowledge Israel's right to exist.

Instead of arguing with Carter, Begin agreed to stop Israeli overflights of Saudi Arabia and indicated he was making tentative plans for direct meetings with Anwar Sadat. This may have been the first time Carter became aware that Egypt's shrewd President was also doing his homework, and had also become convinced that, as a strong and self-assured leader, the uncompromising Begin might be able to make an agreement that a weaker Israeli leader could not.

Carter's memoirs record some wry afterthoughts on the visit which seemed to be going surprisingly well:

"Begin gave me his views about the historical nature of Israel, which was interesting this time, although I was familiar with most of what he said from my studies of the Old Testament and more recent history. I had no idea then how many times in the future I would listen to the same discourse . . .

"The feeling of optimism had a short life. As soon as Begin returned to Israel, he recognized as permanent some of the settlements on the West Bank. Predictably, this act was the most important item of discussion at my next news conference. Shortly thereafter, when Secretary Vance traveled through the area, he sent generally favorable reports about the attitude of President Sadat and the other Arab leaders, but he was extremely discouraged after talking with the Prime Minister in Jerusalem. My colleagues and I decided to develop a reasonable proposal based on Cy's extensive talks, hoping that public opinion and the general desire for peace might be decisive."[23]

The pot was boiling now, and Carter's ideas were picking up momentum. On August 11 former Supreme Court Justice and U.S. Ambassador to the UN Arthur Goldberg, a staunch friend of Israel who had been U.S. Ambassador to the United Nations at the time Resolution 242 was drafted, visited the White House. He urged that Carter proceed aggressively and suggest another meeting of the Middle Eastern leaders at Geneva, with both Carter and Soviet Chairman Brezhnev presiding over the initial sessions. The problem in carrying this out was how to deal with the problem of Palestinian representation.

"Whenever the State Department even explored the question of how to involve the Palestinians," Carter writes, "the Israelis objected very strongly. Yet somehow the plight of these people had to be addressed if there was ever to be permanent peace."[24]

In his diary entry for August 29 Carter records:

"Assad in an interview in *The New York Times* proposed that the PLO not participate in

---

23. Carter, Jimmy, *Keeping Faith: Memoirs of a President*, Bantam Books, New York, 1982, p. 291.
24. *Ibid.*, p. 292.

the Geneva Conference, but that the Arab League might substitute for them. We'll pursue this idea!"[25]

In the Middle East, however, something else was brewing. In July, according to subsequent Israeli newspaper accounts, Begin was informed by his intelligence service of a Libyan-inspired plot to assassinate President Sadat. Begin did not simply sit on the information or turn it over to U.S. intelligence for relay to Egypt, as might have been done in the past. Instead, Begin had one of his intelligence officers pass the information directly to the Egyptians at a secret meeting in Morocco.

According to Israeli press accounts, the initially skeptical Egyptians caught the plotters red-handed. When Egypt retaliated against Colonel Qaddafi by launching a brief border war against Libyan troop concentrations and communications, Begin let it be known that Israel would do nothing to disturb the Egyptians in Sinai so long as they were preoccupied in Libya.

Meanwhile, the Carter Administration was proceeding down its chosen track toward a comprehensive solution. Carter writes:

"When Israeli Foreign Minister Moshe Dayan came to Washington to discuss the peace process with me on September 19, I expected a difficult session. I had great personal respect for Dayan, because I knew he was striving to end the Israeli military occupation on the West Bank and at the same time retain adequate security for his country. However, I was then convinced that some of Israel's recent actions were the main obstacles to progress on the peace talks. I told him that I thought the gratuitous endorsement of a new group of settlements, the recent Israeli invasion of Lebanon, and the failure to make any reasonable proposals or counterproposals on the question of Palestinian representation were almost insuperable obstacles.

"I asked Dayan to respond, and he said I was wrong. He promised that no more civilians would go into the settlements, but only people in uniform into the military sites. (This was a major concession, not to be honored later by Prime Minister Begin.) On Lebanon, the six tanks sent in over the weekend would be the limit of Israeli involvement, he said. He even showed some flexibility on the Palestinians, proposing that there could be a joint Arab delegation for the opening session at Geneva; afterward PLO members could be part of the Jordanian delegation, provided they were not well-known leaders . . . If Dayan was speaking accurately for Israel, the meeting had been surprisingly productive, possibly enough to let us bring the Arabs around. Since the only forum the United States had to work on was the Geneva Conference under the aegis of the United Nations, we had to get the Soviet Union, as co-chairman, to agree to the format we were so laboriously evolving. On September 23, during my meeting with Foreign Minister Gromyko, he told me, 'if we can just establish a miniature state for the Palestinians as big as a pencil eraser, this will lead to a resolution of the PLO problem for the Geneva Conference.'"[26]

On October 1, the United States and the Soviet Union issued a joint statement calling for a resumption of the Geneva negotiations and setting forth the principles which Carter had decided to pursue and supporting the "legitimate rights" of the Palestinians.

The reaction in Israel was a firestorm of opposition, and this was quickly reflected in the U.S. Congress where 150 members signed a letter criticizing the joint statement

---

25. Carter, Jimmy, *Keeping Faith: Memoirs of a President*, Bantam Books, New York, 1982, p. 292.
26. *Ibid.*, pp. 292-3.

with the Soviets. In the Arab world reaction was generally negative, although Yassir Arafat called U.S. support for Palestinian participation in the negotiations a "turning point" and a "positive step" and Sadat sent a private message urging that nothing be done to prevent Israel and Egypt from negotiating directly with the U.S. as intermediary, either before or after the Geneva Conference was convened. Carter met with Dayan who warned that there would be deep opposition within the Israeli government to resumption of negotiations jointly chaired by the U.S. and USSR, but there was no formal Israeli statement to this effect.

Instead, and not for the first time, it was Syria which expressed the strongest public opposition to the meeting, thus in effect allowing Begin to remain silent and not take the blame as spoiler of the great powers' plans.

Carter was informed by Senate Majority leader Byrd that, despite the letter signed by 150 members of Congress attacking the idea, there was a lot of quiet majority support for the initiative. Carter informed him that "my problem was that it was too quiet."[27]

Sadat contacted Carter on November 2 with a plan of his own for a summit conference in East Jerusalem attended by the Middle East parties plus the permanent members of the United Nations Security Council. This would have added China, the U.K. and France to the group and Carter opposed it on grounds that it would create new problems and stir up still further opposition.

At this point events in the Middle East began moving rapidly down an entirely different track. The July contact between Israel and Egypt reportedly had been followed by a September meeting in Morocco, this time between Foreign Minister Dayan and one of President Sadat's most trusted aides.

On November 9, President Sadat told his Parliament, "I am ready to go to the Israeli Parliament itself to discuss peace." Egyptian Foreign Minister Ismail Fahmy resigned in protest. The Israelis quickly issued an invitation, and on November 19, 1977, President Sadat landed at Ben Gurion International airport. His meetings with Israel's leaders, his magnanimous address in the Knesset and Begin's cautious reply, and the Egyptian President's return to a tumultuous welcome at home were televised to a fascinated world, and are now part of Middle East history.

The Sadat initiative was coldly received by the other Arabs. Syria broke diplomatic relations with Egypt. Syrian, Iraqi and Libyan officials all were quoted as calling for Sadat's assassination. Most important, however, was the negative reaction by Saudi Arabia, whose leaders feared that Sadat's initiative was in fact simply an attempt to get his own Sinai territory back from Israel as the price of a separate peace, leaving the Palestine problem to fester unsolved.

Carter had braved considerable domestic opposition to develop momentum for a comprehensive settlement, but there was little question of opposing the direct Egyptian-Israeli initiative, and Carter slowed his own efforts toward an international conference.

Sadat followed up his Jerusalem initiative with an invitation to hold the multinational peace conference which the U.S. and USSR had planned for Geneva in Cairo

---

27. Carter, Jimmy, *Keeping Faith: Memoirs of a President*, Bantam Books, New York, 1982, p. 296.

instead. The Arabs and the USSR refused, leaving only the U.S. and Israel willing to accept the invitation. Carter sent Vance on another round of Middle East visits, and then asked Begin to make some reassuring gesture concerning the Palestinians and the occupied territories. Begin brought his plans to Washington where Carter found him far more forthcoming on Sinai than any of his Labor party predecessors, but not so in his "autonomy plan" for the West Bank which Carter described as "not acceptable" but "a step in the right direction." In discussions about it, however, Carter writes, "Begin sounded much more flexible regarding the West Bank than I had expected, but I was to discover that his good words had multiple meanings, which my advisers and I did not understand at that time."[28]

There was intense U.S. popular interest in the follow-up meeting December 20 between the defense ministers of Israel and Egypt and in the climactic visit, on Christmas Day, 1977, by Prime Minister Begin to President Sadat in Egypt.

Begin, meanwhile, was playing his own game with the U.S. media. He seized on Carter's cool but correct characterization of Begin's autonomy plan as a "good beginning." The comment was intended to prompt an Israeli re-examination of the plan. Instead, in a move reminiscent of the manner in which Israel's supporters had sometimes forced the hands of American presidents starting with Franklin Roosevelt, the Israeli Prime Minister pretended to believe that he had a U.S. endorsement. The U.S. press also insisted on interpreting a year-end statement by Carter that he opposed the creation of a Palestinian state as an endorsement of the Begin plan. Questioned by newsmen before he had seen the full Carter statement, Sadat commented that he was "embarrassed." A chill seemed about to envelop U.S.-Arab relations.

Carter, however, was still sounding out other Middle Eastern leaders on whether to support Sadat's initiative, or to try to re-open comprehensive negotiations in Geneva. In Tehran, on New Year's Eve, he met with both the Shah and King Hussein of Jordan. On January 1, 1978 he recorded in his diary:

"All three of us agreed that we ought to give Sadat our support; that the basis for a Middle East peace settlement should be UN Resolutions 242 and 338; that there should be some minor modifications of the 1967 Israeli borders; that the people in the West Bank-Gaza area should have self-determination but not the right to claim independence . . . Both the Shah and King Hussein said that they want to go after I do to Saudi Arabia and to Egypt to try to express support for Sadat."[29]

Carter met on January 3 with King Khaled of Saudi Arabia and Crown Prince Fahd and reported that he "found the Saudis interested and constructive." He continues:

"They expressed their unequivocal support for Sadat, because they wanted peace and stability in the region, but merely smiled when I urged them to make this known through their public statements; they did not want to alienate the more militant Arabs. The Saudi leaders were knowledgeable, tough negotiators, surprisingly frank and good-humored. They made it obvious to me that they would accept some minor modifications in the 1967 Israeli borders, but they

28. Carter, Jimmy, *Keeping Faith: Memoirs of a President*, Bantam Books, New York, 1982, p. 300.
29. *Ibid.*, pp. 301-2.

were adamant in their commitment to an independent Palestinian state. They were the only Arab leaders I had met who maintained this strong position even in private."[30]

Now Carter was determined to deal with Begin's statements implying that Carter was willing to sell out the Palestinians, and the embarrassment this had caused Sadat. Carter's plane made an unscheduled stop in Egypt where he set matters straight. Two months later, in February 1978, President Sadat spent six triumphal days in the U.S., meeting with Carter and members of Congress, participating in U.S. network television interviews, and giving a televised speech at the National Press Club. On that visit President Carter described Sadat as the "world's foremost peacemaker."

On March 6, 1978, exactly one month after President Sadat's televised speech at the National Press Club, Mark Siegel, a White House deputy political adviser, resigned his position as Administration spokesman to the Jewish community. It was a protest at what he saw as a Carter tilt away from Israel. Two weeks later Prime Minister Begin arrived in Washington for meetings on March 21 and 22 with President Carter and members of Congress. The *New York Times* quoted an anonymous Administration official on that visit as follows:

"It was a turning point for us. When Begin left, everyone was frustrated, not just in the White House but on Capitol Hill. He left behind heavy footprints and a lot of frustration. That's the first time I saw a break in the solid support base for Begin on the Hill."

What followed may or may not have resulted from the Begin visit. In any case, it too was a turning point in Israel's influence in the Congress. For the first time in history, Israel's lobby in Washington took a strong stand on a bill, and then lost in the Congressional voting.

It started because U.S. Middle East specialists were concerned that Sadat's initiative had derailed their own efforts to get all of the moderate Arabs together behind a settlement initiative. Now a gulf seemed to be opening between the U.S. and Egypt on the one hand and the rest of the Arabs on the other. Officials at the Department of State and the Pentagon wanted to demonstrate both to Sadat and to the other Arabs that moderation could pay off, quickly and tangibly. Therefore, the Carter Administration proposed on February 18, 1978 the sale of 60 F-15 long range fighters to Saudi Arabia and an additional 15 to Israel; 50 F-5E fighter bombers to Egypt; and 75 F-16 fighter-bombers to Israel.

There was a probability that, if left to its own devices, the Senate would approve only the sales to Israel. To forestall that, the Administration made it clear to Congress that the sales were firmly linked in an all-or-nothing package. In his visit to Washington, Begin had not discussed the package and the Israeli government reacted slowly. It apparently hoped it could obtain its own portion while its American lobby, by now engaged in an all-out effort, prevented the Saudi and Egyptian sales. Belatedly, Israel accepted the fact that Carter had linked all the sales together inseparably. Israeli Embassy officials began to contact Senators personally. They were too late, however, to kill the

---

30. Carter, Jimmy, *Keeping Faith: Memoirs of a President*, Bantam Books, New York, 1982, pp. 304-5.

proposal in committee as they hoped to. Instead, an eight-to-eight tie vote in the Senate Foreign Relations Committee allowed the proposal to reach the Senate floor.

The Democratic Administration, meanwhile, had received strong assistance from two Republicans. Senate Minority Leader Howard Baker and former Secretary of State Henry Kissinger offered to speak up in support of the package on two conditions: that it include 20 more F-15 fighters for Israel and that the bomb racks be removed from the Saudi planes to limit their offensive, but not their defensive, capability.

When the Senate finally approved the sale, however, the decisive support came from Democratic Senator Abraham A. Ribicoff. Of the five Jewish senators, he was the only one to vote for the package. During a 10-hour closed debate on the bill, he and Senator Jacob Javits exchanged angry words, both citing their Jewish heritage. In the end there was little doubt that the Ribicoff vote for the package swung enough others with it to carry the day.

Senator Ribicoff, for years one of Israel's staunchest supporters in Washington, had in 1978 visited Saudi Arabia and Syria. He said that the visit to Saudi Arabia, where his delegation met knowledgeable and efficient American-trained Saudi ministers clearly anxious to maintain their American ties, completely changed his image of that country. The visit to Syria he described as a "shocker." Whatever his previous thoughts about Egypt, he found himself defending President Sadat's initiative against Syrian charges that it betrayed the Arab cause and Syrian predictions that, in any case, Israeli intransigence would make the Sadat initiative fail. Ribicoff returned, he said, with a whole new perception of what the United States must do in the Middle East.

"It was a tough position to take," he reported. Lifelong friends were now "very critical of me." However, after the vote, he told the *Washington Post* :

"There's nothing I have ever done in the Senate that has ever met such an overwhelming approval . . . not only from people who voted on my side, but by people who voted on the other side. . . . I had a lot of senators tell me 'Abe . . . we're ashamed. We agree with you and we know what it means for you to do this and the pressure you must have been under. We've been under pressure and we have voted the opposite way.' It was very interesting to me to get that reaction."

In the spring of 1978, there was other bad news from the United States for the Begin government. Led by Professor Leonard Fein, editor of the Boston Jewish monthly *Moment*, 36 distinguished American Jews sent a letter of solidarity to Israel's "Peace Now" movement, which had turned out an estimated 300,000 demonstrators to protest the Begin hard line. The signatories included such articulate supporters of Israel as sociologists Daniel Bell and Seymour Lipset, authors Saul Bellow and Irving Howe, historian Walter Laqueur and editors Martin Peretz and Jesse Lurie. In Israel, the *Jerusalem Post* commented on the letter:

"Fear of showing division and dissent to a hostile Gentile World is deeply etched into Jewish history. What was perhaps acceptable for unobtrusive internal debate was considered dangerous and illegitimate if displayed to general view. . . . That now a group of such responsible American Jewish personalities has broken through the constraint of public unity testifies to the depth of their concern."

Carter has written of his own growing concern throughout this period:

"The Israelis were not honoring the commitment Dayan had given me about their settlement policy, but were building up those enclaves in the occupied territories as rapidly as possible. Whenever we seemed to be having some success with the Arabs, Begin would proclaim the establishment of another group of settlements or make other provocative statements. This behavior was not only very irritating, but it seriously endangered the prospects for peace and Sadat's status both in Egypt and within the Arab world. The repeated Israeli invasions or bombing of Lebanon also precipitated crises; a stream of fairly harsh messages was going back and forth between me in Washington and Begin in Jerusalem."[31]

His diary reveals that Carter was soon moving firmly toward resuming the initiative himself in the Middle East. As early as February 3, 1978, he had written:

"We had quite an argument at breakfast, with me on one side and Fritz, Cy, Zbig, and Ham on the other. I think we ought to move much more aggressively on the Middle East question than any of them seem to, by evolving a clear plan for private use among ourselves . . . discussing the various elements with Sadat, one by one, encouraging him to cooperate with us by preventing any surprises in the future, and by inducing him to understand Begin's position. The plan that we evolve has got to be one that can be accepted by Begin in a showdown if we have the full support of the American public . . . I don't know how much support I have, but we'll go through with this effort."[32]

On February 4, accompanied by their wives, the Presidents of Egypt and the U.S. had traveled to Camp David. Sadat bitterly told Carter that Begin was rejecting advice from Dayan and from Ezer Weizman for a moderate position and was instead yielding to pressure from Ariel Sharon, the military firebrand and truce breaker, who was now Minister of Agriculture in Begin's cabinet. Sharon was advocating a program to settle hundreds of thousands of Jews in the West Bank. It was at that point that Carter had talked Sadat out of breaking off talks with Israel and returning to the policy of Pan-Arab solidarity against any deal with Israel. The result had been Sadat's successful campaign with the U.S. media.

However, U.S. media sympathy for an Arab leader did not influence events in the Middle East. Carter writes:

"On the afternoon of March 11, I received word that PLO terrorists had launched an attack on the Israeli coast, killing 35 people. All but two of these victims were civilians . . . Three days later the Israelis retaliated with an invasion of Lebanon. In the fighting, more than a thousand noncombatants were killed and more than a hundred thousand left homeless. Israeli invasion forces remained in Lebanon. To me this seemed a terrible overreaction by the Israelis, and I instructed Cy to tell them we would introduce a resolution in the United Nations calling for their withdrawal from Lebanon and the establishment of a United Nations peacekeeping force there; and that I was particularly disturbed because American weapons, including extremely lethal cluster bombs, had been used in the operation, contrary to our agreement when they were sold."[33]

---

31. Carter, Jimmy, *Keeping Faith: Memoirs of a President*, Bantam Books, New York, 1982, p. 306.
32. *Ibid.*, pp. 310-11.
33. *Ibid.*, p. 311.

The Israeli army was still in Lebanon when Prime Minister and Mrs. Begin arrived in Washington on March 21, 1978. Carter records that in a private "intense, sometimes emotional discussion about the Middle East" he succeeded in "narrowing down the points to sharp issues for the first time in my relationship with Israel."[34]

Begin used the opportunity, however, to claim he was "wounded in the heart" when his December plan for the Palestinians had first received words of praise which Carter later withdrew.

After comparing notes with Vance, who had been talking with Dayan while Carter was talking to Begin, Carter records that "we decided it was time to fish or cut bait." The next day Carter and his aides met with Begin and the Israelis who had accompanied him. Carter writes:

"I then read to Begin and his group my understanding of their position: not willing to withdraw politically or militarily from any part of the West Bank; not willing to stop the construction of new settlements or the expansion of existing settlements; not willing to withdraw the Israeli settlers from the Sinai, or even leave them there under UN or Egyptian protection; not willing to acknowledge that UN Resolution 242 applies to the West Bank-Gaza area; not willing to grant the Palestinian Arabs real authority, or a voice in the determination of their own future to the extent that they can choose between the alternatives outlined above. Although Begin said this was a negative way to express their position, he did not deny the accuracy of any of it. These became known as 'the six no's.' "[35]

Carter writes of that meeting that "it was clear to everyone on both sides of the table that, unless he changed his positions, Begin was becoming an insurmountable obstacle to further progress. This was a heartbreaking development, and I began to inform the Congressional leaders who supported Israel about our failure, being careful to describe the positions of Sadat and Begin as accurately as I could, checking each point with my personal notes. Some of them met with Prime Minister Begin and confirmed 'the six no's.' They, too, were discouraged."[35]

Israeli soldiers raise their flag on Mount Hermon overlooking Syrian highlands during October, 1973 war.

---

34. Carter, Jimmy, *Keeping Faith: Memoirs of a President*, Bantam Books, New York, 1982, p. 312.
35. *Ibid.*, pp. 313-4.

Israel Office of Information

As it became increasingly clear that some of Israel's leaders did not intend to hand back the Arab territories conquered in 1967, West Bank Palestinians realized they had little control over their destiny. Above, Israeli soldiers in Jerusalem evict Arab occupants of the former Jewish quarter of the old city before bulldozing the houses. Houses rebuilt on the site were turned over to Jewish occupants. Below, left, Palestinians evicted from the West Bank in 1967 begin to dig in for a long stay at Jebel Joffe, a squatter's colony on the outskirts of Amman first set up by Palestinian refugees in 1948. Below, right, Israeli soldiers search a Palestinian who remained behind in the West Bank.

UNRWA   PLO

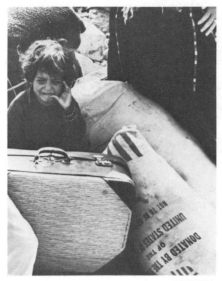

UNRWA   UNRWA

Early in his first term President Carter said there would be neither peace nor justice in the Middle
East until the Palestinians had a homeland of their own. It was an irony of history that at exactly
the period when an American President became deeply and personally concerned with the problem, and Egypt had a leader prepared to make the compromises necessary for a lasting Arab-
Israeli peace, Israel was led by Menachem Begin, who had no intention of returning any part of
the West Bank to its Palestinian inhabitants. Above, left, Palestinian girl arriving on East Bank
of Jordan in 1967. Above right two Palestinian children at Karamah emergency camp in east
Jordan Valley. Below, first and third refugee generations. The grandfather in 1948 lost his home
in present-day Israel. Now he and his grandson are refugees in Jordan from the West Bank.

UNRWA

CHAPTER XVIII

Camp David

"The more I dealt with Arab leaders, the more disparity I discovered between their private assurances and their public comments. They would privately put forward ideas for peace and encourage us in any reasonable approach. However, the peer pressure among them was tremendous. None of them — apart from Sadat — was willing to get out in front and publicly admit a willingness to deal with Israel."[1]

Jimmy Carter, 1982

"There was also a private-public disparity, though of a different nature, among the leaders of the many organized groups in the American Jewish community. In our private conversations they were often supportive and, like the Arab leaders, urged us to explore every avenue that might lead to peace. They would deplore Israeli excesses, travel to Jerusalem to seek out moderate leaders who shared the same goals, and give generously of their time and money to any peaceful or benevolent cause. But in a public showdown on a controversial issue, they would almost always side with the Israeli leaders and condemn us for being 'evenhanded' in our concern about both Palestinian rights and Israeli security."[2]

Jimmy Carter, 1982

"It was business as usual after Begin came to power. The only real difference was that Begin was honest about his intentions. Those who ruled before him were hypocrites and liars who deceived their own people first and then the world."[3]

Yassir Arafat, 1984

1. Carter, Jimmy, *Keeping Faith: Memoirs of a President*, Bantam Books, New York, 1982, p. 286.
2. *Ibid.*, pp. 286-7.
3. Hart, Alan, *Arafat: Terrorist or Peacemaker?*, Sidgwick and Jackson, London, 1984, p. 406.

"The brightest success of the Carter Administration was its peacemaking effort in the Middle East. After being surprised by Anwar el-Sadat's dramatic voyage to Jerusalem in November 1977, Jimmy Carter engaged the United States as a 'full partner' in the tortuous diplomacy of peace negotiations. The Camp David accords were the result of skillful and tenacious efforts by President Carter, and a peace treaty between Israel and Egypt was concluded in March 1979. No American President has ever had so crucial and detailed a role in a successful mediation between third parties. Egypt recovered its territories, and Israel gained peace with its most formidable foe. It was a spectacular victory for international conciliation. The terms of this treaty, however, did not unravel the Palestinian issue, which was left to future negotiation."[4]

Abba Eban, 1983

"Carter's stature as President peaked in September of 1978 with the Camp David accords on the Middle East. The announcement in the East Room with Anwar Sadat and Menachem Begin attending was the high point of the term."[5]

Joseph A. Califano, Jr., 1981

His open break with Israel was having serious domestic repercussions for Jimmy Carter. Two Democratic Party fund-raising banquets in New York and Los Angeles had to be postponed because so many Jewish Democrats cancelled their reservations to attend.

In June, 1978, a group of experienced Democratic Party leaders advised Carter to "stay as aloof as possible from direct involvement in the Middle East negotiations; this is a losing proposition." By the end of July, however, Carter had decided to ignore their advice. He writes:

"There was no prospect for success if Begin and Sadat stayed apart, and their infrequent meetings had now become fruitless because the two men were too personally incompatible to compromise on the many difficult issues facing them. I finally decided it would be best, win or lose, to go all out. There was only one thing to do, as dismal and unpleasant as the prospect seemed—I would try to bring Sadat and Begin together for an extensive negotiating session with me."[6]

On August 8, 1978, Carter, Begin and Sadat made joint announcements about the forthcoming meeting. Carter was "deluged with warnings from my closest advisers and friends," but he went ahead, poring over everything the U.S. government could provide him on the personalities, predilections, and positions of the two men he was determined to bring and hold together. His greatest problems, he records, were keeping the two of them from making negative statements about each other prior to the meeting, and getting his own media advisers to agree to the total exclusion of the press from Camp David during the negotiations.

4. Eban, Abba, *The New Diplomacy: International Affairs in the Modern Age*, Random House, New York, 1983, p. 71.
5. Califano, Joseph A., Jr., *Governing America: An Insider Report from the White House and Cabinet*, Simon and Schuster, Inc., 1981.
6. Carter, Jimmy, *Keeping Faith: Memoirs of a President*, Bantam Books, New York, 1982, p. 316.

Jimmy Carter has written his own dramatic and insightful account of the 13 days the three leaders spent on a mountaintop hammering out the Camp David agreements. It is ironic that the agreements eventually led to a Nobel peace prize for Sadat and Begin. Originally a majority of the committee in Sweden wanted to give the prize to Sadat alone, but one member insisted that Begin be included as well. Begin, however, took advantage of the peace he had concluded with Egypt to launch his forces into an 'anti-terrorist' sweep of Southern Lebanon which cost an estimated thousand lives. Later, in 1982, he launched another, major invasion of Lebanon in which another 20,000 Lebanese and Palestinians died, and which also cost the lives of more than 600 Israeli soldiers and some 250 American military personnel.

In doing this, Begin vindicated Sadat's critics, who said that rather than providing a framework for Middle East peace, by making a separate peace that pulled Egypt out of the Arab camp, he had made another Arab-Israeli war inevitable. Whether one blames Begin's actions, or the U.S. failure to stop them, only three years after the Camp David summit, Sadat was killed by a group of Islamic fundamentalists.

Even a cursory reading of Carter's account makes it clear that *Sadat's* prize was earned. If it was to be shared, the other recipient should have been Jimmy Carter himself in recognition of the time, thought and persuasion he devoted to that 13-day ordeal. The following account of the meeting and all of the quotations are based upon Carter's writings, published in the Oct. 11, 1982 issue of *Time* magazine and in his book, *Keeping Faith: Memoirs of a President*, Bantam Books, New York, pages 319 to 402.

On the first day, Tuesday, September 5, 1978, Carter records:

"Despite my efforts to the contrary, expectations had built up to a fever pitch. My only hope was that in the quiet and peaceful atmosphere of our temporary home, both Begin and Sadat would come to know and understand each other better, and that they would trust me to be honest and fair in my role as mediator and active negotiator. It was soon to be obvious that Sadat seemed to trust me too much, and Begin not enough."

In an initial meeting with Carter, Sadat explained that he was eager to conclude an agreement settling all of the issues, and not just establish procedures for future negotiations. Since Sadat believed Begin did not want an agreement and would therefore try to delay, Sadat's second preference was for an agreement with Carter that would be so good for Israel that Begin would be condemned in Israel and the U.S. if he rejected it. Sadat added that he had 'here in my pocket' a comprehensive settlement plan, and that he was prepared to be flexible on everything but land and sovereignty.

In Carter's first meeting with Begin, however, both were ill at ease as the Georgian tried to establish an atmosphere of informality, and Begin pursued a deliberate and methodical approach. Carter writes:

"I knew that his preoccupation with language, names and terms could severely impede free-flowing talk . . . Unlike Sadat, Begin was planning for an agreement at Camp David only on general principles, which might then serve as a basis for future meetings . . . I told him that Sadat had expressed a concern about Begin's preoccupation with details at the expense of major issues. Begin looked up and said, 'I can handle both.' "

Carter noted from the beginning a serious difference over the phrase from

U.N.Security Council Resolution 242 "inadmissibility of the acquisition of territory by war." The Egyptians insisted that Israel acknowledge the applicability of this principle in any treaties signed, because of its implication that lands occupied by Israel during the six-day war have not changed hands legally. Working from the same premise, Begin said he would agree only if the word "belligerent" were inserted before the word "war." He was seeking to lay the groundwork for a case that although Israel had struck first in the 1967 war, it had been a pre-emptive attack and the lands therefore had been seized in a defensive war. Carter writes also:

"Begin had repeatedly promised full autonomy for the West Bank Palestinians, and I pushed him on how much freedom they would have. He replied that the only powers they would not be able to exercise would be those relating to immigration of Palestinian refugees and the security of Israel. This sounded good, but later the Israelis would seek a veto over almost anything of substance the Palestinians could decide, even claiming that road construction and water supplies affect the security of Israel"

On the second day Sadat explained that Egypt must have every inch of its land returned with unequivocal sovereignty over it, and that other nations from which Israel had taken land should be treated in the same manner. He told Carter that there were recognized international boundaries for Sinai, all of which belonged to Egypt, and for the Golan, all of which belonged to Syria. Carter writes that when he asked who had sovereignty over the West Bank and Gaza, Sadat replied:

"Sovereignty rests among the people who live there, not in either Jordan or Israel."

When Begin rejected Sadat's request that Israel pay for the Egyptian oil it was pumping from occupied Sinai, an argument ensued as to who had conquered whom. Sadat accused Begin of only being interested in retaining occupied land. Begin replied that of 24,000 square miles of territory involved, he was offering to return more than 90 percent of it to Egypt, and merely postponing the question of sovereignty over the other 2,340 square miles, a figure Carter assumed referred to the West Bank and Gaza. Sadat rejoined that the inadmissibility of the acquisition of territory by war was the essence of the question, and could not be ignored.

Sadat said that for 30 years the Israelis had desired full recognition, no Arab boycott, and security. Now he was offering all of that, Sadat said. and Begin was ignoring the offer.

"Premier Begin, you want land," Sadat charged. Continuing, Sadat repeated to Begin what he had told Carter. Neither Israel nor Jordan could claim sovereignty over the West Bank. Self-determination by its residents was the only measure of sovereignty and ultimately would lead to creation of a Palestinian state. Such a state would not be independent or have military forces, but should be linked to Israel or Jordan, Sadat said. His own preference was Jordan.

Almost every discussion in which both Sadat and Begin participated deteriorated into an unproductive argument, Carter notes. Feeling pressed, Sadat would move away from details and into broad principles or concepts. Begin would react in exactly the opposite manner, shifting to "minutiae or semantics, with an inclination to recapitulate ancient history or to resurrect an old argument."

As a result, Carter writes, he developed his own technique to keep the negotiations going:

"I would draft a proposal I considered reasonable, take it to Sadat for quick approval or slight modification, and then spend hours or days working on the same point with the Israeli delegation. Sometimes, in the end, the change of a word or phrase would satisfy Begin . . . On any controversial issue, I never consulted Sadat's aides but always went directly to their leader. It soon became obvious, however, that (Moshe) Dayan, (Ezer)Weizman or Attorney General Aharon Barak could be convinced on an issue more quickly than the Prime Minister, and they were certainly more effective in changing Begin's mind than I ever was."

By the end of the second day the goals of the two leaders were also clear to Carter:

"Begin wanted to deal with the Sinai, keep the West Bank and avoid the Palestinian issue. Sadat was determined to address all three. I sided with Sadat, of course, and stated that the principals must address all the controversial issues . . . Sadat said . . . 'I will not sign a Sinai agreement before an agreement is also reached on the West Bank.' Sadat was to prove adamant on this.

By the third day, Thursday, September 7, Carter was in heated discussion with the Israeli delegation, informing them that "the key question was: 'Are you willing to withdraw from the occupied territories and honor Palestinian rights, in exchange for adequate security assurances, including an internationally recognized peace treaty?' "

Begin, he says, was evasive, proposing that everyone simply live together with the question of sovereignty to be decided later. Carter writes:

"The expanding settlements were creating doubt that the Israelis were bargaining in good faith concerning any reduction in Israeli influence on the West Bank. This was the root of Sadat's distrust of Begin's motives, and I admit that I shared the belief that the Israeli leader would do almost anything concerning the Sinai and other issues to protect Israel's presence in 'Judea and Samaria.' "

In the afternoon when Carter, Begin and Sadat met together, Carter writes, the Israeli Prime Minister proposed that the meeting avoid the difficult problems:

"He said that regarding the Sinai issues, including settlements and airfields, we should turn the problem over to the military leaders, who could resolve the differences and report back to the heads of government for approval. Sadat quickly replied that this would be a complete waste of time. Without specific direction from the top, there would be no way that his Defense Minister could negotiate for Egypt . . . Begin asked about whether Sadat would keep his commitment that the Strait of Tiran would be an open international waterway. Sadat replied, 'Of course. I said so before and I will keep my promise.' "

Sadat confided at the meeting that "I still dream of a meeting on Mount Sinai of us three leaders, representing three nations and three religious beliefs. This is still my prayer to God." Begin agreed with the proposal and added that the hospitality with which Sadat had been received by the people of Israel showed the depth of their desire for peace.

On the fourth day, despite Begin's objections, Carter told him the U.S. would present a comprehensive proposal for peace:

"It will not surprise either you or Sadat. When it is finished tomorrow, I will present it to you first and then to the Egyptians. I can see no other possibility for progress."

Of the fifth day, Carter writes:

"There were more than 50 distinct issues to be resolved . . . I knew that Sadat and I could come up with a reasonable agreement that a majority of Israelis would gladly accept. My major task was to convince Begin . . . The only thing that would succeed was a proposal that was patently fair, that did not violate Sadat's broad principles and that we could sell to the other Israelis. From daybreak Saturday, the entire American delegation bent to this task, and shortly after midnight the document was ready to be put into final form."

By this time each group had fallen into its own patterns. Sadat dressed carefully but casually, took his meals in his cottage, paced himself and exercised meticulously in the mornings, preferring not to begin substantive business before 10 a.m. Begin dressed formally, spent a great deal of time with his staff, and ate in the common dining room with most of the members of the Israeli and American delegations. Carter, despite his liking for outdoor exercise, wasn't getting much of it as he took the lead in personally drafting compromise proposals.

On Sunday, the sixth day of the Camp David summit, Carter's discussions with Begin took a bad turn when Begin again insisted that the language in Resolution 242, "inadmissibility of the acquisition of territory by war," was unacceptable. Carter told him angrily, "What you say convinces me that Sadat was right – what you want is land."

Begin, Carter writes, responded:

"The problem of security also involves territory. We are willing to return Sinai; for the time being we are conceding our legitimate claims of sovereignty over Judea, Samaria and Gaza."

In the evening when Begin again proposed to delete all references to Resolution 242, Carter told him:

"If you had openly disavowed Resolution 242, I would not have invited you to Camp David or called this meeting. Israel has repeatedly endorsed 242 but now you are not willing to respect the language. If you don't espouse 242, it is a terrible blow to peace."

When the Israelis suggested alternative language for Carter's proposal concerning the Palestinians, Carter told them: "What you want to do is make the West Bank part of Israel."

"The whole idea is to let the people govern themselves," U.S. Secretary of State Vance added. "You are retaining a veto!"

"We want to keep the right to do so," Begin responded, "but we don't intend to do so."

"No self-respecting Arab would accept this." Carter said. "It looks like a subterfuge. We are talking about full autonomy – self control. You are not giving them autonomy if you have to approve their laws, exercise a veto over their decisions and maintain a military government. If I were an Arab, I would prefer the present Israeli occupation to this proposal."

On the seventh day Sadat disappointed Carter by rejecting the idea of Egypt taking title to the Sinai settlements while Israelis continued to live in them. Carter writes:

"When I asked him if he would permit Jews from any nation, including Israel, to live in Cairo or in Aswan, he replied, 'Of course.' I pointed out to him that in that case it was not logical to exclude them from the Sinai settlements. Sadat said, 'Some things in the Middle East are not logical or reasonable. For Egypt this is one of them.' He was firm—they would have to leave. He wanted the withdrawal of all Israelis from the Sinai to be completed within two years. I preferred three, to accomodate Israeli needs, and he agreed."

Carter's account of the eighth day on the mountain top depicts the contrasting styles of the two Middle Eastern leaders:

"I worked that afternoon on the terms for an Egyptian-Israeli treaty . . . writing the proposed agreement on a yellow scratch pad. Within three hours I had finished and walked over to Sadat's cottage to go over the draft with him. I began to read it aloud, but he reached for the pad, read it, made two changes that would make it more pleasing to Israel and handed it back. 'It's all right,' he said. Our meeting had lasted less than 20 minutes.

"I ate with the Israelis in the dining hall, and during the meal Begin said he wanted to see me as soon as possible for the most serious talk we had ever had. He came to my cottage at about 8 p.m. Then he went into an impassioned speech about the use of Resolution 242 language in the text of our Camp David agreements. He said, 'Israel cannot agree under any circumstances to a document which includes this phrase (inadmissibility of acquisition of territory by war) and I will not sign it.'

"He claimed that he sincerely wished he could sign my proposal, but the will of the Israeli people must be represented by him as their Prime Minister.

"I pointed out that I had seen public opinion polls every two or three weeks in which a substantial majority of the Israeli people were willing to accept a peace treaty with an end to the settlements, the removal of Israeli settlers from the Sinai and the yielding of substantial portions of the West Bank. I was distressed by his attitude and, perhaps ill-advisedly, said that my position represented the Israeli people better than his.

"It was a heated discussion, unpleasant and repetitive. I stood up for him to leave, and accused him of being willing to give up peace with his only formidable enemy, free trade and diplomatic recognition from Egypt, unimpeded access to international waterways, Arab acceptance of an undivided Jerusalem, permanent security for Israel and the approbation of the world—all just to keep a few illegal settlers on Egyptian land."

The ninth day Carter started on a new framework draft, working directly with Aharon Barak of the Israeli delegation and Egyptian Under Secretary for Foreign Affairs Osama El-Baz. Things went well. They worked hard on a paragraph about Jerusalem, about which Carter writes:

It referred to Jerusalem as the city of peace, holy to Judaism, Christianity and Islam, and stated that all persons would have free access to it, free exercise of worship and the right to visit and travel to the holy places without distinction or discrimination. We agreed that Jerusalem would never again be a divided city, that the holy places of each faith should be under the administration and full authority of their representatives, that a municipal council drawn from the inhabitants should supervise essential functions in the city, and so forth."

If the ninth day had been an upper for Carter, the tenth was a downer. He writes:

"Dayan and Weizman came by, and soon it all boiled down to the settlements . . . I could not think of any way to resolve this fundamental difference. We began to make plans to terminate the negotiations. That evening I began to list the differences between the two nations and was heartbroken to see how relatively insignificant they really were."

On Friday, Sept 15, the eleventh day of negotiations, Carter was discussing with his staff a plan to collect proposals from Sadat and Dayan, summarize the unresolved differences, and prepare a final communique explaining them when Vance burst into the room to announce that Sadat and his aides had packed and requested a helicopter to take them back to the capital. Carter describes his feelings in this "terrible moment":

"I sat quietly and assessed the significance of this development–a rupture between Sadat and me, and its consequences for my country and for the Middle East power balance. I envisioned the ultimate alliance of most of the Arab nations to the Soviet Union, perhaps joined by Egypt after a few months . . . I looked out to the Catoctin Mountains and prayed fervently that somehow we could find peace. Then I changed into more formal clothes before going to see Sadat.

"He explained the reason for his decision to leave: Dayan had told him the Israelis would not sign any agreements. This made Sadat furious. . . . His own advisers had pointed out the danger in his signing an agreement with the U.S. alone (on the basic principles on which a Middle East peace should be based). Later, if direct discussions were ever resumed with the Israelis they could say, 'The Egyptians have already agreed to all these points. Now we will use what they have signed as the original basis for all future negotiations.'

"It was a telling argument. I told him that we would have a complete understanding that if any nation rejected *any* part of the agreements, *none* of the proposals would stay in effect. Sadat stood silently for a long time. Then he looked at me and said, 'If you give me this statement, I will stick with you to the end.' "

On the twelfth day Carter and Sadat reviewed the Sinai proposal and "found no significant disagreement except over the Israeli settlements–and no disagreement at all between myself and Sadat." Regarding the comprehensive framework, Carter says, "we were also very close." They agreed to an exchange of letters. The U.S. would reconfirm its historic position that East Jerusalem was part of the West Bank. Sadat would confirm that the Wailing Wall should always be retained exclusively by the Jews. The conversations with Begin again hung up on the need for him to agree to a withdrawal of Jewish settlers from the Sinai. Carter describes the scene:

"I thought the discussion would never end. Begin was shouting words like 'ultimatum,' 'excessive demands' and 'political suicide' . . . We then had a surprisingly amicable discusion about the framework for peace. On Jerusalem, I told the Israelis that Sadat wanted a separate exchange of letters so that each nation could make public its own different ideas. On the West Bank settlements, we worked out language that no new Israeli settlements would be established after the signing of this framework and that the issue of additional settlements would be resolved during the negotiations. Begin later denied that he had agreed to this, and claimed that he had promised to stop building settlements only for a three-month period. My notes are clear–the settlement freeze would continue until all negotiations were completed."

On Sunday, September 17, 1978, the thirteenth day, Carter decided with Sadat that the entire paragraph on Jerusalem would be deleted and each country would submit its own separate view in an exchange of letters that would become part of the official record of the meeting. But, Carter writes:

"A serious problem erupted with the Israelis. Vance had just shown them a copy of our draft letter that would go to Sadat, restating the U.S. position on Jerusalem, which had been spelled out officially in U.N. debates over the years. There was an absolute furor, and Begin announced that Israel would not sign *any* document if we wrote *any* letter to Egypt about Jerusalem . . . I told him I had drafted a new version . . . I suggested he read it, but that there was no way that I could go back on my commitment to Sadat to exchange letters. Any future talks might depend on his and Sadat's assessment of my integrity, and I could not violate a promise.

"I walked back . . . very dejected. Sadat was there, dressed to go back to Washington. I asked everyone else to leave and told Sadat what was happening. We realized that all of us had done our best, but that prospects were dim indeed.

"Then Begin called. He said, referring to the new version . . . 'I will accept the letter you have drafted on Jerusalem.' I breathed a sigh of relief. It seemed that the last obstacle had been removed . . .

"We arrived at the White House at about 10:15 p.m. and went directly to the East Room, where our signing of the documents and some brief remarks pre-empted the new prime-time TV shows. The Framework for Peace in the Middle East and the Framework for the Conclusion of a Peace Treaty Between Egypt and Israel were two major steps forward.

"We had no idea how far we still had to go."

UPI

One of the first of Israel's West Bank settlements was Elon Moreh. In this 1977 photo a gun-toting Israeli settler walks to car for his daily drive from Elon Moreh on the West Bank to his job in Israel.

NYT Pictures

Jimmy Carter left Camp David believing he had a pledge from Prime Minister Begin to freeze further West Bank and Gaza settlement activity pending negotiation of a peace agreement. On this, Carter has written, "my notes are clear." Begin, however, said he had agreed to freeze the settlements for only 90 days. After that he resumed Israel's expensive program of "creating facts" in Jerusalem and the West Bank according to the map on the adjacent page. Above, apartment projects for commuters to Jerusalem dominate the skyline. Below, apartments in the West Bank settlement of Ariel are available to Jewish settlers for a quarter of the price they would pay for the equivalent in Israel proper.

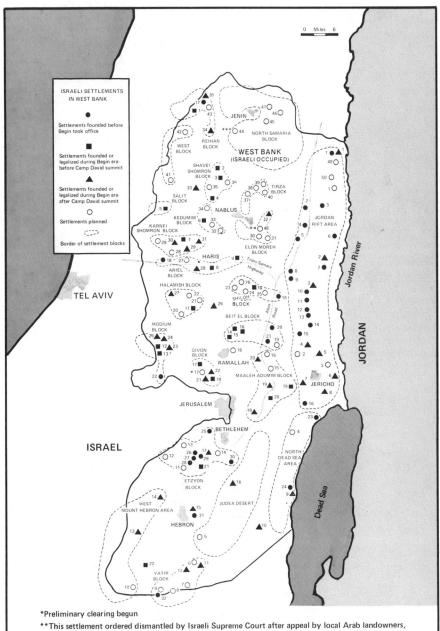

ISRAELI SETTLEMENTS IN WEST BANK

● Settlements founded before Begin took office

■ Settlements founded or legalized during Begin era- before Camp David summit

▲ Settlements founded or legalized during Begin era- after Camp David summit

○ Settlements planned

⌐ ⌐ Border of settlement blocks

0 Miles 6

WEST BANK (ISRAELI OCCUPIED)

JENIN

NORTH SAMARIA BLOCK

REIHAN BLOCK

WEST BLOCK

SHAVEI SHOMRON BLOCK

SALIT BLOCK

NABLUS

KEDUMIM BLOCK

KARNEI SHOMRON BLOCK

TIRZA BLOCK

JORDAN RIFT AREA

ELON MOREH BLOCK

HARIS

ARIEL BLOCK

HALAMISH BLOCK

Trans Samaria Highway

SHILOH BLOCK

TEL AVIV

MODIUM BLOCK

BEIT EL BLOCK

GIVON BLOCK

RAMALLAH

MAALEH ADUMIM BLOCK

Allon Road

Jordan River

JORDAN

JERICHO

JERUSALEM

ISRAEL

BETHLEHEM

NORTH DEAD SEA AREA

ETZYON BLOCK

JUDEA DESERT

WEST MOUNT HEBRON AREA

HEBRON

Dead Sea

YATIR BLOCK

*Preliminary clearing begun

**This settlement ordered dismantled by Israeli Supreme Court after appeal by local Arab landowners, but is listed on later versions of Drobles blueprint as a planned settlement.

***A nahal (military settlement) training site is located in military base near here. While this does not yet constitute a settlement, it is in area earmarked for a planned settlement on Drobles blueprint.

Life cycle of a settlement. Since West Bank Palestinians are unwilling to sell their land, the first stage in creating a settlement is expropriation of Arab-owned land "for security purposes." The land is fenced and marked as a military outpost like that above. Later, the land is released by the military and civilian housing like that below is created for rent or sale at bargain prices to Jewish Israelis, many of whom continue to commute to their jobs in Israel proper.

NYT Pictures

CHAPTER XIX

After Camp David

"On the West Bank settlements, we worked out language that no new Israeli settlements would be established after the signing of this framework and that the issue of additional settlements would be resolved during the negotiations. Begin later denied that he had agreed to this, and claimed that he had promised to stop building settlements only for a three-month period. My notes are clear—the settlement freeze would continue until all negotiations were completed. "[1]

Jimmy Carter, 1982

By the end of the Carter Administration, the intensity of cross-pressures on American interests in the Middle East was profound. America's commitment to the survival of Israel remained strong, yet that survival could be ensured in the long term, in the view of many American leaders, only by a comprehensive solution of the Palestinian issue. Such a solution would require a convergence by the Arab states and Israel toward a central position. This was not feasible while Arab leaders ruled out compromises with Israel and while the Begin government was frankly immobile on issues that required territorial concessions to Palestinian nationalism. The United States, moreover, continued to have significant interests in the stability of moderate regimes in the area, particularly in Egypt and Saudi Arabia. "[2]

Abba Eban, 1983

---

1. Carter, Jimmy, *Keeping Faith: Memoirs of a President*, Bantam Books, New York, 1982, p. 397.
2. Eban, Abba, *The New Diplomacy: International Affairs in the Modern Age*, Random House, New York, 1983, p. 71.

"Instead of using the Sadat statesmanship as an opportunity for peace, Begin used it to take the Egyptian Army out of the Middle East equation. If that caused immense difficulties for Sadat among his Arab brothers, Begin seemed not to care."

William Raspberry, *Washington Post*, July 22, 1981

"It is time for all Palestinian leaders to forego the use of violence and to recognize Israel's right to exist in peace. And it is time for the Israeli military occupation to end and for freedom and full autonomy to be granted to Palestinians who live either in the West Bank and Gaza or as refugees from their homeland. This is what was promised at Camp David."

Jimmy Carter, August 9, 1981

"It was Arafat, his Palestinian people, and the Lebanese who were to pay the full and terrible price of Sadat's separate peace with Israel. Within one month of the signing of the separate peace, with Egypt officially neutralized by it, Israel began a five-month blitz on the Lebanon. Some 50,000 Palestinian refugees fled northwards as their camps were being bombed and strafed by Israeli jet fighters, and sometimes pounded by long-range artillery; 175,000 Lebanese fled from the south and became refugees in their own land; thousands, Palestinians and Lebanese, were killed. In Beirut Western diplomats openly admitted they were shocked and sickened by the scale of the Israeli attacks and the apparent indifference of their governments."[3]

Alan Hart, 1984

As they stood before massed microphones in the White House that euphoric Sunday night, Presidents Carter and Sadat and Prime Minister Begin held not one but two agreements. One was called "A Framework for the Conclusion of a Peace Treaty Between Egypt and Israel" and the other was "A Framework for Peace in the Middle East."

The former agreement called for an Israeli-Egyptian peace treaty to be signed within three months, major Israeli withdrawals within three to nine months after that, the normalization of all relationships between the two countries within a year, and a complete Israeli withdrawal from Egyptian territory within three years.

The latter embodied agreements concerning Palestinian "autonomy," the Jewish settlements on the West Bank, and the linkage between the two framework agreements. The Jerusalem problem had been deferred by exchanges of letters in which each of the three countries simply stated its position, without accepting the positions of others.

Carter spent Monday afternoon working on an address to Congress about the Camp David agreement, but he sent Vice President Mondale to Sadat to see if the Egyptian President wanted the U.S. to use any particular statements or phrases that might help secure cooperation from the Palestinians and other Arabs. Sadat's advice was "Just do not aggravate the Israelis, some of whom are quite excitable and unpredictable people."[4]

---

3. Hart, Alan, *Arafat: Terrorist or Peacemaker?*, Sidgwick and Jackson, London, 1984, p. 406.
4. Carter, Jimmy, *Keeping Faith: Memoirs of a President*, Bantam Books, New York, 1982, p. 404.

Carter writes in his memoirs:

"That same afternoon we heard reports that Prime Minister Begin was making negative statements to Jewish audiences concerning the arrangements for Jerusalem, withdrawal from the West Bank, new settlements in the occupied territories, Palestinian refugees, and future relationships with Israel's other neighbors. When we were together at the Capitol for my report to Congress, I discussed with Sadat and Begin what a serious problem this was. Begin's statements were certain to alienate the moderate Arabs and the Palestinian leaders, and to impede any further progress on the Palestinian and West Bank issues. It seemed that suspicions at Camp David were proving well founded. Begin wanted to keep two things: the peace with Egypt — and the West Bank."[5]

Carter prudently decided that now that he had been vindicated in his determination to make peace between Israel and its largest — and most dangerous — neighbor, the time was ripe to mend some domestic fences. His diary for September 19 recorded:

"Had a meeting of key Jewish leaders, along with Fritz and others. We reminisced about the extreme strain between them and me and the rest of the Jews in the United States. I pointed out in a nice way that the controversies that I had put on the table that caused the strain had been the source of ultimate success, and hoped that they would not only work to repair the political damage, but to restrain Begin, who is acting in a completely irresponsible way."[6]

"The meeting was delightful," Carter writes in his memoirs, "full of fun and good cheer, and we welcomed it because it was so rare. All of us were happy about the Camp David accords. But the respite was to be quite brief, because Begin continued to disavow the basic principles of the accords relating to Israel's withdrawal of its armed forces and military government from the West Bank, negotiations on an equal basis with the Palestinians and other Arabs, and the granting of full autonomy to the residents of the occupied areas. His statements, which were in sharp contrast to those of the American and Egyptian delegations, soon created understandable confusion among those who were intensely interested in the Middle East."[7]

Before Begin left Washington, Carter had one more private talk with him of which the U.S. President writes:

"I talked to him privately about the good prospects for cooperation from some of the other Arab leaders, and warned that his remarks were making it almost impossible for them to join in any future discussions. His reply was evasive and non-committal, and I had a feeling that he really did not want any early talks involving the Palestinians and other Arabs. The next day in New York, Begin continued his disruptive comments."[8]

It was not all bad news, however. Initially Carter thought he detected cautiously positive reaction from both the Saudis and King Hussein.

Then, on September 27, he learned that the Knesset had voted to support the Camp David agreement and remove Israeli settlers from Sinai. "This," Carter wrote in his

---

5. Carter, Jimmy, *Keeping Faith: Memoirs of a President*, Bantam Books, New York, 1982, p. 405.
6. *Ibid.*, p. 405.
7. *Ibid.*, pp. 405-6.
8. *Ibid.*, p. 406.

diary, "was a remarkable demonstration of courage, political courage, on the part of Prime Minister Begin, who had to go against his own previous commitments over a lifetime, against his own closest friends and allies who sustained and protected him during his revolutionary days."[9]

The Russians opposed the agreements, saying the Israelis had won everything and the Egyptians and other Arabs had gained nothing. Then Begin began taking actions that only strengthened their case. He announced plans to expand the West Bank settlements and to move his office to East Jerusalem. When Carter demanded an explanation, Begin told him the actions on the settlements were designed to appease his political allies, who were turning against him. Carter shrewdly surmised that Begin was using "the settlements and East Jerusalem issues to prevent the involvement of the Jordanians and the Palestinians" by strengthening their growing suspicion that Camp David was only a separate peace between Egypt and Israel.

At a summit meeting in Baghdad, the Saudis joined the "rejectionists" in condemning the Camp David agreements. Then Begin told Carter that the Israeli cabinet had agreed to accept the draft treaty but had ruled out any timetable for agreement on the West Bank. Sadat's position was now beginning to harden, as he saw his isolation from the other Arab countries growing.

On December 17, 1979, Secretary Vance wearily ended a six-day shuttle with the news that, although the specified three months had passed since the Camp David agreements were signed, no peace treaty was in sight. The Egyptians complained of excessively legalistic maneuvers by Israel, while the Israelis charged "zigzagging" by Sadat.

Perhaps the sharpest complaint was by Menachem Begin himself, who angrily told Vance that the U.S. had abandoned the role of honest broker and was siding with the Egyptian position. His complaint once again brought Israel's U.S. supporters into action. Of the 36 American Jewish intellectuals who only eight months earlier had shocked the Begin government by supporting the Israeli peace movement, 33 now stated in a message to President Carter that the U.S. position was "unacceptable" and that Israeli objections to "the proposed Egyptian revisions are reasonable."

A three-way impasse, first between Egypt and Israel, then between Israel and the U.S., and finally between pro-Israel Americans and the Carter Administration, continued for three more months. In March, 1979, Carter himself set out on a six-day mission to Cairo and Jerusalem. Few thought he could bridge the gulf between Egypt and Israel concerning the Palestinians. American editorial writers complained that U.S. Presidents are expected to preside over signing ceremonies for treaties already negotiated, and not to expend their efforts and prestige in trying to reconcile the irreconcilable. Once again the world was prepared for a letdown.

By this time, however, there was little that could happen to Carter in either Egypt or Israel that had not happened to him before. In his March diary entry from Cairo he records:

---

9. Carter, Jimmy, *Keeping Faith: Memoirs of a President*, Bantam Books, New York, 1982, p. 407.

"In my private visits with Sadat he emphasized again and again that his main concern was about me . . . It was imperative to him that the United States and Egypt stand together, no matter what might be the outcome of the negotiations. He reviewed briefly the result of his trip to Jerusalem and our Camp David talks, and the fact that the agreements we reached there comprised the first progress for Palestinians in 30 years . . . I reminded Sadat that Begin . . . had gone much further than the other Israeli government leaders who had preceded him; that in Begin's mind he went too far at Camp David. Sadat understands that Begin may wish to back out if he gets a chance, or wait until after 1980 when there is a President in the White House who may not be so equally balanced between the Israeli and Arab interests. Sadat understands that it's important to conclude the negotiations now." [10]

On March 10, from Jerusalem, Carter records:

"Then I asked Begin if he wanted to go into the study, because I was prepared to give him a report on my meeting with Sadat, review the outstanding issues, and hopefully expedite his acceptance of the treaty terms, arrange for the signing ceremonies, and have a conclusion of my trip to the Mideast without any further interruptions.

"He seemed to show little interest in my conversations with Sadat. We arrived at the point that Sadat wanted him to come to downtown Cairo and for Sadat to come to Jerusalem for the signing ceremonies. Begin told me then for the first time that he could not sign or initial any agreement . . . I couldn't believe it. I stood up and asked him if it was necessary for me to stay any longer. We then spent about 45 minutes on our feet in his study. I asked him if he actually wanted a peace treaty, because my impression was that everything he could do to obstruct it, he did with apparent relish. He came right up and looked into my eyes about a foot away and said that it was obvious from the expression on his face that he wanted peace as much as anything else in the world. It was almost midnight when I left. We had an extremely unsatisfactory meeting, equivalent to what we'd had the previous Saturday night at the White House." [11]

Writing later in his memoirs, Carter records his emotions:

"Rarely have I been so frustrated as I was that evening. I was convinced that Begin would do everything possible to block a treaty and to avoid having to face the problem of the full autonomy he had promised to the Palestinians on the West Bank. He was obsessed with keeping all the occupied territory except the Sinai, and seemed to care little for the plight of the Arabs who were having to live without basic rights under Israeli rule." [12]

In the course of the next day's activities in Jerusalem, however, Carter actually presided over a meeting of the Israeli cabinet where, he records, "in spite of many interruptions I finally completed my remarks . . . We spent hours talking about the difference between 'derogate,' 'is not consistent with' and 'contravene.' " Carter also spoke to the Knesset on that visit and notes "There was quite a buzz among them when I said that the people were ready for peace, but that the leaders had not yet shown that they had the courage to take a chance on peace. Begin apparently resented this comment, but it was accurate and needed to be said. When Begin got up to try to speak, he was interrupted constantly by shouts and rudeness. He seemed to take delight in it, beam-

---

10. Carter, Jimmy, *Keeping Faith: Memoirs of a President*, Bantam Books, New York, 1982, p. 418.
11. *Ibid.*, p. 421.
12. *Ibid.*, p. 421.

ing with pleasure every time it occurred. One of the women members of the Knesset, Mrs. Cohen, was expelled."[13]

It was only on the morning of his departure that Carter got a commitment from Begin to sign a treaty if Sadat would agree to some rewording of the draft text. Sadat agreed within minutes of Carter's arrival for a farewell call in Cairo. Carter was airborne again when word was flashed jubilantly from the President's homeward-bound plane that at the last moment agreement had been reached. On March 26, the Israeli-Egyptian peace treaty was signed by President Sadat and Prime Minister Begin in televised ceremonies before a huge audience on the White House lawn.

During the signing ceremonies, Palestinians were protesting across the street from the White House in Lafayette Square. The bitterness they felt in Washington that day was only a mild foretaste of what was to come. While inviting the Palestinians (but not their PLO representatives) to discuss "autonomy" for the people of the West Bank, the Begin government continued to exhibit every sign of preparing for a long, perhaps permanent, occupation of their land.

The settlements proliferated. Whereas they were initially corrugated shacks and mobile homes set on bleak mountain tops, now hundreds of expensive, modern concrete villas and apartments extended row upon row, across hills and the valleys in between. Some were occupied by religious fanatics, many of whom were from the United States. They appeared all over the West Bank, Uzi machine guns slung across their shoulders. They were eager to lecture before television cameras about their God-given rights to the land, or to burst into Arab homes or schools after any minor incident in obvious efforts to frighten away the Arab neighbors from whom the land they occupied had been taken. Other "settlers," however, were simple Israelis, a great many of them either "Oriental" Jews or their descendants. They were attracted not by Begin's politicized theology but rather by the low costs at which these West Bank houses were made available to them. They still commuted to office jobs in Jerusalem or Tel Aviv, but lived in homes purchased for one quarter the price of the same home just a few miles away in Israel proper. The Israeli government made up the difference and it was rapidly bankrupting Israel.

Demonstrations by West Bank Arabs were broken up with escalating Israeli military brutality. The endless war with the Palestinian guerrillas across the Lebanese border was fought with increasing ferocity, and with weapons supplied by the U.S. on the condition that they be used solely for Israel's defense.

Israeli withdrawals from Sinai continued in accordance with the Israeli-Egyptian agreement, although sometimes it appeared that Begin was seeking to provoke Sadat into renouncing the agreement before all of the Sinai was gone. As for Sadat, he seemed grimly determined to keep his own people quiet, and to ignore the increasingly vocal criticism from much of the Arab World. Clearly, his objective was to get the Israelis off every last inch of Egyptian soil before he took up the Palestinian cause too vociferously. After that, who could say how the Israeli-Egyptian peace would turn out?

---

13. Carter, Jimmy, *Keeping Faith: Memoirs of a President*, Bantam Books, New York, 1982, p. 422.

In the U.S. there was increasing sympathy for the Palestinians, and some under-standing of the rejection by the other Arab countries of the Camp David agreement, but there was perplexity too. If the Arabs were so sure that Begin would not give back the West Bank and East Jerusalem, why did they not let some Palestinians go to the peace table and demonstrate Israeli intransigence before the world? There lingered in American minds a suspicion that the Arab refusal to test the Camp David plan was based not on the certainty that it would not work, but on the fear that it might.

Since Begin ruled out negotiations with the PLO, it could not, and Hussein would not, join the autonomy talks. Therefore Begin was never really tested. The situation smacked of the easy Jewish victories of the Mandate era, when Jewish settlers would testify eloquently before Royal Commissions of inquiry, and the absent Palestinians were represented only by well-meaning but ineffectual friends.

By anyone's reckoning, the Palestinians, as usual, were the losers. But so was Jimmy Carter. He badly needed a triumph before the 1980 election campaign.

Carter's attention throughout his last year in office was focused on non-Arab Iran, but the Arab-Israel dispute still caused him a series of small problems. It cost him his old political comrade-in-arms, the U.S. Ambassador to the UN, Andrew Young. Young was forced to resign after the Israeli government made an issue of a secret meeting between Young and the PLO observer to the UN. It was not Young's first breach of discipline, but the U.S. Black community saw it as a clear decision by Carter that Jewish support was more important to him than black support. Blacks set out to disprove this in the election to come.

Then, just before the June, 1980, New York Democratic primary, Carter reversed a U.S. vote for a UN resolution condemning Israeli settlements on the West Bank. It was a serious error. In the minds of Americans who knew nothing about the Middle East, the switch made him look like a bumbler. To Americans who understood, it make him look no better than his predecessors, surrendering to the Israel lobby in an election year. And he lost the Jewish vote in New York anyway to Senator Edward Kennedy, who had a long record of unquestioning compliance with any request from the Israel lobby.

Secretary of State Cyrus Vance, a good soldier to the end, took the blame for a "failure of communication" leading to the bizarre U.S. reversal of position on the UN vote. He was openly unhappy, however, about Carter's increasing election year con-cern with Jewish opinion on the Middle East and bitterly opposed the appointment of former Democratic National Chairman Robert Strauss as President Carter's special Mid-dle East Ambassador. Vance resigned a short time later over Carter's unsuccessful at-tempt to rescue American hostages in Iran by force.

There were no more triumphs to be wrung out of the Middle East. Carter probably never had a chance to defeat Ronald Reagan, short of simultaneously turning the U.S. economy around and getting the U.S. hostages safely out of Iran. However, Carter almost went down in history as the only U.S. President to turn the Arab-Israeli dispute to his own political advantage. With all of the others, up until then, it had been largely a matter of containing the damage.

President-elect Ronald Reagan gave little sign that he was deterred by any of this.

In fact, prior to assuming office, he gave little sign that he realized he might need to re-examine the hardline pro-Israel views he had been enunciating for years in Southern California film circles, where they were extremely popular. The next four years promised to be a chapter of a whole new kind in the delicate U.S. relationship to the Arab-Israeli dispute.

UPI

Invasion begins. Villagers in Southern Lebanon hold white flags as Israeli tanks (above) roll across a Lebanese border that had been quiet for 10 months preceding the June 6, 1982 invasion of Lebanon. Stated purpose was to round up Palestinian guerrillas within 24 miles of the Israeli border. Below, Arabic-speaking Israeli soldiers interrogate Palestinians near Sidon.

Wide World

CHAPTER XX

President Reagan and Strategic Consensus

"The administration acted prudently in fulfilling the commitments of its predecessors on the AWACS sale. The damage of a negative vote to our position in the Middle East, to a moderate evolution of the area and to a constructive peace process would be grave, perhaps irretrievable. The Congress must not undermine the President's authority in international affairs by a rejection of the sale; the consequences would haunt us for many years in many fields. We cannot afford this—especially after a decade and a half of domestic division. "[1]

Former Secretary of State Henry Kissinger, October, 1981

"Defeat on AWACS would be a serious embarrassment to Reagan, both at home and abroad. Israel's friends should not be under any illusion that they help Israel's cause by embarrassing and undermining the authority of their indispensable friend in the White House. . . . Those who worry about the deal ought to trust the President, the Secretary of State and the Secretary of Defense. "[2]

Former President Richard Nixon, October, 1981

"In the Middle East alone the new Administration struck out in new directions. For over a year it abstained from any initiative designed to carry the Camp David accords beyond the Carter Administration's achievement in sponsoring a peace treaty between Egypt and Israel. The assassination of President Anwar el-Sadat and the early efforts

---

1. Kissinger, Henry A., "Don't Make the AWACS Sale a Test of Strength," *Washington Post*, October 6, 1981, p. A-21.
2. Nixon, Richard M., in statement released October 4, 1981 and reported in the *New York Times* of the same date, p. 1.

of Hosni Mubarrak to consolidate his rule contributed to this American passivity. Secretary Haig made a visit to the Middle East in an attempt to persuade friendly states that the central issue was Soviet expansion. This effort was a failure, partly because Arab states showed more concern about Israel than about the Soviet Union, and partly because the thesis about the primacy of the Soviet threat was not borne out by any evidence."[3]

Abba Eban, 1983

"Solutions are always fiercely controversial, and easy prey to partisan politics; hence a powerful impulse at the start of any new administration to innovate. Richard Nixon tried studied neglect until the area exploded into the October 1973 Arab-Israeli war. Only then did he turn to the hard business of Henry Kissinger's shuttle diplomacy. Jimmy Carter, thinking big, went for the sweeping 'comprehensive' solution by trying to bring the Soviets into the act. That backfired by outraging the Israelis. But it also encouraged the breakthrough in Jerusalem that lead to the considerable, though more modest, Camp David breakthrough. Thinking even bigger, the Reagan Administration came on strong, initially, with an approach that seemed to shove the Arab-Israeli conflict aside, as a matter of secondary importance to what an official State Department spokesman was describing, in advance of the Haig tour, as 'the deteriorating position of the West vis-a-vis the Soviet Union.' The East-West element was to be given 'the highest priority in the region at this time.' "[4]

Philip Geyelin, 1981

"When Israel attacked Iraq's nuclear research facility on June 7 and a month later sent its U.S.-supplied aircraft against Palestinian terrorists in a densely populated residential district in Beirut, the Reagan-Haig 'strategic consensus' was critically wounded."[5]

Rowland Evans and Robert Novak, 1981

"Israel might have sincerely believed it was a defensive move."[6]

President Ronald Reagan, 1981

"Within hours of Weinberger's persuasive argument at the secret June 10 National Security Council meeting for a strong American response to the raid, Begin had been informed. The spectacle of a foreign leader attacking one of Reagan's Cabinet chiefs for advising the President at an NSC meeting did not sit well in Reagan's White House."[7]

Rowland Evans and Robert Novak, 1981

---

3. Eban, Abba, *The New Diplomacy: International Affairs in the Modern Age*, Random House, New York, 1983, p. 77.
4. Geyelin, Philip, *Washington Post*, April 20, 1981.
5. Evans, Rowland and Novak, Robert, *Washington Post*, July 24, 1981.
6. Reagan, President Ronald, Presidential Press Conference, June, 1981.
7. Evans, Rowland and Novak, Robert, *Washington Post*, June 24, 1981.

"Will (President Reagan) accept that the best way to blunt a Soviet push in the Middle East is to do what is necessary to ease the Israeli-Palestinian dispute?"[8]
Stephen S. Rosenfeld, *Washington Post*, August 7, 1981

"If the arms flow to Israel continues, in the face of the proprieties of American law, the distrust of American motives and of its intended role as honest broker in resolving Arab-Israeli differences will be significantly heightened."[9]
Former Defense Secretary James R. Schlesinger, 1981

"Begin, without question, is making it difficult to assist Israel."[10]
William C. Clark, Deputy Secretary of State, 1981

"Now we are trying once again to pick up the pieces of our diplomacy, shattered by another in the weary cycle of Israeli surprises."[11]
Former Undersecretary of State George Ball, 1981

Prior to his 1976 inauguration, Jimmy Carter had seriously considered appointing George Ball as his Secretary of State. Ball was Undersecretary of State during the Kennedy and Johnson Administrations and then had served as U.S. Ambassador to the UN. After returning to his Wall Street investment firm, Ball remained an articulate and activist speaker and writer on foreign affairs. Carter was talked out of the appointment by partisans of Israel, and thus deprived himself of a particularly experienced and self-confident statesman who might have taken enough of the burden of world affairs off Carter's shoulders to enable him to produce some of the foreign policy triumphs he needed at re-election time.

Now, as President-elect Ronald Reagan huddled with his own "kitchen cabinet," made up of long-time supporters and aides from his days as California governor as well as more recently-acquired national campaign advisers and fund-raisers of the self-made-man stripe, he faced the same dilemma. Reagan wanted and needed one of his most experienced and wisest supporters, Caspar Weinberger, in his cabinet. He also wanted George Shultz, a former University of Chicago economics professor who had acquired a reputation as a low-key, no-nonsense problem solver in previous Republican administrations. Both, however, were officers of the Bechtel Corporation, a giant, San Francisco-based construction company with contracts all over the world. In Saudi Arabia the company was building two entirely-new industrial cities at either end of a trans-Arabia oil and gas pipeline.

Supporters of Israel maintained that Bechtel executives were far too personally involved in Middle East affairs for two of them to hold the two top-level positions in the Reagan Administration. Israel's American friends were aware that Reagan—perhaps

---

8. Rosenfeld, Stephen S., *Washington Post*, August 7, 1981.
9. Schlesinger, James R., Former Defense Secretary, *Washington Post, June 12, 1981.*
10. Clark, William C., Deputy Secretary of State, July 22, 1981.
11. Ball, George, Former Undersecretary of State, *Washington Post*, June, 15, 1981.

more than any President-elect since World War II – had a reputation for delegating the big issues to trusted aides, and then acting on the advice they gave him. The result was that Caspar Weinberger, an Episcopalian and former Budget Director and Secretary of Health, Education and Welfare, became Secretary of Defense, clearly the top job in the new Administration. George Shultz, also a former Budget Director and Secretary of Labor and of the Treasury, was left outside looking in. Shultz, characteristically, said nothing about it in public, but he was deeply hurt and disappointed.

Reagan instead appointed General Alexander Haig as his Secretary of State, and the Washington establishment, which feared Reagan's rich conservatives and populist "California crazies" just as much as it had feared Carter's "Georgia Mafia" four years earlier, breathed a collective sigh of relief. Haig, a "political general," had come to national prominence as Kissinger's deputy in the National Security Council. Once, early in the Nixon Administration, a reporter had asked Kissinger how it was that the lights burned late in his National Security Council offices night after night, and yet the press was asked to believe that Kissinger was a "secret swinger" pursuing *la dolce vita* with a succession of glamorous women. "If someone's working late in my office," Kissinger had replied airily, "it's probably Haig."

Just how true that was became obvious after Kissinger was appointed Secretary of State and Haig succeeded John Haldeman as White House Chief of Staff. It was the period of deepest Watergate travail for President Nixon, and sometimes it had seemed that Haig wielded an extraordinary share of Presidential authority as Nixon became increasingly preoccupied with the defense of his embattled Presidency. It was Haig who had warned Jerry Ford to prepare for the sudden transition from Vice President, informing him that evidence on recently-subpoenaed tapes would inevitably lead to President Nixon's resignation or impeachment. It was Haig who was suspected by the media of offering a "deal" to Ford: Nixon's resignation for a promise of pardon. It was also Haig who saw to security precautions during that 1974 transition to prevent any foreign power or domestic element from taking advantage of the chaos in Washington.

Ford, wishing to reward Haig for loyal service to Nixon, while staffing the White House with his own team, had sent Haig off to the position of NATO commander, against the wishes of most of America's NATO allies who did not want the alliance headed by a "political general" so closely associated with a disgraced President. Haig, however, by hard work and application to his NATO job, had earned a large measure of respect in Europe. He had also narrowly escaped a bomb assassination attempt there. Reasoning that none of this would hurt him politically, upon his retirement from the Army he had briefly probed his chances for the 1980 Republican Presidential nomination. He had decided, however, that the other Republican candidates were too strong for him to overtake.

With all this already behind him, the Washington and New York foreign policy establishment was generally pleased at Haig's selection. It even supported his early attempts to establish himself "vicar" of U.S. foreign policy, and thus prevent end-runs around the Secretary of State of the kind he had watched Kissinger perform for the four years they were together in the White House.

Haig made it clear from the beginning that he expected to be in charge of Reagan

Administration foreign policy and that he would brook no interference from White House staff or Presidential friends. A "transition team" of Reagan campaign supporters had appeared at the Department of State in December, 1980, to oversee the changeover from the Carter Administration. When its work was finished, the team leader, Robert Neumann, a former UCLA professor who had already served as U.S. Ambassador to Afghanistan and to Morocco, was appointed Reagan's Ambassador to Saudi Arabia. To their astonished disappointment, Haig dismissed all of the other team members with polite thanks, but no job offers.

Then, only a few weeks after Neumann had arrived in Saudi Arabia, Haig publicly dismissed him as well. Neumann, who had prepared position papers on foreign affairs for the Reagan campaign and had helped prepare Reagan for his televised election debates with President Carter, had committed what Haig defined as the cardinal sin, sending advice directly to the President through "back channels." In publicly crucifying a Reagan Administration political Ambassador, the vicar was making it clear that there would be no second-guessing of his own policy, and that none of the tricks he had watched his old boss, Henry Kissinger, play on William Rogers would be committed against *this* Secretary of State.

Only weeks after his inauguration, President Reagan was wounded by a would-be assassin's bullet. Haig rushed from the Department of State to the White House pending the arrival in Washington of Vice President George Bush, who had been on a speech-making trip. Asked by a television reporter who was "in charge" in the momentarily chaotic White House, a tense, white-faced Haig had said, without further explanation, "I am." Since he was not, legally or de facto, in charge, the incident unnerved the press and an audience of millions who saw it on television. In a way it may have strengthened him with the President and the President's long-time cronies, however. They probably wrote Haig off that day as a man capable of upstaging the boss. Unfortunately, Haig had a considerably different self-image and it soon became apparent that, in his own mind, he was using his position as Secretary of State to run for the Presidency.

Normally a Secretary of State is expected to take the blame for unpopular decisions, as had Vance for Carter, and to save the popular ones for the President to announce. He also is expected to labor tirelessly but quietly in a field that has no built-in special interest support or national constituency. Haig's style was the opposite in every respect. Therefore, from the first, Haig and Reagan were on a collision course of which neither was fully aware.

Traditionally, the position of Under Secretary of State is a political one, usually held by a trusted incumbent party functionary or friend of the President, there to see that the scenario outlined above is played properly, and to take some of the ceremonial burden off the Secretary. Under Carter the job had been held by a Los Angeles attorney who was also a good administrator. Under Reagan the job was turned over to Judge William Clark, a wealthy California attorney and rancher who had spent much of his life promoting Ronald Reagan's political career. Clark's most recent position had been Chief Justice of the California Supreme Court. He was intelligent, loyal and was considered highly conservative. Reagan's supporters wanted him in the State Department to keep an eye on Haig and also on the career officials of what, in Southern California conservative circles, was considered a bastion of suspect internationalism, soft-headed liberalism, and occasional outright appeasement.

At first both Haig and the State Department professionals noted only that Judge Clark was low-key, did not seem interested in second-guessing them, and that he spent less time than they had expected at the White House talking to the President. They overlooked the fact that he was amiable, a quick study, and possessed of a large measure of common sense, all qualities that made him particularly valuable to an aging President who had no intention of changing his style of delegating not only the technical aspects of his job, but also much of the policy making.

Nevertheless, the Reagan Administration policy pronouncements concerning the Middle East were confusing. Persons knowledgeable about the area could not take them seriously.

By the end of the Carter Administration, foreign affairs professionals had been making no secret of their conviction that Israel was a rapidly-growing strategic and political liability to the United States. The new Reagan Administration now seemed to be trying to wish away the realities apparent to anyone who had made even the most casual study of the Middle East. On February 13, 1981, only a month after he had assumed office, the new U.S. Secretary of State's approach to the Middle East was bluntly described in the *Washington Post* by syndicated columnists Rowland Evans and Robert Novak, who already had the reputation of being well connected with the ultra-conservative wing of the Republican Party, as well as being particularly knowledgable about the Middle East in their own right. They wrote:

"Haig looks at Israel not in terms of American constituency-group politics but as an American ally with strategic strength to offer Washington, much like Saudi Arabia and other U.S. allies in the Arab World." [12]

Only three weeks later, in a CBS "Face the Nation" interview on March 8, Defense Secretary Caspar Weinberger, in remarks more in line with Middle East realities, emphasized the need for U.S. allies in the Middle East but conspicuously omitted any mention of Israel in this regard:

"It is essential we have a presence in the Middle East or, as it is being called, Southwest Asia. We need some facilities and additional men and material there or nearby, to act as a deterrent to any Soviet hopes of seizing the oil fields or interdicting the line." [13]

As the months passed, and press statements accumulated, it became increasingly clear that the Administration's new Middle East policy, called "strategic consensus," was not shared by Weinberger. In fact it was a Haig idea based upon a false premise. Haig believed that the U.S. could build a strong and useful three-country Middle Eastern alliance based upon its existing bi-lateral ties with Israel, Egypt, and Saudi Arabia without solving the Palestinian problem that divided them. Haig's approach ignored

---

12. Evans, Rowland and Novak, Robert, *Washington Post*, February 13, 1981.
13. Weinberger, Caspar, U.S. Secretary of Defense, in remarks on "Face the Nation," CBS interview, March 8, 1981.

completely the fact that Saudi Arabia was deathly afraid that in any future Middle East flare-up Israel would seize upon any pretext to "take-out" the vast oil-fields and installations in the Saudi Eastern province that were the source of Saudi diplomatic and financial power, and which Israel blamed for many of its own problems. Egypt was equally afraid that, in the absence of any further action to implement the promises concerning the Palestinians made by Begin to Sadat at Camp David, growing discontent both within Egypt and among Egypt's Arab and Muslim neighbors would bring down the Sadat regime. Now, instead of addressing these over-riding obstacles to stability in the Middle East, Haig was proposing to ignore them and instead engage American allies in the Arab World in the U.S. preoccupation with the threat of Soviet encroachment into the Middle East oil fields on both the Iranian and Arabian shores of the Gulf.

Haig's strategic consensus idea obviously had originated with Israel, which was eager to have U.S. military equipment stockpiled on Israeli soil. Although the supplies would ostensibly be for the use of an American Rapid Deployment Force to be airlifted directly from the U.S. in case of trouble in the Gulf region, having the supplies under its control would ensure Israel freedom to pursue its own military ends in any future Middle East war. If Israel used the opportunity of such a war to fulfill old plans regarding Jordanian or other Arab territory, there would no longer be the danger of a U.S. cutoff of supplies. An idea so clearly made in Israel was unacceptable to both Saudi Arabia and Egypt. Haig went right on talking it up, however, while America's Arab allies went on politely ignoring it.

Meanwhile, Prime Minister Begin began making full use of the unaccustomed freedom a pro-Israel U.S. Secretary of State provided. The Begin government had fallen in early 1981. The issue was primarily the downward spiral of the Israeli economy. Although economic mismanagement and favoritism had been a problem under Labor, the downhill slide had worsened under Begin. Inflation was accelerating, productivity decreasing, and Begin seemed heedless of it all as he spent heavily upon his settlements. U.S. economic and military assistance was what kept the country going, and Begin was now spending some 10 per cent of that on settlements in territories that the U.S. still insisted must someday be handed back to the Palestinians.

The Labor opposition forced a vote of no-confidence and early elections. Labor was confident of victory, and already Labor coalition leaders were hinting to U.S. Jews both inside and outside of the Reagan Administration that they might use their new lease on the government to reach a political agreement with the Arabs. At least one, and perhaps several unofficial middlemen, began shuttling between Israeli Labor coalition leaders and moderate Palestinians to sound out possibilities of a quick settlement which both sides could sell to their constituencies while Labor was still riding the crest of its expected victory.

Begin had other plans, however. First he loosened foreign exchange controls, allowing Israelis to import a flood of the foreign-made consumer products they had increasingly been doing without. Then he began a series of confrontational military moves that included air strikes against Palestinians all over Lebanon, combat in Southern Lebanon between Israel's surrogate Lebanese forces and UN peacekeeping troops, and the shooting down by Israel of two Syrian troop-carrying helicopters in northern Lebanon during fighting there between Syrian soldiers and Israeli-armed and trained Maronite Christian militiamen. The Reagan Administration, closely supported by Saudi Arabia, found itself engaged in putting out military brush fires being ignited by Begin all around Israel's borders.

When the joint U.S.-Saudi efforts apparently had succeeded in quieting the situation in Lebanon, Begin further fanned the flames of Israeli nationalism with a sudden air raid on a French-assisted Iraqi nuclear reactor just south of Baghdad. In the course of the raid, Begin made very clear to the world, his planes had violated with impunity the air space of two of the closest U.S. friends in the Arab World, Saudi Arabia and Jordan. Begin claimed the nuclear research being done in Iraq was weapons-related. Iraq, unlike Israel, is a member of the International Atomic Energy Agency and as such regularly opens its facilities to IAEA inspectors. They had said no military research was going on there. One French technician was killed in the raid. The action, therefore, set off protests in the Middle East, Europe and the United Nations. Begin had propelled the Reagan Administration into a no-win situation where, if it remained silent about the violation of Saudi and Jordanian air space, it risked alienating two of its most important Middle Eastern allies. This was the topic U.S. Ambassador to Saudi Arabia Neumann was said to have discussed with the White House, prompting his dismissal by Haig. On the other hand, U.S. Ambassador to Israel Samuel Lewis warned that U.S. condemnation of Israel's action would cause Israelis to "circle the wagons" and thus strengthen election support for Begin.

Reagan equivocated. Pressed by American journalists to comment on Israel's seemingly reckless and aggressive actions, the U.S. President said lamely that perhaps Israel "thought" they were defensive. Within hours Reagan learned that Begin was quoting his words in election rallies as proof that the United States supported Begin's hardline policies. At the same time Begin told Israeli voters that statements in both Western and Eastern Europe condemning the violations of international law involved in the raid on Iraq were proof that European anti-Semitism was not dead. By this time, in Israel a vote for Begin had become a patriotic statement. Against all the odds of only two months earlier, he was re-elected by a narrow margin.

There is no doubt that most U.S. Jewish supporters of Israel were deeply chagrined by the Begin victory. It was hard to envision any American President, even one as seemingly unconcerned with day-to-day events as Reagan, putting up much longer with the Begin policy of plucking the eagle's feathers to delight his economically deprived, poorly-educated and xenophobic followers in Israel, while at the same time brusquely and even defiantly demanding ever-increasing handouts from the U.S. taxpayer. One long-time and usually fervent Jewish supporter of Israel, Joseph Kraft, suggested in his nationally-syndicated column for July 14, 1981:

"American officials ought to take Begin up on his repeated insistence that everything is different now because the United States and Israel are allies. The fact is that Israel has not recently behaved as a good ally should behave. It has acted as though that alliance meant an American blank check for everything Begin considered to be in his country's national interest. It has created situations at times – notably the raid on the Iraqi nuclear installation – that were harmful to American interests." [14]

From sources inside the Reagan Administration Roland Evans and Robert Novak wrote in their July 24, 1981 syndicated column:

"Some Presidential intimates have cautioned Reagan that the timing of Begin's air raid may have been deliberately planned to weaken U.S. ties with its essential Arab allies – particularly Saudi Arabia. He has listened closely. . . . Against his will, his instinct and a lifetime of emotional support for Israel, President Reagan is reappraising the U.S.-Israel connection to preserve his 'strategic consensus' in the Middle East against Soviet penetration." [15]

Even after he had watched Begin deliberately set up a series of bloody and dangerous confrontations with the Arabs in order to come from behind to win re-election, Reagan at first seemed caught by surprise when Begin's confrontational tactics were turned against the Reagan Administration itself. The problem had begun when the Carter Administration decided to sell five airborne early-warning aircraft to Saudi Arabia, primarily to protect the Arab oil-producing states against the increasingly menacing gestures of the Ayatollah Khomeini's Iran. The Carter Administration had postponed the legally-required notification to Congress of the sale until after the 1980 national elections.

After Carter lost, he offered to send the notification to Congress during the final two months of his Administration. In that manner Carter would spare Reagan's incoming Administration a bruising fight with pro-Israel Congressmen in its first weeks in office.

U.S. military planners felt the sale was absolutely necessary to the protection and stability of the oil-producing areas. Nevertheless, they knew that – as in all matters affecting Israel – a number of Jewish members of Congress would take highly emotional positions, and a much larger number of Congressmen would want to be recorded as opposing the sale for the record, even if they hoped it eventually would take place.

The offer of the lame-duck Carter Administration to "take the heat," therefore, was magnanimous, reflecting the outgoing President's discovery during his four years in office that Middle East affairs were far too important for partisan politics. Amazingly, the incoming Reagan Administration declined the offer, saying it needed time to study the matter. Clearly at that time there was no one who understood Middle East realities in charge. If nothing else it indicated that, up to the time of his inauguration, Reagan probably sincerely believed his own campaign statements about Israel's strategic value to the United States, and honestly did not understand how essential cooperation by the moderate Arabs was to U.S. global strategy.

Now, having "studied" the matter, the Reagan Administration had come to the conclusion that if the Arab countries of the Gulf were to be protected from Iranian and, perhaps, even Soviet-instigated incursions, the $8.5 billion AWACS sale must be concluded.

Israel, predictably, went all out to oppose the sale. Its potent Washington lobby,

---

14. Kraft, Joseph, *Washington Post*, July 14, 1981.
15. Evans, Rowland and Novak, Robert, *Washington Post*, July 24, 1981.

the American Israel Public Affairs Committee (AIPAC), started its campaign in Congress to stop the sale by having its Congressional and media disciples quote back pro-Israel Reagan campaign rhetoric.

The Reagan Administration, however, staunchly maintained, in the words of then National Security Adviser Richard Allen, that "the five AWACS aircraft that would be sold to Saudi Arabia" were the minimum required "to maintain one AWACs (plane) continuously in the air" and that "AWACS and the other air defense equipment would make a substantial contribution to the security interests of the United States in a vital part of the world without endangering the security interests of Israel." [16]

As leaders from both political parties, including all three living ex-Presidents, came out strongly in favor of the sale, the Israeli campaign in the U.S. became more shrill. There were invocations of the European Holocaust and charges that the U.S. valued Arab oil over Jewish blood and that proponents of the AWACS deal were guilty of "tactical anti-Semitism." Israel's powerful lobby now made the issue a test of strength, vowing openly to punish any Congressman who did not toe the line, and claiming that the United States was acting against the best interests of Israel. AIPAC normally contends that the interests of the two countries are inseparably linked, but in this case that pretense was abruptly abandoned, and it was made clear to Congressmen that those who did not support the wishes of Israel on this issue could expect to pay dearly at election time. (It was a vow Israel's friends spent millions, with partial success, to fulfill in 1982 and 1984.)

The power of Israel's persuasion was demonstrated in a 301-111 vote in the House of Representatives to disapprove the sale. Since both houses of Congress had to disapprove in order to block the sale, however, the Administration concentrated its efforts on the Senate. Few Senators wanted to be recorded as voting against Israel's desires. Nevertheless, the Administration felt from the beginning that when the voting began, patriotism and personal integrity would produce just enough Senators to support a move which respected leaders in both parties said was essential to U.S. interests. Although President Reagan's faith apparently never wavered, Senator Howard Baker admitted that he was not sure of victory until a week before the vote. Most of the Washington press corps predicted a Reagan defeat until only a few hours before a resolution disapproving the sale was defeated 52-48. At the last moment a handful of Senators, including some publicly on record against the sale, found reasons, such as the tragic assassination of President Sadat by anti-Western Islamic fundamentalists a few days earlier, to reverse their public stands and to support the Administration. After the votes had been counted, however, there were few in the Reagan Administration who still believed that further strengthening Israel, or keeping moderate Arab regimes weak, was somehow in the national interest.

Meanwhile, Saudi Arabia was taking an initiative from the Arab side toward peace. In the fall of 1981, then-Crown Prince Fahd, who was soon to become King of Saudi Arabia, enumerated eight principles for a peaceful settlement of the Arab-Israeli dispute.

---

16. Allen, Richard V., former Assistant to President Reagan for National Security Affairs, "Why the AWACS Sale is Good for Us," *Washington Post*, September 9, 1981.

These principles were in fact those of U.N. Security Council Resolution 242, with two additional features tailored specifically to meet often-reiterated Palestinian objections to the U.N. plan. Resolution 242 calls only "for achieving a just settlement of the refugee problem." In his principles the Saudi Crown Prince defined such a "just settlement" in terms he believed would be acceptable both to the Palestinians and to the United States and other western powers. The Saudi plan specified, first, that after a U.N. trusteeship period, the Palestinians must have their own independent state in the West Bank. Second, it called for repatriation or compensation for all Palestinians who had lost their homes. Despite Menachem Begin's comment that the Saudi plan is a model of "how to liquidate Israel in stages," U.S. and European officials found nothing to criticize in it. Instead President Reagan called the plan a "hopeful sign." He pointed out that the Arab recognition of Israel implicit in the Saudi plan was in fact a major breakthrough toward eventual peace. Even the pro-Israel Haig said "There are aspects in the eight-point proposal made by Crown Prince Fahd by which we are encouraged." Israel's response was to use Knesset members to campaign against the Saudi plan and Saudi Arabia itself in the U.S. The Israeli rhetoric was becoming harsher.

For one week in November 1981 it seemed possible that Western perceptions of the respective roles of the Arabs and the Israelis would have to be reversed. As Arab heads of state, including PLO Chairman Yassir Arafat, assembled in Fez, Morocco, to discuss whether to unite behind the Saudi plan, the Israelis were threatening to veto British, French, Italian and Dutch participation in the international force being assembled by the United States to supervise the final Israeli withdrawal from Egyptian territory in the Sinai. It seemed that just as the Arabs finally were prepared to unite behind a concrete peace proposal conforming to Resolution 242, and thus to European and American positions on a settlement, the Israelis were laying the groundwork for a renunciation not only of any Western European support, but possibly even a renunciation of the Camp David commitments Israel had made to Egypt under U.S. auspices. However, the role reversals did not come to pass at that time.

At Fez the scenario changed. Although Arafat had earlier indicated he could support the Saudi plan, his own PLO executive committee, consisting of representatives not only of Arafat's majority Al Fatah but also of other more radical Palestinian groups, would not back him in this bold move. When he arrived in Fez he had to resume his familiar zig-zag tactics, refusing to confirm in public what he was reported to have said in private in support of the Saudi plan. President Hafez Al-Assad of Syria cancelled his attendance at the conference entirely. The decision was so sudden that a Moroccan delegation actually was on hand at the airport to meet him when it received the news that he would not be arriving. After five hours of debate, with the usual Arab extremists in opposition and neither Syria nor the PLO offering the hoped-for support for the Saudi plan, King Hassan of Morocco abruptly adjourned the Arab summit meeting. It was a tactical move to keep the plan alive and viable for reconsideration at a subsequent Arab summit meeting, rather than letting it go down to defeat in Fez.

Meanwhile, the U.S. and Israel, in the words of columnist Philip Geyelin of the *Washington Post*, "apparently agreed on at least a tentative trade-off of a new 'strategic' military relationship between the two countries in return for Israeli acceptance of Europeans in a Sinai peace-keeping force."

It had been a difficult negotiation, however, with Israeli Defense Minister Ariel Sharon seeking a "strategic cooperation agreement" that would place U.S. bases, troops and military supplies in Israel, and the U.S. seeking to limit any agreements to vaguely defined consultation, coordination, and joint military maneuvers. The resulting agreement, was, therefore, a grudging U.S. payment-in-advance to induce Israel to follow through on its final Sinai withdrawal commitment under the Camp David treaty with Egypt.

After it was signed, Begin made it clear to the U.S. that it contained far less than he had wanted, while at the same time he seemed to be trying through Radio Israel's broadcasts in Arabic to make the Arabs believe that it contained far more than it did.

As early as the summer of 1981, *Washington Post* columnist William Raspberry had suggested that in repeatedly seeking to settle Israel's domestic and foreign political problems with his U.S.-supplied warplanes, Menachem Begin was demonstrating that "America has a madman for an ally." What followed the signing of the U.S.-Israeli memorandum on strategic cooperation seemed only to confirm this. On Saturday, December 13, 1981, the Polish Army unexpectedly declared a state of martial law and arrested the entire leadership of the Solidarity free trade union movement in that country. The following morning, Sunday, December 14, Prime Minister Begin suddenly checked out of the hospital where he had been recovering from a broken hip joint. He proceeded directly to an emergency cabinet meeting he had convened in his home. Within 90 minutes the Cabinet had approved annexation of the Golan Heights areas seized from Syria in the 1967 war, and lost and then recaptured by Israel in 1973. An emergency session of the Knesset ratified the annexation on the same day.

Although world attention was fixed on Poland, there was an angry global reaction to Israel's flagrant violation of international law. To the chagrin of Israel, the U.S. joined in a 15-to-0 U.N. Security Council vote that declared the Golan annexation null and void. The U.S. press reported that President Reagan's anger was aroused by the obvious Israeli attempt to repeat its 1956 success, when it had invaded Egypt while the rest of the world was preoccupied with the bloody Russian repression in Hungary. Begin's precipitate move on December 14, 1981 seemed timed solely to take advantage of world distraction over the surprise "coup" by Poland's Communist Party and army. Unfortunately, it also gave the Russians an opportunity to distract Third World attention from Poland by conspicuously coming to the support of Syria, and it heightened the tension in a developing Soviet-U.S. confrontation.

Only later did American newsmen realize that Begin's actions had been even more Machiavellian than the press had realized. Secretary Haig had been in Europe and was scheduled to visit Israel over the weekend on which the annexation was announced. Haig had cancelled his trip to Israel at the last moment and returned directly to the United States, only because of the declaration of martial law in Poland. Had Haig not suddenly cut short the trip, Begin would have been able to carry out his surprise move while Haig was in the country or just after he had departed. It was the ploy Begin had used earlier in the year when he traveled to Egypt to meet with President Sadat and then, later in the week, ordered the bombing of the Iraqi nuclear reactor. This had falsely signaled the world that Egypt had acquiesced in advance in the bombing of Iraq, and further exacerbated Egypt's estrangement from other Arab countries. The same tactics in regard to the Golan annexation might have estranged the Arab world from the United States, perhaps even bringing about the destruction of U.S. embassies in the Middle East and a denunciation of the U.S. by Saudi Arabia, clearly Israel's top foreign policy goal throughout 1981.

The American reaction to such transparent trickery by Israel was slow in coming, reflecting divided counsel within the Reagan Administration, but strong on arrival. The U.S. suspended the recently-concluded U.S.-Israeli memorandum of understanding on strategic cooperation. It also suspended further discussion of three U.S. military "sweeteners" for Israel for 1982. These would have authorized the Defense Department to make purchases of up to $200 million a year from Israel; permitted Israel to spend part of its U.S. military financing credits on purchases from Israeli domestic defense industries rather than from American industries; and would have permitted other countries receiving U.S. military aid to use part of that aid to buy equipment and services from Israel instead of from the United States. Such unique and vitally important concessions to Israel have always been over and above the high levels of direct U.S. military and economic aid to that country. The Reagan Administration's action to suspend such hidden benefits, as well as the overt benefits watched by the public in both countries, seemed to signal its intention this time to make the U.S. punishment fit the Israeli crime.

The Begin reaction, if not that of a madman, at least made plain what Middle Eastern specialists had long known. He was not as interested in courting American support as in playing to the Israeli man in the street, who loved the spectacle of the tiny country's feisty Prime Minister telling off the world in general and the U.S. superpower in particular.

Begin simultaneously summoned American Ambassador Samuel Lewis to his residence, and journalists to the Israeli Foreign Ministry. Lewis for years had followed the time-honored approach of American ambassadors in Tel Aviv. Over and over he had declared that strong U.S. admonitions to Israel only make Israelis rally around whoever is leading their government at the time. The Carter Administration generally had followed Lewis' advice, and nevertheless had been the target of steadily escalating Begin abuse. The Reagan Administration had, for 10 months, sought to do likewise, with identical results.

Even Lewis' monumental patience seemed momentarily at an end. He had been kept completely in the dark about Israel's annexation move and the U.S. government had been severely embarrassed by, and in the eyes of the world almost implicated in, the illegal Israeli action. Now Lewis found himself listening to a denunciation of his government which, though it may have sounded like the ravings of a maniac, in fact was being read from carefully-prepared notes.

Lewis, who told an aide "I've seen better political theater before, but never to a smaller audience," was wrong about the size of the audience. By the time he got back to his embassy to report the tirade to Washington, Lewis found that his own report was unnecessary. The newsmen summoned to the Foreign Ministry already had received a Ministry press release describing in minute detail Begin's statement to the American ambassador. It was summarized by *Time* magazine as follows:

"You declared that you are 'punishing' Israel. What kind of talk is that, 'punishing' Israel? Are we a vassal state? A banana republic? Are we 14-year-old boys that if they don't behave they have their knuckles smacked?

"You have no moral right to lecture us on civilian casualties. We have read the history of [World War II], and we know what happened to civilians when you carried out military operations against the enemy. We also read the history of the Vietnam war and your term 'body counts.'

"You cannot and will not frighten us with 'punishment and threats.' Threats will fall on deaf ears.

"You are trying to make Israel hostage to the memorandum of understanding. No sword of Damocles will be hanging over our heads. The people of Israel have lived for 3700 years without a memorandum of understanding with America and will continue to live without it for another 3700 years.

"You have imposed upon us pecuniary sanctions, and in the process you have broken the word of the President. What do you want to do? Hit us in the pocket?

"Nobody will succeed in intimidating [American Jews] by anti-Semitic propaganda. They will stand by us. This is the land of their forefathers – they have the right and duty to support us.

"The word rescind is a concept from the time of the Inquisition. Our forefathers went to 'the stake' rather than rescind their faith. We are not going to the stake."

This time the images truly had reversed. Israel's Prime Minister was playing to the xenophobic mob, reviling both the U.S. and all its Western allies, making it difficult for Israel's American partisans to support him without incurring charges of turning on their own country, and publicly upbraiding an American ambassador who for years had worked patiently for understanding between Israel and the United States.

The performance was reminiscent of President Nasser in his most self-destructive years, or of the contemporary Colonel Qaddafi. Although leaders of virtually every national Jewish organization eventually spoke out dutifully in Begin's defense, the statements were cautious and half-hearted. The press had already reported that when Senator Claiborne Pell denounced Israel's annexation of the Golan, he received a standing ovation from a B'nai B'rith audience in Rhode Island.

Even Israel's redoubtable Ambassador Evron, the same Israeli diplomat who long ago had carefully developed ready access not only to President Johnson, but also to top CIA leadership, sounded tired and dispirited as he repeatedly defended his government's actions on U.S. television and in press interviews. He was only two months short of retirement and his scheduled replacement was Philadelphia-raised Moshe Arens, one of the most outspoken hardliners in the Israeli Knesset, whose most notable difference with Begin had been in March, 1979 when Arens voted *against* the Camp David agreements because he had wanted Israel to *keep* Sinai.

For a time U.S.-Israeli relations seemed as cool as they had been in 1956 and 1957 when President Eisenhower had threatened to use U.S. economic power to make Israel withdraw from the lands it had seized in the Suez attack. As before, however, because of the self-destructive abstention by Syria that kept the Saudi principles of peace from being adopted by the Arab states at Fez, there was no positive Arab initiative to which Reagan could turn.

Reagan's basic instincts, built up over a lifetime in films and politics, remained pro-Israel, although he was furious with Begin. Secretary of State Haig, though careful not to push his "strategic consensus" ideas any longer, also remained strongly pro-Israel. The man who might have goaded either into exploring further initiatives with the Arabs, Judge Clark, had moved from the Department of State to the White House to replace National Security Advisor Richard Allen. But, although "strategic consensus" had run its course, he apparently did not feel secure enough in the foreign affairs field to call for new Middle East ideas on his own. Therefore, under a Secretary who got the job originally only because Israel had not vetoed him, no new idea emerged from the Department of State. And with the dead hand of the Arab rejectionists still throttling political initiative in the Arab world, no initiative emerged from that quarter. In Israel, however, something big was stirring.

UPI

Muslim parents feed their injured child intravenously as they negotiate on foot the dangerous crossing between beseiging Israeli army and encircled West Beirut July 15, 1982.

Wide World

Victims (above) of Israeli air raids on Beirut June 11, 1982, during first week of the invasion of Lebanon. Israeli tank en route to Beirut (below) fires into residential apartment at coastal town of Jiye on second day of the Israeli invasion of Lebanon.

George Azar

CHAPTER XXI

The Invasion of Lebanon

"The United States has not given a 'green light' to Israel to undertake any military actions in Lebanon."
State Department Spokesman Dean Fischer, April 29, 1981

"When Israeli forces moved deep into Lebanon in June 1982 to destroy the infrastructure of the PLO, the United States illustrated its ambivalence in a series of changing attitudes. It began by opposing the expedition but then drew attention to the 'opportunities' that the invasion had opened for a stable Lebanon and a Palestine movement shorn of the PLO's radical and militant leadership. The U.S. representative, Philip Habib, negotiated an agreement for the PLO to leave Beirut, but the United States expressed strong opposition to the bombardment, shelling and siege of Beirut which the Israeli government considered vital as a means of pressure on the PLO. Yet, later, when many Israelis were expressing opposition to their government's militant policy, the United States was giving the impression of acquiescence."[1]
Abba Eban, 1983

"Let us suppose for the sake of argument that you are Hitler. You give the order to liquidate a people who happen to be Jews by killing them in gas chambers. Now let us suppose that I am Begin or Sharon. I give the order to liquidate a people who happen to be Palestinians by bombing and strafing their refugee camps and by dropping cluster and fragmentation bombs among them. Am I really any different from you, any better than you, because I am liquidating a people by more conventional means, more

---

1. Eban, Abba, *The New Diplomacy: International Affairs in the Modern Age*, Random House, New York, 1983, p. 76.

acceptable means? What is the crime . . . is it liquidating a people or the means by which a people is liquidated? Are we really saying it's okay to liquidate a people by some means but not by others?"[2]

Yassir Arafat, 1984

"The soldiers . . . brought back with them stories about families of up to 10 relatives helping each other to survive amid collapse and panic. Stories about children completely different from the rocket-launching children who were the only ones mentioned by official Israeli propaganda. Lost children of 10 or 12 caring for their younger brothers, and for old people, begging food for their families; children who didn't cry, who don't engage in mischief because they already have somber seriousness of age. They met Palestinian youths who served as volunteers in hospitals, who have friends, who want to have children some day, and, who, like the Israelis, dream of a motorcycle, of a girl; youths who are also proud of being unafraid of death and who also mourn the death of others. They brought back stories of nurses who remained with the wounded, of doctors who did not flee; and they encountered Palestinian youths who, like themselves, did not ask for mercy and did not humble themselves. These soldiers saw that Palestinian youths, like themselves, feel pride in their identity . . . The soldiers . . . did not hear the Palestinians utter more painful or complex questions than those that cause them such anguish in Israel. When they heard Palestinians speak of that country which they will have some day, they heard faint echoes of the reminiscences of their own parents and grandparents about earlier times in Israel. Or, hearing such dreams, perhaps they felt a tinge of envy."[3]

Jacobo Timerman, 1982

On July 17 and 18, 1981 Israel had sent its American-supplied planes to bomb what it called a PLO headquarters building in a heavily-populated residential district of Beirut. The resulting carnage was awesome, even by Lebanese standards. Between 100 and 300 persons were killed in their Beirut apartments, and twice as many injured. The U.S. should have investigated to determine whether its own laws had been broken, since weapons supplied to Israel as well as to other U.S. military aid recipients are, by American law, to be used strictly for defensive purposes.

President Reagan made no effort to determine whether bombing Palestinian residential quarters in Beirut was "defensive," but he directed Philip Habib, a State Department Far East specialist of Lebanese ancestry, to negotiate a binding cease-fire between Israel and the PLO leaders in Lebanon. Habib, who despite chronic heart problems had returned from retirement to become the President's special envoy to the Middle East, and who became known for his salty language, his fair-minded dealings with subordinates, and his clear-headed approach to problems, delivered the cease-fire agreement on July 24, 1981. It was scrupulously honored by the PLO, which did not fire

2. Hart, Alan, *Arafat: Terrorist or Peacemaker?*, Sidgwick and Jackson, London, 1984, p. 439.
3. Timerman, Jacobo, *The Longest War: Israel in Lebanon*, Alfred A. Knopf, New York, 1982, p. 104.

a single shot across the Lebanese border, despite repeated Israeli provocations, for the next 10 months.

Also in the summer of 1981, Ariel Sharon became Israel's Minister of Defense. By his own admission, he began planning an invasion of Lebanon from the day he took office.

His motivation was unchanged from that of his previous cabinet assignment when, as Minister of Agriculture, he set in motion a plan to settle one million Israelis in the West Bank over a 30-year period. While most critics felt the plan was economically unfeasible, Sharon brushed aside economic objections. He considered the PLO the only major obstacle to carrying it out. The PLO was the nucleus around which Palestinian nationalism had crystalized, and it was Palestinian nationalism that was impeding his plan by motivating the Arabs to stand their ground and not abandon their West Bank homes and lands. To remove that PLO nucleus, Sharon was determined to go to Beirut and "decapitate" the PLO leadership. He would kill as many Palestinian leaders as he could, and disperse the others. He was not really concerned about the level of PLO terrorist activities within the West Bank and Israel, a certain number of which he probably considered useful in keeping Israelis militant and motivated. He certainly was not awed by whatever military power the PLO retained in fractured Lebanon, especially since it was no longer being used across the Lebanese-Israeli border. But he was deeply worried that continued observance of the cease-fire by the PLO was changing Arafat's image in Western Europe from that of a military to a political leader, and was keeping nationalism alive among Palestinians on the West Bank.

In his memoirs, former Secretary of State Haig reveals that he was first told by Prime Minister Begin, while both men were attending President Sadat's funeral in October, 1981, that Israel was coı•ᴣmplating a move into Lebanon. Begin said the Israelis would be careful not to involve Syria in the conflict. Haig warned Begin that "unless there is a major, internationally recognized provocation, the United States will not support such an action."

"In the months ahead," Haig subsequently wrote, "the subject would arise again and again." In February, 1982, the head of Israeli military intelligence briefed Haig on a general plan for an invasion of Lebanon. Haig insisted that the Israelis do nothing before they had completed their withdrawal from Sinai, scheduled for April.

Sharon, who was described by Israelis by this time as "a war waiting to happen," was becoming increasingly anxious to start his invasion. His vision by now had expanded still further. He hoped not only to drive the Palestinian leaders out of Lebanon, but also all of their followers and families, using the same terror tactics so successfully followed in 1947 and 1948 in present-day Israel. Sharon reasoned that if he could frighten the Syrians into letting them pass, most of the fleeing Palestinians would end up in Jordan, which already had a population almost evenly divided between Palestinians and East Bank Jordanians. The incoming flood of Palestinian refugees from Lebanon, Sharon believed, would ultimately destabilize King Hussein's regime. A Palestinian state could be set up in its place, perhaps with some military help from Israel. Then, Sharon reasoned, there would again be a "Palestine," and Israel would be able on some pretext to push into it a million Palestinians living in the West Bank and Gaza, and

250,000 Palestinians living in Israel proper. This, Sharon told his followers, would make Israel truly a Jewish State, miraculously "cleansed" of its original Palestinian inhabitants, all of whom would be ensconced in a new homeland of their own on the East Bank of the Jordan river in the former Hashemite Kingdom of Jordan.

Sharon's plan was consistent with Begin's life-long struggle to seize and hold the West Bank for Jewish occupation. Sharon convinced Begin that the best way to carry out the plan was to link up with the Maronite Phalange militia of Bashir Gemayel. By this time Gemayel's troops owed most of their weapons, ammunition and training to Israel. Sharon hoped to use the Phalange to hunt down the PLO leaders in the streets of Beirut.

Sharon wanted to make his link-up with the Phalange well before August 23, 1982, the day that Lebanese Presidential elections were scheduled. It was part of his plan that the younger son of Phalange Founder-Leader Pierre Gemayel be elected President of Lebanon on that day, since Sharon believed that Bashir Gemayel was the only Maronite leader sufficiently bold and ruthless to carry out the plan in its entirety.

Sharon outlined his invasion plan personally to Haig. He later claimed that, by not opposing it, Haig had given him the "green light." The *New York Times* had by then also carried a detailed and fairly accurate account of it. U.S. correspondents meanwhile filed to their newspapers several accounts of Israeli attempts to provoke the PLO fighters into firing, from their well-fortified position in Beaufort Castle in Southern Lebanon, across the border into Israel.

Sharon obviously was taking seriously Haig's condition that there must be an "internationally recognized provocation" before Israel could invade.

On April 21, the Israeli air force bombed what it called PLO positions in Lebanon, killing 23 persons, in "retaliation" for the death of an Israeli officer killed by a land mine in the portion of Southern Lebanon patrolled by Israeli surrogate Major Saad Haddad's troops. There was no PLO response. On May 9, after a bomb attack on a bus in Jerusalem, Begin renounced the cease-fire agreement and Israeli aircraft killed 11 persons and wounded more than 50 in what were termed reprisal raids on Palestinian camps in Lebanon. This time the PLO broke the cease-fire briefly, firing exactly 100 Katyusha rockets into Israel before Yassir Arafat personally ordered the barrage to stop. It was the first, and only, time Palestinians had responded to the Israeli air attacks with cross-border shelling. Israeli troops and armor, however, began assembling along the Lebanese border.

On June 4 Shlomo Argov, the Israeli Ambassador to the U.K., was wounded in London in an assassination attempt. Sharon seized upon it as the pretext for another series of devastating air raids on Lebanon.

The British Government, aware of what Sharon was doing, quickly announced that the would-be assassins had been arrested and interrogated. They were from an Iraqi-funded group headed by Sabri Al Banna, known as Abu Nidal, a Palestinian who had broken with and sworn to kill Yassir Arafat. The PLO representative in London was also on their "hit list," British police said.

Begin ignored the British statement and convened his cabinet so that Sharon could outline a plan to send Israeli ground forces 25 miles into Lebanon and put all Israeli territory beyond the range of PLO artillery. When cabinet members asked for a briefing by an Israeli intelligence officer concerning the London incident, Sharon banned the intelligence officer from attending the meeting, so that he could not corroborate the British report absolving the PLO of responsibility for shooting Argov.

With Israeli aircraft preceding them, Israeli tank columns then rolled across the Lebanese borders on June 6, 1982. It was a three-pronged drive which was never intended to stop short of Beirut. One column, heading up the center of Lebanon, encountered heavy Palestinian resistance at Beaufort Castle. A column proceeding up the coast road moved rapidly behind air strikes that frightened most of the population of Tyre out of the city and buried many of the Palestinians living in Sidon's suburbs in their homes and schools. A third column, far inland, headed directly for the Beirut-Damascus road, which was heavily defended by Syrian troops.

The middle column was bogged down by suicidal Palestinian resistance. The inland column ran into bloody fighting with well-placed Syrian troops who were finally pushed back only because the Israeli Air Force used, and thereby revealed to the Soviet Union, every bit of its superior U.S. electronic technology to blast the Syrian Air Force out of the Lebanese skies. But Syrian resistance nevertheless stopped the Israeli inland column far short of the Beirut-Damascus road. The column traveling up the coast, however, soon reached the southern suburbs of Beirut. It bypassed the western, Muslim-held areas to link up with the Maronite militias in the northern and eastern areas of the city. Beirut was surrounded, and southern Lebanon was a charnel house with between 10,000 and 20,000 persons killed, and hundreds of thousands homeless.

Israeli author Jacobo Timerman, a hero of the democratic resistance against Argentina's military dictatorship of the mid-70s, was taken on a tour of the newly-conquered areas of southern Lebanon. After viewing shattered Tyre and Sidon he wrote:

"Two cities demolished in a painless and insipid operation. Neither blood nor a bad taste in the mouth. We could look but it was impossible to see. To see . . . we should have talked to mothers seeking sons lost when the Israeli Air Force bombed open cities. . . . We should have sifted through the rubble and touched carbonized bones."[4]

The invasion had moved so rapidly that journalists were able to photograph the still smoking rubble, and the bodies of hundreds of civilians being pulled out of it. Israeli military censors banned the transmission of photos and censored accounts of what was going on. But journalists who could not transmit their stories from Israel could transmit them from Damascus, which was only 65 miles away from besieged Beirut. Once again the images were reversed. During past Middle East wars, journalists could transmit in relative freedom from Tel Aviv and Jerusalem. In 1982 it was the Arab capitals that opened their communications outlets to foreign journalists. The world began to see a new side of the Middle East wars. Instead of smiling Israeli pilots and soldiers, they began to see the thousands of terrified, fleeing Arab refugees, charred Arab corpses, and Palestinian militiamen standing their ground until they were liter-

4. Timerman, Jacobo, *The Longest War: Israel in Lebanon*, Alfred A. Knopf, New York, 1982, p. 25.

ally buried under an avalanche of shells and murderous cluster bombs, fired from U.S.-supplied tanks and planes.

Until the Lebanese Civil War began, Beirut had been one of the most beautiful and modern cities in the world. It was home to a huge foreign community including between 5,000 and 10,000 Americans, many of them life-long residents. As Israeli forces tightened the noose on Beirut, shocking images appeared nightly on American television screens: Israeli soldiers, reclining in tank turrets, laughing as, from the heights around Beirut, they rained death down on frightened civilians below; Israeli jets swooping down on the undefended city to pour a stream of rockets into residential apartments; Israeli gunboats circling lazily just outside rifle range, firing shells into former beach clubs, luxury hotels and seaside villas.

To their credit, the decent people of Israel were the first to react. Timerman, now safely back in a seaside apartment in Israel, only a few miles south of the carnage, wrote:

"I know the significance of those helicopters that each minute head north or return from the north. They go to kill in Beirut or to bring back the wounded. They enrage me. So do the Palestinians, because they were so stupid. . . . And I'm angry, too, with us, with the Israelis, who by exploiting, oppressing, and victimizing them made the Jewish people lose their moral tradition, their proper place in history."[5]

At a Peace Now rally in Israel in which 100,000 Jews protested the invasion, Timerman stood with his two-year-old grandson on his shoulders and wondered "How many years remain for me to try to stop the war that the state army will send my grandson to fight?"[6]

Americans, too, began to react to the Israeli atrocities, literally for the first time in the decades since the endless Israeli-Palestinian war had begun. A mass demonstration wound through downtown Washington, protesting the arrival of Prime Minister Begin to explain the war to President Reagan, and rallied on the elipse behind the White House. In front of the White House, Washington Jews had organized a welcoming demonstration. Both the pro and anti-Begin demonstrations dispersed at approximately the same time and participants in each found themselves walking back to their parked cars and buses side by side. The atmosphere was tense but there was no violence that day. It may have been one of the last times that partisans and opponents of Israel in the U.S. would mingle without violence on American streets.

A vigil every evening to protest the invasion was organized by Arab-American groups on busy Connecticut Avenue near the Israeli Embassy. Soon there was a Jewish counter vigil, organized by local synagogues, across the avenue each evening. Twice, when one or two women arrived early for the Arab-American protest vigil, hoodlums broke out of the Jewish group, rushed across the street and seized the signs carried by the women. Several other times when Jewish vigilantes crossed the street, the protestors quietly stood their ground until police appeared and the pro-Israel partisans returned to their own area. Every Friday evening American Jewish supporters of Israel's Peace

5. Timerman, Jacobo, *The Longest War: Israel in Lebanon*, Alfred A. Knopf, New York, 1982, p. 103.
6. *Ibid.*, p. 34.

Now movement appeared at the Israeli Embassy to join the Arab-American protest group. Increasingly the Arab-Americans were augmented by Americans with no Middle Eastern ethnic ties. The Jewish peace activists also appeared weekly to join a candlelight vigil held each evening near the White House by the Arab Women's Council, a group originally formed by wives of Arab diplomats in Washington but soon joined by other Washington women, some of them wives of U.S. diplomats who had served in the Middle East. Similar demonstrations and counter-demonstrations occurred in other U.S. cities.

The U.S. Government was slow to react, and the paralysis reflected increasing confusion within the Reagan Administration, which was becoming polarized between diehard supporters and increasingly outspoken detractors of Israel. When the Israeli attack began on June 6th, the U.S. had supported the initial U.N. Security Council resolution calling for a cease-fire. Israel rejected the resolution. Two days after the invasion a stronger resolution was introduced at the U.N. condemning the invasion and calling for sanctions. President Reagan was in England but, on the recommendation of a crisis management team headed by Vice President George Bush in Washington, the President authorized a U.S. vote in favor of that U.N. resolution as well. In England, where both were with the President's party, National Security Adviser William Clark told Secretary of State Alexander Haig about the President's decision. Haig went immediately to the President and insisted that, instead of supporting the resolution, the U.S. must veto it. Then, to make sure that his demand was carried out, he personally telephoned U.S. Ambassador Jeane Kirkpatrick at the United Nations.

"With only minutes to spare," he writes in his memoirs, "I telephoned Mrs. Kirkpatrick and instructed her to veto the resolution, regardless of any other instructions she may have received, whether or not Israel was named in the resolution."

Despite Haig's determination to support the Israeli invasion, for which he must have felt some personal responsibility, Reagan was acting to stop it. The President appealed to Begin on June 9 to accept a cease-fire and on the following day sent a similar appeal to President Assad of Syria. Assad indicated he would accept a cease-fire if Israel would withdraw unconditionally. Begin, however, refused a cease-fire until Israeli objectives had been achieved. Reagan then signed a letter prepared for him by Clark calling upon Begin to withdraw his forces from Beirut. Again Haig protested.

By this time, with the bloody seige of Beirut in full swing, even Americans who had never before been involved in Middle East affairs were becoming concerned at American inaction. So were members of President Reagan's inner circle, who believed that unless the U.S. stopped it, one of the great massacres of modern history was about to take place. The PLO rank and file were firmly entrenched in the great steel-reinforced apartment buildings that made up West Beirut. They were standing their ground against tanks and aircraft. The Israelis were unwilling to take the massive losses that would have resulted had they sought to advance further into the city with ground forces. Bashir Gemayel, meanwhile, was making it clear that, after seven years of intermittent civil war in which his militia had lost virtually every engagement it had fought against the Palestinians and their Lebanese Muslim supporters, his Phalange militiamen were not going to try to take West Beirut for the Israelis. The Israelis, therefore, shut off food and, for some of the time, water to the hundreds of thousands trapped in West Beirut, and continued raining down fire and steel from the skies, the hills and the sea around the city.

As the struggle within the U.S. Government continued, a poignant interview took place in the White House. Judge Clark, Secretary of Defense Weinberger and the other Californians were not the only people in Washington who had decided that somehow the Haig veto on U.S. action had to be broken. Among the leaders of the Arab Women's Council, which by now had set up a 24-hour-a-day vigil in Lafayette Square across from the White House, was Nouha Alhegelan, Syrian-born wife of the Saudi Ambassador in Washington. Articulate, strikingly attractive, and fluent in English, the red-haired Mrs. Alhegelan had begun appearing on U.S. television and radio talk shows to tell Americans that the "defensive" weapons they had sent to Israel were being used to destroy Lebanon and its people.

On June 18, she visited the White House and spoke about the suffering in Beirut with the President's wife, Nancy, who, by the end of the interview, was openly weeping. Judge Clark, who was present for that session, arranged a follow-up meeting between the President and Saudi Ambassador Faisal Alhegelan. Judge Clark was authorized by the President to enter into direct back channel communication with the Saudi Government which, in turn, could and did communicate directly with the PLO leaders in Lebanon.

In the past, whenever he suspected that a member of the Administration was influencing U.S. foreign policy decisions or was establishing direct liaison with foreign governments, Secretary Haig had not merely threatened but had actually submitted a draft letter of resignation to the President. Members of the White House staff made certain now that Haig learned of Judge Clark's direct line between President Reagan and the Saudi royal family and awaited the customary letter of resignation from Haig. This time it was agreed that when he submitted it, the President would accept it. Haig, it seems, was tipped off not only as to what was happening, but why. Therefore, although he demanded an appointment with the President, he did not make any threats nor did he submit the expected resignation letter in advance. When he saw the President there still was no draft letter in the President's hands. Reagan, nevertheless, assured the stunned Haig that he had decided to accept the Secretary of State's resignation when it arrived, and that a successor had already been contacted.

In short, Haig was fired. It was none too soon. That day the first of what became a series of protest demonstrations was held outside the State Department. Among the hundred or so demonstrators who stood in blistering summer sun outside the diplomatic entrance was a scattering of retired diplomats. As other protestors, many of them students and faculty members from nearby universities, watched in amazement, first a trickle and then a steady stream of State Department officials began pouring across the street to shake the hands of their protesting, retired colleagues.

One on-duty diplomat told the demonstrators "Speaking for myself, I admire what you're doing and if this goes on much longer I believe some of us will be out here on the street with you."

"Let's hope it doesn't come to that," a retired U.S. Ambassador on the picket line replied. It didn't. Two hours later Secretary Haig returned from the White House, assembled the top officers of the Department of State, and informed them that the White House had accepted his resignation.

When Haig was slow to vacate his office, Reagan told him that his presence was no longer needed to smoothe the transition. Although the arrival of George Shultz, two and a half years after Reagan had been dissuaded by pro-Israel advisers from appointing him, signaled major changes of policy, they were not immediately apparent. The seige of Beirut was in full swing. Begin had no intention of lifting it until the PLO had been destroyed. And, although Beirut was being destroyed, the securely dug in PLO was not. Reagan sent Philip Habib to Beirut to seek to negotiate an end to the violence that was now filling U.S. television screens night after night with sickening scenes of slaughter.

A cease-fire in place was established on August 3 to enable Habib to negotiate the PLO's departure. Sharon, who had built his military reputation in Israel's previous wars through lightning advances after each cease-fire, broke this one on its first day. He intensified his bombardment and tried, unsuccessfully, to push his forces into West Beirut. That day Reagan finally spoke out, calling the Israeli bombardment "disproportionate" and, for the first time during the nearly two months the war had continued, questioning whether or not Israel was using its American weapons for "legitimate self-defense," as required by U.S. law. The President also called for a return by Israeli forces to the cease-fire line of the previous day. In a repeat of the denouement of every previous Israeli war, Begin seized upon the fact that the U.S. President had finally broken his silence and called upon Israel to honor its cease-fire promise of a day earlier. He set out to denounce the President to American Jews.

"Nobody should preach to us," Begin told a group of 190 American Jewish leaders who had been brought to Jerusalem. "Nobody is going to bring Israel to its knees. You must have forgotten that the Jews kneel but to God." At the same time, Israeli officers began giving background briefings about the dire and "unpredictable" consequences any kind of U.S. pressure on Israel would unleash.

A U.S. plan for evacuation of the PLO fighters was accepted by Israel on August 11, while Arafat equivocated, fearing for his freedom of action and possibly his life if he were sent to Syria. On August 12 Sharon mounted his most ferocious attack of the entire war, starting with a dawn artillery barrage that continued throughout an 11-hour air attack on the helpless city. Despite the fact that most of West Beirut's population by then was huddled in deep cellars under the strongest buildings, some 300 people died in the Muslim areas of the city during that one day.

Israeli Journalists Ze'ev Schiff and Ehud Ya'ari, in their excellent account of the invasion entitled *Israel's Lebanon War* have written:

> "What made 'Black Thursday' so terrifying was the sense of brute violence run wild, given the sharp contrast between the progress in the negotiations and the savage attack on the city. The wife of (Lebanese) Prime Minister Wazzan declared a hunger strike to protest the action, and the Muslim leaders of West Beirut phoned the American Embassy with harrowing descriptions of wanton destruction and frantic cries for help."[7]

7. Schiff, Ze'ev, and Ya'ari, Ehud, *Israel's Lebanon War*, Simon and Schuster, New York, 1984, p. 225.

Alerted by Habib as to what was happening, President Reagan tried to telephone Prime Minister Begin. The call was put through to the Prime Minister only after the barrage had halted. When the U.S. President finally reached Begin, Reagan called the bombings "unfathomable and senseless," saying that if the Israelis did not observe the cease-fire he would pull Habib out and cancel the U.S. mission.

The Israeli cabinet met that day and Sharon asked it for permission to take advantage of the new cease-fire and again advance further into West Beirut. Instead he faced a near rebellion by the cabinet with Begin and all but one minister demanding that the shooting stop so that the PLO evacuation could begin. In an unprecedented action reminiscent of Golda Meir's dramatic personal intervention to get Sharon under control nine years earlier, the cabinet withdrew Sharon's authority over the Air Force.

That same night Arafat gave in to pleas that he agree to evacuation of his forces from Beirut. Because he had delayed the agreement earlier by saying that he would not be safe in Damascus, the U.S. prevailed upon Tunisia to accept him and his followers. With this accomplished, Muslim political leaders in Beirut told Arafat that for their sake he must agree to leave as soon as possible. After a frantic search by telephone to locate Habib, Arafat announced his acceptance of an agreement to evacuate all of the PLO fighters to eight Arab countries under the supervision of U.S., French and Italian troops. The agreement also guaranteed the safety of the "law-abiding and noncombatant Palestinians who remain in Beirut." Habib offered his personal word on this, after first securing an Israeli assurance that Palestinian civilians in the city would not be harmed.

PLO fighters were ordered to report to their respective headquarters and were issued new uniforms. The various PLO organizations paid their debts to Beirut's merchants. Then the first unit of PLO fighters left Beirut by ship on August 21. As the evacuation continued, by truck to Syria and ship to the other Arab countries, both the Palestinian and Israeli soldiers treated the operation as a victory. The Israeli soldiers thought it meant they would soon be going home. The Palestinians were celebrating the fact that an Arab army had fought the Israeli army, with all of its American-suppplied weapons and air power, to a draw, evacuating only to spare the civilian population of Beirut further death and destruction.

Israeli troops were supposed to stay off the routes being used by the evacuees. They did not, however, and could often be seen among the Maronite crowds jeering the departing Palestinians. Surprisingly, the exchanges between the Israeli and Palestinian fighters themselves were not uniformly unpleasant. Troops of both sides were photographed flashing victory signals back and forth. Perhaps, while claiming victory, the troops of both sides were beginning to realize that in their half century of intermittent warfare there had been many losers and survivors, but as yet no winners.

Since Philip Habib and his Arabist deputy, career Foreign Service Officer Morris Draper, had negotiated so many cease-fires that had been broken by Sharon's aerial and artillery bombardments of defenseless civilians, his personal relationship with the two Americans had plumbed the depths. When Sharon told Habib that Israelis who had taken part in the operation should receive a decoration to be called the "expulsion medal," Habib responded that yellow might be the appropriate color.

Schiff and Ya'ari, who reported that vignette, describe another incident that almost set off hostilities between Israeli forces and the U.S. Navy. Sharon had ordered the evacuation halted when one PLO unit boarded a Greek evacuation ship with its jeeps, contravening the terms of the agreement. Draper, who was present at the port when Sharon gave the order, pointed out that French troops overseeing the area had checked and passed the vehicles, after removing forbidden weapons. There was no way, therefore, to make the Palestinians debark. Sharon nevertheless refused to allow the ship to depart. As news of the impasse reached Washington, orders were flashed to two Sixth Fleet destroyers standing off Beirut to enter the harbor and escort the Greek ship and its Palestinian passengers out of the port, by force if necessary.

U.S. Ambassador Samuel Lewis in Israel then appealed directly to Begin, pointing out that the U.S. aircraft carrier and two destroyers anchored off Beirut were prepared to extricate the Greek ship, no matter what the military cost. Begin, who had never before in his life given in to U.S. pressure, reluctantly conceded, to the evident astonishment and relief of his own foreign ministry officials. One of them told the shaken U.S. Ambassador afterward, "this time you've honestly earned your salary."

The evacuation continued until more than 14,000 Palestinians and Syrians, including some women and children, had left West Beirut. Of these, 8,000 Palestinians traveled by sea and 6,000 Syrians and members of the Syrian-officered Palestinian Liberation Army traveled overland to Damascus.

Although he had failed to kill the Palestinian leaders, Sharon had succeeded in his plan to root the armed Palestinians out of Beirut, where they had been securely ensconced for more than a decade. Now he turned his attention to the remainder of his plan to get the Palestinians out of Lebanon and on their way to Jordan.

The first stage was to have Bashir Gemayel nominated for the Presidential election. Sharon hoped, after Gemayel was elected, that he would become the second Arab leader to sign a peace treaty with Israel. While the Israelis were negotiating with Gemayel, the U.S. decided not to press its luck. U.S. troops had been included in the multi-national force supervising the evacuation only at the insistence of Israel and over the objections of U.S. Secretary of Defense Weinberger who wanted troops from traditionally neutral nations to do the job. The U.S., therefore, withdrew its troops from Lebanon to the carrier offshore. The sudden departure of the U.S. forces caught others in the international force, which by now also included a British support unit, by surprise. They had expected to stay for the full 30 days specified in the evacuation agreement until their positions could be taken over by the shattered Lebanese Army. However the other participants in the international contingent followed the U.S. lead and withdrew their troops.

Then, on September 14, 1982, after Bashir Gemayel's nomination but before his election as President of Lebanon, a time bomb devastated his East Beirut headquarters. It was generally conceded that the bomb was carried in by the son of the owner of the building, who was known to Gemayel's guards. The question was who had put him up to it? There were three obvious suspects. One was Israel, since Sharon had obviously been disappointed in Gemayel. He had originally sized up Bashir as fiercely anti-Muslim, fanatically anti-Palestinian, and easily intimidated by the Israeli advisers with whom he had been meeting since 1976. Bashir, however, had refused to commit his militiamen to the capture of West Beirut. He had met with the Israelis the day before his death. He may then have refused to commit himself to making peace with Israel after he assumed the Presidency.

Another suspect was Syria, which had a long history of seeking to dominate Lebanese leaders of all sects and parties. Syria was generally believed to have been behind the ambush assassination of the stubbornly independent Druze Leader, Kamal Jumblatt, in 1978. The Syrians may have concluded that Bashir Gemayel had the makings of another stubbornly independent Lebanese leader.

Still another obvious suspect was former Lebanese President Suleiman Franjieh. After Franjieh had completed his term of office in 1976, during Lebanon's Civil War, his son, daughter-in-law and granddaughter had been massacred by Bashir Gemayel's militiamen in a surprise attack on their home in Northern Lebanon. Franjieh, who had vowed to kill Bashir after that, quickly ended speculation that he was behind the bombing. Instead of celebrating Bashir's death as expected, he publicly lamented the fact that someone else had gotten to Bashir first.

Whether Syria or Israel is guilty may never be known. History is written by the victors. Syria will be blamed by Israel's partisans. Nevertheless, Sharon moved with such speed that it is almost impossible to believe that he had no foreknowledge at all of the assassination plan.

The explosion had occurred in early afternoon and, as dead and wounded occupants of the building were loaded into ambulances, word spread that Bashir Gemayel, although wounded, had survived. Even as the reports that he had survived continued to be broadcast on the Phalange radio, however, Israeli transport planes loaded with arms and ammunition were arriving in a steady stream at Beirut airport. By the time late that night that stunned Lebanese finally understood why they had not heard Bashir's voice on the radio or seen him alive on television, new ammunition supplies and new orders had been issued to the Israeli forces poised all around Beirut. At dawn they rolled into West Beirut, now stripped of its Palestinian defenders and complacent under the international guarantees of its inviolability.

The small remaining Muslim militias, totaling perhaps 1000 men in various uncoordinated and generally undisciplined units, assembled to defend their own immediate neighborhoods. The attack was so sudden, however, that whatever resistance they offered generally delayed the attackers for only minutes, or at most hours. There was no attempt by the militias to coordinate their defenses. As usual, the heaviest casualties were suffered by civilians who had left for their offices before they realized that West Beirut was being invaded, and who were caught in the crossfire as they sought to return to their homes.

As the fighting continued, block by block, in West Beirut, the Israelis began assembling groups of Maronite militiamen. The bulk of them were Phalangists from East Beirut. But other militiamen also appeared, apparently driven or flown to Beirut from Major Saad Haddad's Israeli-directed force guarding the Israeli border. All of the militiamen were loaded into trucks and driven to the sprawling Sabra and Shatilla Palestinian refugee camps late in the day that the invasion of West Beirut had begun, and just after the areas around the two contiguous camps had been secured by Israeli soldiers. Either the militiamen themselves or the Israeli troops surrounding the camps set up initial covering fire. A contingent of Maronite officers moved into an Israeli command post in a five story building overlooking the camps. Then the Maronite militiamen began entering the camps, which had been established for so long that they were almost indistinguishable from nearby Lebanese slum areas. The population, in fact, was partly Lebanese and partly Palestinian, reflecting the fact that the two peoples had been mingling and inter-marrying throughout the 34 years that had elapsed since the Palestinians arrived in Beirut as refugees from a homeland that had suddenly become Israel.

Because the camps had been in or near the front lines during the years of civil war and also during the Israeli seige of Beirut, the occupants had long since learned how to take cover in their homes and in improvised shelters to survive shell fire. Although the only remaining male residents were old men or teen-aged boys, some of the latter still had small arms, even though heavy weapons had been turned over to authorities at the time of the PLO evacuation.

It was not long, therefore, before the Christian militiamen withdrew after encountering small arms fire. They again ordered heavy covering fire laid down throughout the camps. The next time they went in the boys had hidden themselves or fled, and the militiamen did not come out, except as their units were relieved by fresh units which were carefully checked in by the Israeli soldiers guarding all exits from the camp. Instead, as darkness fell the militiamen requested Israeli units to supply illuminating flares, which the Israelis did throughout the next two nights.

Soon Palestinians began reaching the exits, pleading with the Israelis to allow them to escape. The Israelis turned them back, firing warning shots when necessary. Individual Israeli soldiers began leaving their posts, however, to report to their officers what they could see as they looked down the long streets or peered into the camps from the higher buildings around them. There were no able-bodied young men left in the camps, but a systematic massacre was being conducted by the Phalangist militiamen of old men, women, children and infants. Even horses, dogs and cats were being shot or stabbed to death. The soldiers, unfortunately, were reporting nothing the Israeli officers didn't already know. They had heard the Phalangist officers, from their joint command post, ordering their men to kill everyone they encountered in the camp. Within an hour of the time his forces had entered the camp, Israeli officers heard Phalange militia commander Elie Hobeika angrily shouting into his walkie talkie when a squad leader asked him what to do with the women and children, "That's the last time you're going to ask me. You know what you have to do with them.' "

As the Maronite militia units rotated in and out of the camp they boasted to the watching Israeli soldiers not only about how many victims they had killed, but how they were raping the women before killing them. The massacre and its lurid details were briefly reported in the U.S. and very widely reported in Europe and the Middle East. Since most U.S. editors seemed reluctant to print anything about Israeli complicity in the massacre, few Americans are aware that it was only Begin and Sharon's fear of exposure by the press and by the U.S. Government that finally brought it to a halt. This became clear, however, in the inquiry by the Israeli Government's Kahan Commission, set up to assuage both international and internal Israeli outrage. As is the case with most investigation commissions appointed by governments, however, its desire to protect the national image heavily outweighed its desire to uncover the truth. The commission's final report reveals enough, however, to establish the shocking extent of Israeli complicity.

In fact Israeli soldiers guarding every entrance to the camps knew what was happening from the time it began. It was the Palestinians inside, isolated and dug into their hovels and shelters, who did not realize until it was too late that it was not just a routine firefight or bombardment that was occurring around them, but a systematic, house-by-house massacre of the occupants. Even the hospitals were not safe. The medical staffs of two hospitals, including many Europeans, for a time treated a steady stream of wounded Palestinians who sought refuge within the hospitals when they could not get out of the camps. However, Phalangists eventually reached both hospitals and herded the medical staffs out at gunpoint. They never saw the patients again. Some Palestinian nurses were raped and killed and male Palestinian medical personnel were separated from the foreigners, led away and shot.

The two surviving bands of foreign medical personnel, one from each hospital, were eventually turned over to Israeli Brigadier General Amos Yaron, who professed horror when they told him what was happening, but made absolutely no move to stop it. His horror, in fact, seems to have stemmed from the realization that such a large number of foreign doctors and nurses had witnessed parts of the massacre. The Israelis apparently had no idea when they trucked the Phalangist militiamen to the two camps that there were some two dozen Western Europeans and North Americans inside.

At the exact time the massacre began on Thursday night, Morris Draper and Samuel Lewis were complaining, in Jerusalem, to Ariel Sharon about Israel's violation of its promise not to send Israeli forces into West Beirut, but rather to let the Lebanese Army, when it was ready, occupy and disarm the city. By 7:50 a.m. Friday, Israeli Military Correspondent Ze'ev Schiff records in his book on the Lebanon invasion, he had heard that a "slaughter" was taking place in the camps. He tried to telephone a friend in the Israeli Government, Communications Minister Mordechai Zippori.

At the same time an Israeli tank commander who was later willing to testify to the Kahan Commission became aware that Phalangists were executing groups of people very close to his position. He drove his tank up on an embankment just in time to witness the murder of five women and children. When he started to report the incident on his radio members of his tank crew said they already had heard other Israeli soldiers reporting such incidents to their battalion commander over the battalion radio network, but the only response had been "it's not to our liking." At 4 p.m. that day when a militiaman passed their tank, the Israeli crew asked him why he was killing women and children. The Phalangist responded that "women bear children and the children grow up to be terrorists."

By 11 a.m. Schiff had gone to Zippori's office in Tel Aviv. Zippori telephoned Foreign Minister Yitzhak Shamir, who was scheduled to meet that afternoon with Sharon and with Morris Draper, and told Shamir about the reports. Shamir did nothing about it and, in the subsequent investigation, even denied that he had received the report of the massacre, apparently unaware that Schiff had been seated in Zippori's office throughout the latter's telephone conversation with Shamir.

By this time Israeli Television's military correspondent, Ron Ben-Yishai, had heard about the massacre from an Israeli officer at the Beirut airport. He asked for details and learned that fresh Maronite militiamen were being assembled and permitted to go into the camps to join the militiamen already there.

By 4 p.m. Friday three U.S. journalists had visited the U.S. Embassy in Beirut to tell diplomats that the Phalangists had been turned loose in the camps. The Embassy passed the report on to Morris Draper and also telephoned Amin Gemayel, elder brother of the slain Bashir, to ask him about it. Gemayel telephoned back almost immediately to confirm that Phalange militiamen were in the camps. He said, however, that they would soon be withdrawn.

By this time truckloads of Palestinian women were being driven through the streets of Christian East Beirut while Phalange militiamen shouted to the crowds that they were newly-created Palestinian widows. Some were released near Muslim areas to seek refuge. Others were not seen again.

By 6 p.m. when two Israeli Brigade commanders had begun discussing over the military communications network what women and children who had escaped from the camps were telling people outside, they were told by Israeli Paratroop Commander Amos Yaron, the same officer who had received the foreign medical personnel, to stop discussing the matter on the radio.

By this time Morris Draper was complaining to Amin Gemayel that his promise to get the Phalangist militiamen out of the camps still had not been honored. An hour and a half later, at 7:30 p.m., he passed to the Israeli Foreign Ministry representative in Beirut a complaint from Lebanese Prime Minister Wazzan that Phalangist militiamen were in Shatilla and were murdering patients in the Acre hospital there. Draper told the Israeli official that more Phalange militiamen had been seen assembling at the Beirut airport and warned that "contriving to employ the Phalangists in West Beirut could lead to terrible consequences."

By 8:30 p.m. a group of Israeli officers had visited Ben-Yishai at the Beirut apartment he was using as Israeli Television headquarters. They said they had specific atrocity stories to tell him. They had passed these stories up their own chain of command. It was the subsequent absence of orders to withdraw the Phalangists from the camps that moved them to go to the press. Ben-Yishai reached Sharon by telephone at Sharon's home at 11:30 p.m. Friday night. Sharon asked if Ben-Yishai had any details of the murders and Ben-Yishai related that the Israeli soldiers had seen murders taking place in a section close to the Israeli division headquarters outside Shatilla. Sharon thanked him for the information and, since it was the Jewish new year, wished him a happy new year before hanging up. By this time so many Phalange militiamen had gone into the camps that the Israelis guarding the exits had lost all track of the numbers inside. They were still turning away Palestinians who pleaded to be allowed out, however. Two bulldozers had also been allowed into the camp, along with another borrowed from the Israeli Army by the Phalangists, who had requested that the IDF markings be obliterated.

At 8 a.m. Saturday morning Ron Ben-Yishai arrived at the camps with a film crew in time to see a long line of old men, women and children, many covered with dirt and blood, being driven ahead of them at a run by Phalangist militiamen. The victims shouted at the camera crew to tell them what was happening. The militiamen tried to chase the television crew away. Only at this point, with Phalangists threatening to shoot Israeli cameramen, did an Israeli officer intervene, telling the Phalangists to leave the area and the Palestinians to return to their homes. The arrival of the Israeli television crew had forced the Israeli Defense Forces to step in and stop the massacre they had been watching, hearing, supplying and supporting for 36 hours.

By 10 a.m. Morris Draper was on the phone to Bruce Kashdan of the Israeli Foreign Ministry dictating in a voice that betrayed his fury a message for Sharon: "You must stop the acts of slaughter. They are obscene. I have a representative in the camp counting the bodies. You should be ashamed! The situation is absolutely appalling. They're killing children! You have the field completely under your control and are therefore responsible for that area."

Although there are reports that surreptitious killings continued in the camps throughout the day and perhaps even on Sunday, the full-scale massacre effectively ended as more and more journalists began arriving on the scene Saturday morning. Some saw what the bulldozers had been used for since their arrival in the camp the previous evening. One with its scoop full of bodies was proceeding toward a mass grave, while another was pushing earth over bodies even as the world press stormed in.

There was an immediate, unseemly scramble by Israelis to blame the Phalange, and by the Phalange to blame Haddad's troops. Prime Minister Begin had gone to the synagogue on Saturday, the day the massacre was revealed, and remained unavailable for immediate comment throughout the day. Subsequently he tried to dismiss it with the wisecrack that "when goyim kill goyim, they hang the Jews."

With the U.S. press minimizing the affair, and particularly Israel's responsibility for it, and with his usual self-righteous indifference to European outrage, Begin apparently hoped the matter would blow over in Israel itself. It did not, however. In fact, eventually a crowd estimated at 400,000 people, 10 per cent of Israel's population, turned out in Tel Aviv to demand an investigation, Begin finally yielded and appointed a commission headed by Israeli Chief Justice Yitzhak Kahan. The report was a whitewash, but not completely. While it was reluctant to implicate the dozens, or perhaps hundreds, of Israeli military men who knew the massacre was proceeding but did nothing to stop it, the commission did charge Ariel Sharon personally with "indirect responsibility" for the massacre and recommended that if he did not "draw the appropriate conclusions" (resign), Begin should dismiss him.

The Kahan Commission was not the only official body to whitewash the affair, however. By this time Amin Gemayel had been elected President of Lebanon in his dead brother's place. The official Lebanese Government commission he appointed confirmed only that there had been a massacre, minimized the number of victims, and did not even speculate as to who had carried it out. Even the PLO has never blamed the Maronites, other than to admit that a few of Haddad's men may have served as "guides" for the Israeli forces it alleges committed all of the murders. And Beirut's Muslim leaders, although they knew that Maronite militiamen rather than Israeli soldiers had done the actual killing, decided that to admit it would make the Muslim-Maronite breach in Lebanon unbridgeable. Veteran Beirut Sunni Muslim leader Saeb Salam explained that "sometimes it is better to lie for your country."

Israel's Kahan Commission put the total of dead at 700 to 800. The Palestinian Red Crescent put the number of dead at more than 2,000. Lebanese authorities issued death certificates for more than 1,200 people by name. They were for persons whose disappearance at the time of the massacre was attested by relatives who could produce three witnesses. Given the fact that whole families, including infants, were wiped out, it seems likely that the actual number of victims is far higher than that admitted by Israel, perhaps somewhere between the Lebanese and Palestinian estimates.

The massacre had an epilogue that augured badly for the future of Israel, now polarized by the Lebanese invasion and its aftermath between "Oriental Jews" who generally supported Begin and Sharon, and "European Jews," who generally supported peace with the Arabs. Sharon refused to "draw the appropriate conclusions" and Begin could not summon up the courage to fire him. The Israeli "Peace Now" organization therefore again organized a protest march. This time a grenade was thrown into the crowd, killing one Israeli, Emil Grunzweig, and injuring 10 others including the peace activist son of an Israeli cabinet minister. The Israelis, who by then were responsible for the deaths of some 20,000 Palestinians, Lebanese and Syrians during the summer of 1982 in Lebanon, seemed almost as upset at the loss of their cherished self-image as a democratic nation where dissent by anyone is tolerated by all, as they had been at the loss in Lebanon of their image as a moral one.

Begin, therefore, finally made a gesture to the protesters. He accepted Sharon's resignation as Minister of Defense, but allowed Sharon to remain in the cabinet as a minister without portfolio.

It is perhaps best to let the two Israelis, Schiff and Ya'ari, sum up the internal and external damage to their country from the massacre. They write:

"The Kahan Report notwithstanding, it is difficult to say that Israel has truly and ultimately come to grips with the events at Sabra and Shatilla. In many ways, the government is still treating the entire affair as a freak historical accident or a matter of abominable luck; not once has it been acknowledged that dispatching the Phalangists into West Beirut, and particularly into the refugee camps, was a cornerstone of the war policy from June 15 onward and that, in discussions at both the General Staff and more restricted forums, Ariel Sharon repeatedly urged his officers and aides to have the Phalangists 'clean out' West Beirut. . . . If there is a moral to the painful episode of Sabra and Shatilla, it has yet to be acknowledged."[8]

8. Schiff, Ze'ev, and Ya'ari, Ehud, *Israel's Lebanon War*, Simon and Schuster, New York, 1984, pp. 284-5.

George Azar

Since Beirut had no effective defenses against aircraft attacks, Israeli aircraft supporting the 1982 invasion were able initially to pinpoint and demolish PLO-occupied buildings such as the one pictured above in West Beirut. Later, when Israelis found they could not root out the Palestinians from their strong points in the city, the Israelis turned to terror bombing in hopes of turning the Lebanese of West Beirut against the Palestinian fighters. Below, relatives of Lebanese and Palestinians buried in rubble of destroyed building watch rescuers dig for victims.

Wide World

U.S. Marines and French soldiers (above) watch as PLO fighters travel to port for evacuation by sea from Beirut on August 25, 1982. Mother and father (below) bid farewell to Palestinian fighter being evacuated. As a condition for withdrawing PLO forces, Yassir Arafat received a personal guarantee for the safety of Palestinian families left behind from U.S. Presidential Envoy Philip Habib. Within two weeks U.S. forces had left, Israeli forces had broken their promise not to move into West Beirut, and between 1,000 and 2,000 Palestinian civilians had been massacred there, principally at the Sabra and Shatilla refugee camps.

Wide World

Israeli Northern Corps commander Major General Amir Drori (above, left) passes a truckload of Palestinian Liberation Army soldiers evacuating Beirut by road for Syria August 26, 1982. With Palestinian armed fighters gone, and immediately after the departure of U.S. Marines and French and Italian troops overseeing the evacuation, General Sharon violated his pledge to let the Lebanese army assume control in West Beirut by moving in his own forces. Israeli troops met only light resistance, with most of the casualties sustained by civilians like the Lebanese motorist below.

Wide World

CHAPTER XXII

The Reagan Plan

"Reagan's attempt to move the Camp David negotiations forward in September 1982 was well conceived, and initial Israeli opposition was not likely to endure. Reagan had proposed a resumption of the Camp David negotiations for the purpose of establishing a regime of 'full autonomy' for the Palestinians in the West Bank and Gaza; he had added that in such negotiations the United States would advocate a permanent solution under which the Palestinians in the West Bank and Gaza would form part of a Jordanian-Palestinian state, while secure boundaries between Israel and the Jordanian state would be fixed by negotiation. This proposal had been rejected by the Begin government almost before it had been promulgated, since it conflicted with the aim of maintaining all the territories under Israeli rule. The large sectors of Israeli opinion that were favorable to a compromise praised Reagan's initiative, but internal Israeli contention became irrelevant when the PLO, under Yassir Arafat's frightened leadership, declined to give King Hussein of Jordan the necessary authority to lead a Jordanian-Palestinian delegation . . . The United States has immense importance for Israel's security and economy, is the chief mainstay of Jordan, and ensures the defense of Saudi Arabia, but in a crucial test it was unable to enlist any of those three governments on behalf of an enlightened diplomatic initiative that would have brought no harm to any of the three and would have advanced the interests of regional stability."[1]

Abba Eban, 1983

"I would not want to pick the date today, but in a realistic way, that (U.S.-PLO) dialogue has to take place. . . . There are some responsible preconditions and it may need some

---

1. Eban, Abba, *The New Diplomacy: International Affairs in the Modern Age*, Random House, New York, 1983, p. 77.

negotiations as to their (the PLO) attitude vis-a-vis Israel . . . and it may take some actions by Israel vis-a-vis the PLO. But as you go down the road at some point that dialogue has to take place and I think that (it) will happen."[2]

Former President Gerald R. Ford, 1981

"There is no way for Israel ever to have an assured permanent peace without resolving the Palestinian issue. . . . So I think Jerry is certainly right in saying these discussions have to be done. The problem is the recognition of the PLO as a political entity by the United States before the Palestinians were willing to acknowledge that Israel is a nation that has a right to exist. So any mechanism that can be found to resolve that difficulty would be a very successful step forward."[3]

Former President Jimmy Carter, 1981

"The Palestinian Liberation Organization's ultimate inclusion in the peace process could be for Reagan, in a sense, what the China opening was for Richard Nixon—one of those unthinkable about-faces that Republican presidents, more so than Democratic presidents, seem uniquely able to execute."[4]

Philip Geyelin, 1981

On September 1, 1982, the day the last PLO fighters were evacuated from Beirut under the protection of U.S., French, Italian and British soldiers, President Reagan went before the television cameras to talk to the American people about the Middle East. What he unveiled was a total about-face from the Haig era. This time his Administration had a positive policy for the Middle East that clearly was made in the U.S. rather than, as in the beginning of his Administration, made in Israel.

The product of the State Department's Middle East experts, approved and vetted by both the new Secretary of State, George Shultz, and National Security Adviser William Clark, it seemed to presage a new, activist era in U.S. Middle East diplomacy. Building on the Camp David Accords, it addressed the portions of those accords which had never been implemented, those dealing with the Palestinians, the West Bank and Gaza. In essence it was U.N. Security Council Resolution 242 with a significant addition. Whatever Palestinian entity emerged to govern the Palestinians in the West Bank and Gaza was to be linked with Jordan. During his first month in office Shultz had told the Israelis that President Reagan was determined that destruction of the PLO's power in Beirut must be followed by a solution to the Palestine problem, or a new PLO would arise.

Begin's reaction, nevertheless, was a predictable and almost instant tantrum. The day after Reagan proposed his plan Begin went before the Knesset to attack the plan as a "lifeless stillborn." He told the Knesset that Israel would never relinquish control

---

2. Ford, Former President Gerald, in interview October 10, 1981 aboard U.S. Air Force plane returning from the funeral of President Anwar Sadat in Cairo, Egypt.

3. Carter, Former President James E., in interview October 10, 1981, aboard U.S. Air Force plane returning from the funeral of President Anwar Sadat in Cairo, Egypt.

4. Geyelin, Philip, *Washington Post*, August 20, 1981.

of the West Bank and Gaza. "We have no reason to get on our knees," he shouted. "No one will determine for us the borders of the Land of Israel." The Knesset voted 50 to 36 to reject the plan.

To make sure that Reagan understood who was up and who was down in his version of the Israeli-U.S. relationship, Begin took the occasion to announce a far-reaching expansion in his settlements program. The Ministry of Defense would convert four military outposts into permanent civilian settlements. This was in line with the strategy whereby land which Arabs refused to sell was expropriated "for military defense purposes." Then, after fencing off and occupying seized lands with a military vehicle or two or perhaps some quonset huts, the army turned over each area to the civilian authorities for a settlement. The Arab farmers were compensated for land they didn't want to sell at all with money made available because tax-free funds could be raised in the U.S. Under this unique system, there were no losers except the Arab farmers and the American taxpayers.

Begin also announced on the day he rejected the Reagan Plan that 42 new Israeli settlements would be established in the West Bank within the next four years, and 100,000 additional Jews would be moved into the West Bank over the next five years. Further, Begin announced, 20,000 Jews would be settled into the Golan areas he had annexed from Syria a year earlier, and 10,000 would be settled in Gaza, already one of the most crowded areas in the world because of the concentration of Palestinian refugees there. Begin also announced plans for an increase in settlements within Israel itself, in the Galilee and Negev areas, which had heavy Arab populations.

Given Israel's lack of resources and lack of people willing to move into these contested areas, the plans sounded like those of a madman, and many took them with a grain of salt feeling that it was the only way Begin could think of to show his own people his scorn for Reagan and his defiance of American power. However, the plans were in fact part and parcel of Sharon's grandiose dreams for "cleansing" the West Bank of Palestinians and driving them into Jordan. At the same time Begin was announcing them, Sharon was saying that his war in Lebanon had ended all possibility of West Bank autonomy for the Palestinians.

The PLO, predictably, also attacked the Reagan Plan on the basis that it seemed to leave no place for the PLO itself in the Palestinian future. But, in a reversal of their performances only a decade earlier when Arab nations tended to react negatively at first and only accepted U.S. plans when it was too late, the moderate Arabs this time bided their time.

At another meeting in Morocco, from which Syria abstained, all of the Arab countries attending adopted the Saudi seven principles for Middle East peace they had declined to act upon a year earlier. The Fahd Plan thus became the Fez Plan, setting out a positive Arab peace plan for the first time in the history of the Arab-Israeli dispute.

What followed was more positive Arab diplomacy. Having at last agreed on a peace plan of their own, the Arab summit participants then turned to a consideration of the Reagan Plan. While not endorsing it over their own, they announced that it was "not inconsistent" with the Fez Plan, and that the two together could therefore form a working basis for Middle East peace.

Meanwhile the public opinion fallout from the summer of Israeli carnage visited upon Lebanon, climaxed by the Sabra-Shatilla massacres, was showing up in U.S. polls. Liberal American journalists who had never before written a critical word about Israel had, almost without exception, criticized what they portrayed as a betrayal of U.S. confidence in the Jewish state. U.S. public opinion, as sampled in an October, 1982, *Washington Post-American Broadcasting Corporation* poll, for the first time in history recorded an even split in American public support for the Arabs and the Israelis. Sadat's positive efforts of earlier years, and the Begin-Sharon negative activities of 1982, had finally yielded a measurable impact after a summer in which Americans had followed Middle Eastern events closely. With a positive U.S. policy clearly enunciated in the Reagan Plan, the time seemed ideal to move forward toward peace negotiations, whether Begin and his deeply-divided government wanted them or not.

Unfortunately, if U.S. foreign policy under George Shultz was back on track in regard to the Palestinians, it was following a dead-end street in Lebanon. In his condolence call on Pierre and Amin Gemayel right after Bashir Gemayel's death, Morris Draper had assured Amin Gemayel that, if he chose to stand for President in Bashir's place, he would have U.S. support. American diplomats in Lebanon had always been more comfortable with Amin Gemayel than with his younger brother. Amin Gemayel was reserved and correct, where his younger brother had been flamboyant and emotional. And Amin had always kept his lines open to the Arab camp in general and Syria in particular, while Bashir was making overtures to the Israelis and encouraging them to arm and train his Phalange militia.

The U.S. was therefore pleased when Amin Gemayel was elected President of Lebanon on September 21, 1982, with the support of Muslim leaders who might have withheld it from Bashir. The Israelis, who had had a new, preferred candidate of their own completely outside the Gemayel family, were unhappy and Sharon immediately tried to circumvent the U.S.-Gemayel relationship with direct "secret negotiations" between himself and Amin Gemayel for an Israeli-Lebanese peace agreement. To his dismay he found Gemayel was keeping the U.S. fully informed of the conversations. The U.S. had also resumed an activist role in Lebanon, although not without misgivings. Shultz had supported the return of U.S. troops to Lebanon after the Israeli invasion of West Beirut and the breakdown of law and order and massacres. Weinberger, who had a clear idea of the limits of U.S. military power, and of the problems of small unit military operations in a politically-unstable area such as Lebanon, opposed the return of U.S. forces as part of the multi-national force there. Shultz, supported by National Security Adviser Robert (Bud) MacFarland, a career Marine officer, prevailed, however. Soon, in addition to U.S. Marines there were U.S. military advisers and trainers in Lebanon committed to a two-year program of strengthening the Lebanese Army to take over the policing and defense of the country.

It has been a curious truism that Russians and Arabs working together, even on a well-conceived project such as the Aswan Dam, generally do not get along. Americans and Arabs generally do. Now another facet of the interplay of national characteristics in the Middle East was becoming obvious to American newsmen in Beirut. While the American trainers and their Lebanese military students, of whatever sect, generally worked easily together, the U.S. and Israeli troops stationed at adjacent checkpoints did not. The same phenomenon had long been apparent at the U.S.-operated early warning station separating Israeli and Egyptian forces in the Sinai desert. No matter what Americans thought when they arrived, after a few weeks on the job they almost routinely entered into angry confrontation with the Israelis, while their contacts with Egyptian military personnel from adjacent posts routinely evolved from polite correctness to warm friendship. The explanation offered then was that the Israeli military forces, for reasons of their own, were engaged in daily probing of the alertness of U.S. technicians and the sensitivity of their equipment, while the Egyptians seemed content to trust the Americans to do their job.

Perhaps the same factors were at work in Beirut. The mission of the U.S. Marine units when they returned was to replace the Israeli units in sensitive positions around the airport, which also happened to be close to the Muslim areas which had suffered the most during the brief Israeli occupation. But the Israelis seemed extremely reluctant to leave. Even after they withdrew, there were almost daily incursions by Israelis taking "short-cuts" through the U.S.-controlled areas they had been forced to evacuate. Obviously they were skeptical of the ability of U.S. Marines to prevent guerrilla infiltration through the Marine-controlled areas, and were seeking to prove that the Marines were not alert.

The U.S. Marines began to react strongly and the open resentment came to a head in successive incidents. In one of them a Marine captain, brandishing only his 45-caliber revolver, stood in front of an intruding Israeli tank that had ignored orders to halt at a Marine check post. The tank commander threatened to roll right over the captain if he did not step aside. U.S. Marines watching the impasse began to make their own preparations to destroy the Israeli tank. The Israelis literally backed off, but the incident was widely reported in the U.S. press.

The contrast in the way it was handled by different U.S. newspapers was an interesting demonstration of how news about the Middle East is frequently slanted, distorted or suppressed by biased American editors. Some newspapers presented the incident, via misleading headlines, as if the U.S. officer were the aggressor or had been drinking. In fact his action had been correct, was recognized as such by his superiors, and was taken to end repeated Israeli provocations. The upshot was more meetings by U.S. and Israeli officers in the field to contain such incidents, and fewer attempts by the Israelis to return to the areas around the Beirut airport which they had relinquished to the U.S. Marines.

It was perhaps his concentration on resolving these and a series of other U.S. problems in Lebanon that caused Shultz to neglect the most important aspect of the Reagan Plan. At the same time that King Hussein was negotiating intensively with Yassir Arafat for, in effect, the PLO's power of attorney for peace negotiations, Menachem Begin was rapidly expanding his settlements on the West Bank.

Begin's message was clearly one of continued defiance for President Reagan. In vain, Hussein waited for a sign from Reagan that he was serious about his own plan for returning the West Bank to its Palestinian inhabitants, implementation of which would be obstructed by the settlements Begin was feverishly opening and expanding.

A few Congressmen proposed that the U.S. reduce its aid to Israel by exactly the amount it was calculated Israel was spending upon the settlements. Instead, inexplicably, Reagan increased U.S. aid to Israel. Hussein was dismayed, and Arafat became increasingly skeptical about the sincerity of U.S. support for Hussein and the strength of U.S. resolve to stand up to Israel.

At this time Shultz was saying he did not expect to deal seriously with the West Bank and the Palestinian problem until agreement had been negotiated between Lebanon and Israel for withdrawal of Israeli forces from Lebanon. He seemed to believe that such an Israeli withdrawal would result in the withdrawal from Lebanon of Syrian forces and would thus be a long-awaited foreign policy truimph for the U.S.

In fact, things worked just the other way. Whatever Begin's long-term intentions vis-a-vis Lebanon, he clearly intended never to withdraw from the West Bank. Now Shultz's misplaced priorities, putting solution of the Lebanon problem before the Palestine problem, were making Israeli non-cooperation on the West Bank easier for Israel to handle without an open clash with the U.S. Every day that Begin stalled, niggled and nit-picked over the withdrawal of his forces from Lebanon bought him a day free from U.S. pressure to negotiate over the West Bank.

No one was better suited than Begin for the role of stalling and nit-picking except perhaps Sharon. By this time Sharon had supplemented his on-going "secret negotiations" with Amin Gemayel for an Israeli-Lebanese peace agreement with a series of sub-conspiracies. He was secretly arming the traditional enemies of the Maronites, the Druze. He was secretly conspiring with Fadi Frem, head of the Phalange militias, to deprive Gemayel's government of its major source of revenue, the customs duties levied on goods unloaded in the Port of Beirut. And he was upgrading the militia of Israel's puppet Maronite, Saad Haddad, into a territorial brigade and deploying it over a larger section of Lebanese territory. He also visited President Amin Gemayel's father, Sheikh Pierre Gemayel, and told him that, if his son did not sign the agreement worked out in their "secret" negotiations, he would limit Amin Gemayel's effective reach to the Lebanese Presidential Palace grounds.

If things were not going well in Lebanon, despite U.S. concentration on that country, they were even worse in the area the U.S. was neglecting. To the world's surprise, King Hussein and PLO Chairman Arafat struck a deal whereby Hussein would be authorized to represent Palestinian interests, with Arafat's blessing, in peace negotiations with Israel based upon the Fez and/or Reagan Plans. Arafat flew off to Kuwait for a meeting with his Executive Committee and there he had the rug pulled out from under him. The Committee would not approve the agreement he had made. The wildly-mismatched groups still loosely gathered under the PLO umbrella would not agree on anything remotely resembling a compromise peace plan. Hussein, feeling let down first by Reagan and then by Arafat, broke off further negotiations.

From that moment things started to fall apart all over the area. Syrian President Hafez Al-Assad deeply resented what he now correctly interpreted as a U.S. effort to deal Syria out of the Middle East equation. If Amin Gemayel thought he was having troubles with Israel, Assad decided to teach him the true meaning of trouble. If the U.S. was punishing Syria as a "spoiler," he would show the U.S. what a spoiler could do. And if Arafat was thinking seriously about ignoring Assad and joining Hussein in a peace initiative, Assad would once and for all destroy Arafat.

First Syria fomented a rebellion within the PLO ranks that broke into open fighting wherever Palestinian forces were stationed in Syrian-controlled territory. Gradually Arafat's forces were pushed toward the sea. In April, 1983, a suicide bomber crashed a pick-up truck through a police checkpoint and blew up the U.S. Embassy in Beirut. More than 60 persons, including 17 Americans, were killed. Among the dead were Robert Ames, a top CIA official visiting from Washington who was reported by the Israeli press to have been for a time the American side of a direct line of contact between the White House and Yassir Arafat, and Janet Stevens, an American writer who had remained in Beirut during the Israeli invasion and who was writing a book about the Sabra-Shatilla massacre. Other victims included Lebanese employes of the Embassy who had until then been unscathed through eight years of civil war, a young American Embassy wife on her first day of duty as an Embassy employe in her own right, and a number of visitors and visa applicants. The bombing was attributed to Iranian-directed Shia fundamentalist extremists, but the U.S. made no secret of its belief that the plot had been organized through the Iranian Embassy in Damascus, and that the Syrians could have stopped it had they chosen to.

During the month of the Embassy tragedy, Secretary of State Shultz set out to complete what was supposed to be his first tangible foreign policy accomplishment, a withdrawal agreement which was to rid Lebanon first of the Israeli forces, who would retain rights to leave observers in certain key points in Southern Lebanon, and then the Syrians. The Lebanese-Israeli withdrawal agreement was approved by the Lebanese Parliament by a majority of 80 votes. Syria, however, would not abide by any agreement that "rewarded Israeli aggression" or that put Syrian forces, which had been invited into Lebanon by the Lebanese Government in 1976 to end the civil war there, on a par with Israeli forces which had rolled over the Lebanese borders in the 1982 invasion. Shultz returned to the U.S. with an agreement that was meaningless without Syrian cooperation. By all accounts he was now as unhappy with Assad as Assad was with the U.S.

In June, Arafat, who had returned from Tunis to Lebanon to put down the rebellion within his forces, was invited to Damascus to talk with President Assad's brother, Rifaat. The talks went well. Arafat, following his usual security procedures to conceal his movements, sent his car back to Tripoli, Lebanon, but secretly remained in Damascus, planning to travel via another means. His vehicle was ambushed and many of those accompanying it killed. The next day Assad expelled Arafat from Damascus. There was no doubt in Arafat's mind that the Syrians had tried to kill him.

In August, 1983, stung by continuing losses to their forces in Lebanon, the Israelis withdrew their forces from the Shouf mountains, which throughout the civil war had been the scene of uneasy but peaceful co-existence between the Druze, led first by Kamal Jumblatt and, after his death, by his son, Walid, and Maronites loyal mostly to Camille Chamoun. With arms supplied by both the Israelis and the Syrians, the Druze took over 60 Maronite villages, killing perhaps 1,000 Maronites and dispossessing 50,000. It was the single biggest territorial loss suffered by any sect in Lebanon during eight years of civil war.

244 A CHANGING IMAGE

In September, Arafat returned by sea to Tripoli to join his loyal forces for a last stand against the encroaching Syrians. Palestinians loyal to Abu-Moussa, a former Al Fatah military leader who had split with Arafat after the seige of Beirut, and belonging to the various Palestinian organizations organized and funded by Syria, did the fighting. But the Syrians provided artillery, ammunition and transportation. They had pushed Arafat's loyal troops into the huge Nahr al Barid refugee camp outside Tripoli by the time Arafat reached his surrounded forces. With Assad's forces now closing in for the kill, and the Israelis preventing Arafat's escape by sea, it appeared that the Palestinian leader with the incredible luck that had saved him from death so many times, had come to the end of the line. Though Arafat had never seemed capable of evolving a long-range strategy for the Palestinians on the international scene, he was at his best in inter-Arab politics. With Syrian shells crashing around him just as heavily as Israeli shells had rained down upon him in Beirut the previous summer, Arafat sent out a challenge to the Saudis and to other moderate Arabs, whose subsidies paid both PLO and Syrian expenses.

Who is to be the leader of the PLO, Yassir Arafat or the President of Syria? The tactic worked. Assad had by then pressed Arafat into the city of Tripoli itself. But the Saudis and other Arabs insisted that Arafat and his 4,000 loyal fighters be allowed to evacuate Tripoli on September 24 on Greek ships. The Israelis were warned by Egypt and the U.S. not to try to stop the evacuation.

The worst blow of all to the U.S. and other powers seeking to reduce the level of tension in the area was still to come, however. With internal security in Lebanon rapidly deteriorating, the mission of the U.S. Marines at the Beirut International Airport had become increasingly ambiguous. They were frequently caught in the crossfire of battles between Lebanese Army units stationed nearby, and Druze and Shia militiamen in the hills and forest areas around them. The Marine commander felt it would reduce their exposure to stray bullets and shrapnel if he brought his men in from their outposts around the airport when they were not on duty. The posts were guarded at all times, but off-duty troops slept in the large concrete office building the Marines were using as a headquarters.

In the early morning of October 23 the Marines on guard duty outside the barracks heard the whine of a heavy truck approaching them. They were not alarmed since they were stationed on the main road to the airport terminal and heavily-laden trucks stopped at their checkpoint frequently. This truck did not stop, however. Instead it turned suddenly, shifted into a lower gear, and headed straight through flimsy barriers toward Marine headquarters. As the guards raised their rifles, the truck, packed with explosives, disintegrated before their eyes, sending the sentries sprawling backward to the ground. The concrete Marine headquarters settled inward upon itself, collapsing into a pile of rubble. Two hundred and forty-one U.S. Marines, sailors and soldiers were killed. At the same time a similar attack was carried out against a French military outpost in the city. Subsequently another truck bombing destroyed an Israeli military headquarters in the south, killing a great many of Israel's Arabic-speaking intelligence personnel. Once again all three truck bombings were attributed to Iranian-directed Shia fundamentalist groups, headquartered in the Bekaa valley in areas loosely controlled by Syrian Army units.

With perhaps a fifth of its military personnel in Lebanon killed in one explosion, the U.S. was in a state of shock that was ameliorated only slightly by the news that a relieving battalion of Marines, which had already embarked for Lebanon, had been diverted at sea to join in the invasion of the tiny Caribbean island state of Grenada, where an eccentric leftist President had just been murdered by extremists within his own movement.

When the relieving battalion finally arrived in Beirut to replace the survivors of the ill-fated previous battalion, the reinforcements were already wearing a combat ribbon awarded for an almost bloodless victory in Grenada. They were soon to start paying more dearly for their next ribbon.

When the first shells and bullets had begun hitting Marine positions, their officers had explained that, since they were close to a Lebanese Army unit that was engaged in frequent fire-fights with Druze units in the hills above, the Druze were firing "not because of who we are but because of where we are." Now, however, the Marines were also taking sniper fire from Shia positions in the slums between the airport and the city.

Nabih Berri, leader of the largest Shia militia, called Amal, was considered a moderate and, in fact, had been married to an American woman and had children living in the U.S. He was also closely aligned with Syria. He assured the Marines that his men were not doing the sniping, and that whenever it began he was sending his own militiamen to chase away the perpetrators. Suspicion fell again on extremist Shia gangs whose primary loyalty was to the Ayatollah Khomeini in Iran. The Marines, therefore, began to fire back and, with their sniper scopes and infra-red sights capable of penetrating darkness, they soon had hit a few of their tormentors. The victims generally turned out to be children, and this increased the tension. Now Marines were taking fire from the blackened shells of buildings in Shia suburbs all around the airport. Some of the perpetrators were, literally, children on their way home from school. And many of the Marines who fired back at them were not much more than children themselves.

Things were beginning to turn out just as Defense Secretary Weinberger had predicted they would when he argued against sending in U.S. military forces except for short and carefully defined missions. The Democratic leadership in Congress briefly flirted with the idea of politicizing the issue, asking what, exactly, was the mission of the U.S. forces in Beirut. The PLO had been evacuated a year earlier. The Israelis had withdrawn far to the south. The combatants remaining had little or nothing to do with the big issues of U.S. foreign policy. The Republicans responded that the Marines were supporting the elected government of Amin Gemayel. This only made matters worse, since both Berri's militiamen around the Marines and Walid Jumblatt's Druze in the hills above were seeking to overthrow the Gemayel government.

Another complication was the fact that the U.S. was perceptibly drawing closer to Israel again. Begin, though a fanatic who had employed violence and terrorism to accomplish his political goals, was also an intelligent man. He could see that in falling in with Sharon's plans to realize their joint dream of taking over the West Bank he had caused the deaths of at least 600 Israeli soldiers and many thousands of Lebanese and Palestinians, had polarized Israel and wrecked its economy. He was also devastated by the death of his wife. It is not clear whether the national catastrophe or his personal loss weighed most heavily upon him, but the combined burden was more than he could carry.

Begin stepped aside in favor of his Foreign Minister, Yitzhak Shamir, a terrorist rival from the war of independence days when Begin headed the Irgun Zvai Leumi underground organization and Shamir was a leader of the even more intransigent and violent Stern Gang. Begin retreated into his home, closed the door behind him, and disappeared from public view. Shamir set out to tackle Israel's problems.

The military accord with the United States, mutually suspended in the recriminations that followed Begin's annexation of the Golan Heights, was revived and the next month Shamir headed to the U.S. to collect increased military and economic aid. He was closely followed by Gemayel, who left puzzled by the political advice offered by the Reagan Administration but fortified by promises of more aid. All of this only turned up the battlefield temperature around the increasingly bewildered Marines, who still prided themselves on the close and friendly liaison they maintained with leaders of the contending Lebanese units around them, but who nevertheless were taking heavier casualties in an increasingly hostile military environment.

The Reagan Administration judged Syria to be behind the escalating level of violence. After Israeli aircraft struck at Syrian ground to air missile sites in the Bekaa valley, U.S. reconnaisance F-14 aircraft flew over the same area and received heavy Syrian anti-aircraft fire. Whether the U.S. deliberately provoked the confrontation, or unknowingly blundered into a situation where its planes were bound to be taken for Israeli jets returning for another raid is not clear.

In any case, the next day the U.S. launched two wings of navy fighter aircraft to attack Syrian missile positions in Lebanon. Although the Israelis had done it with impunity over and over again, two U.S. aircraft were shot down on the first American try. One U.S. pilot was fatally injured. Another bailed out and was taken prisoner by the Syrians. It appeared that American military efforts to intimidate Syria were no more effective than had been the U.S. political offensive of the preceding months.

The issue even began to take on domestic political significance as election year approached. The Reverend Jesse Jackson, a Black leader seeking the Democratic Presidential nomination, offered to go to Syria to seek the release of the surviving Navy flier, an Annapolis graduate who also was black. American Jewish supporters of Israel, aware that Jackson had for several years been calling for improving U.S. ties with the Arabs in general and the Palestinians in particular, either attacked or ridiculed the idea. Assad, however, was also aware of Jackson's previous record. Jackson was invited to visit Damascus and returned with a smiling Navy flyer, released unconditionally by Syria.

The incident only pointed up the increasing irrelevance to U.S. interests in the Middle East of the U.S. military presence in Beirut, where Marines were being killed for no obvious reason except that they were there. The disagreement within the Reagan Administration broke into the open. Weinberger wanted to withdraw the Marines from their exposed position ashore. Shultz and MacFarland argued that they should stay or, if they were withdrawn, that the U.S. should use some of its other weapons to "punish" the Syrians and their Lebanese allies for what was becoming an increasing American humiliation. Reagan's confusing public statements seemed only to reflect the views of the adviser to whom he had spoken last. On December 14, Reagan said that he would withdraw the Marines if there were a "collapse of order" in Lebanon. This apparently was protested by Shultz. On February 3, therefore, Reagan was quoted as saying he was not prepared to "surrender" in Lebanon and that if the U.S. were to leave under Syrian pressure, "that means the end of Lebanon."

By that time, however, Reagan's White House aides had already agreed with Weinberger that U.S. ground forces must be withdrawn immediately from their untenable positions on Lebanese soil. On February 7, as the Lebanese Army was once again collapsing and the Shia and Druze militias were seizing abandoned Lebanese Army positions both in West Beirut and all around the Beirut airport, the White House announced that the Marines would soon be "redeployed" to the U.S. ships offshore. Within a few days, and without further harassment, they were gone.

Shultz had the final word, however. The Marines departed not with a whimper but with a bang. As soon as they were safely "redeployed," the battleship New Jersey opened up with its huge guns. American residents of Beirut described how the entire city shook as giant U.S. shells passed overhead on their way to the ridgeline above Beirut, dotted not only with gun enplacements but also with Druze villages. When one of the huge missiles hit a house or apartment building in such a village, it brought the entire structure down upon the occupants. This final paroxysm of destructive rage only pointed up U.S. frustration. Once the foremost protectors of Lebanon, Americans now seemed unable to understand that, after providing the weapons used for Lebanon's destruction, they had forfeited the trust and respect their ancestors had earned a century earlier. The bombardment by the New Jersey, a particularly shocking event in the tragic history of a country not easily shocked, casts a long shadow over future U.S.-Lebanese relations.

Even Amin Gemayel, who had started turning to Syria for support even before the spectacular American withdrawal, made official his rejection of his former U.S. mentors. On March 5, 1984, Lebanon cancelled the Lebanese-Israeli withdrawal agreement of May 17, 1983. It was the end of the era when even the most powerful Lebanese politicians sought an American protector. Now, the humblest U.S. citizen seeking to live, work or even travel in Lebanon needed a Lebanese protector, and most of those were of little value to the long-term American residents. Only the bravest or the most foolhardy Americans dared remain in what had once been a comfortable and hospitable second home to virtually every American who lived or worked anywhere in the Middle East.

Lebanese (right) run for shelter under concrete apartment building as shells start to fall during summer, 1982, Israeli seige of Beirut. Israeli spotter (below) directs artillery fire on Burj al Barajna Palestinian refugee camp from hills above Beirut.

Wide World

Wide World

CHAPTER XXIII

The Revolt of the Moderates

"Looking back on the four years of my presidency, I realize that I spent more of my time working for possible solutions to the riddle of Middle East peace than on any other international problem. I have asked myself many times if it was worth the tremendous investment of my time and energy. The answer will depend on the wisdom and dedication of the leaders of the future. Only history will reveal if my hopes and prayers are to be answered, or if another round of bloody confrontations will ultimately lead to an international tragedy."[1]

Jimmy Carter, 1982

"From the beginning (Arafat) has been the only Palestinian leader who could talk about dealing with Israel and not be killed the next day for saying so."[2]

Brian Uruquart, 1984

"There is no Jordanian option. There are no options. There is a reality. Palestine and the Palestinians . . . and the proper and only representative is the Palestine Liberation Organization."

King Hussein of Jordan, January 30, 1981

"It is not Israel that has to be secure. It is the Arab countries that have to feel more secure if they are to maintain their thrust toward a peaceful settlement of the Palestinian problem."

Prince Saud Faisal, Foreign Minister of Saudi Arabia, June, 1981

---

1. Carter, Jimmy, *Keeping Faith: Memoirs of a President*, Bantam Books, New York, 1982, p. 429.
2. Hart, Alan, *Arafat: Terrorist or Peacemaker?*, Sidgwick and Jackson, London, 1984, p. 450.

"We, the Israelis, remain. They, the Palestinians, remain. After forty years, after several wars, after so many alliances and unutterable sufferings, so many political shifts, the protagonists remain. Israelis as well as Palestinians, the same dying ones. The political boundaries have been altered several times, but basically both of us remain in the same place. We have denounced and insulted each other, we have murdered, persecuted, and beaten each other, but we remain the same, and we are stuck in the same place."[3]
Jacobo Timerman, 1982

In September, 1984, surrounded in the northern Lebanese city of Tripoli, it had seemed that Yassir Arafat's remaining days on earth were numbered. Syrian shells rained down on the ancient Lebanese city and its leaders begged Arafat and his 4,000 PLO loyalists to leave to spare the city further bombardment.

There was no way to escape by land. His old enemy, Syrian President Hafez Al Assad, wanted his scalp, and quickly. Israeli gunboats, meanwhile, circled offshore like hungry sharks. Then something extraordinary happened.

Arafat appealed to Saudi Arabia, which bankrolled Syria, the PLO and Jordan's King Hussein as well. It was not the first time that Saudi-funded armies had fought each other. It had happened in Jordan in 1970 and 1971 when the Jordanian Army fought the PLO. It had happened again in Lebanon in 1976 when the Syrian Army had intervened to stop the PLO from routing the Maronite Phalange militia. The Saudis had, however, been as timorous about trying to re-direct the mutual destructiveness of their clients as was the U.S. when Israel, totally dependent upon massive U.S. economic assistance, made huge financial outlays to build West Bank and Golan Heights settlements and thereby thwarted U.S. peace efforts, or used its U.S.-supplied weapons to level cities and towns in Lebanon, once a virtual U.S. protectorate.

In response to Arafat's appeal, however, the Saudis acted with uncharacteristic forcefulness. They told President Assad that, if he did not let Arafat and his PLO loyalists leave in safety, they would cut off Syria's economic subsidy. Since Assad's cold war with Iraq and the hot war in Lebanon had deprived Syria of other sources of foreign exchange, Assad stopped the shelling.

Israeli gunboats still blocked Arafat from freedom, however. It seemed they might succeed in killing Arafat where Syria had failed. Now another Arab leader stepped out of character. Egypt's President Hosni Mubarrak, a pragmatic former fighter pilot, had been conscientiously carrying out the pro-western foreign policy that had cost the life of his predecessor, Anwar Sadat. Mubarrak, however, decided that this policy, based upon maintaining at least a "cold peace" with Israel regardless of the cost to his relations with other Arab states, had its limits. He told the Israelis that if they denied Arafat safe passage out of Tripoli, it was the end of "normalization" of relations between Egypt and Israel. The PLO force was evacuated by sea and was not harassed by Israel as it headed for the safety of Egyptian waters. In Egypt, Arafat disembarked and proceeded directly to Cairo to thank Mubarrak for his timely intervention.

3. Timerman, Jacobo, *The Longest War: Israel in Lebanon*, Alfred A. Knopf, New York, 1982, p. 112.

Since most of the Arab countries had severed diplomatic relations with Egypt at the time of Sadat's 1977 journey to Jerusalem, Arafat's gesture set off a storm of protest from the "rejectionists," both among the Arab states and among component groups within the PLO. Arafat's own Al Fatah guerrilla group was both the largest, by far, and the most politically moderate of the diverse assemblage of Palestinian organizations then sheltering under the PLO umbrella. It is not clear whether Arafat fully anticipated the strong and protracted reaction to his reconciliation with Egypt, but it had a profound effect on the subsequent composition of the PLO.

The cluster of tiny but noisy and dangerous Marxist guerrilla groups which had for so long put the Palestinians at odds with the U.S., Western Europe, and more moderate Arab countries all walked out of the PLO and joined the Syrian-directed anti-Arafat front. Gone was Ahmad Jibril's PFLP-GC, which had kidnapped, robbed and occasionally murdered foreigners as well as Lebanese and other Palestinians during Lebanon's civil war. Gone was Nayef Hawatmeh's Syrian-based and Soviet-directed PDFLP, and gone was George Habash, the Marxist medical doctor whose specialists in sky-jacking and international terrorism had for a generation been the single most effective exhibit in Israel's campaign to dehumanize the Palestinians in the eyes of the world. It was Habash's PFLP that had precipitated the 1970 confrontation with the Jordanian Army that resulted in the PLO losing its Jordanian base. He nevertheless had retained a strong ideological hold on the Marxist "all-or-nothing" Palestinians who had made a profession out of losing for so long. Habash's departure from the PLO, therefore, gave Arafat and his more moderate followers some freedom to adopt a practical strategy for recovering a part of their lost land without being called traitors for not demanding it all.

Wisely, Arafat never looked back. He knew that, whatever the outside world thought of him, among the rank-and-file Palestinians in Israel proper, the West Bank and Gaza, and in their diaspora, at least 80 percent would follow his lead. The point was no longer whether or not they thought he was the best leader or even whether they endorsed his relatively moderate policy. The point was that the Palestinian rank and file had finally recognized, before many of their contending leaders, that if they wanted the world to take them seriously, they had to demonstrate that they could accept the discipline required to unite behind one national leader, even if as individuals they disagreed with some of his policies.

It was a revolt of the moderates, first by Saudi Arabia against Syrian manipulation of the Palestinians, then by Egypt against Israeli intransigence, and finally by Arafat against the PLO's left-wing lunatic fringe which had for so long set his international agenda. This revolt was about to transform completely the Arab side of the Palestinian-Israeli dispute.

Arafat made the first move. He called a November, 1984, meeting, in Amman, of the Palestine National Council. The PNC was, in effect, a national parliament for the Palestinians, containing representatives of all the scattered communities and individuals who make up the four million-strong Palestinian community worldwide. As such it is the only body that can confer legitimacy on Palestinian leaders.

Once again both the Israeli and Syrian governments set out to thwart this decisive attempt by the Palestinians to take over direction of their own destiny. Syrian President Al-Assad revoked the passports of all PNC members living in Syria and Lebanon. Similarly, Israel banned travel by the 181 PNC members living under Israeli occupation, prompting Israeli peace leader Uri Avnery to comment that "the Israeli government clearly prefers an extremist PLO because the existence of a moderate PLO would require Israel to negotiate about the West Bank."

Virtually all PNC members who could, however, traveled to Amman to provide a quorum. Among them were PNC members from North and South America, including not only naturalized Americans but at least one PNC member born in the United States of Palestinian parents. The heavy-handed steps of the governments of Israel and Syria to sabotage the meeting were more than offset by firm support from King Hussein. Wavering PNC members who were residents of Jordan but who were reluctant to support Arafat until they felt sure he would win were told that life in Jordan might be complicated for them in the future if they did not stand up to be counted now.

Arafat got his quorum, enabling the meeting to approve resolutions in the name of Palestinians everywhere. King Hussein then told the body that, if the Palestinians would agree to negotiate on the basis of U.N. Security Council Resolution 242, their representatives in a joint delegation with Jordan would be representing the PLO in its own right. Resolution 242, with the loss of nearly four fifths of the original Palestine Mandate it implies, was a bitter pill for the Palestinians assembled from all over the world. The debate was long and impassioned, prompting Arafat's resignation at one point. An interesting sidelight was the fact that, since Jordan Television carried the proceedings live, Palestinians living in the West Bank, Gaza, and in Israel itself were able to watch what indisputably was *their* government engaged in genuine open debate of a kind not often seen in any third world country.

Arafat emerged from the debate undisputed leader of the Palestinians. Whether his following was 80 percent, as conservatively estimated, or upwards of 90 percent as estimated by his ecstatic followers, the numbers would be the envy of any leader in a Western democracy, or in Israel. It made future efforts from either quarter to question Arafat's legitimacy as leader of the Palestinians ironic, since they would come from leaders who could command no such majority among their own peoples.

With his mandate renewed, Arafat signed on February 11, 1985, an agreement to work with King Hussein on putting together a team to negotiate with Israel on the land-for-peace basis. This time there was no backsliding, as there had been when Arafat had unsuccessfully sought backing from his own supporters for a similar agreement a year earlier. The absence of the nay-sayers was proving a tonic to Palestinian prospects to retrieve at least a portion of their lost lands.

Although still unwilling to recognize Israel until it defined its boundaries and recognized the PLO as the government, within defined boundaries, of the Palestinians, Arafat made it clear that the PLO was willing to be represented at an international peace conference with Israel. The conference would be based upon putting all of the principles of Resolution 242 into action and it would be understood that the Palestinians would set up their own state – in confederation with Jordan, in deference to the Reagan Plan – in the territories vacated by Israel. It was an historic concession for the PLO.

It was Ralph Waldo Emerson who said that "events are the master of man" and nowhere is this more true than in the Middle East. The giant step forward toward peace represented by the Hussein-Arafat agreement was followed by a whole series of setbacks. This time it was, perhaps, no coincidence that extremists in Syria, Israel, Iran and Libya all seemed to be colluding to discourage both the Palestinians and the United States from continuing their progress toward a negotiated peace.

Israel's successful contribution to raising the level of Middle East tension was called "Operation Iron Fist." It was carried out in conjunction with a withdrawal of Israeli forces from what virtually everyone but Ariel Sharon himself now agreed had been a catastrophic debacle for Israel in Lebanon.

The Shia of Southern Lebanon, who had suffered heavily in the cross border fighting between the PLO and the Israelis prior to the cease-fire of 1981, had almost welcomed the Israelis as liberators at the beginning of the 1982 invasion. After two years of almost incredibly insensitive treatment by Israeli occupation forces, and blatant Israeli divide-and-rule sponsorship of local toughs and militias that made the PLO look almost benevolent in retrospect, the Shia had begun to make Israeli troops pay a fearful price. Any teen-ager in an automobile, riding a donkey, or even afoot and carrying a pack might turn into a human bomb, destroying everyone near whatever checkpoint he or she approached. Since the end of the invasion in the summer of 1982, the toll of Israeli soldiers killed in Lebanon had doubled.

Therefore the Israelis decided to withdraw their combat troops entirely from Lebanon, leaving only "advisers" to their puppet militia, now commanded by General Antoine Lahad, who had taken over upon Major Saad Haddad's death from skin cancer. In order to minimize casualties during the delicate process of dismantling their positions in Lebanon and transporting their men and equipment back to Israel, the Israeli Defense Force launched a series of lightning dawn raids upon Shia villages in the territory to be vacated. Called "Operation Iron Fist," the raids were characterized by ostentatious and heavy-handed brutality, intended to cow the villagers both for the present and the future.

Israeli tanks would set up hidden ambushes on all sides of a village to be raided. Then armored personnel carriers would rumble into the village, unloading heavily-armed Israeli soldiers who called upon the villagers to assemble in the main square. Those who sought to escape from the village, as many of the young men and boys did, would be cut down by gunfire from the tanks stationed in ambush outside. There were no questions asked. The tank crews mowed down anyone who moved. The entire area around the village being raided became a "free-fire zone." After the first two or three such raids, most of the young men took to sleeping in the hills. But those who did not, and who therefore were trapped in their villages, were hauled off to Israel in trucks.

How many others were killed in "Operation Iron Fist" is unknown. Glimpses into the savagery with which it was carried out were provided in European and even the U.S. media. Journalists, after hearing rumors of the dawn killings as Israelis surrounded villages and the young men tried to slip out, began racing to the scene whenever they learned that such an operation was taking place. Generally they arrived after the shooting but while houses were being searched, and sometimes looted, and while occupants were still being held at gunpoint in the village center.

The Israeli Army began "arresting" non-Israeli journalists of any nationality who sought to approach a village under siege. When that did not deter journalists, they fired at an NBC camera team seeking to reach a village surrounded by Israeli troops.

A few days later, on March 21, 1985, an Israeli tank put a burst of gunfire through the motor and windshield of a vehicle being driven by Lebanese journalists. The occupants climbed out of the disabled car and other following journalists heeded the warning and stopped their vehicles nearby.

When members of a CBS camera team began filming the bullet-shattered car, the tank crew that had fired the first burst fired a shell at them at almost point-blank range. CBS Cameraman Toufiq Ghazawi and Soundman Bahij Metni were killed instantly. Their driver lost both legs. The Israeli Government made no excuses. It said the journalists should not have been in an area where anyone who moved was likely to be mistaken for a "terrorist." There was little further television coverage of Operation Iron Fist. But by the time it was over 1,150 Lebanese and Palestinians had been hauled across the border into Israel where they were held in a concentration camp as hostages against the safe withdrawal of Israeli forces from their part of Lebanon.

Meanwhile, fundamentalist Iran was doing its part to keep the Middle East pot boiling. The U.S. Embassy in Beirut had been moved from Muslim West Beirut to a Christian-controlled area where once again it was bombed, but with a much lower casualty toll. Then in December, 1984, terrorists hijacked a Kuwaiti airliner to Tehran. The purpose of the hijacking was to secure the release of 17 Iraqis and Lebanese being held in Kuwait. They had been convicted of bombing the U.S. and French Embassies in Kuwait, along with various Kuwaiti government buildings and residential areas, one year earlier in December, 1983. All of the bombers had been Shia extremists, except for one Lebanese Maronite who had been hired to rig the car and truck bombs employed.

The Muslim prisoners were members of Al Dawa, a shadowy Shia fundamentalist organization directed and funded by Khomeini's Iran. It was organized to carry out sabotage operations against Iran's opponents, using Shia nationals of Iraq and Lebanon.

The arrival of the hijacked Kuwaiti plane at the Tehran airport started a charade in which Iranian authorities pretended to be negotiating with the hijackers, who in fact seemed free to come and go as they wished. There were several Americans on the plane, including three U.S. AID officials. The hijackers and the Iranian government apparently expected the U.S. to react to this by pressuring Kuwait to release its 17 prisoners.

The U.S. reaction was low-key, however. The Kuwaiti Ambassador in Washington, Sheikh Saud Nasir Al-Sabah, made himself available to U.S. journalists, explaining that the 17 prisoners had been convicted after a fair trial in Kuwaiti courts, with five actually sentenced to death but with no date set to carry out those sentences. He also noted that neither the Embassy bombings nor the hijacking had taken place in a vacuum. Such tragedies would inevitably continue, he pointed out, so long as the basic Middle East grievances remained unresolved.

Iran finally released the plane, but only after two of the U.S. AID officials, Charles Hegna and William Stanford, had been shot dead at point blank range in an effort to force Kuwait to capitulate.

In June, 1984, a similar tragic drama began when two Shia extremists who had boarded a Trans World Airlines flight in Athens seized the jumbo jet and forced it to shuttle between Algiers and Beirut, dropping off some passengers at each stop. After two visits to Algiers, and on its third stop in Beirut, serious negotiations began. By this time a 23-year-old American Navy diver, Robert Stethem, who had been returning home after completing underwater harbor repair work at an American base in Greece, had been beaten, shot at point blank range, and his body dropped on the Beirut tarmac.

This time, however, the hijacking took a different turn from that in Kuwait six months earlier, although both were committed by Shia fundamentalists. The controlling power in Beirut is Syria, not Iran, and Syria was not anxious to give either Israel or the U.S. an opportunity for a rescue operation, which could have set off another round of Israeli-Syrian warfare. Shia militiamen of Nabih Berri's Al Amal militia, which was increasingly controlled by Syria, "reinforced" the Shia extremists already aboard the plane. The original two hijackers vanished, but some of their Shia fundamentalist comrades remained aboard the plane, side by side with the more moderate Berri's men.

The other difference between this Beirut hostage drama and the earlier one in Kuwait was that the demands of these hijackers were basically reasonable. Instead of linking the fate of their American hostages to that of prisoners convicted in a court of law, they asked that some 766 Shia hostages remaining from the 1,150 Israel had originally taken from Southern Lebanese villages in Operation "Iron Fist," be freed. They too were innocent hostages being held in defiance of international law and without charges.

The nearly impotent Lebanese airport authorities could not prevent western television crews from going out on the tarmac and actually interviewing the pilot in his cockpit, or the hijackers on the ramp. By this time all non-American passengers and all of the American women and children as well as elderly or sick men had been released, either in Algiers or Beirut. The others reported their new, Amal captors were treating them well. Finally the hostages were taken off the plane entirely and dispersed in various parts of Muslim Beirut to thwart a U.S. rescue attempt.

During the hijacking drama relations between Israel and the U.S. grew increasingly strained. After Israel had completed its withdrawal from Southern Lebanon it had begun releasing its Lebanese hostages in small groups. It was apparent from the beginning of the hijack drama that the U.S. wanted the Israelis to expedite freeing all of the remaining Shia hostages. Instead, Israel stopped freeing them altogether. Israeli Defense Minister Rabin, a dour character at the best of times, apparently was speaking for Israeli domestic audiences when he told newsmen that, if the U.S. wanted Israel to do something to ease the situation, it should ask.

This was exactly what the U.S. could not do if it was to maintain its world-wide stance of never negotiating with kidnappers or terrorists. Even the simplest U.S. journalist understood this. Criticism in the U.S. press grew, reluctantly but steadily, based on the premise that "friends shouldn't have to be asked." Israel, with characteristic stubbornness, stood its ground for a few days while it slowly dawned on the U.S. public — which for once seemed to comprehend the situation in its entirety — that Israel was waiting for the promises of U.S. arms and money which normally accompany any U.S. request to the Jewish state.

Americans grew increasingly irritated, and American Jewish supporters of Israel telephoned, cabled and in some cases flew to Israel to deliver frantic appeals to Prime Minister Shimon Peres to abandon what seemed to be either a gratuitously abrasive or transparently greedy stand against the obvious and fervent desires of the Reagan Administration and the U.S. public as a whole.

Syria, and the Amal militia, sensed a good thing when they saw one. The remaining hostages began to appear at Beirut restaurants, in the custody of well-armed Amal militiamen but nevertheless available to talk with western journalists. Further, some of the hostages were Americans who lived and worked in the Middle East, understood what was going on, and told western journalists that such outrages would continue until the U.S. addressed the basic grievance that had polarized the area. One hostage was actually filmed asking another why their captors seemed to hate the state of New Jersey. The explanation, on camera, was that the Lebanese gunmen were talking about the U.S. battleship of the same name, whose bombardment six months earlier had killed some of their relatives.

Israel's friends in the U.S. began to realize that their cause was starting to suffer the worst U.S. press treatment since the televised destruction of Beirut in the summer of 1982. The journalists who steadfastly defended Israel through this 17-day ordeal became progressively fewer, and shriller. Had the U.S. government listened to their demands that it get tough and send in airborne troops, hundreds of innocent people in Beirut might have been killed and few, if any, U.S. citizens would have emerged alive. Therefore the Reagan Administration negotiated seriously and urgently with Syria's Assad, and he in turn put increasing pressure on the Shia groups. By this time it had become apparent that although Amal's captives were being well treated, a smaller group, including U.S. servicemen from the plane, were being held out of sight by the original fundamentalist captors. Finally both groups were driven overland to Damascus and released to U.S. authorities there. It was no secret that, based on U.S. assurances, President Assad had personally guaranteed to the Shia captors that, after they had released their American hostages, Israel would over a short period release all of the Lebanese hostages it was still holding. The Israelis, apparently attempting to discredit all Arab leaders who cooperated with the U.S. in the operation, then delayed releasing their hostages throughout most of the summer.

This however was almost overlooked in Lebanon where new fighting had broken out between Nabih Berri's militiamen and remaining, or returning, supporters of Yassir Arafat in the Palestinian camps. It seemed to be another attempt by Assad to thwart Yassir Arafat, but it backfired. After watching Syrian-supplied shells kill nearly 1000 of their Palestinian kinsmen, the Syrian-funded Palestinian rebels could stand it no longer. They turned their own Syrian-supplied artillery on their Lebanese Shia tormentors and broke up the seige. Arafat emerged immeasurably strengthened.

The skyjacking threw the media spotlight on eight other Americans who had been kidnapped in Beirut by Shia extremists over the previous year and a half. They also were being held as hostages for the safe release of the 17 prisoners in Kuwait. One, Cable Television Correspondent Jeremy Levin, had either escaped or been allowed to escape from the house where he was kept blindfolded and chained to a radiator for

11 months in Lebanon's Bekaa Valley near the Shia town of Ba'albek. He and his wife and the relatives of the other still-missing hostages were able to generate some media pressure on the U.S. government to seek their release as well.

Subsequently another of the American prisoners, the Reverend Benjamin Weir, was released. He reported that he had seen four other missing Americans alive, but that all were in danger if there was no progress concerning the Lebanese and Iraqi Shia prisoners in Kuwait.

The problem was the same that bedeviled the U.S. during the Kuwait hijacking, however. The 17 were extremists who had killed Kuwaitis and foreign residents of Kuwait, and they had been convicted in a court of law. If they were released, what restraint would there be on terrorists anywhere?

As pressure built upon the U.S. to address the basic Middle East problem by solving the Arab-Israeli dispute, a renewed cycle of international violence in the fall of 1985 only underlined the need for a solution.

For a year individual attacks against Jews within both Israel and the West Bank had gradually increased. It was clear that although the PLO, unlike the fringe Palestinian groups, was avoiding violence on the international stage, it had not abandoned what it called "armed struggle" and Israel called "terrorism" within Israel and the occupied territories.

Further, young Palestinians on the West Bank had drawn some conclusions from the almost spontaneous Shia revolt against Israeli occupation of Southern Lebanon. The Lebanese Shia had inflicted such severe casualties on Israeli troops that the Israelis had withdrawn the bulk of their forces from Southern Lebanon.

There followed a rash of attacks on Israelis, mostly on the West Bank but also in Israel itself. Israeli civilians were kidnapped and shot in remote areas, or stabbed in crowded markets. How much resulted from a spontaneous upsurge of Palestinian nationalism and how much was actually planned from abroad is not clear. However, when three Israelis, two men and a woman, were killed aboard a yacht in Cyprus by three supporters of the Palestinians, one of them an English volunteer who for a time was said to have served in Yassir Arafat's Al Fatah, the Israelis struck.

Eight of their American-supplied aircraft took off from Israel and were refueled somewhere over the Mediterranean. They flew to Malta and then, dropping to an extremely low level to avoid radar detection, they headed directly west to strike and obliterate the building being used as Arafat's headquarters in Tunis. Some 70 Palestinians and Tunisian policemen, gardeners, neighbors and passersby, were killed.

The raid caused a flurry of charges and counter charges. First, the Israelis charged that Arafat's PLO had killed the three Israelis in Cyprus and that this was retaliation for his resumption of international terrorism. Palestinians said the three Israelis were intelligence agents charged with spotting Palestinian attempts to smuggle guns and fighters into Israel, and that in any case Arafat's PLO had not done the killing.

They charged further that Yassir Arafat had been scheduled to meet with members of the PLO Executive Committee in his headquarters at the exact moment when the raid was carried out. Arafat and his advisers were spared only because the meeting had been postponed when Arafat was called to meet with Tunisian Government officials instead. Whether or not the Israeli raid was aimed at such a meeting, it was Arafat's office that was destroyed, and once again he was saved from assassination only by his incredible good luck.

Even before the charges and counter charges could be fully aired, an Italian cruise ship, the *Achille Lauro* was hijacked at sea by three young men belonging to a Palestinian fringe group. Egyptian authorities talked them off the ship by promising that they would be released unharmed from Egypt. After they left the ship, however, it was discovered that they had killed an elderly, crippled American tourist, Leon Klinghoffer, and dumped his body overboard. The Egyptians nevertheless sent the hijackers off on an Egyptian plane, supposedly to Tunis where the Egyptians said Arafat had agreed to receive and punish them.

The plane was denied permission to land by Tunisian authorities, and four American Sixth Fleet jets, guided by a radar-bearing U.S. aircraft that had been screening all commercial air traffic while looking for it, swooped in and forced the Egyptian plane to land at a U.S. base in Sicily. Italian authorities arrested the shipjackers. Since, despite his denials, many suspected that a fringe group loyal to Yassir Arafat was behind the *Achille Lauro* affair, the PLO leader appeared with President Mubarrak in Cairo to pledge publicly that PLO armed actions would be confined to Israel and the occupied territories.

A victim of terrorism within the U.S. was 41-year-old Alex Odeh, a Palestinian-born U.S. citizen who was Southern California regional director for the American-Arab Anti-Discrimination Committee (ADC). Mr. Odeh, a writer and poet who had been on television during the *Achille Lauro* affair to explain how unlikely it was that Arafat's followers would be involved, was killed by a bomb triggered to explode and kill whoever first entered his ADC office in Santa Ana, California, the morning of Oct. 11, 1985. He became the first American to be killed on American soil as a direct result of the Arab-Israeli dispute since the assassination of Robert Kennedy 17 years earlier.

More tragedies in Europe followed in December when Palestinian followers of Arafat's bitter rival, Sabri Al Bana (Abu Nidal), allegedly funded by Iran, trained in the Syrian-controlled Bekaa Valley of Lebanon, and using passports supplied by Libya, killed 15 persons in Rome and 3 in Vienna in attacks on airport offices of Israel's El Al Airline. The fact that five Americans died, including Natasha Simpson, an appealing 11-year-old, focused both U.S. Government and U.S. media attention on international terrorism.

When Israel spoke of punishing the PLO, the Reagan Administration privately forwarded a strong warning to Israel not to seize upon the attacks as an excuse to attack PLO offices in Jordan. At the same time Administration spokesmen began, for the first time, to focus public attention upon the differences between Arafat's relatively moderate policies and tactics and those of extremists like Abu Nidal who, when he had been turned out by Iraq several years earlier, put himself at the service of the remaining 'rejectionist' states opposing a compromise peace. For the first time, Americans began to learn from their own government and media something of Yassir Arafat's relative moderation within the Palestinian camp.

As President Reagan and Libya's Colonel Qaddafi traded insults over the Abul Nidal outrages, however, it clearly was Secretary of State Shultz who was advocating the use of military force and Secretary of Defense Caspar Weinberger who was arguing against getting bogged down in military action in the Middle East.

Disarray in the Reagan Administration was reflected within the moderate Arab Camp. Alarmed when he realized the Administration was not working to overcome Congressional objections to selling defensive arms to Jordan, King Hussein held a series of intensive meetings seeking formal PLO acceptance of UN General Assembly Resolutions 242 and 338 in return for U.S. agreement to a UN-hosted peace conference to be attended by Israelis and Palestinians. The PLO also wanted formal U.S. acknowledgement of the Palestinian right to self-determination. In February, King Hussein acknowledged failure and placed much of the blame upon the PLO. Yassir Arafat treated the matter as a temporary difference with Jordan, but King Hussein closed PLO offices in Amman, perhaps to forestall an Israeli attack upon them.

Israel, meanwhile, was also in disarray. Labor Prime Minister Peres spoke of peace negotiations, perhaps only to provoke a Likud walkout and new elections before his deadline for turning over the Government to the Likud in late 1986.

In March, 1986 the U.S. Sixth Fleet moved into the Mediterranean Gulf of Sidra for what had become a bi-annual confrontation over Libya's claim that the area is within its territorial waters, and the U.S. claim that it is not. Charging that Libya attacked its ships, the U.S. sank a Libyan patrol boat, damaged another, and fired missiles at a Libyan radar station. In April, a bomb killed a U.S. Army sergeant and a Turkish woman in a West Berlin nightclub, and the U.S. charged Libyan complicity.

President Reagan sent Navy aircraft from carriers and Air Force attack bombers from England on a night strike against what the U.S. described as five Libyan military targets. Two U.S. pilots were killed. Among at least 37 Libyan dead were Qaddafi's adopted 15-month-old daughter, Hanna. Among some 93 wounded were his two youngest sons. Libyan authorities showed American newsmen that one of the "military targets" was the Aziziya Barracks in Tripoli, where Qaddafi lived with his family.

Americans were divided. Many thought Qaddafi had left Reagan no choice. Others believed the action strengthened the Libyan. Some said the violence lowered the U.S. to Qaddafi's level. Europeans generally expressed the latter view. Retaliatory killings of British hostages and an American in Lebanon added bitterness to the debate.

It is axiomatic that when momentum toward peace slows, the Middle East drifts toward war. The Reagan Administration's retreat from its own Middle East peace plan seemed to be further radicalizing the Arab world, turning the Muslim fifth of the world's population against the United States, and loosening the ties between the U.S. and its European allies. At home, the FBI reported that of seven terrorist acts in the U.S. in 1985, four had been directed against Arab Americans by Jewish extremists. By mid-1986, after the actions against Libya, newspapers were filled with denunciations and defenses of the influence of American Jews and Israel's U.S. lobby in Washington.

Midway in his second term President Reagan was learning what so many of his predecessors had learned too late: No matter how difficult the obstacles to Middle East peace, its absence is far, far worse.

Wide World

A bulldozer (above) scoops earth over the mass grave of hundreds of Palestinian victims of heavy Israeli air attacks on refugee camps on the outskirts of Sidon during the first week of the 1982 Israeli invasion. Israeli soldier (below) disperses families outside internment camp where Palestinians arrested in the Sidon area are being held.

UPI

CHAPTER XXIV

A Word About Lobbies — Carrots and Sticks

"Ethnic advocacy represents neither a lack of patriotism nor a desire to place foreign interests ahead of American interests; more often it represents a sincere belief that the two coincide. Similarly, resistance to the pressures of a particular group in itself signals neither a sellout nor even a lack of sympathy with a foreign country or cause, but rather a sincere conviction about the national interest of the United States. There is a clear and pressing need for the reintroduction of civility into our public discussions of these matters."[1]

Senator Charles McC. Mathias, Jr. (R-Md.), 1981

"For this generation of Americans, the news from the Middle East, and indeed from most of the Muslim world, has tended more and more to merge with the sociology of what happens at home—the results of oil embargoes, energy crises, and the impassioned efforts of Jewish-Americans, Arab-Americans, Greek-Americans, Armenian-Americans and others to make ethnocentric views prevail in a willing, hostile or more often than not, simply indifferent public opinion and Congress."[2]

John Cooley, 1981

"The ability of pro-Israel groups to marshall and maintain the support of the mass media, mass public opinion, and broad cross-sections of associational life in this country such as organized labor and non-Jewish interest groups have enabled them to amplify and

---

1. Mathias, Senator Charles McC., (R.MD), *Foreign Affairs*, Summer, 1981.
2. Cooley, John K., "The News from the Mideast: A Working Approach," *The Middle East Journal*, Autumn, 1981, pp. 465-6.

disseminate their policy preferences far beyond the limits of their own organizational structures. "[3]

Robert H. Trice, 1977

"There is a strong Jewish lobby. I do not understand why the Jewish community should resent it being labeled as such. They are a very effective lobby. "[4]

Rep. Paul M. (Pete) McCloskey (R-California), 1981

"Fear undoubtedly is the greatest single factor accounting for Jews' high level of political activity. "[5]

Steven D. Isaacs, 1974

Since the creation of Israel, the popular American perception of the resulting conflict has been that of a Jewish David repeatedly vanquishing an Arab Goliath. In describing the relative size of the informational and educational efforts supporting the Middle Eastern antagonists in America, it is tempting to reverse the image. In the battle of pro-Israel and pro-Arab groups in the United States, Goliath wears the Star of David and, until recently, no one had ever come near him with a stone.

In both the Middle East and the United States, however, Israeli victories are no longer absolutely predictable. The October War of 1973 was, technically, a draw. But Israel's total dependence upon a massive U.S. resupply effort after only a few days of fighting shattered the myth that Israeli armed forces by themselves were of any significance in geopolitical terms. Similarly, in the United States the pro-Israel Goliath among U.S. lobbies finally suffered its first defeat in the spring of 1978 when it opposed the Carter Administration plan to tie the sale of F-15 fighters to Saudi Arabia and F-5Es to Egypt to sales of F-15s and F-16s to Israel. Senate approval for the package came despite strenuous, though tardy, Israeli objections. Then, in case anyone thought the Israeli defeat was a one-time exception, the Israel lobby was defeated again in the 1981 Senate vote on AWACS for Saudi Arabia. This time the lobby had started its campaign long before the Administration had begun its own spade work.

Again, in the 1984 election year, the lobby was unable to put through its campaign for a Congressional resolution recognizing Jerusalem as Israel's capital after Congressmen realized that the resolution would not only flaunt international law barring the acquisition of territory by force, but also would needlessly jeopardize American exports and perhaps even American lives in countries occupied by more than 800 million Muslims.

Just as the 1973 military standoff in the Middle East completely altered the attitudes of many of the Arabs and Israelis there, there are indications that the defeats of the Israel lobby in its own favorite arenas, the U.S. Senate and House of Representatives,

---

3. Trice, Robert H., "Congress and the Arab-Israeli Conflict: Support for Israel in the U.S. Senate, 1970-1973," *Political Science Quarterly*, Fall, 1977, p. 463.
4. McCloskey, Rep. Paul M. (R-CA) July 7, 1981.
5. Isaacs, Steven D., *Jews and American Politics*, Doubleday, N.Y., 1974.

have altered its tactics. They are now seen to be increasingly extreme, both in terms of lavishly rewarding Congressmen who do the lobby's bidding, and savaging those who do not.

There is no countervailing "Arab Lobby" in terms of a U.S. group that supports Arab causes per se. There are, however, small Arab-American ethnic organizations, some business groups comprised of U.S. exporters to Middle East markets, public relations firms hired to lobby on behalf of specific Arab countries, and one or two small "think tanks" specializing in Middle East affairs.

Such groups, whether pro-Israeli or pro-Arab, have one thing in common that strikes a visitor to their offices immediately: tight security. Getting past the closed-circuit television cameras and electronically controlled doors to enter the Washington offices of AIPAC (rhymes with hay-pack), the American Israel Public Affairs Committee, is only slightly less awesome than being admitted to an Israeli or Arab embassy in Washington. Security at the pro-Arab groups was not as tight until mid-1985. Then a policeman was severely injured while seeking to deactivate a bomb placed outside the Boston office of the American Arab Anti-Discrimination Committee (ADC).

In October, 1985, a bomb placed inside the ADC office in Santa Ana, California, killed Southern California Regional Director Alex Odeh. The following month an apparent fire bomb gutted the lower three floors of a building housing ADC national headquarters on Connecticut Avenue in Washington, D.C. An ADC employe working in the fourth and fifth floor area occupied by ADC was unhurt. Whether this marked the arrival in the U.S. of the Israeli and Arab extremist assassination squads that have stalked each other through the Middle East and spilled over into European cities and towns is not yet clear. It may just be American home-grown violence. There are in the U.S. some disturbed and extremely dangerous people on both sides.

Young storm troopers of the Jewish Defense League, founded in the U.S. by the Rabbi Meir Kahane before he emigrated to Israel and was elected to the Knesset, have been successfully bombing homes and automobiles in the U.S. with impunity for more than a decade. They have broken up campus meetings with bicycle chains, and telephoned death threats to Arab as well as Russian diplomats in the United States. Their victims have included persons accused of World War II crimes against Jews in Europe, members of Jewish peace groups, and U.S. university faculty and students accused of being hostile to Israel.

In New York, terrorists claiming to represent the Jewish Defense League actually have fired into houses and apartments occupied by families of Soviet diplomats assigned to the United Nations, missing two sleeping children by inches in one case. One JDL member arrested by Israeli authorities in Israel was planning a free-lance assassination mission against an Arab speaker then touring U.S. universities. As a result, service in the U.S., particularly New York, is a nightmare for many Arab diplomats and during times of tension some have chosen to send their families home.

On the Arab side, some years ago international terrorists of Dr. George Habash's Marxist-line Popular Front for the Liberation of Palestine carried out successful recruiting activities among Arab students at American universities, but for missions abroad.

The only allegations of violent activities in the United States stemming from the

Arab side centered on charges that Libyan "Cultural Attaches" have incited or at least discussed madcap acts of violence to keep their own students studying in the U.S. in line. The one documented case was the serious wounding in Colorado of a Libyan student leader opposed to the regime of Colonel Muammar Qaddafi. Although any such actions carried out so far in the U.S. were intended to terrorize or discipline students or opposition figures from their own countries, developing such a capability in the U.S. means there could eventually be a threat to Israeli diplomats or their U.S. supporters.

The current terrorist actions being perpetrated against Arab-American activists, whether by U.S. Jewish extremists or by one of the several Israeli intelligence organizations specializing in "dirty tricks," are almost certainly intended to provoke reprisals against American Jews that can then be attributed to Arab countries or Arab extremists.

Such lunatic fringe actions are so far outside the acceptable bounds of American political activity that they can only have extremely negative repercussions on U.S. public opinion. They are reminiscent of the activities of Dr. Habash and his PFLP "Director of Operations," the late Wadi'a Hadad, who mindlessly killed passengers and innocent bystanders in aircraft and air terminals in Europe, or the savage assassinations by Abu Nidal (Sabri Al-Bana) of Israelis and PLO moderates in Europe. In their heyday, such actions created an extremely negative world opinion toward the Palestinian cause as well as its tactics, which persists strongly in the United States to this day.

Madmen and fanatics aside, after the visitor has penetrated the closed circuit television monitors and combination door locks designed to protect the legitimate pro-Israel and pro-Arab organizations, there is much similarity in the perceptions of both sides of who is well organized and well funded and who isn't, how they can most effectively go about their work, what their organizational strengths and weaknesses are, and how the battle for American public opinion is going.

Ronald Koven, then a foreign editor of the *Washington Post*, summarized it nicely in an interview in 1975:

"I think there is a cultural factor involved. The Israelis are of European origin and they have an advanced public relations sense. They know how to speak our language. They understand how we reason, and they are able to use that to their advantage. The Arabs as a group have not even really played the public relations game.

"Moreover, there is a cultural barrier. People of European origin and Arabs think differently. The Israelis, for example, have been able to use to very good effect statements by Arabs which are intemperate. It has taken a long time for the American and European press to realize that in Arab culture rhetoric is often just rhetoric, something which exists by itself and does not necessarily imply actions.

"Now I think things are changing, both because the American press is finally beginning to pay better attention to the Arab world and because the Arab world is beginning to understand public relations. Of course, if you are looking at the pro-Arab and pro-Israel forces within the U.S., you have to take into account the fact that while there are two million people of Arab origin in the U.S., for the most part they tend to be low on the economic scale—the workers of Detroit and not the opinion leaders.

"The Jewish population in the United States, on the other hand, is three times as large and probably twice as rich for all sorts of historical reasons. Having worked with the political system, they know how it functions and are in positions of influence out of proportion to their number, especially on the Democratic side."[6]

Zionist Archives

On a triumphal visit to the United States in 1951, Israel's first Prime Minister, David Ben Gurion, is welcomed (above) to an Israeli bond rally and (below) presents a menorah to President Harry Truman (left) on the latter's 67th birthday as Abba Eban (center) Israeli Ambassador to the U.S. and the U.N. looks on.

Zionist Archives

6. Ghareeb, Edmund. Exerpted from interview with Ronald Koven, Middle East editor for the *Washington Post*, in "The American Media and the Palestine Problem," *Journal of Palestine Studies*, Autumn 1975/Winter 1976, pp. 132-3.

Zionist Archives

Touching all bases. Above, left to right, Israeli Prime Minister David Ben Gurion (in chair) talks with two visiting U.S. Democratic Party leaders (on couch), Franklin D. Roosevelt Jr. and Senator John F. Kennedy, soon to be President of the United States. Below, Ben Gurion with U.S. President Dwight D. Eisenhower (center) and Secretary of the Treasury C. Douglas Dillon.

CHAPTER XXV

The Israel Lobby – Where Goliath Works for Little David

"You can conjure a situation where there is another oil embargo and people in this country are not only inconvenienced and uncomfortable, but suffer. They get tough-minded enough to set down the Jewish influence in this country and break that lobby. . . . It's so strong you wouldn't believe now. We have the Israelis coming to us for equipment. We say we can't possibly get the Congress to support that. They say, 'Don't worry about the Congress.' Now this is somebody from another country, but they can do it."[1]

General George S. Brown, Chairman, Joint Chiefs of Staff,
October 10, 1974

"I've never seen a President—I don't care who he is—stand up to them . . . They always get what they want. The Israelis know what is going on all the time. I got to the point where I wasn't writing anything down. If the American people understood what a grip these people have got on our government, they would rise up in arms."[2]

Admiral Thomas Moorer, Former Chairman, Joint Chiefs of Staff,
1984

"Whatever resentment many congressmen may inwardly entertain about the pressures of the lobby, the American system itself predestines them to yield. Israel possesses a

1. *Time* ; November 25, 1974, report on extemporaneous comments by General George S. Brown, Chairman, Joint Chiefs of Staff, at Duke University question and answer session October 10, 1974.
2. Moorer, Admiral Thomas, Chief of Naval Operations, 1967-70; Chairman, Joint Chiefs of Staff, 1971-74, quoted in *They Dare to Speak Out*, Findley, Paul, Lawrence Hill, Westport, Conn., 1984, p. 161.

powerful American constituency, the Arabs do not, and despite their wealth, the oil companies as well are unequal to the impact of ethnic politics. "[3]

Edward Sheehan, 1976

"We have to respect the views of our Jewish citizens, but not be controlled by them. "[4]

Rep. Paul N. McCloskey (R-CA), 1981

"When an issue of importance to Israel comes before Congress, AIPAC promptly and unfailingly provides all members with data and documentation, supplemented, as circumstances dictate, with telephone calls and personal visits. Beyond that, signs of hesitation or opposition on the part of a Senator or a Representative can usually be relied on to call forth large numbers of letters and telegrams, or visits and phone calls from influential constituents. "[5]

Senator Charles McC. Mathias, Jr. (R-MD), 1981

"Support for Israel is indeed the highest single priority on the Jewish agenda and nobody should feel the slightest embarrassment or awkwardness or guilt in proclaiming this priority. "[6]

Hyman Bookbinder, 1985

"We are single-minded about a single issue. "[7]

Thomas Dine, 1985

General Brown's words surfaced in press reports of a supposedly off-the-record question and answer session at Duke University which earned him a reprimand from President Ford. His comments were also the subject of indignant editorials across the nation which concentrated on an inaccurate reference to Jewish ownership of banks, and a debatable reference to Jewish ownership of newspapers which, though inaccurate in terms of sheer numbers of Jewish versus non-Jewish publishers, was close to the mark in terms of real national influence. The editorial writers generally ignored General Brown's references to Congress and "that lobby," and thus saved themselves possible embarrassment on both counts only seven months later when 76 U.S. Senators, at the urging of "that lobby," signed a letter to President Ford aimed at torpedoing his Administration's major "reassessment" of its policy toward Israel. How did an ethnic lob-

3. Sheehan, Edward, "Step by Step in the Middle East," *Foreign Policy*, Spring, 1976, p. 58.
4. McCloskey, Representative Paul M., (R. CA) July 7, 1981.
5. Mathias, Senator Charles McC., (R.MD) *Foreign Affairs*, Summer, 1981.
6. Bookbinder, Hyman, Washington Director, American Jewish Committee, at 54th General Assembly, Council of Jewish Federations, reported in *Jewish Telegraph Agency* daily bulletin, November 21, 1985.
7. Dine, Thomas, AIPAC Executive Director, at 54th General Assembly, Council of Jewish Federations, reported in *Washington Report on Middle East Affairs*, December 2, 1985, p. 7.

by develop such power that it can repeatedly cajole a majority of Congressmen to defy the President on major foreign policy issues?

Jewish fund-raising organizations in the U.S. go back at least to the 19th century and more than 235 autonomous central Jewish community organizations cover 800 communities in North America. Their United Jewish Appeal annual drives are designed to fund charitable activities in Israel, the U.S., and elsewhere in the world, in about that order, since far more than half of the total funds raised are passed to the United Israel Appeal for charitable, educational, and development work in Israel. The remarkable success in fund-raising also means that Israel's extraordinarily effective network of advocacy organizations in the U.S. is well financed. Further, because the flow of money is from American citizens, and the board of directors is made up of American citizens, Israel's principal lobbying organization in the U.S., which openly backs the policies of the Israeli government across-the-board and takes its cues directly from Israel's Ambassador, does not register as a "foreign agent."

Thus, although Israeli Embassy personnel are extremely good at their jobs and are very well attuned both to the U.S. media and to individual members of Congress, their efforts largely duplicate activities carried out on their behalf by the various American organizations. A spokesman for the New York-based Conference of Presidents of Major American Jewish Organizations, an umbrella group representing 34 separate Jewish organizations in the United States, made no apologies in stating to the author that "it is our policy to support any democratically-elected government of Israel, and we feel that what is good for Israel is good for the United States."

Among the many constituent organizations with their own separate Washington and New York offices are the B'nai B'rith, with some half million members worldwide, and the 40,000-member American Jewish Committee, which publishes *Commentary* magazine. Both organizations are also extremely active in mobilizing support for Israel, although the emphasis varies. The American Jewish Committee is frankly concerned about the effect of increasingly intransigent Israeli positions in the Middle East on the perceptions by American Gentiles of American Jews. The Anti Defamation League of the B'nai B'rith, on the other hand, is quick to label any doubts expressed by non-Jews about Israel or its actions as "anti-Semitism."

Of all the Jewish organizations separately engaged in one or more activities in support of Israel, the only one actually registered to lobby in Congress on Israel's behalf is the American Israel Public Affairs Committee. Founded in 1954 as an outgrowth of the American Zionist Council, AIPAC was expanded to include representatives of the other Jewish organizations on its board, and to utilize their grassroots resources for its lobbying activities. Administered by a highly professional and dedicated staff, it provides an extensive library and research services heavily utilized by the Washington media and Congressional staffers.

AIPAC purchases and distributes to large numbers of opinion makers copies of any book that is favorable to Israel. It turns out, rapidly and in large quantities, reports on current Israel-related questions for distribution to members of Congress, its own membership, and others on its 50,000-name mailing list.

Most important, perhaps, is its computerized listing of supporters of Israel in every state and congressional district. As a result, a member of Congress who is undecided or hostile on a matter of great concern to Israel can routinely expect to receive letters and telegrams not merely from a scattering of leading citizens in his own constituency, but perhaps also from past and potential campaign contributors. Legend has it that one New York Representative who told pro-Israel lobbyists in 1977 that he would have to hear from taxpayers at home before he voted to bring the U.S. aid appropriation to Israel up to the $1.7 billion level, received 3,000 telegrams and letters supporting the bill from his constituents in only two days.

AIPAC has "power of attorney" from many of the supporters in its computerized files. When a pending matter is urgent, a Congressman may see telegrams from his constituents, billed to their home telephone numbers, even before some of the constituents themselves know the telegrams or mailgrams have been sent over their names.

AIPAC was for years synonymous with Isaiah "Si" Kenen, a well-connected, genial lobbyist of a back-slapping era when Americans were less knowledgeable about the Middle East. Its second Executive Director was Morris Amitay, a foreign service officer for seven years and a legislative assistant on Capitol Hill for five more. Under his active stewardship, AIPAC still was able to keep Congress in line until the 1978 Egyptian, Saudi, Israeli aircraft package vote. The geniality had gone out of its approach, however. Instead of using only the carrots of generous speaking honoraria and campaign contributions, it also resorted to the stick. Congressmen knew that AIPAC would turn off the contributions, and voters, if they did not shape up. However, in his effort to corral votes to defeat the 1978 bill on the floor, Amitay apparently overextended himself and lost credits that could not easily be recouped. After his former Capitol Hill employer, Senator Abraham Ribicoff of Connecticut, who was not standing for reelection, voted for the package, the Senator criticized the pressure tactics of the AIPAC lobbyists, saying "they do a great disservice to the U.S., to Israel, and to the Jewish community." Amitay resigned in 1980.

Thomas Dine, the new AIPAC Executive Director, also a long-time Capitol Hill legislative assistant, had the reputation of being a low-key manager. In fact, until he accepted the position, he was not particularly identified by his colleagues with Israeli issues. At first he seemed to rely as much on providing timely information to Congressmen and the media as on putting pressure on them directly.

Events in Israel have become increasingly difficult to explain, however, and its catastrophic financial problems have become unmanageable without the steadily increasing economic transfusions from the U.S. that have, at this writing, reached an annual total of nearly four billion dollars, all of it in outright gifts. To carry out its annual assault on the U.S. Treasury, AIPAC, under Dine, has adopted tactics that make the Amitay era seem almost somnolent in retrospect. AIPAC now sets out openly to "punish" Congressmen who don't toe the line by lavishing on their opponents what Dine calls "early money, middle money, late money." At the same time, concentrating on members of appropriations, military and foreign affairs committees, AIPAC has orchestrated extraordinarily generous campaign contributions for the incumbents who have produced the steadily increasing economic and military appropriations for Israel. AIPAC's successes, both in unseating "enemies" and re-electing "friends" in Congress,

Dine boasted after the 1984 elections, "have defined Jewish power in America for the remainder of this century."

Perhaps the most remarkable thing about the vast congeries of pro-Israeli organizations is not the money they have raised, nor even the political support they have rallied for Israel, but rather the manner in which they have maintained a public unity of purpose in supporting Israel within the American Jewish community, despite the factionalization and fluidity that now characterize Israeli domestic politics. The chairmanship of the Conference of Presidents rotates automatically from one constituent organization to the next. AIPAC staffers actually write many of the pro-Israel statements inserted into the Congressional record by pliable Congressmen. They may also write the speeches delivered to Jewish organizations by Congressmen who choose to supplement their incomes with the generous honoraria these organizations provide to members of Congress who deliver their votes when Israel needs them.

It was an ironic coincidence that, just prior to the election that made Menachem Begin the first right-wing Prime Minister of Israel, the chairmanship should have devolved upon Rabbi Alexander Schindler, an outspoken liberal who was an early opponent of the Vietnam War and who, prior to assuming the position, had expressed dovish views on the Palestinians and the occupied territories.

The drama that followed demonstrates the determination of mainstream American supporters of Israel, and particularly Rabbi Schindler as the then "leader of organized American Jewry," to sweep dissension within the American organizations supporting Israel, or between American Jewish leaders and Israeli leaders, behind a screen of public unity. According to reports that preceded their first meeting after Begin's election, Rabbi Schindler strongly disapproved of the Gush Emunim West Bank settlements, which were avowedly not based upon security concerns but rather "on the right of Jews to settle anywhere in the land of Eretz Israel." Yet the official Israeli government statements following that first meeting implied that the American Jewish leader had endorsed such settlements.

"I pretty well knew what I was going to say before I went," Rabbi Schindler reported subsequently. "I knew he was the only Prime Minister Israel had; that there was a danger of fragmentation within the American Jewish community; that I had at least the obligation to keep the community united in order to give this man a chance to form a government." Since then the annual report of the Conference of Presidents of Major American Jewish Organizations has added:

"Dissent ought not and should not be made public . . . when Jewish dissent is made public in the daily press or in the halls of government, the result is to give aid and comfort to the enemy and to weaken that Jewish unity which is essential for the security of Israel."

A subsequent president, Howard Squadron, regularly rallied behind Menachem Begin's actions publicly. But he made no secret of his concern that, even if a majority of American Jews remain doggedly supportive of Begin's Israel, non-Jewish support for Israel has suffered a dramatic erosion. Events in 1981, when Israel repeatedly bombed civilians in Lebanon, in 1982 when the Israeli invasion cost the lives of 20,000 Lebanese and Palestinians and culminated in the Sabra-Shatilla massacre, and in subsequent years when harsh Israeli actions have subjected American diplomats, service personnel, businessmen and even tourists to reprisals have put an increasing strain on the U.S. Jewish community's relationship to American gentiles. There have been a number of hurried visits by American Jews to Israel to plead with Israeli leaders to be more forthcoming, but their doubts seldom surface outside the Jewish media. What the long-term effect on the perceptions of their gentile countrymen of this "my country right or wrong" attitude by American Jews will be is hard to assess. Israel, after all, is not their country.

The current dilemma posed for American Jews by the simultaneous increase of Israeli financial dependence and Israeli extremism has been succinctly summed up by one Arab-American activist who admitted freely that his community will never reach the cohesion or effectiveness of American Jews. However, he added, "It's the first time in the history of the Israel lobby that their people over there are burning bridges faster than their friends over here can build them."

Zionist Archives

The assumption of power in Israel in 1977 by Prime Minister Menachem Begin blunted the most effective weapon of Israel's U.S. lobby. Heretofore the Arabs had been depicted as ''terrorists'' and Americans were left to assume that Israelis were not. When Begin became the elected Prime Minister of Israel, Americans learned that his right-wing extremist underground Irgun Zvai Leumi had in fact been using terrorist methods almost since its inception. Pictured is the King David hotel, British headquarters in Jerusalem, after it was blown up by Begin's followers with the loss of many Jewish as well as British and Arab lives. After the British withdrawal Begin's irregular soldiers used similar methods against the Arabs. News of their massacre of the inhabitants of the Palestinian village of Deir Yassin, near Jerusalem, was credited by Israelis with the ''opening of the land'' as residents of many other Arab villages fled before advancing Jewish soldiers both before and after the proclamation of Israeli independence on May 15, 1948.

CHAPTER XXVI

Jewish Dissenters — Cranks or Prophets?

"How sad it would be if Israel used its privileged position merely to ward off pressure and postpone a settlement to an indefinite date. When that settlement comes, not only will its terms have worsened for Israel, but Israel's influence within the U.S. will have decreased as that of others grows."[1]

Guido Goldman, May, 1978

"[Rabbi Moshe] Levinger is the tail that wags the Israeli dog that in turn wags the United States. He is the personification of the settlement controversy, a zealot who takes orders from the Bible, certainly not from Menachem Begin or Jimmy Carter or Anwar Sadat. . . . What the Rabbi Levingers of Israel would do is turn their country into a permanent occupying power, squandering Israel's moral mandate in the process."[2]

Richard Cohen, *Washington Post*, April, 1980

"The Holocaust and the moral content of the Jewish tragedy have suffered a grave degradation in the hands of those who have used them to justify the invasion of Lebanon in particular, and Israeli foreign policy in general."[3]

Jacobo Timerman, 1982

---

1. Goldman, Guido, *New York Review of Books*, May, 1978.
2. Cohen, Richard, Column entitled "An Unseeing Course for a Man of Vision," *Washington Post*, April, 1980.
3. Timerman, Jacobo, *The Longest War*, Alfred A. Knopf, New York, 1982.

"Some think we are naive, but there is increasing concern among Jews about Israel's settlements in the West Bank, and an increasing wish that Israel would take an initiative to test the Palestinian willingness to make peace."[4]

Mary Appelman, April, 1985

"We are Jews who oppose Zionism, who deplore Israeli oppression and aggression, who fear that Judaism may not survive Israel. We are probably a majority of Jews, but no one knows this because we have been effectively intimidated and suppressed by the Zionist minority."[5]

Roberta Strauss Feuerlicht, May, 1985

Not all American Jewish supporters of Israel accept the philosophy that dissent must stay within the Jewish community. Nor do they accept the accompanying maxim that, although American supporters are the lifeline of Israel, they have no business advising Israelis on matters of diplomacy or security, because "Israeli lives, not ours, are on the line." Pro-Israel but also pro-peace sentiment is freely expressed within a small but articulate and active segment of the Jewish community. It is centered primarily on the campuses of major U.S. universities and among young Jewish professionals, many of them veterans of the campus-based "new left" movements of the 60s and 70s. Although these trends increased noticeably after the assumption of power by the Likud government headed first by Menachem Begin and then by Yitzhak Shamir, they were already evident under the previous Israeli Labor governments, and they have not disappeared with the reappearance of a Labor coalition Prime Minister. There is, in fact, a long history of American Jewish dissent toward Israel. Its diversity of motives, however, has mitigated against this Jewish dissent having any major impact, as yet, on organized U.S.-Jewish support for Israel.

Support for beleaguered Jewish communities abroad has been characteristic of American Jews almost since they themselves became firmly established in the United States. Yet an influential segment of Jewish opinion in the United States, as in Western Europe, has traditionally viewed the Zionist movement with great reserve. In the U.S., during the first half of the 20th Century, support for political Zionism originally was most likely to be found among the newer American Jewish communities of Eastern European origin. The descendants of earlier waves of immigrants, many of German origin, were more likely to be concerned with Jewish assimilation into American life. Representatives of this earlier group had already achieved great distinction in U.S. public life by the early twentieth century. Like their counterparts in France and Britain, they saw the creation of a specific Jewish "nationality," as distinct from Jewish religious adherence, as a serious threat to the increasingly secure status of Jews in the United States and in the Western European democracies.

4. Appelman, Mary, Chairman, America-Israel Council for Israeli-Palestinian Peace, quoted in *Washington Report on Middle East Affairs*, April 29, 1985, p. 7.
5. Feuerlicht, Roberta Strauss, author of *The Fate of the Jews*, writing in *The Washington Report on Middle East Affairs*, May 27, 1985, p. 3.

One such distinguished American Jew was Henry Morgenthau, Sr., who was U.S. Ambassador to the Ottoman Empire during World War I. He provided vital assistance to the Jewish community in Palestine, just as he did to other religious and ethnic minority groups impoverished and threatened by the drawn-out fighting between Arab-assisted British forces and the Ottoman Turkish armies. By personally intervening to save the tiny Jewish community from starvation and possible extinction in Palestine, he preserved it for the ultimate creation of a Zionist state, which he came to believe was a "stupendous fallacy" and "blackest error." After his return to the U.S., Ambassador Morgenthau remained a life-long opponent of a separate political homeland for the Jews in Palestine. Similarly, members of the Jewish Sulzberger family, owners of the *New York Times*, were reluctant to put their newspaper's full support behind a movement they had long opposed, until some time after Israel had become a *fait accompli*.

However, American Jewish support for a Zionist state in Palestine grew steadily during World War II. Most of the once significant anti-Zionist sentiment in the American Jewish community was silenced by the rise of Adolf Hitler in Germany, and much of the rest faded away in the face of dramatic, successful moves to transport the survivors of Nazi death camps, legally or illegally, to Palestine, and the even more dramatic defense in 1948 by Jews in Palestine of their newly-created state against what was perceived in the U.S. as an invasion by the combined armies of Egypt, Jordan, Iraq, and Syria, as well as the indigenous Palestinians who were being displaced.

Today, although she writes movingly and sympathetically of Ambassador Morgenthau, her grandfather, historian Barbara Tuchmann is a convinced Zionist. And although the *New York Times*, through its columns and editorials, may sometimes mildly criticize specific Israeli government policies or leaders, one would look in vain for any doubt as to the wisdom or validity of the existence of Israel as a nation.

Nevertheless, vestiges of that original Jewish dissent from the establishment of Israel are still active and articulate. The American Council for Judaism for many years sent groups of prominent American Jews to the White House to protest the concept of "the Jewish people" as a legal entity and, as the welcome there wore thinner, to the Department of State to protest new manifestations of U.S. support for Israel. Finally, in the wake of the Six-Day War of 1967, the Council dropped its active opposition to Israel and its long-time executive director, Rabbi Elmer Berger, set up a new organization in New York, American Jewish Alternatives to Zionism, Inc. He still issues regular newsletters and speaks to interested groups. His audiences frequently are composed of non-Jews and Arab Americans, and he has visited most of the Arab countries as well as attending numerous United Nations activities concerned with the Arab-Israeli problem.

Rabbi Berger's colleague in the early days of the anti-Zionist movement, Dr. Alfred M. Lilienthal, also maintained an office in New York for many years, and subsequently moved it to Washington. Until 1985 he published a newsletter and traveled extensively, speaking around the United States and at U.N. meetings abroad, and visiting Middle Eastern countries. He has conducted a great deal of historical research into all aspects of the Zionist movement and also into modern Arab history and the tangled history of U.S. support for Israel. The result has been, over 30 years, a stream of articles in his own publications and in national magazines. He also has written four books: *What Price Israel?*, *There Goes the Middle East*, *The Other Side of the Coin*, and, in 1979, *The Zionist Connection: What Price Peace?* The latter book, updated and reissued regularly and nearly 900 pages long, is probably the most comprehensive report on Zionist activities ever published in the U.S.

These veteran Jewish anti-Zionists have American followers in many walks of life, but limited following within the organized Jewish community. Their presence in so many Middle Eastern-oriented activities has effectively prevented the anti-Zionist movement from taking an anti-Jewish tilt, however, and their complete acceptance by Arab-American and other activist groups has certainly encouraged other anti-Zionist Jews to follow the same course. As for their lasting influence, the final verdict is not in. It is certain, however, that since both Rabbi Berger and Dr. Lilienthal have traveled and lectured so frequently in the Middle East, they have made a major contribution to Jews everywhere by demonstrating conclusively to the Arabs that there are prominent American Jews who do not support Israel. Beneficiaries of their example have been members of Jewish communities in such Arab countries as Egypt, Syria and Morocco and, particularly, the many American Jews who regularly travel to or work in Arab countries.

Although there is an ideological gulf between Jewish anti-Zionists and the growing number of American Jewish intellectuals who criticize Israeli policies rather than the state itself, many of those under forty in both camps have one thing in common. They have been identified with, or at least exposed to, the campus activism of the 1960s and 1970s. After early immersion in idealistic social programs, the anti-Vietnam war movement, environmental causes, and, especially, opposition to the pervasive and insidious influence of special interest groups on American political life, it is difficult for many politically-aware young Jewish professionals to accept everything they see (and many have visited Israel in person as summer Kibbutzniks, students, tourists, or all three) happening today in Israel. They see the tiny country now almost submerged by the economic burdens of creating West Bank "settlements," and of maintaining a huge number of Israelis in uniform to conduct the long-term military occupation of the West Bank and Gaza. This occupation they find particularly paradoxical not only because of the brutalities that occur so regularly when any group oppresses another, but also because it keeps within Israel's extended frontiers a captive Arab population that, together with the Arabs living inside Israel's pre-1967 boundaries, someday may outnumber the Jewish inhabitants of Israel.

Because of the precept even among Zionist dissenters that American Jews do not advise Israelis on how best to defend themselves, such currents of dissent within the American Jewish community seem to coalesce around movements, or visitors, from Israel itself. The Breira (Hebrew for "Alternative") movement, which emerged after the October 1973 war, brought Israeli doves, many with impeccable military records, to the U.S. to meet with Jewish groups on and off campus. Its speakers called for Israel to make peace with the Palestinians before a fifth war, and perhaps a shift in the relative strength of the combatants, made such a peace impossible. Breira did not last even until the end of the 70s, however, and the circumstances of its demise created much bitterness. Members of the Jewish mainstream might say that the Breira leaders were drawn from the campus counterculture and that their goals were those of the New Left; that their fatal mistake was to put too much emphasis upon the supposed moderation of the PLO; and that predictably the reaffirmation of hardline statements by the diverse and contending PLO leaders cut the ground out from under Breira. These critics might or might not admit that Breira's final, unpardonable sin was to take the argument outside the Jewish community through invitations to non-Jews to hear their speakers and through paid advertisements in non-Jewish publications.

Breira sympathizers might counter with charges of McCarthyism by such hawkish American writers as Jean Rael Isaac of "Americans for a Safe Israel" and by the American Jewish Committee's popular monthly *Commentary*, which commissioned its own article on Breira to reiterate the Isaac charges and to add some of its own. They speak not only of Jewish Defense League violence against Breira meetings, but also of reprimands and threats of dismissal received by young rabbis who provided a forum for Breira speakers, thus eventually closing off Breira from such natural constituencies as university campus Hillel groups.

History aside, since the problem remains, the Shalom Achshav (Peace Now) movement in Israel, which has mounted massive protests in Israel against the occupation of Lebanon, now provides a new nucleus for American Jews concerned about the consequences of uncritical support for present Israeli policies. In the United States the New Jewish Agenda is a group that routinely and publicly challenges current Israeli policies as part of an activist stand on many U.S. social issues.

There are in the U.S. several groups, frequently drawn from New Jewish Agenda members, who concentrate on Middle East issues. These groups coalesced in opposition to the policies of Menachem Begin and Ariel Sharon, but at this writing virtually all are sponsoring speaking tours in the U.S. for Israeli peace activists, or joint appearances before Jewish and Gentile groups of Palestinian and Israeli speakers. The theme of most of these speakers is that Israel must make peace with the Palestinians, and that Yassir Arafat's PLO is the only group that presently can negotiate a peace with Israel that Palestinians everywhere will accept. One such group is the America-Israel Council for Israeli-Palestinian Peace, the U.S. sister organization of an Israeli organization bearing the same name. Another such U.S. group is the Washington Area Jews for an Israeli-Palestinian Peace, which is active in the U.S. capital and which has co-sponsored events with Palestinian-American groups.

Veterans of the campus activist movements of the 60s and early 70s are now older, and many have "dropped out" of dissenting activities under the pressure of jobs, family opposition, and increasing uncertainty as to what is the best course for Israel as the Arab world grows perceptibly stronger. Though some still predict a significant new wave of dissent from inside rather than outside American Zionist ranks, only time will determine whether such movements will also follow the path of diminishing public impact already taken by their anti-Zionist Jewish predecessors.

There is one major difference between the two movements, however. The anti-Zionist assimilationists still represented by Dr. Lilienthal and Rabbi Berger were concerned about the effect of support for Israel on the American Jewish community. If every Jew, they asked, were automatically accepted as a citizen of Israel, would any Jew still be accepted by other Americans as a citizen whose primary loyalty was to the United States?

Some of the current American Zionist dissenters describe an entirely different concern. It is not so much what Zionism might do to their own seemingly secure status in the U.S. that worries them, but what militarism and occupation duty is doing to Israel, the Israelis, and the Zionist ideal.

The dualism of deep misgivings about the new Israeli reality, combined with profound devotion to the Zionist ideal, was eloquently expressed by Professor Leonard Fein, editor of the Boston Jewish monthly, *Moment*, in an article describing his experiences as an outspoken American visitor to Israel in 1979.[6] Fein describes the plight of Israeli doves concerned about their government's support of West Bank settlements; the problems of the chairman of the Conference of Presidents of Major American Jewish Organizations, who had come to tell the Prime Minister American Jews find the settlements policy "difficult to explain," and Prime Minister Begin's angry comment about another prominent American Jewish fundraiser for Israel: "Does he think that his subsidies and donations entitle him to influence our policies and actions?"

Fein is one of the American Jewish intellectuals who publicly protested Begin's policies in the spring of 1978, and then with equal vehemence protested "unacceptable" U.S. Government criticism of Begin's policies in December of the same year. In his eloquent way, Fein typifies the dilemma of U.S. Zionist intellectuals today: alternately critical of Israeli policies, and then of non-Jewish Americans who voice essentially the same criticisms.

UPI

General Ariel Sharon shares lunch with an Israeli reservist during the first week of the June, 1982, Israeli invasion of Lebanon. "Sharon's War," as Israelis called it, brought to the surface the deep ambivalence within Israel concerning the direction in which the country is headed. Is it always to be militaristic, expansionist and at war with its neighbors, or will it eventually seek a compromise peace with all of the Arabs and integrate itself into the Middle East? The answer may depend upon the United States, and American Jewish supporters of Israel, whose blind devotion to any elected Israeli government, moderate or extremist, is to a large extent responsible for the plight in which present-day Israelis find themselves.

6. Fein, Leonard, "Israel, Summer 1979: A Visitor's Journal," *Moment*, January, 1980, pp. 27-8.

CHAPTER XXVII

The Arab Lobby — Wherever It Is

"Numerous stories have appeared recently about some sort of powerful 'Arab Lobby,' under whose auspices a massive grand propaganda plan has supposedly been designed to brainwash the American public. A recent rundown also appeared in newspapers identifying several lawyers who were lobbying for the Arabs, listing their salaries. I asked the reporter why no corresponding story appeared about the Israeli lobby and his response was that he had written the piece based upon who was registered as a foreign agent. He could not respond to my statement that nearly every Jewish organization in the U.S. lobbied directly for Israel without registering as foreign agents."[1]

Senator James Abourezk, 1976

"You may put it down as a matter of fact that any criticism of Israel will be met with a cry of anti-Semitism."[2]

James Reston, 1975

"When we lost the country in 1948, I was studying at the University of Chicago, and I could not go home. The tragedy has shaped my life ever since."[3]

Dr. Hisham Shirabi, 1980

---

1. Abourezk, Senator James (D-SD) in talk at the "Arab and American Cultures Conference" of the Middle East Institute, Washington, D.C., September, 1976.
2. Reston, James, quoted by Edmund Ghareeb in "The American Media and the Palestine Problem," *Journal of Palestinian Studies*, Autumn 1975/Winter 1976, p. 130.
3. Shirabi, Dr. Hisham, quoted by Milton Viorst in "Building an Arab-American Lobby," *Washington Post Magazine*, September 14, 1980.

"My friends and I had all been admirers of Nasser, and we couldn't understand what had happened. The (1967) war gave us a sense of Israel's dynamism and of its scientific, military, technical and intellectual prowess. At the same time, we saw the inability of the Arabs to work together. We did a lot of soul-searching in the months after the war."[4]

Dr. Edward Said, 1980

"The war of 1967 was a shock to all Arabs. Unlike the Jews, we never saw it as a defensive war by Israel but as aggression by a force unwilling to settle outstanding claims. It was an insult to us to hear Arthur Goldberg, the U.S. delegate, vilify Arabs on the floor of the United Nations. He seemed to be talking about me."[5]

James Zogby, 1980

"I want to emulate the Jews. If we hadn't seen a need to compete with the Jews, the Arab-Americans would still have no political organizations."[6]

Richard Shadyac, 1980

"We're here as Americans talking about America's Middle East policy . . . trying to shape ideas and ensure that there is a discussion of the kind of policies that we think make sense for the region."[7]

David Sadd, 1985

"Our clients don't think about the United States every day. We remind them to say something nice . . . We keep them focused on how their interests here are affected by what they say and do at home."[8]

Les Janka, 1985

"Israel bashing is a bad business for the Arabs . . . and (Arab-American organizations) make a mistake when they attack Israel."[9]

Denis M. Neil, 1985

---

4. Said, Dr. Edward, quoted by Milton Viorst in "Building an Arab-American Lobby," *Washington Post Magazine*, September 14, 1980.
5. Zogby, James, quoted by Milton Viorst in "Building an Arab-American Lobby," *Washington Post Magazine*, September 14, 1980.
6. Shadyac, Richard, quoted by Milton Viorst in "Building an Arab-American Lobby," *Washington Post Magazine*, September 14, 1980.
7. Sadd, David, quoted by Christopher Madison in "Arab-American Lobby Fights Rearguard Battle to Influence U.S. Mideast Policy," in *National Journal*, August 31, 1985, p. 1935.
8. Janka, Les, quoted by Christopher Madison in "Arab-American Lobby Fights Rearguard Battle to Influence U.S. Mideast Policy," in *National Journal*, August 31, 1985, p. 1938.
9. Neil, Denis M., quoted by Christopher Madison in "Arab-American Lobby Fights Rearguard Battle to Influence U.S. Mideast Policy," in *National Journal*, August 31, 1985, p. 1935.

"They would like us to forget about Israel but we won't. They're clobbering our people over there."[10]

Senator James Abourezk, 1985

Very few Americans who follow Arab activities in the United States would agree that there is an "Arab lobby" at all. There are Arab-American groups, some political and some not, but few have significant membership. There are American and Arab-born "Middle East experts" in "think tanks" in various parts of the United States willing and able to explain quite accurately to Americans Middle Eastern history, events and perceptions. And there are attorneys and public relations firms, mostly in Washington, hired by individual Arab countries to represent their interests not only in the courts, but also in Congress and with the press.

If this, in toto, comprises a lobby, the quotations above reveal that its leaders are diverse in their backgrounds, motives, methods and even their messages. When they work together at all, it is uneasily. Most feel almost impotent in the face of what they consider a generally successful media conspiracy to keep their messages from reaching the American man in the street. All feel outraged at what they see as out-and-out bribery of Congress by Israel's lobby and its hundreds of allied Jewish groups to produce huge sums of money for Israel, some of which finds its way back to further fuel the Israel lobby.

Some of the academic "Middle East experts" suffer unremitting professional intimidation from militant Jewish students and faculty colleagues who bombard University board members and department heads or local school board members with complaints that they are "pro-Arab" or "anti-Israel" on the basis of "evidence" that would make even the 1950's red-hunting Senator Joseph McCarthy blush. Virtually all of the Arab-Americans feel physically intimidated by the militant Jewish Defense League and even more violent splinter organizations. And the publicists and think tanks are harassed not only by an almost uniformly hostile press, but also by manipulation of the IRS, the courts and other government agencies from within by hidden partisans of Israel.

If pressed, however, even the gloomiest member of this extraordinary, ad-hoc, non-coalition will admit that American attitudes are changing. And if the change is monumentally slow, at least it is steadily toward a more open-minded, and less Israel-centered attitude toward the Middle East. If pressed further, scholars and lawyers and Arab Americans alike will agree that the change is in spite of actions by Arab radicals like Muammar Qaddafi and the various Marxist and anti-Arafat Palestinian groups, has little to do with the work of any component of the so-called "Arab lobby" in the U.S., and is only partially attributable to the actions of the Arab moderates who, for domestic reasons, hide or obscure the fact that increasingly their interests and those of the U.S. coincide.

The change, in fact, is because Israel has gone into an increasingly obvious and accelerating economic, military and moral tailspin that forces its American lobby to

---

10. Abourezk, Senator James, quoted by Christopher Madison in "Arab-American Lobby Fights Rearguard Battle to Influence U.S. Mideast Policy," in *National Journal*, August 31, 1985, p. 1936.

levy increasingly exasperating demands upon the U.S. Treasury, the Pentagon, the press, academia and, of course, Congress. The cost in credibility to Israel's lobby, and to the U.S. Jewish community which supports it, increases each year. The ultimate beneficiary can only be the message borne by the diverse elements of the "Arab lobby," which is that long-term U.S. and Arab interests have always coincided, and that short-term differences arise only because of U.S. favoritism for Israel. If it seems surprising that it is taking so long to get this simple message across, a closer look at the unlikely messengers may help explain why.

Between 100,000 and 200,000 Lebanese and Syrians have immigrated to the United States over the past century, more than half of them between 1890 and 1920. The early immigrants had little formal education and were primarily interested in making enough money to alleviate the poverty of their families in the Middle East. However, they brought with them large measures of optimism, energy, thrift, and business acumen. They were strongly individualistic and tended to go into business for themselves, starting as itinerant peddlers. As a result of not concentrating in ethnic ghettos, their children assimilated more rapidly than the children of many earlier and larger immigrant groups. They also acquired considerably more formal education and professional and technical skills than had their parents. Thus, when Arab-Americans attained political or community leadership, it generally was on the basis of local achievement and local issues, not ethnic identity or support. Whatever ethnic identity remained coalesced largely around their churches or family social activities rather than politics or occupations.

In 1932 a number of regional groups formed the "National Association of Syrian and Lebanese-American Organizations." Some regional federations grew large enough to permit the formation of a National Association of Federations, which in the early 1950s sponsored a convention in Lebanon and Syria, but subsequently declined and disappeared. Even though some vestiges of regional federation leadership remained, particularly in the Midwest, conditions were changing. New groups of immigrants were coming to the U.S. from many parts of the Middle East. Their social composition ranged from unskilled workers from the Yemen to members of the entrepreneurial classes of Egypt, Iraq, and Syria, fleeing the socialist experiments then under way in their countries. Muslims made up a much higher percentage of this new wave of immigrants. Students, mostly Muslim, came from virtually every Arab country to study in American universities. Some married Americans and remained in the U.S. Others eventually returned to the U.S. after finding little market for their specialized technical skills in certain Arab countries with still under-developed economies or unstable governments.

As the new Arab-Americans, more diverse in terms of national origin and religion, joined the children of the older Lebanese-Syrian immigrants, some differences developed between some of the less Americanized newcomers and the totally assimilated children and grandchildren of the first-comers. This dichotomy persists in the political activities of the Arab-American community.

Raised with strong assimilationist goals and suspicious of changeable and sometimes radical Arab regimes, the American-born Arab-Americans, and some of the newer Christian Arab immigrants as well, are frankly uneasy in political organizations without strong and obvious American identity, flagged by the "American" in organizational titles. Some also welcome the non-ethnic leavening that has occurred in their groups through the addition of non Arab-American spouses, friends and associates. This is an inevitable development in all portions of the Arab-American community, because its members adhere to religions that cross ethnic lines. Whether they are Sunni or Shia Muslims or Catholic, Orthodox or Evangelical Christians, most Arab-American families, through marriage of some members outside the Arab community, begin the process of ethnic assimilation within a generation.

Among the largest Arab-American groups are those based upon regional origin. They are only marginally active on the political scene. Examples are the Ramallah and El-Bireh societies, whose members trace their ancestral roots to two adjacent Palestinian towns, one Christian and one Muslim.

The oldest and still one of the two best known Arab-American political organizations is the National Association of Arab Americans (called "N triple A"). It is the only Arab-American group registered as a lobby and, although it operates with only a quarter of the staff and a vastly smaller membership, it clearly was inspired by the success of the American Israel Public Affairs Committee (AIPAC), NAAA's pro-Israeli counterpart. Any resemblance stops there, however. NAAA suffers periodically from the three-cornered nature of its support. There has been persistent Lebanese-Palestinian tension among its members, meaning that while many of its leaders sought to keep NAAA focused upon the Palestinian grievance, some of the rank and file were more concerned about the deterioration of conditions in Lebanon. Among those with a Lebanese orientation, there was also tension reflecting the problems within that divided country itself. While NAAA has continued to work on raising Congressional consciousness concerning the basics of the Palestine problem, it has spent a great deal of its time on specific questions such as arms sales to Saudi Arabia and Jordan, loss of American jobs and exports resulting from Congressional restrictions on compliance with Arab boycott laws, and the disastrous economic and diplomatic results of gratuitous insults to Arabs and Muslims such as the bill raised perennially in Congress to move the U.S. Embassy from Tel Aviv to Jersalem. Although few Arab Americans would take exception to any of the projects listed, the differing priorities of the elected officers have taken their toll on the organization.

By far the largest politically-oriented Arab-American membership group is the American Arab Anti-Discrimination Committee (ADC), founded in 1980 by former U.S. Senator James Abourezk and patterned after the Anti-Defamation League of B'nai B'rith. Again, the resemblance stops after the names. While the ADL is extremely well-funded and has world-wide membership, ADC's funding is precarious, its regional offices are tiny and often housed in donated space, and its spartan and under-staffed Washington headquarters is crammed into two floors of a building which had seen better days even before it was fire-bombed in late 1985. ADC has some 15,000 members, however, and extremely active chapters in some cities with large Arab-American communities. Perhaps because it is personally directed by its founder, it has somehow avoided the pitfalls of the Lebanese-Palestinian, foreign-born versus American-born, Christian-Muslim dichotomies that hamper other Arab ethnic groups. In addition to its main function, which is to protect Arab Americans of any religious background against local discrimination, the ADC has strongly supported the Palestinians, sponsored relief drives for Lebanese maimed or displaced by war, and from its beginning has emphasized coalition building with other groups. It welcomes non Arab-Americans as full members, and has thus enrolled dozens, perhaps hundreds, of former U.S. government officials, educators, businessmen and missionaries who have lived in the Middle East and become concerned with improving U.S. understanding of the Arabs. Despite its rising membership, however, ADC remains under-funded and suffers from high staff turnover.

The third nation-wide, politically-oriented Arab-American group is the Arab American University Graduates organization. Also founded in 1980 by members of the NAAA who were dissatisfied with what they felt was an insufficiently forceful stand on the Palestine problem, it tends to take a considerably more partisan stand on Middle East political issues and probably a much higher percentage of its membership is foreign born.

Its membership consists of politically-oriented Arab intellectuals in the U.S. and its positions are more closely attuned to those of the PLO than are those groups with primarily American-born leadership like the ADC and NAAA, which tend to campaign for U.S. even-handedness abroad.

The newest such ethnic-based organization is the Arab American Institute, founded in 1985 by James Zogby, a former executive director of the Palestine Human Rights Campaign and a co-founder with Senator Abourezk of the ADC. AAI's goal is to encourage Arab-American participation in mainstream U.S. political activities via both the Republican and Democratic parties. Zogby, American-born and of Lebanese descent, also heads a relief organization called Save Lebanon.

An organization which is active on university campuses, now concentrates also on work with U.S. clergymen, and frequently introduces visiting West Bank Palestinians to Congressmen is the Palestine Human Rights Campaign, directed by the Reverend Donald Wagner, and headquartered in Chicago. It is typical of a category of small organizations concerned with Palestine which are not primarily based upon ethnicity.

In the same category but purely charitable in nature are American Near East Refugee Aid (ANERA) and the Musa Al Alami Foundation. In the cultural field there are the American Arab Cultural Foundation and some other groups concentrating on distribution of Palestinian handicrafts, books, paintings, and music, and whose goals are both to raise funds for relief activity and to help preserve Palestinian institutions and the Palestinian heritage.

Individual Arab countries have paid lobbyists in Washington, some on permanent retainer and others contracted to coordinate a specific project such as an arms purchase that needs Congressional approval. These may be public relations firms, usually with some political ties to a past or present occupant of the White House, or law firms. One firm, Dennis Neil Associates, is registered to represent several moderate Arab countries, including Morocco, Egypt and Jordan. A lawyer and registered foreign agent is Fred Dutton, who has for several years represented Saudi Arabia in Washington. Mr. Dutton, who formerly directed Congressional relations for the U.S. AID program, is in fact an adviser to each incoming Saudi Ambassador concerning the complexities of getting things done in Congress and in the U.S. Capital in general. Saudi Arabia also retains two public relations firms, Cooke Ruef & Associates and Gray and Company, one with Democratic and one with Republican party connections.

The academic scene is more widely dispersed among some 20 to 30 Middle East studies centers fairly evenly distributed around the United States and described in more detail in this book's chapter on universities. There are also a number of think tanks concentrating on Middle East subjects and publishing, and varying from small to very small, in major U.S. urban centers.

In Washington one of the two most venerable is the Middle East Institute which conducts an active program of lectures, book and occasional paper publishing and language (Arabic, Hebrew, Persian and Turkish) teaching and publishes a specialized quarterly, *The Middle East Journal*. Amideast, originally called the American Friends of the Middle East, is another veteran organization which, when it changed its name after 1967, switched from political activities to educational, training and student counseling projects in the Middle East and publishing in the U.S. within the same carefully defined field.

Newer Washington institutions in order of appearance are the Institute of Palestine Studies, with a mostly Arab-born staff that moved from Beirut after 1976; and three groups founded and directed by retired U.S. foreign service officers. These are the Islamic Studies Institute (formerly Islamic Centennial Fourteen) of the American University, which publishes and produces educational material and educational films and slide shows; the American Arab Affairs Council which publishes an academic quarterly, *American Arab Affairs*, and conducts regional seminars around the United States; and the American Educational Trust which publishes books (including this one), a mass-circulation and highly topical newsletter, *The Washington Report on Middle East Affairs*, operates a press and periodical clipping service, the *Middle East Clipboard*, produces educational films and videotapes, and conducts a speaker's program. The newest such Washington organization, headed by an academic and including former foreign service officers on its advisory board, is the National Council on U.S. Arab Affairs. It provides speakers, conducts seminars, and publishes studies in an occasional papers series oriented toward academia.

In New York the U.S.-Arab Chamber of Commerce publishes a magazine concerning U.S.-Arab trade for circulation both to its U.S. membership and through its regional offices in the U.S., as well as through Chambers of Commerce in the Arab countries. It has semi-autonomous regional offices in several U.S. cities. Also in New York, Americans for Middle East Understanding distributes a quarterly theme newsletter, *The Link*, to a very large list of recipients. Claremont Publications, near the campus of Columbia University, maintains extensive archives, issues a very comprehensive Middle East clipping service, and publishes reference compilations of key press clippings on topical subjects.

In Boston, besides the extensive publishing program of the Arab American University Graduates, the American Middle East Peace Research Institute commissions or supports research and publishing activities focusing on Palestine by scholars around the U.S.

In the Los Angeles area the News Circle publishing company of Glendale, California, issues two magazines, one aimed primarily at Arab-Americans in the Southern California area, and another aimed at a national audience concerned with doing business in the Middle East. In the Bay area of Northern California Najda, which began as an organization of wives of Arabs living in the U.S., now raises funds for relief activities, distributes handicrafts made in refugee camps, and has an active publishing program varying from Middle East cookbooks to a topical newsletter. Its officers are also deeply involved in evaluating books, films and other academic aids for teaching about the Middle East in U.S. schools at all levels.

There are some small politically-oriented groups seeking Middle East peace which fall squarely between groups described in this chapter and those described under Jewish dissenters. Like nearly all of the groups described in both chapters, their membership is diverse but their primary interest is in a compromise settlement in the Middle East that will bring about a lasting peace.

There is another category of political groups with strong campus ties whose focus is Middle Eastern but whose orientations range from mildly to straight party-line Marxist. They use the term "solidarity group" to distinguish themselves from the non-Marxist organizations. The largest such U.S. group is the November 29 Coalition, based in San Francisco. A publishing group in the mildly Marxist category is the Middle East Research and Information Project, with editorial offices in Washington and business and circulation offices in New York.

The November 29 Coalition has been able to bring surprising numbers to pro-Palestinian demonstrations using volunteers from other "solidarity" groups focusing on other causes such as halting U.S. intervention in Central America. The November 29 Coalition, like Marxist Palestinian commando organizations, is extremely critical of traditional Arab regimes. Its goal is social revolution in the Arab World, and its members justify using the Palestinian grievance to further that goal by declaring that there can be no justice for the Palestinians until all of the traditional Arab systems have been replaced with Marxist regimes. Although leaders of the non-Marxist groups described previously generally avoid any association with these "solidarity" groups, there is some casualness on university campuses at both the faculty and student level, and also among Palestinian students in the U.S., about supporting both.

The 1984-85 shakeout in the Arab camp, in which the Palestinians have divided into a Syrian-supported, Marxist-oriented anti-Arafat minority and a Saudi, Jordanian, Egyptian-supported pro-Arafat majority, may eventually be clearly reflected among groups supporting the Palestinians in the U.S. The Arab cause in the U.S. will be better served when its Marxist and non-Marxist supporters can be clearly distinguished, since the rhetoric of the Marxists has contributed toward the confusion and negativism in American popular perceptions of the Palestinians, their leaders, and their cause.

In the past decade in the U.S. there have been literally scores of smaller organizations established along educational, political and commercial lines, all based upon the hope of substantial support from U.S. corporations or from the Arabs themselves. While few received much support at any time, the decline in Middle East oil revenues has affected prospects for all of them adversely. Originally envisioned to serve or attract support from U.S. businessmen looking for Middle Eastern markets, they have seen their funding dwindle as Arab trade with the U.S. has dropped. Even among the organizations named above, few have more than two or three paid staff members in their offices. They are heavily dependent upon student interns, unpaid fellows or associates, and volunteers to carry out their activities.

As expectations within some of these organizations for serious U.S. business participation in anything remotely resembling political activity have died, many have cast a desperate eye toward Arab governments, thinking they might become parties to something like the close relationships between the Government of Israel and its partisans in the U.S. Such hopes have gone largely unfulfilled. Although some Arab businessmen, and a few individual members of prominent Middle Eastern families undoubtedly have dabbled from time to time in support for one organization or another, few lasting ties have developed. A survey of the field shows that while one group or another may occasionally exhibit temporary affluence, poverty is the general lot. An Arab who wishes to endow a U.S. institution with funds is more likely to pick the university whose diploma hangs on his wall. Universities like the University of Southern California or the University of Texas, from which thousands of Arab students have graduated, are far more likely to benefit from Arab oil money than are Middle East-oriented U.S. think tanks.

There seems to be a cultural block in operation here. The Middle East is hierarchical. In the past, what the tribal leader believed, his followers were expected to accept. The principle was transferred intact to Arab nations. Although Arabs who have lived and studied in the U.S. have come to understand that Congress responds to public opinion (and financing) from the hinterlands, and not vice versa, there are few in authority in any Arab country who can accept the idea that an investment in American public opinion would be worthwhile. Instead, they consider it demeaning to themselves.

Whatever changes take place in U.S. perceptions of the Arabs will, therefore, have little to do with the work of an Arab lobby, if one is ever created. Instead, they will have a great deal to do with the successes in the U.S. of Israel's American lobby, or the failure abroad of the cause it represents.

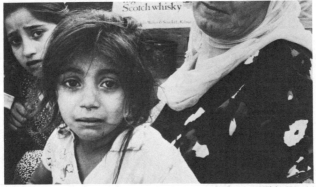

Wide World

Fear and shock are etched into the faces of these children as they emerge on August 2, 1982 during a brief cease fire in the Israeli seige of West Beirut.

Palestinian men (above), blindfolded and with bound hands and feet, await transport to Israeli prison camp near Sidon from Barouk in Lebanon's Bekaa Valley, where they were seized during the second week of the 1982 Israeli invasion of Lebanon. Palestinian women (below) congregate outside an Israeli detention center seeking information from Israeli guard about missing husbands, brothers and fathers.

Wide World

CHAPTER XXVIII

American Business and
The Arab Cause

"A curious thing is that the archives contain little or no evidence of the oil company pressure which is so often alleged by the Zionists to have taken place. It was to be expected that the companies having an interest in petroleum concessions in the Arab countries, particularly Saudi Arabia, would be opposed to the creation of a Jewish state in Palestine. They undoubtedly were, but I recall no instances where the representatives of ARAMCO or any other oil company came into the Department and urged that our government follow a particular line regarding Palestine, nor could I find any letters to that effect in the files. Those of my colleagues whom I have consulted on this point, notably Loy Henderson, Gordon Merriam, and Fraser Wilkins, likewise can recall no pressure on the part of the oil companies. It is of course possible that the oil companies made oral representations at a higher level, but if they did so we were not aware of it. In any event, if there was oil company pressure, it failed of its objective."[1]

Evan M. Wilson, 1979

We can no longer doltishly ignore the prime political reality of the Palestinian issue. So far we have persistently approached the Middle Eastern problem from the wrong side, spending enormous political capital to settle the Israeli-Egyptian quarrel, which has little to do with oil, while in the process inflaming the Israeli-Palestinian dispute, which critically affects our relations with oil-producing countries. . . . Let there be no mistake about it. So long as we delay a frontal attack on the Palestinian issue, we

---

1. Wilson, Evan M., *Decision on Palestine: How the U.S. Came to Recognize Israel*, Hoover Institution Press, Stanford, 1979, p. 152.

290 A CHANGING IMAGE

are alienating the whole Muslim world, as our shattered embassies have demonstrated."[2]

George Ball, 1980

"As the British sit back and contemplate the blessings of the Saudi arms package for their economy–and, we suspect, quietly discuss what can be done to develop new sales to Jordan–we in the United States need to reflect on what has been lost to the American economy. The U.S. Department of Commerce estimates that $1 billion in exports supports 25,000 jobs in direct and indirect employment in the U.S. manufacturing sector. Therefore, the loss of the Saudi contract and the ban on American sales to Jordan could possibly mean a loss of over 175,000 jobs to American industry . . . If American sales of civilian goods and services were booming, it could be said that the loss of military sales was not really that important. Unfortunately, the U.S. merchandise trade deficit surged to $15.5 billion in September, 1985, its highest level in history, with the manufacturing sector–in the black as recently as 1981–bearing the brunt of the deficit . . . Continually declining exports to the Middle East and North Africa account for a significant part of the U.S. trade deficit."[3]

John Haldane, 1985

Looking for the relationship between political activities of the Arab lobby and the U.S. oil companies and other large American corporations doing business in the Middle East is a little like the country bumpkin looking for the pea in the carnival shell game. Even a rube realizes, after turning the shells over often enough, that the pea probably is not there at all.

U.S. corporations have provided little financial assistance for pro-Arab political causes. This is obvious to anyone who visits the various pro-Arab organizations. The president of one such organization remarks to visitors who come panting up the stairway to his fourth floor office in a Washington building with no elevators, "It's a young man's game."

It is a stark contrast with the large, new multi-windowed buildings occupied by various components of the "Israel Lobby," such as AIPAC, which has its headquarters almost in the shadow of the Capitol dome.

This is not to say that the big companies have no interest in impressing the Arabs, or in international economics issues such as income tax allowances for overseas Americans or U.S. regulations concerning the Arab boycott of Israel. These same U.S. companies, however, have no interest whatsoever in providing domestic critics with excuses to call them anti-Israel, anti-Semitic, or anti-anything that can be avoided. They are well aware that there are vigilant friends of Israel in all walks of American life, including positions on their own boards of directors, who would rapidly alert a host of federal regulatory agencies to any pro-Arab activities that had even the appearance

---

2. Ball, George, "Our Threatened Lifeline," *Washington Post* Outlook Section, January 20, 1980.
3. Haldane, John, "Trading Jobs for Votes," *Washington Report on Middle East Affairs*, December 2, 1985, p. 6.

of conspiracy, illegality, or irregularity. Further, Jewish consumers can be mobilized quickly for an economic boycott, as the Mexican tourism industry discovered a few years ago after the Mexican delegate to the United Nations supported an anti-Zionist resolution.

Whatever the desires of the Arab countries in which they operate, the oil companies are not going to use up their Congressional credits on the Arab-Israel dispute. They have legitimate, and to them more immediately important, battles to fight in such areas as oil depletion allowances, windfall profits taxes, and tax exemptions.

By saving their credibility, the oil companies and other U.S. concerns in the Middle East were able to move fairly effectively in the case of U.S. anti-boycott legislation, which threatened to cripple American companies in their competition with European and Japanese firms for Middle Eastern markets. Working through the Business Roundtable, U.S. businessmen with interests in the Middle East reached an agreement with Israel's American partisans, represented by B'nai B'rith, on what legal measures were appropriate to prohibit "secondary" and "tertiary" boycott measures as distinguished from the internationally acceptable "primary" Arab boycott of Israel. The results were incorporated into an administration bill before it became the subject of Congressional debate. The bill has made it considerably more difficult for American companies to do business in the Middle East, costing the U.S. at least $1 billion per year. But at least the modifications worked out by the Business Roundtable and the B'nai B'rith have not totally shut U.S. contractors and exporters out of profitable Arab markets.

Similarly, businessmen have been influential in lobbying against some federal income tax levies on allowances that would, for all practical purposes, make it impossible for American contracting firms in the Middle East to employ Americans rather than foreigners for work ranging from engineering positions through clerical and blue-collar jobs. Here again, a modicum of reason has ultimately prevailed. A balance of payments loss in the billions, and a U.S. employment loss in the hundreds of thousands, has been partially averted. This took place, however, only after extensive lobbying by "big business" against federal tax measures so destructive to long-range American economic interests that it was hard to envision what purpose the drafters could have had other than to drive all U.S. firms and workers completely from the Middle East. It is to keep their powder dry for such challenges, however, that large American companies have stayed as far as possible from the Arab-Israeli dispute.

As tokens of esteem for their Middle Eastern hosts, businessmen find it far more prudent to subsidize the publication of books on Arab art, literature, and culture, or to underwrite traveling cultural exhibitions or performances from the Middle East. A public television showing of a controversial film on Saudi Arabia, "Death of a Princess," provided an opportunity for Mobil Oil to purchase advertisements opposing the showing. But the dispute had nothing directly to do with Israel. Mobil subsequently has taken other public positions on controversial Middle East matters, but to date it is almost the only U.S. oil company to do so.

American companies also give funds to American and non-American organizations for use in refugee relief, education, and vocational training programs. Even such actions on behalf of Palestinian refugees, however, are subject to criticism by some pro-

Israel partisans. A $2.2 million gift to American Near East Refugee Aid (ANERA) by Gulf Oil immediately after the war of October 1973 reportedly resulted in a virtual boycott of Gulf by some U.S. Jewish groups.

In the case of the Middle East, even the time-honored idea of grants for academic projects is not totally free of risk for large companies. As discussed elsewhere in this study, the University of Southern California recently returned to American companies all initial contributions aimed at supporting a Middle East Studies Center after a local press campaign alleged possible Saudi control and after the contributors were subjected to careful SEC scrutiny concerning the conditions under which contributions had been solicited from U.S. firms doing business in the Middle East.

The lengths to which even small businessmen go to avoid U.S. domestic problems while seeking to impress favorably the countries of the Middle East is described by veteran anti-Zionist author Alfred Lilienthal, who in 1979 published *The Zionist Connection: What Price Peace in the Middle East*? An American businessman purchased 20 copies of the book. Instead of distributing them to American opinion-makers who might be in a position to do something about Zionist activities, however, he then prudently shipped all 20 copies to the Middle Eastern country in which his firm was working. There the books were distributed to local government officials, a classic case of preaching to the converted and thereby offending no one.

One might expect U.S. companies doing business in the Middle East to purchase large and expensive advertisements in the publications of pro-Arab U.S. lobbying organizations, such as those described above, or to purchase and distribute to interested parties in the media or academia books that reflect favorably on the Arab cause, just as AIPAC does in the case of pro-Israel books. Apparently, however, most feel the risks of criticism from within the U.S. far outweigh whatever vague or intangible public relations advantages might accrue to them in the Middle East. Subsidizing non-political charitable, cultural, or educational activity is less controversial and just as impressive.

The October 1981 Congressional battle over approval of the sale of AWACS to Saudi Arabia, however, provided a conspicuous exception to the timidity usually shown by American industry and business on such questions. Led by representatives of the companies which would benefit directly from the sale, proponents mustered a potent coalition of private corporations and political conservatives to contact individual Senators who seemed to be wavering over the vote.

Richard M. Hunt, director of government for NL Industries, a manufacturer of petroleum equipment, assembled an *ad hoc* group of Washington representatives of some 40 companies with Middle East interests to support the sale. Leading members were the Boeing Company, which faced the closure of its AWACS production line if the sale were not approved, and Pratt and Whitney, maker of the engines for AWACS. Others included Exxon and Mobil from the petroleum industry and Brown and Root and Bechtel representing major U.S. construction firms. Some of the *ad hoc* group's meetings were held in the Washington offices of the Business Roundtable, although that business lobbying group did not take a formal stand on the sale.

A similar *ad hoc* coalition of 34 conservative organizations was coordinated by

Richard Sellers, Washington director for the Coalition for Peace Through Strength and director of Congressional relations for the American Security Council. Supporting groups included the Veterans of Foreign Wars, the American Military Retirees Association, Catholics for Christian Political Action, Young Americans for Freedom, the Conservative Victory Fund and the National Christian Action Committee.

Representatives of groups in both the political and industrial categories worked on individual Senators, stressing both the national security aspects and the economic advantages of the sale. The president of Boeing sent telegrams to 1600 of his firm's subcontractors urging their support through their own representatives. Brown and Root supplied position papers to Senators from states in which the firm and its affiliates are located. The president of Pratt and Whitney sent telegrams predicting that a Senate veto of the President's plan would only force the Saudis to turn to non-American aircraft producers and "would cost the U.S. both exports and jobs."

Summing up the effort, which may well have been crucial to the close Senate vote which made the sale possible, a businessman explained it had "created the environment" which enabled key Senators to drop their uncommitted positions and support President Reagan.

If the effort was a harbinger of better things to come for U.S. business however, the future was deferred during the second Reagan term. When pressure began to build for another Congress-Administration eyeball-to-eyeball confrontation in mid 1985 over another aircraft package for Saudi Arabia, it was the Reagan Administration that blinked. It postponed submitting the proposal to Congress and the Saudis then turned to the United Kingdom for an initial $4.5 billion order, with more training and some parts contracts to follow. U.S. business, never very aggressive in seeking out new markets overseas, seemed to have lost the capacity to defend its Middle East markets even at home.

A man who survived the Sabra Shatilla massacre (below left) shows photos of his wife and daughters killed by Phalangist militiamen trucked to the site by the Israeli Army after it had surrounded and secured the camps. Body of a massacred child (below right) lies by her dead mother's outstretched hand.

Wide World

At the time journalists burst into the Sabra-Shatilla camps some 36 hours after the September, 1982 massacre began, they found bulldozers transporting bodies in their scoops and covering them in mass graves. Not all of the 1,000 to 2,000 victims were buried, however, and Red Cross workers above assembled bodies of many of the victims for identification. A surprise for the killers was the unexpected presence of a large contingent of European and North American doctors and nurses in the two camp hospitals. Below, medical personnel from Norway, West Germany and France tell the press how they were forced at gunpoint to abandon their patients and how the Phalangists separated and shot the Palestinian doctors and nurses before turning the foreign medical personnel over to an Israeli officer.

Wide World

CHAPTER XXIX

Arab Diplomatic Activities

"The Arabs have been their own worst enemies when trying to reach the American media and the American people with their arguments about Middle East questions. The Israelis, on the other hand, have been the most effective spokesmen for a foreign nation I have dealt with."[1]

Lee Eggerstrom, Ridder Newspapers, 1975

"Although a good deal of attention and publicity are periodically attracted by the activities of foreign lobbyists or agents, a close examination of their activities shows that those lacking strong indigenous support acquire only limited or transient influence on American foreign policy."[2]

Senator Charles McC. Mathias, Jr., 1981

"The disparity between American and Arab culture lends support to Americans' impression of the Arab world, an impression, I must say, that is helped very little by Arab attitudes toward what we call public relations. I once told a Kuwaiti Cabinet Minister that the Arabs ought to try to explain their position to the American people. Indignantly, he said, 'Why should we tell the Americans anything, because we have the truth.'"[3]

Senator James Abourezk, 1976

1. Eggerstrom, Lee, of Knight-Ridder Newspapers, quoted by Edmund Ghareeb in "The American Media and the Palestine Problem," *Journal of Palestine Studies*, Autumn 1975/Winter 1976, p. 144.
2. Mathias, Senator Charles McC. Jr., (R.MD.), "Ethnic Groups and Foreign Policy," *Foreign Affairs*, Summer, 1981.
3. Abourezk, Senator James (D-SD), in a talk delivered to the "Arab and American Cultural Conference" of the Middle East Institute of Washington, D.C., September, 1976.

All 21 Arab League members as well as the Palestine Liberation Organization are represented in the United States or at the United Nations. Only a few, however, conduct active information programs, and few of those are deeply concerned with the Arab-Israeli dispute. Among those that are, the most active are the PLO, Saudi Arabia, Egypt, Jordan, Kuwait and the Arab League Information Program.

After many years of essentially negative initiatives, simplistically depicting U.S. support for Israel as an imperialist plot rather than trying to explain the Palestinian cause to Americans, over the past decade the Arab League Information Center has greatly modified its message. Its early leaders, as eager for confrontation as for understanding, have been replaced by U.S.-educated Arab personnel well attuned to the American mentality. Its budget, however, is extraordinarily modest, and its spokesmen are still handicapped by the fact that they work for 21 masters, many of whom have strongly differing perceptions not only of the best means of dissemination, but of the message itself.

Palestinians once met even constructive American criticism with statements to the effect that "our cause is just, and if you cannot understand that, it's your problem, not ours." Some now assume more responsibility for U.S. perceptions. A few still publicly defend the necessity of a stage of violence as a means of bringing their cause to world attention. Yet most probably realize that the years of international violence and terrorism, presumably now past for all but Soviet, Iranian, Syrian and Libyan-funded fringe groups, were lost years concerning promotion of their cause in the U.S. While some may still cite "Jewish control of the media" as justification for inaction in the U.S., others continue to reprint and distribute whatever favorable articles about their cause do appear in the U.S. and British press. Arab League Special Ambassador Clovis Maksoud, a strong and indefatigable speaker, travels the U.S. lecture circuit as do some of the local Arab League Information office directors. If outnumbered 100 to 1, their cause is nevertheless on the upswing abroad, and the repercussions of the shifting balance overseas are all in their favor at present.

It is too soon to assess the new PLO information offices in New York and Washington, but they maintain close relations with the Arab League and other Arab diplomats. From the initial evidence, they have learned tremendously from the mistakes of Palestinian spokesmen of past years. Their U.S. staffs are well-educated, soft-spoken and tireless in projecting an image of reasonableness, moderation and patience.

Saudi Arabia has an active information program and its Ambassador takes a keen interest in positive relations with the U.S. media. It has also dispatched some extraordinarily effective Saudi spokesmen on speaking tours of the U.S., selecting highly-intelligent U.S.-educated government officials, and briefing them carefully on current American sensitivities. Their messages focus on the benefits to Americans of the economic relationship between Saudi Arabia and the United States. By carefully marshalling facts, they seek to allay American fears that the Saudis may use their investments to control any sector of the U.S. economy. Their well-briefed spokesmen have been particularly cautious not to link Saudi economic power with Saudi political concerns in their public statements, having learned how easily such linkage brings charges of "economic blackmail." In general, these speaking programs have been efficiently conducted to counteract an aggressive long-range effort openly directed by the Israeli Embassy in Washington to arouse hostility toward Saudi Arabia among Americans.

Egypt, after the 1967 to 1974 hiatus in diplomatic relations, embarked on an active cultural program of displaying Egyptian films, works of art, and musicians. Given the close political relations developed by Anwar Sadat, and the attention devoted to maintaining them by Hosni Mubarrak, Egypt enjoys a very favorable image among Americans.

Libya for a time took American groups, composed primarily but not exclusively of Arab-Americans, to Libya to see and hear for themselves about current economic and political developments. Relations have deteriorated in recent years to the point where few Americans would go. In the case of Iraq, formerly cold relations have warmed with re-establishment of diplomatic relations in late 1984, and an extremely active Ambassador and press attache have conducted an effective program of inviting influential Americans to visit Iraq in order to assess personally its current attitudes toward the U.S.

Though very small, the Jordanian and Syrian embassies have had skilled personnel in the U.S. for many years. Jordan maintains an active and effective information office which distributes a handsome magazine about Jordan and sponsors a number of exchange programs and invitations to U.S. scholars to participate in seminars in Jordan. Kuwait maintains experienced information and political officers in the U.S. and conducts a program of distributing Kuwaiti publications in English and Arabic to interested Americans. The smaller oil-producing members of the Gulf Cooperation Council also maintain press attaches in Washington, but their function is confined largely to collecting U.S. press comments and reactions concerning Gulf affairs, rather than actively seeking to influence U.S. opinions.

For many years King Hussein of Jordan seemed uniquely successful in his ability to communicate with Americans. Even when differences arose over the Camp David agreements, his positive image in the U.S. was undiminished.

After President Sadat's journey to Jerusalem and his regular U.S. press and television interviews, he became so personally popular in the U.S. that President Carter could get an appreciative laugh from American audiences by saying how grateful he was that he did not have to run for re-election against Anwar Sadat.

Both of these Arab leaders, King Hussein in the 1960s and 1970s and President Sadat from the early 1970s until his death in 1981, clearly understood the power of American television and the American press. Each used those media with great effect to send his message directly to the American public. More recently a number of Saudi officials have made themselves available to U.S. television and journalists, and polls have recorded almost immediate positive results. The ultimate persuader, however, was not the medium, but the message: Moderation, reasonableness, and a willingness to compromise on small matters in order to get on with important concerns. In short, each leader seemed to tell Americans that he wanted to do just what Americans hoped he would do: Go at least 50 percent of the way toward peace with each of his neighbors in the Middle East.

Their successes, in their own times and without the support of the bulk of the Arab information programs in the U.S., illustrate the basic problem the Arabs face in explaining themselves. No matter how skilled they may eventually become, Arab spokesmen in the U.S. will not make politically significant inroads into uncommitted American public opinion until the Arab countries themselves can publicly agree on unified policies.

In terms of population, Libya may be one of the smallest and least significant Arab countries. But so long as the suspicion remains that it supports international terrorism as an instrument of national policy, the entire Arab image is severely tarnished. When Saudi Arabia, Egypt, Syria, and Jordan briefly seemed to move in tandem after the 1973 war, and American friends of the Arabs could speak confidently of a "moderate Arab camp," American perceptions of the Arabs began to change. Later, when Syria seemingly embarked on a radically separate course, old American stereotypes quietly resumed their places.

After all has been said about the relative strengths of the Israeli and Arab lobbies, the accessibility of the media, and east-west cultural differences, the overriding importance of Arab leadership and Arab policies is still evident. When PLO Chairman Yassir Arafat first went before the United Nations, every American turned on his television set to see the "terrorist" in the flesh. Had he chosen to address popular American concerns rather than the concerns of the Third World and radicals within his own Palestinian constituency, the U.S. would almost certainly be engaged in a constructive dialogue with the PLO today.

If the PLO Chairman had been able to extricate all of the American hostages in Iran in 1979, or if after he succeeded in securing the release of some black and female hostages he had persisted in efforts to rescue others, he would have struck at the heart of the American people in their moment of vulnerability. Such an action would have revised in a season years of negative perceptions.

Had the Saudi principles for a Middle East settlement been accepted at the Arab summit conference in Fez in late 1981, the Arab information effort would suddenly have had a "salable" program for U.S. audiences. The U.S. political climate might have altered sufficiently to make the Israelis think again before invading Lebanon in 1982. (It is interesting to note that prior to the Fez meeting Israel described the Saudi principles as a "plan for the liquidation of Israel." Immediately after the plan was rejected, and Israel had "annexed" the Golan Heights, the Israelis used Syrian rejection of the Saudi plan as one of the justifications for the Israeli annexation action).

It is no fault of the Arab information programs in the U.S. that, despite the changes recorded in recent years, American perceptions of the Arab-Israeli dispute are still basically one-sided. For all practical purposes, only three Arab countries have, since World War II, set out systematically to influence American public opinion favorably, regardless of the consequences in their own countries or elsewhere in the Arab world. The polls in each case recorded almost immediate success in terms of high U.S. regard for Jordan, Egypt and Saudi Arabia. By contrast, prior to the incumbency of Menachem Begin, Israel's leaders never lost sight of the crucial importance of U.S. public opinion for their cause.

CHAPTER XXX

Christian Churches — Peace or Armageddon?

"Whatever formula for the peace process develops, there should be reciprocal recognition of the right of self-determination. The Jewish people have claimed and exercised their right to self-determination in the state of Israel. The Palestinian people claim and seek to exercise their right of self-determination by creating a Palestinian entity, including the option of a sovereign state."

Middle East Policy Statement Adopted by the Governing Board,
National Council of Churches of Christ in the U.S.A.,
November 6, 1980

"The right and power of Palestinian people to self-determination by political expression, based upon full civil liberties for all, should be recognized by the parties in the Middle East and by the international community . . . Whatever political expression the Palestinians achieve, they should subscribe to the conditions requisite for the recognition and security of other states and peoples in the area."

The Middle East Conflict: A Presbyterian Report, 1974

"As a member of a recent interfaith peace mission to Israel and the Occupied Territories under the sponsorship of the American Friends Service Committee and the Fellowship of Reconciliation, I had the opportunity to talk at length with Israeli and Palestinian leaders. I came away alarmed at the escalating cycles of violence and repression on the West Bank and in the Gaza Strip, and the reports of Israeli mobilization for an invasion of Lebanon. I became distressed at the evidence of a pervasive and growing pattern of exploitation of Palestinians by Israeli citizens on the West Bank, the rapid expansion of Israel's settlements, the arming of settlers and Village Leaguers, the expulsion and deportation of elected leaders, the confiscation and appropriation of Arab

*property, the demolition of Arab homes, the restriction of academic activities in Pales-
tinian universities, the meeting of civil strife with deadly force. At the same time, I
became aware of moderating trends in the Arab world, of clear signals that Palestinian leadership was turning away from violent solutions, of a growing determination
among Palestinian people to seal self-determination, not at the expense of Israel, but
in co-existence with Israel."*

Bishop C. Dale White, United Methodist Church,
in Congressional briefing, June 23, 1982

*"God deals with nations in relation to how nations deal with Israel . . . I believe God
blesses America and has blessed America because we have blessed Abraham and have
blessed the Jews. I think if America, for example, turned against Israel, our value to
God would cease to be."*

The Rev. Jerry Falwell, founder of the Moral Majority, in copyrighted
article in Tyler (Texas) *Courier-Times-Telegraph*, February 6, 1983

*"The Christian has a major responsibility to stand by Israel, to defend her divine right,
to vote with her . . . Christians cannot stand by and witness the PLO, the Communists,
and Islam doing again to the Jews what was done to their land in the first century."*

From advertisement in the *New York Times*
by "Twentieth Century Reformation Hour Broadcast," 1977

*"I feel that America is tied with the spiritual umbilical cord to Israel. . . . The Judeo-
Christian concept goes all the way back to Abraham, and God's promise to Abraham
which I believe also included America. Because God still says I will bless those that
bless Israel and I will curse those that curse Israel. And thank God the United States
of America still stands supreme today. And I believe firmly (this is) because we've stood
behind Israel and I pray God we always will stand behind Israel."*[1]

Radio Evangelist Jimmy Swaggart

*"We must not allow ourselves to make the theological presuppositions found in Fun-
damentalist communities. We must not turn Israel into an unreal theological phenomenon
that takes us away from realistic discussion of concrete realities."*

The Rev. John T. Pawlikowski, Catholic Theological Union, Chicago, in address
to Eighth National Workshop on Christian-Jewish Relations, November, 1984

*"In the past 2500 years the falling away and restoration of the 'people of Israel' has
occurred many times and been announced even more. Nevertheless, 20th century fundamentalists believe that the words of Amos, as they believe with all words and all
prophecies of the Bible, apply to all times. By doing so they discount any and all historical
references. As evangelical Christian Dewey Beegle remarked in* Prophecy and Predic-

---

1. Dehmer, Alan, "Unholy Alliance, Christian Fundamentalism and the Israeli State," *ADC Issues*,
April 1984, p. 7.

tion, *such a methodology employs a double standard: literalism for the interpretation of prophecy and relativism for the interpretation of history.*"[2]

Alan Dehmer, 1984

"I've been to Israel and Egypt. I went to Lebanon for a couple of weeks and met with Yassir Arafat. I also talked to our ambassador and to churchmen and leaders on both sides of the issue. Arafat challenged me to go back to Los Angeles and find a bookstore where there's even one book about the Palestinians. I went to Pickwick, Vroman's and everywhere and found not one book, not even a pamphlet. But there were literally hundreds of titles on the Israelis. This is the greatest country in the world for information flow, yet we have almost no information at all about the problem which most plagues us."[3]

Mel White, Christian educator and filmmaker, 1981

"Why does organized American Jewry continue its flirtation with the Christian right? We know the reasons of course. Most Jewish leaders are willing to forgive anything so long as they hear a good word about Israel."[4]

Rabbi Alexander Schindler, head of the
Union of American Hebrew Congregations, 1983

"You know, I turn back to your ancient prophets in the Old Testament and the signs foretelling Armageddon, and I find myself wondering if—if we're the generation that is going to see that come about. I don't know if you've noted any of those prophecies lately, but, believe me, they certainly describe the times we're going through."

President Ronald Reagan in remark to Thomas Dine, executive director
of the American-Israeli Public Affairs Committee, October 18, 1983

Christianity in America reflects the diversity of the immigrants who brought it with them from all parts of Europe, Asia, Latin America and the Middle East. It also encompasses uniquely American elements, including the cerebral transcendentalism of New England, the sometimes bizarre or "primitive" fundamentalism of the American South, and native American theologies such as that of the Latter Day Saints of the Mid and Far West.

It is not surprising, therefore, that American Christian approaches to the Israeli-Palestinian problem should reflect such diverse elements as "mainline" Protestant concern with human rights, traditional Catholic concern with the interests of Christians in the Middle East, and Protestant fundamentalist preoccupation with Israel as the fulfillment of Biblical prophecy.

---

2. Dehmer, Alan, "Unholy Alliance, Christian Fundamentalism and the Israeli State," *ADC Issues*, April 1984, p. 7.
3. White, Mel, "Please, Church, Look at This One," *World Vision*, October, 1981, pp. 12-13.
4. Dehmer, Alan, "Unholy Alliance, Christian Fundamentalism and the Israeli State," *ADC Issues*, April 1984, p. 10.

It follows therefore, that the establishment Protestant churches which once strongly supported the immigration into Israel of Jewish refugees from Nazi persecution now, increasingly, express concern about the denial of self-determination to the Palestinians, and recognition to the PLO. Nor is it surprising that Christian fundamentalists, particularly those who rely for a following upon sensationalism and shock in their message and on radio or television as the messenger, have for many years sought to relate each new political or military development in the Middle East to the fulfillment of Biblical prophecy, and convince their scattered flocks that Israel's "ingathering of the Jews in Jerusalem" heralds the imminence of Armaggedon, the second coming, and salvation for those who have accepted Jesus Christ as their personal savior.

What *does* surprise many Americans, and especially, perhaps, liberal American Jews, is the Israeli courtship, begun by former Prime Minister Begin, of the Reverend Jerry Falwell of Lynchburg, Virginia, founder and leader of the Moral Majority. Falwell is a prototype of the highly politicized, right-wing electronic evangelist, and in unguarded moments will joke that a Jew "can make more money accidently than you can on purpose." Yet Falwell's support for Begin was so absolute that he split openly with at least one Moral Majority local chapter leader in the Washington, D.C. area who would not go along with it. Even Falwell's most loyal followers must have been concerned when, after Begin's American-furnished warplanes killed 300 civilians in one afternoon raid in Beirut in July 1981, the fundamentalist clergyman telephoned the Israeli Prime Minister to "cheer his spirits."

The 1982 invasion of Lebanon and subsequent massacres of Palestinians in the Sabra and Shatilla refugee camps did not cool Falwell's ardor. "I don't believe the Israeli Government was in any way involved," he said. His explanation was that PLO sympathizers killed their own families and neighbors "to turn world opinion against Israel." Followers who stuck with him after that could hardly be surprised at his subsequent support for South African apartheid and the Marcos regime in the Philippines.

The Falwell-Begin episode has highlighted a serious controversy within the American Jewish Community. In the past, the Christian side of Christian-Jewish cooperation generally focused on liberal "establishment" churches, and it extended to joint activism on behalf of a wide spectrum of social concerns. Now Israel, and American Jews for whom Israel is the *only* issue, are looking to fundamentalists as the last great reservoir of U.S. Christian support.

In the words of Rabbi Arthur Hertzberg, however, "The continuing interest of the Jew is in exactly the kind of society that makes Mr. Falwell uncomfortable."[5]

Howard Squadron, a former chairman of the Conference of Presidents of Major American Jewish Organizations, thinks the gain for Israel is worth the price of supporting Christian fundamentalists:

"They strongly support a lot of things I think are dreadful for the country. But I'm not going to turn away their support of Israel for that."[6]

5. Hertzberg, Rabbi Arthur, quoted in "Lobbying and the Middle East," *Congressional Quarterly Weekly Report*, August 22, 1981, p. 4.
6. Squadron, Howard M., Chairman of the Conference of Presidents of Major American Jewish Organizations quoted in "Lobbying and the Middle East," *Congressional Quarterly Weekly Report*, August 22, 1981, p. 4.

For Americans who had followed closely the long shadows cast in the U.S. by the Arab-Israeli dispute, the warm relationship between Falwell and Israel came as no surprise. For as long as Israel has existed, and before, many fundamentalist Christian clergymen could be counted upon for support by pro-Israel lobbying groups or Jewish religious leaders. Some of these Christian fundamentalists have visited the Holy Land many times, often with some degree of Israeli sponsorship or support. Most consider the creation of Israel as the fulfillment of Biblical prophecy. There is no question that Falwell and certain other fundamentalist U.S. clergymen are just as emotional, if not always so subtle, on Israel's place in the Middle East as are Israeli religious leaders themselves.

It is difficult to estimate whether most members of fundamentalist churches are as passionate about Israel as some of their clergymen. It is certain, however, that large numbers of Americans who believe that the Old Testament is the literal word of God have been told by electronic evangelists like Jimmy Swaggart and Jerry Falwell that the establishment of Israel, as well as its territorial expansion, is prophesized in the Bible. Relating these contemporary political events to Biblical prophecy implies that the day of judgement is almost at hand. It may also prompt a desire to give generously to a Falwell or a Swaggart, while there is still time. A Christian fundamentalist minister, while doing good for Israel, therefore, can also do well by himself.

When poll responses concerning the Middle East are broken down by religion, Protestants are slightly more likely to be positive about Israel than are Catholics. Similarly, there is evidence indicating higher favor for Israel in areas where fundamentalist churches are strong.

Mr. Falwell's belief that "God deals with nations in relation to how nations deal with Israel," is not original. Lyndon Johnson had an aunt in Texas who told her nephew that from the moment President Truman helped in the creation of Israel, he was certain to win the 1948 election. The point of her advice to President Johnson was that he should be on the lookout for similar opportunities to pile up future credits.

Over the years other self-proclaimed Christian fundamentalists have not hesitated to issue blatantly political appeals for support of Israel against the Arabs. On November 15, 1977, at the time of President Sadat's journey to Jerusalem, readers of the *New York Times* were confronted with a full-page advertisement headlined "Fundamentalists Vote with Israel" and paid for by "The 20th Century Reformation Hour Broadcast" of Collingswood, New Jersey. It read, in part:

"The Old Testament belongs to Jews and Christians alike. Here we learn that the Holy Land is the 'Land of Promise' for Israel and the Messiah. We are called fundamentalists because we believe the Bible to be the very word of God and that it is to be taken literally on its every representation. The covenants made with Abraham, Isaac and Jacob and their descendants by Almighty God are not myth or legend. These are clear and from God a land grant and divine deed. . . . Israel's immediate adversary today is . . . the descendants of Esau, the Palestinians, and the Arabs. The world is back again to Jacob and Esau. Esau is claiming Jacob's land. . . . The Christian has a major responsibility to stand by Israel, to defend her divine right, to vote with her. . . ."

On October 26, 1981, two days before the Senate AWACS vote, a group calling itself "Christians United for American Security" and chaired by a longtime friend of

Israel, Dr. Franklin H. Littell, published a full-page advertisement in the *Washington Post* headlined "U.S. Secrets in Saudi Hands Threaten American Security." The advertisement charged the Saudi regime is "anti-American . . . vulnerable to subversion from within" and has "provided massive funding for PLO terrorism . . . reviled President Sadat . . . and sworn jihad (holy war) against Israel." The advertisement described Israel as "our one democratic friend and reliable ally in the region" and urged "the U.S. Senate to reject the plan to feed the Saudi appetite for more military hardware." It was signed by 29 "responsible Christian leaders" including such diverse public figures as the Rev. Jerry Falwell and the Rev. Father Robert Drinan, former Congressman and president of Americans for Democratic Action.

As Israel continues to use American fundamentalists to accomplish its political goals in the Middle East, American Jews, and liberal Christians as well, might ponder some observations by David Graybeal in the February 24, 1982 issue of *Christian Century*:

"Conservatives who are so clear about the separation of church and state in America rejoice in their conviction that today Judaism and the nation of Israel are identical once again in the Holy Land. This uncritical pro-Semitism toward Israel, which can exist untroubled alongside an anti-Semitism toward American Jews, can be understood only within the context of an eagerness for the rapture of the endtime on the part of people for whom the Book of Revelation is history yet to be enacted . . .

"Although in the short run the symbiotic relationship between the United States and Israel has some obvious advantages for both, in the long run that relationship is filled with tragic possibilities . . .

"The tragic consequence for the United States is that our identification with an Israel which has had occupying armies in Egypt, Jordan and Syria for 14 years increasingly reveals the cynicism in our commitments to human rights, to international law, and to the United Nations . . . "

"The tragic possibilities for Israel are also large. Jews seem blithely oblivious of the degree to which many Christians, especially fundamentalists, believe that Israel is an expendable instrument of God's purpose . . .

"The mixture of fundamentalist images about the end-time is complex, but support for the establishment of Israel, the encouragement for it to occupy the land fully up to its Biblical borders (which would mean annexing the West Bank and Gaza) seems to be clearly part of it. But just at the moment when that occurs, the apocalyptic countdown starts, according to this view, and the time for caring about Israel, or the United States for that matter, is over. In the eschaton, God cares about the elect in Christ.

"Israelis and American Jews would be well advised to pay attention to the way this double-mindedness toward Israel on the part of fundamentalist Christians works. If they do, they will be a bit more restrained in their enthusiasm for the current mystique about Israel held by these Christians."

More significant for the long run, perhaps, are actions of various major U.S. Christian denominations in providing a hearing for Arab speakers, or even sponsorship as is the case with the American Friends Service Committee. It is ironic that the more liberal Protestant churches, which in the past have often allied themselves with Jewish groups in defense of separation of church and state in the United States, now frequently find themselves at odds with the same Jewish groups because of their opposing stands on the Palestinian question. There have been frequent difficulties between Jewish organizations and the National Council of Churches, and some Protestant denominations—generally but not always of liberal persuasion—continue to provide both the hall and the audience for Palestinian speakers. This has also been true of the Roman Catholic Church in the U.S., and of course of the Orthodox church groups with which many Christian Arab-Americans are affiliated.

Increasing support for letting the Palestinian viewpoint be heard, despite the mainstream U.S. media blackout, is not the only crusade of major U.S. denominations. The Catholic Church and many major Protestant denominations have set up task forces to study the Middle East problem. The Friends and Mennonites concentrated on relief work in the West Bank and Gaza, and thereby gained a lot of first hand information while incurring the long-term animosity of the Israeli Government. The Presbyterians have also devoted a great deal of attention to the problem, perhaps because their denomination has lost so much in terms of schools and hospitals it operated in the Middle East before the establishment of Israel created present anti-U.S. attitudes. The Presbyterian Church has issued study kits and organized workshops at the local level both to understand the problem and also to do something about it. Workshop participants even examine the failure of the U.S. media to provide adequate information about the Palestine problem, and are encouraged at the end of the seminars to share their personal conclusions with national officials and their representatives in Congress.

The National Council of Churches of Christ in the USA has also probed carefully into the problem and on November 6, 1980 issued a carefully-reasoned policy statement. One recommendation:

"Steps toward peace which would make possible direct negotiations between Israel and the Palestinians must include official action by the Palestine National Council, the deliberative body of the Palestine Liberation Organization, including either an amendment of the Palestine National Covenant of 1968 or an unambiguous statement recognizing Israel as a sovereign state and its right to continue as a Jewish state. At the same time, Israel must officially declare its recognition of the right of Palestinians to self-determination, including the option of a sovereign state apart from the Hashemite Kingdom of Jordan and of the acceptance of the Palestine Liberation Organization as a participant in the peace negotiations . . . These reciprocal initiatives will remove doubts about the acceptance by the two parties of each other's right to a national existence."[7]

Reading such statements, which belatedly reflect for the United States some of the serious concern and thoughtful recommendations previously expressed by the World Council of Churches and many European Catholic and Protestant leaders, lends poignancy to the apocryphal tale of a UN negotiator who pleaded with adamant Arab and Israeli colleagues to "sit down together and settle this thing like good Christians."

The mainline churches, inhibited first by the strong residual sympathy for Jewish refugees from Nazism and by fear of being labeled "anti-Semitic," and later by the uncompromising Arabic rhetoric of the 1950s and 60s, have been woefully slow to address themselves to what is obviously a moral issue of immediate concern to Christians

7. Policy Statement on the Middle East, National Council of the Churches of Christ, USA, November 6, 1980.

the world over. Nevertheless, despite the late start, the near total failure of the U.S. media and other national institutions to address the Israeli-Palestinian issue fully opens up an almost unprecedented opportunity for American Christianity to prove its relevance toward one of the most complex, and potentially dangerous, issues of the second half of the 20th century.

It has become almost trite to say that the Middle East, because of the overlap and immediacy of both U.S. and Soviet national interests there, is the area where major confrontation is most likely to break out. Even if nuclear disaster in such a confrontation is somehow averted, there are, in *Christian Century* author David Graybeal's opinion, serious implications for U.S. society and the way in which the American Christian majority regards its tiny but politically-overweening Jewish minority. He writes:

"Suppose that the United States does get involved in a devastating Middle East war for whatever reasons, and suppose that history in some sense does continue. In the aftermath of that conflict, when the inevitable question arises as to who got us into it, Christians may conveniently forget their former fascination with Israel and instead point to the Jews in our midst. There is enough latent anti-Semitism around to make that possibility dangerous."[8]

On balance, one might say that within the liberal Protestant denominations, sympathy for the newly-perceived Palestinian underdog is to some extent offset by traditional concern for good relations and dialogue with neighboring Jewish congregations. Within the fundamentalist denominations, support for Israel as the fulfillment of Biblical prophecy is similarly offset to some extent by accompanying conservative reservations against foreign political involvement. Within both the Catholic and Orthodox Christian churches in the U.S., the concern of local parishioners with ethnic ties to Arab countries and clergy who have become partisans of the Arabs through service in the Middle East is somewhat offset by ties between Christian and Jewish leadership at the national level, and also by concern for the Catholic church institutions now operating with Israeli sufferance both in Israel proper and in the militarily-occupied areas.

All of these pluses and minuses do not quite add up to zero, however. Given the relative strength of the two camps in the United States, any support in the form of audiences provided for Arab spokesmen by Christian organizations may be a significant part of the total of such activity in the United States. By contrast, Christian support for Israel, though probably equal or perhaps even greater in terms of total sympathetic audiences, resolutions, paid advertisements, and so on, is nevertheless an almost insignificant portion of the total pro-Israel political activity in the United States.

---

8. Graybeal, David M., "The U.S. as Israel's Godparent," *Christian Century*, February 24, 1982, pp. 198-9.

Wide World

One alliance, two perspectives. A military policeman of the Lebanese Christian Phalange militia (above) directs Israeli soldiers toward their positions encircling West Beirut in June, 1982. When Palestinian forces withdrew from the battered city in late August, their safety and that of their families was internationally guaranteed. After the withdrawal of U.S. Marines, however, the Israelis moved into West Beirut, in violation of their pledge not to do so, and turned the Palestinian refugee camps over to the Phalange. Palestinian girls (below), murdered in Sabra camp.

Wide World

PLO

One people, two perspectives. Above, Israeli rescue workers search for injured after Palestinian guerrillas blew up vehicles in downtown Tel Aviv on June 30, 1967. Below left, Palestinian woman works on traditional handicrafts in UNRWA vocational training center in Gaza strip. Below right, Palestinian girls studying to be teachers in UNRWA women's training center in Ramallah during the same period.

UNRWA   UNRWA

CHAPTER XXXI

The Media —
Copout or Conspiracy?

"Let me warn here that I am not one of those who believes that Jews own all the newspapers. That statement is both racist and inaccurate. What I do believe is that a great sympathy for Israel exists in the American media, among both Jews and non-Jews. I also believe that journalists like to write what is fashionable."[1]

Senator James Abourezk, 1976

"It is my personal belief that if the media as a whole in the Western world had done an adequate job in reporting from the Middle East, it would not have been necessary for the Palestinians to resort to violence to draw attention to their case."[2]

James McCartney, 1975

"I had previously covered Latin America, the Soviet Union, Asia (including Vietnam), and Europe. In none of these extremely complicated places did I have comparable inner difficulties. For the fair-minded journalist, as for so many others, the Middle East involves a special confrontation—a confrontation with oneself and one's previous prejudices, as well as with a new and ever-fascinating culture."[3]

Georgie Anne Geyer, 1980

---

1. Abourezk, Senator James, from address at the "Arab and American Cultures Conference" of the Middle East Institute, Washington, D.C., September 24, 1976.
2. Ghareeb, Edmund. Excerpted from interview with James McCartney, Ridder Newspapers, quoted in "The American Media and the Palestine Problem," *Journal of Palestine Studies* Autumn 1975/Winter 1976, p. 140.
3. Geyer, Georgie Anne, "The American Correspondent in the Arab World," in *The American Media and the Arabs*, CCAS, Georgetown University, 1980, p. 65.

"I will not name them, but there are top figures in the profession with long records of championing Israel and Jewish people who complain bitterly in private that if they dare to express one word of sympathy for Palestinian Arab refugees, they are flooded with Jewish hate mail accusing them of anti-Semitism."[4]

I.F. Stone, 1980

Probably no one in the world would disagree with the statement that there will be no peace in the Middle East until the great powers approach the Arab-Israeli conflict as a problem to be solved rather than as a problem to be exploited. Nor would informed observers disagree with the statement that the Soviet attitude toward the Israeli-Palestinian problem has always been ambivalent. There have been periods, such as just prior to the 1967 war, when the Soviet attitude has seemed adventuresome, aimed at fomenting and then exploiting trouble. There have been other times, such as during the 1973 war, when the Soviet Union has been reasonable and conciliatory. At such times clearly the fear that a Middle Eastern confrontation could lead to a nuclear exchange with the U.S. outweighed the desire to exploit Arab fears of Israel and its American patron.

It has been one of the great tragedies of our era that, on those occasions when the Soviet Union clearly was ready to cooperate on achieving Middle East peace, the normally peace-loving United States was not. A major reason has been a nearly total lack of understanding of the problem on the part of the American people.

Had Americans understood that by 1973 the problem was not that of a beleaguered Israel fearful of being pushed into the sea, but rather that of an expanding Israel reluctant to return Arab lands seized in 1967, they might have forced Henry Kissinger to stop playing 19th century great power politics and get on with a comprehensive settlement. Tens of thousands of Lebanese, Palestinian, Egyptian, Israeli and American lives would have been saved. Similarly, in 1980, when Menachem Begin had resumed building West Bank settlements, contravening his Camp David understanding with President Carter to freeze the settlements, the U.S. President might have felt strong enough to ignore traditional election year politics and crack down on Begin had Carter felt the U.S. public understood the issue. Instead, with the media at least as likely to side with the Israeli as with the U.S. version of the Camp David understanding on settlements, Carter let the whole matter slide until after the election. It meant, in effect, the destruction of the Camp David agreements. The same situation prevailed when Begin rejected the Reagan Peace Plan and announced a huge new expansion of Israeli settlements. Had the U.S. media kept the American public informed, and had any U.S. President felt confident that the media would support him in a difficult confrontation with Israel, the Middle East might be much closer to peace today.

Two U.S. institutions are primarily responsible for the unwillingness, or unpreparedness, of the United States to assume a responsible role in the Middle East, and to treat each aspect of the Arab-Israeli dispute, and each party to the dispute, on

---

4. Stone, I.F., quoted in Lord Caradon, "Images and Realities of the Middle East Conflict," *The American Media and the Arabs*, CCAS, Georgetown University, 1980, p. 80.

its merits. Congress, out of fear of Israel's U.S. lobby, has failed the American citizenry it represents. But the other institution, the media, must shoulder an even larger share of the blame. It has failed to inform the American people about the Middle East, and that information void is what has left Congress defenseless. In the absence of an informed American public opinion on the Middle East, there is no way for an individual Congressman to build up any kind of counter-force to resist a ruthless, well-funded and single-minded pro-Israel lobby.

In 1975 James McCartney, in the paragraph quoted at the beginning of this chapter, blamed the western media for Palestinian violence. The European media, on the whole, have rectified their errors of omission. In the U.S., although the situation is complicated, things are in fact worse than at the time McCartney spoke. A much higher percentage of American newsmen writing on foreign affairs understand the truth of Middle Eastern matters, but they are at least as reluctant as ever before to write or speak it. It is no exaggeration to say that, in 1986, the U.S. media bears a major share of the blame not just for past Palestinian violence, but for the continuation of Middle East bloodshed as a whole.

How in this day and age has U.S. journalism, considered by most Americans to be the most advanced mass communication system in the world, failed so abysmally in its responsibility to inform Americans about basic Middle Eastern realities? Is it the result of a conspiracy or Jewish "gentlemen's agreement?" Is it the result of benign neglect? Or is it mostly because, of all the peoples of the world, the Arabs seem to have the least understanding of modern public relations and of how to persuade rather than antagonize?

Since journalists like nothing better than writing about themselves, and probably 75 percent of informed U.S. journalists would agree with everything written so far in this chapter, it perhaps is best to let them speak for themselves, medium by medium.

NEWSPAPER EDITORIAL POSITIONS

"The subtlety of the pressures concerning the Middle East for a newspaper in the city with the world's largest Jewish population is revealed in the following comment about a former New York Times *editorial writer: 'It was not a case of his being pressured to write something that he did not believe, but rather a case of not being able in every case to say quite as much as he might wish to say about the issue.' One suspects that it is this subtle pressure—certain tacit assumptions about the Middle East 'reality' and the probable reaction of one's superiors, colleagues, and readers—that may account in part for the seeming 'tilt' of editorial writers, layout editors, headline writers, and reporters."[5]*

Michael C. Hudson, Washington, D.C., 1980

---

5. Hudson, Michael, "Room for Improvement," in *The American Media and the Arabs*, CCAS, Georgetown University, 1980, p. 93. (Inner quote is from "Zionist Lies on American Editorial Pages," p. 138, and refers to former *New York Times* Editor James Brown.)

"The duty of the mass media, the duty of journalism, is to educate—to tell the truth. But your American mass media are not telling the truth. You are covering up."[6]

Yassir Arafat, Beirut, 1981

"You see it time and time again. The image of Palestinians as Russian agents, as terrorists, versus the image of Israelis as a people who make the desert bloom. Believe me, if I had all the money in foreign aid Israel had from the U.S., and all the European technicians who emigrated there, I could make trees grow out of cement. But while they create and reinforce a good image we sit back and complain that the Western media is biased. The fault is ours."[7]

Rami Khouri, Amman, 1981

The print media are still the primary sources of information for American leaders and opinion makers. In considering both newspapers and news magazines, a distinction must be made between the editorial pages and political columns, which are of great importance to decision makers, and the news pages, which may have a greater influence on the informed general public.

Since newspaper editorials take distinct positions, the bias of each newspaper's editorial pages can be measured over a period to provide a general portrait of American press attitudes toward the Arab-Israeli dispute. This was done for an eight-year period from 1966 to 1974 by Robert Trice, subsequently director of arms transfer policy of the Department of Defense, while he was on the Ohio State University faculty. Trice coded a total of 2,924 editorials from 11 dailies which he described as "the American elite press." They were the *New York Times, Washington Post, Chicago Tribune, Los Angeles Times, Denver Post, Atlanta Constitution, Christian Science Monitor, St. Louis Post-Dispatch, Wall Street Journal, Louisville Courier Journal*, and the *Dallas Morning News*. Among his conclusions:

"As American involvement in Indochina wound down, the Arab-Israeli conflict emerged to join U.S.-Soviet relations and Sino-American relations as one of the few foreign policy topics to garner the sustained interest of the press. . . . In terms of the possible roles played by the opinion makers of the prestige press, the evidence . . . provides hints that American editors may have been predisposed to follow the lead of the American government to adopt an open-minded, cautiously supportive stance toward Israel, and to approach the actions of all others with a jaundiced outlook that ran the gamut from skepticism (in the case of the UN) to open antipathy (in the case of the Palestinians). . . .

"It is significant that through all these periods of crisis between successive Administrations and virtually every other relevant party—Arab governments, Israel, the Soviet Union and American pro-Israel groups—the press provided steady support for the actions of the U.S. government. . . . The unwavering if qualified editorial support shown toward the United States stands in sharp

6. Weisman, John, Excerpted from interview with PLO Chairman Yassir Arafat quoted in "Why the Palestinians are Losing the Propaganda War: An on-the-Scene Report," *TV Guide*, October 24-30 and October 31-November 6, 1981, Part 2, p. 8.
7. *Ibid.*, Excerpted from interview with Amman Editor Rami Khouri, Part 2, p. 12.

contrast to press opinion concerning other major actors. Support for Israel was greatest in 1970 during the War of Attrition and was particularly strong during the final third of that year in the wake of Egyptian-Soviet violations of the cease-fire agreement. However, the elite press was critical of a number of Israeli actions over the years, particularly those concerning the annexation of Jerusalem, policies toward the occupied territories and the Israeli retaliatory raid policy.

"The Arab governments were never able to elicit much sympathy from American newspapers. . . . However . . . after the end of the War of Attrition the press was less critical of the Arabs than in preceding years. The Soviet Union was consistently treated as the major villain in the Middle East. With the exception of 1969, when hopes ran high that a solution could be hammered out in the Big Four and Big Two talks, the Soviets always received more criticism from the American press than any other government actor. . . .

"Editorial opinions on most foreign policy issues are a function of the persuasiveness of the arguments presented by the U.S. government as well as other governments; the cultural, religious and political belief systems of the editorial staffs, and their perceptions of the opinions of significant individuals and groups in the domestic and international political environments. . . . Israel received moderately favorable editorial treatment on most issues over the nine-year period. Two of the most important issues on which it enjoyed the support of the American elite press concerned preconditions for a negotiated peace, and demands for recognized and secure national boundaries. . . .

"The Arab states did not fare as well as Israel in the competition for American editorial support. In particular, perceived Arab aggression, support for Palestinian military activities, policies toward Arab Jews (particularly in Iraq), and the 1973-74 oil price rise and embargo aroused strong criticism from U.S. newspapers. . . .

"The United States government was able to rally editorial support for its position on most issues. However, the degree of enthusiasm shown by the elite press varied considerably from issue to issue. Successive Administrations found strong backing for almost any peace initiative, cautious support for U.S. aid policy to Israel (whether generous or stingy), and general skepticism about the wisdom of providing economic and military aid to the front-line Arab states. . . .

"The dominant themes running through the editorials on American Middle East policy were the need for the government to defend U.S. 'national interests,' to act in an 'even-handed' manner, to avoid being dragged into a confrontation with the Soviet Union, and, interestingly, the need for Soviet-American cooperation. . . .

"It is possible to cast editorial coverage of Palestinian-related issues in two different lights. On the one hand, it is quite accurate to say that the irregular military activities of Palestinian groups received almost universal condemnation from prestige American newspapers. Palestinians were the target of more criticism on the issue of their commando and terrorist attacks than any other single party or any other issue that arose during the 1966-1974 period. On the other hand, American editors would also frequently refer to Palestinian demands for the right of self determination. And, more often than not, they would at least grudgingly admit that Palestinian demands, however intolerable their methods, were legitimate, and that a resolution of the 'Palestine problem' was a pre-requisite to a lasting Middle East settlement. . . .

" . . . As a group, America's prestige newspapers were more supportive of most Israeli policies and actions than those of the Arab states. However, we were a bit surprised to find that both support for Israel and criticism of the Arab states were considerably weaker than we had anticipated. The Palestinians and the French rivaled the Soviets as consistent targets of strong editorial attacks on most issues.

"There were also some variations in the orientation of different elite newspapers toward the Middle East conflict. The *Christian Science Monitor* and the *St. Louis Post-Dispatch* were the only newspapers that were 'net critics' of Israel, and the *Monitor* was alone as a 'net supporter' of the Arab states. Although there were substantial differences in their enthusiasm, all 11 papers showed overall support for the policies and actions of the U.S. government. . . . The clear message sent to policy makers by the opinion shapers and transmitters of the elite press was that they would support any reasonable U.S. initiative to bring about an equitable and permanent settlement as long as it avoided the prospect of direct U.S. military involvement. We suspect that the general trends established during the 1966-1974 period have changed only slightly since then. If the time frame of the analysis were extended through 1978 the data would probably show increasingly similar general levels of support for Israel and the Arab governments (particularly Egypt, Jordan and Saudi Arabia), increased recognition of the importance of Palestinian self-determination as an element in any stable peace, and continued condemnation of Palestinian commando and terrorist activities. . . ."[8]

NEWSPAPER NEWS COVERAGE

"According to former Washington Post *reporter Stephen Isaacs, 'of the 1,748 daily newspapers in the United States in 1972, 3.1 per cent were owned by Jews . . . Those newspapers (owned by Jews) published 8 per cent of all the newspapers printed each day in the country'. . . . The situation of the prestige press is different. These newspapers have unusual resources, including their own foreign correspondents. The two most prestigious U.S. newspapers,* The New York Times *and* The Washington Post, *are both owned by Jewish families and both have been subjected to considerable journalistic scrutiny themselves on the question of alleged pro-Israel bias."*[9]

Michael Hudson, 1980

"Amos Elon, the famous writer of The Israelis, *told me once in Jerusalem that the way the Americans eulogized the Israelis after the 1967 war was the worst thing that we could have done. It gave them, he said, a totally unreal confidence and idea about the world, and led directly to the 1973 war. I strongly agree. Whenever a nation is unfairly portrayed, an imbalance is created that is bad for everyone. This is why press coverage must be* fair, *not complimentary."*[10]

Georgie Anne Geyer, 1980

"Daily we have air raids; daily we have sea raids; daily we have shelling. If this were happening in Maalot it would make headlines. . . . Why don't you see both sides of the coin? Why do you cover the news only from the Israeli angle?"[11]

Yassir Arafat, 1981

8. Trice, Robert H., "The American Elite Press and the Arab-Israeli Conflict," *Middle East Journal*, Summer 1979, pp. 310-325.
9. Hudson, Michael, "Room for Improvement," *The American Media and the Arabs*, CCAS, Georgetown University, 1980, p. 96.
10. Geyer, Georgie Anne, "The American Correspondent in the Arab World," in *The American Media and the Arabs*, CCAS, Georgetown University, 1980, p. 67.
11. Weisman, John. Excerpted from interview with Yassir Arafat in "Why the Palestinians are losing the Propaganda War, *TV Guide*, October 24-30 and October 31-November 6, 1981, Part I, pp. 7, 10.

"I call it the audience factor—in this case a tremendous interest in and sympathy for Israel. It's a factor in how editorial judgments are made."[12]

Steve Bell, *American Broadcasting Company*, 1981

So much for the official editorial positions of America's elite newspapers. What about the impressions conveyed in the news columns of those papers, read by a far greater audience and subject to almost imperceptible manipulation by reporters, copy readers, headline writers, and editors? In the absence of a scholarly critique, it is useful to rely on some comments by those in the best position to keep score, the media personnel themselves. In 1975, a Lebanese-American journalist, Edmund Ghareeb, interviewed prominent U.S. news personnel for the *Journal of Palestine Studies* about American media coverage of the Palestine problem and the Arab-Israeli conflict. The individuals offered sometimes conflicting but generally forthright comments:

Lee Eggerstrom, Ridder Newspapers

"It is correct that the U.S. news media have been generally pro-Israeli and anti-Arab. Until the October 1973 War and the resultant Arab oil embargo, the U.S. citizen and the media paid little attention to the Arab states. The Middle East was an area where the creation of Israel was watched with great interest, fostered by an effective interest group within the U.S. . . . The Arab oil embargo made many changes in the U.S. One significant result was a 'new discovery' of the Arab nations by the American news media. I have no way of citing statistics, but I believe it is a safe assumption to say that the news media stories about the Arab nations and datelined from Arab states since the October War equal the total news coverage out of those countries since 1948 . . .

"The treatment of Palestinian commandos, or guerrillas, represents in my opinion the best example of the American news media's lack of understanding about what is really happening in the Middle East. Good reporters . . . can write provocative and informative articles about Middle East altercations and developments. The headline over their stories, however, will end up stating something like 'Arab Terrorists Strike Again.' It is unfortunate that desk editors and newsroom personnel do not know the difference between the various Arab ethnic and national groups. It is unfortunate for the American people, who must rely on the news media to inform them of wars of liberation for homelands abroad and what the issues are."[13]

---

12. Weisman, John. Excerpted from interview with Steve Bell of the American Broadcasting Corporation, quoted in "Why the Palestinians are losing the Propaganda War: An on-the-scene Report," *TV Guide*, October 24-30 and October 31-November 6, 1981, Part 1, p. 12.
13. Ghareeb, Edmund. Excerpted from interview with Lee Eggerstrom, Ridder Newspapers, quoted in "The American Media and the Palestine Problem," *Journal of Palestine Studies*, Autumn 1975/Winter 1976, pp. 142-3.

James McCartney, Knight Newspapers

"It is my belief that because of the large Jewish populations in major cities, where there is a kind of built-in audience for what's happening in Israel, the automatic reaction of some of our editors was to view the situation in terms of what those readers would want to know. And what they would want to know was: How was Israel doing? . . . There is an immensely large Jewish community in New York City, and there is no doubt that the *New York Times* is owned by a Jewish family. But I am not willing to make the possible inference that this leads to slanted reports on the Middle East, which would impugn the integrity of the *New York Times*. I believe that they believe they are objective within their intellectual frame of reference. But I think that there are certain questions any newspaper should ask itself in the reporting of any controversial situation in which there are known divergent views. I think the *Times* should perhaps increase its own credibility by not assigning Jews to play a major role in covering Middle East issues. And I think in many newspapers with Jewish staff who have a great interest in Israel, there is sometimes a certain degree of bias."[14]

Ronald Koven, *Washington Post*

"Historically, the American press has been a reflection of its society. The press has been a way for immigrant groups to be upwardly mobile. Up until about 1950 or earlier, newsrooms of major metropolitan newspapers on the East Coast had large numbers of people of Irish origin in dominant positions. About that period the Irish were accepted into our society in a different way, so journalism didn't seem to be so desirable as a profession. They went on to places where they made more money and had more prestige. In the same way the next wave in American journalism was the Jews. For that reason there were and are disproportionate numbers of Jews in the American media, relative to the population. . . . I think the next wave after the Jews — you can just see the thin edge of the wedge — are blacks. . . . I want to put the question of the presence of Jews in the media in its historical perspective; it's not a Zionist plot."[15]

TELEVISION NEWS

"Television is now the first and most dramatic shaper of public information on the Middle East. Where television coverage of the region is now skewed, technological and time constraints and especially the lack of access granted by countries in the region can most often be blamed."[16]

Robert Hershman (PBS) and Henry Griggs, Jr. (NBC), 1981

---

14. Ghareeb, Edmund. Excerpted from interview with James McCartney, quoted in "The American Media and the Palestine Problem," *Journal of Palestine Studies*, Autumn 1975/Winter 1976, pp. 138-140.
15. *Ibid.*, from interview with Ronald Koven, Foreign Editor, *Washington Post*, pp. 136-7.
16. Hershman, Robert and Griggs, Henry L., Jr., "American Television News and the Middle East," *Middle East Journal, Autumn, 1981, p. 471.*

"We have a terrible problem of balance. The network has a very good bureau in Tel Aviv, and the ability to satellite news directly out of Israel. But there is a continuing problem of access in Arab nations."[17]

Steve Bell, ABC, 1981

"The Arabs just don't give us access. And they pay the price for that—and they have never seemed to figure out that they'd have a lot more people in this country sympathetic to them if they'd opened up to us over the years. . . . The Israelis know how to feed the press."[18]

Sanford Socolow, CBS, 1981

"While American attitudes toward Israel are affected by American-Israeli relations, Israel and its supporters, especially Zionists in the United States, have some ability to manipulate American opinion. For instance, it was found that both the Eichmann trial and the NBC showing of the presentation 'Holocaust' generated added sympathy and support for Israel."[19]

Michael Suleiman, 1980

"From the Arab point of view, television is something that can be exploited . . . It is a vehicle that can be used to transmit views, ideas, opinion and expose genuine injustices to the rest of the world. One cannot exploit it simply by asking to have a live camera set up in front of one's office and expecting to be able to make propagandistic statements without being challenged on them."[20]

Barry Dunsmore, 1980

"In television there is a control room, there is a policy. Sometimes we find the TV studios open for us. Then when we want to expose something, the lines go dead. As if somebody upstairs just pushed a button. You talk to us about changing our image. It is not our image that should be changed, but your American mentality."[21]

Shafiq al-Hout, Palestine Liberation Organization, 1981

17. Weisman, John. Excerpted from interview with Steve Bell of the American Broadcasting Corporation, quoted in "Why the Palestinians are losing the Propaganda War: An on-the-scene Report," *TV Guide*, October 24-30 and October 31-November 6, 1981, Part 1, p. 8.
18. Weisman, John. Excerpted from interview with Sanford Socolow of the Columbia Broadcasting System, quoted in "Why the Palestinians are Losing the Propaganda War: An on-the-scene Report," *TV Guide*, October 24-30 and October 31-November 6, 1981, Part 1, p. 14.
19. Suleiman, Michael W., "American Public Support of Middle Eastern Countries: 1939-1979" in *The American Media and the Arabs*, CCAS, Georgetown University, 1980, p. 36.
20. Dunsmore, Barry, "Television Hard News and the Middle East," in *The American Media and the Arabs*, CCAS, Georgetown University, 1980, p. 76.
21. Weisman, John. Excerpted from interview with Shafiq al-Hout of the Palestine Liberation Organization, quoted in "Why the Palestinians are Losing the Propaganda War: An on-the-scene Report," *TV Guide*, October 24-30 and October 31-November 6, 1981, Part 2, p. 14.

As with the press, there are two significant dimensions to television coverage of the Arab-Israeli dispute, formal coverage in news and documentary shows and informal impressions created by television entertainment programs. According to Robert Trice, "studies have shown that there are virtually no differences in foreign policy news coverage among the three national television networks that dominate the electronic media."[22]

If this is the case, comments by two prominent network reporters to Edmund Ghareeb may be representative of foreign correspondents and "anchor persons" in general. One, former ABC Middle East correspondent Peter Jennings, said:

"I spent five years off and on in the Middle East, and I probably did more reporting in the Arab world than any other television correspondent. I was never 'politically' edited by ABC no matter what kind of story I covered, or what I had to say. At present, on the broadcast 'A.M. America' that I am engaged in, I've seen no sign whatever that anyone has resisted me presenting an Arab point of view when it was justifiable, just as nobody has prevented me from presenting an Israeli point of view when it was justifiable."[23]

However, asked to comment on a statement by political columnist James Reston that, "you may put it down as a matter of fact that any criticism of Israel will be met with a cry of anti-Semitism," Jennings agreed:

"That's quite true. The editor of an article in *Commentary* Magazine labelled me, along with Reston and others, as being notably pro-Arab or notably anti-Semitic. I think it is extremely unfortunate and misguided to suggest that because someone happens to disagree with . . . the politics of Israel, he should be regarded as anti-Semitic."[24]

Marilyn Robinson, then an NBC Washington reporter, had similarly mixed comments:

"I think there is a great deal of anti-Arab bias, especially in the magazines, where you have caricatures. They have to be a little more careful on television. . . . I used to do 'cut-ins' on the *Today* show. . . . At 7:25 and 8:25 every morning, the local stations cut in and do their own local news for five minutes and then go back to the *Today* show in New York. Well, I was the girl in charge of the local cut-ins for Washington during the time when Yassir Arafat was supposed to come over here to the United States . . . and I led with Arafat every day. When I began to introduce my copy about Arafat, I would never refer to the Palestinians as Palestinian terrorists. I'd even up the copy. Now, when Arafat went to the United Nations I was evening up the copy and I was using a lot of tape on Arafat, letting him have a chance to talk. But when we cut back to New York at 7:35, the guy who did the national news was doing the same story and he didn't even up the copy. He would repeat the same story that I had read locally, using

---

22. Trice, Robert, "The American Elite Press and the Arab-Israeli Conflict," *Middle East Journal,* Summer 1979, p. 306.
23. Ghareeb, Edmund. Excerpted from interview with Peter Jennings of the American Broadcasting Corporation in "The American Media and the Palestine Problem," *Journal of Palestine Studies, Autumn 1975/Winter 1976, p. 129.*
24. *Ibid.*, p. 130.

words like 'terrorists,' which means that everybody who was listening to the local cut-in and listening to the national news right after heard me even up the copy and heard him leave the copy as it came straight over the wire. . . . I got a lot of phone calls from Jewish people saying that I had no business reading national news on a local cut-in. That is, they knew that I was supposed to be doing local news but I was doing national news. But they also knew I was evening up the copy, and they didn't like it. And they wrote to the news director. Within a week I was told never to do national news in the local cut-ins again. Not one Arab between here and the Mississippi River called in to say 'Thank you, Miss Robinson, for being fair.' Not objective, but just fair. Now nobody can do national news on the local cut-ins. . . .

"The Jewish people know, instinctively, how to manage the press. . . . They're at home with media and communications, and are very good. The Arabs, on the other hand, are not at home with communications. They are afraid when a reporter comes up to them. They don't know that if there is something anti-Arab on the air and enough Arabs call and say, 'We're not going to take this,' it will stop."[25]

Five years after the *Journal of Palestine Studies* article on "The American Media and the Palestine Problem" was written, *TV Guide* commissioned author John Weisman to conduct a series of interviews and prepare an article concerning treatment of the Arab-Israel dispute by American television.

PLO Chairman Yassir Arafat told Weisman that "the duty of the mass media, the duty of journalism, is to educate — to tell the truth. But your American mass media are not telling the truth. You are covering up."

The *TV Guide* investigation "seems to confirm Arafat's opinion," Weisman reported. In his article, "Why the Palestinians Are Losing the Propaganda War: An on the Scene Report," he wrote:

"There is, of course, the unshakable fact that some Palestinians have engaged regularly in acts of terrorism, trying to slaughter Israeli civilians as a way to draw attention to their cause. Yet, without discussing the merits of that cause, it is undeniable that, in covering the conflict between Palestinians and Israelis, the U.S. networks are much more likely to give the Israeli perspective than they are to voice Palestinian concerns.

"*T.V. Guide* reviewed 10 months of coverage on the nightly news shows from logs and tapes supplied by the Vanderbilt University Television News Archive — from July 1980 through April 1981. There were 38 reports of raids and retaliations by both sides; 24 of the 38 were Israeli raids on Palestinian targets in South Lebanon. Only three of these reports — for a total of one minute, 10 seconds — showed pictures of the effects of the Israeli attacks. None showed any Palestinian victims. On the other hand, of the 14 reports of Palestinian raids and attacks on Israel during the period, 11 included pictures of Israeli victims, and the filmed reports totaled some 17 minutes.

"Not that the Israelis have been exempt from criticism. Coverage of military actions on the West Bank has caused them embarrassment. And our survey using the Vanderbilt Archive does not encompass the events of this past summer: Israel's bombing of Iraq's nuclear reactor in June and the intensified fighting between Israeli and Palestinian forces that reached its height when the Israelis bombed Beirut on July 17, killing, some say, more than 300.

---

25. Ghareeb, Edmund. Excerpted from interview with Marilyn Robinson of the National Broadcasting Corporation in "The American Media and the Palestine Problem," *Journal of Palestine Studies*, Autumn 1975/Winter 1976, pp. 146-147.

"During the pre-July 17 crescendo, American networks all showed pictures of Israeli victims. What Americans did not see until the bombings in Lebanon became too serious to ignore were the Palestinian and Lebanese civilians who had borne the brunt of attacks on settlement camps and the Lebanese cities. It took an event of the magnitude of the Beirut bombing – with its resultant Lebanese civilian dead – to bring extensive coverage to American TV."[26]

During the Israeli invasion of Lebanon in June, 1982, however, the situation was reversed. The Israelis did not allow journalists to accompany their troops for several days and when they did, they were subject to heavy censorship. Journalists based in Beirut, however, had the run of the battlefront, at their own risk, and had little trouble transmitting from either Beirut or Damascus. Since journalists based in Lebanon traditionally lived and worked in predominantly Muslim West Beirut, as the Israelis closed the net around that part of the city and began shelling and bombing its inhabitants while periodically shutting off water and electricity, television cameras were there, among the victims.

Yassir Arafat, for years his own worst enemy with the media, finally began to use television effectively to tell his story to the world. While he was not a master of the medium, as was Anwar Sadat, nevertheless his daily walks among the besieged people of Beirut, and his unstaged gentleness with the children who crept out of the city's basement shelters to see him, finally began to convey something of the courage and grace under fire with which his followers had long been familiar, but which was an entirely new dimension of Arafat and the Palestinians to the outside world.

Night after night, television brought scenes of indescribable carnage into American living rooms, as Ariel Sharon's Israeli air, naval and artillery assault sought to reduce one of the great modern cities of the world to rubble. The Israelis, seeking to finish a barbaric task before U.S. public opinion forced them to stop, made in three months every mistake the Palestinians had made over the previous 15 years. Menachem Begin, who finally seemed to be running out of words, sought to hide from the cameras. Ariel Sharon, glorying in the slaughter, strutted and blustered before the cameras like the Third Reich's Marshal Goering. By the end of the summer, and after the Sabra-Shatilla massacres which were also reported, at least briefly, on U.S. television, basic sympathy for Israel in a Gallup poll taken in October, 1982, had for the first time declined to a level (32 per cent) just above that of basic sympathy for the Palestinians (28 per cent).

It was an interesting demonstration of how quickly intensive, even-handed coverage of the Arab-Israeli dispute could change basic American perceptions. It also demonstrated how even-handed coverage could come about. First, TV camera access was at least as good on the Arab side as on the Israeli side. Second, the Palestinians were for the first time dealing more intelligently with the international media than were the Israelis. And finally, with Beirut the top world news story day after day in the summer of 1982, there was no way for unseen hands to push forward stories unfavorable

26. Weisman, John, "Why the Palestinians are losing the Propaganda War: An on-the-scene Report," *TV Guide*, October 24-30 and October 31-November 6, 1981, Part 1, p. 8.

to the Arabs and bury stories unfavorable to Israel. The world spotlight was on the story and Americans were closely informed about it. Therefore, attempts by any one network to downplay its significance, as seemed occasionally to happen with CBS, caused audiences to switch to the competition.

In the subsequent four years, much of the public impact of that three months of concentrated U.S. media coverage of the Middle East has been lost. The Israelis began a series of well-planned damage-control public relations operations, while the Arabs, with seemingly limitless capacity for self-destruction, resumed some of their previous public infighting. But, although the raw numbers on public opinion polls had, within a year, returned approximately to three or four to-one sympathy by Americans for Israelis over Palestinians, in fact the Israelis had lost, perhaps permanently, a key element of their public opinion support. Begin, Sharon, and the siege of Beirut lost the support of American media liberals for Israel. It was a loss that could cost Israel dearly in future years.

John Cooley, long-time *Christian Science Monitor* correspondent in the Middle East and now in London with ABC, is highly respected by his American foreign correspondent colleagues and also by the leaders of Middle Eastern countries whom he has interviewed over the years. In his article, "The News from the Mideast: A Working Approach," published in the Autumn 1981 issue of the *Middle East Journal,* Cooley cites lack of access to the Arab side as a major factor in the unbalanced television coverage depicted in all of the studies quoted. So do Henry L. Griggs, Jr., foreign producer of "NBC Nightly News," and Robert Hershman, former Middle East correspondent for the MacNeil/Lehrer Report on the Public Broadcasting System and associate producer of "CBS Reports," in their article "American Television News and the Middle East," also published in the Autumn, 1981 issue of the *Middle East Journal.*

If the Arab explanation for lack of balance in U.S. television coverage of the Arab-Israeli dispute were narrowed down to one word, it would be "conspiracy." If the explanation by most American professional television reporters were also boiled down to one word, it would have to be "access." The situation in Beirut in the summer of 1982 supports the Americans. The reversion to Israel-centered TV coverage of the Middle East since that time supports the Arabs. The truth, perhaps, lies somewhere in between.

All, however, agree with Hershman and Griggs that in the United States "televison now is the first and most dramatic shaper of public information on the Middle East." They also seem unanimous in declaring that for many years U.S. television, with the single exception of the summer of 1982, has not provided Americans with balanced information on the Middle East in general, and the Israeli-Palestinian dispute in particular.

It is the duty of the U.S. Government to formulate foreign policies which support U.S. interests and which take into consideration traditional American concerns for human rights, self-determination, and political and social justice. However, such policies can neither be adopted nor carried out without strong and continuing public support. How can such essential support be engendered if the principal medium of American public information about the Middle East, over a period of many years, consistently presents an unbalanced picture of events there?

It is a question all concerned Americans must ponder.

TELEVISION ENTERTAINMENT

"To be an Arab in America today is to be an object of contempt and ridicule by television under the guise of entertainment. To me this anti-Arab image on entertainment manifests itself in the politics of America."[27]

Jack Shaheen, 1978

"No other ethnic group in America would willingly submit to what Arabs and Muslims in general have faced in the United States media."[28]

John Cooley, 1981

"No religious, national and cultural group . . . has been so massively and consistently vilified."[29]

Nicholas Von Hoffman, 1981

"We must remember that if one group is under attack we all are under attack. If Jews are not safe, then Arabs are not safe. If Blacks are not safe, then neither are Chicanos, or Poles, or Irish or whatever ethnic group you can think of."[30]

Former Senator James Abourezk, 1980

Entertainment programs are the other side of the television coin. Here, until very recently, Arab-Americans have been surprisingly quiescent in the face of racial slurs and jokes that would have drawn torrents of protest had they been directed at any other ethnic minority in the U.S. Professor Jack Shaheen, of Southern Illinois University at Edwardsville, has followed the treatment of Arabs on U.S. television programs for more than a decade, and has written a book entitled *The TV Arab*, published in 1984 by Bowling Green State University Popular Press. He writes:

"Because Arabs and Arab civilizations are held in contempt by many in Hollywood, many Americans and their political representatives have few if any positive feelings about Arabs. Their impressions are based in part on the clouded image of the TV screen. . . . Stereotyping tends

27. Shaheen, Jack, "The Arab: TV's Most Popular Villain," *Christian Century*, December 13, 1978.
28. Cooley, John, "The News from the Mideast: A Working Approach," *The Middle East Journal*, Autumn 1981, p. 468.
29. Von Hoffman, Nicholas, *Washington Post*, quoted in American Arab Anti-Discrimination Committee (ADC) publication, May 3, 1980.
30. Abourezk, James, Former U.S. Senator, in remarks at founding meeting of ADC, May 3, 1980.

to be self-perpetuating, providing not only information but, as Walter Lippmann wrote, 'pictures in our heads.' These pictures of Arabs reinforce and sharpen viewer prejudices. Television shows are entertainment, but they are also symbols."[31]

"As any television fan knows, a villain is needed in conflicts that pit good against evil. Today's villain is the Arab, simplistically and unfairly portrayed. . . . Depicted as the murderous white-slaver, the dope dealer, the fanatic, or, more sympathetically, as the spoiled rich kid who thinks money can buy love, the television Arab, as seen on entertainment programs, is about as close to being a real Arab as Rudolph Valentino was. . . . To make matters worse, programs stereotyping the Arab are sold in syndication to foreign countries. Thus America's TV image of the Arab is marketed throughout the world."[32]

This picture may change with continued efforts by the American Arab Anti-Discrimination Committee, described elsewhere in this study, and with Dr. Shaheen's work. The former is sensitizing Arab-American viewers, and showing them how to protest specific ethnic slurs directly to the television networks. Dr. Shaheen is sensitizing the networks themselves, through his interviews and correspondence with them and his book on the subject.

CARTOONS

"Mark Twain described Palestine as a bleak, barren land, where even the sky and the landscape are dreary, a country peopled by rather greasy, hook-nosed Arabs, pronounced of course Ay-rabs by Twain's enlightened traveller. . . . In some of the characters of Innocents Abroad *you can almost recognize the ill-intentioned Ay-rabs of today's cartoons of a Bill Mauldin or a Herbert Block."*[33]

John Cooley, 1981

"During my first visit to the Middle East, I became apalled at the unfairness of the picture presented in the American press of the 'dirty street Arab,' or the Arab with knife in his teeth, or the fat and lazy desert shaykh. The cartoonists were and are particularly culpable on this, although the Arab terrorists give them quite enough fodder. Nevertheless, what one saw in the American press at that time, because of a combination of liking for Israel, emotional reaction to the Holocaust, and the limited nature of Arab efforts to present their position, was one of the most grotesque characterizations in journalistic history."[34]

Georgie Anne Geyer, 1980

31. Shaheen, Jack, "The Arab: TV's Most Popular Villain," *Christian Century*, December 13, 1978.
32. Shaheen, Jack, "Do Television Programs Stereotype the Arabs?" *The Wall Street Journal*, October 12, 1979.
33. Cooley, John, "The News From the Mideast: A Working Approach, the *Middle East Journal*, Autumn 1981, p. 468.
34. Geyer, Georgie Anne, "The American Correspondent in the Arab World," in *The American Media and the Arabs*, CCAS, Georgetown University, 1980, p. 67.

Perhaps because they were the greatest sinners against the Arabs, American political cartoonists have demonstrated, even more obviously than the editorial writers of their newspapers, a new readiness to see the Arab side of Middle Eastern problems, particularly since President Sadat's Jerusalem initiative. Nevertheless, the leering, hand-rubbing Arab oil sheikh, with a line of fat veiled wives trailing behind his dirty robes, has become a familiar fixture to American newspaper readers. This is especially true in the nation's capital where, since the creation of Israel, the *Washington Post's* Pulitzer prize-winning cartoonist, Herbert Block, has waged an almost continuous one-man war against the Arabs. His targets included the late Egyptian President Anwar Sadat, even after the latter's journey to Jerusalem. Block's racism is simply the reverse side of a pro-Israel mindset that, as Israel has moved steadily toward the extreme right, has put Block at war with himself – still a liberal and civil rights advocate on domestic matters, but a near-fascist on international matters involving Israel, and ruthless hatchetman when dealing with American political figures who at one time or another have criticized Israeli policies. Another near psychotic for many years when it came to Arabs was Bill Mauldin, the champion of the dogface infantryman in World War II, whose view of what was happening in the Middle East seemed permanently blocked by the Holocaust. Since the 1982 invasion of Lebanon, however, Mauldin's cartoons have caught up with the times. If he is still critical of Arabs, he is also critical of Israel. He is typical of the non-Jewish (and sometimes Jewish as well) U.S. liberals, who, after 1982, became even-handed.

Leonard Davis, a thoughtful lobbyist for Israel in Washington, has described the style of portraying a hook-nosed Arab, either armed to his jagged teeth or fondling the gas pump to which his camel is tethered, as a manifestation of anti-Semitism just as vicious as anything ever directed against the Jews in the U.S. in earlier eras. Thomas Stauffer, a frequent writer on Middle East affairs, and a Harvard University faculty member, cites close parallels in technique between depictions of Arabs by American cartoonists and anti-Jewish cartoons from the Nazi era in Germany.

Meg Greenfield, columnist for *Newsweek* and editorial page editor for the *Washington Post*, describes the "two pillars of our misunderstanding" of the Arab: "One is our own cultural insularity. The other is the general willingness of Arab leaders to let their purposes be defined by the aberrant and extreme." The result, she says, has been "an Arab caricature in our culture." She continues:

"That caricature, incidently, is one of the very few 'ethnic jokes' still indulged in by our cartoonists and stand-up comics. It is somehow considered permissible where comparable jokes are not, and I do not think this is wholly owing to the absence of a big enough Arab-American political constituency to raise hell. There is a dehumanizing, circular process at work here. The caricature dehumanizes. But it is inspired and made acceptable by an earlier dehumanizing influence, namely, an absence of feeling for who the Arabs are and where they have been."[35]

---

35. Greenfield, Meg, "Our Ugly-Arab Complex," *Newsweek*, December 5, 1977, p. 110.

OVERVIEW

In a country as vast as the United States, and a field as diverse as its media, it is difficult to reach clear-cut conclusions as to why the media have not served the public adequately in the case of the Middle East. Well-informed Americans divide on this question, with some attributing the problem to a blatant Zionist media conspiracy, and others attributing it to having Jewish representation at all levels and in all branches of the U.S. media. As evidence of the relative spontaneity of the situation, a look at a specific western U.S. city is instructive. What is atypical about that city, which here must remain unnamed, is the fact that the handful of local partisans of the Arabs have relatively few complaints about media bias. They feel that pro-Arab speakers who appear locally usually receive adequate press coverage.

There is, however, an obvious explanation for the unusual situation in that western city. There is a veteran daily newspaper reporter of partial Lebanese descent there who for many years was a newspaper TV editor and columnist. If the sponsors of a talk on the Middle East asked that reporter's newspaper for coverage, the reporter would personally cover the event even if it meant giving up an evening with the reporter's family. As long as the event itself was newsworthy and the time spent covering it did not detract from the reporter's regular responsibilities, the coverage of pro-Arab speakers was generally, although not always, accepted and printed by the newspaper's editors.

Unfortunately, this heartening example of journalistic freedom and media accessibility to all points of view gives rise to one obvious question. If, in that western city, there is one skilled and experienced reporter who, by an accident of birth, is personally committed to the proposition that visiting pro-Arab spokesmen should receive fair and accurate coverage in the reporter's newspaper, how many similarly skilled and experienced reporters (or editors, or copy-readers) are there in the same city who are equally committed to the full and fair presentation of each pro-Israel program in that city? And what of all the other American cities, where there may be not a single friend of the Arabs, but many friends of Israel, on the local newspaper city desks?

The odds against equal time for the Arab viewpoint are further illustrated by the perfectly logical methods used by one daily newspaper in the same western city for selecting the letters to the editor to print on its editorial pages. To avoid charges of bias, the newspaper prints letters in strict arithmetical proportion to the number received on each side of any given subject. Thus, on a specific issue, if 100 letters supporting Israel's position and 10 letters criticizing it are received, the paper might print the 10 most logical, or literate, or interesting pro-Israel letters, and the best one of the anti-Israel letters. The methods are fair to those who write to the newspaper. In a sense, they also reward industry and keep readers informed of opinion trends in their community. But is it really fair to the uninformed reader who may just want to hear all of the arguments on both sides and then make up his own mind? Given this overwhelming flood of opinion on one side, and only token representation of the other, can the general reader judge U.S. Middle Eastern policies intelligently and constructively? And what happens when not even 10, or not even one, letter presenting the Arab viewpoint is received?

The picture is further complicated by advertising. Every newspaper editor is familiar with the angry letter from a reader so offended by an article that he cancels his subscription. Even on small newspapers, such letters are accepted philosophically. You can't please all of the readers all of the time. But there also are advertisers, or managers of advertising agencies, who echo the same complaints and the same threats. To a small town daily, to lose one or two supermarket chain accounts for a year may be the difference between operating in the black or in the red. For a national magazine, loss of a major account, or alienation of a number of advertising agencies, can have the same effect. There is no question but that advertiser pressure, exercised through the publisher, is a factor in editorial decisions, no matter how vociferously the editor may deny it.

Does this apply at the level of the major U.S. dailies? Let's examine the *Washington Post*. During the summer of 1982 its coverage of the Lebanon invasion was at least as complete and graphic as was the network television coverage. It stood in marked contrast to the coverage in the *New York Times* which, like CBS, seemed somehow to be minimizing or playing down the horrors being perpetrated against a civilian population with American weapons supplied to Israel for defensive purposes only.

The Israelis orchestrated a great deal of protest against the *Washington Post* after that turbulent summer. Subsequently, the *Post* has been remarkably circumspect about its coverage of major Middle Eastern events which reflect badly upon Israel. Some or all of the concerned editors clearly have decided that bad news about Israel does not please their publisher.

Both the *Times* and the *Post* have regular columnists who speak out forcefully on Middle East questions, however. On the *Times*, Anthony Lewis, who is Jewish, has been particularly outspoken about Israeli excesses on the West Bank and in Lebanon. On the *Post* the syndicated Evans and Novak column has been a major channel of accurate information not only on the Middle East, but also on Administration thinking about the problem. (This was true in the Carter as well as the Reagan era.) Syndicated columnists Philip Geyelin, Mary McGrory, Richard Cohen, William Raspberry and Carl Rowan have also on occasion been outspokenly critical of Israel or its actions. But *Post* editorials almost never are.

Nevertheless, an increasing tendency among rank and file journalists, liberal and conservative, to put aside the rose-colored glasses through which so many viewed Israel prior to 1982, seems to have initiated a reaction among die-hard supporters of Israel. This is to found new publications, such as *The National Interest* launched in 1985, or to buy up older, respected U.S. publications. The new owners, while continuing coverage of other areas almost unchanged, openly use the publication to build up Israel, tear down the Arab nations, and to publish laudatory material about U.S. political leaders friendly toward Israel.

The American Jewish Committee many years ago developed its magazine, *Commentary*, into a mainstream U.S. publication, objective on issues outside the Middle East, and openly biased regarding Israel. Old-line readers were surprised, however, when the once highly respected liberal monthly *New Republic* suddenly became more uncritically pro-Israel than *Commentary*. During the Begin era, when *Commentary* expressed grave reservations about where Likud-bloc right-wing extremism was taking Israel and its Jewish backers in the U.S., *New Republic* support remained undiluted.

The story behind the change has been told in an article by Robert Sherrill entitled "The New Regime at the *New Republic* " in the March/April 1976 issue of *Columbia Journalism Review*. Martin Peretz, a wealthy bankroller of left-wing causes, was once a major backer of *Ramparts* magazine, almost the flagship of the New Left campus revolt of the 1960s. When *Ramparts* prepared an editorial critical of Israel, however, Peretz objected vociferously, was faced down by the entire staff, and subsequently withdrew all his money from the magazine. He then purchased the venerable *New Republic* in 1974. Stanley Karnow, foreign editor at the time Peretz took over, told Sherrill how Peretz differed from the previous owner, Gilbert Harrison:

> "Harrison tries to approach things from a very rational viewpoint. Peretz, by contrast, is a very emotional guy. He has certain great passions in life, one of which is Israel. I hate to keep bringing in the Israeli thing, because I consider myself just as pro-Israel, but it colored his whole view of the world."

Since that time, other prestige magazines and newspapers have been taken over by financiers who have made their money in other fields but who seem equally determined to turn their publications into American voices for Israel. Among them are *U.S. News and World Report* and *The Atlantic Monthly*. Meanwhile *Newsweek*, owned by the *Washington Post* Publishing Company, has evolved steadily into an apologist for Israel and an opponent of the Arab states, while the *Washington Post* follows discreetly in the same direction, but at a more dignified and, perhaps because of staff resistance, uncertain pace.

Although eventually such abuse of a familiar masthead discredits the publication, as has been the case with the *New Republic*, it takes many years for the public as a whole to become aware that a publication which has long seemed to be independent has, in fact, been transformed into a voluntary propaganda organ for Israel. Meanwhile, the fact that the actively pro-Israel majority within the Jewish community rapidly becomes aware of the change helps the publication's circulation and advertising receipts.

With the increasing number of wealthy Muslims and Arabs living and working in the United States today, it would seem natural that a media counter lobby would develop. In fact it has not happened and almost certainly will not happen, given the ethnic diversity of that heterogenous community, its divergent political interests, and the fact that many of its members are not yet really integrated into U.S. political life. Therefore, despite events in the Middle East which are forcing individual American news people to reassess their preconceptions and stereotypes, and which to a surprising extent are making them individually even-handed in their approach to the Israeli-Palestinian problem, the coverage as a whole in the U.S. media is not becoming more balanced. Given the trend toward purchases of prestigious U.S. media outlets by extreme partisans of Israel, the picture may even be darkening.

When a delegation of Arab journalists visited the National Association of Arab Americans in 1977, one Arab journalist asked how the NAAA could work effectively in the face of "an American media conspiracy to exclude Arab viewpoints." His NAAA host told him then that there is no conspiracy blocking access to the American media. "The levers are there to be used by anyone who knows how to pull them," the NAAA representative explained. The problem *then* was that there were far too many skilled hands willing to pull those levers for one side, and far too few for the other.

As Israel's situation worsens, however, and its dependence upon the U.S. taxpayer increases, its American partisans are becoming increasingly concerned and, perhaps, desperate. The problem *now* is that the formerly spontaneous efforts of tens of thousands of individual Jewish subscribers, advertisers, reporters, editors and publishers seem gradually to be coalescing into something very much akin to the Zionist media conspiracy which even Arab-Americans once doubted existed.

Zionist Archives

One war, two perspectives: Americans read, saw and heard a great deal in their media about the six-day Arab-Israeli war of 1967. Emphasis was on the efficiency and audacity of Israeli military personnel like those pictured above boarding their tanks. There was far less in U.S. media about the human toll of that same war, paid by young victims like these children crossing into Jordan from the West Bank to an uncertain future in Palestinian refugee camps.

UNRWA

CHAPTER XXXII

The Universities — The Great Fear

"A major effort to counter the anti-Israel campaign is being mounted by AIPAC's Political Leadership Development Program, working with the existing campus pro-Israel infrastructure centered in the B'nai B'rith Hillel Foundations and in cooperation with other organizations. The central purposes of this effort are to restore balance to the campus discussion of the Middle East, and to support the development of America's future pro-Israel leadership."[1]

American-Israel Public Affairs Committee College Guide, 1984

"The Israeli lobby pays special attention to the crucial role played by American colleges and universities in disseminating information and molding opinion on the Middle East. Lobby organizations are concerned not only with academic programs dealing with the Middle East, but also with the editorial policies of student newspapers and with the appearance on campus of speakers critical of Israel. In all three of these areas of legitimate lobby interest and activity, as in its dealings on Capitol Hill, pro-Israeli organizations and activists frequently employ smear tactics, harassment and intimidation to inhibit the free exchange of ideas and views."[2]

Paul Findley, 1985

"When I give a talk at a university or elsewhere, it is common for a group to distribute literature, invariably unsigned, containing a collection of attacks on me spiced with

---

1. Kessler, Jonathan S., and Schwaber, Jeff, *The AIPAC College Guide:Exposing the Anti-Israel Campaign on Campus*, AIPAC, Washington, D.C., 1984, p. vi.
2. Findley, Paul, *They Dare to Speak Out*, Lawrence Hill and Company, Westport, Conn., 1985, p. 180.

'quotes' (generally fabricated) from what I am alleged to have said here and there. I have no doubt that the source is the Anti-Defamation League, and often the people distributing the unsigned literature acknowledge the fact. These practices are vicious and serve to intimidate many people. They are of course not illegal. If the ADL chooses to behave in this fashion, it has a right to do so; but this should also be exposed."[3]

Noam Chomsky, 1985

"Our research and that of the Anti-Defamation League and American Jewish Committee evaluated the materials on the Arab-Israeli conflict as biased, propagandistic and having a strong pro-Arab and anti-Israel slant. Our responsibility in Tucson is part of a national challenge to counter a powerful, well-financed effort to promote the Arab cause while attempting to undermine the legitimacy of Israel. The price of Jewish security has always been vigilance."[4]

Carol Karsch, Co-Chairman,
Tucson Jewish Community Council Community Relations Committee, 1982

"The charges of the Tucson Jewish Community Council are irresponsible and its tactics reprehensible: secret tape recordings; vicious slander and innuendos against the director and outreach coordinator; leaks to the press when it serves its purpose; planting of 'spies' in classes . . ."[5]

Michael Bonine, Executive Secretary, Middle East Studies Association
in 1982 letter to University of Arizona President Henry Koeffler

". . . It's an awful lot like the McCarthy period. And I include not only the Near Eastern Center (controversy) but the whole line taken on Israel."[6]

Professor Jerrold Levy, University of Arizona, 1985

Nowhere are the partisans of the Israelis and the Arabs forced into closer proximity than in American universities, where those who teach Middle Eastern history or political science or Semitic languages must deal with both of these ethnically, linguistically, and culturally related peoples. In a series of off-the-record discussions on the subject with educators of widely divergent views, all of whom were involved in teaching some aspect of modern Middle Eastern history, politics or economics, it came as no surprise to hear each declare vehemently that he or she had not compromised personal academic or intellectual integrity, "despite what others may have done." For those who were Jewish, or who were sympathetic to Israel, or both, the subject usually ended there. For those who were none of those, however, it continued along disturbing lines. Many, perhaps most, declared flatly that they seldom lose the feeling that they are being

3. Findley, Paul, *They Dare to Speak Out*, Lawrence Hill and Company, Westport, Conn., 1985, pp. 184-5.
4. *Ibid.*, p. 231.
5. *Ibid.*, p. 225.
6. *Ibid.*, pp. 236-7.

watched — by students, faculty colleagues, university administrators, and the community at large, including the state legislators or private donors upon whom their universities depend.

Those faculty members who did not have university tenure found the situation highly threatening or inhibiting. They worried that their statements would be reported out of context to their superiors, perhaps via complaints from influential members of the community. Those with tenure were less concerned, and dismissed the possibility that they could be intimidated by such happenings. Nevertheless, some stated that openly expressing their true beliefs on Middle Eastern affairs ultimately could affect, or in some cases had affected, their positions or influence within their university departments.

It is difficult for an outsider to evaluate these comments. Just as a scholar is unlikely to declare that he got ahead by intellectual dishonesty, neither is he likely to attribute not rising higher in his field to personal limitations if there are other possible factors involved. Therefore, it seems best to refer first to a cautious and thorough report prepared in mid-1979 by a distinguished diplomat and scholar in Middle Eastern affairs, Dr. Richard H. Nolte. Dr. Nolte was commissioned by Esso Middle East to visit and assess 18 Middle East study centers, to many of which the company, a division of Exxon, had made support grants.

The centers, all established after 1946, are generally interdisciplinary committees of professors from various departments rather than separate faculties. Only a few give separate degrees. As a rule, their function is to encourage or improve the teaching of Middle Eastern languages and to interest history, political science, or related departments in hiring Middle East specialists. The centers use whatever funds are available to them to assume part or all of the costs of such experts. They also organize lectures and conferences around foreign specialists. Such Middle East centers, Dr. Nolte reported, include some 500 full and part-time faculty members teaching some 16,000 undergraduates, including more than 1,000 majoring in Middle East studies, and about 1,300 graduate students in fields related to the Middle East.

Federal money for such foreign language and area centers has steadily diminished since it reached a peak in the 1969-70 academic year. The Ford Foundation, which devoted millions of dollars in seed money to the creation of study programs and centers for various areas, also considers its role ended. Thus, in a period of academic belt-tightening, and given a tradition of "last in, first out" when the academic environment faces financial stress, Middle East centers are now particularly concerned with finding new sources of funds. They therefore seem unusually vulnerable, via the purse strings, to anyone who seeks to limit or channel their activities. It is against this background that Dr. Nolte wrote the portion of his report concerning the Arab-Israeli dispute. It is quoted in full below:

"Foreign disputes often have echoes on U.S. campuses, sometimes of considerable though temporary vehemence. None has generated as much intensity of feeling over so long a period, however, as the Arab-Israel issue. One might think that the Middle East centers, precisely the focus of those most involved with the Middle East, would be vulnerable to partisan disruptions and that instruction would be impaired. Not so. In every center without exception, the director, faculty and students of every faith and ethnic background were unanimous that in their program, academic objectivity was scrupulously observed, political feelings were excluded from the classroom, relationships were open and friendly, and instruction was in no way impaired.

"Underlying this unexpected unanimity one sensed an almost urgent awareness that the self-interest of each demanded that the scholarly canon be maintained by all. On a few campuses (Arizona, Utah, Texas) the unanimity was there but the sense of necessity was missing; the Arab-Israeli issue seemed remote, the protagonists of Israel were relatively few, other causes appeared more important.

"The apolitical virtue of one's own center, however, was not the whole story. It was freely acknowledged at some universities that center-connected professors exercising their citizen's right outside the academic programs to express extreme views or engage in political activity, had on occasion created difficulties for center directors.

"Again it was not unknown for students and even faculty members unconnected with the Middle East Program (who were better informed) to indulge in invective and noisy discourtesies of one kind or another—shouting down a guest speaker for example.

"Another curiosity: the commonly held view that while the home program was 'clean,' other centers had been politicized, 'Center X has been taken over by the Zionists' or 'Center Y is 100 per cent pro-PLO.' Both untrue, but such views, which have a certain wishful quality about them, seem to have inordinate staying power."[7]

It is with some trepidation that one from outside the academic world takes issue with a report by a scholar on an academic subject. Yet, this writer's own observations after conversations at nine of the same centers visited by Dr. Nolte, and with scholars from three others, differ in one major respect. Comments indeed centered on the suppression of dissent and takeovers by partisan groups at *other* university centers. Nevertheless, many of the persons with whom I spoke were not so sanguine about the situation at their *own* centers or universities. It may be that, talking to a member of their own profession, they were weighing their words carefully, and that, in talking to me, they were blowing off steam. Or it may have been naive of Dr. Nolte to expect his respondents to criticize the situation at their own centers. Such criticism could reflect upon the personal integrity of the respondent himself who, after all, is employed there. Criticism might also jeopardize future funding prospects for the respondent's institution, since Dr. Nolte was compiling information for one potential sponsoring organization and writing a report that very likely would serve as a guide to many others. Perhaps, as a complete outsider conducting totally off-the-record interviews, it was natural that I would hear enough about each interviewee's own institution and colleagues to convince me that a majority of Middle East center faculty members believe that complete freedom of expression on the Arab-Israeli dispute exists at few such centers on American campuses today.

At the University of Michigan, a Jewish graduate student reported that his Arab-American faculty adviser warned him away from a Palestine-oriented and toward an Egypt-oriented dissertation topic so that he would not jeopardize his chances of future unversity employment by acquiring the reputation of being anti-Israel. At a prestigious Ivy League university, an outspoken faculty critic of Zionism, not of Arab descent,

7. Nolte, Richard H., Report for Esso Middle East on "Middle East Centers at U.S. Universities," May, 1979.

asserted that "only my tenure and the conspiracy laws protect me in an institution where more than half of my colleagues are Jewish and where almost no one else, Jew or Gentile, dares to speak frankly about Israel."

Some center directors and faculty members maintain vehemently that they and their colleagues enjoy total freedom of expression on the Arab-Israeli dispute, and that their publications conclusively demonstrate this. I can only report that of the strong partisans of the Israeli cause and the Arab cause with whom I spoke, nearly all of the former report that they are satisfied with the academic environment in which they work, and a majority of the latter report they are not.

A French scholar, Dr. Irine Errera-Hoechstetter, who visited American Middle East study centers in 1970, reported afterward that "political cleavages in the Middle East" have "strong partisan echoes in the U.S." which "put the canon of inter-disciplinarity in jeopardy" and "could result for some of the centers in actual dissolution."[8]

Her prediction was fulfilled at the University of Southern California. This second-largest private university in the United States has graduated large numbers of students from Middle Eastern countries. Members of the leading Saudi Arabian families began going to USC shortly after World War II, and by now there is hardly a government ministry in Riyadh that could not organize a USC alumni association chapter. Some years ago, the University received a $1 million endowment from the late King Faisal of Saudi Arabia for a chair in Middle Eastern studies. The gift was generous, but not inordinately so for a private university that played a pioneering role in educating many of the most prominent leaders of Saudi Arabia.

In 1978, however, after a vote by the University Board of Trustees approving the organization of a Middle East Studies Center, in which two members of the Board abstained and one vote negatively, a firestorm of criticism broke out over the University when one of the dissenting board members took his objections to the press. Leaders of the large Los Angeles Jewish community, and the *Los Angeles Times*, focused their criticism on the center director, who had held the King Faisal chair since its founding. They charged that his dual role as Center Director and chairman of its fund-raising arm, the Middle East Center Foundation, in effect gave him—and possibly through him, the Saudis—undue influence over University programs. Members of the University faculty charged that the Center would usurp faculty prerogatives and compromise academic integrity. The Securities and Exchange Commission launched an investigation to determine under what circumstances funds for the foundation had been solicited from American companies, and whether the donors had received the impression that the size of their donations might influence the degree of cooperation their representatives received in Saudi Arabia. The University subsequently dissolved the fund-raising Middle East Center Foundation and returned all the contributions it had received to the donor companies. The Center continued to exist on paper, but no longer in fact.

Whatever the merits of the various allegations, one fact impresses even the uninformed. The Center and its fund-raising foundation were structured almost identically with other similar semi-autonomous organizations at private universities in the United

8. Nolte, Richard H., Report for Esso Middle East on "Middle East Centers at U.S. Universities," May, 1979, pp. 22-3.

States. The agreement of the heavily-endowed Annenberg School of Communications with USC was the model for the Middle East Center's agreement with the University. But the Annenberg School continues its existence on the same campus without community, faculty, or media concern about its funding, programs, or effect on academic integrity.

Similar disputes have brought controversy to other universities. An article entitled "Arab Money and the Universities," published in the American Jewish Committee periodical *Commentary* in April, 1979, cited Middle East programs that had fallen through at MIT, the University of Alabama, and the University of Pennsylvania. The magazine also pointedly equated a Duke University program in Islamic and Arabian Development Studies, which had received a $20,000 grant from Saudi Arabia, with the program discontinued at USC.

A Swarthmore College alumnus, Former Assistant Secretary of State Willis Armstrong, after his retirement had become secretary treasurer of the Triad Foundation established by Saudi entrepreneur Adnan Kashoggi. In 1977 he proposed a $590,000 Triad Foundation grant, to be paid over three years, to Swarthmore and two other prestigious small colleges, Bryn Mawr and Haverford. The three sister schools were all located in affluent Philadelphia suburbs and they already shared a Russian studies program.

The Triad proposal was to use one quarter of the grant to finance a rotating professorship and the remainder to expand the colleges' Middle East book collections, strengthen existing Middle East-related courses, and provide scholarships for needy Arab foreign students. The three colleges would have complete freedom to choose the visiting professors, the books to be added to their collections, and the students to admit.

A Swarthmore political science professor, James Kurth, contacted the American Jewish Committee (AJC) about the proposal, however. What followed was a story not unlike dramas acted out at the other universities cited above. What is unique is the fact that a confidential memorandum outlining AJC strategy has become available. Excerpts from it are quoted in Former Congressman Paul Findley's *They Dare to Speak Out: People and Institutions Confront Israel's Lobby* and are reproduced below:

"Professor Kurth brought these facts to our attention and asked for AJC help in blocking the implementation of the program. We discussed the matter and agreed that it would make most sense to try to kill the program through quiet, behind-the-scenes talks with college officials, before 'going public;' and that protests against the program need not be based solely or particularly on Jewish opposition to Arab influence. Instead, we thought it should be possible to generate concern about the program based on its sponsorship by Khashoggi and its evident public relations aims, not appropriate for colleges of the stature of these three schools . . . I immediately sent Professor Kurth a folder of information on Khashoggi, the Triad Corporation and the Triad Foundation which was compiled by the AJC Trends Analysis Division. I also notified the AJC Philadelphia chapter of these developments so that they could be in touch with Professor Kurth to assist in getting some local Philadephia Jewish community leaders, alumni of the schools or otherwise associated with them, to raise questions about the proposed grant."

Subsequently an article appeared in the Swarthmore student newspaper, falsely charging that Khashoggi "was under indictment by a federal grand jury." On the evening of the day the article appeared, a petition was circulated in the Swarthmore College dining hall referring to Khashoggi as a "munitions monger." At almost the same moment the Philadelphia Jewish Federation delivered a letter to the Swarthmore College president.

"It all happened in about eighteen and a half minutes," one Swarthmore observer subsequently told Findley. "It was like the Great Fear sweeping across France during the French Revolution."

Articles in the Philadelphia press and the student newspapers of the other two colleges followed. The Jewish Community Relations Council, the American Jewish Committee and the Anti-Defamation League of B'nai B'rith issued a joint statement, concentrating on Kashoggi as the source rather than the merits of the academic and scholarship program itself. Even Congressman James Scheuer, a Jewish Swarthmore alumnus, called the Swarthmore College President demanding the telephone numbers of members of the College's Board of Managers so that he could contact them. Haverford, sensitive to the 'munitions monger' charge, was the first to bow out. Next was Swarthmore. Bryn Mawr, however, continued to pursue the grant and its President, Harris Wofford, a former Peace Corps Director, asked in the Bryn Mawr/Haverford student newspaper:

"Wouldn't it be prejudice to accept a donation from Lockheed, for example, which *was* found guilty of improper practices, while refusing it from Triad, whose donor (contrary to the Swarthmore *Phoenix's* allegation) has not been indicted let alone convicted of anything?"

By this time, however, Adnan Kashoggi apparently had had enough. He gave up the foundation and with it the offer to the three colleges. Sadly, Triad Foundation Officer Willis Armstrong wrote to the president of Swarthmore College:

"Swarthmore seems to me to have taken leave of its principles and to have yielded all too quickly to partisan and xenophobic pressure from a group skilled in the manipulation of public opinion. I am at a loss to think how the United States can promote peace in the Middle East unless we can gain Arab confidence in our understanding and objectivity. For a Quaker institution to turn its back on an opportunity to contribute to this understanding is profoundly depressing."[9]

Ira Silverman, who took credit for orchestrating the entire campaign, has the last word in the American Jewish Committee's secret memorandum:

"Our participation was not widely known on the campuses and not reported in the public press, as we wished. This is a good case history of how we can be effective in working with colleges to limit Arab influence on campuses — although in view of the school's Quaker background and Khashoggi's cloudy reputation as an arms merchant, its happy ending is not likely to be replicated easily in other cases."[10]

(An interesting postscript is that the American University in Washington, D.C., a chronically under-endowed institution in sharp competition for students with a number

---

9. Findley, Paul, *They Dare to Speak Out*, Lawrence Hill and Company, Westport, Conn., 1985, p. 194.
10. *Ibid.*, p. 195.

of other major four-year universities in the national capital and adjacent Maryland and Virginia suburbs, has solicited and received a major endowment from Adnan Kashoggi to fund a University sports center. Kashoggi funding, applied to sports rather than to upgrading Middle Eastern area and language studies, became welcome rather than menacing.)

Commentary saved its severest criticism for Georgetown University, which in 1977 accepted a gift of $750,000 from Libya to endow a chair at the Washington, D.C. Catholic institution's Center for Contemporary Arab Studies, a grant of $50,000 from Iraq, and other donations from Saudi Arabia, Egypt, Qatar, Jordan, the United Arab Emirates, and the Sultanate of Oman. Columnist Art Buchwald publicly accused the University of accepting "blood money from one of the most notorious regimes (Libya) in the world today." In a subsequent exchange, he wrote: "I don't see why the PLO has to have a PR organization when Georgetown is doing all their work for them." After sustained public criticism, a new President of the University, Father Timothy Healey, returned both the Iraqi and Libyan contributions over the public protests of the Center Director and his deputy. They had originally solicited the donations with the full approval of the University's previous president. At no time were there serious allegations that the funds from either country came with strings attached.

Ironically, in subsequent outside evaluations of Georgetown University, the Center for Contemporary Arab Studies has been cited for excellence in its field and is now one of the University's major areas of concentration. Its faculty members were instrumental in helping another Catholic institution, Villanova University in Pennsylvania, establish the only other U.S. university center devoted exclusively to Arab studies. That center, directed by Father Kail Ellis, an Augustinian priest of Lebanese descent, was also the subject of an organized pressure campaign, which Villanova University successfully overcame. Of that campaign, Professor John Ruedy, Director of Studies at the Georgetown Center, said:

"It was the Zionist issue, but nobody said it. I could tell because I'd been there before. The first line of opposition is on academic grounds. But when you get around all these and answer all the questions, then they bare their fangs and say, 'This is anti-Israel, This is anti-Semitic, and it will be against the interests of the University. And we have to relate to Jewish donors,' and so on. This is precisely what happened at Villanova."[11]

Demonstrating that no issue is too mundane or routine to ignite the glowing coals of campus Middle East partisanship, a dispute on a faculty appointment at the University of Texas was catapulted into the pages of the *Wall Street Journal* even before the local Texas newspapers had heard of it. The University's well-funded Middle East Studies Center had offered to pay half the costs of a jointly-approved appointment to the history department, so that the department could offer courses in modern Arab history. When the Middle East Center did not approve on academic grounds an Israeli-born candidate who did not have a Ph.D., what seemed a routine exercise of the Center's prerogative

---

11. Findley, Paul, *They Dare to Speak Out*, Lawrence Hill and Company, Westport, Conn., 1985, p. 202.

was suddenly escalated, via the press, into a confrontation. Charges of discrimination were leveled against the Center's acting director. The ultimate decision was to hire two persons, one at history department and one at Middle East Center expense, to handle what administrators from both the department and the Center agree is less than a normal teaching load for even one instructor.

The longest-running academic dispute, however, took place in Tucson, Arizona, focused on the outreach program of the University of Arizona's Near East Center. It was the 1958 National Defense Education Act (NDEA) that made possible the federal funding of university centers offering languages judged critical to national defense and foreign policy. In 1976, new guidelines provided that NDEA centers would be required to spend at least 15 per cent of their federal funds on "outreach" to share their language and area expertise with the general public. Although these included lectures and workshops for faculty and students at the University, in general outreach was expected to comprise lectures, concerts, and art exhibits for the public at large, adult education classes, workshops for businessmen, and curriculum development and in-service training for teachers in area schools.

In 1980 representatives of the Tucson Jewish Community Council (TJCC) visited the chairman of the University's Oriental Studies Department to charge that its Near East Center Director, Dr. Ludwig Adamec, and his Outreach Coordinator, Sheila Scoville, "had an anti-Israel bias."

The subsequent persecution of these two educators, with active participation and perhaps even the complicity of the local press, continued for more than three years and was so vicious and patently unfair that it is hard to believe that fair-minded Americans would allow it to continue, much less participate in it. Yet, year after year as the battle continued, those who cooperated in harassment of the University as a whole and the center in particular received annual TJCC "man and woman of the year" awards.

Dr. Jerrold Levy, a Jewish professor at the University, has tried to convey the atmosphere which made it possible for the TJCC "investigation" to continue for so long, despite the fact that University officials and finally an outside committee looked into and rejected charge after charge:

"I don't depend on Jewish funds for my academic work or for my livelihood. It's the people in the professional classes, doctors, lawyers, who feel intimidated. The friends I have within the (Reform) congregation are very, very close to the chest on political matters. I know a professional man who is very liberal, but now that he's got a well-established business, he's not coming out against the TJCC. There are some concerned people who are not saying anything. We're up against a very well-organized group of co-religionists here . . . It's an awful lot like the McCarthy period. And I include not only the Near Eastern Center (controversy) but the whole line taken on Israel. It's an awful lot like Germany in the thirties too. It's a lot like what we Jews have been yelling about, that we want to be free from. And then who starts doing it again? It's a very scary business." [12]

12. Findley, Paul, *They Dare to Speak Out*, Lawrence Hill and Company, Westport, Conn., 1985, pp. 236-7.

Although the University was at first almost unduly compliant, suspending the work of the outreach program until the charges could be investigated, gradually officials at the several levels of the University involved took increasingly firm stands.

The TJCC in turn contacted Arizona Congressmen, seeking to intimidate the University administration, and the U.S. Department of Education, seeking to stop funding for the Near East Center. The vice chairman of the TJCC allegedly told members of the University's Department of Judaic Studies that Dr. Adamec was a "member of the German Wehrmacht during World War II." He told a University official that Adamec had been "arrested as a Nazi."

It was true that Adamec had been arrested as a teenager. But the Nazis had done the arresting, throwing him into jail for trying to escape from his native Austria into Switzerland. He had spent the remainder of World War II in a Nazi concentration camp.

A four-member investigating committee, made up of Middle East scholars from other universities and approved jointly by the University and the TJCC, issued a report stating in part:

"The TJCC has exercised its right to question the University and the University has responded fully and adequately. The TJCC is entitled to disagree with the University position and to make that disagreement known. To insist, however, that the case can be closed only after the University takes actions in line with the TJCC demands is to cross a clearly demarcated line. It is to go beyond the legitimate right to question and to be informed, moving into the illegitimate demand to control and to censor."[13]

Among the TJCC charges against Sheila Scoville was one that she had given teachers a map of the Middle East that did not include Israel. In fact it was a map of the Ottoman Empire, which had ceased to exist 30 years before Israel was created.

Because the TJCC was accusing her of anti-Israel bias, Scoville confined her Middle East survey course for teachers to the historical and cultural background of the Middle East, avoiding the post-World War II period entirely. This did not provide relief. The TJCC then complained that she had redesigned the course because she did not wish to acknowledge the existence of Israel. When all charges concerning her professionalism broke down under scrutiny of the University and the committee of outside scholars, the TJCC tried to make Scoville's personal life the subject of the inquiry.

The University belatedly took the kind of strong stand that might better have been taken at the beginning. In October, 1982, Robert Gimello, head of the Oriental Studies Department, wrote:

It happens that both scholars deny the accusations in question, but more important than the truth or falsity of the accusations is the fact that they are irrelevant and out of order. Members of our department are entitled to whatever political views they may choose to hold . . . The University in any free and open society is by design an arena of dispute and contention, and it does not cease to be such an arena when it engages in community outreach . . . For all of these reasons, we have resolved not to close our outreach program. Neither will we discard any of the books we use in that program, or keep them under lock and key, or burn them."[14]

---

13. Findley, Paul, *They Dare to Speak Out*, Lawrence Hill and Company, Westport, Conn., 1985, p. 216.

14. Ibid, p. 216.

If the University statement awarded the moral victory to the academics, nevertheless the campaign against them left the University profoundly changed. Dr. Adamec resigned as Director of the Near East Center and Ms. Scoville resigned as Coordinator of the Outreach Program. At a Middle East Studies Association meeting she remarked:

"The other coordinators think they can work with these pressure groups. My experience is you simply cannot. I fear that the future outreach programs inevitably will take on a political bias and cease to serve educational purposes."

The Middle East Studies Association, the major U.S. professional organization for educators in Middle East subjects (which the TJCC also sought to investigate), was able to join the battle on the side of the University, and is still headquartered in Tucson.

But the TJCC also claims victory, pointing to Adamec's voluntary resignation and Scoville's self-imposed limitations on controversial subject matter. It is a strange kind of victory, however. Where no anti-Semitism existed, much surely has been created among observers of the persistent and unfair personal vendetta conducted by the TJCC.

It is ironic, too, that two of the bitterest engagements in American academia's re-enactment of the Middle East's endless war have taken place at the Universities of Arizona and Texas, both cited in the Nolte Report as campuses where "the Arab-Israeli issue seemed remote."

Given the cultural differences between the Arab countries and the U.S., and the sensitivities of the American Jewish community, it is obvious that no American university should accept Middle Eastern gifts casually. If they are from American companies doing business in the Middle East, it is appropriate to look into the circumstances under which the donation was solicited. If the gift comes directly from a Middle Eastern country, the expectations and conditions of the donor, if any, should be carefully examined, frankly dealt with, and fully explained to the university community. That done, however, there should be no further stigma attached to a university faculty honestly striving to familiarize American students with a critically important and little-understood part of the world.

There are many more students of Hebrew in the United States than there are students of Arabic. There are many more students enrolled in courses on various aspects of modern Israel than there are in courses on the Arab countries. And for every donation to an American university by an Arab country or by an individual who may support an Arab cause, there surely are many sizable donations from Jewish institutions or wealthy Americans who enthusiastically support Israel. Yet there is no record of public protest or university refusal of any such gift for Hebrew, Judaic, or similar studies. Equal treatment for gifts to strengthen scholarship and knowledge about all parties to the Arab-Israeli dispute would be the best evidence that true freedom of inquiry into and expression about that dispute exists on American campuses.

"SAM and DELILAH"

RELAX, HONEY— REMEMBER, I'M YOUR ONLY TRUE FRIEND IN THE MIDDLE EAST!

Reprinted by permission: Tribune Media Services.

ISRAEL'S ECONOMY
WEST   BANK

Copyright, 1985, Ranan Lurie. Reprinted with permission of Univeral Press Syndicate.

THE PALESTINIAN ARAB MOST DEFINITELY HAS A STAKE IN OUR FUTURE

Reprinted by permission: Tribune Media Services

U.S. ASSISTANCE   U.S. LOANS & GIFTS
APOLOGIES FOR SPYING AGAINST U.S.

SO... WE'RE STILL BUDDIES, RIGHT?

ISRAEL

Danziger in The Christian Science Monitor © 1985 TCSPS

BUY OURS NOT THEIRS   DIET

ISRAELI GOVT. ADMITS HIRING SPIES IN U.S.

"Are we paying for this with foreign aid or private donations?"

By permission of Bill Mauldin and WIL-JO ASSOCIATES, INC.

ISRAEL SPY CASE

Wailing Wall

By Tony Auth. Reprinted by permission of Universal Press Syndicate.

For many years Israel could do no wrong and the Arab states could do little right so far as American cartoonists were concerned. Since 1982, however, cartoons critical of Israel are being turned out by some leading U.S. cartoonists, though few are picked up by clients other than the cartoonist's home newspaper.

CHAPTER XXXIII

Congress – For Sale or Rent

"Don't look to Congress to act. All we know is how to increase aid to Israel."
Representative Lee Hamilton, (D-IN) 1984

"The death of U.S. Senator Henry Jackson has been one of the greatest losses Israel has suffered during the past 10 years . . . He was a one-man Israeli Army."
Editorial in Israeli newspaper Yediot Aharonot, November 9, 1983

". . . It is no overstatement to say that AIPAC has effectively gained control of virtually all of Capitol Hill's action on Middle East policy. Almost without exception, House and Senate members do its bidding, because most of them consider AIPAC to be the direct Capitol Hill representative of a political force that can make or break their chances at election time."[1]
Paul Findley, Former Representative, (R-IL) 1985

"Long ago I decided that I'd vote for anything AIPAC wants . . . I don't need the trouble (pro-Israel lobbyists) can cause. I made up my mind I would get and keep their support . . ."[2]
Representative Clarence D. Long, (D-MD) 1982

---

1. Findley, Paul, *They Dare to Speak Out*, Lawrence Hill and Company, Westport, Conn., 1985, p. 25.
2. *Ibid.*, p. 38.

"There are a lot of American Jews with lots of money who learned long ago that they can achieve influence far beyond their numbers by making strategic donations to candidates . . . No Arab population here plays such a powerful role."[3]

Carl Rowan, 1981

"Through a combination of persistence and persuasion, we were able to provide Israel with an increase in military-economic aid in one year alone which is the equivalent of almost three years of contributions by the national United Jewish Appeal."[4]

Representative Stephen J. Solarz, (D-NY) 1980

"What is tragic is that so many Jewish people misconstrue criticism of Israel as anti-Jewish or anti-Semitic . . . It is easier to criticize Israeli policy in the Knesset than it is in the U.S. Congress."[5]

Representative Mervyn M. Dymally, (D-CA) 1985

"I am a supporter of Israel and Israel's right to exist, and I have the same sensitivity to the people in the diaspora who are the people of Palestine. I continue to support the right of the Palestinian people to a homeland today."[6]

Representative Walter Fauntroy (D-DC), 1985

"We've got to overcome the tendency of the Jewish community in America to control the actions of Congress and force the President and the Congress not to be evenhanded (in the Middle East)."

Representative Paul N. (Pete) McCloskey, (R-CA) July 7, 1981

"At the State Department we used to predict that if Israel's prime minister should announce that the world is flat, within 24 hours Congress would pass a resolution congratulating him on the discovery."[7]

Donald Bergus, Former U.S. Ambassador to Sudan, 1985

If some Presidents have abdicated their responsibility for formulating sensible U.S. Middle East policy, and many journalists have failed in their responsibility to explain Middle East realities, virtually all sitting Congressmen have abandoned any pretext of balance in the Middle East. As one Congressman in late 1985 told a Pentagon expert who was explaining the need to sell U.S. arms to Jordan, if that country was expected to play a constructive role in the peace process, "the facts don't matter."

---

3. Findley, Paul, *They Dare to Speak Out*, Lawrence Hill and Company, Westport, Conn., 1985, p. 67.
4. *Ibid.*, p. 70.
5. *Ibid.*, p. 77.
6. *Ibid.*, pp. 63-4.
7. *Ibid.*, p. 27.

The Congressional bias for Israel has a long history, but it was not always so evident in the 1950s when Israel had other sources of arms such as the USSR, France, and Britain, and other sources of economic assistance, such as West German reparation payments. But as Israel's political, military and economic situation has worsened, its dependence upon the United States has increased to the point where it quite literally receives all of the privileges, but assumes none of the responsibilities, of a 51st state.

Congress in the 1980s provides more than $1,000 per Jewish Israeli per year in military and economic grants; transfers to Israel military equipment that is in short supply even for U.S. units; and, by helping Israel build up aircraft and weapons production, literally takes skilled jobs away from Americans to provide employment for Israelis.

All of this is done, year after year, despite open and acknowledged Israeli violations of U.S. law and of the terms under which the grants are made. For example, Israel is prohibited by U.S. law from using American weapons for anything other than defensive purposes. Yet it has used U.S. aircraft in offensive strikes as far from its borders as Baghdad and Tunis. It has rained U.S. bombs and shells by the thousands on the villages, towns and cities of Lebanon. It has repeatedly dropped extraordinarily deadly U.S. cluster bombs, capable of killing every living thing in an area as large as a football field, over Palestinian refugee camps. Israel has continued to spend vast sums, made possible by generous U.S. aid, on Jewish settlements the U.S. calls illegal in the occupied West Bank. It has violated international law in all of the territories it has occupied, and it has ignored the human rights of Arabs within its own borders and within all of the occupied territories. Yet Congress has not investigated any of these violations, reported regularly by U.S. journalists and diplomats, and often acknowledged by Israel itself.

Admiral Thomas Moorer, former Chairman of the Joint Chiefs of Staff, the highest military position in the U.S. Government, illustrates Congressional squeamishness about incurring Israeli wrath by contrasting its handling of the North Korean seizure of the *USS Pueblo* with the death of one crew member, and the Israeli attack on a sister ship, the *USS Liberty*, with the deaths of 34 crew members:

> "When the *Pueblo* was seized by the North Koreans, I spent weeks over on the Hill testifying about the *Pueblo* in the most minute detail. But nothing like that's ever been done for the *Liberty* . . . The difference in the way these two events were handled is mind boggling."[8]

Instead of investigating Israeli transgressions of the laws Congress itself has enacted, most members of Congress annually rubber stamp assistance for Israel at a level which is contrary to the interests and wishes of a majority of their own constituents and which privately many, perhaps most, members of Congress deplore. It is clear, therefore, that the methods used by Israel's U.S. lobby to assure compliance with Israel's demands are as effective as any ever devised by any lobby in U.S. history.

As discussed in an earlier chapter, the American Jewish community's power over

---

8. Moorer, Admiral Thomas H., Chairman of the Joint Chiefs of Staff, 1971-74 and Chief of Naval Operations, 1967-70, from remarks at December 11, 1985 press conference at National Press Club, *The Washington Report on Middle East Affairs*, December 30, 1985, p. 7.

Congress is wielded primarily through the American Israel Public Affairs Committee (AIPAC), Israel's principal lobbying organization, with more than 50,000 members of its own, and with representatives of most U.S. major national Jewish organizations on its board. However, several of the other national Jewish organizations which once were the principal pro-Israel lobbying groups still assist in the effort. These include the Anti-Defamation League of B'nai B'rith, the American Jewish Committee, and the Conference of Presidents of Major American Jewish Organizations. These groups have always resorted to a combination of carrot and stick to maintain their power over Congressmen. In recent years the carrot has grown enormously in size, and so has the stick.

Perhaps the best known early victim of the stick was Senator William Fulbright. When, in the 1960s, as Chairman of the Senate Foreign Relations Committee, he began to express doubts openly about the wisdom of a no-questions, no-strings, no-obligations policy of increasing aid to Israel, and his committee held hearings on the pressure groups seeking to influence U.S. Middle East policies, he was targeted for defeat by the several Jewish organizations then comprising the lobby. The campaign took two tracks, both indirect, because Senator Fulbright was at the time greatly admired by American liberals, including many U.S. Jews, for his strong stands against increasing U.S. involvement in Vietnam and other examples of what he called "the arrogance of power."

One track in the campaign to deprive him of his Senate seat was an orchestrated series of press attacks, particularly in the *New York Times*. Such attacks almost never referred to the Senator's concerns about the Middle East. Instead they pounced upon any comments the Senator might make which could weaken him either with his own conservative border-state constituents or with the national liberal establishment. Thus in the time of highly emotional national debate that preceded and accompanied enactment of U.S. civil rights legislation and enforcement by U.S. courts of that legislation, the *New York Times* carefully reported to its national audience anything Senator Fulbright said during his campaigning in Arkansas that could mark him as a hypocrite, adapting to provincial if not downright racist sentiments at home. Similarly, speeches made to groups like the World Affairs Council in New York were carefully culled for "internationalist" sentiments which could be passed via wire service reports to Arkansas newspapers. The point was to tarnish the Senator's national stature and at the same time convince Arkansas voters that their Senator had lost touch with the desires and interests of his constituents and had become more cosmopolitan in outlook than Arkansas voters might desire. The Senator's defeat by Arkansas Governor Dale Bumpers became one of the lobby's first big triumphs, but his stature as a revered elder statesman mitigated against public gloating over his defeat outside trusted, well-defined, pro-Israel circles.

Perhaps the lobby's next big trophy was Representative Paul Findley, a hard-working and highly intelligent and idealistic Republican who had served his Illinois constituency for 22 years. Findley had become involved in Middle East affairs by chance when he traveled personally to the People's Republic of Southern Yemen to bring back safely an imprisoned constituent. In several months of seeking Arab support for his one-man assault on the most pro-Russian, anti-American country in the Arab World, Findley became acquainted with Syrian President Al-Assad and PLO Chairman Yassir Arafat. Afterward, with full encouragement from both the Ford and Carter administrations, Findley tried to parley his success in South Yemen into a personal effort to make both the Syrian President and the PLO leader less extremist and more cooperative with U.S. peace efforts. Although he failed with Assad and enjoyed only partial success with Arafat, Findley had broken the lobby's unwritten but strictly-enforced rule for Congressmen. Only Jewish Congressmen are to become deeply involved in Middle East matters. The lobby warned Findley to desist. When he didn't, it openly set out to get him. It took six years. The first two attempts to find and subsidize a Republican who could beat him in the primaries and/or a Democrat who could beat him in the general election failed. After the re-apportionment of Illinois congressional constituencies so that Findley's district no longer included essential Republican areas or even one of the two towns in which he had lived, however, the lobby mounted a major effort. It flooded the constituency with Jewish student and housewife volunteers who went to Southern Illinois to go from door to door canvassing for Findley's opponent, and it collected immense amounts of out-of-state money for Findley's opponent. The third try was successful when Findley lost by 1.407 votes, less than one per cent of the total cast, in 1982.

Like a local pool hall hustler, the lobby began dramatically calling its shots in advance. It proclaimed that it would "get" Representative Paul (Pete) McCloskey in 1982 if he sought a Senate seat from California. McCloskey, a much-decorated Marine veteran of World War II and Korea, had opposed the war in Vietnam long before it became a campus crusade, and had beaten former child film star Shirley Temple Black in the Republican primaries for a seat in the House of Representatives. After that he had set out with a distinctive brand of personal courage and commitment to principle to, among other things, restore an even-handed balance to U.S. Middle East policies. Among his many proposals to do this was one that the U.S. reduce its annual economic assistance to Israel by exactly the amount Israel was spending each year on its illegal West Bank settlements.

As it mounted a truly massive campaign against the liberal California Republican, the lobby solicited pro-Israel donations from all over the United States for McCloskey's Republican opponent in the California Senatorial primary, San Diego Mayor Pete Wilson. Although McCloskey carried Northern California, Wilson won in more populous and conservative Southern California and, having secured the Republican nomination, went on to win the Senate seat in the general election. McCloskey went back to practicing law in the San Francisco bay area, where he has been subjected to personal and professional harassment from extremist members of California's powerful Jewish community.

In the 1984 general elections the lobby publicly targeted two powerful Senatorial "enemies." One was North Carolina Senator Jesse Helms who, as a vociferous critic of all U.S. non-military foreign aid, was probably the only long-term member of the Senate who had never cast what the lobby would call a "positive" vote for Israel. The other lobby target was Illinois Republican Charles Percy who, as Chairman of the Senate Foreign Relations Committee, had voted for Israel more than he had voted against it, but who often took an independent attitude in his comments about Palestinian rights, and Israeli violations of them, and who had voted in 1981 to approve the Administration's sale of advanced F-16 aircraft to Saudi Arabia. It was this vote that was cited repeatedly by the lobby in an extraordinary effort centered on written appeals from Jewish businessmen, movie stars and financiers to raise immense amounts of money all over the United States for Percy's opponent, former Illinois Representative Paul Simon.

That 1984 campaign also revealed how the carrot had grown. Formerly, pro-Israel Senators and Representatives could be rewarded adequately through speaking engagements for sevices rendered to Israel. Jewish civic or religious organizations would invite the Congressman who was to be assisted. If he wished, AIPAC writers would prepare his speech for him. If he was busy, they would even deliver it for him. But in any case he received a $1,000 or $5,000 or even greater speaking fee. This was useful for rewarding friends but unwieldy when it came to punishing enemies. In any case, it was so abused by the pro-Israel and many other lobbies that Congressional ethics committees felt forced to impose limits on the amount of outside income that a Congressman could earn.

As a direct reaction to this limitation on Congressional earnings, and to a rule that an individual can donate only $1,000 to a candidate, an entirely new means of raising money for Congressional campaigns was devised. It is called the political action committee (PAC). A PAC, incorporated as a non-profit fund-raising and fund-dispensing organization, could provide up to $10,000 each to an unlimited number of candidates. A wealthy donor, who by law can give no more than $1,000 to any single candidate, can give up to $5,000 each to any number of PACs. By using enough PACs advocating a particular point of view, that donor can donate as much as he wishes to the candidates agreeing with the point of view.

By 1984, the lobby was working openly not just to defeat Percy and Helms, but also to reward all of the faithful friends of Israel on appropriations, military and foreign affairs committees, and punish "enemies" of Israel on those committees by funding the campaigns of their challengers.

The results were mixed. The lobby spent three times as much as it did on any other House contest on the campaign of Maryland Democrat Clarence (Doc) Long. As chairman of the House Appropriations Committee, Long boasted that he could and did get Israel whatever economic aid it asked for. He was beaten by Helen Delich Bentley, who had built up sizable local support through years of service in Baltimore and Maryland politics. Despite massive Jewish PAC and individual donations to North Carolina Governor Jim Hunt, he too was beaten by Jesse Helms. Safely back in the Senate, however, Helms went to great lengths to mend his fences with Israel, literally recanting or contradicting everything he had ever said about the Middle East prior to 1984.

Pro-Israel PACs provided more than $140,000 for the successful campaign of Senator Carl Levin of Michigan. "He's always voted for money for Israel and that's important for pro-Israel PACs," Gordon Kerr, Levin's administrative assistant, explained. "He's a member of armed services."

The lobby's biggest triumph, however, was the defeat of Percy, who after setting up a law practice in Washington, D.C., told an audience in the national capital:

"The day after the election last year, I said that if I had known that my vote in support of the sale of AWAC's or my criticism of the Israeli invasion of Lebanon would have determined whether I was re-elected, I would not have changed my vote or a single word of my criticism of the invasion . . . The administration has submitted to Congress preliminary notification of its intention to sell arms to Jordan. But before the notification was even received on the Hill, more than 70 of my former colleagues had signed a resolution opposing any arms sales to Jordan. I'm not in the business of second guessing my former colleagues, but I must say that in this instance, more than 70 of them are wrong."[9]

Edward Roeder, whose Capitol Hill-based Sunshine News Services publishes an annual directory of political-action committees entitled *PACs Americana*, is not a specialist in Middle East affairs. Prior to the 1984 elections, however, in the course of routinely identifying and writing a description of every PAC in the United States for his all-inclusive directory, he was puzzled by a rapidly-growing group of PACs that seemed not to fit into any of the three most common categories. Normally a PAC is established to serve the purposes of a company like Johnson's Wax or Westinghouse, a registered industrial or business lobby like Real Estate Mortgage Bankers, avocado growers, or the National Rifle Association, or a cause like environmental protection or family planning. Its purpose is defined by its title. Every now and then, however, Roeder would come across well-heeled, vaguely-defined PACs with non-descriptive titles such as National Political Action Committee, Joint Action Committee for Political Affairs, Citizens Organized Political Action Committee, Roundtable PAC, Desert Caucus, Florida Congressional Committee, or San Franciscans for Good Government. At the same time he was struck by an omission. Suddenly, after 1983, there were *no* PACs that mentioned Israel, Judaism, Zionism or the Middle East in their titles. A PAC which had been founded as "Texans for a Sound Middle East Policy" had changed its name in 1983 to TxPAC. It wasn't hard to connect the disappearance of Israel-related PACs to the sudden proliferation of PACs with no visible affiliation or cause. Telephone calls bore out the connection.

Robert Golder, President of the "Delaware Valley PAC," explained to Roeder that "This PAC is a group of American Jewish people working for a stronger American position on Israel." He also explained why his PAC was contributing $10,000 each to the election opponents of Senators Helms and Percy:

"This guy (Helms) has never voted for Israel. Whether it's foreign aid or airplanes or economic aid or grants, he votes against Israel . . . As president of a PAC, what matters to me is that as a Senator with a vote, he is 100 per cent against Israel and we are interested in helping the state of Israel."[10]

Golder also told Roeder that "Senator Percy is a very powerful Senator . . . Unlike Helms, he is a moderate, and people listen when he talks . . . He has not been 100

9. Percy, Charles, "An Opportunity for Peace," remarks delivered September 27, 1985 at the Annual Conference of the Middle East Institute, reported in *The Washington Report on Middle East Affairs*, October 7, 1985, pp.5-6.
10. Roeder, Edward, *Financing the Elections of the 99th Congress: Pro-Israel PACs*, Sunshine Press, Washington, D.C., 1984, p. 3.

per cent pro-Israel. We would be very much happier with Paul Simon who is 100 per cent pro-Israel."

Golder, who was considerably more open than many of the officers of the 54 PACs Roeder positively identified in 1984 as pro-Israel fund-disbursing organizations, also explained:

"I don't know that it's necessary for outsiders to know who we are. It's a small group of Jewish fund-raisers raising money from mostly Jewish contributors and we can explain who we are to them."

In an interview with another caller Golder said:

"Look how much we can get from the United States Government by being politically active . . . we're trying to get those candidates [elected] who will vote 'yes' on foreign aid."[11]

The 54 pro-Israel PACs Roeder discovered spent some $5 million on the 1984 elections alone. Roeder also looked for overt or covert pro-Arab or anti-Israel PACs. He found one that had been briefly active and then had closed down, and another that had registered but had never raised or disbursed any funds. Since Roeder published his findings in mid-1984, Arab-American groups claim to have discovered as many as 70 secret pro-Israel PACs. One Capitol Hill insider predicts that more than 90 will be active in the 1986 elections. Their existence is openly discussed in U.S. Jewish publications, with Jewish national leaders suggesting certain guidelines to coordinate their activities. One suggestion is to support Congressional incumbents on the key committees who have voted 100 per cent in favor of Israel, even where the incumbent is not Jewish and a challenger is. Non-Jewish Congressmen must feel assured, it is explained, that if they support aid to Israel consistently, Israel's lobby will support them consistently.

There apparently still are no active pro-Arab PACs, nor even a PAC just supporting even-handed U.S. Middle East policies.

Direct donations from individuals, together with carefully targeted and coordinated PAC contributions to candidates on key committees, comprise the Israel lobby's carrot and stick to keep Congress in line in the 1980s, just as direct donations from individuals and groups and speaker's fees did the same work in the 1970s. Political scientists have recorded how the lobby has used such tools, and who were the most susceptible Congressmen, almost since the establishment of Israel. The researchers' methods differed, and the time frames within which they worked were widely separated, but their conclusions are remarkably similar. Perhaps two statements from separate 1977 studies tell the story:

"Congress' foreign affairs role is typically marginal, but American-Israeli relations are an exception. Historically Congress' role has been large in this issue-area, and Congress is consistently more supportive of Israel than is the executive branch."[12]

---

11. *Findley, Paul, They Dare to Speak Out*, Lawrence Hill and Company, Westport, Conn., 1985, p. 44.
12. Garnham, David, "Factors Influencing Congressional Support for Israel During the 93rd Congress," *The Jerusalem Journal of International Relations*, Spring 1977, p. 25.

"There is a moderate positive association . . . between the amount of money received by Senators for speaking to Jewish groups and their voting records on Israel-related issues."[13]

If these comments indicate that little has changed between 1977 and 1986, nevertheless, as the Arab-Israeli dispute has evolved, so has the manner in which it affects the U.S. Government. At the time when U.S. support was crucial for U.N. approval of the 1947 plan to partition Palestine, the struggle was waged to some extent between State Department officials who had worked in the Middle East on the one hand, and official and unofficial White House advisers close to the American Jewish community on the other.

The State Department officials saw no peaceful way to carry out the plan and they feared the consequences for U.S. interests in an area where educational ties had long been close, and where promising postwar economic ties were developing rapidly.

The White House advisers were equally adamant that the European Jews who had survived Hitler's extermination camps should find a refuge and national home in Palestine. President Truman expressed impatience alternately with the persistent pressures applied to him by proponents of the Jewish state, and with the efforts of the State Department "lower echelons" to steer the U.S. away from supporting creation of such a state. In each case, President Truman made the ultimate choice among the sharply opposed alternatives submitted by his advisers, and historians will be able to argue for all time whether he was pulled by compassion for the homeless death camp survivors or pushed by the passionate dedication to their cause of a large portion of America's politically powerful Jewish leadership.

Since that time support for Israel has coalesced in the Congress, while concern for Arab positions and reactions is still voiced most clearly in the Departments of Defense, State, Treasury and Commerce. The White House staff itself can go either way, given the presence there of both domestic liaison officers to the U.S. Jewish community, and National Security Council advisers who are Middle East specialists. Recent U.S. Presidents have found themselves frequently under attack domestically for reaching out to acquire and hold Arab allies, and almost continuously under attack in the Middle East for their support of Israel. Increasingly, they have let Congress follow its own historic tendencies to lavish military and economic aid generously on the Jewish state.

Votes of individual Congressmen on Middle East issues have been tracked exhaustively. Scholars have then analyzed the characteristics shared by those Congressmen who consistently support Israel, regardless of the administration's position. The results of these studies are so consistent, from Congress to Congress, and from scholar to scholar, that they are simply recorded on the following pages in the words of their authors. Appropriate credits go to Robert H. Trice, for his analysis of support for Israel in the U.S. Senate from 1970 to 1973, published in the *Political Science Quarterly*; David Garnham, for his analysis of the 93rd Congress, published in the *Jerusalem Journal of International Relations*; and David Logan, for his analysis of the 95th Congress, published by the National Association of Arab Americans.

---

13. Trice, Robert H., "Congress and the Arab-Israeli Conflict:Support for Israel in the U.S. Senate, 1970-1973," *Political Science Quarterly*, Fall 1977, p. 460.

The historical bias of Congress on issues related to Israel was demonstrated anew by all of these studies. Support for Israel does not seem to be based on party politics. Roughly equal percentages of Republican and Democratic members have supported Israel in the key votes that have been analyzed. In earlier years support did correlate quite closely, however, to liberal voting records. Congressional liberals supported Israel more consistently than did Congressional conservatives. Regional differences have also had some importance in determining how a Congressman will vote on the Middle East. In the words of Dr. Trice:

"The bases of pro-Israel support are strongest in the heavily industrialized, urbanized states of the Northeast, and weaker in the South and the less populous heartland of the country. Particularly striking is the weak support for Israel shown by senators from the Rocky Mountain states relative to all other regions." [14]

Trice's study finds some evidence supporting three popular explanations for the pro-Israel bias in Congressional voting patterns. One of these is the impact of the "Jewish vote." He writes:

"According to the standard argument, Jews offset their numerical weakness as a voting group because they, more than other ethnic minority, tend to vote as a bloc. It is contended that legislation that in any way affects Israel is of high salience to American Jews, and they are quick to articulate their policy preferences to their representatives in Congress (and) tend to vote in accordance with the policy demands of Jewish community leaders. Over time, Congressmen come to anticipate reactions of organized Jewry. . . . Direct pressures by Jewish voters become less necessary, and the support of Congressmen from states with sizable Jewish populations for pro-Israeli legislation becomes more automatic." [15]

Trice notes also that other studies of Jewish voting patterns in Presidential elections confirm that Jews do tend to vote as a bloc, but that party differences rather than the policies of the individual candidates seem to be the most important factor in capturing the Jewish vote. On the national level, a Democratic candidate generally does better than a Republican with Jewish voters . . . Even if the popular perception of how Jewish votes are cast is incorrect, however, it apparently is shared by Congressmen. Trice reports:

"Senators who come from states with relatively larger percentages of Jewish voters are, on the whole, more likely to vote in favor of Israel's interests than are those with smaller Jewish constituencies. . . . The implication is that very small Jewish populations—in some cases as small as two per cent or less of a state's total population—were capable of generating and maintaining consistent support for their policy preferences from their respective Senators." [16]

Turning to a second popular explanation for the pro-Israel bias in Congress, Trice writes:

---

14. Trice, Robert H., "Congress and the Arab-Israeli Conflict: Support for Israel in the U.S. Senate, 1970-1973," *Political Science Quarterly*, Fall 1977, pp. 452-3.
15. *Ibid.*, p. 456.
16. *Ibid.*, pp. 457-8.

"Critics of pro-Israel interest group activities frequently charge that American Jews extend their political leverage well beyond the limits of their voting strength by means of their willingness to give generous financial assistance to Congressmen who are sympathetic to their policy preferences. There is some evidence to support the contention that Jews as a group do contribute heavily to Congressional and Presidential campaigns. However, it is not possible to determine accurately the size or the recipients of these campaign contributions. There is, however, another common form of financial assistance that is measurable, and that may serve as a surrogate for campaign contributions. It is an accepted practice of domestic interest groups to assist supporters in Congress by inviting the Congressman to speak to their conventions or working groups, and to pay these speakers honoraria for their remarks.

. . . "The question is whether such financial assistance affects the voting behavior of the recipients. There is, of course, a 'chicken and egg' problem. . . . Critics of the pro-Israel lobby may argue that giving Senators honoraria amounts to little more than an attempt to buy support for Israel. Supporters of pro-Israel group efforts, however, may argue that the honoraria represent a perfectly legitimate and widely used means of giving financial backing to those incumbents who have already demonstrated their willingness to vote in favor of Israel's interest . . . There is a moderate positive association . . . between the amount of money received by Senators for speaking to Jewish groups and their voting records on Israel-related issues."[17]

Trice also states that even the combined positive correlations between pro-Israeli voting and all three of these factors—higher percentages of Jewish constituents, financial support from Jewish groups, and liberal voting records—are not sufficient to explain the variations in Senatorial voting records. He therefore lists some additional factors which probably influence the Congressional bias for Israel significantly even if they are not measurable.

"One important factor is the direct lobbying efforts of domestic interest groups. While it is not possible to measure precisely the relative influence of pro-Israel and pro-Arab groups, there is little doubt that the greater organizational strength and activity level of domestic pro-Israel groups has resulted in considerable political payoffs in terms of Congressional receptivity and willingness to make public statements in support of Israeli positions. . . . Some analysts argue that a major source of strength for the pro-Israel movement is the network of Congressional aides who are openly supportive of Israel's interests and who work hard to convince their bosses and their bosses' colleagues to support Israel. In the absence of any strong countervailing pressure from pro-Arab groups we might expect those Senators with only marginal interest in the dispute to follow the path of least political resistance and vote as their staffs and colleagues suggest. . . .

"For some Senators, however, the Arab-Israel conflict is likely to be a very salient issue. Congressmen with Presidential aspirations are likely to be sensitive to the fact that as they become more nationally prominent their voting records on Israel-relevant issues will be closely and publicly scrutinized by pro-Israel groups. A mixed record of support for Israel in the past may be sufficient for some Jewish groups to question a Congressman's willingness to support Israel if elected President. Such doubts could result in the withholding of Jewish financial and electoral support.

"The actual strength of domestic pro-Israel forces is not nearly as relevant as the political constraints that potential Presidential candidates may perceive. Few men with either immediate

17. Trice, Robert H., "Congress and the Arab-Israeli Conflict: Support for Israel in the U.S. Senate, 1970-1973," *Political Science Quarterly*, Fall 1977, pp. 458-60.

or long-term visions of national office are likely to run the risks associated with openly challenging the political muscle of pro-Israel groups. The lack of any readily-observable political benefits for assuming an anti-Israel stance, coupled with the prospect that such a position would be likely to alienate an identifiable bloc of American voters, may explain the support for Israel displayed by some Senators.

"Beyond these identifiable and separable sources of support looms the entire domestic political environment that surrounds the governmental policy-making system. The ability of pro-Israel groups to marshall the support of the mass media, mass public opinion, and broad cross-sections of associational life in this country such as organized labor and non-Jewish interest groups has enabled them to amplify and disseminate their policy preferences far beyond the limits of their own organizational structures . . . (F)or whatever reasons a particular Congressman supports Israel, he is likely to be well in the mainstream of opinion in his home district or state." [18]

The Garnham study was based on seven Senate votes between December 20, 1973 and October 1, 1974, and two House votes on December 11, 1973. It produced generally similar conclusions. Garnham found that 75 per cent of the Representatives had voted in favor of Israel and only eight per cent had voted against Israel on both bills. In the Senate, 38 per cent of the Senators had voted in favor of Israel on all seven issues, while only two Senators had opposed Israel on all seven votes. Some of Garnham's conclusions are excerpted below:

"Future Congressional support for Israel is likely to remain high, but it may decline somewhat from past levels. Since the Yom Kippur War, many U.S. officials and scholars have concluded that the heterogeneous Middle Eastern interests of the United States are served best by a policy which continues close ties with Israel but seeks to improve relations with the Arabs. . . . Congressional support may decline also because of negative reaction to Israel's intrusions into domestic U.S. politics." [19]

Garnham stated that Senators were more likely to adopt pro-Israeli stances regardless of the percentage of Jewish constituents in their states, while the stances of Representatives correlated more closely with the percentage in their districts. He explained:

"It is more probable that a Senator will have Jewish constituents, and given the high level of Jewish political activity, Senators are more likely to be exposed to articulate pro-Israel arguments. This point has been made by Morris Amitay, the executive director of the American Israel Public Affairs Committee. . . . 'You look about at who the Jewish constituents are from sparsely inhabited states. They're teachers, they're doctors, they've invariably been involved some way in politics. They're usually respected people in the community, so you don't have to pitch it at the level of I contributed $10,000 to your campaign—unless you do this you'll make me unhappy and I'll contribute to your opponent next time. At most it's implicit, and it's not even implicit a large percentage of the time.' " [20]

---

18. Trice, Robert H., "Congress and the Arab-Israeli Conflict: Support for Israel in the U.S. Senate, 1970-1973," *Political Science Quarterly*, Fall 1977, pp. 462-3.
19. Garnham, David, "Factors Influencing Congressional Support for Israel During the 93rd Congress," *The Jerusalem Journal of International Relations*, Spring 1977, p. 27.
20. *Ibid.*, p. 34.

Like Trice, Garnham notes that:

"Potential Presidential candidates appear to support Israel more ardently than other Senators. This would partially explain why Jewish population is a less powerful explanation of Senate voting. Given the more national orientation of Senators, and the much larger number of potential aspirants, more Senators are inclined to support Israel regardless of the size of their own State's Jewish population."[21]

Garnham concludes his study as follows:

"The perspectives of Congress and the executive branch are significantly different. The Congress is much more supportive of assistance to Israel while the executive branch is more concerned with offering inducements to Arab governments . . . The executive branch has been consistently less supportive of Israel and relatively more concerned with Arab-American relations. At least in part this reflects the perspective of career officers of the Departments of State and Defense."[22]

In his study of the 95th Congress, Logan found no significant contradictions with the earlier studies cited above. However, his conclusions point to an evolution in the role of Congress with regard to the Middle East. He writes:

"First, Middle East policy is becoming increasingly complex. It is no longer valid to look at American Middle East policy solely through eyeglasses oriented towards the Arab-Israeli conflict. There are now many other issues involved. These include oil, strategic concerns and worry about Soviet influence, Arab-to-Arab relations, and Arab conflicts with other Arab states. The votes of the 95th Congress reflected this growing complexity; the range of issues was wider and the voting patterns less consistent than in previous Congresses. . . .

"Finally, it was found that there has been no real decrease in support for Israel, but that there has been an increase in support for other factors in the Middle East. The 95th Congress also gave Arab states, particularly Egypt and Saudi Arabia, more than any Congress had before. As one Senate staff aide put it, 'People now realize that what is good for the Arabs doesn't have to be bad for Israel."[23]

In fact time has not validated that optimistic assessment. Whatever individual members of Congress may have decided, Israel's lobby seems determined that Israel is to be the only American ally in the Middle East. The Reagan Administration's initial tendency under Secretary of State Alexander Haig to let Israel make U.S. Middle East policy, and the subsequent uncertain Middle East leadership of George Shultz, made it almost impossible for individual Congressmen to follow either the dictates of their own consciences or of common sense, if those were in conflict with AIPAC wishes.

Representative Daniel Rostenkowski (D-ILL), the present Chairman of the House Ways and Means Committee, was startlingly frank after he voted against the AWACS

---

21. Garnham, David, "Factors Influencing Congressional Support for Israel During the 93rd Congress," *The Jerusalem Journal of International Relations*, Spring 1977, p. 27.

22. *Ibid.*, p. 41.

23. Logan, David, "The 95th Congress and Middle East Policy: Voting Patterns and Trends," study prepared for and published by the National Association of Arab Americans, April 23, 1979, pp. 4-5.

and F-15 aircraft package for Saudi Arabia. He told a Chicago radio station that, although he personally favored the sale, he voted against it because he feared the "Jewish lobby." His vote against his better judgement didn't matter, he hastened to add, because the House majority against the sale (301 to 111) was overwhelming in any case and the only chance of approving the sale was in the Senate.

Former Representative Paul Findley explains that in the House of Representatives "most committee action, like the work of the full House, is open to the public and nothing occurs on Israeli aid without the presence of at least one representative of AIPAC. His presence ensures that any criticism of Israel will be quickly reported to key constituents. The offending Congressman may have a rash of angry telephone messages to answer by the time he returns to his office from the hearing room."[24]

Conservative political analyst Paul Weyrich, a former Senate staff aide, confirms that Israel lobby practices are similar in the Senate:

"It's a remarkable system they have. If you vote with them, or make a public statement they like, they get the word out fast through their own publications and through editors around the country who are sympathetic to their cause. Of course it works in reverse as well. If you say something they don't like, you can be denounced or censured through the same network. That kind of pressure is bound to affect Senators' thinking, especially if they are wavering or need support."[25]

How totally this system controls Congressional voting on the Middle East is well illustrated by the record for 1985, a non-election year when Congressmen might be a little less concerned with AIPAC censure. Nevertheless, the Congress was so hostile toward Reagan Administration feelers about new military aircraft sales to Saudi Arabia that the Administration decided not to submit the package to Congress. Saudi Arabia therefore ordered $4.5 billion worth of aircraft from British manufacturers. British officials expect the ultimate value of the order will be twice that amount when spare parts, training, updating and maintenance contracts are added to the initial purchase.

If, as estimated by the U.S. Department of Commerce, each billion dollars in lost sales means a loss of 25,000 U.S. jobs, the total cost to American workers of that Congressional action is more than 100,000 jobs. Strangely, the cost to Israel will be high as well. U.S. planes are sold to Saudi Arabia without bomb racks and certain offensive equipment and the U.S. does not permit their use at the Tabuk Air Base, near Israel. British planes, however, come with no such equipment or basing restrictions. Apparently, loosening political ties between the United States and its moderate Arab allies is Israel's highest policy priority, higher even than Israel's current military security.

Another Congressional accomplishment in 1985 was raising U.S. assistance to Israel for the 1986 fiscal year to $1.8 billion in foreign military sales credits and $1.2 billion in economic support funds. This, together with the second half of an "emergency supplemental" aid package approved by Congress the previous year brought total direct

---

24. Findley, Paul, *They Dare to Speak Out*, Lawrence Hill and Company, Westport, Conn., 1985, p. 51.
25. *Ibid.*, p. 36.

U.S. government aid to Israel to $3.75 billion, all in grants rather than partially in grants and partially in loans as in previous years.

Early in 1985 a group of Senators, led by Presidential aspirants Jack Kemp (R-NY) and Edward Kennedy (D-MA), had circulated a letter insisting that the Administration not sell arms to Jordan until King Hussein had entered into direct peace negotiations with Israel. The action in fact ensured that peace talks would be postponed since the only real impediment to talks at that time was Israel's insistence upon excluding any Palestinian negotiators it did not individually approve. Late in the year Congress voted to defer the $1.9 billion Jordan arms package until 1986. Since the arms would be paid for by the U.S., the nearly 50,000 jobs involved were not such a clear-cut loss to U.S. industry as in the aborted Saudi deal, but the action effectively undercut another long-term friend of the U.S. in the Arab world at a time when King Hussein was being heavily pressed by Syria, which is armed by the Soviet Union.

Also in 1985, the Congress voted to conclude a Free Trade Agreement with Israel, although no major U.S. business or trade organization supported it and a large number of such American industrial associations had testified that it would eliminate American jobs in their industries.

Having therefore effectively voted away between 150,000 and a quarter million American jobs and close to $4 billion in taxpayer money for Israel in 1985, one would expect Congressmen would have some explaining to do to constituents when they went home at the end of the year. It does not work that way, however, when the Administration does not press its differences with Congress, and when the press virtually ignores sacrifices Congress imposes upon unsuspecting Americans on behalf of Israel. In fact, it is more likely that members of Congress who opposed Israel-backed programs will have to explain themselves to AIPAC.

In 1983 Representative Nick Rahall, a West Virginia Democrat of Lebanese descent, sought to rescind a provision in the Fiscal 1984 appropriation for Israeli military purchases which permitted the Israelis to use U.S. funds to develop production in Israel of the Lavie fighter plane, based upon U.S. technology.

"Approximately 6,000 jobs would be lost as a direct result of taking the $250 million out of the U.S. economy and allowing Israel to spend it on defense articles and services which can just as readily be purchased here in the United States," Rahall told fellow members of Congress. "Americans are being stripped of their tax dollars to build up foreign industry. They should not have to sacrifice their jobs as well."

Rahall's amendment was defeated 379 to 40 but in May, 1984, Rahall told Findley:

"Almost all of those who voted with me have told me they are still catching hell from their Jewish constituents. They are still moaning about the beating they are taking."[26]

That is the background to the response by Representative Lee Hamilton (D-IN) quoted at the beginning of this chapter. He was asked in 1983, after a car bomb attack had killed 241 U.S. Servicemen in Beirut, whether Congress might take action if the Administration did not withdraw U.S. Marines to Navy ships offshore. "Don't look to Congress to act," Hamilton said. "All we know is how to increase aid to Israel."

---

26. Findley, Paul, *They Dare to Speak Out*, Lawrence Hill and Company, Westport, Conn., 1985, p. 80.

Money buys television time and television time creates votes. Therefore funding appeals have grown increasingly strident in recent years both for self-proclaimed friends of Israel, and to defeat candidates alleged to be Israel's enemies.

The Evidence of the Polls: 1946-1986

"While anti-Jewish sentiment was evident among some Americans in the 1930s and 1940s, anti-Arab feelings are quite evident in the 1970s. Thus, in 1975, around 50 per cent of the American public and about 75 per cent of Jewish Americans thought of Arabs as backward, underdeveloped, greedy, arrogant, and even 'barbaric'. . . . Public opinion on the Middle East is changing, but very slowly. It is influenced by U.S. relations with the regimes in the area and by how the Administration in office views the situation. As the Palestinians became a significant factor in the Middle East and the strategic importance of the Arab World to the United States grew more pronounced, a more 'balanced' American approach was advocated. At this juncture, the 'reasonableness' of Sadat is contrasted with the 'intransigence' of Begin — hence the slight but visible changes in public attitude."[1]

Michael W. Suleiman, 1980

"National polls show that the American public's attitude toward the Arab-Israeli conflict has featured five major distinctions in recent years: (1) considerably greater 'sympathy' for Israel compared to the 'Arab nations'; (2) a distinctly more favorable image of Israel than of Israeli governments and policies; (3) increased differentiation in viewing Arab countries (for example, Egypt is now seen about on a par with Israel in terms of 'favorableness,' and Saudi Arabia is seen at least on a par with Israel in terms of 'importance' to U.S. interests; (4) concern for Israel's security greater than sympathy for Palestinian claims to a national homeland; and (5) a much more favorable image of the Palestinian than of the PLO, which is viewed as not representative of most Pal-

---

1. Suleiman, Michael, "American Public Support of Middle Eastern Countries 1939-1979," in *The American Media and the Arabs*, CCAS, Georgetown University, 1980, p. 36.

estinians and not entitled to a role in negotiating a Middle East peace settlement until it recognizes Israel and disavows use of terrorism.[2]

Alvin Richman, 1983

Introduction

Those who are skeptical of polls in general have expressed particular suspicion of polls pertaining to the Arab-Israeli dispute. They reason that American polls on the Middle East may have been tainted either by partisanship among those who prepare the questions or among the polltakers themselves. It seems likely, however, that major polling organizations would take all reasonable precautions against such problems, to protect their own credibility. This is borne out by Department of State analysts who for several years have examined the results obtained by the media and commercial polling organizations on all foreign policy questions. On Middle East affairs they have recorded a high degree of consistency among the various major polling organizations, both in the public attitudes recorded, and in the evolution of those attitudes over 35 years. Although wording of a question as well as the ethnic or religious background of the person asking the question can significantly influence responses, it nevertheless would be foolish to ignore the polls. They reveal a great deal not only about current American attitudes, but also about the factors that influence those attitudes positively and negatively. A number of different polls are presented in this appendix, adapted and updated from the author's 1980 case study for the Department of State's Foreign Service Institute: *Too Often Promised Land—American Public Opinion and the Arab-Israeli Dispute.*

After 40 years in the American public consciousness, the Arab-Israel dispute has become a "mature issue." This means that in the absence of major new developments, there are no major opinion swings, and even after such a swing occurs, opinions over time gradually tend to return to their long-term levels. In fact, through all the years that polls have been taken, only two events have ever caused sudden, major swings in American public opinion on the Israeli-Palestinian dispute. Those were President Anwar Sadat's journey to Jerusalem in 1977, and the Israeli invasion of Lebanon culminating in the Sabra-Shatilla massacre in 1982.

The Sadat era more than doubled American support for the Arabs, and resulted in still further increase of support for Egypt beyond support for the other Arabs. Over the long run, however, the swing toward the Arabs was not enough to offset the declining, but still overriding, popular support for Israel. The Lebanon invasion resulted in a sharp increase of support for the Arabs and also a decline in support for Israel. The undifferentiated support for the Arabs had vanished within a year, but moderate Arab states and leaders individually retained some gains. Support for Israel changed from that time, with Americans still approving "Israel," but likely to disapprove "recent actions of the Israeli Government."

---

2. Richman, Alvin, U.S. Department of State, "American Attitudes Toward the Middle East Since Israel's Invasion of Lebanon," paper presented at the American Association of Public Opinion Research meeting, May, 1983.

There have, however, been other significant changes within American public opinion. When American polls on the Arab-Israeli dispute began in the late 1940s, better-educated Americans were more favorably inclined toward Israel than were other Americans. Today that is no longer true. While shifts away from blanket support for Israel and toward support for specified, moderate Arab countries are small in terms of overall American opinion, they are significant if one assumes that opinions of better-educated Americans "trickle down" to less educated or less informed Americans over time. University-educated Americans have shifted from basic sympathy toward Israel to ambivalent feelings toward Israel and more carefully differentiated feelings toward the Arab states in remarkable numbers, particularly after the Sadat journey. Where there have been setbacks to this trend, they seem directly attributable to incidents of Arab or Iranian terrorism. It is in such responsiveness among the better-educated Americans (and also among the more affluent and those in executive and professional positions) toward more conciliatory positions taken by certain Arab leaders that hope for eventual American even-handedness lies. It should be the subject of careful attention not only by leaders of Israel and the Arab countries, but also by U.S. leaders responsible for putting into effect an American foreign policy which can enhance the prospects for Middle Eastern peace.

Before the creation of Israel, three Gallup polls provided the first insights into American opinion on Palestinian events. In the first two, respondents were asked if they had been following specific Palestinian developments. Only those who answered affirmatively were asked to give their opinion. The results: In January 1945 the 55 per cent who said they had "followed the discussion on permitting Jews to settle in Palestine" gave these opinions:

Favor the idea	76%
Favor if Jews do	4
Against the idea	7
Favor leaving it up to the British	1
Favor leaving it up to the Arabs	1
Miscellaneous	3
Don't know	8

In May 1946, the 50 per cent who said they had "heard or read about the Jewish migration into Palestine" were asked: "Do you think it is a good idea or a poor idea to admit 100,000 Jews to settle in Palestine?" The answers:

Good idea	78%
Poor idea	14
No opinion	8

The last of the three pre-Israel Gallup polls made no effort to weed out those who had not been following events. The results therefore cannot be compared with those above. But the differing results from exactly the same respondents for two differently worded questions during this October 1947 poll are worth considering. They illustrate not only the manner in which wording can influence answers, but also how flexible U.S. opinion on the subject was at the time.

Question: "The UN has recommended that Palestine be divided into two states-one for the Arabs and one for the Jews—and that 150,000 Jews be permitted now to enter the Jewish state. Do you favor or oppose this idea?"

Favor	65%
Oppose	10
No Opinion	25

Question: "If war breaks out between the Arabs and the Jews in Palestine, with which side would you sympathize?"

Jews	24%
Arabs	12
Neither	38
No Opinion	26

The significance of these early polls is that, although Americans overwhelmingly favored allowing large numbers of Jewish survivors of the World War II European Holocaust to settle in Palestine, most of those same Americans had not yet taken sides between the region's Arabs and Jews. Pioneer Jewish settlers, attracted by the Zionist slogan of "a land without a people for a people without a land," reported their surprise upon arriving in Palestine to find it heavily populated by Arabs. From the polls above, it seems likely that in the 1945-1947 period few Americans realized that the Jewish immigration into Palestine they supported might result in a forced Arab emigration. In any case, in 1947 only one in four Americans identified with the Jewish side, half that number identified with the Arab side, and the remaining 64 per cent had no opinion or said they were neutral.

There were no more comparable Gallup polls until the six-day war of June 1967. Those who said they had been following developments in the Middle East had risen by that time only a few points to 59 per cent. Among those who said they had followed developments, however, sympathy for the Israelis had more than doubled to 59 per cent and sympathy for the Arabs had dropped to an almost insignificant 4 per cent. Something important had happened to American public opinion in the 21 years between 1947 and 1967. Many more Americans had taken sides in the Middle East dispute, and although in 1947 American supporters of Israel outnumbered supporters of the Arabs by two to one, in 1967 Americans supported Israel over the Arabs by fifteen to one.

Through the following years, with Israel increasingly perceived as an occupying power rather than a nation of refugees in danger of being pushed into the sea, support for Israel gradually dropped to figures of 50 and 44 per cent in 1969 and 1970 respectively. But U.S. public support for the Arab camp, still led by mercurial President Nasser and still perceived as under the influence of such abrasive personalities as Ahmad

Shukairy, the PLO spokesman-leader who was forced to resign after the 1967 debacle, remained insignificant at five per cent in 1969 and three per cent in 1970. Regardless of sympathies, however, most Americans did not want the U.S. to become involved with either side if war should break out. In 1967, 41 per cent of respondents said the U.S. should "stay out" of the conflict and by 1970 this percentage had risen to 58.

Perhaps the most significant change in American public opinion recorded by Gallup during the six years between the June 1967 war and the October 1973 war was in the percentage of Americans who said they were following events in the Middle East. From the 59 per cent of 1967 it had risen to 85 and 86 per cent in the 1969 and 1970 polls.

The first Gallup poll in 1973 was taken from October 5 to 8, encompassing the day before and the first three days of the three-week October war. Americans following events in the Middle East had increased still further, to 90 per cent. Of those, 47 per cent, a three per cent increase over 1970, supported Israel while six per cent supported the Arabs, double the 1970 figure.

Two months later in December, 1973, just six weeks after many Arab nations had imposed an embargo on oil shipments to the United States, another Gallup poll found that Americans following events in the Middle East had climbed to an all-time high—before or since—of 97 per cent. This perhaps bore out the Arab adage of the time that Americans sitting in gas lines at last had sufficient time to think about the Middle East.

However, the thoughts of Americans during the oil embargo did not follow the patterns the Arabs had intended. Support for Israel had climbed seven per cent in two months to 54 per cent, only one per cent below the high point reached during the June war of 1967. Support for the Arabs had also climbed from six to eight per cent—a 25 per cent increase. However, although militant Arabs sought to credit this increase in support for the Arabs to the oil embargo, there were other significant factors at work. Americans were impressed by the new military prowess demonstrated by the Egyptian and Syrian armies. They were aware that Egyptian military communiques had been accurate, in contrast to Israel's. And, in contrast to 1970 when Nasser's Egypt had openly cheated on cease-fire terms by moving ground to air missiles into the Suez Canal area for many hours after the stand-still deadline, this time, as in 1948 and 1956, it was Israel which continued movement for days after the armies had been pledged to halt. This flagrant Israeli cheating had nearly triggered direct Russian intervention to rescue the Egyptian Third Army which was cut off from Egypt by Israeli troops under General Sharon advancing long after the cease-fire deadline.

Thus there were several simultaneous reasons for the increased level of interest by the American public, and the resulting tendency of more individual Americans to side with both the Israeli and Arab causes. The following years, with more frequent polls and with fewer events occurring between polls, provide clearer indications of what makes American public opinion change, and what does not.

The first half of 1974 saw the fall of the Golda Meir government in Israel, the shuttle negotiations by U.S. Secretary of State Henry Kissinger that eventually led to the Sinai I agreement, the lifting of the Arab oil embargo against the U.S. on March 18, visits by President Nixon to Arab countries and to Israel, restoration of diplomatic relations between the U.S. and Syria, and finally the resignation of President Nixon.

Surprisingly, there were few public opinion polls to record the effects that these momentous events had on American public opinion. The American Jewish Committee commissioned the Daniel Yankelovich organization to carry out three polls in April, July and October of 1974, each containing a different question designed to elicit readiness by the American public to blame Jews for (1) the gasoline shortage; (2) "this whole movement to get rid of Mr. Nixon" and (3) the state of the economy. Two fixed questions, asked in each poll, concerned readiness to vote for a Jew for President, and perceptions of the relative closeness of American Jews to Israel and to the United States.

For purposes of this study, the only question comparable with the Gallup questions previously asked was included in the October 1974 poll, just one year after the outbreak of the 1973 war and the resulting oil embargo. Asked with whom they would identify if war should break out in the Middle East, respondents answered:

Israel	55%
Arabs	9
Both	5
Neither	17
Don't know	14

Support figures, therefore, were just one percentage point higher for both Israel and the Arabs than the figures recorded by Gallup 10 months earlier. Other conclusions of the 1974 surveys were summarized in an American Jewish Committee report as follows:

"While things are not so bad as one had feared, they are not so good as one might hope. Three quarters of the American public see Israel as a viable and necessary state. Although there is no enthusiasm for military aid, this can be seen as an aspect of a reserve about foreign aid in general, rather than as anti-Israel in particular, since there is even less enthusiasm for aid to most other countries. When blame is placed for trouble in the Middle East, Israel and the Jews are low on the list, with the Arabs and Russia high. What seems to warrant concern is that almost a third of the American people would not want a Jewish President and see Jews as being closer to Israel than to the United States. When those who express uncertainty about these matters are added to the antis, the total becomes uncomfortably large."[3]

In the second half of 1974, with President Nixon replaced by his Vice President Gerald Ford, U.S. attention stayed focused on the Middle East as leaders of Israel, Egypt, Syria and Saudi Arabia visited Washington, and Secretary Kissinger continued his shuttle negotiations. At a meeting in Rabat, Arab heads of state designated the PLO, not King Hussein, as spokeman for the Palestinians, and on November 13 PLO Chairman Arafat made his first appearance before the UN General Assembly. The shuttle finally broke down in March 1975, with President Ford and Secretary Kissinger seem-

---

3. Rosenfield, Geraldine, "Attitudes of the American Public Toward Israel and American Jews: The Yankelovich Findings," The American Jewish Committee Information and Reference Services, December, 1974.

ing to place the blame on Israel. Arms shipments to Israel were suspended during an Administration "reassessment."

As these events took place, public opinion support for Israel took a precipitous tumble as measured in two Gallup polls for the period. It had crested at 54 per cent in the Gallup poll taken in December 1973, immediately after the October War and during the oil embargo. By January 1975 it had slipped to 44 per cent. In April, immediately after the Administration had scarcely concealed its displeasure with Israel over the shuttle failure, it bottomed out at 37 per cent. Support for the Arabs, by contrast, neither rose nor fell, holding at 8 per cent in all three polls of December 1973 and January and April, 1975.

Although basic sympathy for the Arabs neither rose nor fell, American feelings about the Arab oil boycott were negative, even belligerent, in the January 1975 poll taken 10 months after the embargo was lifted. The Gallup question, and answers totalling 129 per cent because of multiple responses, were:

"If the Arab nations impose another oil boycott on the United States, what policy do you think the United States should follow?"

Try to become self-sufficient		35%
(Develop new energy resources	15)	
(Conserve energy, don't waste	12)	
(Ration gasoline	5)	
(Use other forms of fuel, coal, etc.	3)	
Economic Sanctions: Put embargo on Arab nations, don't send food, other items		24
Military intervention		10
Seek oil from other nations		3
Negotiate/have international conference with Arab nations		4
Meet Arab demands/meet terms		2
Other responses (including those who oppose military intervention)		18
No opinion		33

In the second half of 1975 the Kissinger shuttle resumed and resulted in the signing of the Sinai II agreement in September.

No more Gallup polls record U.S. public opinion reaction in the period of U.S.-Israel tension that preceded the signing of the agreement, and the era of improved relations that followed it. However, the privately commissioned Yankelovich polls to elicit public attitudes on Israel, U.S. Jews, and the Middle East continued. One was taken in January 1975 and another in January 1976. Conclusions reflected a great deal of confusion about the Middle East in American minds, but they were not out of line with previous Gallup poll results. In a memorandum the sponsoring American Jewish Committee summarized the findings as follows:

"If war should break out between the Arabs and Israel, more than half of those questioned would still identify with Israel and three-quarters would still see Israelis as people they can get along with. Almost as many (73 per cent) described the Palestine Liberation Organization as terrorist and undemocratic. But, as in last year's survey, only a little under one third (31 per cent) support Israel's refusal to negotiate with the PLO. As many (31 per cent) think it is wrong of Israel to refuse, and 38 per cent say they do not know.

"The one conspicuous shift in attitude appears in the question about too much influence over United States Middle East policy. Whereas in April 1974 those seeing American Jews as having too much influence were 29 per cent of the total, in January 1976 their percentage was 49. But respondents selecting organized labor as having too much influence over U.S. Middle East policy rose in the same period from 24 to 45 per cent. The public seems to have become more aware of interest groups in general.

"By contrast, the question asking about too much power in the United States shows a drop of 11 per cent among those who believe Jews have too much power (34 per cent in January 1975, 26 per cent in January 1976). This may indicate that the question is interpreted as relating to domestic policy which concerns most Americans more than foreign policy. In domestic matters, Jews are not perceived as being a special-interest group, while in foreign affairs Jews are perceived – if only because of the media – as vigorous partisans of Israel.

"The one question that was asked in all five surveys is, 'Do you feel most of the Jewish people in the country feel closer to Israel or to the United States?' In the latest poll just under half think them closer to Israel, and a quarter are not sure. These percentages have been essentially stable since 1974."[4]

U.S. initiatives in the Middle East traditionally come to a halt in an election year and 1976 was no exception. As Carter was defeating Ford in the U.S., in the Middle East the Lebanese civil war also had stopped all progress. There were no Gallup polls during 1976 relevant to the Arab-Israeli dispute. However, after the U.S. election, a Louis Harris survey asked whether respondents expected "the new Carter Administration will do a better job, not as good a job, or about the same kind of job in helping to negotiate a settlement in the Middle East?" The answers could not have been more neutral. They were: Better, 22 per cent; not as good, 20 per cent; about the same, 40 per cent; and not sure, 17 per cent. Based on its surveys, the Harris organization reported "it is possible that the country is witnessing a profound change in attitudes toward foreign policy. The public seems increasingly convinced that foreign policy will become an area of essentially bi-partisan effort, and that a new Administration, even of the opposite party, will be fully capable of carrying on as well as the predecessor."

President Carter seized the Middle East initiative almost from his first day in the White House at the beginning of 1977. He declared that the Palestinians were entitled to a homeland; that Israel must eventually return captured Arab territory; and he set out to meet with all the concerned Arab and Israeli leaders. When the election of Menachem Begin in Israel seemed to set back peace prospects, Egyptian President Sadat's dramatic journey to Jerusalem set them forward again. In such a year it is difficult,

---

4. Rosenfield, Geraldine, "Attitudes of the American Public Toward Israel and American Jews: The Yankelovich Findings," The American Jewish Committee Information and Reference Services, March 1976, pp. 1-3.

but not impossible, to relate U.S. public opinion shifts to specific events. Gallup polls in June and October 1977 drew a clear picture of U.S. public opinion prior to the Sadat initiative. In June those who said they had been following events had climbed back up from 1975 levels to 86 per cent, and support for Israel had risen from the all-time low of 37 per cent, recorded after the Ford Administration blamed Israel for the shuttle breakdown two years earlier, to 44 per cent. Support for the Arabs, for the fourth time in nearly four years, had been measured at 8 per cent. In October 1977, with the U.S. apparently moving the parties toward Geneva negotiations, 79 per cent of those asked said they were following events. Among those support for Israel had climbed two more points to 46 per cent, and support for the Arabs had made its first rise in four years, from 8 to 11 per cent.

Other 1977 surveys pinpointed specific U.S. attitudes. A February Roper survey reporting American sympathy for Israel at 47 per cent versus sympathy for the Arabs at 6 per cent found a clear majority of 55 per cent favoring a compromise in which Israel would give up conquered territory for a peace settlement. A Harris poll of the same period found 68 per cent in favor of the U.S. "keeping the lead in trying to get negotiations going" toward a peaceful settlement, with only 15 per cent opposed and 17 per cent not sure. Of Jews polled on that question, an even higher 87 per cent favored the U.S. initiative. More than half of elite, informed, respondents to a Foreign Policy Association poll opposed the idea of "tilting" toward either side and recommended instead that the U.S. follow an evenly-balanced approach.

That was the situation on the eve of the Sadat visit to Jerusalem, which not only broke the old rules of play but also changed American perceptions of the players. The first polls showing altered American perceptions of the Middle East players were taken even as the drama was unfolding. The Harris organization asked in early December 1977 for an evaluation of Middle East protagonists. The results are juxtaposed below with answers in parentheses to the same questions posed by Harris interviews in October, just before the Sadat visit to Jerusalem:

	Wants a Just Peace		Reluctantly Wants Peace		Doesn't Want Peace		Not Sure	
	12/77	(10/77)	12/77	(10/77)	12/77	(10/77)	12/77	(10/77)
Israel	47	(55)	30	(20)	11	(6)	12	(19)
Egypt	52	(37)	26	(27)	10	(9)	12	(27)
Jordan	23	(34)	30	(23)	17	(7)	30	(36)
Saudi Arabia	24	(29)	27	(23)	19	(11)	30	(37)
Syria	15	(22)	26	(25)	27	(11)	32	(42)
Libya	14	(21)	24	(20)	25	(13)	37	(46)
PLO	11	(13)	15	(15)	47	(35)	27	(37)

After the Sadat initiative 52 per cent of Americans believed Egypt wanted a "just peace," a 15 point increase in two months. Israel's rating on the same question dropped eight points to 47 per cent, putting it behind Egypt for the first time since Israel was created. Based possibly on their negative reactions to the Sadat initiative, ratings for all other Arab countries also dropped, but in the case of every Arab country there was a partially offsetting increase in the "reluctantly wants peace" column. Only the PLO, already lower in the ratings than any Arab country, showed little loss in the "wants a just peace" column and none in the "reluctantly wants peace" category, possibly because both already were so low relative to any of the others named.

The Harris poll also documented a rise in positive ratings for President Carter's effort to achieve peace from 34 per cent to 62 per cent and a belief by 85 per cent of the public that direct Arab-Israel talks would be more effective for achieving peace than use of third countries such as the U.S. In short, whatever its original plans or the misgivings of its Middle East experts, the Carter Administration was firmly compelled by public opinion to climb on the Sadat initiative bandwagon. Those, like Israel, who showed misgivings suffered a slight drop in U.S. public esteem. Those who actively opposed the initiative, like the other Arab countries, suffered a much sharper drop.

In an effort to seize the peace-making initiative from President Sadat, Prime Minister Begin had brought to Washington his own plan for the West Bank in December, 1977. Carter's reserved comment that it was a "good beginning" was mistakenly seized upon by both Begin and the U.S. media as an endorsement. A chill in U.S.-Egyptian relations seemed inevitable. However, on a return flight from Saudi Arabia President Carter made an unscheduled stop in Cairo and successfully set the record straight. In February, President Sadat spent six days in the U.S., not only meeting with Carter and members of Congress, but also participating in U.S. television interviews and giving a televised speech at the National Press Club in Washington. He was hailed by President Carter as the "the world's foremost peacemaker."

The results of these activities were reflected in the February 1978 Gallup poll. Among the 79 per cent who said they were following events, support for Israel had tumbled 13 per cent in four months to a new low of 33 per cent. Given no chance to single out Egypt for a separate rating, respondents gave the Arabs as a whole an unprecedented 14 per cent rating. This was a six point (75 per cent) climb in eight months, half of it achieved before before and half after the Sadat initiative.

The impact of the Sadat initiative on more specific points was revealed by other polls. A January, 1978 Harris poll contrasted American opinions of the Egyptian and Israeli leaders as well as opinions about their two countries. The question and answers:

"If . . . there was a difference between (1) Egypt and Israel or (2) President Sadat of Egypt and Prime Minister of Israel, on a peace settlement in the Middle East, whom would you trust more?"

(1) Israel vs. Egypt		(2) Sadat vs. Begin	
Israel	43%	Sadat	32%
Egypt	20	Begin	32
Not Sure	37	Not Sure	36

In a January 1978 NBC poll on their performances in "handling peace negotiations in the Middle East" respondents rated the Egyptian leader considerably higher than the Israeli leader. The results:

	Sadat		*Begin*
Excellent	30%	Excellent	16%
Good	35	Good	33
(Subtotal)	(65)	(Subtotal)	(48)
Only Fair	21	Only Fair	31
Poor	3	Poor	5
Not Sure	11	Not Sure	15

For the first time in more than 30 years of U.S. public opinion polling, an Arab leader had decisively outscored an Israeli leader. The American public jumped ahead of the negotiators to render its verdict on their causes as well. A January 1978 Gallup poll asked the two-thirds of respondents who said they had been following Middle Eastern developments, "Do you think Israel should or should not withdraw its military forces and civilian settlements from the Sinai Peninsula?" A 40 to 29 per cent plurality said Israel should withdraw, while 31 per cent said they had no opinion in the settlement issue, a high level of indecision for a group claiming to be attentive.

At this stage it appeared that the change in U.S. opinion was not at the expense of the Palestinian parties to the dispute. A December 1977 NBC poll asked: "Do you agree or disagree that the Palestinian Arabs should have their own country?" The answers: Agree, 55 per cent; disagree, 25 per cent; not sure, 20 per cent.

Opinions held by the educated elite are generally believed to be precursors of opinions of the general public. Therefore possibly the most significant development of the period was a dramatic reversal in the perceptions of the Middle East protagonists by university-educated Americans, who in earlier years were stronger supporters of Israel than the public at large. In the October 1977 CBS poll above, they still backed Israel over the Arabs 49 to 34 per cent. By April 1978 the tables had turned. University graduates supported the Arabs over Israel by 40 to 36 per cent. Answers to two other CBS questions, in mid-March and in April, brought out a similar shift in opinions by university graduates in favor of Sadat and Egypt and away from Begin and Israel:

"In general, do you approve or disapprove of Egyptian President Anwar Sadat's/Israeli Prime Minister Menachem Begin's handling of Arab-Israeli relations?"

March 1978	*General Public*		*College Graduates*	
	Sadat	*Begin*	*Sadat*	*Begin*
Approve	57%	34%	80%	33%
Disapprove	27	46	12	55
No Opinion	16	20	8	12

"Israel and Egypt are trying to negotiate a peace settlement. Do you think Israel/Egypt has made too many concessions, not enough, or the right amount?"

April 1978	General Public Israel	General Public Egypt	College Graduates Israel	College Graduates Egypt
Too many	12%	6%	7%	4%
Not enough	50	43	63	34
Right number	19	40	19	51
No Opinion	19	11	11	11

The polls did not indicate how much the Sadat initiative, while clearly diminishing support for Israel and enhancing support for Egypt, affected American opinion about the Arabs as a whole. Already the American public, and college graduates in particular, seemed well aware of the growing divergence of opinion in the Arab camp, as revealed by this April 1978 CBS question:

"Do you think the other Arab states feel as Sadat does or do you think that Sadat speaks only for Egypt?"

	Total Public	College Graduates
Sadat speaks only for Egypt	65%	73%
Others feel as Sadat	16	12
No Opinion	19	15

The period of intense effort and frequent disagreements between negotiation of the Camp David agreements in September 1978 and the treaty signing on the White House lawn in March 1979 provided several impressions of what the American public thought of the activist American role. In late December, 1978, a Harris poll found that most Americans, specifically including American Jews, wanted the U.S. to remain even-handed, at least when the question indicated the President was tilting toward Egypt:

"Do you think (President Carter) was right to back Egypt or should he have backed Israel or should he not have backed either side?"

	Shouldn't Back Either	Right to Back Egypt	Should Back Israel	Not Sure
Total Public	59%	22%	6%	13%
Jews	68	14	12	6
Catholics	61	24	5	10
Protestants	56	23	7	14

A January 1979 Gallup question found strong majorities of the total public, Israel sympathizers, and Arab sympathizers in agreement that U.S. policy toward Israel and Egypt was even-handed:

"Do you think President Carter is leaning too much in favor of Israel . . . Egypt . . . or treating both sides fairly?"

	Total Public	Pro-Israel Public	Pro-Arab Public
Treating both fairly	62%	61%	68%
Favoring Israel	11	10	18
Favoring Egypt	10	17	5
No Opinion	17	12	9

Another January 1979 Gallup poll demonstrated that even pro-Israel sympathy did not preclude criticism of Israeli policies. A majority 54 per cent of those who expressed sympathy for Israel said Israel was "not doing all it should" to achieve peace, while 36 per cent of Israel's sympathizers disagreed. The same Israel sympathizers were only slightly more critical of Egypt than they were of Israel, with 62 per cent saying Egypt was not doing all it should.

Those polls, at a time of maximum U.S. involvement in the Egyptian-Israeli negotiations, indicated that although many Americans were not abandoning old loyalties, they were nevertheless willing to criticize specific actions of either side and were supportive of an activist U.S. policy to achieve a peace treaty, so long as they perceived it to be even-handed and fair.

Between 1977 and 1982, U.S. public opinion movements became almost too minor and subtle to track. Continuing acts of violence in Israel and Lebanon were reported in the U.S. media, but through sheer repetition they had lost some of their former impact in arousing American public opinion against the perpetrators. Disturbances in the West Bank, and the killing of Palestinian demonstrators, showed Americans an unfamiliar, ugly side of Israel. They may have been a significant factor in the already-visible shifts among better educated and better informed Americans. However, negative images from these events were no doubt offset to varying degrees by other Middle East events.

The taking of American diplomatic hostages in Iran was depicted by partisans of the Arabs at the time as the "latest disaster" for U.S. public opinion. They noted that in the immediate aftermath of the Tehran Embassy seizure, angry American demonstrators made no ethnic distinctions, apparently confusing Iranians with "Arab oil sheikhs" in their signs and slogans. If the role of Algeria in retrieving the hostages improved popular U.S. perceptions of the Arabs, the actions of Colonel Qaddafi did not.

Developments within the U.S. also had little apparent effect on opinion, except within the American Black community. There the resignation of President Carter's representative to the United Nations, Andrew Young, had a visible effect on perceptions of the Arab-Israeli dispute. Blacks felt that only Israel's insistence turned a relatively routine matter into a cause for Young's resignation. Among American Jews with the same perception, there were some private bitter comments at Israel's apparent heedlessness of the ultimate cost to U.S. Jews in terms of their relations with American Blacks.

The issue had considerable repercussions as Black delegations visited both sides in the Middle East. Some, like the Reverend Jesse Jackson and the Southern Christian Leadership Conference, focused their attention on West Bank Palestinians and the PLO. Others, like Vernon Jordan's Urban League, concentrated on fence-mending visits with Israeli leaders. There were angry words in the wake of these trips, with individual Jewish financial backers of Black and civil rights organizations vowing "never again," and Blacks depicting the fracas as still another manifestation of the Black-Jewish tensions which had crystallized over affirmative action and ethnic quotas. These were perceived by Blacks as a tool to pull themselves up, and were perceived by Jews as a threat that could hold them down in the fluid American social structure.

Black delegations to the Middle East, no matter whether they seemed to favor the Palestinians or the Israelis, all espoused similar messages of non-violence. So long as the PLO refused to play its "last bargaining chip," recognition of Israel's right to exist, there was little chance that American public perceptions of the PLO, as distinct from the Palestinians, would change radically. There was also little evidence that the PLO, engrossed as it was in Third-World, inter-Arab and intra-Palestinian politics, really thought a change in American public opinion very important to it at that time.

For that period the Gallup polls are the most instructive, since they were directly comparable to all the preceding years. By January 1979 Israeli support had risen again to 42 and in August 1981 to 44, about the median for all the gyrations since the October War. The Arab support meanwhile reached an all-time high of 15 per cent in 1979 and 11 per cent in 1981, still far below support for Israel but significantly higher than at any time before late 1977. The number of Americans who told Gallup interviewers they had been following Middle Eastern events reached 93 per cent in November 1978, 92 per cent in January 1979, and slid back to 81 per cent in 1981.

With the end of the Carter Administration and the beginning of the Reagan Administration, events in the Middle East tended to strengthen three growing public perceptions. Although in Israel emphasis moved from Jewish religious settlements in the West Bank to Israel's fulfillment of its Camp David commitments, nevertheless Israeli actions in the West Bank and Lebanon made Israel seem increasingly pugnacious and militaristic. In Egypt, until his assassination in 1981, President Sadat continued to project an image of moderation and statesmanship. Finally, the rest of the Arab world seemed from the U.S. vantage point to remain essentially negative, refusing to offer peace terms or conditions of its own.

The result was almost no movement in American public opinion, despite such sensational events as Israel's bombing of the Iraqi nuclear reactor, the bombing of a residential area in Beirut with the reported loss of 300 lives, and finally the tragic assassination of President Sadat.

Perhaps the most striking evidence that Americans are moved positively by evidence of conciliation and moderation such as that exhibited by President Sadat in late 1977, and negatively or not at all by pressure such as the Arab oil boycott in late 1973, is provided by a series of Roper polls over a nine-year period. Respondents were asked exactly the same question in each poll:

"At the present time do you find yourself more in sympathy with Israel or more in sympathy with the Arab nations?"

Sympathize	8/81	7/81	4/80	5/78	1/78	3/77	12/74	11/73
More with Israel	39%	35%	37%	35%	37%	43%	41%	47%
More with Arab nations	10	10	9	10	5	5	5	7
Egypt, but not other Arab nations (volunteered)	3	2	2	1	1	–	–	–
Both equally (volunteered)	10	11	15	15	16	13	13	10
Neither	23	22	21	22	24	23	25	18
Don't know	16	19	15	18	16	16	18	17

The second major event which abruptly changed U.S. public perceptions of the Arab-Israeli dispute was the Israeli invasion of Lebanon. Apparently very few Americans realized that the Lebanese-Israeli border had been quiet for 10 months prior to the invasion, under terms of a U.S.-brokered cease-fire agreement. For that reason, the actual questions are presented here, since they indicate either a lack of information about the situation on the ground by the polling organizations themselves, or possibly the beginnings of a trend by some organizations to manipulate their responses to mask a growing public skepticism about Israel.

During the first month the U.S. public was closely divided in appraising the June 1982 invasion. Following are the results of three polls during that period:

Gallup June 11-14, 1982 question asked of 92 per cent of the public who claimed to have "heard or read " about the situation in the Middle East:

"Israel recently began military operations in Southern Lebanon to stop Palestinian artillery attacks on settlements in Israel. Do you approve or disapprove of this action by Israel?

Approve – 40%   Disapprove – 35%   No Opinion – 25%

CBS-*New York Times* June 26-27, 1982 question asked of 76 per cent of the public who said they had heard or read something about "the recent fighting by the Israeli Army in Lebanon:"

"Some people say Israel is right to fight in Lebanon in order to stop the PLO – the Palestinian Liberation Organization. Others say that Israel is wrong to go into Lebanese territory. Do you think Israel is right or wrong to fight in Lebanon?"

Right – 34%   Wrong – 38%   No Opinion – 24%
Other volunteered comments – 4%

Los Angeles Times June 29-July 7, 1982 questions:

"Do you think the Israeli Army should or should not remain (in Lebanon) until a buffer zone is established between Southern Lebanon and Northern Israel – or haven't you heard enough about it yet to say?"

Should – 51%   Should not – 18%
Not sure – 11%   Unaware – 20%

"Do you think the Israeli Army should or should not have attacked Lebanon to begin with – or haven't you heard enough about it yet to say?"

Should – 24%   Should not – 50%
Not sure – 13   Unaware – 13

As the summer wore on, and the fighting continued, concern arose about whether Israel's security needs justified its actions. Three Harris polls presented the same question:

"Let me read you some statements about Israel's move into Lebanon. For each, tell me if you tend to agree or disagree . . . Israel was wrong to go to war and kill thousands of Lebanese civilians."

	June 13-22	*July 9-14*	*August 5-10*
Agree	49%	52%	63%
Disagree	41	35	29
Not Sure	10	13	8

It was the revelations concerning the Sabra-Shatilla massacre, however, that dramatically changed U.S. perceptions, causing many pro-Israel respondents to abandon their justifications of Israeli actions on grounds of military necessity.

A Gallup/*Newsweek* September 22-23, 1982 poll asked the 87 per cent of the public who said they had heard about "the massacre of Palestinians in Beirut refugee camps by Lebanese Christian militia . . . which of the following comes closest to your view?"

	Aware Public	*Pro-Israel Public*	*American Jews*
Israel is very much responsible because it let Christian militia soldiers into the Palestinian camp	32%	16%	11%

Israel must bear partial responsibility because its troops had taken control of the area where the massacre occurred	49	60	54
(Total Israel responsible)	(81)	(76)	(65)
Israel cannot be held responsible for the massacre because it was carried out by Lebanese Christian militia	8	16	28
Don't know	11	8	7

A Harris October 29-November 1, 1982 poll also assessed post-massacre sentiment with the following statements:

	Agree	Disagree	Not Sure
Israel was **wrong** to allow the Lebanese troops to go into Palestinian refugee camps and kill civilians	71%	23%	6%
Israel was **wrong** to move into West Beirut, where the PLO leadership was dug in, because it meant heavy bombing of a major civilian center	50	41	9
Israel was **right** to move into Lebanon in the first place, since PLO and Syrian bases there were regularly shelling Israel	49	42	9

As for lasting effects, the raw data shows a reversion to basic and long-term attitudes within a year of the beginning of the invasion.

An ABC/*Washington Post* poll asked the same question at regular intervals:

"In the Middle East situation, are your sympathies more with Israel or more with the Arab nations?"

	3/3-9 1982	8/17 1982	9/24-26 1982	1/18-22 1983	2/25-3/2 1983
Israel	55%	52%	48%	47%	52%
Arab Nations	18	18	27	17	16
Neither, both (volunteered)	13	16	12	15	13
Don't know	14	14	13	21	19

The Gallup Poll, the only one that has measured U.S. public opinion based upon responses to the same question ("In the Mideast situation are your sympathies more with Israel or the Arab nations") ever since 1967, reflected a remarkable near-even split in basic sympathies for Israel (32 per cent) and the Arabs (28 per cent) on September 22 and 23 immediately after the Sabra Shatilla massacre. This was a 100 per cent jump in sympathy for the Arabs from any figure previously recorded. By January, 1983, however, the figures recorded had reverted to almost pre-invasion levels of 49 per cent for Israel and 12 per cent for the Arabs. A chart presenting these Gallup figures over an 18-year period is printed at the end of this appendix.

The Gallup/*Newsweek* September 22 and 23, 1982 poll also tried to measure changes in public perceptions of both Israel and the Palestinians in the light of the massacres. The complete table:

Relation Between Perception of Israel's Responsibility for Beirut Massacre and Change in Sympathies Regarding Middle East:

	Total Public		Pro-Israel Sympathizers	
	Israel Respons.	Israel Not Respons.	Israel Respons.	Israel Not Respons.
	81%	8%	23%	5%
Sympathy Toward Israeli Position Compared to One Year Ago:				
More	19%	65%	34%	62%
Less	60	20	47	24
Same (Vol.)	10	8	14	11
Don't know	11	7	5	3
Sympathy Toward Palestinian Position Compared to One Year Ago:				
More	46%	8%	40%	14%
Less	27	48	36	54
Same (Vol.)	16	18	16	27
Don't know	11	26	8	5

Events in the summer of 1982 also had a noticeable effect on U.S. perceptions of Israeli Prime Minister Menachem Begin, as measured by four ABC/*Washington Post* polls between March 1982 and March 1983:

	March 1982	Mid-August 1982	Late Sept. 1982	February-March 1983
Favorable	39%	33%	26%	23%
Unfavorable	22	32	47	34
No Opinion	39	35	27	43

Evidence of increasing differentiation by Americans among Middle East countries was provided by polls which separated the Arab nations into named individual states. An August, 1983 Gallup poll asked the following question on nations of the Middle East and South Asia:

"I would like you to rate your opinion of several countries. Using a scale of one to seven where seven represents a country you *like* very much and one represents a country you *dislike* very much, how would you rate your opinion of the following countries?"

The listing, from most liked to most disliked:

Egypt	4.8	Lebanon	3.6
Israel	4.7	Pakistan	3.5
India	4.3	Syria	3.3
Jordan	4.2	Iraq	2.7
Saudi Arabia	3.8	Iran	2.0
Afghanistan	3.7		

In assessing these results the Gallup organization pointed out that Libya had been covered in a survey of African nations and had been ranked lowest, comparable to the ranking on *this* survey for Iran. The high rating for India was accounted for by Gallup with the explanation that Mrs. Gandhi had recently visited the U.S. and, even more important perhaps, the academy-award winning film *Gandhi* was enjoying a tremendous box-office success in the U.S. at the time of the survey. The indifferent rating given Saudi Arabia, Gallup says, probably reflects continued resentment over U.S. dependence upon Saudi petroleum, and the still-vivid memory of the 1973 oil boycott.

Two other examples of differentiation closely following officially-proclaimed U.S. Government attitudes are provided by an October 23 to 27, 1985 Harris poll. One question asked:

"If peace negotiations between Israel and the Arabs take place, would you favor or oppose (read each item) being included in the negotiations?"

	Favor	*Oppose*	*Not Sure*
Israel	84	13	3
Egypt	77	18	5
Jordan	72	20	8
U.S. (as a sponsor of negotiations)	71	25	4
Palestinian leaders not affiliated with the PLO	64	29	7
Syria	59	31	10
PLO	41	54	5
Russia (as a sponsor of negotiations)	27	69	4

The second question asked:

"I'm going to read off some countries and groups and for each one I'd like
you to tell me if you feel it has leadership which is now reasonable and
which will really work for a just peace settlement in the Middle East, or
if it has unreasonable leadership that probably will make it impossible to
work out a peace settlement."

	Reasonable	Unreason.	Not Sure
Israel	72	22	6
Egypt	69	22	9
Jordan	55	28	17
Saudi Arabia	51	37	12
Syria	30	52	18
PLO	10	82	8

An indication of where the Arab-Israeli dispute stands in terms of public opinion
priorities was provided by a February 1981 Roper poll. It asked respondents about the
use of U.S. troops in eight different situations. The poll showed only 26 per cent of
Americans would favor use of U.S. troops even in case of an invasion of Israel by
Arab countries. The results:

Sending U.S. Troops . . .	Favor	Oppose	Don't Know
If U.S. Embassy employes were taken hostage again in some other country	64%	24%	12%
If Soviet troops invaded Western Europe	51	35	14
If the Soviet Union invaded West Berlin	46	41	13
If Cuban troops were involved in a Communist takeover of a Central American country	42	42	16
If Arab forces invaded Israel	26	58	16
If Soviet troops invaded Poland	23	58	19
If North Korea invaded South Korea	20	63	17
If Soviet troops invaded Iran	17	69	14

The lack of American public support for the Palestinians has long puzzled Arabs
familiar with the U.S. tradition of sympathy for the underdog. It is less puzzling if
one examines closely the answers to slightly different questions on the subject. The

U.S. public is not so basically pro-Israel and anti-Palestinian as superficial consideration might imply. In fact, it was PLO use of what seemed to Americans to be terrorist methods in support of the Palestinian cause, rather than the cause itself, that bothered Americans.

Between 1977 and 1982 the Roper organization asked: "As you may know, the Palestinian Liberation Organization in the Middle East – known as the PLO – wants to establish a homeland for Palestinians on territory occupied by Israel since 1967. Do you think the PLO is right or wrong in wanting to establish a Palestinian homeland in Israel (in 1980 this was changed to 'in Israeli-occupied territory'), or haven't you paid much attention to it?"

The results (in percentages):

	July 1977	Oct-Nov 1979	Aug 1980	Aug 1981	Aug 1982	Oct 1982
Right	21	26	19	17	18	19
Right, but their methods are wrong (volunteered)	9	14	8	11	11	12
(Total right)	(30)	(40)	(27)	(28)	(29)	(31)
Wrong	20	17	25	24	34	31
Haven't paid much attention	33	33	31	31	25	25
Don't know	17	10	16	17	12	13

To the 1980 poll Roper added this question: "If the PLO agreed to recognize the existence of Israel and also stopped its military raids on Israel, do you think Israel should agree to the idea of a homeland for Palestinians on territory now held by Israel, or don't you think they should agree to such a Palestinian homeland?" When the Palestinian homeland was coupled with PLO recognition of Israel, 39 per cent per cent said they thought "Israel should agree." This 39 per cent of respondents was then asked: "Suppose the PLO agrees to recognize Israel and stop its raids, but Israel won't go along with the idea of a Palestinian homeland. In that case, do you think we should or should not reduce U.S. military supplies to Israel until it agrees with the idea of a Palestinian homeland?"

Responses to the two questions:

Israel should agree to a Palestinian homeland if the PLO recognizes Israel	39%
(Favor strong pressure on Israel to accept it	19)
(Oppose strong pressure	15)
(No opinion about pressure	5)
Israel should not agree to a Palestinian homeland	21
No opinion about a Palestinian homeland	40

From these answers one can reach a number of conclusions about U.S. public opinion and the Palestinians. First, support for a Palestinian homeland peaked in 1979, when it clearly enjoyed the support of a U.S. President (Carter). This was a period close to the Sadat initiative and the generally favorable upturn of American feeling about the Arabs that followed it.

Second, most polls show that more Americans think the idea of a Palestinian homeland is right than think it is wrong, but only if one includes those Americans who disassociate the idea of a Palestinian homeland from the methods of the PLO.

Finally, if PLO recognition of Israel is included in the question, then Americans favoring a Palestinian homeland outnumber those opposing it by nearly two to one.

Significantly, although Democrats and Republicans hardly differed in their opinions about a Palestinian homeland, those who were better educated, executives and professionals, and those who were in higher income brackets were significantly more favorable to the idea. Some 50 per cent of university-educated respondents, of executives and professionals, and of those earning more than $25,000 annually, said Israel should agree to a homeland for the Palestinians if the PLO recognized Israel. About 25 per cent from the same categories said Israel should not agree.

No more than one quarter of any population group approved U.S. pressure on Israel to accept a Palestinian homeland. University-educated respondents, however, were more willing to pressure Israel than those without a university education, by 24 to 15 per cent.

Juxtaposing a number of Gallup and Harris surveys reveals that the U.S. public consistently views "the PLO" more negatively than it views "the Palestinians." When Israel is contrasted with the PLO, therefore, it rates higher in U.S. sympathies than when it is contrasted with the Palestinians.

The question asked by the two polling organizations was the same except that sometimes it referred to "the PLO" and sometimes to "the Palestinians." On two Harris polls both were referred to, with the expected widely differing results.

The question asked was:

"In the dispute between Israel and the Palestinians (or Palestinian Liberation Organization—PLO), which side do you sympathize with more—Israel or the Palestinians (PLO)?" The responses (with don't know omitted):

	Israel	Palestinians	Neither, Both (Volunteered)	Israel	PLO	Neither, Both, (Volunteered)
Nov. 1982 (Gallup)	40%	17%	27%	Not Asked		
Aug. 1982 (Harris)	Not Asked			59%	15%	12%
June 1982 (Harris)	Not Asked			60	16	13
Aug. 1981 (Harris)	47	15	13	59	14	9
July 1980 (Harris)	47	14	23	65	6	17
Oct. 1979 (Harris)	Not Asked			55	14	12
Nov. 1978 (Gallup)	39	12	23	Not Asked		
Dec. 1974 (Harris)	44	14	26	Not Asked		

As indicated in the introduction to this appendix, many Middle East specialists and virtually all partisans of the Arabs in the U.S. consider results obtained on Middle East questions by the traditional American polling organizations suspect. They cite Jewish ownership and/or operation of the polling organizations themselves, and bias in favor of Israel by the American media, who are the primary purchasers of polls.

They also cite the fact that wording of questions, emphasis or tone of voice, and, of course, the timing of the poll in relation to major news stories all can influence results. Some of these improper influences can easily be spotted, such as the inaccurate reference to cross-border shelling in two of the previously-cited questions about causes of the Israeli invasion of Lebanon in 1982. Others, such as the fact that a poll was made just after an inflamatory event like a hijacking in which American passengers have been killed are clear at the time the poll is published but are often overlooked in presentations of long-term trends. Other factors such as the personal prejudices or the tone of voice used by the questioner are impossible to uncover.

Motivated by these concerns, Arab-American scholars have commissioned polls, using methods conforming to the code of ethics of the American Association for Public Opinion Research, but with questions written in what they maintain is a more neutral manner. The results are interesting in themselves, and also interesting for the somewhat different light they shed on the Gallup, Harris, Roper and Yankelovich poll data previously cited. Here are a few of the results of a February, 1985, poll conducted by the Survey Research Center of the Institute for Social Research at the University of Michigan. The poll was commissioned by the International Center for Research and Public Policy in Washington, D.C. All of the results reproduced below were published in the summer, 1985 edition of the *Journal of Palestine Studies*.

Question: "In the Middle East Conflict, do you think the United States should favor Israel, favor the Arab countries, or should the U.S. not favor one side or the other?"

Favor Israel	20%
Favor neither side	70
Favor Arab countries	0.2
Don't know, N.A., other	12

This indicates an overwhelming American majority for an even-handed rather than a pro-Israeli policy.

Question: "How important is it that the U.S. maintain friendly relations with Israel?"

Very important	48%
Somewhat important	39
Not important	6
Don't know/other	8

Question: "How important is it that the U.S. maintain friendly relations with the Arab countries in conflict with Israel?"

Very important	44
Somewhat important	42
Not important	6
Don't know/other	9

The answers to these two questions show that Americans recognize that the Arab countries are as important to the U.S. as is Israel.

Question: "I will read two statements and then I would like to know which of the two you agree with more:

"The first statement is: Peace in the Middle East will come only when the Palestinian people have a state of their own on the West Bank.

"The second is: A Palestinian state on the West Bank would be a threat to the security of Israel. Which statement do you agree with most?"

(The order of the statements was reversed in half of the interviews to eliminate question-order bias.)

Pro-West Bank State	55%
Anti-West Bank State	27
Both	2
Neither	7
Don't know	6
No answer	7

Here the placing of the question into the context of a step toward peace results in a significant increase in public support of a Palestinian state.

Question: "The U.S. Government has agreed to give Israel $2.6 billion a year in military and economic aid. Do you think this aid is the right amount, too much, or not enough?"

Too much	54.2%
Right amount	30.7
Not enough	3.9
Don't know/no answer	11.4

Question: "The U.S. Government has agreed to give Egypt 2 billion dollars a year in military and economic aid. Do you think this aid is the right amount, too much, or not enough?"

Too much	55.6%
Right amount	30.3
Not enough	3.9
Don't know/no answer	10.4

Although U.S. public opinion is almost identical regarding aid to Israel and aid to Egypt, not long after this question was asked, aid to Israel was increased to nearly $4 billion, and aid to Egypt decreased to about $1 billion. Aid figures set by the Administration and Congress apparently have little to do with public opinion.

Question: "Some people suggest that an international conference including the U.S., the Soviet Union, Israel, Syria, Jordan, Egypt and the PLO should convene and try to settle the Arab-Israeli conflict. Do you think the U.S. should participate in such a conference?"

Yes	66%
No	25
Don't know/not sure	10

U.S. Government reluctance over a period of several years to allow the Soviet Union to become involved in Middle East peace negotiations, therefore, apparently has little basis in U.S. public opinion.

A final area of surprising findings from this especially-commissioned poll concerns American perceptions of Middle Eastern leaders. These February, 1985, results, arranged from most positive at the top to most negative at the bottom, show that, after U.S. disillusionment with Menachem Begin, Israeli leaders no longer get a free ride in U.S. public opinion. Instead they are judged as cautiously and suspiciously as are individual Arab leaders.

U.S. PERCEPTIONS OF MIDDLE EAST LEADERS

	Favorable	Unfavorable	Don't recognize	Other
Hussein of Jordan	45	20	20	17
Mubarrak of Egypt	41	11	34	17
Peres of Israel	41	11	32	18
Fahd of Saudi Arabia	41	15	28	18
Assad of Syria	24	37	25	17
Arafat of the PLO	11	65	13	13

U.S. EVALUATIONS OF LEADERS' PEACE RECORDS

	Seeking Peace	Blocking Peace	Don't know	Other
Mubarrak	30	6	59	8
Fahd	28	9	57	8
Hussein	26	13	56	8
Peres	19	7	67	8
Assad	10	23	61	8
Arafat	9	26	60	8

UPI

This Palestinian girl poses a challenge to all Americans, who are beginning to realize that the irresponsible exercise of power is the enemy of both justice and peace in the Middle East.

ROPER POLL RESULTS 1973 - 1981

PARTISANS OF ISRAEL OR THE ARABS

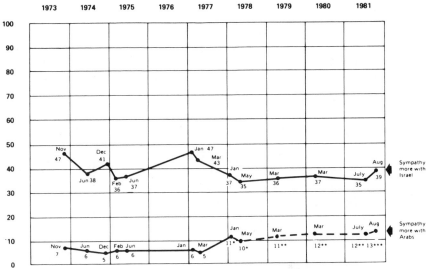

*Includes one percent volunteering sympathy for Egypt alone, but not the other Arab states.

**Includes two percent volunteering sympathy for Egypt alone, but not the other Arab states.

***Includes three percent volunteering sympathy for Egypt, but not the other Arab states.

RESPONDENTS EXPRESSING NO PREFERENCE BETWEEN ARABS OR ISRAELIS

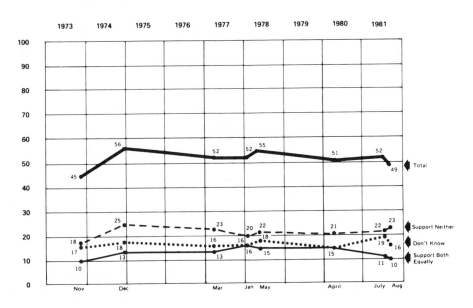

GALLUP POLL RESULTS 1967 - 1983
AMERICAN SUPPORTERS OF ISRAEL OR THE ARABS

AMERICAN RESPONDENTS CLAIMING TO BE FOLLOWING MIDEAST EVENTS

Index

ABC, 161, 313, 316, 319
ABC Poll, 371-2
Abd al-Hadi family, 17
Abd al-Illah, Regent of Iraq, 22, 59
Abourezk, Senator James, 279, 281, 283, 295, 307, 320
Abu Nidal (Sabri Al Banna), 222, 258-9, 264
Abu Musa, 244
Acheson, Dean, 28, 36
Achille Lauro, 258, 375-6
Adamec, Dr. Ludwig, 335-7
Afghanistan, 207, 373
Agnew, Spiro, 128
Al-Assad, President Hafez, 113, 153-4, 171, 175, 213, 225, 242-4, 246, 250, 252, 256, 342-3, 381-2
Al-Assad, Rifaat, 243
Al Dawa, 254
Al Fatah, 76, 112, 209, 213, 244, 251, 257
Algeria, 46, 65-6, 68, 73, 83, 128, 133, 255, 367
Alhegelan, Ambassador Faisal, 226
Alhegelan, Nouha, 226
Al-Hout, Shafiq, 316
Al-Husayni, Al Haj Muhammad Amin, 16
Aliyah, first, 12-3; second, 13
Allen, Richard, 207, 212, 217
Allon, Yigael, 41; Allon Plan, 104
Al-Sabah, Sheikh Saud Nasir, 254
Al-Said, Nuri, 28, 59
Amal, 245, 255-6
America-Israel Council for Israeli-Palestinian Peace, 277
American Arab Affairs Council, 285
American Arab Anti-Discrimination Committee (ADC), 258, 263, 321
American Arab Cultural Foundation, 284
American Council for Judaism, 275
American Educational Trust, 285
American Friends of the Middle East, 285
American Friends Service Committee, 299, 304-5
American Israel Public Affairs Committee (AIPAC), 174, 268-70, 301, 327, 339-353
American Jewish Alternatives to Zionism, 275
American Jewish Committee, 7-8, 66, 159, 172-4, 269-71, 302, 324, 342, 360-2
American Military Retirees Assn., 293
American Near East Refugee Aid (ANERA), 284, 292
Americans for Mid East Understanding, 285

American Security Council, 293
American University, 4, 333-4
American University of Beirut, 35, 110
American University in Cairo, 67
American Zionist Council, 269
Ames, Robert, 243
Amitay, Morris, 270, 350
Anderson, Robert, 44-5, 72, 80
Angleton, James, 74, 98
Annenberg School of Communications, 332
Anti-Arab bias, 355, 357-8, 367
Anti-Defamation League, 90, 269, 283-4, 328, 333, 342
Anti-Semitism, 12, 16, 106, 134, 154, 159, 210, 212, 216, 269, 279, 290, 305-6, 308, 316, 322, 334, 337, 340
Antonius, George, 11-2
Appelman, Mary, 274
Arab-American Institute, 284
Arab-Americans, 224-5, 252, 261-4, 275-6, 279-287, 321-23, 326, 346, 351, 379
Arab boycott of Israel, 283, 290
"Arab Cold War," 56
Arab embassies and diplomats, 263
Arab Israeli wars, 2, 71, 167. 1948: 54, 82, 103-5, 275-7. 1956: 51, 72, 77-8, 82, 85, 103-4, 127. 1967: 7-6, 81, 83, 85-100, 103-5, 107, 111, 113, 125, 127, 167, 173, 187, 214, 275, 280, 308, 312, 358-9; War of Attrition: 110, 311. 1973: 1, 5, 7, 122-148, 154, 159, 188, 204, 214, 262, 276, 292, 298, 308, 312-3, 350, 359-61, 368
Arab League, 7, 176, 296
Arab Legion, 34, 47, 59, 76, 85, 158
Arab Lobby, 263-4, 268, 279-87, 298, 346, 349
Arab nations, 18, 58, 102, 104, 137, 195-7, 200, 209-10, 217, 239, 276-7, 295-8, 315-6, 342, 347, 355-60, 371-2, 380
Arab rejectionists, 217, 258
Arabs, 11, 49, 55, 58, 66, 116-8, 154, 156, 167, 171, 225, 240-1, 280, 295-8, 309, 311-3, 315-8, 321-3, 325, 355-66, 375-8
Arab Women's Council, 225-6
Arafat, Yassir, 156, 165, 177, 185, 196, 209, 213, 219-22, 227-8, 237, 241-5, 250-3, 256-9, 286, 298, 301, 310, 317-8, 342-3, 381-2
ARAMCO, 289
Arens, Moshe, 216
Argentina, 223

381

Argov, Shlomo, 222-3
Arif, President Abd al Salam, 59, 68
Armstrong, Willis, 332-3
Association of Arab American University
   Graduates, 284-5
Aswan High Dam, 44-7, 190, 240
Atherton, Alfred L. Jr., 1-2
Atlantic Monthly, 325
Attlee, Earl Clement, 37, 75
Austin, Senator Warren, 30-1, 33
Australia, 5, 22, 88
Austria, 258, 336
Avnery, Uri, 252
AWACS, 203, 211-2, 262, 292, 304, 345,
   351-2

Ba'ath, 68
Badeau, Ambassador John, 64
Baghdad Pact, 46-7
Baker, Sen.Howard, 180, 212
Balfour, Arthur, 11, 13, 15; Balfour Declara-
   tion, 13, 15-6
Ball, George, 2, 5-6, 39, 115, 158, 205, 290
Barak, Aharon, 189, 191
Beaufort Castle, 222-3
Bechtel Corporation, 205
Beegle, Dewey, 300-1
Begin, Menachem, 4, 6, 9, 18, 170-1, 173-93,
   195-200, 204-5, 209-11, 213-6, 219, 221-2,
   224-5, 227-9, 231, 234-5, 237-41, 245-6,
   271, 273-4, 277-8, 298, 302, 308, 318, 324,
   355, 362, 364-5
Bell, Daniel, 180
Bell, Steve, 313
Bellow, Saul, 180
Ben Bella, Ahmed, 66, 68
Ben Gurion, David, 16-8, 22, 33, 39, 41, 43-6,
   48, 51, 57, 78, 99, 117, 163
Bennett, Max, 42
Bentley, Rep.Helen Delich, 344
Ben-Yishai, Ron, 233, 235
Berger, Rabbi Elmer, 275-7
Bergus, Donald, 116, 119, 340
Bernadotte, Count Folke, 18
Berri, Nabih, 245, 255-6
"Big Lie" (1967 war), 83
Biltmore Program, 22
"Black Thursday," 227
Block, Herbert, 321-2
B'nai B'rith, 216, 269, 283, 291, 327, 333, 342
Boeing Company, 293
Bonine, Michael, 328
Bookbinder, Hyman, 7, 268
Boumedienne, Col.Houari, 128
Bourguiba, Habib, 66
Bowles, Chester, 63
Brandeis, Justice Louis, 36
Breira (Alternative) peace movement, 276-7

Brezhnev, Leonid I., 1, 76, 89, 132-4, 141-8,
   175
British Mandate for Palestine, 15-6, 33-4, 112,
   167, 170, 201, 252
Brookings Institution, 167-8
Brown, General George S., 267-8
Bryn Mawr/Haverford, 332-3
Brzezinski, Zbigniew, 168, 181
Buber, Martin, 75
Buchwald, Art, 334
Burgess, W. Randolph, 55
Bush, Vice President George, 207, 225
Business Roundtable, 291-2
Byrd, Robert, 177
Byrnes, James, 28

Califano, Joseph, 186
Camp David, 172, 181, 186, 196-9, 201, 209,
   213-4, 216, 297, 308, 366-8
Camp David Agreements, 6, 186-204, 237-8
Canada, 22, 78
Caploe, David, 8-9
Caradon, Lord Hugh, 105
Carmel, Hesi, 41-2
Carter, President Jimmy, 162, 165-82, 185-93,
   195-202, 204-7, 211, 238, 249, 273, 297,
   308, 362-4, 378
Carter Administration, 1, 3, 6, 165, 172-4, 176,
   179, 186, 195, 198, 203, 207-8, 211, 215,
   262, 343, 364, 367-8
Carter, Rosalynn, 166, 169-70, 181
Cartoons, 321-2
Castro, Fidel, 64-6
Catholics, 8, 303, 305-6
Catholics for Christian Political Action, 293
CBS, 208, 254, 315-6, 319, 324, 369
CBS poll, 366
Celler, Rep.Emmanuel, 21
Center for Contemporary Arab Studies, 334
Central Intelligence Agency, 74-6, 98-100, 106,
   128, 144, 216, 243
Chamoun, President Camille, 58-60, 163, 243
Chehab, Com.Fuad, 60
China, 177, 238
Chinese People's Republic, 45, 136,
Chomsky, Noam, 328
Christian Arabs, 3, 13-4, 58, 61, 112, 156, 163,
   210, 282-3, 305-6, 370
Christian Century, 304
Christian Churches, 162, 166-7, 283, 299-306
Christian fundamentalists, 300-6
Christian Science Monitor, 319
Christians United for American Security, 304
Church, Sen.Frank, 128
Churchill, Winston, 13, 23, 46
Claremont Publications, 285
Clark, William C., 205, 207-8, 217, 225-6, 238
Clifford, Clark, 32

Coalition of Peace Through Strength, 293
Cluster bombs, 182, 219, 224, 341
"Coca Cola" invasion, 60
Cohen, Richard, 273, 324
Columbia Journalism Review, 325
Commentary, 8, 269, 277, 316, 324-5, 332, 334
Conference of Presidents of Major American Jewish Organizations, 269, 271, 278, 302, 342
Cooley, John, 261, 319-21
Cox, Archibald, 136
Crane, Charles, 15
Crusaders, 12
Cuba, 64-6, 68, 124, 376
Cyprus, 50, 257
Czechoslovakia, 34, 44

Davis, Leonard, 322
Dayan, Moshe, 18, 42-3, 74, 81, 96, 98-9, 116, 118-9, 127, 129, 153, 163, 176−7, 181-2, 189, 191
Deacon, Richard, 90
Dehmer, Alan, 300-1
Democratic Party and Democrats, 3, 5, 8, 22, 32, 40, 64-6, 72, 81, 88, 99, 103, 117-8, 121, 163, 186, 201, 265, 285, 343, 348, 378
Derogy, Jacques, 41-2
Detente, 4, 204
Diaspora, 12, 36, 340
Dine, Thomas, 268, 270-1, 301
Dinitz, Simcha, 126-30, 142, 145, 161
Dobrynin, Anatoly, 107, 125, 132, 143
Dominican Republic, 76
Draper, Theodore, 124, 228-9, 233-4, 240
Dreyfus Affair, 12, 41, 98
Drinin, The Rev. Fr. Robert, 304
Druzes, 58, 163, 230, 242-5, 247
Dual citizens, 84, 97, 263
Duke University, 268, 332
Dulles, John Foster, 5, 39, 45, 47-8, 51, 54, 66, 71, 73, 75, 78-9, 106
Dunsmore, Barry, 315
Dutton, Fredrick G., 284-5
Dymally, Rep. Mervyn M., 340
Eban, Abba, 53, 63, 71, 78-80, 109, 123, 186, 195, 204, 219, 237
Eddy, William, 32
Eden, Anthony, 46-8, 50-1, 56-7, 78
Eggerstrom, Lee, 295, 313
Egypt and United Arab Republic, 3, 6, 18, 34, 40-8, 50-60, 64, 67, 71-86, 89, 91-2, 94-107, 110-147, 152-62, 170-3, 175-82, 186-193, 197-203, 213-6, 241, 244, 250-1, 258, 270, 275-6, 282, 284, 286, 296-8, 301, 304, 308, 312, 318, 330, 334, 359, 362-6, 373-6, 381
Egyptian Jews, 42-3, 276

Eisenhower, President Dwight D., 39-41, 43-54, 57-61, 64-7, 72-80, 103, 158, 216
Eisenhower Administration, 39, 43, 52, 55-6, 61, 64, 73-4
Eisenhower Doctrine, 55-6, 58, 71, 75
Elath (Epstein), Eliahu, 32-3
El Baz, Osama, 191
El-Bireh, 283
Ellis, Father Kail, 334
Elon, Amos, 312
Ennes, James M., Jr., 88, 93, 96-7, 99
Erlichman, John, 103
Ernst, Morris, 22
Errera-Hoechstetter, Dr. Irine, 331
Evans, Rowland, 6, 204, 208, 211, 324
Eveland, Wilbur Crane, 87, 98
Evron, Ephraim, 73-5, 79, 90, 92, 216
Exxon, 329-32

Fahd, King of Saudi Arabia, 133, 172-3, 212, 381-2
Fahmy, Ismail, 177
Faisal, King of Saudi Arabia, 15, 35, 48, 104, 128, 133-7, 249, 331
Faisal II, King of Iraq, 48
Fallaci, Oriana, 117, 122
Falluja Pocket (1948 war), 41, 51
Falwell, the Rev. Jerry, 300, 302-4
Farouk, King of Egypt, 40, 56, 116
Fauntroy, the Rev. Walter, 340
Fein, Leonard, 180, 278
Feinberg, Abe, 81
Feuerlicht, Roberta Strauss, 10, 274
Fez Plan, 239, 242, 298
Findley, Rep. Paul, 327-8, 332-6, 339, 342-3, 352-3
Fischer, Dean, 219
Fisher, Max, 158
FLN, 65-6
Ford, President Gerald, 109, 130, 143, 151, 155-62, 206, 238, 268, 360
Ford Administration, 156-7, 159-62, 343, 361, 363
Ford Foundation, 329
Forrestal, James, 28
France, 12, 39, 42-7, 49-6, 58, 65-6, 85, 89, 92, 97-8, 104-6, 177, 210, 213, 228-9, 238, 254, 274, 311, 333, 341
Franjieh, President Suleiman, 230
Frankfurter, Felix, 36
Freedom of Information Act, 96
Free Trade Agreement with Israel, 353
Frem, Fadi, 242
Fulbright, Sen. William, 158, 342

Galbraith, Ambassador Kenneth, 63
Gallup polls, 357-373, 378-9
Garment, Leonard, 103, 108

Garnham, David, 347, 350-1
Gaza, 34, 41, 43, 46, 53-4, 91, 178, 182, 188, 196, 221, 237-9, 251, 276, 299, 304-5
Gemayel, President Amin, 233-4, 240, 242, 245-7
Gemayel, Bashir, 163, 222, 225, 229-30
Gemayel, Pierre, 163, 222, 240, 242
Geneva Peace Conference, 176-8
Georgetown University, 334
Germany, 68, 122, 275, 321, 335, 341, 376; East Germany, 143-4
Geyelin, Philip, 7, 204, 213-4, 238, 324
Geyer, Georgie Anne, 307, 312, 321
Ghareeb, Edmund, 313, 316-7
Ghazawi, Toufiq, 254
Gibli, Col.Benjamin, 42
Gimello, Robert, 336
Giscard d'Estaing, President Valery, 171
Glubb Pasha, 47
Golan Heights, 86, 89, 122, 125, 129, 188, 214-5, 239, 246, 250, 298
Gold, Bertram, 158-9
Goldberg, Arthur, 158, 175, 280
Golder, Robert, 345-6
Goldman, Guido, 273
Grand Mufti of Jerusalem, 16-9
Grayball, Rep. David, 304, 306
Great Britain, 13-5, 17, 29, 32, 39, 41-4, 46-56, 59, 61, 67, 74, 83, 102, 104, 106, 129, 132, 177, 213, 222, 229, 238, 274, 290, 293, 341, 352, 357
Greece, 44, 229, 244, 255
Greenfield, Meg, 322
Greneda, 245
Griggs, Henry, Jr., 314-5, 319
Gromyko, Andrei, 176
Grunzweig, Emil, 235
Gulf Cooperation Council, 297
Gulf of Aqaba, 51, 54, 71, 78, 80
Gulf of Tonkin Resolution, 99
Gulf Oil Corporation, 292
Gur, Gen. Mordechai, 85
Gush Emunim, 271

Habash, Dr.George, 112-4, 251, 263-4
Habib, Philip, 219-20, 227-8
Hadad, Wadi'a, 264
Haddad, Maj. Saad, 222, 230, 234-5, 242, 253
Haig, Alexander, 6, 125, 130, 136, 143-5, 204, 206-9, 214, 217, 221-2, 225-6, 238, 351
Haldane, John, 290
Haldeman, John, 206
Hamilton, Rep. Lee, 339, 353
Hammarskjold, Dag, 49
Harmon, Avraham, 79, 92
Harris Poll, 362-4, 371, 373, 378-9
Harrison, Gilbert, 325
Harsch, Joseph C., 2

Hart, Alan, 152, 183, 196
Harvard University, 8, 330-1
Hassan, King of Morocco, 213
Hawatmeh, Nayef, 251
Healey, Father Timothy, 334
Hegna, Charles, 254
Hejaz, 14
Helms, Sen. Jesse, 343-6
Helms, Richard, 105
Heren, Louis, 78-9
Hersh, Seymour, 101-2, 118
Hershman, Robert, 314-5, 319
Hertzberg, Rabbi Arthur, 302
Herzl, Theodor, 12, 17
Hijackings, 112, 254-6, 258
Hitler, Adolf, 17, 27, 37, 73, 122, 219, 275, 347
Hobeika, Elie, 231
Holocaust, 8, 18, 21, 167, 212, 273, 321, 347; film, 315
Hopkins, Harry, 73
Hot Line, 86
Howe, Irving, 180
Hudson, Michael, 309, 312
Hughes, Emmet John, 47, 49-50
Hughes, Thomas, 78
Humphrey, Vice President, Hubert, 80, 103, 174
Hungary, 49-52, 55, 144, 214
Hunt, Gov. Jim, 344
Hussein, King of Jordan, 47-8, 60, 76, 83, 85, 91-2, 112-4, 121, 128, 154-6, 159, 169-70, 178, 197, 221, 237, 241-3, 249-50, 252, 259, 297, 353, 360, 381-2
Hussein, Sherif of Mecca, 14-5

Ibn Saud, King Abd al-Aziz of Saudi Arabia, 21, 23-4, 28
Imam Badr, 67
India, 170, 373
Institute of Palestine Studies, 285
International Atomic Energy Agency (IAEA), 210
International Center for Research and Public Policy, 379-82
Iran, 6, 132, 156, 163, 201, 209, 211, 253-5, 296, 298, 367, 375-6
Iraq, 15, 19, 28, 48, 50, 57-60, 68-9, 83, 129, 133, 170, 177, 204, 210-11, 215, 222, 250, 254, 257-8, 275, 282, 297, 311, 334, 373
Iraqi nuclear installation, 210-11, 215, 341, 368
Ireland, 65, 68
Irgun Zvai Leumi, 18, 170, 246
Isaac, Jean Rael, 277
Isaacs, Steven, 262, 312
Islam, 3, 58, 104, 114, 191, 300
Islamic Studies Institute, 285
Ismail, Hafez, 120, 126, 133, 138

Israel, 1-2, 6-7, 18, 24, 29, 31, 33-4, 39, 41, 50, 52-5, 60, 64-7, 71, 73-81, 85, 87-99, 101-7, 109-13, 115-121, 123-4, 127, 130, 151-60, 165-71, 185-93, 195-201, 203-5, 208-16, 219-235, 237-41, 249–58, 262-3, 268, 279-81, 290, 299-305, 308, 312-5, 317-9, 323-8, 334, 336-7, 339, 349, 359-6, 373-4, 376-9; occupation of Lebanon, 253; withdrawal from Lebanon, 237-9, 242-3, 247; Israel-Lebanon peace, 240; U.S.assistance, 2, 3, 239, 250, 255, 310-1, 339-48, 380-1; U.S.public opinion, 119, 253-4, 355-6, 372-3
Israelis, 36, 46, 48-9, 51, 56, 115, 156-7, 185, 194, 221-31, 250-5, 295-8, 301, 305, 308, 315, 318, 322, 341, 375; Israeli-Egyptian peace, 116; Israeli Defense Force, 253
Israeli Embassy in Washington, 224, 263, 297
Israeli intelligence, Mossad, 41-2, 74-81, 89-91, 98, 113, 221, 223, 264
Israel Labor Coalition, 107, 117, 170-1, 178, 209-10, 274
Israel Likud Bloc, 173, 274, 324
Israel Lobby, 7, 39, 44, 73, 128-9, 157, 203, 211-2, 216, 261-4, 267-9, 281-2, 287, 290, 309-10, 324, 326-37, 339-52
Israeli setttlements, 152, 175-6, 181-2, 189-192, 200, 209, 221, 239, 241-2, 271, 274, 276, 278, 299, 308, 341, 343, 357, 365, 368
Italy, 44, 106, 145, 213, 228, 258, 375-6; peacekeeping in Lebanon, 238

Jabotinsky, Vladimir, 16, 18, 170
Jackson, Sen. Henry, 118, 129, 339
Jackson, The Rev. Jesse, 246, 367
Jacobson, Eddie, 30
Janka, Les, 280
Japan, 5
Jarring, Sec. Gen. Gunnar, 106
Javits, Sen. Jacob, 174, 180
Jennings, Peter, 316
Jerusalem, 1, 18, 34, 76, 83, 85, 92, 104, 107, 162, 169, 171, 175, 177, 181, 185, 191-3, 196-201, 204, 222-3, 227, 262, 283, 304, 311-2, 322
Jerusalem Journal of International Relations, 347, 350-1
Jerusalem Post, 180
Jewish Agency, 32-3, 67, 158
Jewish Defense League, 263, 277
Jewish Dissent, 271, 273-8
Jews, European, 12-3, 156, 167, 219, 264, 310, 347, 358; Oriental, 170-1, 200, 235
Jews, U.S., 45, 54-7, 73, 79, 89, 103, 106, 108, 112, 157-9, 169-70, 172-4, 180, 183-4, 197, 200, 203, 216, 224-5, 227, 261-4, 267-71, 273-6, 296-7, 300-2, 307-9, 311-2, 314, 316-7, 322-6, 312, 314-7, 323-6, 327,

332-40, 350, 355, 361-2, 365, 379; White House Liaison, 108; Jewish vote, 22, 29, 32, 48-9, 64-5, 85, 88, 103, 118, 157, 162, 166; bloc vote, 348; Jews in Congress, 183, 211, 343
Jibril, Ahmad, 251
Johns Hopkins University, 4
Johnson, President Lyndon B., 55, 64, 71-5, 85, 89-90, 94, 99-100, 113, 216, 303
Johnson Administration, 5, 72, 75, 83, 88, 106, 205
Jordan, 3, 6, 15-6, 34, 42, 46-8, 57, 59-60, 76-7, 83, 85, 87, 92, 98, 104, 106-7, 112-4, 120-1, 128-9, 152-6, 162, 167, 169-73, 176, 188, 193, 198, 209-10, 221-2, 229, 237-9, 249-52, 258, 275, 283-4, 286, 290, 296-8, 312, 334, 363, 373-5; arms, 340, 345, 353; "Jordanian-Palestinian State," 237
Jordan, Hamilton, 181, 194
Jordan, Vernon, 367
Journal of Palestine Studies, 9, 313, 316-7, 379
Judaism, 86, 191, 274-8
Jumblatt, Kamal, 230, 243

Kabbani, Ambassador Sabah, 165
Kahan Commission, 231-5
Kahane, Rabbi Meir, 263
Karami, Rashid, 61
Karnow, Stanley, 325
Karsch, Carol, 328
Kashdan, Bruce, 234
Keating, Kenneth, 138, 139, 141
Kemp, Rep. Jack, 353
Kenen, Isaiah "Si", 73, 270
Kennedy, Sen. Edward, 201, 353
Kennedy, President John F., 63-7, 69, 72
Kennedy Administration, 5, 64, 205
Kennedy, Joseph Jr., 65
Kennedy, Sen.Robert, 68, 258
Khalid, King of Saudi Arabia, 178
Khalidi, Walid, 35, 110
Khomeini, Ayatollah, 211, 245, 254
Khouri, Fred J., 54
Khouri, Rami, 310
Khrushchev, Nikita, 49
Kidd, Admiral I., 88
King-Crane Commission, 15-6
King, Henry C., 15
Kirkpatrick, Jeane, 6, 225
Kissinger, Henry, 44, 102-3, 107, 109-10, 113, 115-6, 120, 123-38, 141-5, 152-60, 162, 167-8, 180, 203-4, 206-7, 308, 359-61
Klinghoffer, Leon, 258
Knesset, 177, 197, 199, 213-4, 216, 238-9, 263
Knowland, Sen.William, 73, 75
Koeffler, Henry, 328
Korea, 5, 45, 343, 376
Kosygin, Alexei, 86, 133

Koven, Ronald, 264, 314
Kraft, Joseph, 4, 210
Krim, Mathilde, 81
Kurth, James, 332
Kuwait, 112, 133-4, 242, 254-7, 295-7

Lafayette Square, 199, 226
Lahad, Gen. Antoine, 253
Laird, Melvin, 105
Laqueur, Walter, 35, 180
Lasker, Mary, 81
"Lavon Affair," 41, 43, 96, 98; Lavon, Pinchas, 43, 73-4, 98-9
Lawrence of Arabia, 14
League of Nations, 15
Lebanon, 53, 57-61, 114, 120, 163, 209-10, 238-47, 254-8, 273-282, 353, 366, 373; Israeli invasion, 176, 181, 219-23, 232, 235, 253, 271-2, 298-323, 341, 345, 356, 369-70, 379; civil war, 163-4, 224-5, 230-1, 243; Lebanese army 229, 232, 240, 247
Levin, Sen. Carl, 344
Levin, Jeremy, 256-7
Levinger, Rabbi Moshe, 273
Levy, Jerrold, 328, 335-7
Lewis, Anthony, 324
Lewis, Ambassador Samuel, 210, 215, 229, 231
Libya, 157, 176-7, 253, 258, 264, 296-8, 334, 363, 373, 375
Lilienthal, Alfred, 23, 37, 275-6, 292
Lippmann, Walter, 321
Lipset, Seymour Martin, 8, 180
Littell, Dr. Franklin H., 304
Logan, David, 347, 351
Long, Rep. Clarence (Doc) Long, 344
Los Angeles Times, 310, 331, 370
Lurie, Jessie, 180

MacArthur, Gen.Douglas, 30
MacFarland, Robert, 240, 246
MacMillan, Harold, 55-6
McCain, Adm. John, 88
McCartney, James, 9, 307, 309, 314
McCloskey, Rep. Paul N. (Pete), 262, 268, 340, 343
McGonagle, William, 88, 93-6
McGrory, Mary, 324
McMahon, Sir Henry, 14, 16
McNamara, Robert, 80
McPherson, Harry, 75
Maksoud, Amb. Clovis, 158, 296
Malta, 50
Mansfield, Sen. Mike, 157
Marcos, President Ferdinand, 302
Maronites, 58, 163, 210, 222-3, 228-31, 233, 235, 242-3, 250
Marshall, Gen. George, 28, 30, 32-3
Massachussetts Institute of Technology, 332

Mathias, Sen. Charles, McC., 39-40, 261, 268, 295
Mauldin, Bill, 321
Meir, Golda, 55, 105, 108, 117-8, 120-2, 124-5, 127, 135-43, 145, 147-8, 152-4, 228, 359
Metni, Bahij, 254
Mexico, 291 (Jewish boycott)
Middle East Center Foundation, 331
Middle East Institute, 285
Middle East Journal, 285, 319
Middle East Study Associations, 292, 328, 337
Miller, Merle, 36, 71, 73, 75, 79, 81
Mobil Oil, 291
Mohieddin, Zakaria, 81
Mollet, Guy, 46, 48, 51
Moment, 180, 278
Mondale, Sen. Walter F., 1, 172, 181, 196-7
Moorer, Adm. Thomas, 87, 94, 131, 144, 267, 341
Morgenthau, Henry, Sr., 14, 275
Morocco, 46, 133, 148, 156, 170, 176-7, 207, 239, 360; Fez conference, 213, 216, 276, 284, 298
Moyne, Lord, 18
Mubarrak, Hosni, 204, 250, 258, 297, 381-2
Murphy, Robert, 60-1
Muslim Arabs, 3, 12-4, 104, 172
Muslim Brotherhood, 42
Muslims, 18-9, 21, 49, 58, 61, 112, 122, 156, 163, 170, 172, 209, 223, 225, 227-8, 230, 240-1, 262, 283, 320, 325; Shia, 163, 243-5, 247, 253-7, 375; Sunni, 163, 243-5
Naguib, Gen.Mohammad, 40, 42
Nagy, Imre, 51
Najda, 286
Nasser, President Gamal, 39-45, 47-8, 50, 53, 55-61, 64, 67, 73-9, 83-4, 104, 106, 114, 116, 120, 127, 216, 280, 358-9
Nathanson, Philippe, 42-3
National Association of Arab Americans (NAAA), 325-6, 347
National Council of Churches, 305
National Council on U.S.-Arab Affairs, 285
National Defense Education Act (NDEA), 335
National Pact (Lebanon), 58, 61
National Press Club, 179, 364
National Security Agency (NSA), 90-2, 102, 110, 238, 240
National Security Council, 101, 105, 107, 119, 125, 144, 168, 204, 206-7, 347
Nationalist Chinese, 45
NATO, 40, 53, 65-6, 206
Nazi persecution of Jews, 18, 24, 28-9, 97, 275, 305, 321, 336
NBC, 156, 254, 315-6, 319
NBC Poll, 365
Negev, 81, 239

Neil, Denis M., 280, 284
Nessen, Ron, 157
Netherlands, 80, 213
Neumann, Ambassador Robert, 207
New Jewish Agenda, 277
Newsweek, 322, 325
Newsweek Poll, 370-1
New York Post, 159
New York Times, 53-4, 159, 161, 175, 179, 222, 275, 300, 303, 309-10, 314, 324, 342, 369
New Zealand, 5
Niles, David, 24, 32, 37
Ninio, Victorine, 42-3
Nixon, President Richard M., 64, 101-3, 106, 109, 113, 116, 118-21, 124-5, 127-8, 130, 132-6, 138,143-7, 153-5, 203-4, 206, 238, 359-60
Nixon Administration, 5, 102, 106-7, 116-18, 125, 134, 155, 206
Nobel Peace Prize, 185
Nolte, Dr. Richard, 329-30, 337
North Korea, 91, 341
Novak, Robert, 6, 204, 208, 211, 324
November 29 Coalition, 286
Nutting, Anthony, 47

Oberlin College, 15
Odeh, Alex, 258, 263
Oil, 5, 115, 123-4, 130, 132-6, 153, 171, 208-9, 267, 289, 311, 313, 351; Oil embargo, 359-61, 368, 373
Oman, 334
O'Neill, Speaker Thomas (Tip), 168
Operation "Iron Fist," 234, 253-5
Oswald, Lee Harvey, 67

"Package aircraft sale," 262
Pakistan, 373
Palestine, 3, 11-8, 21-5, 27-9, 31-7, 40, 59, 102, 110-7, 120, 167, 172, 178-9, 208, 219, 264, 275, 283-4, 289, 321, 325, 330, 340, 347, 357, 380
Palestine Human Rights Campaign, 284
Palestine Liberation Organization, 112-3, 120, 156, 168-9, 172-3, 176, 181, 199-201, 213, 219-23, 226-8, 234-5 , 237-9, 241-5, 250-3, 257-8, 264, 277, 296, 298, 302-5, 330, 334, 342-3, 355, 358-60, 362-4, 367-9, 371-7, 381; Palestine National Congress, 242-3, 251-2, 257, 305; U.S.dialogue, 237-8
Palestinians, 7, 17-8, 29, 31, 34-6, 54, 68, 76-7, 110-4, 117, 120, 152, 158, 163-4, 168–73, 175-9, 182, 186-9, 195-201, 204, 213, 219-225, 237-40, 242-3, 250-4, 256, 271, 282-4, 286, 291-2, 296, 298, 307-13, 317-9, 321, 325, 340-1, 355-6, 360, 362, 367-9, 372-80; homeland, 365, 377-80; "issue," 186, 188, 195, 208, 238, 246, 249-50, 259, 343-4; terrorism, 317-9

Pan Arabism, 45, 56, 58-9, 114, 116, 181
Pawlikowski, Rev. John T., 300
PBS, 315, 319
Peace Now (Shalom Achshav), 180, 224-5, 235, 277
Pearl Harbor, 15
Pearson, Anthony, 88, 91, 97
Pearson, Lester, 78
Peel Royal Commission to Palestine, 12
Pell, Sen. Claiborne, 6-7, 216
Percy, Sen. Charles, 343-6
Peres, Shimon, 74, 99, 256, 259, 381-2
Peretz, Martin, 180, 325
PFLP, 112, 114, 251, 263-4
Phalange, 163, 222, 225, 230-5, 240, 242, 250
Philippines, 29, 302
Poland, 12, 49, 68, 214, 376
Political Action Committees (PACs), 344-53
Political Science Quarterly, 347-51
Porter, Ambassador William J., 65-6, 68
Powell, Jody, 166
Pratt and Whitney, 293
Protestants, 8, 299-306

Qaddafi, Col. Muammar, 157, 176, 216, 258-9, 264, 281, 367
Qassim, President Abd al-Karim, 59-60
Qatar, 334
Quandt, William, 168

Raab, Earl, 8
Rabin, Yitzak, 106, 117, 155, 157, 160-1, 168, 170, 174, 255
Radio Israel, 214
Rahall, Rep. Nick Joe, II, 353
Ramallah Society, 283
Ramparts, 325
Randall, John, 94
Rapid Deployment Force, 209
Raspberry, William, 196, 214, 324
Rayburn, Speaker Samuel, 71, 75
Reagan, Nancy, 226
Reagan, President Ronald, 201-17, 220, 224-8, 237-9, 241-2, 247, 258-9, 293, 301, 375-6; The Reagan Plan, 238-42, 252, 308
Reagan Administration, 3, 6, 74, 203-12, 246, 256-9, 293, 351-3, 368, 381
Republican Party and Republicans, 3, 5, 8, 40, 55, 65-6, 72, 78, 99, 158, 205-6, 285, 342-3, 348, 378
Reston, James, 279, 316
Revisionists, 16, 18, 22, 104, 170
Riad, Mahmud, 101, 119-20
Ribicoff, Sen.Abraham, 180, 270
Richardson, Elliot, 105, 136
Richman, Alvin, 355-6
Robinson, Marilyn, 316-7
Roche, John P., 79-80
Rockefeller, Nelson, 102

Roeder, Edward, 345-6
Rogers, William, 101, 103, 105, 111, 117-9, 126, 207; Rogers Plan, 101, 105-8
Rokossovsky, Konstantine, 49
Romans, 12
Romulo, Gen. Carlos, 29
Roosevelt, Eleanor, 22, 24, 33, 73
Roosevelt, President Franklin D., 21-4, 31-2, 48, 73, 78, 178
Roosevelt, Kermit, 40
Roosevelt, Theodore, 40
Roper Polls, 363, 374, 376-7
Rosenfeld, Stephen S., 205
Rosenfield, Geraldine, 362
Rostenkowski, Rep.Daniel, 351-2
Rostow, Dr. Eugene V., 5, 72, 79-80, 92, 158
Rothschild, Lord Nathaniel, 11, 13
Rowan, Carl, 324, 340
Ruedy, Prof. John, 334
Rusk, Dean, 33, 37

Sabra-Shatilla refugee camps, 231, 233, 240, 243, 302, 318, 356, 370-2
Sabri, Ali, 116
Sadat, President Anwar, 4, 116-26, 132-3, 135-6, 138, 141-9, 154-7, 161, 166, 168-9, 172, 175-81, 185-93, 196-200, 203, 209, 212, 214, 221, 240, 273, 297, 303-4, 318, 322, 355-7, 364-8; Sadat initiative, 363-4; Journey to Jerusalem, 251, 304, 362-3
Sadat, Jihan, 166, 181
Sadd, David, 280
Said, Dr.Edward, 280
SAM missiles, 110-11
Samuel, Sir Herbert, 17
Saud, (Prince Saud Al Faisal), 249
Saudi Arabia, 4, 6, 14, 21, 28, 32, 35, 57, 67, 104, 112, 115, 128, 133-6, 148, 155, 157-8, 162, 175, 177-80, 195, 197-8, 205, 207-12, 226, 237, 239, 244, 249-51, 262, 270, 283-6, 289-90, 292-3, 296-7, 304, 312, 331-4, 351, 355, 360, 363-4, 373-4; Saudi Peace Plan, 213, 298; aircraft sale, 262, 344, 352
Scali, John, 144
Scheuer, James, 333
Schiff, Ze'ev, 227, 229, 233, 235
Schindler, Rabbi Alexander, 271, 301
Schleifer, Abdullah, 72
Schlesinger, James, 126-30, 133, 205
Schneider, William, 8
Scoville, Sheila, 335-7
Scowcroft, Gen. Brent, 144
Scranton, William, 103, 121, 153
Sellers, Richard, 293
Sephardic Jews, 12
Shadyac, Richard, 280
Shah of Iran, 6, 132, 156, 178

Shaheen, Prof. Jack, 320-1
Shamir, Yitzhak, 6-7, 18, 246, 274
Sharabi, Hisham, 279
Sharett, Moshe, 41-3, 46, 152
Sharon, Gen.Ariel, 152-3, 181, 214, 219, 221-2, 227-235, 239-40, 242, 246, 253, 277, 318-9, 359
Sheean, Vincent, 11, 15-6
Sheehan, Edward, 5, 268
Sherrill, Robert, 325
Sh'ma, 9
Shukairy, Ahmad, 358-9
Shultz, Sec. George, 205-6, 227, 238, 240-3, 246-7, 351, 375
Siegel, Mark, 179
Silver, Rabbi Abba Hillel, 37
Silverman, Ira, 333
Simon, Rep. Paul, 344, 346
Simpson, Natasha, 258
Sinai, 6, 39, 49, 51, 53-4, 71, 73, 75, 77-8, 82, 88, 91-2, 99-100, 107, 110, 116, 127, 132, 157, 159-62, 176-8, 182, 188-91, 197, 199-200, 213-4, 216, 221, 241; withdrawals, 116, 127, 156, 213-4, 365; agreements, 359, 361
Sisco, Joseph, 105, 107, 113, 117, 119-20, 124
Sixth Fleet, 93
Smith, Thomas, 94
Socolow, Sanford, 315
Solarz, Rep. Stephen J., 340
Solidarity Free Trade Union (Poland), 214
Sorenson, Theodore, 64, 67
South Africa, 302
Southern Christian Leadership Conference, 367
Southern Illinois University, 320
Spain, 12, 116, 216
Squadron, Howard, 271, 302-3
Stalin, Joseph, 23, 44
Stanford, William, 254
Stauffer, Thomas, 322
Stern Gang, 18, 246
Stethem, Robert, 255
Stettinius, Edward R., Jr., 23
Stevens, Janet, 243
Stevenson, Adlai, 40, 63
Stone, I.F., 308
Straits of Gibralter, 7
Straits of Hormuz, 7
Straits of Tiran, 49, 54, 71, 77-80, 89, 126, 189
"Strategic Consensus," 204, 208-9, 211, 217
Strauss, Robert, 201
Sudan, 83, 104
Suez Canal, 13-4, 23, 39, 41-2, 47-57, 82, 86, 103, 110-12, 116-7, 122, 124-6, 133, 135, 138-9, 144, 152, 156, 161, 216, 359; nationalization, 46, 49
Suleiman, Michael, 315, 355
Sulzberger family, 275

Swaggart, Jimmy, 300
Swarthmore College, 332-3
Sweden, 106, 185
Switzerland, 171, 336
Sykes-Picot Agreement, 14
Symington, Stuart, 117
Syria, 4, 6, 15, 28, 50, 57-9, 67, 76-7, 82-3,
    86, 89, 91, 98, 106, 112-4, 120-9, 133,
    152-5, 157, 162, 164-5, 171-2, 175, 177,
    180, 188, 209, 213-6, 221, 223, 225,
    228-30, 235, 239, 242-7, 250-3, 255-6,
    275-6, 282, 296-8, 342-3, 353, 359-62, 371,
    373-4, 381

Taft, Sen. Robert, 40
Tahmass, 95
Taylor, Alan R., 4
The *Nation*, 8
The National Interest, 324
The New Republic, 324-5
The *Washington Post*, 6, 7, 180, 208, 213-4,
    264, 273, 304, 310, 312, 314, 322, 324-5,
    371-2
Time Magazine, 159, 187, 216
Timerman, Jacobo, 220, 223-4, 250, 273
Toth, Joseph and Steven, 91, 93
Toynbee, Arnold, 37
Triad Foundation, 332
Trice, Dr. Robert, 262, 310, 316, 347-51
Tri-Partite Agreement, 46
Truman, President Harry S, 27, 29-32, 34,
    36-7, 48, 54, 65, 72, 75, 151, 158, 303,
    347
Tuchmann, Barbara, 275
Tucker, Robert, 4-5
Tucson Jewish Community Council Community
    Relations Committee (TJCC), 328, 335-7
Tunisia, 46, 66, 148, 228, 243, 257-8, 341
Turkey and Ottoman Empire, 3, 11-5, 59, 157,
    170, 275, 336; Byzantines, 12
TV Guide, 317

United Arab Emirates, 334
United Jewish Appeal, 159, 269, 340
United Nations, 18, 24, 33-4, 36, 39, 41,
    47-51, 53-6, 59-60, 65, 76-80, 86, 104-6,
    110, 112, 127-30, 142-9, 155-6, 161;
    Security Council, 107, 134, 139, 145, 165,
    168, 176-8, 181-2, 201, 205, 209-10, 213-4,
    225, 275, 280, 291, 296, 298, 310, 363;
    General Assembly, 29, 55, 124-5;
    diplomats, 263; Partition Plan, 29, 31-4, 36,
    105, 112, 347, 358; peacekeeping force,
    181, 209, 213, 229
UN Security Council Resolution 242 – 102, 105,
    112, 116, 148, 133-6, 173, 175, 178, 181-2,
    188, 190-1, 213, 238, 252; Resolution
    338 – 137, 140, 153, 178

Universities: University of Alabama, 332;
    Arizona, 335-7; Michigan, 330; Penn-
    sylvania, 332; Southern California, 331-2;
    Texas, 330, 334-5; Utah, 330, Villanova,
    334
Uranium Processing Plant, Pennsylvania, 97
Urban League, 367
Uruquart, Brian, 249
U.S. Arab Chamber of Commerce, 285
U.S. Arab ties, 246, 264, 347, 351-3, 355-6,
    358-9
U.S. Assistance to Israel, (including weapons):
    106, 110-11, 121-30, 151, 158, 160-63,
    179, 181, 200, 204-5, 209, 214-5, 220, 224,
    226-8, 242, 250, 255, 262, 270-71, 310-11,
    339-353; help with weapons production,
    353; aircraft, 262; F-16, 262
U.S. Blacks, 201, 246, 367-8
U.S. Congress: House, 8, 11, 14, 45, 52, 55,
    72, 80, 87, 90, 98-9, 118, 128-30, 155,
    157, 159, 169, 172-4, 179-82; Senate, 67,
    72, 103, 151, 160-1, 196-7, 203, 211-3,
    242, 245, 261-3, 267-70, 281, 283-5, 287,
    291-3, 304, 309, 327, 339-53, 364, 381;
    PAC money, 344
U.S. Department of Commerce, 290, 347, 352
U.S. Department of Defense, 29, 88, 90, 105,
    126-7, 206, 215, 282, 310, 347, 351
U.S. Department of State, 24, 27, 29, 31, 36,
    43, 57, 65, 67, 78-9, 84, 92, 98, 101, 103,
    106, 108, 110, 117, 119, 129, 161, 169,
    175, 179, 204, 207-8, 210, 217, 219, 226-7,
    238, 275, 289, 336, 340, 347, 351, 355,
    367
U.S. Department of the Treasury, 55, 72,
    270-1, 282, 347
U.S. Elections: 1940, 22-3; 1948, 303; 1952,
    40; 1956, 39, 52; 103; 1968, 103; 1972,
    118, 121; 1976, 159, 162, 362; 1980, 2,
    201, 205, 211; 1982, 212, 246; 1984, 2,
    212, 262, 342; bloc voting, 7-8, 348-9; con-
    tributions, 350, 362
U.S. Embassies, 243, 254
U.S. Information Service, 42; Voice of
    America, 84
U.S. Intelligence, 74-6, 79-80, 96, 99, 113-4,
    122, 176
U.S. Interests, 83, 116, 153, 156, 173,
    195-202, 211-2, 219, 237-9, 253, 259, 261,
    271, 273, 282, 297, 337
U.S. Israel Strategic Cooperation Agreement,
    214-5
U.S. Marines, 60, 240-1, 244-7, 343, 353
U.S. Media, 3, 43, 45, 89, 119, 129-30, 154,
    178, 206, 210, 212, 214, 223, 234, 240,
    253-9, 261, 295-8, 307-26, 364, 379
U.S. Navy, 72, 83, 88-91, 94, 98-100, 125,
    229, 247; ships: USS Andrew Jackson, 97;
    USS FDR, 145; USS Liberty, 87-8, 91-9,

113, 341; USS Little Rock, 93; USS New Jersey, 247, 256; USS Pueblo, 91, 341
U.S. News and World Report, 325
U.S. Policy, 9, 362, 375, 377, 381
U.S. Polls, 261-2, 318, 325-6
U.S. Press, 223, 240-1, 253-9, 281, 307-14, 323-6, 341
U.S. Public Opinion, 8-9, 318, 323, 325-6, 340, 377-80
U.S. Securities & Exchange Commission, 292, 331
U.S. Sixth Fleet, 93, 125, 247, 258
U.S. Television, 60-1, 224, 240, 291, 314-9; Entertainment, 320-3
USSR, Soviets, 4-5, 12, 19, 34, 39-40, 44, 47, 49-57, 74-84, 89, 91, 94, 96, 98, 101-8, 110-4, 116, 119-20, 123-5, 127, 132, 135-7, 141-8, 153, 167, 173, 176-8, 192, 198, 204-5, 208, 211, 214, 240-1, 263, 296, 307-8, 310-11, 351, 353, 359-60, 373, 376, 381; arms to Mid East, 44-6, 106, 110, 124, 126-8, 131-3, 144, 156, 160, 223, 341

Vance, Cyrus, 165, 168, 173, 175, 178, 181-2, 190, 192-3, 198, 201, 207
Veterans of Foreign Wars, 293
Vietnam, 49, 63, 65, 71-2, 75-6, 86, 89, 102, 110, 120, 128, 136, 145, 166, 216, 271, 276, 307, 310, 342-3
Von Hoffman, Nicholas, 320
Wagner, The Rev. Donald, 284
Waldheim, Sec. Gen. Kurt, 139, 153
Wallace, Henry, 32
Wall Street Journal, 334
Washington Area Jews, 277
Watergate, 99, 121, 125, 136, 143-5, 154, 166, 206
Wazzan, Shafiq, 277, 233
Weinberger, Sec. Caspar, 204-6, 208, 226, 229, 240, 245-7
Weir, The Rev. Benjamin, 257
Weisl, Edwin Jr., 73
Weisman, John, 317-8

Weizman, Ezer, 181, 189, 191
Weizmann, Dr. Chaim, 13, 16-18, 30-2, 41
Wells, Sumner, 24
West Bank, 6, 41, 48, 76, 83, 85, 91-2, 104, 107, 112, 152, 155-6, 170-1, 173, 175-6, 178, 181-2, 188-92, 195-9, 213, 221, 237-9, 241-2, 245, 250-2, 257, 276, 278, 299, 304-5, 308, 318, 324, 341, 364, 367-8, 380
Western Europe, 5, 50, 251, 274, 376
Weyrich, Paul, 352
White, Bishop C. Dale, 299-300
White Paper, 18
Will, George, 179
Wilson, Evan, 27-8, 35, 289
Wilson, Harold, 78
Wilson, Rep. Pete, 343
Wilson, President Woodrow, 11, 14-5, 31
Wofford, Harris, 333
Wolf, Rabbi, Arnold Jacob, 9
World Bank, 44
World War I, 13-4, 30, 59, 275
World War II, 17-8, 22, 29, 31, 34, 40, 51, 60, 65, 206, 216, 263, 275, 298, 331, 336, 358

Ya'ari, Ehud, 227, 229, 235
Yalta Conference, 23
Yamani, Sheikh Ahmed Zaki, 133
Yankelovich Poll, 360-2, 379
Yaron, Gen. Amos, 233
Yemen, North, 57, 67, 104, 170, 282; South, 342-3
Yost, Charles, 80
Young Americans for Freedom, 293
Young, Andrew, 201, 367

Zionism, 11, 13, 16, 22, 32, 35-6, 98, 274-8, 334-5
Zionists, 8, 12-3, 15-8, 22-4, 27-8, 30-1, 91, 273-8, 289, 358; organizations, 11; American Zionists, 29, 31, 37, 315, 323, 326
Zippori, Mordechai, 233
Zogby, James, 280, 284